European Union Politics

European Union Politics

SECOND EDITION

Michelle Cini

OXFORD
UNIVERSITY PRESS

Great Clarendon Street, Oxford OX2 6DP

Oxford University Press is a department of the University of Oxford.
It furthers the University's objective of excellence in research, scholarship, and education by publishing worldwide in

Oxford New York

Auckland Cape Town Dar es Salaam Hong Kong Karachi
Kuala Lumpur Madrid Melbourne Mexico City Nairobi
New Delhi Shanghai Taipei Toronto

With offices in

Argentina Austria Brazil Chile Czech Republic France Greece
Guatemala Hungary Italy Japan Poland Portugal Singapore
South Korea Switzerland Thailand Turkey Ukraine Vietnam

Oxford is a registered trade mark of Oxford University Press in the UK and in certain other countries

Published in the United States
by Oxford University Press Inc., New York

First published 2003
Second edition 2007

British Library Cataloguing in Publication Data

Data available

Library of Congress Cataloging in Publication Data

European Union politics / [edited by] Michelle Cini.—2nd ed.
p. cm.
ISBN-13: 978–0–19–928195–4
1. European Union—Textbooks. 2. European Union countries—Politics and government—Textbooks. I. Cini, Michelle.
JN30.E9419 2006
341.242′2—dc22 2006033145

Typeset by Newgen Imaging Systems (P) Ltd., Chennai, India
Printed in Great Britain
on acid-free paper by
Bath Press Ltd, Bath

ISBN 0–19–928195–5 978–0–19–928195–4

10 9 8 7 6 5 4 3 2 1

Preface

This second edition of *European Union Politics* builds on the success of the first, published in 2003. A great deal has changed in the European Union over this period, and this has led to the introduction of some new chapters – for example, on the constitutional treaty, and on public opinion – alongside the updating of contributions that were published in the first edition. Also new to this edition is a concluding chapter by Alex Warleigh, which looks to the future of European integration, providing interesting insights on the EU's global role.

Originally this edited book aimed to offer teachers and students of EU politics an introductory text that would be both accessible to and challenging for undergraduates coming to the subject for the first time. It came as something of a surprise that the book was also being used by more advanced students – in some cases in conjunction with journal articles or more in-depth texts. Even so, the principles upon which the first edition was based – the assumption of no prior knowledge and clarity of expression, with more difficult concepts explained in boxes and in a glossary – have been maintained in this edition. This is not evidence of a 'dumbing-down'; it is, rather, a concerted effort to make the book an appealing prospect for students who might otherwise be deterred from further study of the European Union.

As noted first time around, the large number of chapters in this volume (27 in this edition) should not be taken to imply that the book is comprehensive; but it does provide a solid overview of a range of topics, falling loosely under the rubric of EU politics. Other textbooks focus more specifically on history, theories, institutions, policies, and (albeit to a lesser extent) on issues. This book aims to give a taste of all of these five areas of EU study. Again, it should be stressed that for many students the chapters in this book will be the starting point for their work on the EU. It would be disappointing if this were the only book they read on the subject.

Finally, a debt of gratitude goes to Ruth Anderson at OUP for her efficient handling of the project and her encouragement throughout the process. Thanks are also owed to the contributors, without whom this book really would not have been possible. Finally, I would like to thank the University for providing me with a University of Bristol Research Fellowship over 2005–6, *and* my Department for giving me the space to get on with my research – and this book project – during that year.

MC

Preface

[illegible]

Contents

Detailed Contents

Guided Tour of Learning Features

This text is enriched with a range of learning tools to help you navigate the text material and reinforce your knowledge of the European Union. This guided tour shows you how to get the most out of your textbook package and do better in your studies.

Reader's Guides

Reader's Guides at the beginning of every chapter set the scene for upcoming themes and issues to be discussed, and indicate the scope of coverage within each chapter topic.

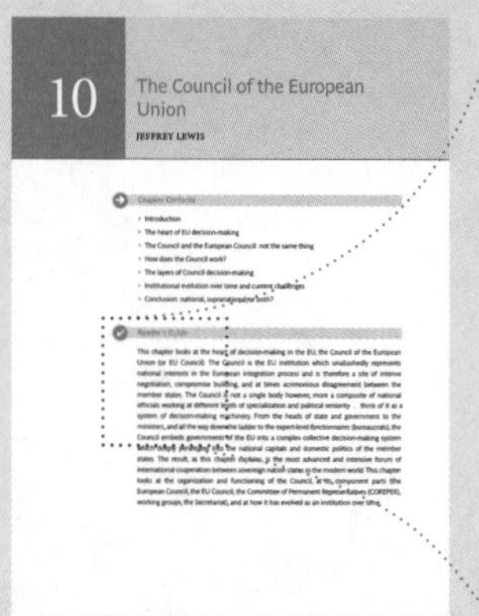

Reader's Guide

This chapter looks at the hea
Union (or EU Council). The
national interests in the Euro
negotiation, compromise buil
member states. The Council
officials working at different le
system of decision-making m
ministers, and all the way dow
Council embeds governments

Boxes

A number of topics benefit from further explanation or exploration in a manner that does not disrupt the flow of the main text. Throughout the book, boxes provide you with extra information on particular topics that complement your understanding of the main chapter text.

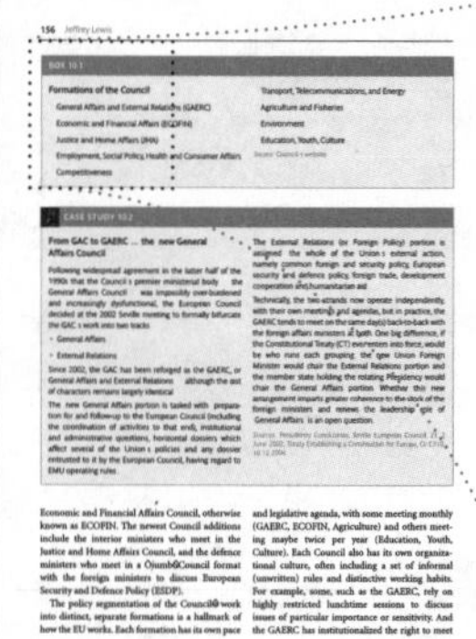

BOX 10.1

Formations of the Council

General Affairs and External Relati
Economic and Financial Affairs (E
Justice and Home Affairs (JHA)
Employment, Social Policy, Health
Competitiveness

Glossary Terms

Key terms are bold-faced in the text and defined in a glossary at the end of the text, to aid you in exam revision.

Consociational(ism): a political r
together distinct communities i
making, whilst protecting the inter

Constitutional Treaty: the Treaty s
the EU Constitution, which was si
2004, but which has not been ratifi
of 'No' votes in referenda in France
in 2005.

Constitutionalization: the formali
the game, which in an EU conte

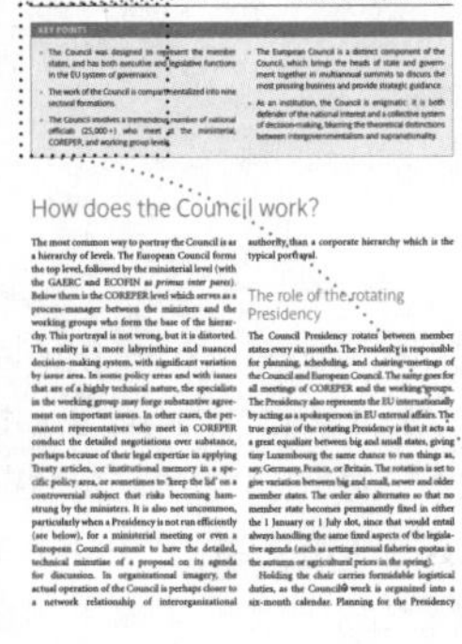

KEY POINTS

- The Council was designed to re
states, and has both executive an
in the EU system of governance.
- The work of the Council is compa
sectoral formations.
- The Council involves a tremendo
officials (25,000+) who meet
COREPER, and working group leve

Key Points

Each main chapter section ends with a set of Key Points that summarize the most important arguments developed within each chapter topic.

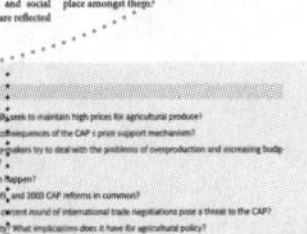

QUESTIONS

1. Why did the CAP originally
2. What were the negative co
3. How did European policy-
etary costs in the 1980s?
4. Why did the 1992 reform h
5. What have the 1992, 1999,
6. To what extent does the cu

Questions

A set of carefully devised questions has been provided to help you assess your comprehension of core themes, and may also be used as the basis of seminar discussion and coursework.

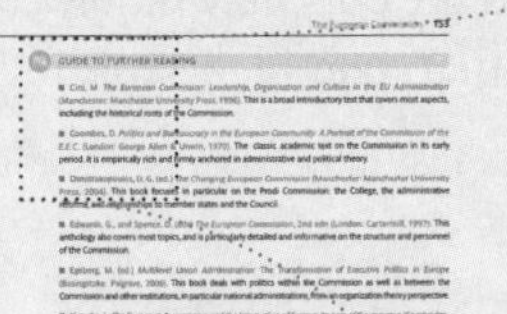

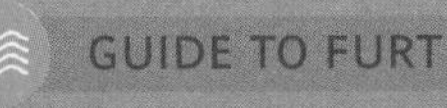

GUIDE TO FURTHER REA

- Cini, M. *The European Con*
(Manchester: Manchester Univ
including the historical roots of
- Coombes, D. *Politics and Bu*
E.E.C. (London: George Allen &
period. It is empirically rich and
- Dimitrakopoulos, D. G. (ed.)
Press, 2004). This book focuse

Further Reading

To take your learning further, reading lists have been provided as a guide to find out more about the issues raised within each chapter topic and to help you locate the key academic literature in the field.

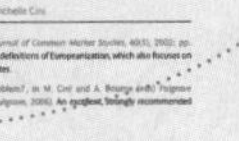

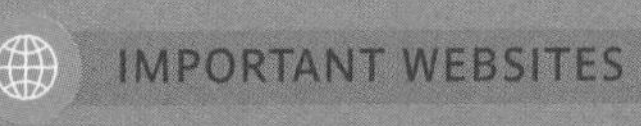

IMPORTANT WEBSITES

- http://www.qub.ac.uk/sch
PaperSeries/EuropeanizationP
University Belfast.
- http://www.arena.uio.no/
Europeanization.

Important Websites

At the end of every chapter you will find an annotated summary of useful websites on the European Union which will be instrumental in further research.

Guided Tour of the Online Resource Centre

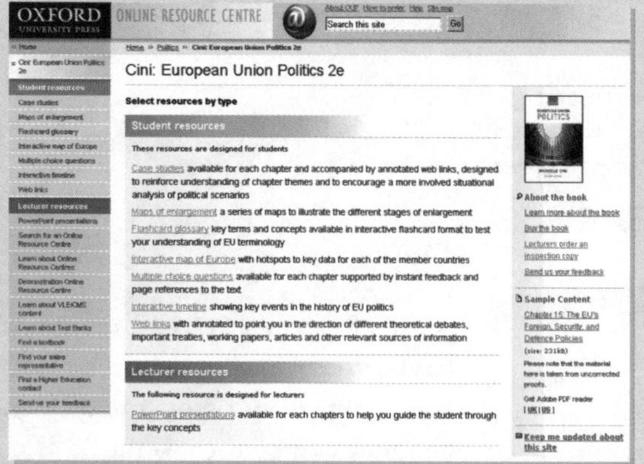

The Online Resource Centre that accompanies this book provides students and instructors with ready-to-use teaching and learning materials. These resources are free of charge and designed to maximise the learning experience.

www.oxfordtextbooks.co.uk/orc/cini2e/

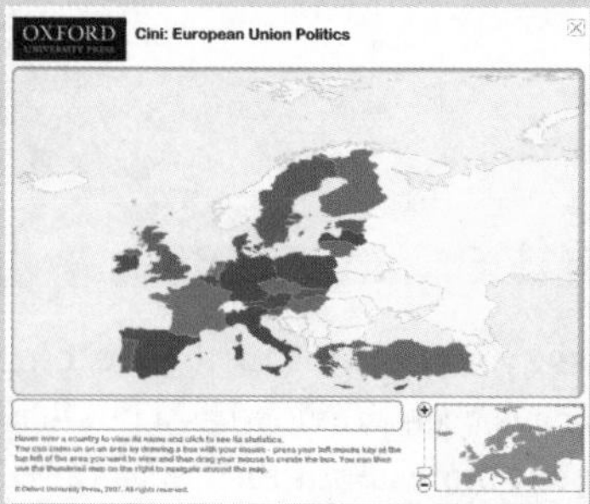

Interactive map of Europe

An interactive map of Europe is provided with 'hot-spots' on each of the member countries. Simply click on the member state you are interested in knowing more about, and read the pop-up window containing vital social and political facts about that state and its role in EU politics.

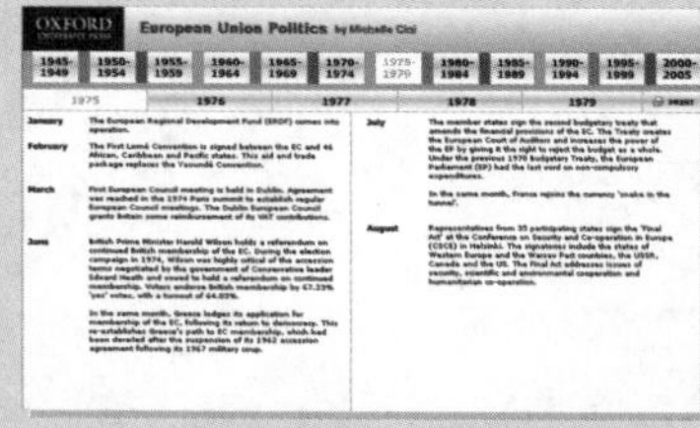

Interactive Timeline

An interactive timeline has been provided so that you can find out about the key events in the history of European Union politics. You click on the date you want, and can read through what happened in different months in that particular year.

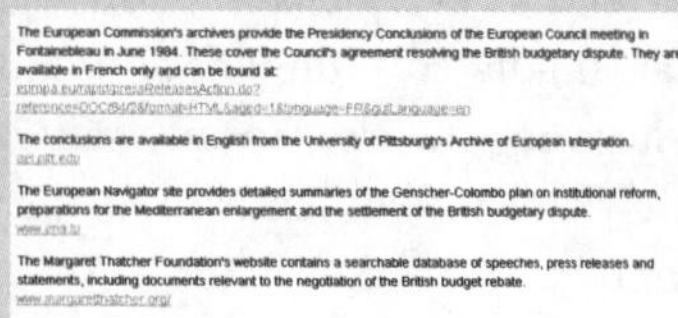

Web Links

A series of annotated web links have been provided to point you in the direction of different theoretical debates, important treaties, working papers, articles and other relevant sources of information.

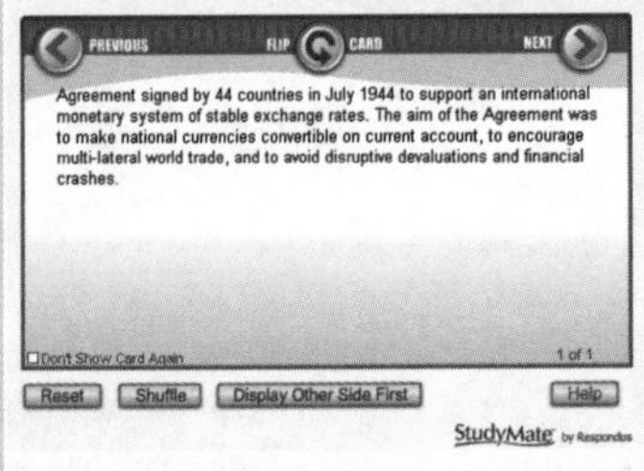

Flashcard Glossary

A series of interactive flashcards containing key terms and concepts have been provided to test your understanding of European Union terminology.

Drafting the Constitutional Treaty

- The Origin of the Constitutional Project
  - The 'future of Europe' debate in 2000
  - the Laeken Declaration in 2001
- Convention on the Future of Europe
  - Duration: from Feb 2002 to June 2003
  - President, conventionnels, civil society
- The IGC and the European Council meetings in Dec 2003 and June 2004
- The signing of the Constitutional Treaty on 29 Oct 2004 by 25 member states and 3 candidate countries

PowerPoint Slides (instructors only)

These complement each chapter of the book and are a useful resource for preparing lectures and handouts. They allow lecturers to guide students through the key concepts and can be fully customized to meet the needs of the course.

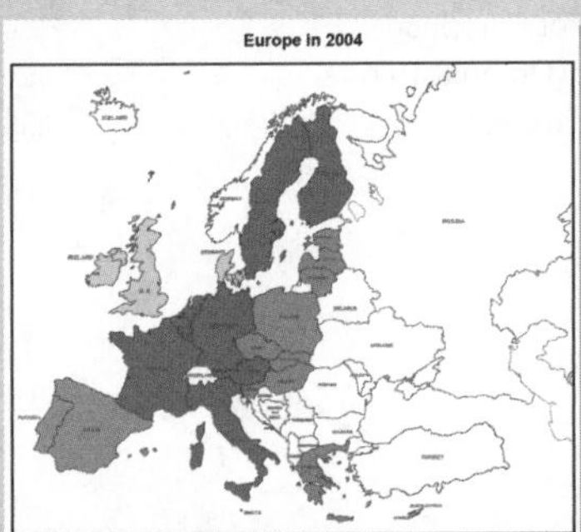

Maps

A series of maps have been provided to show you the different stages of EU enlargement.

Case Studies

Each chapter is supplemented by a short case study that is accompanied by annotated web links, designed to reinforce students' understanding of chapter themes and to encourage them to undertake more involved situational analyses of political scenarios.

Question 2

Which institutional reforms were necessary to implement the single market programme?

- a) Qualified majority voting in the Council
- b) A directly elected European Parliament.
- c) Creating a three pillar structure of the European Union.
- d) All of the above

Multiple Choice Questions

The best way to reinforce your understanding of the European Union is through frequent and cumulative revision. As such, a bank of self-marking multiple-choice questions have been provided for each chapter of the text, and include instant feedback on your answers and cross-references back to the main textbook.

List of Figures

List of Boxes

CHRONOLOGIES

KEY CONCEPTS AND TERMS

CASE STUDIES

OTHER BOXES

List of Tables

About the Contributors

Ian Barnes is Jean Monnet Professor of European Economic Integration in the European Policy Research Centre, Faculty of Business and Law, University of Lincoln, UK.

Pamela Barnes is Jean Monnet Principal Lecturer in European Political Integration in the European Policy Research Centre, Faculty of Social Sciences and Law, University of Lincoln, UK.

Angela K. Bourne is Lecturer in the Department of Politics at the University of Dundee, UK.

Michael Burgess is Professor of Politics, Director of the Centre for European Union Studies (CEUS), and Jean Monnet Professor of European Integration in the Department of Politics and International Studies at the University of Hull, UK.

Dimitris Chryssochoou is Associate Professor of International Organization in the Department of Political Science of the University of Crete, Greece.

Clive Church is Emeritus Professor in the Department of Politics and International Relations, University of Kent, UK.

Michelle Cini is Reader in European Politics in the Department of Politics at the University of Bristol, UK.

Robert Dover is Lecturer at King's College London, UK.

Michelle Egan is Associate Professor in the School of International Service at the American University, Washington DC, USA.

Morten Egeberg is Professor of Public Policy and Administration, Department of Political Science, at the University of Oslo and ARENA, Norway.

Rainer Eising is Professor of European Studies, Friedrich-Schiller University of Jena, Germany.

Gerda Falkner is Professor and Head of the Department of Political Science at the Institute for Advanced Studies, Vienna, Austria.

Eve Fouilleux is Chargée de Recherches, CNRS, Centre de Recherches sur 1'Action Politique en Europe, IEP de Rennes, France.

Kerstin Junge is a Researcher-Consultant at the Tavistock Institute, London, UK.

Ilias Kapsis is a former graduate student in the Law Department at the University of Bristol, UK.

Jeffrey Lewis is Assistant Professor in the Department of Political Science at Cleveland State University, USA.

Lauren M. McLaren is Lecturer in the School of Politics, University of Nottingham, UK.

Machiko Miyakoshi is a graduate student in the Department of Politics, University of Bristol, UK.

Mari Neuvonen is a graduate student in the Department of Politics, University of Bristol , UK.

David Phinnemore is Senior Lecturer in European Integration, and Jean Monnet Chair in European Political Integration, in the School of Politics, International Studies and Philosophy, Queen's University, Belfast, Northern Ireland.

Lucia Quaglia is Senior Lecturer in Contemporary European Studies in the Sussex European Institute, University of Sussex, UK.

Ben Rosamond is Professor of Politics and International Studies in the Department of Politics, and Senior Research Fellow in the Centre for the Study of Globalisation and Regionalisation at the University of Warwick, UK.

Roger Scully is Reader in International Politics in the Department of International Politics, University of Wales Aberystwyth, UK.

Michael Smith is Jean Monnet Professor of European Politics in the Department of Politics, International Relations and European Studies, Loughborough University, UK.

Carsten Strøby-Jensen is Associate Professor, Department of Sociology, University of Copenhagen, Denmark.

Emek M. Uçarer is Associate Professor of International Relations in the International Relations Program at Bucknell University, USA.

Derek W. Urwin is Professor of Politics and International Relations at the University of Aberdeen, UK.

Amy Verdun is Professor, Jean Monnet Chair in European Integration, and Director of the European Studies Program in the Department of Political Science at the University of Victoria, Canada.

Alex Warleigh-Lack is Professor of Politics and International Relations at Brunel University, UK .

Abbreviations

ACP	African, Caribbean, Pacific Countries
AER	Assembly of European Regions
AFSJ	Area of Freedom Security and Justice
AG	Advocate-General
AMCHAM	American Chamber of Commerce
AoA	Agreement on Agriculture
APEC	Asia Pacific Economic Cooperation
ARNE	Antiracist Network for Equality in Europe
ASEAN	Association of Southeast Asian Nations
BEUC	European Consumers' Bureau
BLEU	Belgium Luxembourg Economic Union
BSE	Bovine Spongiform Encephalopathy (Mad Cow Disease)
BTO	Brussels Treaty Organization
BUAV	British Union for the Abolition of Vivisection
CALRE	Conference of European Regional Legislative Parliaments
CAP	Common Agricultural Policy
CARDS	Community Assistance for Reconstruction, Development and Stability in the Balkans
CCP	Common Commercial Policy
CCTV	Closed-circuit television
CDU	Christian Democratic Union (Germany)
CEAS	Common European Asylum System
CEDEC	European Federation of Local Public Energy Distribution Companies
CEE	Central and Eastern Europe
CEEC	Country of Central and Eastern Europe
CEEP	Centre Européen des Entreprises Publics (European Association for Public-sector Firms)
CEFIC	European Chemicals Industry Association
CEN	European Committee for Standardization
CENELEC	European Committee for Electrotechnical Standardization
CEPOL	European Police College
CFI	Court of First Instance
CFSP	Common Foreign and Security Policy
CGS	Council General Secretariat
CIREA	Centre for Information, Discussion, and Exchange on Asylum
CIREFI	Centre for Information, Discussion, and Exchange on the Crossing of Frontiers and Immigration
CM	Common Market
CMO	Common Market Organization
CNJA	Centre National des Jeunes Agriculteurs (French young farmers' association)
CoA	Court of Auditors
CoE	Council of Europe
CONNECCS	The European Commission's database on consultation and civil society
COPA	Comité des Organisations Professionelles Agricoles de la Communauté (European farmers association)
COPS	see PSC
CoR	Committee of the Regions
COREPER	(or Coreper) Committee of Permanent Representatives
CSG	Council Secretariat General
CSU	Christian Social Union (Germany)
CT	Constitutional Treaty
CU	Customs Union
DG	Directorate-General
EAC	European Affairs Committee
EAEC	European Atomic Energy Community
EAGGF	European Agricultural Guidance and Guarantee Fund

EBRD	European Bank for Reconstruction and Development
EC	European Community or European Communities
ECA	European Court of Auditors
ECB	European Central Bank
ECHO	EC Humanitarian Office
ECHR	European Convention on Human Rights
ECJ	European Court of Justice
ECOFIN	Council of Economics and Finance Ministers
ECOSOC	see ESC
ECSC	European Coal and Steel Community
ECU	European Currency Unit
EDC	European Defence Community
EdF	Electricité de France
EDP	Excessive Debt Procedurce
EDU	European Drugs Unit
EEA	European Economic Area
EEB	European Environmental Bureau
EEC	European Economic Community
EESC	see ESC
EFTA	European Free Trade Association
EIB	European Investment Bank
EiOP	European Integration Online Papers
EJA	European Justice Area
EMS	European Monetary System
EMU	Economic and Monetary Union (or European Monetary Union)
EONIA	European Overnight Index Average
EP	European Parliament
EPA	Economic Partnership
EPC	European Political Cooperation (European Political Community)
EPP	European People's Party
ERDF	European Regional Development Fund
ERM	Exchange Rate Mechanism
ERPA	European Research Papers Archive
ERRF	European Rapid Reaction Force
ERT	European Round Table (of Industrialists)
ESC	Economic and Social Committee
ESCB	European System of Central Banks
ESDP	European Security and Defence Policy
ESF	European Social Fund
ETSI	European Telecommunications Standards Institute
ETSO	European Association of Transmission Systems Operators
ETUC	European Trade Union Congress
EU	European Union
EU3	UK, France, and Germany
EUMC	European Union Military Committee
EUMS	European Union Military Staff
Euratom	see EAEC
EURELECTRIC	Union of the Electricity Industry
EURO-C	ETUC's consumer organization
EURO-COOP	European Consumer Co-operatives Association
EURODAC	European fingerprinting system
Europol	European Police Office
EUSA	European Union Studies Association
EWL	European Women's Lobby
FDP	Free Democratic Party (Germany)
FEU	Full Economic Union
FNSEA	Fédération Nationale des Syndicats D'Exploitant Agricoles (French agricultural association)
FPU	Full Political Union
FRY	Federal Republic of Yugoslavia
FTA	Free Trade Area
FYROM	Former Yugoslav Republic of Macedonia
G8	Group of Eight Most Industrialized Countries
GAC	General Affairs Council
GAERC	General Affairs and External Relations Council
GATT	General Agreement on Tariffs and Trade
GDP	Gross Domestic Product
GDR	German Democratic Republic
GEODE	Groupement Européen de Sociétés et Organismes de Distribution d'Energie

GMO	Genetically Modified Organism
GNP	Gross National Product
GWOT	Global War on Terror
HLWG	High-Level Working Group on Asylum and Immigration
ICTY	International Criminal Tribunal for the Former Yugoslavia
IFIEC	International Federation of Industrial Energy Consumers
IGC	Intergovernmental Conference
IMF	International Monetary Fund
IPE	International Political Economy
IR	International Relations
ISAF	International Security Assistance Force
ISPA	Instrument for Structural Policies for Pre-Accession
JAC	Jeunesse Agricole Chrétienne
JHA	Justice and Home Affairs
JNA	Joint National Army (of Serbia)
LI	Liberal Intergovernmentalism
LMU	Latin Monetary Union
MEP	Member of the European Parliament
MFA	Minister of Foreign Affairs
MGQ	Maximum Guaranteed Qualities
MI5	Military Intelligence 5 (British secret service)
MKD	Macedonian Denar
MLG	Multi-level Governance
MoD	Ministry of Defence
MP	Member of Parliament
MTR	Mid-Term Review (CAP)
NAFTA	North Atlantic Free Trade Agreement
NATO	North Atlantic Treaty Organization
NGO	Non-Governmental Organization
NUTS	Nomenclature of Units for Territorial Statistics
NY	New York
OCA	Optimum Currency Area
ODA	Overseas Development Assistance
OECD	Organization for Economic Cooperation and Development
OEEC	Organization for European Economic Cooperation
OJ	Official Journal (of the European Union)
OMC	Open Method of Coordination
OSCE	Organization for Security and Cooperation in Europe
PDB	Preliminary Draft Budget
PES	Party of European Socialists
PESC	Politique Etrangère et de la Sécurité Commune. See CFSP
PHARE	Poland and Hungary Aid for Economic Reconstruction
PJCCM	Police and Judicial Cooperation in Criminal Matters
PLO	Palestine Liberation Organization
PM	Prime Minister
PNV	Partido Nacionalista a Vasco (Basque Nationalist Party)
PPP	Purchasing Power Parity
PSC	Political and Security Committee (also COPS)
QMV	Qualified Majority Voting
REGLEG	Conference of European Regions with Legislative Powers
RELEX	External Relations
SAA	Stability and Association Agreement
SAPARD	Special Accession Programme for Agriculture and Rural Development
SCA	Special Committee on Agriculture
SEA	Single European Act
SEM	Single European Market
SFP	Single Farm Payment
SGP	Stability and Growth Pact
SIS	Schengen Information System
SLIM	Simpler Legislation for the Internal Market
SME	Small and Medium-sized Enterprises
SSC	Scientific Steering Committee
TA	Treaty of Amsterdam
TACIS	Programme for Technical Assistance to the Independent States of the Former Soviet Union and Mongolia
TCN	Third-Country National

TEC	Treaty on the European Community
TEU	Treaty on European Union
UEAPME	European Association of Craft, Small and Medium-sized Enterprises
UK	United Kingdom
UN	United Nations
UNHCR	Office of the United Nations High Commissioner for Refugees
UNICE	Union of Industrial and Employers' Confederations of Europe
UNIPEDE	International Union of Producers and Distributors of Electrical Energy
UNMIK	United Nations Interim Administration Mission in Kosovo
US	United States
USA	United States of America
USSR	Union of Soviet Socialist Republics (the Soviet Union)
VAT	Value Added Tax
VIS	Visa Information System
VOC	Volatile Organic Compounds
WEU	Western European Union
WTO	World Trade Organization
YES	Young Workers' Exchange Scheme

1 Introduction

MICHELLE CINI

Chapter Contents

- Introduction: what is the EU?
- Why was it set up?
- Who can join?
- Who pays?
- How is European policy made?
- The organization of the book

Reader's Guide

This chapter provides a very brief introduction to *European Union Politics*. The aim of the chapter is to help direct those students who are completely new to the study of the EU, by providing some initial building blocks which it is hoped will provide useful background for the chapters that follow. The chapter makes brief comments on what the EU is, why it was set up, who can join, who pays, and how policy is made. The chapter ends by explaining how the book is organized.

Introduction: what is the EU?

The European Union is a family of liberal-democratic countries, acting collectively through an institutionalized system of decision-making. When joining the EU, members sign up not only to the body of EU treaties, legislation, and norms (the so-called *acquis communautaire*), but also to a set of shared common values, based on democracy, human rights, and principles of social justice. Even so, members, and indeed the European institutions, are keen to stress the diversity of the Union – most obviously in cultural and linguistic terms. Since May 2004 the EU has comprised 25 member states (rising to at least 27 or 28 at some point after 2006), and around 450 million people.

Since its establishment in the 1950s, commentators have argued over the kind of body the European Community (now Union) is. While there is a growing consensus that the EU now sits somewhere between a traditional international organization and a state, the question of whether it resembles one of these 'models' more than the other remains contested. Although it might seem fair to claim that the European Union is unique, or a hybrid body, even this point can be contentious where it prevents researchers from seeing similarities between the EU and national systems of government, and international organizations.

The common institutions of the EU, that is the Commission, Parliament, Council, and Courts, along with many other bodies (see Box 1.2) are perhaps the most visible attributes of the European Union. These institutions are highly interdependent; and together they form a nexus for joint decision-making in a now extremely wide range of policy areas. While many argue that the EU Council (comprising the EU's governments and support staff) still predominates as the primary legislator, the importance of the European Parliament has grown substantially since the 1980s, so that it is not unreasonable to talk of it as a co-legislature. Ultimately, however, the member states remain in a privileged position within the EU, as it is they (or rather their governments) who can change the general institutional framework of the Union, through treaty reform; or even – potentially – withdraw from the Union, though it is highly unlikely that any state would take such a dramatic step.

CHRONOLOGY 1.1

The Treaties

The Treaty of Paris, which set up the European Coal and Steel Community (ECSC), was signed on 18 April 1951. It came into force in 1952.

The Treaty of Rome, which set up the European Economic Community (EEC) and European Atomic Energy Community (EAEC or EURATOM), was signed on 25 March 1957. It came into force on 1 January 1958.

Since the 1950s there have been several revisions to these treaties. Note that these are not new (from-scratch) treaties; each revises earlier versions, beginning with the Treaty of Rome. The most important of these came after the mid-1980s.

- The *Single European Act* (SEA, or just 'Single Act') was signed in 1986. It came into force in July 1987.
- The *Maastricht Treaty* (creating a Treaty on European Union, or TEU) was signed in February 1992. It came into force in November 1993.
- The *Amsterdam Treaty* (which revised the TEU) was signed in 1997. It came into force in 1999.
- The *Nice Treaty* (which revised the Amsterdam version of the TEU) was signed in 2000. It came into force in February 2001.

The *Constitutional Treaty* (sometimes referred to as the EU Constitution) was signed in October 2004, after which a ratification process began. In 2005 the citizens of two member states, France and the Netherlands, voted against the Treaty in referenda held in those countries. As a consequence, it has not been possible for this Treaty to enter into force (see Chapters 4 and 23).

Why was it set up?

The European Union was set up as a consequence of the negative experiences of the founding member states during and in the immediate aftermath of the Second World War. Maintaining peace was a primary objective at a time when war amongst the European states seemed almost an inevitability. The general ideas behind the European integration process predated the Second World War, however, as there already existed movements supporting the establishment of some kind of European Community in the 1920s, and even earlier than that.

The objective of peace in (Western) Europe went hand in hand with a desire to ensure that Europe was able to get back on its feet economically after 1945. With the continent as a whole devastated by war, it was essential that the German economy – often thought of as the powerhouse of Europe – reconstruct, even though this might pose a risk to the security of Western Europe. European integration was a means of tying Germany into a unified Europe, that is, to resolve what was called at the time the 'German Question', allowing both peace and economic reconstruction to be pursued simultaneously.

The EU has changed dramatically since the early days of the Community, and some argue that the original objectives of the 1950s are no longer relevant. Certainly, the idea of war between West European states does seem unthinkable now, perhaps demonstrating the success of the integration project. Yet if we consider the original economic ambitions of the Union, the concerns of the post-millennium decade are not so different. The context has altered, both politically and economically, but growth and employment remain at the top of the European Union's agenda.

KEY CONCEPTS AND TERMS 1.2

The 'European institutions'

The term 'European institutions' usually refers to four key EU organizations:

- The *European Commission* (or just 'the Commission'), the executive and driving force of the Union (see Chapter 9).
- The *European Parliament* (or just 'the Parliament' or EP), directly elected and representing the peoples of the Union (see Chapter 11).
- The *Council of the European Union* (the 'EU Council', 'the Council', or the 'Council of Ministers'), comprising the EU's member states/national governments (see Chapter 10).
- The *Court of Justice* (often called the 'European Court of Justice', the 'European Court', or the ECJ), the body that ensures compliance with European law (see Chapter 12).

Other EU bodies include:

- The *Court of Auditors* (the European Court of Auditors or ECA), which ensures the lawful management of the European budget.
- The *Economic and Social Committee* (ESC, EESC, or sometimes 'ECOSOC'), which represents the opinions of organized civil society.
- The *Committee of the Regions* (CoR), which represents the opinions of the regions and local authorities.
- The *European Ombudsman*, which deals with complaints of maladministration against the European institutions.
- The *European Central Bank* (ECB), which takes responsibility for monetary policy and for foreign exchange.
- The *European Investment Bank* (EIB), which finances public and private long-term investment

There are many more agencies and organizations associated with the European Union. See http://europa.eu.int/ for details of these.

Source: http://europa.eu.int/abc-en.htm.

Who can join?

From the very beginning of the project the European Community was open to new members. The criteria for joining were however rather vague. States had to be European, of course, but there was no real definition of what European actually meant (which countries at the margins were included and which were not). There was also an assumption that member states had to be democratic, but again, this was ill defined, and was not included in any treaty until the 1990s.

It was not until the 1990s, and the Copenhagen European Council (summit) of 1993, that a clear(er) set of criteria was established, explaining that countries wishing to join the Union had to meet political and economic criteria, and be able to take on board the Community *acquis communautaire* (the existing body of EU treaties, legislation, norms). These conditions of membership became known as the Copenhagen Criteria.

Although there had been enlargements in the 1970s (with the UK, Ireland, and Denmark joining in 1973) and the 1980s (with Greece joining in 1981 and Spain and Portugal in 1986), the 1990s brought a very different phase in the history of the expansion of the European integration process. The 1990s saw the end of the Cold War, which freed up some West European countries bound by Cold War agreements and/or national preferences, to join the Union. Thus, Sweden, Finland, and Austria became members in 1995. The accession of the former Eastern bloc/Soviet states would take much longer, another decade almost, to complete. It was not until May 2004 that the Czech Republic, Estonia, Hungary, Poland, Latvia, Lithuania, Slovakia, and Slovenia joined, along with two small island states, Cyprus and Malta.

At the time of writing in 2006 the enlargement process is still incomplete. Bulgaria and Romania, unready to join in 2004, will, most likely, join in January 2007, and Croatia, the former Yugoslav state, is particularly keen for the country to join. Other former Yugoslav states are not so far advanced, but eventual membership is not unthinkable. Further East, Ukraine, following the Orange Revolution of 2005, has started discussing a possible roadmap to membership, though this remains a long-term perspective on relations with the West. By contrast, Belarus remains unreconstructed, politically.

Turkey is a special case, as it always has been in its recent relations with the European Union. It has been given a commitment that it may be able to join after 2014, as an incentive to strengthen the hands of reformers within the political elite. However, there is much that needs to be achieved in the meantime. It is likely that Turkey will join the Union, but its prospective membership is controversial in some member states; and there are more general economic and political challenges facing the country as it starts to work towards meeting the conditions that the EU now sets for aspirant members. (See Figure 1.1 for an up-to-date map of the EU, and for more on enlargement see Chapter 26.)

Who pays?

The European Union has its own budget, referred to as either the EU or perhaps more accurately the Community Budget. Unlike national governments, the Union does not have the capacity to tax European citizens in a direct way, which begs the question: from where does this money come? In fact, the Community Budget has more than just one source: it comprises 75 per cent of receipts from

Figure 1.1 Map of Europe

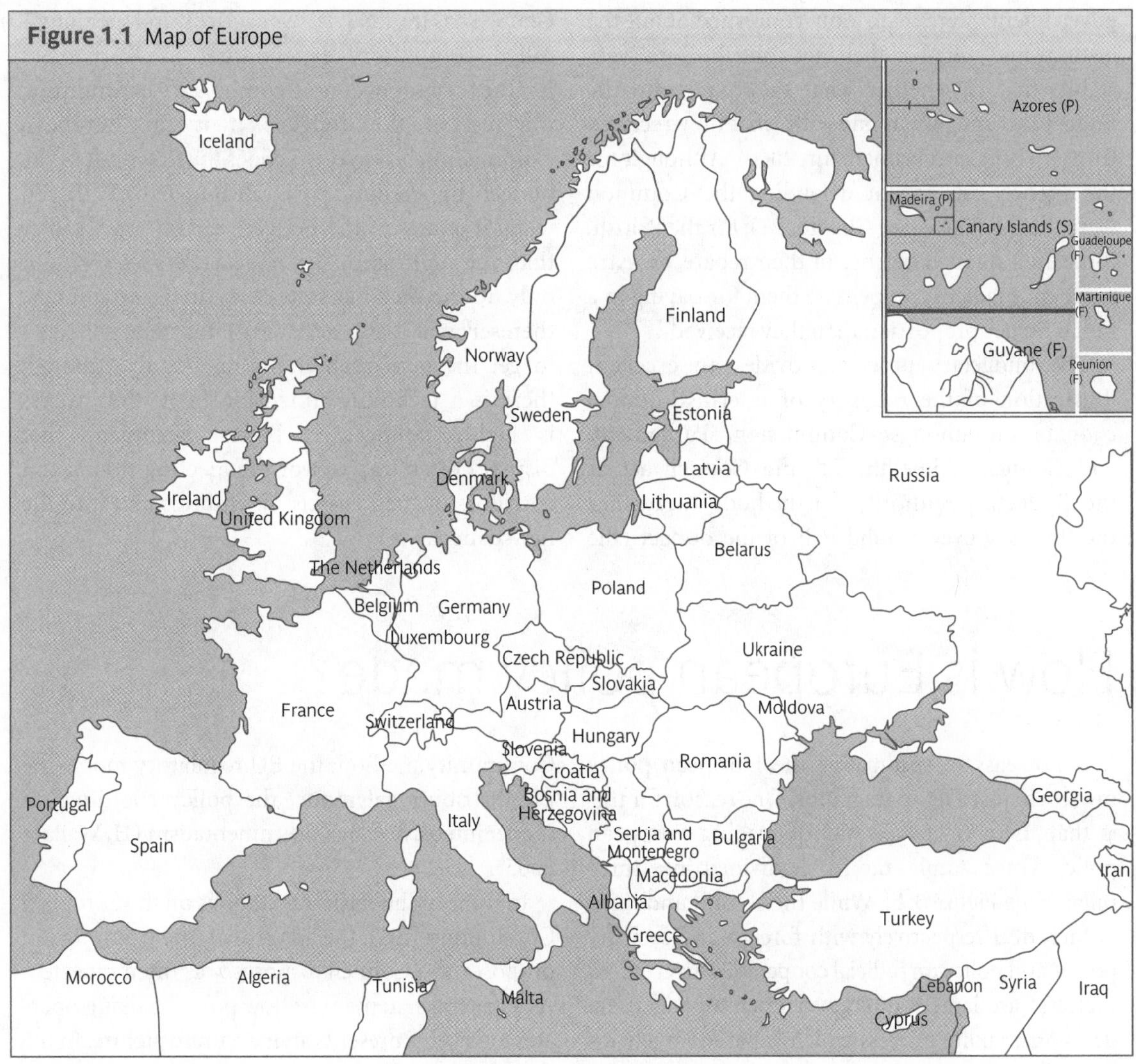

customs duties and sugar levies contributions at the EU's borders, VAT-based contributions (of 0.5 per cent), and national contributions provided by the member states, amounting to 1.25 per cent of **gross national product** (GNP).

To avoid the annual wrangling over the budget, it was decided in the 1980s that the general framework of the budget would be decided on a multi-annual basis. Agreement on this framework, which is known as the **Financial Perspective** is always controversial. It establishes overall levels of funding as well as ceilings for particular policy areas, such as agriculture or regional policy. The 2007–13 Financial Perspective was finally agreed in December 2005 after months of argument. Some countries negotiating, such as German and the Netherlands, were adamant that they would not sanction an increase in the overall budget, which left little room for manoeuvre. The new post-2004 member states were keen to ensure that they benefited from enhanced rights to regional aid, something those countries who had benefited in the past, namely Spain, Portugal, and Greece, were reluctant to concede. In the end, as is often the case, governments were really only concerned about the bottom line; whether their net contributions were stable, that is, whether what they paid into the budget was roughly in line with what they received from it (Begg and Heinemann 2006). Although for the French this meant defending the Common Agricultural Policy (see Chapter 21); for the British, it meant a staunch defence of their rebate, an extra payment made to compensate them for paying in a much higher proportion than they received.

The budgetary process provides an excellent illustration of the necessity of interinstitutional cooperation amongst Commission, Parliament, and Council. While the EP and Council act as the 'Budgetary Authority' for the budget, each has the final say over around half of the budget (the Council has the final say over agricultural spending – called 'compulsory expenditure; the Parliament has the final say over non-compulsory expenditure, the rest of the budget). It is the European Commission however that does the first draft of the budget (the Preliminary Draft Budget or PDB). So when it comes to the budget year on year (rather than the multi-annual Financial Perspective), not only do the member states have to agree amongst themselves, it is also necessary – for most policies – to get the parliamentarians on board. Although there is a technical dimension to it, the process is highly political. It is not surprising that disputes often leap out of the meeting rooms and corridors of the Brussels institutions and into the newspapers.

How is European policy made?

It is not easy to summarize the European policy process in just a few paragraphs. One reason for this is that there is no *one* way of making European policy. For example, the EU is divided into three pillars (see Figure 3.1). While the second and third (which deal respectively with foreign and security policy, and policy on judicial cooperation in criminal matters) are largely intergovernmental, and use a decision-making process which is based largely on government-to-government cooperation, there is much more of a supranational quality to first pillar (EC pillar) decision-making, which accounts for all other European policy areas. Moreover, variation across policy areas is now an important theme within the study of European Union politics. There are several decision-making procedures in operation (see Box 1.3), though the most common now is the codecision procedure (see Figure 1.2). Focusing more on policy types, rather than formal procedures, Helen Wallace has sought to group similar types together, identifying five 'modes' (or types) of European decision-making: the classical Community method; the EU regulatory mode; the EU distributional mode; the policy coordination mode; intensive transgovernmentalism (H. Wallace 2005).

In some of the earliest textbooks on the European Community (EC), the adage that 'the Commission proposes, the Council disposes' was often repeated. As a general statement of how policy-making operates today, this presents an inaccurate picture. In the first (or EC pillar), it is certainly still true that the Commission proposes legislation (see Chapter 9), though this is not a helpful summary of the Commission's role in Pillars 2 and 3. Indeed in Pillar 1, the Commission possesses the exclusive right of initiative: in other words only the Commission can draft legislation. But as we shall see below, the Parliament increasingly plays the role of *co*-legislator in today's European legislative process.

In the EC pillar, it is fair to say that policy now emerges as a result of the interaction of a number of actors and institutions. First amongst these is what is sometimes referred to as the 'institutional

BOX 1.3

Legislative procedures

The *codecision procedure* is the main decision-making procedure for the European Community (the first pillar of the European Union). It is based on the principle of parity: that is, that no European decision can be taken without the agreement of both the EU Council and the European Parliament (see Figure 1.2).

The *consultation procedure* was the original EC decision-making procedure, as outlined in the Treaty of Rome. Consultation allows the European Parliament to give its opinion on Commission proposals, before the Council takes a decision. Once the Parliament's opinion is made known, the Commission can amend its proposal if it sees fit, before the Council examines it. The Council can then adopt the proposal, or can amend it. If they wish to reject it, they must do so unanimously. Under the majority of procedures within the EC pillar **qualified majority voting** now applies to votes taken in the EU Council. The use of **unanimity** is reserved for particularly sensitive political or constitutional issues. It is also in general use (with a few minor exceptions) in Pillars 2 and 3.

The *assent procedure* was introduced in the Single European Act. When this procedure is used, the Council has to get the agreement (or 'assent') of the European Parliament before policy decisions are taken. Under this procedure the Parliament can say 'yes' or 'no' to a proposal, but does not have any right to propose amendments to it. Assent is used in only a relatively small number of policy areas, covering EU enlargement and international agreements, for example.

The *cooperation procedure* was introduced in the Single European Act, and was extended by the Maastricht Treaty. However, at Amsterdam, governments agreed to privilege the codecision procedure and cut back on areas where cooperation was used. It is now used only for economic and monetary union decisions.

triangle' of the European Commission, European Parliament, and the Council of the European Union (the EU Council). However, many other European, national, and subnational bodies, including interest groups, also play an important role in the making of European policy. The functions, responsibilities, and obligations of these actors and institutions depend on the particular rules that apply to the policy under consideration. While there are rather different rules that apply to budgetary decisions (as below) and to the agreement of international agreements, and indeed for Economic and Monetary Union, much of the work of the EC pillar involves a process of **regulation**.

Various legislative procedures govern the way that policy is made (see Box 1.3). The most common of these now is the codecision procedure (see Figure 1.2). The codecision procedure was introduced in 1993, when the Treaty on European Union (the **Maastricht Treaty**) came into effect. Article 251 (EC Treaty) spells out how it should work. This provision was revised in the version of the Treaty called the Amsterdam Treaty (1997). Codecision gives both the Parliament and the Council, as co-legislators, two successive readings of legislative proposals drafted by the Commission. If the two institutions are unable to agree at the end of this process, a 'conciliation committee' is set up. Conciliation involves select members of the Council and Parliament (with the Commission also represented), together trying to hammer out an agreement. Once this is done, the agreement is passed back to the full Council and Parliament for consideration – a third reading.

The procedure used is determined by the so-called **legal basis** underpinning the policy, which involves reference to a specific treaty provision. This provision also determines whether the governments voting in the EU Council need to take their decisions on the basis of unanimity or a qualified majority vote (QMV). The legal basis is decided by the Commission, though the Commission's decision must be based on objective criteria so that it can be challenged through the courts if need be. Where there are grey areas, the choice of legal basis (and hence, legislative procedure) can be extremely contentious. This is because different procedures allow different configurations of actors and institutions a say in the policy process. This is particularly important in determining the relative importance of the Council, Parliament, and Commission in the European policy process.

Figure 1.2 The codecision procedure

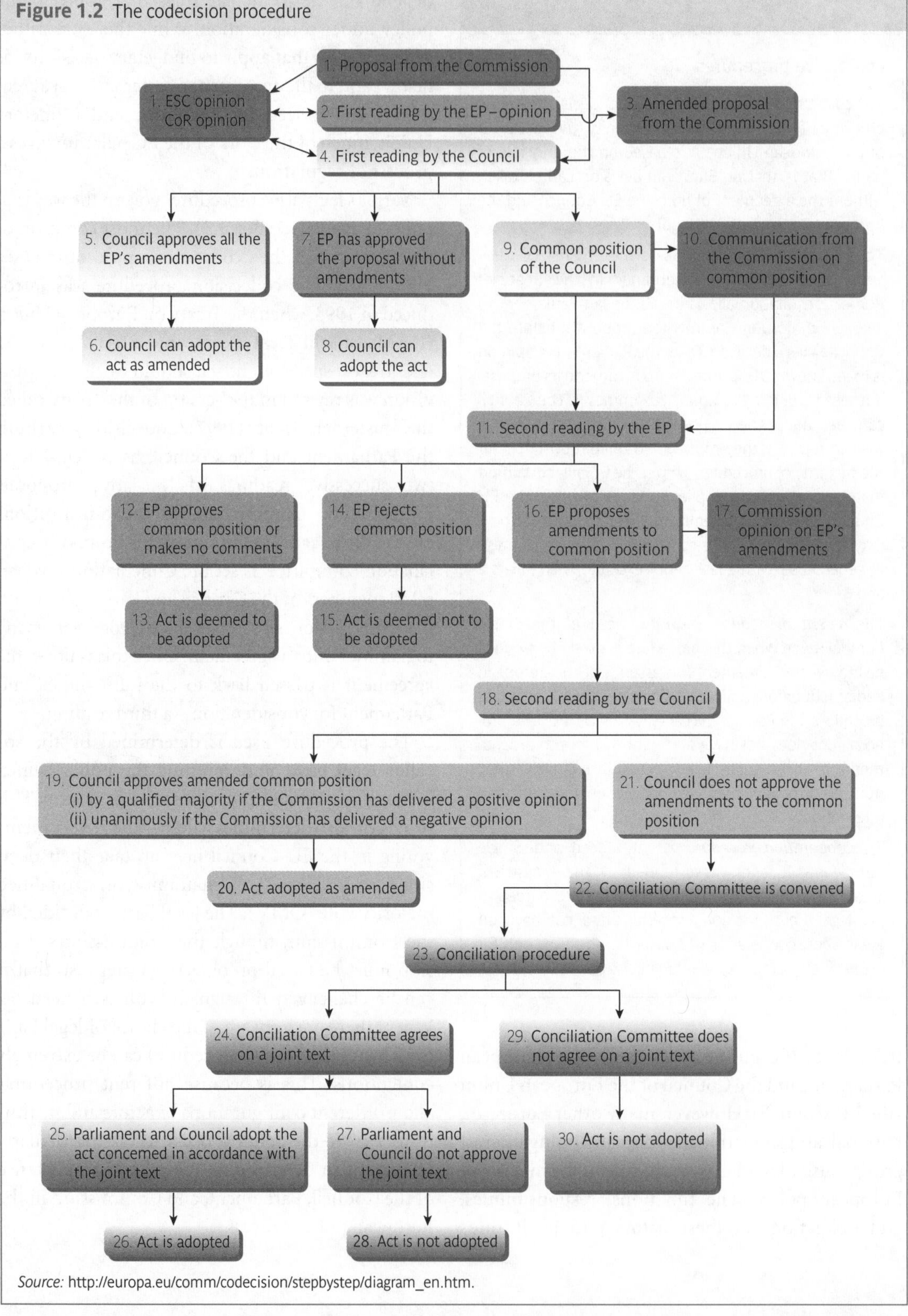

Source: http://europa.eu/comm/codecision/stepbystep/diagram_en.htm.

The organization of the book

The book is organized into five parts. *Part One* covers the historical evolution of the European Community from 1945 to the failure to ratify the Constitutional Treaty in 2005. Chapter 2 focuses on the origins and early years of the European integration process. Chapter 3 covers the period from the Single European Act to the Nice Treaty; and Chapter 4 reviews the Constitutional Treaty.

Part Two covers the theoretical and conceptual approaches which have sought to explain European integration and EU politics. Chapter 5 examines federalism; Chapter 6 reviews the fortunes of neofunctionalism; while Chapter 7 summarizes the key elements of the intergovernmental approaches to European integration. Chapter 8 has a wide remit, focusing on the new (or newer) theories of European integration and EU politics, including work on multi-level governance and new institutionalist approaches.

Part Three deals with the European institutions: the Commission (Chapter 9); the EU Council (Chapter 10); the European Parliament (Chapter 11); and the European Courts (Chapter 12). It also includes a chapter on interest intermediation (Chapter 13).

Part Four covers a sample of European policies, which, though not aiming to be in any way comprehensive, demonstrate the various ways in which such policies have evolved, and – though to a lesser extent – how they operate. Chapter 14 tackles external economic policy; Chapter 15, foreign, security, and defence policy; and Chapter 16, the Single Market. Chapter 17 deals with social policy; Chapter 18 with regional policy; and Chapter 19 with justice and home affairs. Chapters 20 and 21 deal, respectively, with Economic and Monetary Union (EMU) and the Common Agricultural Policy (CAP).

The final part of the book, *Part Five*, comprises six chapters, each of which deals with specific issues related to the politics of the European Union. The first, Chapter 22, is on democracy; the second, Chapter 23, focuses on public opinion; and the third, Chapter 24, is on differentiation (or closer cooperation). Chapter 25 deals with Europeanization and Chapter 26 with enlargement. The final chapter, Chapter 27, provides a forward-looking conclusion to the book, first by examining the kind of model which the EU might reflect in the future; and second by picking up on two earlier themes in the book, the EU's role in world politics – in particular in relation to the USA – and, also, its future reliance, as an enlarged union on the principle of differentiation, that is, the idea that subsets of member states might engage in European projects that do not involve *all* member states.

PART ONE

The Historical Context

2 The European Community: From 1945 to 1985

DEREK W. URWIN

Chapter Contents

Reader's Guide

This chapter reviews the principal developments in the process of European integration from the end of the Second World War through to the mid-1980s. While ideas and arguments in favour of European unity have a much longer history, the war and its aftermath contributed to providing a greater urgency and different context to the issue. In the mid-1980s the European Community took a series of decisions which launched it firmly on a trajectory towards intensive political, economic, and monetary integration. Between these two points in time, neither the support for integration nor the institutional and structural forms it took were preordained or without opposition. The rate and direction of integration depended upon a shifting constellation of forces: the nature of interactions between federalist ideas and their supporters, national governments and their assessments of national self-interest, and the broader international environment. Within these parameters, the chapter looks at the emergence of international organizations in Western Europe in the 1940s, the establishment of the Community idea from the Schuman Plan through to the Treaty of Rome, and the factors that contributed towards the seemingly erratic progress towards ever closer union made by the European Community after 1958.

Introduction

The institutional structure and operation of the European Union (EU) can trace a direct line of descent back to the establishment of the European Coal and Steel Community (ECSC). Indeed, while the intervening decades may have witnessed extensive embellishment and refinement, the broad outline and principle remain those of 1951. However, the idea and dream of a politically integrated Europe possess a much longer pedigree. Across the centuries, numerous intellectuals and political leaders have argued for and have attempted to bring order and unity to the fragmented political mosaic of the European continent. As part of this long-standing dream, an increased intellectual agitation for unity in Europe emerged in the nineteenth century, but almost exclusively by people who were, at best, at the fringes of political decision-making. Their arguments and blueprints held little appeal or relevance for political leaders. However, there did emerge a more widespread recognition that some form of economic cooperation might well contain some potential political advantages for states. Those schemes that did become operative, however, were either short-lived or, like the Zollverein established among German states, highly region-specific and protectionist in their external mien.

The post-First World War peace process, by its emphasis upon national self-determination, made the continental political mosaic even more complex, so leading to a greater urgency for, and difficulty surrounding any process of, cooperation. After 1918, the hopes that had been invested in the League of Nations as a world body dedicated to a cooperative peace quickly foundered in a highly charged atmosphere of economic uncertainty and historic political antipathies. The Low Countries and the Nordic states did explore possibilities of economic cooperation, but with no significant outcome. A few politicians, most notably perhaps Aristide Briand, the French foreign minister, did raise the idea of political integration. But in concrete terms this did not advance beyond the 1930 Briand Memorandum, a generalized proposal advocating a kind of intergovernmental union with its own institutional infrastructures within the League of Nations. Outside political circles, a plethora of associations expounded schemes for cooperation and integration, but failed to achieve any positive results. By the 1930s economic depression and crisis, and the rise of fascism, had led countries to look to their own defences; the outbreak of war in 1939 simply confirmed the absence of any radical change to the European world of states. The history of European integration, therefore, as it is conventionally understood today, essentially begins in 1945. This chapter charts that history, focusing on the period between 1945 and 1985.

The opening moves

The Second World War was a catalyst for a renewed interest in European unity. It contributed to arguments that nationalism and nationalist rivalries, by culminating in war, had discredited and bankrupted the independent state as the foundation of political organization and international order, and that a replacement for the state had to be found in a comprehensive continental community. These ideas were most forcefully expressed in the political vision of the Italian federalist, Altiero Spinelli, who produced a blueprint for a United States of Europe as the overriding priority for the post-war peace. His arguments found strong favour among the various national Resistance movements. However, the new European administrations seemed to give European unity a low priority, concentrating more upon issues of national economic reconstruction. But for several reasons the siren voices of federalism were heard by, and swayed, a larger audience than had been the case in the interwar period, so enabling the possibility and dream of union to survive as an item on the European political agenda (see Box 2.1).

One important factor was the increasingly glacial international political climate. This division of Europe between East and West after 1945, and the subsequent Cold War between the world's two superpowers, the USA and the USSR, fuelled alarm in Western Europe about its own fragile defences in the light of what it feared were the territorial ambitions of the USSR. This led to a deep involvement of the USA in European affairs in the late 1940s. The consequent ideological bipolarization in turn helped propel Western Europe towards defining itself as an entity with common interests. This changing mood was assisted by a general concern over the parlous state of the national economies, a concern which helped generate a widespread belief that economic recovery would require both external assistance from the USA and collaboration on development and trade across the West European states.

It was widely assumed across Western Europe that the lead in any moves towards closer collaboration,

BOX 2.1

Issues and debates in the early years of European integration

Why European integration began, and the reasons why the subsequent plot developed the way it did, have been the subject of intense debate. There has been a tendency, especially among those strongly committed to a federal Europe, to see development moving, if not smoothly, then nevertheless inexorably along a single plane towards a predetermined goal. Yet the history of integration since the formation of the ECSC in 1951 has not been like that. The rate of integrative progress has been far from consistent, and all arguments and pressures for further advances have had to contend with equally powerful countervailing forces pulling in the opposite direction. Nor was there anything preordained about the structural route taken in 1950, or that future developments would revolve largely around a Franco-German axis. There might, both then and later, have been broad agreement about the desirability and principle of a united Europe; but there has rarely been consensus on anything else. As Robert Schuman, the French foreign minister, commented in May 1950 when he unveiled his plan for a pooling of coal and steel resources, 'Europe will not be made all at once, or according to a single plan.'

In reality, the story of integration is complex, with numerous subplots, varying strategies, and different ambitions. As advocated by the federalists, the role of ideas and beliefs has always been central to the progress of integration. Even so, there has been tension within the federalist camp as to the most appropriate strategy to adopt. Simplifying the complex strands of thought somewhat, there have been two competing strategic schools. On the one hand, there are those who have followed the arguments of people like Altiero Spinelli who, in the Ventotene Manifesto of 1940 and his subsequent writings and actions, urged a once and for all 'big bang' solution, an instantaneous and all-embracing transformation into a federal European state. On the other side was a more cautious and pragmatic strategy, encapsulated by the inputs of people like Jean Monnet and Robert Schuman, which envisaged a slower process of steady accretion through a series of limited actions and innovations. But while central and necessary, the force of ideas by itself has not been sufficient. The impact and rate of advance of the federalist impulse has been modified by the input and role of national governments – by their policies and by the degree to which integrative proposals have been seen as fitting with, or at the very least not seeming to threaten, what regimes perceive to be the national interests of their own states. The way in which processes of integration have developed over the past half-century, therefore, is the product of a complex interaction of centripetal and centrifugal pressures, of ideas, principles, and realpolitik scepticism. And all of this intricate dance has occurred within a broader and ever-shifting international political and economic environment which itself has affected, sometimes positively and sometimes negatively, the degree of enthusiasm for, commitment to, and rate of progress of integration.

CHRONOLOGY 2.2

Key dates in European integration, 1947–57

1947	March	Announcement of Truman Doctrine by the USA Signature of Treaty of Dunkirk by the UK and France
	June	Declaration of Marshall Plan by the USA
1948	January	Start of Benelux Customs Union
	March	Signature of Treaty of Brussels by the UK, France, and Benelux
	April	Establishment of Organization for European Economic Co-operation (OEEC) by 16 European states, the USA, and Canada
	May	The federalist Congress of Europe meets at The Hague
1949	April	Signature of the Atlantic Pact and formation of the North Atlantic Treaty Organization (NATO) by 12 states
	May	Treaty of Westminster establishes the Council of Europe
1950	May	Schuman Plan proposes a pooling of coal and steel resources by France, the Federal Republic of Germany, and any other state wishing to join them
	October	Proposal for a European Defence Community (EDC)
1951	April	Treaty of Paris establishes the European Coal and Steel Community (ECSC)
1952	May	Signature of EDC Treaty
	July	ECSC comes into operation
1953	March	Draft Treaty of a European Political Community (EPC)
1954	August	French Parliament rejects EDC. The EDC and EPC plans collapse
	October	Treaty of Brussels is modified to establish West European Union (WEU)
1955	June	Foreign Ministers of the ECSC states meet in Messina, Italy, to consider 'further European integration'
1957	March	Signature of Treaty of Rome establishes the European Economic Community (EEC) and the European Atomic Energy Community (EURATOM)

because of its wartime role, would be taken by the UK, and that, with Germany prostrate and militarily occupied, a British–French alliance would lie at the core of European organization. However, the initial moves towards enhanced collaboration by governments were limited in scope, with the wartime decision by the governments in exile of the Low Countries to establish a **Benelux** customs union an exception. While governments were more typically interested primarily in security arrangements, they did little more than consider mutual aid treaties of the traditional variety. The only formal agreements to emerge were the 1947 Treaty of Dunkirk between the UK and France, and its 1948 extension in the 50-year Treaty of Brussels (formally the Treaty of Economic, Social and Cultural Collaboration and Collective Self-Defence), which incorporated the Low Countries as signatories, and which was later to serve as the basis of the **Western European Union** (WEU). While these treaties listed economic and cultural cooperation as objectives, they were first and foremost mutual security pacts with promises of reciprocal assistance, specifically to guard against possible future German aggression.

While other countries and federalists alike looked to the UK to take a lead, the British attitude towards anything more than cooperation between independent states was consistently negative, at best deeply sceptical, and at worst totally hostile.

By 1948 the Cold War was in full swing. Heightened alarm over events in Central and Eastern Europe helped to consolidate the final marriage between Western Europe and the USA, with the formation of the North Atlantic Treaty Organization (NATO) in 1949. NATO was the conclusion of a programme of American support first outlined in the Truman Doctrine of March 1947, which pledged American assistance for 'free peoples who are resisting subjugation'. It provided a protective shield beneath which Western Europe was free to consider and develop its political and economic options without necessarily having to devote time and scarce resources to military defence. Equally, the USA, itself a federation, saw nothing inherently problematic about closer integration in Western Europe; indeed, also partly because of its own strategic interests, the USA lent its weight after 1947 to proposals for more intensive collaboration. The American commitment was strongly welcomed by the two leading states, the UK and France. But though they were expected to form the vanguard of the European future, neither saw this as leading to radical reconstruction. French European policy was dominated by the need to keep Germany weak and to control its future, a concern met by the military occupation of the country after 1945. The UK was suspicious of anything beyond close collaboration that might diminish its own sovereignty and freedom to act independently.

It was against this backdrop that the protagonists of a federal Europe nevertheless began to receive endorsement from a growing number of senior politicians from several countries (see Chapter 5). Soon, the dominant issue became not whether there should be integration, but rather what form it should take. Governments and political parties took positions on the question of whether this should only be intensive intergovernmental collaboration embedded in formalized treaties and arrangements, or something deeper that would embrace an element of supranationalism and the diminution of national sovereignty. This was the core of the debate at the Congress of Europe in 1948, which led to the establishment of the Council of Europe in 1949 (see Box 2.3).

Political developments were paralleled by activity on the economic front through the introduction of

CASE STUDY 2.3

The establishment of the Council of Europe

The Congress of Europe, a gathering of over 700 delegates or representatives of pro-integration or federalist organizations from 16 countries, along with observers from Canada and the USA, was held at The Hague (in the Netherlands) in May 1948. The Congress was too unwieldy to achieve any practical outcome, not least because it did not speak for governments. But in calling for a European federation or union, with its own institutions, a charter of human rights linked to a European court, a common market, and monetary union, it helped place integration more firmly and visibly on the agenda. It stimulated a process of discussion and debate that culminated in May 1949 in the establishment by ten states of the intergovernmental Council of Europe, the first post-1945 political organization on the continent. The Council, however, represented a victory for those, especially the UK, who wished only cooperation, not integration: decisions would require the consent of all its members, and hence it could not enforce any view or policy upon reluctant member states. Federalists accepted the final outcome of the Council only reluctantly, accepting it as a start that would not preclude a search for something better. By contrast, for others it epitomized the totality of what was desirable or necessary. In seeking to accommodate two very contrasting positions, the product was very much a dead end. More importantly, however, the Council of Europe represented a watershed. It convinced the protagonists of a united Europe that they would have to narrow their horizons even further. It brought the curtain down on the willingness to compromise in order to keep reluctant states and governments on board. It was, therefore, the point at which the post-war belief that the UK should and would take the lead in radical political reorganization came to an end.

the European Recovery Programme, or Marshall Plan. The essence of the Plan was an American offer of economic aid to Europe. The aid, however, was contingent upon the administration of the relief programme being collective, in order to maximize its benefits. The USA further insisted that the European participants in the programme had to decide themselves how aid was to be distributed across the countries involved. These were the basic tasks of the Organization for European Economic Cooperation (OEEC), established in April 1948. The OEEC was primarily concerned with macro-economic cooperation and coordination. Like the Council of Europe, it was intergovernmental in nature, only able to operate with the full consent of all its members. Both organizations, however, had to have some permanent institutions to enable them to perform their allotted functions satisfactorily. While limited in scope and bound very much by the principle of voluntary cooperation, both nevertheless reflected a growing realization in Western Europe of the interdependency of states, and that these states, especially against the backdrop of the Cold War, would prosper or fail together. And both contributed significantly to a learning curve among the participants about how one should go about collaborating. Yet it remained the case that both organizations, in terms of the degree of integration and limitations on national sovereignty, operated on the basis of the lowest common denominator of intergovernmental cooperation. While this clearly met the needs of some states and governments, it was a situation that could not satisfy those who believed in the imperative of union (see Hogan 1987).

KEY POINTS

- The Second World War contributed to a new interest in European unity.
- The first post-1945 governments were more concerned with economic issues than with European integration.
- Federalists and supporters of integration expected the UK, because of its wartime role, to take the lead in reorganizing Europe.
- The Cold War heightened West European fears of insecurity and led to a massive American political and economic involvement in Europe.
- The European international organizations established in the late 1940s were all intergovernmental in nature.

The Community idea

If union were to become a political objective, a different path had to be sought, and federalists had to acknowledge that such a path would prove acceptable to only some countries. The radical redirection of effort was provided by the then French foreign minister, Robert Schuman, who in May 1950 cut through the tangled debate to propose a pooling of coal and steel resources. The Schuman Plan was the blueprint for the European Coal and Steel Community (ECSC), formally established in April 1951 as Western Europe's first organization to involve the yielding of a degree of state sovereignty to a supranational authority (Diebold 1959).

That such a scheme could be proposed, drafted, and turned into reality was the outcome of a combination of shifting circumstances. It had an immediately identifiable and concrete goal, making it more attractive to senior politicians than an instantaneous federal transformation, no matter how strongly they might favour intensive integration. The drafter of the plan had been Jean Monnet, whose experiences as the supremo of national economic planning in France after 1945 had confirmed his long-held view that economic development and prosperity could best be achieved at a European rather than a national level, and that therefore the route to political integration was a long road that inevitably lay through economics. Equally importantly, Monnet had also consistently argued that peace and stability in Europe could be achieved only through a rapprochement between the historic rivals, France and Germany; for Monnet the two states had to form the core of any integrative venture. These were views to which Schuman also strongly subscribed. He was able to persuade his governmental colleagues in Paris of their virtues in part because of further changes in the international environment.

Relations between East and West had reached a nadir in 1948. One consequence was the decision by the USA, backed by the UK and a reluctant France, to form a German state out of the western military zones of occupation in the country. This decision and the establishment of an independent Federal Republic of Germany in 1949 destroyed at a stroke the foundation of France's post-1945 European policy. In addition, the compensatory decision to establish an International Ruhr Authority in April 1949 to supervise coal and steel production in West Germany's dominant industrial region failed to satisfy anyone. In 1950, with the Ruhr Authority increasingly ineffectual and on the point of being abandoned, Monnet's ideas offered France a way out of the dilemma, by indicating a strategy by which the new West Germany could be subject to external influence while it was still politically weak. Schuman's proposal proved equally attractive to the West German leader, Konrad Adenauer, who saw it as a potentially valuable element of his policy of tying the Federal Republic firmly to Western Europe politically, economically, and militarily. Submerging the country in European ventures, he hoped, would further reassure his neighbours that West Germany had abandoned the aggressive nationalism of the past. It is not insignificant that Schuman's announcement was for a structure enabling the pooling of French and West German coal and steel resources, which other countries were welcome to join if they wished. He further made it clear that a new structure would be created even if no other state wished to join: 'if necessary, we shall go ahead with only two [countries]'. Be that as it may, the Schuman Plan was overtly about more than just coal and steel: Schuman emphasized that it would set down 'common bases for economic development as a first step in the federation of Europe'.

Hence, the formation of the European Coal and Steel Community (ECSC) was the product of a combination of integrationist impulses and ideas, national self-interest, and international circumstances. Hailed by Jean Monnet as 'the first expression of the Europe that is being born', the ECSC set in motion a groundswell that some 40 years later was to result in the European Union. While an invitation to join the new body was extended to all West European states, and especially the UK, only four other countries – Belgium, Italy, Luxembourg, and the Netherlands – felt able to accept the supranational principle of the ECSC. The institutional structure adopted by the ECSC – which included a supreme judicial authority – was to serve as a model for all future developments. The most innovative (and in the future a highly contentious) feature was the divided executive and decision-making structure: a High Authority vested with significant power to represent and uphold the supranational principle, and a Council of Ministers to represent and protect the interests of the governments of the member states (Poidevin and Spierenburg 1994).

But if the ECSC were to be merely the first step towards full union, more had to be done. Monnet himself saw the ECSC as the opening phase of a process of sectoral integration, where the ultimate goal of political union would be the long-term culmination of an accretion of integrative efforts, of trust and experience, in a sector-by-sector linkage of specific economic areas and activities that ultimately would result in a common economic market (see Chapter 16). Discussions began more or less immediately on what – for example, transport or agriculture – would and should follow on from coal and steel as the next instances of sectoral economic integration.

The ECSC survived as a separate entity until 1967 when the merged European Communities (EC) was created. Its record of economic success, however, was rather mixed. Even though Jean Monnet had been appointed head of the High Authority, the latter failed to bring national coal and steel policies and practices fully under its control, and it had little or no control over or effect on other economic sectors. By themselves, these issues might in time have forced a re-evaluation of the strategy of sectoral integration. In the event, the direction taken by the latter was altogether surprising. The determining factor was a further transformation in the international climate, which had once again changed for the worse as armed conflict broke out in Korea during the ECSC negotiations. Concerned that the Asian war might be a prelude to war in Europe, the USA called for a strengthening of NATO, while simultaneously stressing that because of its global role and commitments, America itself could not provide the necessary additional resources. When the European members of NATO argued that their economies were too weak to bear substantial additional defence costs, the USA proposed a West German military contribution to NATO.

Only a few years after the overthrow of Nazism, the idea of a German army alarmed its neighbours. In France, the possibility of West German rearmament threatened once again to undermine the core of its European policy. Yet, prompted by Jean Monnet, who saw sectoral integration as a solution to the dilemma, the French government proposed a European Defence Community (EDC), modelled upon the ECSC, which would establish a Western European army that would include military units from all the member states, including West Germany. However, the exercise failed when the French National Assembly refused to take a decision to ratify the Treaty in 1954 (see Box 2.4).

The consequences for integration of the EDC debacle seemed to be severe. It proved to be the high-water mark of the sectoral approach to integration. Only the ECSC survived the damage to the integration cause, and there were fears that it too would collapse. A somewhat disillusioned Jean Monnet announced his attention not to seek reappointment as President of the ECSC High Authority in order to pursue the goal of integration as a private citizen. However, there remained across Western Europe a substantial degree of institutional cooperation built up over the previous decade: NATO, OEEC, the Council of Europe, and, of course, the ECSC. Within these networks there had survived in the little Europe of the ECSC Six a strong commitment to further integration. At a meeting of their foreign ministers at Messina in Sicily in June 1955, the six members of the ECSC took a decisive step forward. Taking as their core text the 1952 Dutch proposal for abolition of quotas and tariffs within, and the introduction of a common external tariff for, the Community area, the foreign ministers agreed to launch 'a fresh advance towards the building of Europe'. This set in motion progress towards plans for a **customs union** and, ultimately, a **common market**, plans which culminated in March 1957 with the Treaty of Rome and the formation of the European Economic Community (EEC). Again, however, only the six members of the ECSC were willing to commit themselves to the leap of faith demanded by the Rome treaty.

KEY POINTS

- The Schuman Plan offered both a way in which France and the Federal Republic of Germany could become reconciled with each other, and a path towards integration that went beyond intergovernmental cooperation.
- The European Coal and Steel Community (ECSC) was the first step in an anticipated process of sectoral economic integration. It brought together six states that delegated some aspects of their sovereignty to a supranational authority.
- Hostility to, and the ultimate rejection of plans for, a European Defence Community (EDC) by France led to its abandonment. The failure of the EDC contributed towards a discrediting of the sectoral strategy and threatened to destroy the whole process of integration.
- In 1955 the ECSC states launched a rescue operation and committed themselves to further integration, signing the Treaty of Rome two years later.

CASE STUDY 2.4

The European Defence Community

Under plans for a European Defence Community (EDC) German units would be part of a European army, all falling under an integrated European, and not an independent West German, command. The other member states would have only a proportion of their armed forces within the EDC framework. The EDC proposal was immediately seen by federalists and others as a significant second step towards integration. However, the question of the desirability or necessity of some form of political control over and direction of an EDC soon led to arguments for a European Political Community (EPC), something which would short-circuit sectoral integration by an immediate advance towards creating a comprehensive federation. The Dutch foreign minister, Johan Willem Beyen, took the argument one step further in 1952, suggesting a parallel drive to economic unity. Arguing that sectoral integration by itself was insufficient for economic development and unity, Beyen proposed that the EDC/EPC nexus be extended to embrace the construction of a customs union and common market (see Chapter 16).

Only the ECSC countries were willing to explore these possible new ventures. The UK declined a specific invitation to join the EDC, but because it wished NATO to be strengthened, it indicated support for a European army that would include a West German military contribution. The EPC idea remained at the draft stage, and Beyen's ideas were largely put on hold because it was clear, not least in the minds of supporters of further integration, that any advance down that road was dependent upon the success or failure of ratification of the EDC by the national parliaments of the proposed members. Ironically, the stumbling block was France, where the idea of a rearmed Germany, even within the EDC, remained deeply perturbing. France had originally wanted, and perhaps had expected, the UK to be part of the new organization as an extra guarantee against any possible resurgence of German militarism, the well-known British hostility to anything that smacked of supranationalism notwithstanding. In a sense, the French proposal for an EDC had been, for many of its politicians, a delaying tactic, perhaps even an idea so outrageous in its audacity that it would become mired in years of debate and argument. The extent to which the notion was embraced both within the ECSC states and beyond, and the speed at which the subsequent talks progressed, placed successive French governments, all short-lived, weak, and concerned more with mere survival than innovation, in a quandary. Confronted by strong political and popular opposition, all were unable or unwilling to make the effort to secure a parliamentary majority for EDC ratification (Aron and Lerner 1957).

After almost four years of stalemate France rejected the EDC in 1954 on a technicality (the vote was not on whether the treaty should be approved, but whether the parliament wished to discuss the treaty). With it fell the hopes for an EPC. The vote did not remove the issue of West German rearmament from the agenda. In a frantic search to salvage something from the wreckage, agreement was secured on a British proposal to revamp the 1948 Treaty of Brussels, bringing into it all the projected members of the EDC. A new body, the Western European Union (WEU), was established, linking together the UK and the ECSC states in a defence arrangement within which West German rearmament would occur. In reality, the WEU remained more or less moribund until the 1980s, and a rearmed West Germany entered NATO as a full and equal member. The outcome, therefore, was the one result which France had hoped to avoid by its advocacy of an EDC.

Rome and the stalling of ambition

Because the new organization was to range over an extremely wide area of activity, the provisions of the Treaty of Rome were necessarily complex. Its preamble may have been less prescriptive than that of its ECSC predecessor, yet, in referring to the determination 'to lay the foundations of an ever closer union among the peoples of Europe', its implications were far-reaching. More specifically, the Treaty enjoined its signatories, among other things, to establish a common market, defined as the free movement of goods, persons, services, and capital, to approximate national economic policies, and to develop common policies, most specifically in agriculture. Although the objectives of the Treaty were expressed in economic terms, as the preamble implied, a political purpose lay behind them. In

CHRONOLOGY 2.5

Key dates in European integration, 1958–85

1958	January	Establishment of the EEC and Euratom
1959	January	First tariff cuts made by the EEC
1961	July	Fouchet Plan for a 'union of states' proposed
1961	July–August	The UK, Denmark, and Ireland apply for EEC membership
1962	January	EEC develops basic regulations for a Common Agricultural Policy (CAP)
	May	Norway applies for EEC membership
1963	January	President de Gaulle vetoes British membership; signature of Franco-West German Treaty of Friendship and Reconciliation
1965	April	Treaty merging the executives of the three Communities signed in Brussels
	June	France walks out of the Council of Ministers and begins a boycott of EEC institutions
1966	January	The Luxembourg Compromise ends the French boycott
1967	July	The three Communities merge to form the European Community
	November	President de Gaulle vetoes British membership for the second time
1968	July	The EC establishes a customs union and agrees on a Common Agricultural Policy (CAP)
1969	December	The Hague summit agrees to consider EC enlargement and supports greater policy cooperation and economic and monetary union
1970	October	Werner Report on economic and monetary union; Davignon Report on foreign policy cooperation leads to establishment of European Political Cooperation (EPC)
1972	March	The currency 'snake' established, limiting margins of fluctuation between participating currencies
1973	January	Accession of the UK, Denmark, and Ireland
1974	December	Paris summit agrees to establish the European Council and accepts the principle of direct elections to the European Parliament
1976	January	Tindemans Report published, recommending reform of the EC institutions
1979	March	Establishment of the European Monetary System (EMS)
	June	First direct elections to the EP
1983	June	Signature of Solemn Declaration on European Union by the heads of state and government
1984	February	EP approves the Draft Treaty Regarding European Union
	June	Fontainebleau summit of the European Council agrees to take action on a number of outstanding issues hindering progress on integration
1985	March	European Council agrees to the establishment of a single market by the end of 1992
	June	European Council agrees on a reform of the Treaty of Rome

aiming ultimately to create something more than a common market, the Treaty emphasized the principle that the problems of one member state would be the problems of all.

The institutional structure was modelled on that of the ECSC, with the **quasi-executive** and supranational European Commission intended to be the motor force of integration; its authority was counterbalanced by the Council of Ministers representing the member states. Facing these executive bodies was a much weaker Assembly with little in the way of significant decision-making powers. The Assembly, which quickly adopted for itself the title of European Parliament (EP), was soon engaged in a perpetual struggle to enlarge its own authority, including a demand for implementation of the Treaty provision on direct elections. The final major EEC institution was the European Court of Justice (ECJ) which rapidly, not least by its ruling that EEC law took precedence over national law, asserted itself as a major bonding force. The new EEC shared its assembly and court with the ECSC and the less significant European Atomic Energy Community (Euratom), also set up in 1957 by a second Treaty of Rome to promote collaboration on the development of nuclear energy for peaceful economic purposes. The three Communities retained separate executive structures until 1967 when they were merged to form the European Communities (EC).

The Treaty of Rome set a target for its objectives. Within specified time limits the implementation and completion of a customs union, and then a common market, were to be achieved through a three-stage process. The auguries were initially bright. Under the leadership of a proactive Commission, early progress towards the goals of Rome was satisfactory. By 1961 EEC internal tariff barriers had been substantially reduced and quota restrictions on industrial products largely eliminated. Towards the end of the decade the EEC could proudly claim that the customs union had been implemented ahead of schedule. Internal EEC trade flourished, rates of economic growth were impressive, and work had begun on establishing a common agricultural policy. These positive advances raised hopes among those committed to the establishment of a political union that that goal might also be expedited. Indeed, Walter Hallstein, the forceful West German statesman and economist who served as President of the Commission from 1958 to 1967, could inform journalists that perhaps he should be regarded as a kind of Western European prime minister. The optimism, however, proved to be premature. Broadly speaking, the transformation of the EEC into a common market was scheduled to be spread over a period of 12 to 15 years. By the early 1970s, however, the EEC was seemingly no nearer that goal than it had been a decade earlier. A series of circumstances had led to its derailment.

The issues that the EEC was obliged to confront in the 1960s were issues that have remained central ever since. In simple terms, they related to the **deepening** and **widening** of the Community: the extent to which, and the rate at which, more intensive integration should be pursued, and how these aspects of integration should relate to the **enlargement** of the EEC. The specific context in which these issues emerged in the 1960s had a focal point in the French President, **Charles de Gaulle**. While he was generally supportive of the EEC as a means of retaining French influence in Western Europe, forging in particular a close relationship with **Konrad Adenauer** and the German economic giant across the Rhine in 1963, de Gaulle was suspicious of anything that might affect that influence and undermine French sovereignty. In 1961 he had tried to push the EEC down a somewhat different route, floating the idea of a 'Union of States' that would entail the incorporation of the EEC into a new intergovernmental organization for the coordination of foreign and defence policy. His proposal was given detailed institutional flesh in the subsequent **Fouchet Plan**. But the idea received at best little support outside West Germany, and was rejected in 1962 after a series of acrimonious meetings. While the smaller EEC members were concerned about being presented with some kind of Franco-German fait accompli, the episode merely added extra substance to de Gaulle's long-standing suspicions that the

EEC, or anything like it, might well act as a brake on his ambitions for France.

Two further episodes heightened the mood of crisis. First, the immediate economic success of the EEC as a trading bloc after 1958 had persuaded other Western European states that had previously rejected involvement to revise their opinion and seek membership. The most important candidate was the United Kingdom, which applied for membership in 1961. In 1963, and again in 1967, de Gaulle, against the wishes of his five partners, vetoed the British application on the grounds that the country, because of its Commonwealth links and close relationship with the USA, was not sufficiently committed either politically or economically to Europe or to EEC objectives. Although not subject to a veto, the other applicant states declined to proceed without the UK. Secondly, according to the schedule set by the Treaty of Rome, the EEC was expected to take some decisive decisions in 1966, including a move to an extension of qualified majority voting (QMV) in the Council of Ministers. At the same time the EEC was faced with approving financial arrangements for the Common Agricultural Policy (CAP) and a Commission proposal for enhancing supranational authority by giving more powers to itself and the EP. The latter proposal clearly involved a diminution of national sovereignty, as would any extension of QMV which would reduce the number of areas where unanimity across the member states was necessary. Instead, for many decisions a two-thirds majority would suffice, with the result that a state could be outvoted but not block the decision by exercising a veto. While the Treaty of Rome had envisaged a steady diminution of the right of a member state to exercise a veto, de Gaulle was not prepared to accept the increased risk of France being outvoted in key decisions. In 1965 he provoked a crisis by withdrawing all French participation in Council of Ministers business except for that dealing with low-level and routine technicalities. The EEC almost ground to a halt. The crisis was resolved only by the Luxembourg Compromise of 1966 (see Box 2.6).

CASE STUDY 2.6

The Luxembourg Compromise

The Luxembourg Compromise (or Luxembourg Agreement) is the name often given to the agreement among the then six member states of the European Community, concluding the 'empty chair crisis' of 1965. The agreement stated that in cases of the vital national interest of one of the member states the Council would aim to find a consensus solution, thus creating a de facto veto right.

The Compromise had practical effects for both the Council and the Commission. In the case of the Council, member states were more willing to accept an extension of majority voting, knowing that in the final instance they could invoke the Luxembourg Compromise and veto unwanted legislation. In the case of the Commission, it meant that this institution had to make more of an effort to ensure that its proposals would not impact upon the vital interests of any member state. In so doing, it made the Commission much more cautious in its policy proposals. These effects were felt despite the fact that the Luxembourg Compromise was never recognized by the European Court of Justice as legally binding.

Overall, the results of de Gaulle's actions seemed to indicate that political integration, as advocated by federalists, was off the agenda, and that the future development of the EC would be more as an intergovernmental grouping of independent states. This shift of emphasis and mood seemed to be symbolized by the 1967 resignation of Hallstein as Commission President. To some extent, the early rapid progress after 1958 had been possible not only because of favourable internal and external economic conditions, but also because, apart from the furore over the Fouchet Plan, national leaders had remained relatively uninvolved in EEC business, being content to allow the Commission to push things forward. If, however, future progress was to be governed by the Luxembourg Compromise, a more positive national governmental input would be required. But even that might be insufficient as long as Charles de Gaulle remained in power. Hence, any way forward had to await the French President's retirement in 1969.

KEY POINTS

- The Treaty of Rome (1957) set out a plan and schedule for a customs union and common market as a prelude to some form of political union.
- In the 1960s the European Economic Community (EEC) was faced by issues of deepening and widening the Community structure, with a division of opinion emerging between France and its five partners.
- In 1965 a serious dispute between France and the other member states over institutional change crippled the EEC. It was resolved by the Luxembourg Compromise.

The emergence of summits

In 1969, at a summit meeting in The Hague in the Netherlands intended to discuss the options open to the EC, the six heads of government attempted to restore some momentum to the stalled organization. The Hague summit opened the way for the enlargement of the EC, especially for the British. It agreed to extend the budgetary competence of the European Parliament (EP), and argued for more common policy. It also called for a move towards Economic and Monetary Union (EMU), initially through an exchange rate system for the EC, as an important step towards the ultimate goal of political union (see Chapter 20). In practice, the Hague meeting inaugurated summitry as a new style of EC decision-making, recognizing that integration could develop further only if it was able to reconcile itself with national concerns. Summitry, that is, the use of European summits to set the political agenda of the Community, was to be formalized and placed on a regular footing with the establishment of the European Council in 1974 as a meeting place for the leaders of national governments (see Chapter 10).

Achievement of the objectives declaimed at The Hague was only partially successful. The first enlargement of the EC duly occurred in 1973 with the accession of the UK, Denmark, and Ireland (Nicholson and East 1987). The other candidate for membership in the 1960s, Norway, had already withdrawn from the final negotiations as a result of a referendum in 1972 which, against government advice, had rejected EC membership. Equally, the EC began to be able to assert a more positive and united presence in international affairs. Represented by the Commission, it spoke with one voice in international trade negotiations, and after the 1970 Davignon Report on policy cooperation, the member states, through European Political Co-operation (EPC), developed an impressive and on balance quite successful structure and pattern of collaboration on, and coordination of, foreign policy (see Chapter 15). After the mid-1970s, two structural funds, the European Regional Development Fund (ERDF) and the European Social Fund (ESF), began to play an important role in providing aid for economic and employment restructuring. The CAP had also come fully on stream in 1972, though in its final form it developed as a protectionist device that shielded European farmers from the full impact of market forces and from the necessity of taking markets and demand into account when planning production (see Chapter 21).

However, while the balance sheet around the end of the 1970s did feature many positive aspects, there was also a debit side. The achievements gained could not disguise the fact that on the broader front of the ambitions of the Treaty of Rome the EC still seemed to be marking time. A common market seemed to be as far away as ever, with the prospect of political union even more remote. The major integrative impetus propounded at the Hague summit had been Economic and Monetary Union (EMU). The leaders had set up a committee under the Luxembourg premier, Pierre Werner, to put some flesh on the proposal. The Werner Report of 1970 outlined a three-stage process for the full implementation of EMU by 1980 (see Chapter 20).

The decade, however, had not progressed very far before this rekindling of ambition was thwarted. In 1972 the EC did attempt to establish a European zone of stability by imposing limits on how far EC currencies would be permitted to float against each other (the so-called snake), but this barely got off the ground. Undermined not least by the quadrupling of oil prices in 1973 – the consequence of war in the Middle East – the snake structure was already dead when it was abandoned in 1976. In addition, the EC experienced both rapidly growing unemployment and inflation in the 1970s. The consequent political and electoral pressures forced governments to turn more to national issues and national defence. Some stabilization was eventually achieved after 1979 with the relaunch – sponsored by the European Council – of a monetary policy. The European Monetary System (EMS) did, through an Exchange Rate Mechanism (ERM), have currency stabilization as an objective. However, by itself the EMS could not achieve monetary union. It was a more modest design and could only be a first step on the road back to EMU. In the 1980s the EMS was deemed, perhaps because of its modesty, to have had some success in curbing currency fluctuations, inflation, and unemployment, thereby contributing to the return of EMU to the central EC agenda in 1989 (see Chapter 20).

On the broader integrative front, the initiative had passed firmly to the European Council. Its formation in 1974 confirmed the central role that had to be adopted by the heads of government in determining the future path of the EC. More specifically, it brought to an apogee the Franco-German axis that lay at the core of the EC that had been, two decades earlier, an essential sub-theme for people like Monnet and Schuman. Formalized in a Treaty of Friendship and Reconciliation in 1963, the relationship and its significance for the EC was to become far more overt in the 1970s. While the two states might not always be able to impose their will upon their partners, their active consent was vital for any progress to be made. Although the leaders of the two states, Valéry Giscard d'Estaing and Helmut Schmidt, accepted the need to utilize and develop the EC as an instrument of pragmatic integration, both tended to evaluate ideas in terms of national interest and were seemingly reluctant to pursue an advanced federalist route. That Franco-German drive had to await the arrival in power of François Mitterrand and Helmut Kohl in 1981 and 1982 respectively (Simonian 1985). With the Commission seemingly downgraded and kept firmly on a short leash, the real achievements that were made could not conceal the fact that the EC was not progressing, or at least was doing so only minimally, towards the aims of the Treaty of Rome.

Nevertheless, the EC, and the European Council in particular, continued to pay lip-service to the ideal of full economic and political union. From its commissioning of the 1976 Tindemans Report, which recommended strengthening the EC institutions and the adoption of more common policies, through to its 1983 Solemn Declaration on European Union, the European Council sponsored studies on how to advance the cause of union or rhetorically reasserted its faith in the ultimate goal. In 1974, the Council of Ministers had eventually agreed to implement the Rome requirement that the European Parliament (EP) should be elected directly by the national electorates. The first direct elections were held in 1979. They gave the EP a sense of greater legitimacy, a feeling that it now had a mandate to review existing structures and to urge the EC to progress to a more cohesive and genuine union. With its moves coordinated by the veteran federalist, Altiero Spinelli, who had been elected to the Parliament, the EP produced a Draft Treaty Establishing the European Union. While the European Council took no immediate action on the EP proposals, the Treaty nevertheless provided a working basis for and contributed towards the developments that within a decade led to the establishment of the European Union (EU).

Ultimately, however, initiative and commitment had to come from the European Council. To do so, it needed to deal with a growing number of issues that it had earlier sought to shelve or avoid: the EC's budget and how national contributions to it were determined; the burgeoning costs, problems, and distorting consequences of the Common Agricultural Policy (CAP); the need to consider and develop further common policies; future enlargements; and a more detailed and positive response to how the EC should fit into a rapidly changing international world. Indeed, adapting to the international environment seemed to increase in urgency in the 1980s. European leaders began to worry that in a new economic era of high technology, which required massive investment, Western Europe was already lagging far behind the market leaders of the USA and Japan, Increasingly, the argument was heard that European survival and competitiveness in this brave new world could be achieved only through cooperation and a common front.

Moreover, the EC states had become alarmed in the late 1970s by an increasingly bellicose Soviet foreign policy that it feared might destabilize the West European status quo. After 1980 they became equally alarmed at the aggressive American response, fearing that they might be dragged into conflict by an American policy over which they had no influence. After 1985 and the arrival of Mikhail Gorbachev as leader of the USSR, the two superpowers began to talk to each other about means of reducing tension and accommodating each other's interests. Almost predictably, the EC states began to express concerns that the two superpowers might reach an agreement that would not take their interests into account.

This international background provided, as it often had done in previous decades, a necessary stimulus for more visible activity on the domestic West European front. Partly by choice and partly by necessity, European Council sessions turned to internal matters. At the core of this new activity was President Mitterrand of France. After the failure of his initial attempts to reflate the French economy after 1981, Mitterrand concluded that recuperation could more readily be achieved by means of European integration, especially when working in close harness with West Germany. With the encouragement of Mitterrand and others, there emerged, in short, a new sense of direction and purpose. In 1984 the Fontainebleau summit meeting of the European Council reached agreement on tackling a backlog of issues that had hitherto stalled the integration progress. With these agreements behind them, members of the European Council were able to take a series of decisions intended to advance the cause of union. They agreed to the establishment of a single internal market by the end of 1992 and to a major revision of the Treaty of Rome. In so doing, they pushed the EC decisively towards a more intense economic integration, the Treaty on European Union, and the establishment of the EU (see Chapter 3).

KEY POINTS

- The Hague summit of 1969 opened the way for the admission of new members to the EC and agreed to seek new initiatives in policy cooperation, especially economic and monetary union.
- The practice of summitry was institutionalized by the establishment of the European Council in 1974.
- In 1984 the European Council reached agreement on several important outstanding issues. This permitted it the following year to consider future developments. It committed the EC to a single internal market and a major overhaul of the Treaty of Rome. These initiatives were helped by concerns that Western Europe's international status, both political and economic, had declined.

Conclusion

The story of the events which led to the Treaty of Rome, and then to its reform in the 1980s, do not portray an inevitable and steady progression towards European union. Behind the rhetoric of inexorable progress towards the goal of 'an ever closer union', there lies a rather more complex reality. Thus, it might be more appropriate to liken the story of integration to a roller-coaster ride, where the uphill and downhill gradients that determined the speed of the ride were the product of a multitude of factors.

The history of the formative decades of European integration was the product of an array of complex interactions. The world of ideas and the agitation of committed federalists had to contend with and were counterbalanced by the roles played by national leaders and governments and their assessment of how developments and proposals might impinge upon national self-interest. No matter how intricate the consequent dance, the steps and routines were influenced by and contained within parameters set by the broader flows of the international political and economic environment. And at the heart of this complex product lay the health of the relationship between France and West Germany. When all, or perhaps only most, of these factors were in positive conjunction with each other, progress could be rapid, significant, and impressive. When they were not, the process of integration was more likely merely to mark time.

? QUESTIONS

1. Why did it prove difficult to establish a momentum for integration in the years immediately following the end of the Second World War ?
2. How important was the development of international European organizations between 1945 and 1950 as a necessary condition for European integration?
3. What lessons for the future could be adduced from the strategy of sectoral integration in the 1950s?
4. To what extent does the failure of the European Defence Community (EDC) suggest that there are some areas of policy that are not amenable to integration?
5. How important were the crises of the 1960s in shaping the future development of the European Community?
6. How important was the establishment of the European Council as a mechanism for promoting further integration in the European Community?
7. To what extent was a collaboration between France and the Federal Republic of Germany necessary for a process of integration to begin?
8. To what extent has the international political and economic environment stimulated or hindered processes of integration?

GUIDE TO FURTHER READING

■ **Arter, D. *The Politics of European Integration in the Twentieth Century* (Aldershot: Dartmouth, 1993)**. A broad historical survey which also considers developments in Eastern Europe.

■ **Burgess, M. *Federalism and European Union: The Building of Europe, 1945–2000* (London: Routledge, 2000)**. A detailed revisionist history of the development of integration which highlights the central role of federalist ideas and influences.

■ **Duignan, P., and Gann, L. H. *The United States and the New Europe 1945–1993* (Oxford: Blackwell, 1994)**. A general survey which examines European developments from an American strategic and policy perspective.

■ **Fursdon, E. *The European Defence Community* (Basingstoke: Macmillan, 1980)**. A rigorous and detailed analysis of the EDC proposals, especially from a military perspective.

■ **Milward, A. S. *The Reconstruction of Western Europe 1945–1951* (London: Methuen, 1984); and Milward, A. S. *The European Rescue of the Nation State* (London: Routledge, 1992)**. Two controversial revisionist analyses of the first post-war decades which argue for the pivotal role of national governments and national self-interest as the driving force of integration.

■ **Pryce, R. (ed.) *The Dynamics of European Union* (London: Croom Helm, 1987)**. A collection of useful analyses on specific episodes in the history of the EC when political union was on the agenda.

■ **Stirk, P. M., and Willis, D. (eds) *Shaping Postwar Europe* (London: Pinter, 1991)**. A collection of useful chapters surveying the various arguments and different kinds of integration sought from 1945 up to the formation of the European Community.

■ **Urwin, D. W. *The Community of Europe* (London: Longman, 1995)**. A broad introductory survey of the post-1945 history of European cooperation and integration.

■ **Urwin, D. W. *A Political History of Western Europe since 1945* (London: Longman, 1997)**. A broad historical survey in which EC developments are reviewed in parallel with international issues and national politics.

IMPORTANT WEBSITES

● **www.let.leidenuniv.nl/history/rtg/res1/** Leiden University's History Department has an interesting site on the history of European integration.

● **http://europa.eu.int/abc/history/index-en.htm** The EU's own website includes a good chronology of events in the history of the European integration process.

● **www.iue.it/LIB/SISSCO/UL/hist-eur-integration/Index.html** The European University Institute in Florence has a European integration history project which includes some helpful links.

● **www.lib.berkeley.edu/GSSI/eu.html** The University of California at Berkeley runs this general EU gateway, which includes links to historical documents and research papers on the history of the EC.

Visit the Online Resource Centre that accompanies this book for lots of interesting additional material. http://www.oxfordtextbooks.co.uk/orc/cini2e/

3 Towards European Union

DAVID PHINNEMORE

Chapter Contents

Reader's Guide

The focus of this chapter is the emergence and development of the European Union (EU). Key issues include the significance for the idea of 'union' of the Single European Act (1986), the Treaty on European Union (TEU) (1992), and the pillar structure of the EU. The chapter also examines the origins and impact on the EU of the Treaty of Amsterdam (1997) and the Treaty of Nice (2000), presenting their key reforms and assessing the extent to which they contribute to the idea of the EU as a 'union'. The chapter also introduces the 'Future of Europe' debate launched in 2001, which led to the adoption of the Treaty establishing a Constitution for Europe (2004).

Introduction

The underlying theme of this chapter is that the EU is less than its title implies. This is obviously the case when one considers the use of the term 'European'. There are many different definitions of what 'European' means, not least in the geographical sense. And no matter which definition one adopts, there can be little doubt that the EU in 2006, even now with 25 members, still does not cover all European states. This is something that has been recognized, most obviously in Article 49 TEU, which allows any 'European' state to seek membership of the EU. It is also evident in the prominence given to enlargement over the last decade.

This chapter is not, however, concerned with the question of the EU's membership and geographical coverage (see Chapter 26). Its focus is more on the extent to which the EU is a 'union'. For although it has long been the goal of the member states to create a European 'union', the extent to which it has achieved this is open to question. Indeed, whereas 'union' might conjure up ideas of coherence and uniformity, the EU today is characterized very much by variation and diversity. This is recognized not just by academics and other commentators, but also by the EU's institutions and its member states. Hence, voices are often heard calling for change. It is in part the desire to ensure that the EU behaves and acts as a 'union' that is behind the ongoing process of treaty reform – or constitutionalization – which has dominated the EU's agenda since the mid-1980s. Indeed, since the TEU was agreed in December 1991, a further three treaties have been agreed. All have sought to reform the EU (see Box 3.1).

What this chapter does, then, is discuss the structure of the EU and how this has been affected by certain key developments over the last 15 years. The chapter examines not only the origins of the EU, but also the background to and content of the Treaty of Amsterdam (1997) and the Treaty of Nice (2000). In between discussing how these have changed the EU and impacted on the idea of 'union', consideration is given to the significance of the launch of EMU, a process which simultaneously promoted closer union and differentiated integration within the EU, thus suggesting that member states may integrate in different ways or at different speeds in the future (see Chapter 24). The chapter concludes by introducing the issues that the EU and its member states sought to address as part of the 'Future of Europe' debate that eventually led to the drafting of the Constitutional Treaty (see Chapter 4). Before then, however, the EU as a 'union' and the TEU need to be considered.

CHRONOLOGY 3.1

Key events, 1986–2004

1986	Single European Act signed (17 and 28 February)
1987	Single European Act enters into force (1 July)
1991	Maastricht European Council agrees Treaty on European Union (9–10 December)
1992	Treaty on European Union signed (7 February)
1993	European Union established (1 November)
1996	1996 IGC launched (29 March)
1997	Amsterdam European Council agrees Treaty of Amsterdam (16–17 June) Agenda 2000 published (15 July) Treaty of Amsterdam signed (2 October)
1999	Stage III of EMU launched (1 January) Treaty of Amsterdam enters into force (1 May)
2000	2000 IGC launched (14 February) Nice European Council agrees Treaty of Nice (7–11 December)
2001	Treaty of Nice signed (26 February) Laeken European Council adopts Declaration on the Future of the Union (14–15 December)
2002	Introduction of the euro (1 January) Launch of the European Convention (28 March)
2003	Treaty of Nice enters into force (1 February)

The European Union as a European union

The idea of creating a European 'union' has long been a goal of states committed to European integration. This was made clear in the 1950s when the six original members of the European Economic Community (EEC) expressed their determination in the first recital of the preamble to the Treaty of Rome 'to lay the foundations of an ever closer union among the peoples' (see Box 3.2). They reaffirmed this in 1972 when they expressed their intention to convert 'their entire relationship into a European Union before the end of the decade'. In joining them in the European Communities (EC), new members from 1973 (Denmark, Ireland, and the United Kingdom), 1981 (Greece), and 1986 (Portugal and Spain) also signed up to this goal. And reaffirmation of the commitment was central to the Solemn Declaration on European Union proclaimed at the Stuttgart European Council in June 1983 and, in part, inspired the Single European Act (SEA) of 1986. This, as its preamble noted, was adopted in response to the member states' desire to 'to transform' their relations into 'a European Union', to 'implement' this new entity and invest it 'with the necessary means of action'.

KEY CONCEPTS AND TERMS 3.2

European Union and European union

Note the use of the word 'union' in these two treaty clauses

DETERMINED to lay the foundations of an ever closer union among the peoples of Europe

Preamble, Treaty of Rome (1957)

By this Treaty, the HIGH CONTRACTING PARTIES establish among themselves a EUROPEAN UNION, hereinafter called 'the Union'

Article 1, Treaty on European Union (1992)

The Single European Act (SEA)

The SEA brought about some significant reforms to the Treaty of Rome. In terms of policies, it introduced a range of formally new competences (environment, research and development, economic and social cohesion); established a deadline for the completion of the internal market and facilitated the adoption of harmonized legislation to achieve this; committed the member states to cooperate on the convergence of economic and monetary policy; and expanded social policy competences to include health and safety in the workplace and dialogue between management and labour. As regards the institutions, it expanded the decision-making role of the European Parliament (EP) through the introduction of the cooperation procedure to cover mainly internal market issues and the assent procedure governing association agreements and accession. It also extended the use of qualified majority voting (QMV) in the Council; allowed the Council to confer implementation powers on the Commission; and established a Court of First Instance (CFI) to assist the Court of Justice in its work. In addition, it gave formal recognition to the European Council and European Political Cooperation (EPC), the latter being the forerunner of the Common Foreign and Security Policy (CFSP) and now having its own dedicated secretariat. The fact that neither the European Council nor EPC were technically part of the was reflective of member states' differences on how much supranational integration they were willing to pursue. For some, there was a clear preference for intergovernmental cooperation. Evidently, the desire for a European 'union' was not universal.

The establishment of the EU was not, however, far off. Despite being a very brief document and one that failed in many respects to meet the aspirations

CASE STUDY 3.3

From Intergovernmental Conference (IGC) to Treaty

The European Union and the European Community were both established by constitutive treaties concluded between their founding member states. If the current member states wish to reform the EU or the EC they need to amend the constitutive treaties. This is done via an intergovernmental conference (IGC) where the member states negotiate amendments. Agreed amendments are then brought together in an amending treaty which all member states must sign and ratify. Ratification normally involves each member state's parliament approving the treaty by vote. In some member states, either for procedural or political reasons, treaties are also put to a referendum.

of **integrationists**, the SEA and the launch of the initiative to complete the internal market by the end of 1992 ushered in a period of renewed dynamism for the EC during the second half of the 1980s. At the time, calls for further steps towards European union were being made by senior European leaders such as the French President, François Mitterrand, and the German Chancellor, Helmut Kohl, as well as by the Commission President, Jacques Delors. All this plus the collapse of communist regimes in Central and Eastern Europe in 1989, the end of the Cold War, and the prospect of German unification led in 1990 to the launch of two **intergovernmental conferences (IGCs)** (see Box 3.3), one on EMU and a second on political union. Out of these emerged the Treaty on European Union (TEU).

CASE STUDY 3.4

The Treaty on European Union

The impact of the Treaty on European Union (TEU) on the process of achieving 'ever closer union' was considerable. Most significantly it formally established the EU. In addition it promoted European integration in a whole variety of ways whether through the promotion of cooperation in the two new intergovernmental pillars on foreign and security policy and justice and home affairs or through the expansion of EC activities. Indeed, thanks to the TEU, the EC was given new competences in the fields of education, culture, public health, consumer protection, trans-European networks, industry, and development cooperation. Citizenship of the EU was also established. And, of course, the TEU set out the timetable for EMU by 1999. As for existing competences, some were expanded, notably in the areas of social policy, the environment, and economic and social cohesion, although in an attempt to assuage concerns of over-centralization of power, the principle of subsidiarity was introduced. Moreover, the TEU saw the establishment of new institutions and bodies including the European Central Bank, the Committee of the Regions, and the Ombudsman. As for existing institutions, the powers of the EP were increased, not least through the introduction of the new codecision procedure, greater use of qualified majority voting in the Council was agreed, the Court of Auditors was upgraded to an institution, and the Court of Justice gained the power to fine member states.

The Treaty on European Union

Agreed at Maastricht in December 1991 and entering into force on 1 November 1993, the TEU – often referred to as the 'Maastricht Treaty' – was designed to expand the scope of European integration, reform the EC's institutions and decision-making procedures, and bring about EMU (see Box 3.4). Moreover, the goal of ever closer union was to be furthered by bringing together the EEC – now renamed the European Community, the European Coal and Steel Community (ECSC), and the European Atomic Energy Community (Euratom or EAEC) as part of an entirely new entity, to be called the 'European Union'. This was to be more than simply the existing supranational Communities. Established in 1993, it comprised not just their **supranational** activities, but also **intergovernmental cooperation** in foreign and security policy matters and justice and home affairs.

This mix of supranational integration and intergovernmental cooperation meant that the new EU fell short of what might normally be considered a 'union': a political and legal entity with a coherent and uniform structure. Indeed, in an early assessment of the EU, Curtin (1993) referred to its constitutional structure as a 'Europe of bits and pieces'. Depending, for example, on the policy area, the roles of the relevant institutions involved in decision-making differ. In the early years of the EC, there was essentially one approach, the so-called **Community method**. This would no longer be the case.

That the EU lacks uniformity in terms of its structures and policy-making procedures is evident from the terminology widely used to describe it. For many, whether they are practitioners, academics or others, the EU structurally is akin to a Greek temple consisting of three 'pillars'. The first comprises the original Communities (the EC, Euratom/EAEC, and, prior to mid-2002, the ECSC – see Box 3.5), while the second and third consist of essentially intergovernmental cooperation in the areas of the Common Foreign and Security Policy (CFSP) and, originally, justice and home affairs (JHA) (see Figure 3.1; and Chapter 1). Changes in the relationship between the pillars since 1993 have meant that the boundaries between them have become blurred.

Figure 3.1 The pillar structure after Maastricht

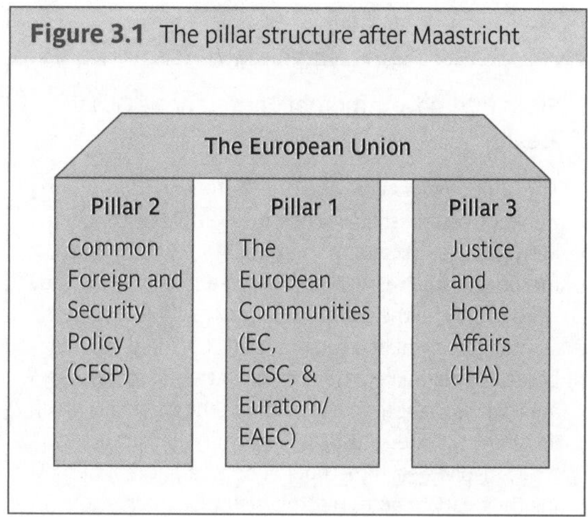

To supporters of supranational integration, the establishment of the EU in 1993 on the basis of three 'pillars' represented a clear setback. This was because the intergovernmental pillars threatened to undermine the supremacy of the Community method, the use of supranational institutions and decision-making procedures to develop, adopt, and police policy. On the other hand, adopting a mix of supranational and intergovernmental pillars merely formalized existing practice. Even prior to the TEU, the member states were pursuing intergovernmental cooperation outside the framework of the EC. The most obvious examples were EPC and **Schengen** activities relating to the removal of border controls (see Chapter 19). These had been taking place since the early 1970s and mid-1980s respectively. All the same, the mix of supranationalism and intergovernmentalism, particularly given that the Community institutions, with the exception of the Council, were at best marginal players in Pillars 2 and 3, meant that the EU, when established, was less of a union than many had either hoped or feared.

BOX 3.5

The European Communities: from three to two

Originally there were three European Communities: the European Coal and Steel Community (ECSC), the European Economic Community (EEC), and the European Atomic Energy Community (EAEC), the EEC being formally renamed the European Community in 1993 thanks to the TEU (though it was often used informally as a shorthand for the EEC before that date). Since then, the ECSC has been disbanded, its founding treaty having expired after 50 years, as envisaged, in July 2002.

The idea of the new EU as a union was also undermined by certain other features of the TEU. First, plans for EMU – the most important new area of EC activity – were set to create a three-tier EU with the member states divided between those which would become full participants, those that would fail to get in (that is, meet the **convergence criteria**), and those – the United Kingdom and Denmark – that either had availed or could avail themselves of opt-outs. Semi-permanent **differentiation** between member states in a major policy area would characterize the new EU. Secondly, it was agreed that closer integration in the area of social policy would be pursued only by 11 of the then 12 member states. Resolute opposition to increased EU competences meant that new legislation resulting from the so-called 'Social Chapter' would not apply to the United Kingdom. Thirdly, Denmark was later granted a de facto opt-out from involvement in the elaboration and implementation of foreign policy decisions and actions having defence implications. All this created the image of a partially fragmented EU.

That the TEU's provisions did not all apply to the same extent to all member states was significant as such differentiation had never been enshrined in the EU's treaty base before. This is not to say that differentiation between member states had never existed (see Chapter 24). But it had been temporary, with new member states given strict time limits for fulfilling the requirements and obligations of membership. Hence, there were fears that the Maastricht opt-outs would set a precedent leading, at worst, to an *à la carte* EU with member states picking and choosing the areas in which they were willing to pursue closer integration. Such fears were initially assuaged when, at the time of the 1995 enlargement, the EU refused to consider any permanent exemptions or opt-outs from the existing ***acquis*** for the new member states. Austria, Finland, and Sweden had to and indeed did accept all the obligations of membership, including those concerning social policy, EMU, and the CFSP, the latter being significant because each of the three countries was still notionally neutral.

KEY POINTS

- Despite 'ever closer union' being a long-established goal of the EC member states, the EU was not created until 1993.
- The EU lacks a uniform structure consisting as it does of one supranational and two intergovernmental pillars.
- The TEU introduced opt-outs from certain policy areas for some member states.

Reviewing the Union: the 1996 IGC and the Treaty of Amsterdam

That the EU, when it was created, was less than its title implied was recognized not only by those studying the EU but also by those working in its institutions and representing its member states. Even those who drafted the TEU acknowledged that what they were creating was not the final product, but part of an ongoing process. In the very first article of the TEU, the member states proclaimed that the establishment of the EU 'marks *a new stage* in the process of creating an ever closer union among the peoples of Europe' (emphasis added). They then proceeded to facilitate the process by scheduling an IGC for 1996 at which the TEU would be revised in line with its objectives. Among these was (and indeed remains) the idea of 'ever closer union'.

The 1996 IGC

Views on the purpose of the 1996 IGC differed. For the less integrationist member states, notably the United Kingdom, it would provide an opportunity to review the functioning of the EU and fine-tune its structures. It was too soon to consider anything radical. For others, a more substantial overhaul was not ruled out. The IGC would provide an opportunity to push ahead with the goal of creating 'ever closer union', something that the EP was particularly keen to see, as its draft constitution of February 1994 had demonstrated. Ever closer union, it was argued, was necessary if the EU wished to rectify the shortcomings of the structures created at

Maastricht and prepare itself to admit an increasingly large number of applicant countries, mainly from Central and Eastern Europe (see Chapter 26). Moreover, several member states were growing increasingly impatient with the reluctance of the less integrationist member states to countenance closer integration. And there was also the need to bring the EU closer to its citizens. Popular reaction to the TEU had shown that more needed to be done to convince people of the value of 'union'. Not only had the Danish people initially rejected the TEU in June 1992, but also the French people had only narrowly approved three months later.

The shortcomings of the EU's structures were highlighted in reports produced by the Council, Commission, and EP in 1995. They all agreed that the pillar structure was not functioning well and that the intergovernmental nature of decision-making in the third pillar was a significant constraint on the development of JHA policy. As for Pillar 2, its inherent weaknesses had been highlighted by the EU's ineffective foreign policy response to the disintegration of Yugoslavia. Such shortcomings needed to be addressed, all the more so since enlargement was now firmly on the agenda. The European Council at Copenhagen in June 1993 had committed the EU to admitting countries once they met the accession criteria (see Chapter 26), so enlargement was set to be a permanent item on the agenda of the EU. Preparations would have to be made, notably where the size and composition of the institutions were concerned. In addition, there was the matter of QMV. Its extension to replace **unanimity** would be necessary if the EU were going to survive enlargement and avoid decision-making paralysis. Also needed within an enlarged EU, at least in the eyes of supporters of closer integration, were mechanisms that would allow those member states keen on closer integration to proceed without the need for unanimous agreement of the others. There was consequently much discussion of ideas concerning a **core Europe**, **variable geometry**, and a **multi-speed** EU (see Chapter 24). It was against this background that preparations for reforming the EU took place. These began in earnest in 1995 with the formation of a 'Reflection Group'. Its report suggested three key aims for the 1996 IGC: bringing the EU closer to its citizens; improving its functioning in preparation for enlargement; and providing it with greater external capacity. In doing so, it also promoted the idea of 'flexibility' mechanisms that would facilitate 'closer cooperation' among groups of willing member states.

The IGC was launched in March 1996 with the early stages of the negotiations confirming expectations that any agreement on reform would not be easily reached. Progress under the Irish Presidency did, however, lead to a draft treaty being produced for the Dublin European Council in December 1996. This though left many issues unresolved. And with a general election due in the United Kingdom in May 1997, it was clear that finalizing agreement on many of these would have to wait until after that had taken place. Certainly the Labour victory did make the job of drawing the IGC to a close easier for the Dutch Presidency. However, differences between other member states now came into the open. Added to this, attention was being distracted away from the unresolved issues on the IGC's agenda by a new French government intent on seeing the EU commit itself to greater action on economic growth and employment.

The Treaty of Amsterdam

What eventually emerged was the Treaty of Amsterdam which was signed on 2 October 1997. It attracted far less popular attention than the TEU in 1992–3. This does not mean that it was an insignificant treaty. It certainly caught the attention of lawyers and practitioners, renumbering as it did all but four articles in the Treaty of Rome and TEU. Moreover, in terms of substantive changes to the EU, it added the establishment of 'an area of freedom, security and justice' to the EU's objectives and – in what is often referred to as communitarization – shifted much of JHA activity from Pillar 3 into the EC pillar (Pillar 1). This meant that, the thrust of cooperation in Pillar 3 was refocused on police and judicial cooperation in criminal matters and the

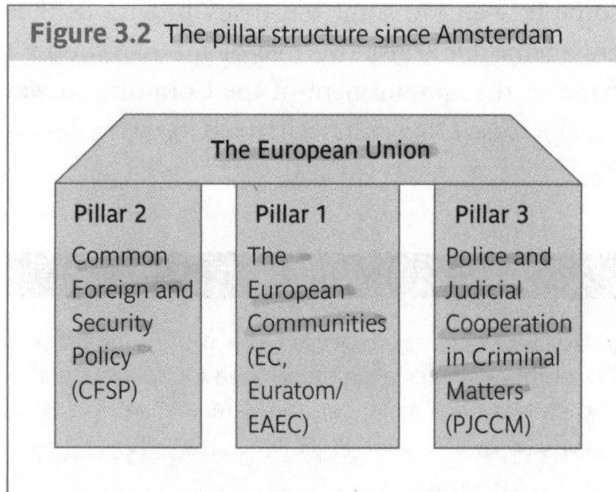

Figure 3.2 The pillar structure since Amsterdam

pillar renamed accordingly (see Figure 3.2). At the same time, provision was made for Schengen cooperation to be incorporated into the EU. These developments meant greater coherence in EU activity. Yet the changes were also accompanied by increased differentiation. The United Kingdom, Ireland, and Denmark gained various opt-outs from both the new 'area of freedom, security and justice' and Schengen cooperation.

There was also the potential for further differentiation with the introduction of mechanisms for 'closer cooperation'. Under these, member states that wished to could use the EC framework to pursue enhanced cooperation among themselves. This was provided the mechanisms were used only as a last resort, that a majority of member states would be participating, and that the cooperation would be open to all other member states. Moreover, closer cooperation could not detract from either the principles of the EU and the *acquis* or the rights of member states. Nor could it be pursued for CFSP matters. Such restrictions, as well as the de facto veto which each member state had over closer cooperation, meant that the provisions would be difficult to use. In fact, as of early 2006, none of the provisions on closer cooperation had ever been used. All the same, the possibility of using differentiation within the EU was being established.

Where the Treaty of Amsterdam lessened differentiation within the EU was in its repeal of the UK opt-out from social policy and the bolstering of the EC's social policy competences (see Chapter 17). Moreover, an employment policy chapter was introduced, in part as an attempt to assuage popular concerns that the EU did not have its citizens' interests at heart. The need to make the EU more citizen-friendly was also behind other new emphases, not least in enhanced EC competences concerning consumer and environmental protection, a new emphasis on transparency and subsidiarity, and a reassertion that EU citizenship does not undermine national citizenship.

In terms of addressing the shortcomings of Pillar 2, the IGC had resisted calls for a communitarization of the CFSP, preferring to maintain existing intergovernmental arrangements. Reforms were, however, introduced in an attempt to improve the consistency of EU action by involving the European Council more, creating the post of High Representative, establishing a policy planning and early warning unit, seeking to develop long-term strategies, clarifying the nature of the different instruments available, defining more precisely the EU's concept of security (the so-called 'Petersberg tasks' of humanitarian and rescue tasks, peacekeeping and crisis management), and allowing for 'constructive abstention' so that member states abstaining would not block CFSP initiatives (see Chapter 15). The desire to deepen integration further was asserted in the renewed commitment to a common defence policy and even a common defence.

Finally, the Treaty of Amsterdam was supposed to prepare the EU institutionally for enlargement. Here, it failed. Rather than agreeing reforms, it simply deferred the resolution of key questions, such as the size of the Commission, the redistribution of votes in the Council, and the nature of majority voting, to a later date. Unanimity was replaced by QMV in some 19 instances, but even here, thanks to German insistence, progress was far less than was either anticipated or desired by many member states. This was underlined in a declaration issued by Belgium, France, and Italy to the effect that further reform should be a precondition for the signing of the first accession treaties with applicant countries. This is not to say that the Treaty of Amsterdam failed totally to introduce institutional reform. The size of the EP was capped at 700 members, and the assent and codecision procedures were extended to some new and to some old treaty provisions thus enhancing the legislative role of the EP. The EP's hand in the appointment of the Commission was also increased, as was its right to set its own rules for its elected members (MEPs).

KEY POINTS

- Early experiences of the EU raised concerns about the functioning of the pillar structure.
- The desire not to be held back by more recalcitrant member states led to mechanisms for closer cooperation between interested and willing member states.
- Despite the acknowledged need to introduce institutional reforms in preparation for enlargement, the Treaty of Amsterdam failed to prepare the EU sufficiently to admit more than a handful of new members.

Preparing for enlargement: the 2000 IGC, the Treaty of Nice, and the 'Future of Europe' debate

With momentum building towards enlargement to include countries from Central and Eastern Europe as well as Cyprus and potentially Malta, the need to introduce institutional reform remained on the EU's agenda. Without such reform it was feared that policy-making could grind to a halt. Moreover, there were concerns that enlargement could challenge the whole idea of 'union'. Admitting 10 countries, most of which had been undergoing processes of wholesale transformation from command to fully functioning market economies was something that the EU had never done before. How to accommodate and integrate the new members became major questions. At the same time, the EU had to ensure that its *acquis* and the notion of 'union' would be neither impaired nor undermined by enlargement, and that its institutions could continue to function as decision-making and decision-shaping bodies. Moreover, confronted with the prospect of what amounted to almost a doubling of its membership, the EU was faced with the challenge of ensuring that the commitment towards 'ever closer union' would be maintained.

Enlargement moves centre-stage

Preparing the EU institutionally for enlargement had been a key objective of the 1996 IGC. The resulting Treaty of Amsterdam failed, as noted, to deliver. Instead, it was decided to postpone reform. A Protocol therefore envisaged that at the time of the next enlargement, the Commission would consist of one national per member state provided that by then the weighting of votes within the Council had been modified either via a reweighting or through the adoption of a dual majority system of voting (see Chapter 10). The idea behind the reweighting was to compensate the larger member states for giving up 'their' second commissioner. The Protocol also provided for an IGC to carry out a 'comprehensive review of . . . the composition and functioning of the institutions' at least one year before the membership of the EU exceeds 20 member states.

In reality the provisions of the Protocol were mainly ignored. For even before the Treaty of Amsterdam entered into force on 1 May 1999, the European Council in 1998 had identified institutional reform as an issue of primary concern for the EU. Then, in June 1999, it agreed to hold an IGC in 2000 to address the key institutional questions left unresolved at Amsterdam. The issues – the size and composition of the Commission, the weighting of votes in the Council, and the possible extension of QMV in the Council – became known as the 'Amsterdam leftovers'.

What pushed the European Council into calling an IGC for 2000 were changes in the EU's handling of the enlargement process. In July 1997, a matter of weeks after the Amsterdam European Council, the Commission had published *Agenda 2000*, its blueprint for enlargement. Following its recommendations, the Luxembourg European Council in December 1997 agreed to launch an inclusive accession process with all applicant states (excluding Turkey) but open accession negotiations proper with only six of the applicants. It was felt at the time that six new members could be squeezed into the EU without necessarily holding an IGC. Within 18 months, however, attitudes towards enlargement were changing and, in the aftermath of the Kosovo conflict of 1999, the decision was taken to open accession negotiations with six more applicant countries and recognize all applicants including Turkey as 'candidate countries'. Opening up the possibility of large-scale enlargement made the need to address the Amsterdam leftovers more urgent. Hence an IGC was called.

The 2000 IGC

The 2000 IGC opened in February 2000 with only a limited agenda. This reflected the preferences of most member states for an IGC focused on the Amsterdam leftovers. Others, including the Commission and the EP, favoured a broader agenda. In a Commission-inspired 'Wise Men's Report' published in October 1999, strong support was voiced for a reorganization of the treaties and the integration of the Western European Union (WEU) into the EU as a step towards a common defence policy. A Commission report in January 2000 also reminded the member states that it was incumbent on them to ensure that the IGC reformed the EU in such a way that it would remain flexible enough 'to allow continued progress towards our goal of European integration. What the Conference decides will set the framework for the political Europe of tomorrow'. The EU, it warned, 'will be profoundly changed by enlargement, but must not be weakened by it'. As for the EP, it came out strongly in favour of a wider agenda, dismissing the 'excessively narrow agenda' adopted by the Helsinki European Council in December 1999 as one which 'might well jeopardize the process of integration'.

Such calls were initially overlooked by the IGC although 'closer cooperation' was added to its agenda by the Feira European Council in June 2000. By this time, however, certain member states were beginning to think more openly about the future of the EU. Hence, negotiations were soon taking place against a backdrop of speeches from the German Foreign Minister, Joschka Fischer, advocating in a personal capacity 'a European Federation' (see Box 3.6), and the French President, Jacques Chirac, championing proposals for a European constitution. Other proposals on the future shape of the EU from, among others, the UK Prime Minister, Tony Blair, and his Spanish counterpart, José-Maria Aznar, soon followed.

Many of the proposals were too ambitious for the IGC, where progress was already proving to be slow not least due to major differences on how best to deal with the Amsterdam leftovers. This was evident from the harsh words exchanged at the Biarritz European Council in October 2000. And the situation was not helped by the heavy-handed manner in which France, now holding the Council Presidency,

BOX 3.6

From confederacy to federation – thoughts on the finality of European integration

Excerpts from a speech by Joschka Fischer at Humboldt University in Berlin, 12 May 2000

Quo vadis Europa? is the question posed once again by the history of our continent. And for many reasons the answer Europeans will have to give, if they want to do well by themselves and their children, can only be this: onwards to the completion of European integration. A step backwards, even just standstill or contentment with what has been achieved, would demand a fatal price of all EU member states and of all those who want to become members; it would demand a fatal price above all of our people. . . .

The task ahead of us will be anything but easy and will require all our strength; in the coming decade we will have to enlarge the EU to the east and south-east, and this will in the end mean a doubling in the number of members. And at the same time, if we are to be able to meet this historic challenge and integrate the new member states without substantially denting the EU's capacity for action, we must put into place the last brick in the building of European integration, namely political integration. . . .

Permit me therefore to remove my Foreign Minister's hat altogether in order to suggest a few ideas both on the nature of this so-called finality of Europe and on how we can approach and eventually achieve this goal. . . .

Enlargement will render imperative a fundamental reform of the European institutions. Just what would a European Council with thirty heads of state and government be like? Thirty presidencies? How long will Council meetings actually last? Days, maybe even weeks? How, with the system of institutions that exists today, are thirty states supposed to balance interests, take decisions and then actually act? How can one prevent the EU from becoming utterly intransparent, compromises from becoming stranger and more incomprehensible, and the citizens' acceptance of the EU from eventually hitting rock bottom?

Question upon question, but there is a very simple answer: the transition from a union of states to full parliamentarization as a European Federation, something Robert Schuman demanded 50 years ago. And that means nothing less than a European Parliament and a European government which really do exercise legislative and executive power within the Federation. This Federation will have to be based on a constituent treaty.

I am well aware of the procedural and substantive problems that will have to be resolved before this goal can be attained. For me, however, it is entirely clear that Europe will only be able to play its due role in global economic and political competition if we move forward courageously. The problems of the 21st century cannot be solved with the fears and formulae of the 19th and 20th centuries . . .

Source: www.auswaertiges-amt.de/www/en/ausgabe_archiv?archiv_id = 1027.

was managing the IGC. Accusations abounded that it was abusing its position as chair by promoting what was essentially a French agenda rather than seeking to broker compromises between the member states. At no point were the accusations louder than at the Nice European Council which, after more than four days, eventually agreed a treaty. Once tidied up, the Treaty of Nice was signed on 26 February 2001.

The Treaty of Nice

What the member states agreed at Nice attracted much criticism. Although it was rightly heralded as paving the way for enlargement, for many it produced suboptimal solutions to the institutional challenges raised by the prospect of an enlarged membership. All the same the Treaty of Nice did equip the EU better to accept new members and avoid decision-making and institutional paralysis. For example, QMV was extended to nearly 40 more treaty provisions, albeit in many instances ones concerned with the nomination of officials rather than policy-making, although some 10 policy areas did see increased use of QMV. Reaching a decision using QMV did not, however, become any easier. Despite a reweighting of votes – each member state saw its number of votes increase with the larger member states enjoying roughly a trebling and the smaller member states roughly a doubling of their votes – the proportion of votes required to obtain a qualified majority remained at almost the same level as before and was actually set to increase. Moreover, a new hurdle was introduced: any decision could, at the behest of any member state, be required to have the support of member states representing 62 per cent of the EU's total population.

The Treaty of Nice also provided for a staged reduction in the size of the Commission. From 2005, each member state would have one commissioner. Then, once the EU reaches 27 members – scheduled for 2008 at the latest, the Commission will be reduced to no more than 26 members. There is, however, a proviso: an equitable rotation system has to be agreed. Staying with the institutions, the cap on the size of the EP was revised upward to 732 and maximum sizes for the Committee of the Regions and the Economic and Social Committee (see Chapter 18) agreed. Reforms were also introduced to the competences and organization of the Court of Justice and the Court of First Instance (see Chapter 12).

The imminence of enlargement coupled with an awareness of existing institutional difficulties also accounts for an enhanced stress on democracy and rights. Hence a 'yellow card' procedure for member states deemed to be at risk of breaching the principles on which the EU is founded was introduced. Thanks to the Treaty of Amsterdam, it had already been agreed that voting and other rights of such member states could be suspended. Moreover, the Treaty of Nice revised the mechanisms for closer cooperation – now referred to as 'enhanced cooperation'. These become easier to use mainly because the number of member states needed to start a project and the opportunities to block such were reduced. Enhanced cooperation could also now be used for non-military aspects of the CFSP. All this opened up the possibility of the EU becoming a less uniform entity.

At the same time, however, the Treaty of Nice arguably gave the EU a greater sense of coherence. In the area of CFSP, and following the development of the European Rapid Reaction Force (see Chapter 15), it made the EU rather than the WEU responsible for implementing the defence-related aspects of policy. It also increased the focus on Brussels as the de facto capital of the EU. With enlargement all European Council meetings would be held in Brussels.

Yet although the Treaty of Nice paved the way for a more 'European' EU by introducing the institutional reforms necessary for enlargement, it did little in terms of the furthering the goal of 'ever closer union'. Integration-minded MEPs were quick to express their concerns, voicing particular criticism at the perceived drift towards intergovernmentalism and the consequent weakening of the Community method (Leinen and Méndez de Vigo 2001). The new Treaty did, however, set in motion a process that drew on the speeches made by Fischer, Chirac, and others in 2000 and after to promote a debate on the future of the EU. To some, the Commission especially, this would provide an opportunity to create a stronger, more integrated EU with a less fragmented structure. Others, however, envisaged greater flexibility, a clear delimitation of competences, and a weakening of commitments to 'ever closer union'.

Beyond Nice: the 'Future of Europe' debate

The initial terms of reference for the debate were outlined in a *Declaration on the Future of the Union* in which the member states called for 'a deeper and wider debate about the future of the European Union'. This would focus, inter alia, on four issues: how to establish and monitor a more precise delimitation of powers between the EU and its member states; the status of the Charter of Fundamental Rights proclaimed at the Nice European Council; a simplification of the Treaties with a view to making them clearer and better understood; and the role of national parliaments in the European architecture. In addition, ways of improving and monitoring the democratic legitimacy and transparency of the EU and its institutions would be sought. The aim was to bring them closer to the citizens. A further IGC and treaty would follow.

The agenda for the 'Future of Europe' debate appeared quite limited. However, by the time the debate was formally launched by the Laeken European Council in December 2001, the reference to 'inter alia' had been seized on and a whole raft of often wide-ranging questions had been tabled for

BOX 3.7

The Laeken Declaration on the Future of the European Union

Excerpts from the Declaration, December 2001

[T]he Union stands at a crossroads, a defining moment in its existence. The unification of Europe is near. The Union is about to expand to bring in more that ten new Member States . . . At long last, Europe is on its way to becoming one big family, without bloodshed, a real transformation clearly calling for a different approach from fifty years ago, when six countries first took the lead . . .

The European Union needs to become more democratic, more transparent and more efficient. It has to resolve three basic challenges: how to bring citizens, and primarily the young, closer to the European design and the European institutions, how to organise politics and the European political area in an enlarged Union and how to develop the Union as a stabilising factor and a model in the new multipolar world . . .

Citizens often hold expectations of the European Union that are not always fulfilled . . . Thus the important thing is to clarify, simplify and adjust the division of competences between the Union and the Member States in the light of the new challenges facing the Union . . .

A first series of questions that needs to be put concerns how the division of competence can be made more transparent. Can we thus make a clearer distinction between three types of competence: the exclusive competence of the Union, the competence of the Member States and the shared competence of the Union and the Member States? At what level is competence exercised in the most efficient way? How is the principle of subsidiarity to be applied here? And should we not make it clear that any powers not assigned by the Treaties to the Union fall within the exclusive sphere of competence of the Member States? And what would be the consequences of this?

The next series of questions should aim, within this new framework and while respecting the 'acquis communautaire', to determine whether there needs to be any reorganization of competence. How can citizens' expectations be taken as a guide here? What missions would this produce for the Union? And, vice versa, what tasks could better be left to the Member States? What amendments should be made to the Treaty on the various policies? How, for example, should a more coherent common foreign policy and defence policy be developed? Should the Petersberg tasks be updated? Do we want to adopt a more integrated approach to police and criminal law co-operation? How can economic-policy coordination be stepped up? How can we intensify co-operation in the field of social inclusion, the environment, health and food safety? But then, should not the day-to-day administration and implementation of the Union's policy be left more emphatically to the Member States and, where their constitutions so provide, to the regions? Should they not be provided with guarantees that their spheres of competence will not be affected?

Lastly, there is the question of how to ensure that a redefined division of competence does not lead to a creeping expansion of the competence of the Union or to encroachment upon the exclusive areas of competence of the Member States and, where there is provision for this, regions. How are we to ensure at the same time that the European dynamic does not come to a halt? In the future as well the Union must continue to be able to react to fresh challenges and developments and must be able to explore new policy areas. Should Articles 95 and 308 of the Treaty be reviewed for this purpose in the light of the 'acquis jurisprudentiel'? . . .

Who does what is not the only important question; the nature of the Union's action and what instruments it should use are equally important. Successive amendments to the Treaty have on each occasion resulted in a proliferation of instruments, and directives have gradually evolved towards more and more detailed legislation. The key question is therefore whether the Union's various instruments should not be better defined and whether their number should not be reduced.

In other words, should a distinction be introduced between legislative and executive measures? Should the number of legislative instruments be reduced: directly applicable rules, framework legislation and non-enforceable instruments (opinions, recommendations, open coordination)? Is it or is it not desirable to have more frequent recourse to framework legislation, which affords the Member States more room for manoeuvre in achieving policy objectives? For which areas of competence are open coordination and mutual recognition the most appropriate instruments? Is the principle of proportionality to remain the point of departure? . . .

[H]ow can we increase the democratic legitimacy and transparency of the present institutions . . . ?

How can the authority and efficiency of the European Commission be enhanced? How should the President of the Commission be appointed: by the European Council, by the European Parliament or should he be directly elected by the citizens? Should the role of the European Parliament be strengthened? Should we extend the right of co-decision or not? Should the way in which we elect the members of the European Parliament be reviewed? Should a European electoral constituency be created, or should constituencies continue to be determined nationally? Can the two systems be combined? Should the role of the Council be strengthened? Should the Council act in the same manner in its legislative and its executive capacities? With a view to greater transparency, should the meetings of the Council, at least in its legislative capacity, be public? Should citizens have more access to Council documents? How, finally, should the balance and reciprocal control between the institutions be ensured?

A second question, which also relates to democratic legitimacy, involves the role of national parliaments. Should they be represented in a new institution, alongside the Council and the European Parliament? Should they have a role in areas of European action in which the European Parliament has no competence? Should they focus on the division of competence between Union and Member States, for example through preliminary checking of compliance with the principle of subsidiarity?

[A] third question concerns how we can improve the efficiency of decision-making and the workings of the institutions in a

Union of some thirty Member States. How could the Union set its objectives and priorities more effectively and ensure better implementation? Is there a need for more decisions by a qualified majority? How is the co-decision procedure between the Council and the European Parliament to be simplified and speeded up? What of the six-monthly rotation of the Presidency of the Union? What is the future role of the European Parliament? What of the future role and structure of the various Council formations? How should the coherence of European foreign policy be enhanced? How is synergy between the High Representative and the competent Commissioner to be reinforced? Should the external representation of the Union in international fora be extended further? . . .

[A further question] concerns simplifying the existing Treaties without changing their content. Should the distinction between the Union and the Communities be reviewed? What of the division into three pillars?

Questions then arise as to the possible reorganization of the Treaties. Should a distinction be made between a basic treaty and the other treaty provisions? Should this distinction involve separating the texts? Could this lead to a distinction between the amendment and ratification procedures for the basic treaty and for the other treaty provisions? . . .

The question ultimately arises as to whether this simplification and reorganization might not lead in the long run to the adoption of a constitutional text in the Union. What might the basic features of such a constitution be? The values which the Union cherishes, the fundamental rights and obligations of its citizens, the relationship between Member States in the Union?

Source: European Council, 'Laeken Declaration on the Future of Europe', 15 December 2001 (via europa.eu. int/constitution/futurum/documents/offtext/doc151201_en.htm).

discussion. In all, the resulting 'Laeken Declaration' contained more than 50 questions. These dealt with matters ranging from the democratic legitimacy of the EU to the future of the pillar structure and cooperation in the area of social exclusion (see Box 3.7). Also, it had been agreed that the debate would not feed directly into an IGC. Instead a Convention comprising representatives of member state governments, members of parliaments, MEPs, and Commission representatives as well as governmental representatives and MPs from the 13 candidate countries would be established to explore how the questions raised in the Laeken Declaration could be answered. Only after the Convention had completed its work would the IGC meet (see Chapter 4).

For supporters of integration disappointed by the Treaty of Amsterdam and the Treaty of Nice, this 'Future of Europe' debate was welcomed as providing a further opportunity to promote the idea of 'ever closer union'. Developments they had in mind included the adoption of a European constitution, something that the EP in particular had long been championing and the French and German governments had publicly endorsed. The EP was also keen to see the communitarization of a strengthened foreign policy and remaining third pillar matters, formal recognition of the EU's legal personality, election of the Commission President, simplification of decision-making procedures, and an extension of its own powers (Leinen and Méndez de Vigo 2001). Many of these ideas were shared by the Commission, which also proposed removing existing opt-outs (European Commission 2002a). They would also be fed, along with a range of other ideas from various sources, into the work of the Convention. The challenge it faced would be to come up with acceptable answers. Whether these would result in a further step along the road to 'ever closer union' remained to be seen.

KEY POINTS

- Changes in the approach the EU was adopting towards enlargement in 1999 gave greater urgency to the need to address the 'Amsterdam leftovers' and agree institutional reform.
- The Treaty of Nice may have paved the way for enlargement, but to many it provided suboptimal solutions to the institutional challenges posed by a significantly larger EU.
- While criticized for potentially weakening the EU, the Treaty of Nice initiated a process designed to respond to calls for a European Federation and a European Constitution.

Conclusion

There has in the history of the EU and its predecessors rarely been a point when ideas for increased integration have not been aired. This has been particularly true of the period since the mid-1980s during which treaty reform and IGCs have become almost permanent items on the agenda of the EU. As a result the EU that was established in 1993 has evolved in a variety of ways. The member states have agreed to expand the range of policies in which the EU has a competence to act; they have increased the decision-making powers of the institutions; and they have embarked on some major integration projects, notably EMU which saw the replacement of 12 national currencies with the euro on 1 January 2002.

Consequently, the EU has many of the characteristics of a union. For some it resembles or is becoming a superstate. Yet for many, particularly supporters of political union, it is a much looser and fluid organization than its name suggests. Its pillar structure embodies a complex mix of intergovernmental cooperation and supranational integration that brings together in various combinations a range of supranational institutions and the member states to further a variety of policy agendas. Adding to the complexity are the various opt-outs that Denmark, Ireland, and the United Kingdom have in certain policy areas as well as the differentiated integration created by the approach adopted towards EMU. Moreover, successive rounds of treaty reform have sought to facilitate a more multi-speed EU through the introduction and refinement of mechanisms for enhanced cooperation. All this raises questions about how uniform and united the EU is.

What the various rounds of treaty reform also reveal, however, is that the EU is taking on more responsibilities and is at least aware of the challenges raised by its complex structure and procedures, particularly given its commitment to enlargement. This is not to say that its member states have warmed to the challenges, introduced appropriate reforms, or decided what the EU's *finalité politique* should be. Debates have continued over what form the EU should take with the latest proposal being the Constitutional Treaty signed in 2004. As the next chapter reveals, this envisages various reforms to the EU. Some would make the EU more like the union that its name implies. Equally, however, the EU would continue to be characterized by a complex mix of supranationalism, intergovernmentalism, and differentiated forms of integration. Reforms brought about by the Treaty of Amsterdam and Treaty of Nice suggest that it is set to remain as such.

? QUESTIONS

1. Is it appropriate to describe the EU in terms of 'pillars'?
2. What is meant by 'ever closer union'?
3. Do opt-outs and mechanisms for enhanced cooperation undermine the EU as a union?
4. What impact did the Treaty of Amsterdam have on the pillar structure of the EU?
5. Why did the 1996 IGC fail to adopt the institutional reforms necessary to prepare the EU for enlargement?
6. Has the Treaty of Nice prepared the EU for enlargement?
7. What impact will enlargement have on the prospects for further integration in the EU?
8. Why was the agenda for the Future of Europe debate expanded between Nice and Laeken?

GUIDE TO FURTHER READING

- Baun, M. J. *An Imperfect Union: The Maastricht Treaty and the New Politics of European Integration* (Boulder, CO: Westview, 1996). An introductory account of the establishment of the EU in 1993 and its early development.

- Church, C., and Phinnemore, D. *The Penguin Guide to the European Treaties: From Rome to Maastricht, Amsterdam, Nice and Beyond* (London: Penguin, 2002). A comprehensive guide to the treaty base of the EU, which reproduces the provisions of the Treaties in their current form.

- Galloway, D. *The Treaty of Nice and Beyond* (Sheffield: Sheffield Academic Press, 2001). A detailed analysis of key reforms introduced by the Treaty of Nice

- Laffan, B., O'Donnell, R., and Smith, M. *Europe's Experimental Union: Rethinking Integration* (London: Routledge, 2000). A challenging and thought-provoking analysis of what the EU is.

- Lynch, P., Neuwahl, N., and Rees, W. (eds) *Reforming the European Union from Maastricht to Amsterdam* (London: Longman, 2000). A volume assessing developments in the EU during the 1990s paying particular attention to the reforms introduced by the Treaty of Amsterdam.

- Monar, J., and Wessels, W. (eds) *The European Union after the Treaty of Amsterdam* (London: Continuum, 2001). An informative collection of studies explaining the significance for the EU of the institutional and policy reforms introduced by the Treaty of Amsterdam

IMPORTANT WEBSITES

- http://europa.eu.int/comm/nice_treaty/index_en.htm Treaty of Nice website.
- http://europa.eu.int/comm/archives/igc2000/index_en.htm Archives of the 2000 IGC.
- http://europa.eu.int/en/agenda/igc-home/ Archives of the 1996 IGC.
- http://europa.eu.int/futurum/index_en.htm Commission website on the 'Future of Europe' debate.
- http://www.europarl.eu.int/europe2004/index_en.htm EP website on the 'Future of Europe' debate.
- http://europa.eu.int/abc/treaties_en.htm The European Treaties.

Visit the Online Resource Centre that accompanies this book for lots of interesting additional material. http://www.oxfordtextbooks.co.uk/orc/cini2e/

4 The Rise and Fall of the Constitutional Treaty

CLIVE CHURCH AND DAVID PHINNEMORE

Chapter Contents

Reader's Guide

This chapter explores the content and significance of the Constitutional Treaty and assesses the reasons for its defeats in referenda in France and the Netherlands. These were partly due to dislike of the actual document but, since many voters were unfamiliar with it or confused it with the existing treaties, they really owed more to a deeper unease about the EU. Yet this was unfair to the Constitutional Treaty which had been negotiated in a new and more open manner and achieved reasonable compromises both between the existing treaties and innovation and between competing views of the EU. Nor did the Constitutional Treaty focus on the issues which apparently worried voters. Nonetheless, while ratification started well enough, the two referenda put the process on hold, causing political disarray and much agonizing over the future of the EU. Hence the chapter ends by considering possible paths ahead for the Constitution and the EU.

Introduction

When the *Treaty establishing a Constitution for Europe* – the Constitutional Treaty – was finally signed on 29 October 2004, the relief that a text had actually emerged from the Convention on the Future of Europe and the succeeding intergovernmental conference (IGC) led to euphoria. For some participants in the process it was a miracle. Indeed, Jan Peter Balkenende, the Dutch Prime Minister, saw it as the start of a new era. In this he was partly right although the era turned out to be very different from what many then expected.

In fact the new reality was that getting the resulting text ratified proved infinitely more difficult than its drafting. Indeed, despite being both more democratically drafted than any previous treaty and aimed at addressing the gap between EU and its citizens, the Constitutional Treaty seems to have widened this dramatically, as evidenced by the 'No' votes in France and the Netherlands in May and June 2005 respectively. The rejections unleashed what for many is a major political crisis which goes far wider than the treaty itself. The votes have been seen as the high-water mark of deep, and continent-wide, integration in Europe, revealing a crisis of legitimacy with much opinion swinging towards opposition to European aspirations and structures. For some it is the biggest crisis in the history of the EU and the most significant event in Europe since 1989. So many observers find it difficult to be optimistic about the outcome.

It is often assumed that all this is due to the document itself. It is, indeed, far from perfect (Church and Phinnemore 2005). First, its title – the Treaty establishing a Constitution for Europe – is a problem. It had to be a treaty because, on the one hand, it was governed by the procedures of the existing treaties on which Union and Community are based, and, on the other, there was resistance to the idea of a constitution for a state-dominated body like the EU. Constitutions were seen, inaccurately, as things only found in states. But common usage has overlooked both this and the careful formulation actually used and talks of the 'European Constitution'. This is easier and reflects the fact that, while the expectation had been of a treaty revision, leaving thoughts of a constitution for later, the Convention decided, early on, to go for something more constitutional. It did so because of ongoing pressure for constitutionalizing the EU so as to make it more effective and democratic and to avoid the over-frequent amendments with which the treaties have been plagued since the mid-1980s. And the text uses constitutional language at many points even though it does not match up to prevailing views of what a constitution is, or should be.

Thus it remains a governance or 'constitutional' treaty. However, while academics can live with the notion that it is both treaty and constitution – something which is not unknown historically – political opinion of all persuasions prefers to ignore the ambiguity and concentrates on one or other dimension, usually the constitutional one. Thus the UK government tended to emphasize the 'treaty' aspect, because this was less frightening, while opponents (and some more enthusiastic supporters) liked to emphasize the 'constitutional' dimension. Uncertainty about its status has polluted debate. This has helped to make the document symbolically controversial.

Secondly, the Constitutional Treaty, though slimmer and somewhat less complex than the existing 20-plus treaties, is not an easy read. Its length – about 160,000 words – is against it. So is its structure, which mixes the new and the old without explanation. Its language remains that of treaties: complicated, legalistic, obscure, technical, and wide ranging. Only lawyers and 'anoraks' can easily understand it. All of which predisposes people against it.

Thirdly, some of its contents, whether the new elements in Part I or the reshaped policy principles in Part III, caused controversy. This is understandable with regard to the new elements, less so where the recycled contents of the existing treaties are concerned. Such attitudes show how unfamiliar people can be with the workings of the EU and have encouraged critics to attack the Constitutional Treaty for introducing other aspects of integration with which they are unhappy. Arguably its complex nature encouraged people to wander off the point.

Clearly the 'No' votes were themselves ambiguous. Indeed, partly because it publicized anew (and more widely) much of the existing treaty base, the Constitutional Treaty served as a catalyst for broader, underlying problems in European politics. As will be seen such wider considerations were the deciding factor in the defeat of the text. Yet, although after the initial excitement the text rather disappeared from view, it still raises many questions. So it remains important to understand it, especially given the limited familiarity with the text and the exaggerated claims made about the 'No' votes.

It is therefore worth remembering how the Constitutional Treaty was actually drafted, a process lasting from early 2002 until late 2004, and what its key elements are. Equally, the many things which the document does not do need to be remembered, given the wide-ranging criticisms made of it. The process of ratification and the reasons why it was rejected in two of the founding member states also need investigation. Finally, an assessment both of the significance of the crisis and of the possible ways ahead is crucial to EU politics.

KEY POINTS

- The constitutional process was derailed in May–June 2005 and has caused a major political crisis.
- The document is both a treaty and a constitution and not simply one or the other.
- It has problems of its own but also serves as a catalyst for deeper concerns about the EU and European integration.

The drafting process

The origins of the Constitutional Treaty are many but its rise owes much to the 'Future of Europe' debate set in motion by the Nice European Council in 2000 and furthered by the Laeken Declaration adopted a year later (see Chapter 3). Although the 'debate' attracted little popular input, while few governments made serious efforts to promote discussion, there was sufficient political support among EU leaders and enthusiasts to proceed towards a further round of treaty reform. This time, in recognition of the need to engage citizens more in the process, the question of how to reform the EU would not be left simply to an IGC. Instead, and drawing on the approach for the Charter of Fundamental Rights in 1999–2000, a 'Convention on the Future of Europe' was established to debate options and make proposals. This 'European Convention' comprised representatives of national governments, members of the European Parliament (EP) and of national parliaments, as well as representatives from the Commission (Michalski 2004). And, not only did representatives come from the member states, but also from the 13 candidate countries. In addition, there were observers from other EU institutions and bodies. Its work was overseen by a chairman, the former French President and MEP, Valéry Giscard d'Estaing, and two vice-chairmen, the former Prime Ministers of Belgium, Jean-Luc Dehaene, and Italy, Giuliano Amato.

The Convention assembled in Brussels for its inaugural session in late February 2002. At the time expectations were mixed. Some doubted whether a disparate collection of politicians, few of whom were particularly well known or knew much about the EU, could produce meaningful ideas on how the future EU should look and function. There were also doubts about the capacity of Giscard, at 76 very much an elder statesman, either to manage the Convention and provide leadership and authority or to ensure that its deliberations reflected the concerns and interests of society more generally. After all, the purpose of the Convention was to ensure a more open, transparent, and democratic process that would ultimately – after the IGC – produce a more legitimate and popular outcome. Technically, the process was open and transparent in so far as formal proceedings were open to the public and all documents, submissions, and speeches were made available online. Yet the Convention failed to attract much media or popular attention. Equally, its efforts to engage people beyond the Brussels-centred cognoscenti were paltry. And with few of the 207 *conventionnels* enjoying much of a public profile – at least until some foreign ministers joined their ranks – the whole exercise remained quite anonymous and restricted to an essentially self-selecting EU elite, skilfully steered by Giscard.

This did not, however, prevent the Convention from confounding doubters' concerns. In fact, it responded positively to Giscard's observation at the inaugural plenary session that the best option was to produce a single text rather than a set of possibilities. This encouraged members to think in terms of a European constitution as they went through processes of listening, study, and drafting (Norman 2005). They did this because they believed, wrongly as it turned out, that this was both more democratic and more likely to encourage people to esteem the EU.

After 16 months' work involving 26 plenary sessions, 11 working groups, and nearly 50 meetings of the praesidium, the Convention was just able to meet its deadline and present the text of a *Draft Treaty establishing a Constitution for Europe* to the European Council in June 2003. Although a number of *conventionnels* opposed the text, calling for a different approach, the fact that the draft represented the outcome of a uniquely open process and had been adopted on the basis of a 'broad consensus' among their colleagues meant that it could not be ignored. This was duly acknowledged by EU leaders at the Thessaloniki European Council which declared that it was a 'good basis' for further negotiations. The latter also allowed for a further period of textual polishing during which otherwise omitted elements of the existing treaties were turned into Part III, something which many now feel to have been an error.

Negotiations were duly opened in the form of an IGC in September 2003. There was therefore barely any time to raise meaningful public awareness of the Convention's draft, let alone promote serious debate on its content. In hindsight this arguably proved costly. Equally, the ambitious Italian goal of concluding the IGC before the end of the year was both rash and naive. Although the Convention's draft enjoyed strong support among the *conventionnels*, none of the member states was willing to adopt it without amendment. Indeed, several had serious reservations about some of its contents. In particular, Spain and Poland objected to a proposed new double majority voting system in the Council. Others either had doubts about, or were opposed to, provisions on the size and composition of the Commission, the role and functions of the proposed Union Minister for Foreign Affairs, the nature and rotation of the Council Presidency, the respective powers of the EP and the Council in deciding the budget, the extension of qualified majority voting, the envisaged revision process, the Danish opt-out in justice and home affairs, and a mutual assistance clause. This should have tempered the Italian Presidency's ambitions.

It did not. Instead, expectations were raised that the European Council in December 2003 would conclude the IGC. Given poor Italian preparation and a general willingness among other member states to defer matters, this was never likely to happen. Nevertheless, media coverage of the meeting in Brussels presented it as a failure for the EU, even though all the member states remained committed to a new treaty. The sense of crisis whipped up by the media and opposition politicians had a partly beneficial effect since it focused minds on the

CHRONOLOGY 4.1

From Nice to a Constitutional Treaty

2001	26 February	Treaty of Nice signed
	7 March	'Future of Europe' debate launched
	15 December	Laeken Declaration
2002	28 February	Inaugural plenary session of the European Convention
	28 October	Praesidium unveils first 'skeleton' constitution
2003	26 May	Praesidium unveils revised text of Part I
	27 May	Praesidium unveils revised text of Parts II–IV
	11–13 June	Convention debates and agrees by 'broad consensus' revised Parts I and II of the *Draft Treaty establishing a Constitution for Europe*
	20 June	Parts I and II of the *Draft Treaty* presented to the Thessaloniki European Council
	9–10 July	Convention debates and agrees by 'broad consensus' revised Parts III and IV of the *Draft Treaty establishing a Constitution for Europe*
	18 July	Complete *Draft Treaty establishing a Constitution for Europe* presented to the President of the European Council
	29 September	IGC opens
	12–13 December	European Council fails to reach agreement on a *Treaty establishing a Constitution for Europe* and IGC negotiations are effectively suspended
2004	24 March	European Council decides to resume IGC negotiations
	17 May	IGC negotiations resume
	18 June	European Council agrees a *Treaty establishing a Constitution for Europe*
	29 October	*Treaty establishing a Constitution for Europe* signed
2005	29 May	French electorate reject the Constitutional Treaty in a referendum
	1 June	Dutch electorate reject the Constitutional Treaty in a referendum
	16–17 June	European Council announces a 'pause' in ratification
	11 November	New German government announces it wishes to revive ratification in 2007
2006	1 November	Scheduled date for the entry into force of the Constitutional Treaty

outstanding issues. It also led to a cooling-off period that allowed the incoming Irish Presidency some time to reflect on how various problems with the draft could be resolved. Its task was made easier by a change of government in Spain in March 2004 and the adoption by the Polish government of a more accommodating position on the double majority issue.

Two months later negotiations were resumed and, within little more than a month, agreement had been reached. The European Council in Brussels in June 2004 duly adopted the *Treaty establishing a Constitution for Europe*. The text – about 90 per cent of which had come from the Convention's draft, despite the IGC making about 80 amendments – was subsequently tidied up and authentic versions produced in each of the 21 official languages of the now enlarged EU. This took much of the summer. The complete version of the Constitutional Treaty along with its protocols and annexes and associated declarations was then signed on 29 October 2004 at a ceremony in Rome, in the same building where representatives of the original six member states signed the 1957 Treaty of Rome.

KEY POINTS

- The European Convention represented a new approach to EU treaty reform.
- Its outcome was then submitted to a difficult renegotiation in an IGC.
- The Constitutional Treaty that emerged from the IGC drew heavily on the text of the Convention's *Draft Treaty establishing a Constitution for Europe*.

Key elements of the Constitutional Treaty

The Constitutional Treaty is a lengthy document introduced by a preamble and divided into four parts. These are supplemented by annexes, protocols, declarations, and a final act (see Box 4.2). To many, particularly those who had hoped – or indeed feared – that the Convention and IGC would produce a short, succinct constitution, it is a disappointing text: complex and impenetrable and doing little to promote transparency and accountability.

Those who read the text closely would beg to differ. For them the Constitutional Treaty represents a significant improvement on the status quo of over 20 dense treaties. In their place we have, more or less, a single text. It has a preamble setting out – admittedly with many rhetorical flourishes – the purpose of the EU; a core Part I outlining the fundamentals of the EU in a new and simpler way; a Part II containing the Charter of Fundamental Rights, now to be legally binding; a Part III containing detailed rules that expand on the provisions of Part I by bringing much of the old treaties into line with them; and a Part IV and a Final Act containing various legal provisions common to international treaties. The protocols, annexes, and declarations provide more detailed specifications and interpretations of what is found in the four parts.

In terms of content, very little of this is new. Much is simply drawn from the existing treaties. Moreover, the text of the Constitutional Treaty is more navigable than what currently exists, thanks to much clearer titles and headings as well as to consolidation. And, in crude terms, everything that one

BOX 4.2

The structure of the Constitutional Treaty

Preamble

Part I

Part II – The Charter of Fundamental Rights

Part III – The Policies and Functioning of the European Union

Part IV – General and Final Provisions

Protocols (36)

Annexes (2)

Final Act

Declarations (50)

BOX 4.3

Part I of the Constitutional Treaty

Title I	Definition and Objectives of the Union
Title II	Fundamental Rights and Citizenship of the Union
Title III	Union Competences
Title IV	The Union's Institutions and Bodies
Title V	Exercise of Union Competence
Title VI	The Democratic Life of the Union
Title VII	The Union's Finances
Title VIII	The Union and its Neighbours
Title IX	Union Membership

KEY CONCEPTS AND TERMS 4.4

The Constitutional Treaty

Simplification: of the overall structure of the EU, by abolishing the pillar structure and creating a new EU with legal personality, but deriving its powers from the member states; of the treaties, by replacing almost all of them with the Constitutional Treaty; of EU decision-making by renaming and reducing the number of procedures and legal instruments.

Competences are: clearly classified through a division into exclusive, shared, and complementary; conferred, it is confirmed, on the EU by the member states; extended slightly.

Democracy is enhanced by: extending the monitoring and decision-making roles of the EP; involving national parliaments more in monitoring EU activities; providing for popular initiatives; stressing the role of political parties; highlighting the democratic input provided by member state governments in the Council; promoting dialogue with social partners and civil society.

Values are: to be promoted more actively by the EU both internally and as part of its external relations; given a new prominence through the incorporation of the Charter of Fundamental Rights as a legally binding document; generally clarified and extended to include respect for human dignity, pluralism, solidarity, tolerance, justice, gender equality, and social inclusion.

Member states: have their role in conferring powers on the EU asserted; gain the option of withdrawal from the EU; have their rights and status clarified; receive confirmation that the EU is to work in their interests as well as those of EU citizens; retain vetoes in key areas such as amendments to the Constitutional Treaty.

Clarification of: competences; legal instruments; the primacy of EU law over national law; the bases of EU power; the aims and principles of the EU.

Efficiency is to be achieved by: introducing a permanent Chair for the European Council and a Union Minister for Foreign Affairs; simpler decision-making rules; easier changes to basic rules; and the strengthening of enhanced cooperation.

needs to know about what the EU does, and how it does this, can be found in Part I. This in turn is divided into nine digestible titles (see Box 4.3) and sets out the core ideas about the nature and purpose of the EU (see Box 4.4).

Such simplification should have made the EU easier to understand. The fact that the Constitutional Treaty sees the abandonment of the existing pillar structure helps simplify matters too. The European Community goes, leaving just the EU, although the much-overlooked European Atomic Energy Community (EAEC) still has a shadowy existence, and the mix of intergovernmentalism and supranationalism persists. The EU takes over treaty-making powers – technically known as 'legal personality' – from the Community while attempts to give the EU more defence and diplomatic influence are also made. The Constitutional Treaty also makes it clear that the EU gets its powers from the member states which 'confer' specific competences on it. In fact the aims and principles of the EU are made much clearer than in the past. At the same time its responsibilities, both to the peoples and states of Europe (and their values), are recognized giving it a dual legitimacy. Values and rights are given a greatly enhanced place in the new text, notably through the formal inclusion of the pre-existing Charter of Fundamental Rights.

Much within this new, essentially single, structure is familiar (Church and Phinnemore 2005). The present main decision-making institutions – Commission, Council, Court, and Parliament – are still there, as is the European Council whose permanence is formally recognized in its new 'institution' status. The European Central Bank remains, as does the Court of Auditors and the two main advisory bodies, the Committee of the Regions and the Economic and Social Committee. Several are reformed, however. From 2014 the Commission is to be reduced in size to the equivalent of two-thirds of the number of member states; a new cap of 750 members is placed on the size of the EP; a permanent President of the European Council is created; a move to team presidencies of the Council is formalized; and a new post of Union Minister for Foreign Affairs is established and to be assisted by a European External Action Service. In a notable departure from the existing practice of limited institutional overlap, the Union Minister for Foreign Affairs will not only chair meetings of the Foreign Affairs Council, but the post-holder will also be a Vice-President of the Commission. This so-called 'double-hatting' – coupled with the fact that the European Council President is also responsible for ensuring the external representation of the EU – is seen in some quarters as a recipe for confusion and undue complexity rather than increasing efficiency.

In terms of how the institutions interact and decide policy, the Constitutional Treaty simplifies matters by reducing the number of decision-making procedures with codecision – renamed the 'ordinary legislative procedure' – becoming the default procedure and by rationalizing and renaming the range of policy instruments. The first of these further increases the input of the EP into policy-making thus, in theory at least, making the EU decisions more democratic. Also introduced in an attempt to enhance democratic input into policy-making is an increased role for national parliaments. They will now receive more information about Commission proposals and have the opportunity to 'yellow card' proposals deemed to be contrary to the principle of subsidiarity. The Constitutional Treaty also envisages citizens' initiatives. Accompanying all this is an extended use of qualified majority voting, although unanimity is still required for a range of sensitive and constitutional issues such as measures relating to tax harmonization, the accession of new members, and revisions to the text of the Constitutional Treaty. A change to what constitutes a qualified majority is also planned. From 2009 a double majority, consisting of 55 per cent of member states representing 65 per cent of the EU's population, will generally be necessary. This should facilitate decision-making. In all this the Constitutional Treaty seeks to make the new EU more efficient than its predecessor.

As to what the EU can do, the Constitutional Treaty clarifies its policy competences. It makes it clearer what the EU's exclusive competences are – customs union, competition, monetary policy for the eurozone, common commercial policy – and identifies those areas where competence is 'shared' with the member states. These include the internal market, social policy, environment, and the area of freedom, security, and justice. In other areas, the EU's role is restricted to supporting, coordinating, and complementary action, all of which are explicitly conferred by the member states and are not the EU's by right. Few new competences are conferred through the Constitutional Treaty. A number of areas – tourism, civil protection, administrative cooperation, energy – are specifically mentioned for the first time in any detail, but each of these is an area where the EU has already been active or has commitments. In other instances, existing competences have been expanded, although not to any great degree. Consequently, the Constitutional Treaty cannot be properly compared with those of its predecessors – notably the Single European Act and the Treaty on European Union (TEU) – which did significantly expand the range of the EU's activities.

Unfortunately, people rarely came to terms with the simplification and restructuring brought about by the Treaty. The text was not easily available and was poorly publicized. And other issues got in the way. Indeed while the Convention and the IGC succeeded in providing one document it did not, as responses and ratification were to show, involve the people and increase the EU's legitimacy in the desired way.

KEY POINTS

- The Constitutional Treaty, while long and complex, does simplify the EU's treaty base and overall nature.
- The pillars of the EU are replaced by a more uniform and coherent structure.
- The Constitutional Treaty also clarifies what the EU can do, and how it does this, without significantly increasing the EU's competences.

What the Constitutional Treaty is not about – an appraisal

Much of the media and popular reaction to the gestation of the Constitutional Treaty showed scant understanding of either the process or the content of the document, let alone its relationship to the existing treaties. Moreover, much comment was fuelled by misunderstandings and myth. This was true not only of tabloid newspapers, but also of reactions in the supposedly 'serious' press and on radio and television. And many politicians, even some of those involved in the Convention, portrayed the document in a light difficult to reconcile with its actual content (Stuart 2003). Added to this, governments did little to promote the Constitutional Treaty positively. When they did discuss the document – which in some cases was only with reluctance – the predominant focus was on what the Constitutional Treaty did not entail as opposed to what it did. This skewed perceptions and put governments on the defensive. It also meant that the agenda was set by scaremongers and others keen to exploit fears of integration for domestic political gain. Consequently, many popular – and to a degree elite – perceptions of the Constitutional Treaty have been informed and shaped more by what it is not.

For some ardent pro-integrationists, the text is a missed opportunity. Motivated by the fears and hesitations of member states it fails either to bring in a proper pedagogic constitution or to move away from the status quo to a radical federal structure with a proper government, bicameral legislature, and majority decision-making and amendment powers. Instead it sticks to the constraining form and details of the old treaties. The reality, of course, was that the Convention and the IGC were never really trying to achieve anything so radical. A related view, often found in the French and Dutch debates, was that the Constitutional Treaty refused to create a true constitutional democracy, failing all the tests of a true constitution, and not moving the EU closer to the people by creating a proper government which could implement the policies they desire. It also places too many restrictions on smaller states and left the continent exposed to US and NATO domination. This overlooks the attempt made to improve the EU's democratic credentials and develop foreign policy potential while making wild assumptions about popular desires and the extent to which the Constitutional Treaty changes the balance between states.

While both views reproach the Constitutional Treaty for not going far enough, most other views make an opposite complaint: that it went far too far. Thus, the majority view in France and the Netherlands was that, at the insistence of the UK government, it would turn the EU into a vehicle for the promotion of Anglo-Saxon and neo-liberal economics, exposing it to rampant forces of globalization and therefore undermining the 'European social order'. Thus it talks more of free markets and undistorted competition rather than of solidarity. And the ECB remains concerned only with price stability and not growth. What supporters of such a view fail to note is that the commitment to the free movement of goods, capital, services, and people and to the liberalization of international trade has been part of the EU's *raison d'être* since the 1950s. The Constitutional Treaty changes little and globalization will impact irrespective of whether the document enters into force or not. Some in France went out of their way to paint the treaty not merely as a social threat but as one which threatens cultural identity. For them, the Constitutional Treaty and Turkish accession were one and the same thing even though the decision to negotiate with Turkey was taken under the existing TEU and talks have continued, albeit uncertainly, since the referendum defeats. Others, mistakenly, saw the Constitutional Treaty as generally taking enlargement too far.

On the Eurosceptic right the Constitutional Treaty is seen as representing a further stage in a move by unelected Eurocrats to assume more powers for themselves. Central diktats thus increasingly rule in ever more areas. All this is at the expense of national rights, interests, and cultures. Such views overlook several realities confirmed by the Constitutional Treaty: powers are expressly conferred on the EU by its member states; membership is voluntary, as shown by the new withdrawal clause; the institutions and the EU as a whole will be more accountable; and subsidiarity is reinforced.

Another perception, found to left and right, is that the Constitutional Treaty constitutes not merely a quantitative change but a qualitative step change, implying the creation of a European 'superstate' with its own constitution. Adherents of such a view see this as the inevitable consequence of the Charter of Fundamental Rights being given legal force, the creation of the Union Minister for Foreign Affairs, and the granting of treaty-making power to the EU as a whole. They also recognize in the provisions on the establishment of the European External Action Service a forerunner of a European diplomatic service to replace national Foreign Ministries and, in the establishment of Public Prosecutor, the harbinger of a new EU legal order displacing national systems. Those on the left see in the supposed superstate opportunities for big business to do away with public services. Such concerns are further fuelled by the references in the Constitutional Treaty to various symbols of supposed statehood (anthem, flag, and currency), the celebration of a 'Europe' day throughout the EU, and the adoption of a motto: 'United in diversity'. Yet, save the last, all these are already there.

A blatant failure to appreciate what the Constitutional Treaty actually says is also evident in the perception of the document as heralding a new socialist menace. Right-wing opponents maintain that a new emphasis on social rights and policy through, in particular, the Charter of Fundamental Rights will lead to greater burdens on business and therefore economic growth. The strict limits on the application of the Charter are conveniently overlooked, as are the complaints that the Constitutional Treaty is a sell-out to international capitalism and simply does not say enough about rights and the need to protect workers. All these views derive ultimately from pre-existing political concerns more than from the actual contents of the Constitutional Treaty. In fact many of the criticisms are directed against what is already in the existing treaties. Were the Constitutional Treaty ever to be brought into effect not a great deal would actually change. In fact it is really another ambiguous product of EU bargaining. The text does not support any of these extreme interpretations because it is such a complicated compromise. Nonetheless, these misapprehensions drove the ratification process.

KEY POINTS

- A lack of familiarity with the content and origins of the Constitutional Treaty has led to ill-informed perceptions of what it means and will entail.
- The Constitutional Treaty is thus accused, from contradictory points of view, of not going far enough and of going too far.
- Were the Constitutional Treaty to be enacted much less would change than critics believe.

Ratification

With little popular and, in many cases, political understanding or appreciation of the Constitutional Treaty, ratification by all 25 member states – a legal prerequisite for its full implementation and a further proof of the document's 'treaty' status – was always going to be a challenge. This was recognized in a Declaration adopted by the IGC that envisaged some member states encountering 'difficulties'. If this were the case, the matter would be referred to the European Council assuming that, by then, four-fifths of the member states had completed ratification. The assumption was that one or more of the Czech Republic, Denmark, Poland, or the United Kingdom would be encountering 'difficulties', particularly since each was committed to hold a referendum as part of the ratification process. As events turned out, it was the French and Dutch popular rejections in May and June 2005 that both forced the issue, prematurely, on to the agenda of the European Council and started the downfall of the Constitutional Treaty, thus ensuring that the new era was much less happy than had been assumed in October 2004.

Before then, however, ratification had been proceeding relatively smoothly even if not in a uniform or coordinated manner. Member states decided for themselves how ratification would take place. All would entail a parliamentary procedure but for many there would also be a referendum. In Ireland, Denmark, and elsewhere, this was a constitutional necessity and there were precedents. In other cases, like the United Kingdom, a referendum was called for reasons of domestic political expediency. In others, there was a sense that the Constitutional Treaty merited popular endorsement. And, in the case of France, President Chirac was in part 'bounced' into holding a referendum by the UK government's decision.

In the autumn many governments started to inform their citizens and to try to be the first to ratify. In the event the Lithuanian parliament led the way, ratifying the Constitutional Treaty in November 2004. It was followed by Hungarian and Slovene legislators before Spain held the first referendum in February 2005 (see Table 4.1). The outcome was, as expected, positive, although low turnout and scant knowledge of the Constitutional Treaty meant the vote was essentially an expression of support for membership of the EU. It was certainly not an informed and ringing endorsement of the latest round of treaty reform. The same could also be said for several, if not most, of the subsequent positive votes in national parliaments.

It was not true, however, of the French referendum when 54.68 per cent of voters – mainly rural, low income, and public-sector based – rejected the Constitutional Treaty. It was equally not true of the Dutch referendum three days later which saw an even larger majority (61.54 per cent) say 'Nee'. Both defeats attracted a high turnout. And the far from overwhelming endorsement in the Luxembourg referendum in July 2005 did little to create a sense that the Constitutional Treaty was a text that commanded popular support, even if in the meantime the Cypriot, Latvian, and Maltese parliaments had voted in favour.

The obvious question arising from the rejections and the generally low levels of support is why? Did voters specifically oppose the Constitutional Treaty or did the referenda simply provide them with opportunity to express more general concerns with the direction and speed of European integration or domestic politics generally? As we have seen the text is problematic in several ways, including its lack of a clear defining purpose or message with which voters can identify. This did not encourage people to read it. And, because it is both riddled with compromises, and often regarded as falling short of their aspirations, many supporters of integration found it hard to sell. The issues it addresses were poorly appreciated, thus making room for other concerns, few of which originated with the authors of the Constitutional Treaty. So, while a significant proportion of those who rejected the Constitutional

Table 4.1 The state of ratification in 2006

As of 20 June 2006	Chamber	Date	Vote			
			Yes	No	Abstentions	Absentees
Austria	Lower	11.05.05	182	1	0	0
	Upper	25.05.05	59	3	0	0
Belgium	Lower	19.05.05	118	18	1	13
	Upper	28.04.05	54	9	1	7
Cyprus	Unicameral	30.06.05	30	19	1	6
Czech Republic*	Bicameral					
Denmark*	Unicameral					
Estonia	Unicameral	09.05.06	73	1	0	27
Finland	Unicameral					
France*	Joint Session	28.02.05	730	66	96	15
	Referendum	29.05.05	44.32%	54.68%	(Turnout: 69.34%)	
Germany	Lower	12.05.05	569	23	2	7
	Upper	27.05.05	66	0	3	0
Greece	Unicameral	19.04.05	268	17	15	0
Hungary	Unicameral	20.12.04	322	12	8	44
Ireland*	Bicameral					
Italy	Lower	25.01.05	436	28	5	61
	Upper	06.04.05	217	16	0	82
Latvia	Unicameral	02.06.05	71	5	6	18
Lithuania	Unicameral	11.11.04	84	4	3	50
Luxembourg*	Unicameral	28.06.05	57	1	0	2
	Referendum	10.07.05	56.52%	43.48%	(Turnout: 90.44%)	
Malta	Unicameral	06.07.05	65	0	0	0
Netherlands*	Unicameral					
	Referendum	01.06.05	38.46%	61.54%	(Turnout: 63.30%)	
Poland*	Bicameral					
Portugal*	Unicameral					
Slovakia	Unicameral	11.05.05	116	27	4	3
Slovenia	Unicameral	01.02.05	79	4	7	0
Spain*	Lower	28.04.05	311	19	0	20
	Upper	18.05.05	225	6	1	27
	Referendum	20.02.05	76.73%	17.24%	(Turnout: 42.32%)	
Sweden	Unicameral					
United Kingdom*	Bicameral					

* Also holding a referendum

Table 4.2 Reasons for rejection

	Netherlands	France
Lack of information	32	5
It will have negative effects on employment/ relocation of enterprises/loss of jobs	7	31
The economic situation in my country is too weak/ there is too much unemployment	5	25
Loss of national sovereignty	19	5
Economically speaking, the draft is too liberal	5	19
Oppose the national government/certain political parties/President	14	18
Not enough social Europe	2	16
Europe is too expensive	13	–
Too complex	5	12
I am against Europe/European construction/European integration	8	4
. . .		
Opposition to further enlargement	6	3
Do not want Turkey in the European Union	3	6

Sources: European Commission, *The European Constitution: Post-Referendum Survey in France*, Flash Eurobarometer, Brussels, June 2005; European Commission, *The European Constitution: Post-Referendum Survey in The Netherlands*, Flash Eurobarometer, Brussels, June 2005. Figures are percentages of those responding to the survey.

Treaty in the Netherlands did so for reasons associated with it, a detailed study of the French referendum makes little reference to the text (see Table 4.2).

It has been widely, and rightly, assumed that popular rejection of the Constitutional Treaty is part of a broader malaise which has at its roots a general dissatisfaction with national governments and a basic alienation from the EU. The former has much to do with domestic political frustration over government strategy, unemployment, threats from globalization, and social welfare difficulties. However, some 'European' issues – albeit unconnected to the Constitutional Treaty – such as the **Bolkestein Directive** on services, Turkey's potential membership of the EU, and the orientations of the Barroso Commission – do feature. All this was given expression as voters used the opportunity presented by the referenda to express unease and dissatisfaction with their national government.

The underlying sense of alienation from the EU is another major problem. The increasing pace of treaty reform and the unsettling implications of enlargement seem to have intensified the malaise. Yet little has been done to address it. This has both allowed the gap to widen and questioned the commitment of political elites to making the process of European integration inclusive. There has been a persistent failure to communicate 'Europe' actively and honestly to the people, with some national governments distorting the reality of the EU for their own political ends and using 'Brussels' as the fall guy for domestically unpopular decisions that they actually support and for which they have often voted. Admittedly, they have not been helped by, in many instances, popular indifference to European issues and by an increasingly populist and sensationalist media ever keen to distort information and provide selective coverage. Even so, communication strategies have been poor and there has been a failure to exploit new media – notably the Internet – to engage people. Attempts by EU institutions to influence opinion have also had little effect and, in many instances, have been treated with circumspection if not outright hostility.

KEY POINTS

- The Constitutional Treaty can enter into force only if it is ratified by all member states.
- 'No' votes in the French and Dutch referenda reflected a range of concerns, not all of which were connected with the Constitutional Treaty.
- Rejection of the Constitutional Treaty highlights yet again the failure of the EU and national governments to engage the people in debates about European integration.

The significance of the Constitutional Treaty and the ratification experience

Although it is probably true that the Constitutional Treaty is best regarded as a further, package deal of treaty reform it is clear that many people see it in a different light. They regard it as symbolizing a qualitative rather than a quantitative change in the EU. This is partly thanks to changes like its title, its incorporation of the Charter of Fundamental Rights, and its institutional innovations. It is also due partly to the way inclusion of Part III makes people more aware of what is in the existing treaties. And holding referenda allows the expression of underlying doubts about the direction, intensity, and speed of European integration.

Hence the 'No' votes in France and the Netherlands have led many to proclaim that the EU is now in a deep crisis of legitimacy, since the EU is decreasingly accepted as a wholly good thing. Some even suggest that the two referendum defeats have made Euroscepticism the dominant political mood in Europe. The defeats are also widely, though not universally, seen as having killed off not only the Constitutional Treaty, but also the European elite's supposedly favourite strategy of seeking integration by stealth. Instead the 'No' votes have started a continent-wide, critical popular debate on Europe. Some would go even further and see the two defeats as the beginning of the break-up of both the euro and the EU. All this is an ironic contrast with the assumption that a constitution would, as Habermas and others suggested, win over the populace.

For others, the 'No' votes were a salutary crisis which would force both rapid renegotiation of the Constitutional Treaty and political change, notably where Turkey, socio-economic policy, and national governments were concerned. And, while these ideas came mainly from opponents of the document, its supporters feared that the defeats would lead to policy blockage inside the EU. This could affect things like economic reform, enlargement, and the EU's foreign policy ambitions. All this does suggest a very real crisis.

However, while the crisis has exposed several weaknesses, its scope has been somewhat exaggerated. And many claims have already been disproved. Thus it has become clear that EU leaders had no Plan B in the event of a defeat. Indeed, rather than engaging in an in-depth analysis of what went wrong in May and June 2005 they preferred to argue about the budget.

So, is there a crisis of legitimacy? It is quite clear that there is a major problem in the old member states of Western Europe whose populations are now much less inclined to identify with the EU than they were. This is because of their economic unease, their lack of confidence in the future and their feeling that their interests are not being taken into account by 'Brussels'. Yet much of the opposition to the Constitutional Treaty came from people who described themselves as good Europeans. Their objections were not to integration as such but to the EU's style and strategy over the last 15 years. And anti-European feelings have not become universal, even if opposition has been encouraged.

Yet, despite the earnest hopes of French and other opponents, the Constitutional Treaty has not been killed off. Nor has there been rapid renegotiation. Nor has any leader yet withdrawn their signature of the document. Moreover, despite assumptions, most evident in the UK, that the Constitutional Treaty is dead and buried, there is still talk about reviving it or returning to it after the French Presidential election in 2007 perhaps during the German Presidency. No alternative text has emerged nor does it seem likely that one will, which suggests that the existing document will have to play a role, whenever institutional and treaty reform is reconsidered. However, it does seem that any treaty changes in future will have to be handled far more publicly than before. A nominated Convention, secretive IGC, and mainly parliamentary ratifications are unlikely to satisfy the majority.

Equally, talk of the demise of the EU is much exaggerated. While there are problems about economic growth in the eurozone, many of these are found at national level and, if anything, will require more rather than less coordination if they are to be solved. Nor have there been moves to wind up the EU, nor are they likely. Indeed the Union has continued to function fairly normally with no major blockages in legislation other than over the budget. Indeed, to the horror of French opponents, the Bolkestein Directive has continued to move forward, while the Commission has indicated that it will do away with some unnecessary legislation, thus seeming to reinforce the dominance of deregulatory ideas.

However, relations between some member states remain soured and party politics in France, in particular, prevent leadership and a sense of direction. Both things owe much to the resentful electoral atmosphere encouraged by the referenda as well as to the developing budgetary crisis, not to mention to the willingness of governments to pander to this and raise questions which go beyond the Constitutional Treaty. So, finally, although many opponents wanted more, it is clear that the referenda have already changed the policy debate. Thus public opinion and political pronouncements have increasingly moved against admitting Turkey, even if accession negotiations are going ahead. Similarly, the French and German governments have clearly listened to their electorates and have moved towards a form of economic patriotism (laced with criticism of the institutions), rather than reform. And attacks on the future of the CAP have apparently been seen off. However, no real debate, let alone a meeting of minds, has emerged on any of this in 2005–6. In other words, the post 'No' situation is as complex and uncertain as the text which supposedly gave birth to it.

KEY POINTS

- The derailing of the ratification process in May–June 2005 has caused something of a crisis in the EU.
- Political attitudes and alignment have been affected by this and some policies show the effects of increased opposition.
- So far there has been little real debate and no formal burying or replacement of the Constitutional Treaty.

Where next for the EU and its treaties?

The response of EU leaders to the 'No' votes in France and the Netherlands was not, as many 'No' voters expected, to abandon the Constitutional Treaty. Instead they called for a 'period of reflection' which would allow a 'broad debate . . . involving citizens, civil society, social partners, national parliaments and political parties' to take place. The plan was for EU leaders to return to the question of how to proceed with ratification in the first half of 2006 and in the light of national debates. This meant that, in the short term, the Constitutional Treaty largely disappeared from view and neither the UK Presidency, nor the majority of member states, were doing anything to promote debate. Most appeared willing to indulge in collective amnesia about the ratification crisis and to assume 'business as usual'. And, without a new text, popular reflection is, in any case, very difficult. Even the EP delayed its report on the subject until December 2005.

The autumn saw slightly more activity, with conferences, suggestions for encouraging popular support, and ideas for the drafting of new compacts. However, none of this had much general impact. So the neglect looked likely to continue with Commission President Manual Barroso declaring that the treaty would not come back for several years. In his view what the EU needed was practical politics, not philosophical musings on the future of Europe. And the Commission also made it clear that its new communication strategy was not meant to be a rescue package for the Constitutional Treaty. Moreover, some hoped that a period of passive euthanasia would ensue during which the Constitutional Treaty would simply pass away. For others, it was simply a cooling-off period and a way out of the ratification crisis would follow. So, by the end of 2005 it looked as though there was little agreement and even less to discuss. Not surprisingly some commentators were talking of 'all pause and no reflection'. And even though there were suggestions that 2006 would see more action – with the Austrian Presidency taking up the cause, including holding a major conference; the French President Jacques Chirac announcing ambitious institutional proposals to come; the EP's debate taking off; the Finnish parliament issuing a report; and even the British Foreign Office thinking about 'brainstorming' – this may not lead anywhere.

To many others, this still leaves open the question of what to do with the Constitutional Treaty. A number of ideas have been canvassed (see Box 4.5), mainly by those who remain committed to it. Thus there has been little support in elite circles for abandonment and certainly not for the proposals from the likes of the Czech President, Vaclav Klaus, who called for the EU's replacement with an ill-defined 'Organisation of European States'. However, Guy de Verhofstadt, the Belgian Prime Minister, has picked this up and suggested that there should be an inner core United States of Europe and an outer circle of less integrated states. Equally French politicians and others have canvassed the idea of an avant-garde, using either the eurozone structures or the flexibility provisions as a base. However, there is considerable opposition, notably amongst opponents of the Constitutional Treaty, to any 'cherry-picking' of parts of the document which could be introduced without an IGC.

Some still hope that the French and Dutch will either come up with a wheeze to resolve the problem or vote again, probably when the political climate has changed. The German Chancellor, Angela Merkel, has suggested tacking on a Declaration on the Social Dimension to the present text to make it more acceptable to Dutch and French voters, an idea which may be taken up during the German Presidency in 2007 which sees rescuing the Constitutional Treaty as one of its main concerns. The majority in the EP is also reluctant to declare the treaty dead and embark on a new process of change, hoping that something will turn up in 2007. However, with the Dutch Prime Minister adamant that the Netherlands will never be asked to revote, especially without moves to reflect the desires of the

BOX 4.5

Options in the case of non-ratification

An obvious option is to declare the Constitutional Treaty 'dead' and for the EU to continue to operate on the basis of the existing treaties. This would respect the outcome of the two 'No' votes but would mean forgoing important institutional reforms contained in the Constitutional Treaty, regarded as vital for the effective functioning of the EU. And few governments are keen to make the large psychological concession involved in burying the document.

Equally there has been no support for replacing the EU by a slimmed-down, nationally controlled body with fewer powers, institutions, and symbols of statehood, as urged by the Eurosceptic group in the EP. This would obviously have some resonance amongst opponents of the Constitutional Treaty but it conflicts with the desires both of left-wing critics of the Constitutional Treaty and of supporters of the EU.

If the Constitutional Treaty and the EU are not killed off, a third option is to keep the ratification process going and, assuming other member states eventually ratify the Constitutional Treaty, make the French and Dutch vote again. There are precedents for this – Denmark in 1993 (TEU) and Ireland in 2002 (Nice) – but the situation is different this time. Not only have voters in two member states rejected the Constitutional Treaty, but the margins were greater than before, the states concerned were founding members of the European Communities, and the reasons for rejection too wide to be resolved by opt-outs. Moreover, most member states have stopped their ratification processes and the symbolism would be bitterly resented.

A fourth possibility is to have a short IGC which would change Article 48 TEU to allow amended treaties to be adopted when approved by a minimum number of states. No member state, however, is likely to give up its control of such amendments.

A fifth option is to introduce – or cherry-pick – agreed elements of the Constitutional Treaty via either informal arrangements or a new, shorter treaty that simply amends the existing treaties. While attractive, there is no guarantee that agreement could be reached among member states on what amendments should be pursued or that the new treaty would be ratified. Moreover, using informal arrangements would smack of integration by stealth and further alienate popular support for the EU.

A sixth option – the Polish 'constitution lite' or 'Nice plus' approach – is to proceed simply with Part I alongside the existing treaties and a non-binding Charter of Fundamental Rights. This would allow a key element of the Constitutional Treaty to be salvaged, but would still require changes to the existing treaties to be agreed by all 25 member states.

A seventh option is to reopen negotiations and conclude a new Constitutional Treaty. This could be either a revised and 'improved' version of the present text or something wholly new. Various scenarios about how this could be done have been proposed. But such strategies would be a bold move, albeit one that could follow a more open, popular, and meaningful 'Future of Europe' debate. In reality reaching agreement on what should go into a new treaty would be difficult given the obvious lack of consensus on what the EU should be doing. And once again, the fate of the new Constitutional Treaty would hang on successful ratification, presumably in all of the signatory states.

An eighth possibility is to pursue some new form or forms of 'variable geometry' or multi-speed Europe. A core Europe, possibly based around the eurozone, or a Europe of various cores could emerge comprising the more integrationist member states whether within the existing EU framework through use of provisions on enhanced cooperation or through the conclusion of new treaties. This might sound attractive to some member states, notably the French who are talking about an avant-garde of six large states, but significant political and legal obstacles would have to be overcome.

A related idea is that something like this might be done by using the existing 'enhanced cooperation' arrangements to apply some of the innovations of the Constitutional Treaty. But this would cause offence in excluded states and the present rules may not allow it.

A final option is actually to have a real debate: encouraging national parliaments to consider the future, inviting citizens to submit their own proposals, or adopting the strategy pioneered by the Irish National Forum on Europe. This would have the advantage of taking the people and their concerns seriously but might not throw up an agreed position and one which would be accepted by the member states.

Dutch 'No' camp, and French politicians like Colonna and Jospin signalling that revoting was very unlikely, it is difficult to see a clear way forward. The idea of a 'Europe of Projects' in which the EU appeals to voters by what it does is not likely to provide this either.

It is also very doubtful that there is the stomach for yet another round of negotiation even if this involves more open and widespread consultation and drafting together with ratification by a Europe-wide referendum. People with very different political views have suggested this, pointing to the fact that the political disagreements which affected both the Convention and the ratification process are just as likely to reoccur in any new negotiation. Given all this, it rather looks as if the EU will have to muddle through, leaving the Constitutional Treaty to one side and hoping that 'something may turn up'. In the meantime it will no doubt occupy itself with other quarrels and policy problems even if a deal on the financial perspective for 2007–13 has been agreed.

KEY POINTS

- The French and Dutch 'No' votes did not herald abandonment of the Constitutional Treaty but a 'period of reflection'.
- Progress on issues on the EU's agenda – such as further enlargement – cannot be wholly divorced from the future of the Constitutional Treaty.
- There are a number of ideas about what should be done about the Constitutional Treaty but most of them seem impossible to achieve.

Conclusion

The situation in which the EU finds itself regarding the Constitutional Treaty is somewhat ironic. Having undertaken the most open ever round of treaty reform to produce a document unanimously agreed by the governments of the 25 member states that both simplifies and clarifies what already exists and does little to increase the powers and roles of the EU, it finds all this cast into considerable doubt by negative votes in referenda in two member states which, historically, have been amongst the strongest advocates of European integration. Improved openness and opportunities for popular engagement clearly failed to deliver popular endorsement of a document that is designed to ensure that the enlarged EU functions more effectively, more efficiently, more democratically, and in a more intelligible manner.

Why it was rejected will be the focus of many future studies. What is clear is that French and Dutch voters used the referendum to vote not simply on the Constitutional Treaty but also on the general pace and direction of European integration, on the performance and standing of their own national governments, and on the nature of the world economy. This is not to deny that there are sound reasons to oppose the Constitutional Treaty but, equally, debates prior to the referenda revealed how little of the actual substance of the document was widely understood or appreciated. The arguments used to encourage people to vote 'No' were often based on misconceptions, false readings, in some cases wilful, and at times hyperbolic. People often forgot, overlooked, or were unaware of the fact that much of what is in the Constitutional Treaty already exists.

Rejection has led to an embarrassing sense of crisis among EU leaders. Few are willing to pronounce the Constitutional Treaty formally dead given the amount of political capital that has been invested in the lengthy debates and discussions in the Convention, the negotiations in the IGC, and the various compromises that resulted. Most member state governments are generally content with what is in the Constitutional Treaty and have not as yet come up with an alternative, which is difficult given the contradictory and often irrelevant criticisms of the text. The generally accepted gains in terms of clarification, transparency, and efficiency that will result from the Constitutional Treaty suggest that this will remain the ghost at the feast for some time.

However, rushing to find a solution to the ratification crisis and the broader question of the future of the EU is neither feasible nor advisable, despite the urgings of the enthusiasts. And success will require both an improved communication policy and proper consultation and involvement of the people. What remains unclear is how the views of the people could and should be canvassed. So far, despite talk of reflection and debate, few except the Commission – and to a lesser extent the French government – have begun to grapple with this problem. Indeed the pause for reflection was extended in June 2006.

And, even if there is better engagement with the people, there is little likelihood of agreement being reached on how the EU should be reformed and what shape it should take. The cheerful belief that, having rejected the Constitutional Treaty, the diverse peoples of Europe will come up with agreed, concise, and workable formulae, whether for a document or a socio-economic order for Europe, is naive. In the end, those who have to work the system are likely to end up with another compromise along the road to constitutionalization. This may mean that the future of the EU will finish up not far from what the Constitutional Treaty suggests it should be. In any case it is likely to inform future choices since it has both support and answers to some of the questions which worried the many voters who did not bother to read it, not to mention lessons about how not to proceed. So its fall may not be as absolute as now appears to be the case.

? QUESTIONS

1. Why was there a Convention on the Future of Europe as opposed to simply an IGC?
2. What is new in the Constitutional Treaty?
3. Why are there such conflicting interpretations of the Constitutional Treaty?
4. Why support the Constitutional Treaty?
5. Why did the French and Dutch people vote 'No' in their referenda on the Constitutional Treaty?
6. What kind of political crisis did these votes cause and why?
7. Why did voters in Spain and Luxembourg vote 'Yes' in their referenda on the Constitutional Treaty?
8. Should ratification of the Constitutional Treaty be continued?

GUIDE TO FURTHER READING

- Church, C. H., and Phinnemore, D. *Understanding the European Constitution: An Introduction to the EU Constitutional Treaty* (London: Routledge, 2005). An accessible discussion of the origins, key themes, and content of the Constitutional Treaty which prints Part I of the Treaty
- Cohen-Tanugi, L. 'The End of Europe?', *Foreign Affairs*, 84 (6) 2005 (available via www.foreignaffairs.org). A short survey of the challenges faced by the EU in addressing the fallout of the two 'No' votes in 2005.

- **Dobson, L., and Føllesdal, A. (eds)** ***Political Theory and the European Constitution*** **(London: Routledge, 2004).** A challenging collection of essays that provides, from the perspective of political theory, critical assessments of the draft Constitutional Treaty produced by the European Convention.

- **Eriksen, E. O., Fossum, J. E., and Menéndez, A. J. (eds)** ***Developing a Constitution for Europe*** **(London: Routledge, 2005).** An academic study of the rationale for a European Constitution and the process that led to the adoption of the Constitutional Treaty

- **European Council** ***Treaty establishing a Constitution for Europe*****, Official Journal of the European Union, C310, 16 December 2004.** The complete version of the signed Constitutional Treaty.

- **Foreign and Commonwealth Office,** ***Treaty establishing a Constitution for Europe: Commentary*****, Cm 6459, London, 26 January 2005 (also available via www.europe.gov.uk).** A detailed article-by-article commentary on how the provisions of the Constitutional Treaty compare with those in the existing treaties.

- **MacCormick, N.** ***Who's Afraid of a European Constitution?*** **(Exeter: Imprint Academic, 2005).** A spirited discussion of selected aspects of the Constitutional Treaty from a legal scholar and former Scottish nationalist MEP.

- **Michalski, A. (ed.)** ***The Political Dynamics of Constitutional Reform: Reflections on the Convention on the Future of Europe*** **(The Hague: Netherlands Institute of International Relations, 2004).** A collection of academic studies on the European Convention and its significance for the reform of the EU's treaty base.

- **Norman, P.** ***The Accidental Constitution: The Making of Europe's Constitutional Treaty*** **(Brussels: Eurocomment, 2005).** A journalist's authoritative account of the European Convention and the intergovernmental conference that produced the Constitutional Treaty.

- **Stuart, G.** ***The Making of Europe's Constitution*** **(London: Fabian Society, 2003).** A UK MP's reflections on the workings and outcome of the European Convention.

- **Usherwood, S. 'Realists, sceptics and opponents: opposition to the EU's Constitutional Treaty',** ***Journal of Contemporary European Research*****, I(2), 2005, 4–12 (available via www.jcer.net).** An article which examines the significance and impact of opposition to the constitutionalization process.

- **van Thiel, S. et al. (eds)** ***Understanding the New European Constitutional Treaty*** **(Brussels: VUB Brussels University Press, 2005).** A supportive series of essays on aspects of the Constitutional Treaty.

IMPORTANT WEBSITES

- **http://european-convention.eu.int/** European Convention website.
- **http://europa.eu.int/constitution/index_en.htm** Constitutional Treaty website.
- **http://europa.eu.int/scadplus/cig2004/index_en.htm** Archives of the 2003 IGC.

Visit the Online Resource Centre that accompanies this book for lots of interesting additional material. http://www.oxfordtextbooks.co.uk/orc/cini2e/

PART TWO

Theories and Conceptual Approaches

5

Federalism and Federation

MICHAEL BURGESS

Chapter Contents

Reader's Guide

When studying theories of European integration, it has been customary for both students and academics to either downgrade or completely overlook the significance of federalism. Even when federal ideas have grudgingly been recognized, they have tended to be subsumed within other theoretical or conceptual categories, such as neo-functionalism, so that until fairly recently federalism has been almost invisible in the study of EU politics (at least in the English language). In the introductory section, the chapter begins by confronting the problems involved in studying the idea of a 'federal Europe'. The following section adds definitional clarity to our subject, while the third section provides a short survey of federal models, with the aim of locating the European Union (EU) in a comparative federal framework. The fourth section involves a detailed investigation of the contribution of Jean Monnet to the goal of a federal Europe, and this is followed in turn by an assessment of the meaning of a federal Europe. The conclusion brings together various strands of conceptual and empirical analysis in order to underline the extent to which the European project has moved 'from quantity to quality'.

Introduction

In contemporary discourse it is common to refer to the phrase 'a federal Europe' when alluding to the ***finalité politique*** (end state) of the European Union). The assumption here is that a federal Europe is the ultimate destination or end point of the European integration process. However, some commentators and observers of the EU believe that this end point has already arrived. This is particularly important since reference to federalism in certain Eurosceptic member states, such as Denmark, Sweden, and especially the United Kingdom (UK) is often couched in gloomy language, intended to convey a strong sense of threat to the autonomy and integrity of the nation state.

Broadly speaking, the phrase a 'federal Europe' refers to a conception of the EU that is constantly changing, but which has at its core a set of basic principles or assumptions which indicate a voluntary union of states and citizens committed to the shared goals of welfare, security, and prosperity, and which is structured in a manner specifically designed to preserve nation state identities, cultures, and interests, where these are consistent with the overall well-being of the union. In practical terms this means that the union is based upon a combination of centralist and decentralist imperatives that facilitate 'common solutions to common problems'. In some policy areas the EU acts on behalf of its constituent members as a whole, while in others it leaves action to the individual member states. This broad conception of a federal Europe, as we shall see, is based upon a simple axiom: 'unity in diversity'. Where and when unity is required by common consent, the EU will act accordingly, while diversity will prevail in cases where and when the member states have agreed to act alone. The EU, it should be remembered, is a voluntary union based upon political consent and legal agreement.

Unfortunately the word 'federal' sometimes serves to muddy the waters. In some countries it has different connotations than in others. To the British, it commonly refers to centralizing tendencies that have the effect of strengthening the European level at the expense of national interests, while in Germany, Belgium, Spain, and Italy, it is understood to refer to a decentralized polity where power is dispersed among the constituent member states. Consequently, a federal Europe means different things to different people at different times and in different political systems. Political elites and mass publics in the EU entertain a variety of preconceptions about different phraseology. For some, to speak about 'European unity', for example, is to suggest something different from 'European Union'; it is to support **cooperation** rather than **integration**. If we follow this distinction, there is a sense, then, in which it is possible to advocate greater unity, but not union. It is therefore important to note that elite use of language, terminology, and definition plays a crucial role in creating images capable of mobilizing EU publics both in support of and against the goal of 'an ever closer union among the peoples of Europe', one of the primary goals of the EU.

This chapter explores the conceptual relationship between **federalism**, **federation**, and European integration in order to explain what is meant by the phrase a 'federal Europe'. This, after all, was the ultimate goal of **Jean Monnet**, the architect of European integration, whose impact on the European Union even today remains indelible. Its purpose, then, is to clarify what is meant by a federal Europe, so that careful analysis and measured reflection can take the place of unthinking knee-jerk reflex reactions to a phrase that operates at different levels of public discourse. In a nutshell, the chapter sets the record straight. We begin with a short survey of the basic conceptual relationship between federalism, federation, and European integration, and then look briefly at a variety of federal models, before exploring the constitutional and political implications of Monnet's Europe.

Federalism, federation, and European integration

In the mainstream political science literature, the terms 'federalism' and 'federation' have usually been used interchangeably. They refer to a particular kind of union among states and citizens. However, the word 'federal' has become a term that embraces a wide variety of different relationships tending toward unity, union, league, and association that range from the domestic arena of trade unions, sports clubs, and parent–teacher associations to the organization of the state, the political system, and governments at the international level. Deriving from the Latin term *foedus*, meaning covenant, the term 'federal' has evolved slowly to refer to different forms of human association. These imply a voluntary agreement or bargain among individuals, groups, and collectivities, in order to maintain their interests, identities, and integrity in pursuit of commonly shared interests and goals. Probably the best shorthand definition of this peculiar set of relationships is Daniel Elazar's allusion to 'self-rule plus shared rule' (Elazar 1987: 12) (see Box 5.1).

It is less important to arrive at a precise definition of the word 'federal' than to underline the core principles which lie at its root. *Foedus* (covenant) and its cognate *fides* (faith and trust) suggest what has been referred to as a 'vital bonding device of civilization' (Davis 1978: 3). And the words which best serve to convey its meaning include the following: mutual respect, recognition and toleration; equality of partnership; reciprocity; compromise; conciliation; and consent. In this sense, the notion of a federal union is founded upon a set of values and beliefs that are rooted in what is intrinsically a moral imperative drawing its intellectual basis from the German term *Bundestreue* ('federal comity' or a federal arrangement made for mutual benefit) (de Villiers 1995: 1–36). This imperative is *moral* in the extent to which it corresponds to a fundamental conviction about the need to work for the interests and benefits of the common weal or welfare. In turn, the political implications of this conviction suggest that the constituent units of such a union or association must always act in the best interests of the whole union. The commitment is therefore a moral commitment that hinges upon the reconciliation of the interests of each individual component

KEY CONCEPTS AND TERMS 5.1

What is federalism?

Federalism can be defined in a number of different ways. Here are some examples:

Federalism (n.) . . . a system of government which unites separate states while allowing each to have a substantial degree of autonomy. A federal style of government usually has a written constitution (e.g. the US) and tends to stress the importance of decentralized power and, in its democratic form, direct lines of communication between the government and its citizens (Oxford English Reference Dictionary, 2nd edn, 2001).

a method of dividing powers of government so that the central and regional governments are within a limited sphere co-ordinate but independent. The test of the principle is: does it embody the division of powers between central and regional authorities, each being independent of the other?

The basic idea behind federalism can be simply stated. It is that relations between states should be conducted under the rule of law. Conflict and disagreement should be resolved through peaceful means rather than through coercion or war (R. Laming: www.federalunion.uklinux.net/about/ federalism.htm).

Federalism is a fragile and dynamic form of political co-operation for sharing power and responsibility among diverse territorial units. In a federalist system, each sphere of government (i.e., the union, states, provinces, counties, municipalities) possesses its own agencies. At the same time, the central government exercises jurisdiction over the citizens of a given state independently of local authorities within the limits of a federal constitution (Mendes and Gall 2000).

part with those of others and of the totality of the union or state.

If we return to the terms 'federalism' and 'federation', we can now appreciate more fully the nature of the union that is inherent in the appellation 'federal'. It is a particular kind of union whose legitimacy rests firmly upon its capacity to sustain the sort of federal values identified above. This statement enables us to focus upon what we mean by federalism and federation. Let us first consider federation. Here it is appropriate for us to take a modestly revised version of Preston King's definition of federation as a basis for our survey. Federation is said to be:

> an institutional arrangement, taking the form of a sovereign state, and distinguished from other such states solely by the fact that its central government incorporates [constituent territorial units into its decision-making procedure] on some constitutionally entrenched basis

(King 1982: 77).

This definition is both precise and comprehensive, and it lucidly expresses the hallmark of all federal states, namely, the notion of 'constitutional entrenchment', that is, the formalization of the division between the centre and the component parts within a constitution. Accordingly, it is not in itself the division of competences that is of pivotal significance, but both the principle and the fact that there is a constitution. Federations vary enormously in how they are structured and in their distribution of powers and competences, but what lies at the core of every federal state is the inviolable right of each constituent unit – whether state, canton, province, or land – to its own constitutional integrity. A federation or federal state, then, is conventionally understood to be a particular kind of state wherein sovereignty is divided and shared between a central (federal) government and the constituent (member state) governments, and rooted in a written constitutional guarantee that can only be amended by special procedures that reinforce legitimacy by maximizing political consent.

The term 'federalism' is much more difficult to conceptualize because it is homonymous, expressing more than one distinct meaning. Federalism is the driving force or dynamic that informs federation and can be construed in three separate ways: (i) as ideology, (ii) as philosophy, or (iii) as empirical fact. It can be *ideological* in the sense that it is a body of ideas that actively promote federation. It can be a *philosophy* of federal ideas and principles that prescribes federation as the good life, or as the best way to organize human relations. Indeed, there exists a rich and well-established European philosophical tradition of federalism that includes such prominent Western political philosophers as Johannes Althusius, Immanuel Kant, Jean-Jacques Rousseau, and Pierre-Joseph Proudhon, as well as more recent contributors such as Alexandre Marc and Denis de Rougemont (see, for example, Carney 1964; Hueglin 1999; Riley 1973, 1976, and 1979; Elazar 1989; and Burgess 2000).

There is, however, a third meaning that can be attributed to federalism, namely, as an *empirical* fact. This pays homage to the complexity of human beings. The reasoning runs in the following way. Since we are each unique human beings that comprise bundles of different identities institutionalized in various forms of *voluntary* human association, it follows that the *formal* organization of human relations must be founded upon 'diversity' as its cardinal principle. Consequently, we require unity but not uniformity. In other words, we require a form of association which recognizes and can accommodate this complexity so that we have the relative autonomy to determine ourselves as individuals, groups, and collective identities within the union while simultaneously promoting the wider interests of the commonwealth. Transferred to the EU, this line of reasoning suggests that the 'ever closer union among the peoples of Europe' should be based upon the federal principle of 'unity in diversity'. Accordingly, the EU must be rooted in Elazar's notion, identified above, of 'self-rule plus shared rule'. The primary building blocks of the EU have already been formally reaffirmed in Article F(1), Title I 'Common Provisions' of the Treaty on European Union (TEU), ratified in 1993, which committed the Union to respect the national identities of its member states. Clearly the principal

KEY CONCEPTS AND TERMS 5.2

Federalism and subsidiarity

Depending on the definitions one uses federalism and subsidiarity may be related concepts. For some subsidiarity is a guiding principle of federalism; whereas for others subsidiarity seems to imply the antithesis of federalism. Although discussed before, subsidiarity was introduced to the EC through the Single European Act of 1987. However, at this point it applied only to the treaty's environmental provisions. It was in the Treaty on European Union, agreed at Maastricht, that the subsidiarity principle became a general principle of Community law. Article 3b of the Treaty reads as follows:

the Community shall act within the limits of the powers conferred upon it by this Treaty and of the objectives assigned to it therein. In areas which do not fall within its exclusive competence, the Community shall take action, in accordance with the principle of subsidiarity, only if and in so far as the objectives of the proposed action cannot be sufficiently achieved by the Member States and can therefore, by reason of the scale or effects of the proposed action, be better achieved by the Community. Any action by the Community shall not go beyond what is necessary to achieve the objectives of the Treaty.

In the Preamble of the Treaty, there was also the suggestion that subsidiarity was related to decentralization. Article A implies that decisions should be taken as closely as possible to the citizen.

However, these provisions leave much room for debate about the implications of subsidiarity. Some see it as little more than a 'rhetorical device' that no one can really disagree with or, more specifically, stress that it is not really about the allocation of competences between national and European levels of governance, but is about how they ought to be exercised (Dinan 2000: 440). Some even feel it should lead to the whole-scale repatriation of European law to either the national or regional/local levels of governance.

After the Maastricht Treaty attempts were made to set out rules to operationalize the principle of subsidiarity (for example, by ensuring the Commission exercises self-restraint when drafting new legislation) – at the Edinburgh European Council meeting of December 1992, most notably. The draft agreed in Edinburgh was incorporated into the Amsterdam Treaty in 1997.

Source: Based on Dinan (1992: 439–41).

focus of 'diversity' in the EU is the 25 member states and the 25 national governments that represent them. In this rather narrow sense, then, the member states constitute one dimension of 'federalism' in the EU. They are, in addition, the constituent units of an emergent federal union.

However, if we were to focus solely upon the EU Council and the European Council (see Chapter 10) to the exclusion of other actors and institutions in the EU, this would approximate not to a 'federal', but rather to a 'confederal' conception of Europe. What then is the difference between the two? The conceptual distinction between federation and confederation is that the latter is a much looser form of union that is much less binding and regulated than the former, and which does not operate directly upon the citizens of the union in the way that federation does. Confederation is, in short, a form of union where the constituent units rather than the central authority remain the decisive force, and institutionalized diplomacy takes the place of federal government (Forsyth 1981).

Nevertheless, this confederal dimension to the EU is also subject to a wide variety of federalist forces and influences at both the EU and member state levels, pressures that emanate from within both the Commission and the European Parliament (EP) at the EU level and from a host of interest groups, public organizations, and civil associations at the member state level. The underlying commitment to building Europe that is evident in this multiplicity of forces – both state and non-state – has as one of its common goals the desire to institutionalize the concrete achievements of integration. Accordingly, this example of 'federalism without federation' impels us to focus upon the peculiar relationship between federalism, federation, and European integration. It is important to look a little more closely at this relationship here before we examine it in more detail in the next section.

The evolution from a 'Community' to a 'Union' (see Chapter 4) corresponds to both a *quantitative* and a *qualitative* change in European integration. If we take the term 'integration' broadly to mean the coming together of previously separate or independent parts to form a new whole, we can see that it is a multidimensional process in that the shift from community to union has led to changes in the legal, economic, social, and political aspects of integration. Indeed, the EU is currently taking great strides in political integration, with the building of a constitutional and political Europe in the wake of the Single European Market (SEM) established by the Single European Act (SEA) and ratified in 1987. As Jean Monnet, the principal architect of the Community predicted, quantity (economic integration) appears to have led to an increasing emphasis upon quality (political integration). In other words, the objective is not just building an economic union whose sole purpose is, say, capital accumulation. Rather, European integration involves the construction of a viable, working political union founded upon peace, order, security, and welfare. In short, the EU as a federal union is supposed to represent a new moral force for good in European and world affairs.

Political elites in the member states and in the central institutions of the EU are now fully engaged in qualitative change, namely institutional reappraisal and constitution building. Consequently, today's EU comprises an institutionalized form of interstate relations, but also represents a radically new departure in the building of a union – a union of states *and* peoples. The EU, we are reminded, acts simultaneously upon *both* states and citizens in what remains Monnet's construction of Europe. We will explore the nature of the relationship between federalism, federation, and European integration a little later when we focus upon Monnet's conception of Europe and its political implications. The next section looks at the variety of federal models, in order to view the EU from a comparative federal perspective.

KEY POINTS

- Federalism is about 'self-rule plus shared rule' and 'unity in diversity'.
- There is an important moral dimension to federalism, as it is all about toleration, mutual respect, and equality of partnership, amongst other principles.
- Federalism also implies an institutional dimension, involving the sharing of powers between the centre and the regions or states, within the framework of an overarching constitution.

The variety of federal models

It is important to understand at the outset that, as Ronald Watts (1999: 1) has emphasized, there is no single, pure mode of federation that is applicable everywhere. Historically, federal states have emerged at different times to suit different circumstances. In some cases they have been the result of long and complicated processes of aggregation, whereby previously separate parts have come together or have been created to form a new state, such as the United States of America (1789) or Switzerland (1848); while in others they have been the product of different kinds of devolution or decentralization, such as Canada (1867), Australia (1901), or India (1950).

The historical origins of federations vary with each different case and the motives for union are not always very clear. Generally speaking, however, two fundamental factors are invariably evident in some form at the creation of most, if not all such voluntary unions. These are, first, the perception of an external threat that precipitates some form of union – as with the early evolution of Switzerland – chiefly for the purpose of security and sometimes called a *Kriegsverein* (military union); secondly, the drive to secure economic welfare – as with the early Dutch and German cases – often guides political and economic elites in their search for markets and trade. This is often called a **Zollverein** (customs union). Sometimes both of these motives are evident simultaneously as with the examples of Canada, Australia, the United States, and, arguably, the EU (see McKay 2001).

Most mainstream studies of federations acknowledge the variation that exists in their internal structures. They recognize that there are broadly three types of federations: (i) the Westminster model; (ii) the republican-presidential model; and (iii) a hybrid type. Examples of the Westminster model, which is based upon representative and responsible government, are found in Canada, India, and Australia as former parts of the British Empire. The republican-presidential model, by contrast, is most closely associated with the United States. Belgium, with its constitutional monarchy and cabinet government responsible to the lower house, the Chamber of Deputies, might be considered by some to be closer to the Westminster model than to the republican-presidential type. Hybrid examples that combine elements of these two models are Germany, Austria, and Switzerland. However, while these groups of comparisons work well from the standpoint of internal structures, we must also consider how they would change if we adopted a different perspective, one which focused on the distribution of powers in federations. This viewpoint alters the comparison in significant ways. Watts (1999: chapter 9) has emphasized that the basic design of all federal models expresses the hallmark of self-rule and shared rule through the constitutional distribution of powers between those assigned to the federal government for common purposes and those assigned to the constituent states for the purposes of local autonomy and the preservation of distinct identities and specific interests.

According to the definition used earlier in this chapter, the EU is clearly not yet a fully fledged federation. Indeed, it is not yet a state and it may never become a state in the sense that we understand conventional federations. It does, however, already possess many state-like characteristics, such as a common currency (the euro), an independent central bank, an embryonic fiscal base, a single market, two distinct levels of government, dual citizen identities, and an evolving Common Foreign and Security Policy, together with a yet incipient Common Defence Policy. And while many important policy sectors remain in the hands of the member governments, the EU also has ultimate authority in commercial transactions, transport, fisheries, and agricultural policies, as well as significant influence in environmental, regional development, and industry sectors. Consequently, the EU is already very close to being a new kind of state, or at least a 'federal-type' union, to the extent that it has increasingly adopted the institutional and policy features that are characteristic of established federations. The conventional strands of government as we know them – the legislative, executive, and judicial branches – are not organized along the same lines as the purported **separation of powers** in the United States, but they were originally arranged in the Treaty of Rome (1957) in such a manner as to balance the interests of individual constituent member states with those of the union as a whole, leaving plenty of scope for the later evolution of an 'ever closer union'. The increasingly complex decision-making procedures, involving cooperation and **codecision** procedures, between the intergovernmental EU Council (the ministers) and the European Council (heads of government), and the supranational Commission and European Parliament are similar in many respects to those of a working federation. These, then, are just a few examples of how and why the EU is often perceived by observers and commentators as approximating to a federal Europe. Clearly there is plenty of evidence to substantiate this public perception.

Before leaving this short survey of the variety of federal models, we turn to their significance for the

EU. What does the federal experience tell us about the EU? This is a question that resonates differently in different member states. Far from having little knowledge and experience of federations, the British have historically been involved in the application of the federal idea to a number of countries. Various federal models were used by the former Colonial Office to resolve an assortment of questions dealing with state building and national integration in the Empire and then the Commonwealth, including India, Australia, Canada, Central Africa, and the West Indies. To the British, then, federations have been practical proposals for export. But they were constructions for others, not for the British themselves. Thus, the federal idea has become associated with the creation of a constitutional and political force whose principal purpose was state and nation building. In short, for the British, the federal idea embodies, rightly or wrongly, connotations of centralization (Burgess 1995).

Given this historical background, it is easy to understand British hostility to the building of a federal Europe. This perspective on federalism in the EU context inevitably pushes public debate and discourse down a road that leads many citizens in Denmark and Sweden, as well as in the UK, to the nightmare scenario of a 'superstate'. But this dystopia is not shared by the citizens of the majority of member states in the EU. Quite the reverse. In most of Europe the perception of the word 'federal' is decentralist rather than centralist and a federal union is a political organization that both divides and shares power rather than concentrating it (as does a unitary state) in one centre.

There are, then, various federal models which furnish us with important lessons for the building of a federal Europe. The context, though, is of pivotal significance. The post-war experiment in European integration and cooperation is based on the territorial dispersion of power and is not designed to replicate, much less to replace, the constituent national and multinational states that comprise the EU. Nonetheless, the EU is greater than the sum of its parts. The genius of the federal idea lies in its simplicity: it seeks to bind the parts together in a way that benefits the whole. Let us now turn to look at Monnet's conception of Europe and its political implications in order to understand precisely how and why the idea of a federal Europe has become a practical proposition.

CASE STUDY 5.3

Federalism 'between the wars'

The federalist movement in Europe emerged in the period between the First and Second World Wars. In the aftermath of the horror of the First World War, Count Richard Coudenhove-Kalergi, an Austrian count, argued the case for a European Union (a pan-Europa) as a way of countering the growing power of the USA and Russia. His plans were picked up by Aristide Briand in the 1920s, who as French foreign minister proposed union as a way of maintaining the peace between France and Germany in 1929. Other proposals for federal union came from the UK, from writers such as Lord Lothian, Lionel Robbins, and William Beveridge, who predicted that Europe would make the same mistakes in the 1930s as it had done before the 'Great War' of 1914–18. Lord Lothian was amongst those who gave their support to the establishment of the Federal Union, which was set up in 1938. By 1940 the Federal Union had recruited 10,000 members in 200 branches (Dedman 1996: 19). Once the Second World War had begun British federalist writings began to have a strong influence on thinking within the European resistance movements whose members, particularly in Italy, even before the war was over, laid out their plans for a new world order. Amongst those influenced was Altiero Spinelli, whose Ventotene Manifesto became a reference point for post-war federalists (Dinan 2000: 231). While imprisoned on the island of Ventotene, Spinelli also translated many of the Federal Union's tracts into Italian.

KEY POINTS

- There are at least three different models of federalism: the republican-presidential, the Westminster model, and a third hybrid version.
- The EU is not yet a fully fledged federal state, though it does have certain federal characteristics.
- British hostility to the federal model owes much to the fact that federalism has been associated with nation building and centralization.

Monnet's conception of Europe and its political implications

Jean Monnet was born in Cognac, France, in 1888 and is considered one of the founders of the European Community. Monnet's conception of Europe was rooted in his desire to remove for ever the causes of war – what he regarded as civil war – that periodically served to tear Europe apart. He sought, in an elemental sense, to identify the forces that drove Europeans to fight each other and, in contrast, to understand those forces that instilled in them a fundamental desire to cooperate with each other. In short, he wanted to persuade Europeans to channel their conflicts into a form of cooperation that would enable them to achieve their goals by seeking out and distilling their common interests. He believed that in every set of circumstances that might conceivably generate conflict there lurked a latent common interest that merely needed to be uncovered. This meant that states, governments, and citizens could be persuaded to transform their rivalries and animosities by changing the context in which these conflicts occurred. It was what he called 'the ECSC method' of establishing 'the greatest solidarity among peoples' so that 'gradually' other tasks and other people would become subject to the same common rules and institutions – or perhaps to new institutions – and this experience would 'gradually spread by osmosis'. No time limits were imposed on what was clearly deemed to be a long, slow, almost organic, process of economic and political integration:

> "We believed in starting with limited achievements, establishing *de facto* solidarity, from which a federation would gradually emerge. I have never believed that one fine day Europe would be created by some great political mutation, and I thought it wrong to consult the peoples of Europe about the structure of a Community of which they had no practical experience. It was another matter, however, to ensure that in their limited field the new institutions were thoroughly democratic; and in this direction there was still progress to be made . . . the pragmatic method we had adopted would . . . lead to a federation validated by the people's vote; but that federation would be the culmination of an existing economic and political reality, already put to the test . . . it was bringing together men and practical matters"
>
> (Monnet 1978: 367).

This extract from Monnet's *Memoirs* throws the relationship between federalism, federation, and European integration into sharp relief. It underlines the interaction between politics and economics as the driving force behind integration. In explaining how Europe could be built by piecemeal, incremental steps – concrete achievements that were tried and tested – Monnet both confronted and confounded his contemporaries with the innovative idea of creating a federation via a hitherto unprecedented route (see also Chapter 6).

Changing the context of international relations in favour of the 'common interest' between states ensured that their energies were diverted from the competitive power politics that led to war, into new areas of unity and cooperation that transcended the state. In consequence, the EU has introduced a rule of law into relations between European countries which, as Duchêne (1994: 405) remarked, has 'cut off a whole dimension of destructive expectations in the minds of policy makers'. It has in practice domesticated the balance of power so that the power politics of the so-called 'realist' school of international relations has been replaced by 'aspirations that come nearer to the "rights" and responsibilities which reign in domestic politics'. In other words, Monnet's approach to the building of a federal Europe meant gradually internalizing what were previously the externalities of the state. This, it hardly needs emphasizing, was a major breakthrough in conventional interstate relations. Nonetheless, in seeking to build a federal Europe principally by means of a series of economic steps,

Monnet was attempting something which had no historical precedent. Indeed, the EC and, since 1993, the EU has evolved in a very different way to other federations. To the extent that it has developed by the gradual 'aggregation' of previously separate political units, it is admittedly similar to the process by which the United States of America was consolidated during the years 1787–9. Here, however, the analogy ends. Past federations have been constructed as a result of treaty-like political negotiations which created a new federal constitution and government. There is no historical precedent for the creation of a multinational, multicultural, and multilingual federation or federal union composed of 25 or more national states, with mature social, economic, political, and legal systems. In this regard the EU is a colossal and original enterprise.

What, then, are the political implications of Monnet's Europe? How did he seek to transform his Europe of incremental economic steps into a federal Europe? And what sort of timescale did he envisage for this grand metamorphosis? The answers to these questions require us to return to some of the assumptions, already identified above, upon which his conception of Europe was originally based. If we recall Monnet's fervent belief in the significance of context and how it was possible to change the nature of problems by changing the context in which they were located, it was his own practical logic that compelled him to give that context a solid form. And it was institutional innovation that answered the call for new habits of thought and action.

The key to understanding the relationship between federalism, federation, and European integration lies in the belief that by forging functional links between states in a way that does not directly challenge national sovereignty in a formal sense, the door to federation will gradually be opened. These so-called 'functional' links were primarily economic activities and they were perfectly expressed in the ECSC initiative of the early 1950s (see Chapter 2). This innovative form of supranational organization was to be the foundation of a European federation that would evolve only slowly to engage national elites in a process of mutual economic interest. These concrete benefits would gradually form that crucial solidarity – the common interest – which Monnet believed indispensable for the removal of physical and mental barriers (see also Chapter 6).

Institutional innovation, then, was vital to the success of European integration. Europeans were limited only by their imagination. If they could develop the vision to look beyond the national state to solve what were actually common problems, they could forge new cooperative links and foster new habits of working together in novel institutional circumstances. And novel institutions also implied novel decision-making processes and procedures to keep the wheels of integration turning. Nothing succeeds like success and as long as the 'Community experiment' yielded results that furnished tangible benefits for its participants, their commitment, based upon their perceptions of the national interest, was assured.

The political implications of Monnet's conception of Europe were and remain far-reaching principally because his particular approach to European integration was the one that succeeded. But Monnet was not without serious competitors in this quest and it is helpful for us to consider his approach from the standpoint of a much more conventional mainstream federalist perspective. Let us put Monnet, as it were, face to face with his main federalist rival, namely, Altiero Spinelli. Spinelli, an Italian, made the goal of a federal Europe his lifelong personal crusade. For our purposes, it is Spinelli's critique of what he called 'Monnet's method' that is of primary concern and we will use his critique to explore what he considered its political implications to be (see Burgess 2000; Pinder 1998b).

The essence of the Monnet method – his political strategy – for European integration was something that eventually came to constitute a major theoretical controversy about federalism, federation, and European integration. It was also the crux of Spinelli's opposition. This was that Monnet's own method of piecemeal, cumulative integration whereby 'political' Europe would be the 'culminating point of a gradual process' contained the huge assumption that at some future undefined point a qualitative change would occur in the constitutional and political relations between states and peoples. But he believed that this would happen only when 'the force of necessity' made it 'seem natural in the eyes of Europeans' (Monnet 1978: 394–5). In short, Monnet's approach to federation rendered constitutionalism – a political Europe – contingent upon the cumulative effect of functional achievements.

It was precisely at this juncture – in the interaction between politics and economics – that Spinelli entered the theoretical debate. Spinelli argued that the weakness of the 'Monnet Method' lay in its failure to deal with the organization of political power at the European level (Burgess 2000: 58). This meant that the political centre would remain weak and impotent, lacking the capacity to go much beyond what already existed. Spinelli's verdict on Monnet's conception of Europe can be succinctly summarized in the following way: it failed according to its own terms of reference. It simply did not possess that inherent sustaining dynamic which Monnet believed, at least initially, would evolve inexorably toward a union of peoples. The predicted shift from *quantity* to *quality* did not occur precisely because of Monnet's excessive reliance upon a functionalist or incrementalist logic. His confidence in such a logic was misplaced because he failed to confront the realities of organized political power. Only strong independent central political institutions could provide European solutions to European problems. Without these institutions, national responses would prevail. Spinelli acknowledged that Monnet had made the first steps easier to achieve, but he had done so by making the later steps more difficult. The building of 'political' Europe based upon economic performance criteria would not necessarily follow according to Monnet's logic, and as a consequence he argued that Europe might very well remain little more than a 'Common Market'.

In retrospect, Spinelli's criticisms of Monnet seem in one sense to have been vindicated. The EC/EU's central political institutions have certainly grown in political influence, but their powers and competences remain weak in certain important respects. The European Parliament, for example, still has only very limited powers of accountability over the Council, while its control over the budget remains only partial and the application of codecision is not yet extensive. These interinstitutional defects and deficiencies, however, are observations that rest on a conventional understanding of what federalism is. Not everybody wishes to see the EP's powers, functions, and role continue to grow exponentially. Indeed, some critics of the EP insist that its place in the institutional scheme of things remains ambiguous (see Chapter 11). Moreover, it could be argued that Spinelli underestimated the political will of the member states, invested in the European Council, that in recent years has taken several crucial steps forward in strengthening the EP and in buttressing qualified majority voting (QMV) in the Council. A series of intergovernmental conferences dating back at least to 1985 have produced the Single European Act (SEA), the Treaty on European Union (TEU), the Treaty of Amsterdam (TA), and more recently the Treaty of Nice, that have each been tantamount to the building of a political Europe. Consequently, there remain certain grounds for optimism concerning Monnet's shift from *quantity* to *quality*. There is some evidence that we have witnessed *both* an expansion of quantity as well as a

KEY CONCEPTS AND TERMS 5.4

Pragmatists vs. radicals

According to Harrison (1974) an important distinction to be made is that between radical federalists and moderates or pragmatists who accept a more incremental approach to unification, but are proud to carry the federalist flag. The radical federalists wanted a 'big bang' approach, creating a federal Europe by creating from the outset federal-type institutions. The more moderate federalists have much in common with neo-functionalists (see Chapter 6), and foresaw a federal outcome from an incremental or gradualist process of functional integration. Using this distinction, Altiero Spinelli was associated with radical federalist ideas, whereas Jean Monnet was a moderate federalist.

shift toward quality. In this respect, then, the political implications of Monnet's conception of Europe remain unclear.

If we move away from the institutional focus for a moment and turn our attention instead to policy matters, the profile of European integration becomes much more substantive and sophisticated. Here *quantity* has shifted unequivocally to *quality*. More and more policy matters that were formerly the exclusive domestic affairs of the member states have gradually been transferred to the EC and then the EU, so that Monnet's Europe has become a de facto polity with conspicuous policy outputs. The combination of an expanding policy arena increasingly subject to majority voting and that is treaty based has therefore corresponded to the transformation of a 'Community' into a 'Union' in which salient supranational, federal, and intergovernmental features coexist, admittedly often uncomfortably, in permanent interplay and reciprocity.

The political implications of Monnet's conception of Europe, then, harbour grounds for both optimism and pessimism. Much depends upon political leadership and the fortunes of the latest highly controversial enterprise, namely, the introduction of the euro in January 2002. The drive toward Economic and Monetary Union (EMU) is unquestionably a political imperative and constitutes yet another incremental step on the road towards a federal Europe. Accordingly, we will turn now to look more closely at what is meant by this ambiguous phrase.

KEY POINTS

- Jean Monnet was one of the founders of the European integration process.
- His federalism vision was an incremental one, constructed upon a functionalist logic.
- The so-called Monnet method, a piecemeal approach to the construction of a federal Europe, contrasted with Spinelli's vision, which involved an immediate shift of political power at the European level.

The meaning of a federal Europe

In certain EU member states, students who are interested in European integration and its current institutional manifestation, namely the EU, are often confronted with the phrase 'a federal Europe' as if it were synonymous with eternal infamy. As we noted in the introduction to this chapter, a conspicuous odium surrounds the word 'federal' and an acute anxiety is often attendant upon references to 'a federal Europe'. The phobia of federalism that is evident in some circles of opinion in the member states must be addressed, because it reflects genuine fears that deserve to be taken seriously. Mindful of such fears and anxieties, let us enter the conceptual world of a federal Europe to try to address the concerns of those who remain firm opponents of the idea for whatever reason.

We have already explained and defined the meaning of federalism, federation, and European integration and we have briefly explored the relationship between these terms. One conclusion that we drew was that in the specific context of European integration, federalism is a particular form of political integration. It is based upon a conception of Europe that implies 'self-rule plus shared rule'. In other words, it refers to a particular way that we might prefer to organize Europe. And this particular conception of Europe has both organizational and institutional implications for the building and design of Europe – a voluntary union, we are reminded, that is to be founded upon liberal democratic principles which recognize, respect, and tolerate difference and diversity. What, then, will this 'federal Europe' look like? How will it be organized and constructed?

Spinelli always claimed that we must begin with what has already been implemented. We cannot go back to the drawing board. Consequently we have to accept Monnet's legacy. We have to build upon the ***acquis communautaire*** – the Community patrimony – and try to transfer as many intergovernmental functions and responsibilities into the *acquis* as changing political circumstances will allow. The EU remains, after all, at the mercy of intergovernmental whims and vagaries. But a federal Europe implies a much more binding and regulated union, where there is a much more equitable working relationship between the EU's central institutions than a purely intergovernmental perspective would allow.

From a federalist perspective, there is currently no institutional *balance* as such, but instead an institutional *imbalance*. The proverbial dice are still loaded in favour of the constituent member states' interests rather than those of the union as a whole. There is therefore a need to review and reappraise the existing institutional framework and its inter institutional relations, powers, and competences.

The *organization* of the EU is predicated upon the existence of a voluntary union with a central authority (in Brussels) that is a creature of its member states. And it is here that federalism and federation, properly understood, constitute the antidote to public misgivings. It is precisely a federal Europe that guards against the feared usurpation of power either by the constituent members of the union or by the new central authority itself. Indeed, one of the purposes of a federal union or federation (as opposed to a unitary, legislative union) is precisely to place formal limits upon the growth of the central authority. But this is not to suggest that there should be no central authority or that it must be prevented from growing at all. There is no such thing as a union characterized by non-centralization. It is rather to accept and acknowledge that the EU must be based upon limited centralization. The organization of the EU based upon federal principles furnishes a guarantee that its increasing strength and capacity to mobilize resources will be limited, controlled, justified, and made persistently accountable.

The construction of Europe is, then, a question of organization. According to federal principles that imply a contractually binding, but limited, form of union in which power is divided and shared between the component states that created it, on the one hand, and the overarching central authority of the union, on the other, there are potentially an infinite number of institutional variations and jurisdictional permutations available. Monnet's approach meant that the architects of Europe had no need to start with a constitution and never had to concern themselves very much with the contentious question of national sovereignty. A federal Europe was to be the culmination, not the beginning, of a long process of economic integration. In view of these circumstances, it is hardly surprising that Monnet should have placed greater emphasis upon the unprecedented institutional innovation of the supranational High Authority rather than the familiar European Assembly when he created the ECSC in 1951.

The institutional framework of the European federal project has always been lopsided, with the dice heavily loaded in favour of the member states represented in the Council, and later the European Council, so that intergovernmentalism has coexisted with supranationalism from the outset. But as the policy commitment of the Community has expanded from the late 1950s, the growing influence and powers of both the EP and the European Court of Justice (ECJ) – in conjunction with an intermittently assertive European Commission – have strengthened the federal elements that sit alongside the confederal European Council of heads of state and government. And it is important that we do not forget that the EU Council (composed of national ministers) and the European Council, in representing the member state governments, are also both *central institutions* of the EU. From our standpoint in this chapter, they are essentially confederal and also constitute an intrinsic part of the EU's constantly evolving institutional composition.

This brings us to the future of institutional reform. Historically it has to be admitted that the EC/EU has merely tinkered with the system so that it has been modified rather than fully reformed. Consequently the central institutions of the EU today that service a union of 25 member states are remarkably similar to those that were established for the six founding members of the EEC in the Treaty of Rome in 1957. From the standpoint of the new millennium, it has to be acknowledged that thus far there seems to be very little millennial thinking about this colossal problem. One significant development, however, has come in the form of evidence of a shift in elite governmental thinking in favour of constitutionalizing the EU. By identifying what each EU institution should do, this would draw firm lines to divide and share powers and competences among the EU's federal and confederal institutions so that both transparency and accountability could be effectively transmitted to both EU elites and mass publics. Accordingly, at the Laeken meeting (see Chapter 4) in December 2001, the member governments took the step, albeit tentatively, towards a new constitution for the EU at the next IGC in 2004. A review of the treaties and the working methods of the EU has already begun, but much remains to be done. Nonetheless, it is beginning to look as if the constitutional and political chickens of Monnet's Europe are finally coming home to roost.

Paradoxically, the meaning of a federal Europe is both simple and complex. At its most elementary level it means 'common solutions to common problems' based upon 'self-rule plus shared rule'. A more sophisticated interpretation compels us to look very closely at the basis of the EU's emerging constitution: its principles, objectives, institutional powers and relationships, and its policy-making and implementation structures. This combination of the simple and the complex means a federal Europe that would constitute a new kind of union of states and citizens. This would rely on both integration and cooperation in an increasingly competitive world of globalized relationships where the familiar 'nation state' competes with rival non-state international actors. In short, the introduction of an EU constitution would simply represent the latest European adaptation to international developments.

KEY POINTS

- To address the extent to which the EU is already federal involves looking at the organization of the Union.
- The EU remains more confederal or intergovernmental than federal.
- The EU is involved in a process of institutional reform, which could lead to the drafting of a European constitution and further moves in a federal direction.

Conclusion: from quantity to quality

This chapter has explained the meaning of a federal Europe by exploring the conceptual interrelationships between federalism, federation, and European integration and by examining the political implications of Monnet's conception of Europe. It has demonstrated that a federal Europe will not be either a United States or Switzerland writ large. It will not replicate the conventional processes of traditional state building and national integration that we associate with the contemporary nation state. Nor will it approximate to the sort of international organizations with which we customarily identify, such as the United Nations. Instead an emerging federal Europe would constitute a new kind of political union in world affairs standing in a long line of voluntary historical unions stretching back several centuries. This new form of union can be described as either 'neo-federal' or 'neo-confederal', but there is no doubt that it represents a new era in the history of interstate relations in Europe (Burgess 2000: chapter 8). In this sense, quantity is about to transform into quality.

? QUESTIONS

1. What is the relationship between federation, federalism, and European integration?
2. What was Jean Monnet's contribution to federal union in Europe after the Second World War?
3. Why did Altiero Spinelli criticize the so-called 'Monnet method' of European integration?
4. Why do the British have a particularly hostile attitude to European federalism?
5. What are the key characteristics of a federal union?
6. Which model of federalism does the EU most resemble?
7. In what sense is there a moral dimension to federalism?
8. How might a confederal union differ from a federal union?

GUIDE TO FURTHER READING

■ Burgess, M. *Federalism and the European Union: Building of Europe 1950–2000* (London: Routledge, 2000). A historical account of the integration of Europe, focusing on the role played by federalist ideas.

■ Burgess, M., and Gagnon, A.-G. (eds) *Comparative Federalism and Federation* (Hemel Hempstead: Harvester Wheatsheaf, 1993). An edited book looking at the concepts of federalism and federation, and including a range of country case studies which identify different traditions of federalism and federation.

■ Elazar, D. J. *Exploring Federalism* (Tuscaloosa, AL: University of Alabama Press, 1987). An excellent study of what federalism means from an authority on the subject.

■ Forsyth, M. *Union of States* (Leicester: Leicester University Press, 1981). A seminal study of confederation. While its focus is on European integration, this book draws on many examples of confederation and federation to explore the process by which states transform themselves.

■ Jeffrey, C., and Sturm, R. (eds) *Federalism, Unification and European Integration* (London: Frank Cass, 1993). An edited book which looks at federalism in the new unified Germany, in a European context, from a variety of different perspectives.

■ Pinder, J. *European Community: Building of a Union* (Oxford: Oxford University Press, 1998). A useful general text on the European integration process, written from a federalist perspective, and the historical process from EC to EU.

IMPORTANT WEBSITES

- www.federalunion.uklinex.net Website of the UK's Federal Union, an organization set up in 1938 to campaign for federalism in the UK, in Europe, and in the world. Lots of useful 'pro-federalist' material.
- www.http://europa.eu.int/comm/public-opinion/archives/eb/eb44/eb44_en.htm Eurobarometer. Some public opinion data on 'The regions and a federal structure for Europe'.
- www.sussex.ac.uk/Units/SEI/oern/index.html Opposing Europe Research Network: academic website, including a number of papers on the phenomenon of Euroscepticism in Europe.

Visit the Online Resource Centre that accompanies this book for lots of interesting additional material. http://www.oxfordtextbooks.co.uk/orc/cini2e/

6 Neo-functionalism

CARSTEN STRØBY JENSEN

Chapter Contents

- Introduction
- What is neo-functionalism?
- A brief history of neo-functionalism
- Supranationalism and spillover
- Critiques of neo-functionalism
- The revival of neo-functionalism
- Conclusion

Reader's Guide

This chapter reviews a theoretical position, neo-functionalism, which was developed in the mid-1950s by scholars based in the USA. The fundamental argument of the theory is that states are not the only important actors on the international scene. As a consequence, neo-functionalists focus their attention on the role of supranational institutions and non-state actors, such as interest groups and political parties who, they argue, are the real driving force behind regional integration efforts. The chapter that follows provides an introduction to the main features of neo-functionalist theory, and to its historical development since the 1950s. It focuses, more specifically, on three theses advanced by neo-functionalists: the spillover thesis; the elite socialization thesis; and the supranational interest group thesis. The chapter also considers the main critiques of the theory to explain why it went out of fashion in the 1970s. The final section scrutinizes the revival of interest in neo-functionalism beginning in the late 1980s and 1990s, as well as providing some examples of how today's neo-functionalists differ from those of the 1950s.

Introduction

Neo-functionalism is often the first theory of European integration studied by students of the European Union. This is largely for historical reasons, as neo-functionalism was the first attempt at theorizing the new form of regional cooperation that emerged at the end of the Second World War. Although few researchers of European integration would now accept all neo-functionalist arguments, the theory remains important because its concepts and assumptions have become part of the so-called **Monnet method** of European integration. Indeed, at times, it has been difficult to separate the theory of integration from the reality of the EC/EU. This has been something of a curse for neo-functionalism, as it has meant that its success as a theory became inextricably tied to the success of the European integration project. But it does mean that it is possible to chart the history of the EC/EU through the lens of neo-functionalism, as we shall see below.

The chapter begins by asking: 'What is neo-functionalism?' The purpose of this first section is to outline the general characteristics of the theory. The second section then summarizes the rise and fall from grace of neo-functionalism between the 1950s and the 1970s. The third section examines three theses which form the core of neo-functionalist thinking. These are: (a) the spillover thesis; (b) the elite socialization thesis; and (c) the supranational interest group thesis. These three arguments help to expose neo-functionalist beliefs about the dynamics of the European integration process. The fourth section reviews the main criticisms of the neo-functionalist school, while the final section turns to more recent adaptations of neo-functionalist ideas, accounting for the renewal of interest in this approach to the study of regional integration at the beginning of the 1990s. The chapter concludes by stressing that although some researchers rediscovered neo-functionalism long after the mid-1950s, its application is very different today, and neo-functionalism is no longer part of the mainstream theorizing of EU developments.

What is neo-functionalism?

The story of neo-functionalism began in 1958 with the publication by Ernst B. Haas (1924–2003) of *The Uniting of Europe: Political, Social and Economic Forces 1950–1957* (Haas 1958). In this seminal book, Haas explained how six West European countries came to initiate a new form of supranational cooperation after the Second World War. Originally, Haas's main aim in formulating a theoretical account of the European Coal and Steel Community (ECSC) was to provide a scientific and objective explanation of regional cooperation, a grand theory that would explain similar processes elsewhere in the world (in Latin America, for example). However, neo-functionalism soon became very closely associated with the EC case and, moreover, with a particular path of European integration. However, some argued that despite the scientific language, neo-functionalism was imbued from the outset with pro-integration assumptions that were not made explicit in the theory.

Three characteristics of neo-functionalist theory help to address the question of what is neo-functionalism. First, neo-functionalism's core concept is that of spillover. This is covered in more detail later in the chapter. It is important to note at this point, however, that neo-functionalism was mainly concerned with the process of integration (and had little to say about end goals, that is, about how an integrated Europe would look). As a consequence, the theory sought to explain the dynamics of change to which states were subject when they cooperated. Haas's theory, then, was based on the assumption that cooperation in one policy area would create pressures in a neighbouring policy area, placing it on the political agenda, and ultimately leading to further integration. Thus, spillover refers to a situation where cooperation in one field necessitates cooperation in another. This might suggest that the process is automatic, that is, beyond the control of political leaders. However, when we look at the various forms of spillover identified by Haas, we will see how this 'automatic' process might be guided or manipulated by actors and institutions whose motives are unequivocally political.

A second, albeit related, point which helps to explain neo-functionalism concerns the role of societal groups in the process of integration. Haas argued that interest groups and political parties would be key actors in driving integration forward. While governments might be reluctant to engage in integration, groups would see it as in their interest to push for further integration. This is because groups would see integration as a way of resolving problems they faced. Although groups would invariably have different problems and, indeed, different ideological positions, they would, according to neo-functionalists, all see regional integration as a means to their desired ends. Thus, one might see integration as a process driven by the self-interest of groups, rather than by any ideological vision of a united Europe or shared sense of identity.

Finally, neo-functionalism is often characterized as a rather elitist approach to European integration. Although it sees a role for groups in the integration process, integration tends to be driven by functional and technocratic needs. Though not apolitical, it sees little role for democratic and accountable governance at the level of the region. Rather, the 'benign elitism' of neo-functionalists tends to assume the tacit support of the European peoples – a 'permissive consensus' – upon which experts and executives rely when pushing for further European integration (see Box 6.1).

KEY CONCEPTS AND TERMS 6.1

Features of neo-functionalism

- Neo-functionalism is a theory of regional integration which seeks to explain the process of (European) integration.
- The theory was particularly influential in the 1950s and 1960s.
- The main focus of the theory is on the 'factors' that drive integration: interest group activity; political party activity; the role of governments and supranational institutions.
- The driving force of integration is deemed to be the self-interest of groups and institutions. They may well have different goals in mind, but the actions they choose, in order to achieve those goals, drive forward the integration process.
- The theory is said to be elitist in the sense that it relies on the 'permissive consensus' of the peoples of Europe. In other words, regional integration is seen as an elite-driven process.
- The concept of spillover is also known as the 'expansive logic of integration'. The 'spilling over' of integration can occur across sectors, but may also involve a shift to a new centre of popular loyalty (at a supranational level).

KEY POINTS

- Neo-functionalism is a theory of regional integration, popular in the 1950s and 1960s.
- The theory deals with the dynamics of the integration process, particularly with regard to the European case. The core concept of neo-functionalism is spillover.
- The theory assumes that integration relies on the self-interest of societal groups. It is also often considered a rather elitist theory.

A brief history of neo-functionalism

Neo-functionalism is very much connected to the case of European integration. Indeed, most neo-functionalist writers have focused their attention on Europe (Lindberg 1963; Lindberg and Scheingold 1970, 1971). This was not their original intention, however. Rather, an early objective was to formulate a general or grand theory of international relations, based on observations of regional integration processes. Political and economic cooperation in Latin America was one of the cases investigated to that end (Haas and Schmitter 1964; Mattli 2005). It was in Europe, however, that political and economic integration was best developed and most suited to theoretical and empirical study. Therefore Europe and European integration became the major focus of neo-functionalists during the 1960s and 1970s.

With the benefit of hindsight the success of neo-functionalism is understandable, as it seemed that the theory explained well the reality of the European integration process at that time. Until the 1970s, neo-functionalism had wide support in academic circles, though after that it lost much of its appeal. Indeed, it almost disappeared as a theoretical and empirical position in the study of European integration. One reason for this was that neo-functionalism lacked a theoretically solid base for its observations. Another reason was that the kind of incremental political integration that neo-functionalism predicted did not take place. From the mid-1970s, political cooperation seemed less compelling, and researchers became more interested in other kinds of theories, especially those that stressed the importance of the nation state. Even Haas was among those who recognized the limitations of neo-functionalism. On this point he wrote that 'the prognoses often do not match the diagnostic sophistication, and patients die when they should recover, while others recover even though all the vital signs look bad' (Haas 1975: 5).

In the late 1980s and during the 1990s neo-functionalism underwent a sort of revival. The new dynamism of the EC/EU, a consequence of the Single Market programme (see Chapter 16), made theories focusing on processes of political integration relevant once again (Tranholm-Mikkelsen 1991). And even traditional critics of neo-functionalism, such as Paul Taylor, accepted the need to examine this approach more closely. On this point, Taylor (1993: 77) wrote that 'The student of the European Community . . . needs to return to the writings of . . . the neo-functionalists – whose writings for many years have been unfashionable. They provide the essential context of theory in which to place the practice of diplomacy and even the speeches of Prime Ministers so that they might be better understood'.

Since this revival of interest in neo-functionalism, a number of scholars have sought to adapt the theory to their own research agendas – whether on the European integration process writ large, on specific policy areas, or on the role of the supranational institutions. Correspondingly there were, in connection with the death of Ernst B. Haas in 2003,

KEY POINTS

- Neo-functionalism was fashionable amongst elites and academics until the 1970s.
- From the 1970s, other theoretical and conceptual approaches seemed to fit the reality of European integration much better than neo-functionalism, and the theory became obsolete.
- From the 1980s and 1990s, with the revival of the integration process, there came also a renewed interest in neo-functionalism. This led to a wave of further research, which used certain elements of the neo-functionalists' conceptual tool-kit.

a number of attempts to evaluate and re-evaluate the importance of the neo-functionalist contribution to the understanding of the development of the European Community (for example, in a special issue of the *Journal of European Public Policy* in 2005). These new approaches and evaluations will be reviewed towards the end of this chapter.

Supranationalism and spillover

The key questions asked by neo-functionalists are whether and how economic integration leads to political integration; and, if it does so, what kind of political unity will result. In this respect neo-functionalism differs from other traditional approaches to international relations theory. Traditionally more realist positions have stressed the power games that occur between states. Among neo-functionalists it was believed that economic integration would strengthen all the states involved, and that this would lead to further political integration. The fundamental idea was that international relations should not be seen as a zero-sum game, and that everybody wins when countries become involved in processes of economic and political integration.

Another important aspect of neo-functionalist theory is related to the development of supranational institutions and organizations. Supranational institutions are likely to have their own political agendas. Over time, neo-functionalists predict, the supranational agenda will tend to triumph over interests formulated by member states. As an example one might look at how the European Parliament (EP) operates. Members of the EP are directly elected within the member states. One would therefore expect it to be an institution influenced very much by national interests. In the Parliament, however, Members of the European Parliament (MEPs) are not divided into groups relating to their national origin. They are organized along party political and ideological lines (see Chapter 11). In other words, social democrats from Germany work together with Labour members from the UK, and liberals from Spain work with liberals from Denmark. According to neo-functionalist theory, MEPs tend to become more European in their outlook, as a consequence of these working practices, though in practice this may be disputed empirically. This is often referred to as 'elite socialization'. The fact that MEPs work together across borders makes it difficult for them to focus solely on national interests. This also makes the EP a natural ally for the European Commission in its discussions with the EU Council, even if the institutions do not always agree on matters of policy.

Political integration is therefore a key concept for neo-functionalists, though it is possible to identify a number of different understandings of political integration in their writings. Lindberg (1971: 59), for example, stressed that political integration involves governments doing together what they used to do individually. It is about setting up supranational and collective decision-making processes. By contrast, Haas tended to see political integration in terms of shifts in attitudes and loyalties among political actors. In 1958 he famously wrote:

> “Political integration is the process whereby political actors in several distinct national settings are persuaded to shift their loyalties, expectations and political activities toward a new centre, whose institutions possess or demand jurisdiction over the pre-existing national states. The end result of a process of political integration is a new political community, superimposed over the pre-existing ones”
>
> (Haas 1958: 16).

Neo-functionalist writers developed at least three different arguments about the dynamics of the integration processes: (a) the spillover thesis; (b) the elite socialization thesis; and (c) the thesis on supranational interest groups. The following subsections set out the content of these theses and the following section presents critiques of these arguments.

Spillover

Spillover is neo-functionalism's best known concept, one which has been widely used both by social scientists and by practitioners. According to Lindberg (1963: 10), the concept of spillover refers to a process where political cooperation conducted with a specific goal in mind leads to the formulation of new goals in order to assure the achievement of the original goals. What this means is that political cooperation, once initiated, is extended over time in a way that was not necessarily intended at the outset.

In order to fulfil certain goals, states cooperate on a specific issue. For example, the original aim may be the free movement of workers across EU borders. But it may soon become obvious that different national rules concerning certification prevent workers from gaining employment in other EU states. For example, nurses educated in one member state may not be allowed to work in another because of differences in national educational systems. As a consequence, new political goals in the field of education policy may be formulated so as to overcome this obstacle to the free movement of labour. This process of generating new political goals is the very essence of the neo-functionalist concept of spillover.

> “Spillover refers . . . to the process whereby members of an integration scheme – agreed on some collective goals for a variety of motives but unequally satisfied with their attainment of these goals – attempt to resolve their dissatisfaction by resorting to collaboration in another, related sector (expanding the scope of mutual commitment) or by intensifying their commitment to the original sector (increasing the level of mutual commitment), or both”
>
> (Schmitter 1969: 162).

KEY CONCEPTS AND TERMS 6.2

Types of spillover

- Functional spillover takes place when cooperation in one sector/issue area 'functionally' creates pressures for cooperation in another related area.
- Political spillover refers to situations characterized by a more deliberate political process, as when actors (national or supranational) make package deals in order to establish common agreement in a range of policy areas.

A distinction is often drawn between different types of spillover: functional (or technical) spillover and political (or cultivated) spillover (Nye 1971; Tranholm-Mikkelsen 1991; Rosamond 2005a; Moravcsik 2005; see also Box 6.2).

An example of functional spillover may be seen in the case of the Single Market (see Chapter 16 and Box 16.3). The Single Market was functionally related to common rules governing the working environment. For example, some of the trade barriers to be removed under the Single Market programme took the form of national regulations on health and safety matters, as different health and safety regulations across the Community prevented free movement. The functional consequence of establishing a Single Market was, then, that the member states ended up accepting the regulation of certain aspects of the working environment at European level (Jensen 2000).

Political spillover refers to situations where policy areas are deliberately linked together, not because they are functionally or technologically related, but for political or ideological reasons (Nye 1971: 202). Special interests are often promoted via so-called 'package deals', where steps are taken to treat a number of apparently discrete issues as a single (composite) item, enabling all (or the majority of) actors to safeguard their interests (Lindberg and Scheingold 1970: 116). For example, if one member state has an interest in a certain policy area, for example to prevent cuts in agricultural spending, while another member state has interests in industrial policy, these member states may agree, formally or informally, to support each other in negotiations. As a result the two policy areas become linked within the bargaining process. Package dealing can often be observed during treaty revisions. Political spillover may also be observed in situations where supranational actors like the Commission try to push forward a supranational or transnational agenda, even where member states are reluctant to accept further integration. In the EU, the Commission often acts as a mediator of national interests in Council negotiations, with the aim of establishing compromises among member states.

Thus, spillover processes may be seen partly as the result of unintended consequences. Member states might deliberately accept political integration and the delegation of authority to supranational institutions on a particular issue. However, as a result of that decision, they may suddenly find themselves in a position where there is a further need for even more delegation. As a result, Lindberg and Scheingold are right to stress that political integration need not be the declared end goal for member states engaging in this process. The latter have their own respective goals, which are likely to have more to do with policy issues than with integration. As Lindberg and Scheingold write: 'We do not assume that actors will be primarily or even at all interested in increasing the scope and capacities of the system per se. Some will be, but by and large most are concerned with achieving concrete economic and welfare goals and will view integration only as a means to these ends' (Lindberg and Scheingold 1970: 117). In this sense the establishment of supranational institutions such as the EU may be seen as the result of unintended consequences of actions among the actors involved in decision-making.

CASE STUDY 6.3

Functional spillover – from Single Market to Economic and Monetary Union

The establishment of the Single Market increased the possibilities for companies in Europe to trade across borders. This generally implied a growth in trade among the countries in the European Community. The increased level of transnational trade in the European Community however made companies (and countries) more exposed to fluctuations in national currencies, which clarified the functional advantages in a common European currency (from that perspective). Economic and Monetary Union can in that perspective be seen as a result of a functional spillover logic connecting growth in trade across borders in the EU with the functional need for a common currency reducing risks related to trade.

Elite socialization

The second aspect of neo-functionalist theory concerns the development of supranational loyalties by participants such as officials and politicians in the decision-making process. The thesis here is that, over time, people involved on a regular basis in the supranational policy process will tend to develop European loyalties and preferences (Pentland 1973). For example, Commission officials are expected to hold a European perspective on problem-solving so that their loyalty may no longer be to any one national polity, but rather to the supranational level of governance.

We can well imagine how participants engaged in an intensive ongoing decision-making process, which may extend over several years and bring them into frequent and close personal contact, and which engages them in a joint problem-solving and policy-generating exercise, might develop a special orientation to that process and to those interactions, especially if they are rewarding. They may come to value the system and their roles within it, either for itself or for the concrete rewards and benefits it has produced or that it promises (Lindberg and Scheingold 1970: 119).

Thus neo-functionalists predicted that the European integration process would lead to the establishment of elite groups loyal to the supranational institutions and holding pan-European norms and ideas. This elite would try to convince national elites of the advantages of supranational cooperation. At the same time neo-functionalists also predicted that international negotiations would become less politicized and more technocratic. The institutionalization of the interactions between national actors, and the continued negotiations between different member states, would make it more and more difficult for states to adhere to their political arguments, and retain their credibility (Haas 1958: 291). As a result, it was expected that the agenda would tend to shift towards more technical problems upon which it was possible to forge agreement.

The formation of supranational interest groups

According to neo-functionalist theory, civil servants are not the only groups that develop a supranational orientation. Organized interest groups are also expected to become more European, as corporations and business groups formulate their own interests with an eye to the supranational institutions (see Chapter 13). As economic and political integration in a given region develops, interest groups will try to match this development through a process of reorganization, to form their own supranational organizations. For example, national industrial and employers organizations established a common European organization, UNICE, in 1958, at much the same time as the European Community was established. In so doing, their intention was to influence future Community policy. Early neo-functionalists also saw a similar role for political parties.

Furthermore, neo-functionalists believed that interest groups would put pressure on governments to force them to speed up the integration process. These groups were expected to develop their own supranational interest in political and economic integration, which would ally them to supranational institutions, such as the European Commission. Thus, 'in the process of reformulating expectations and demands, the interest groups in question approach one another supranationally while their erstwhile ties with national friends undergo deterioration' (Haas 1958: 313).

Before we examine criticisms of the neo-functionalist approach, it is important to stress the following point: neo-functionalism is often compared to or is seen as connected with federalism (see Chapter 5). Federalists argue that the EU should establish strong federal institutions leading in the end to the creation of a federation with some similarities to the USA. Sometimes neo-functionalism is seen as a theoretical approach that supports a federalist agenda. Neo-functionalists, like federalists, talk about processes of political integration, and about the advantages of this process (see Box 6.4). However neo-functionalists like Haas (Haas 1971: 20–1) stressed that neo-functionalism and federalism are very different in several respects. The most important of these, according to Haas, is that federalism is a political position, while neo-functionalism is both theoretical and scientific. Federalists are interested in how things ought to be, while neo-functionalists analyse the processes of integration and disintegration from a scientific point of view. However, critics of neo-functionalism might dispute the claim that neo-functionalism is devoid of a political agenda.

KEY POINTS

- Neo-functionalists believe that there are different types of spillover. Functional and political spillover account for different dynamics of the integration process.
- 'Elite socialization' implies that over time people involved in European affairs shift their loyalties to the European institutions and away from their nation state.
- Neo-functionalists believe that interest groups also become Europeanized, placing demands on their national governments for more integration.

BOX 6.4

Neo-functionalist expectations about the European institutions

Neo-functionalists have formulated theories which they have used to predict the behaviour of the European institutions.

- The European Commission is expected to act as a 'political entrepreneur', as well as a mediator. The Commission will, according to neo-functionalist theory, try to push for greater cooperation between the member states in a direction that leads to more and more supranational decision-making.
- The European Court is expected not only to rule on the basis of legal arguments, but also to favour political integration. In this way, the Court will seek to expand the logic of Community law to new areas.
- The European Parliament is expected to be a supranationally orientated institution and to be a natural ally of the European Commission. Although MEPs are elected by the nationals of their home country, they are divided politically and ideologically in their daily work. Neo-functionalists expect MEPs to develop loyalties towards the EU and the 'European idea', so that they would often (though not always) defend European interests against national interests.
- The EU Council (Council of Ministers) is expected to be the institution where national interests are defended. However neo-functionalists would expect member states from time to time to be influenced by the logic of spillover, which will lead them to argue for more and more economic and political integration, despite their national interests. The member states are also expected to be influenced by the fact that they are involved in ongoing negotiations in a supranational context. This makes it difficult for a member state to resist proposals which lead to further political integration.

Critiques of neo-functionalism

We now review briefly the main criticisms of neo-functionalism made by observers such as Haas (1975, 1976), Moravcsik (1993, 1998, 2005), Taylor (1990, 1993), Keohane and Nye (1975), Keohane and Hoffman (1991), and Schmitter (2005).

Neo-functionalism has been criticized on both empirical and theoretical grounds. At an empirical level the criticism focused on the absence (or slow pace) of political integration in Western Europe during the 1970s and up to the mid-1980s. Neo-functionalism had predicted a pattern of development characterized by a gradual intensification of political integration, a development that by the 1970s had clearly not taken place. The French boycott of the European institutions in the mid-1960s had led to a more cautious phase in the evolution of the Community, and a recognition of the importance of political leaders as constraints on the process of integration. Indeed, with the European Community having suffered numerous crises, it could even be argued that the integration process had reversed. Moravcsik writes that:

> Despite the richness of its insights, neo-functionalism is today widely regarded as having offered an unsatisfactory account of European integration . . . . The most widely-cited reason is empirical: neo-functionalism appears to mispredict both the trajectory and the process of EC evolution. Insofar as neo-functionalism advances a clear precondition about the trajectory in the EC over time, it was that the technocratic imperative would lead to a 'gradual', 'automatic' and 'incremental' progression toward deeper integration and greater supranational influence
>
> (Moravcsik 1993: 476).

Even Haas talked about the possibility that there might be a disintegrative equivalent to spillover, which might be labelled 'spillback'!

However alongside these empirical critiques lie theoretical objections which cover a broader spectrum. Here we shall focus on three main types of criticism. The first set of objections was aimed at the theses advanced by neo-functionalists. An example of this is Taylor's challenges to the elite socialization thesis, and to the idea that supranational loyalties would emerge in institutions such as the Commission. Taylor (1990) pointed out that, rather than integration making officials more European, it was the interests of the member states in having 'national' civil servants in the Commission that increased as political integration intensified. Member states became increasingly aware of the need to ensure that they reached 'their' quota of European civil servants (Taylor 1990: 180) and that their interests were represented. Moreover, it was surmised that European civil servants would become more nationally orientated when vital political issues were on the agenda (see also Hooghe 2001).

Correspondingly Risse (2005) has argued that if the neo-functionalists were right, farmers and women should be among the most EU-supportive citizens in Europe, which is definitely not the case:

> “Haas seemed to have assumed . . . that those who profit most from European integration are also most likely to shift their loyalties toward Europe than others. If this were true, two groups should be more supportive of European integration than they actually are. First, farmers are arguably the one professional group who profit most from the EU . . . Yet, there is no indication that farmers identify with the EU to any considerable degree. Their satisfaction with the EU's performance appears also to be rather low. Second, we would expect women to be in general more supportive of European integration than men, given that it was the EU that pushed gender equality, particularly equal treatment and equal pay in the workplace . . . But there is a gender gap in support for the EU, with men being in general more supportive of integration than women”
>
> (Risse 2005: 297).

The second set of objections was based on criticism of the theories formulated by Haas himself. By the late 1960s Haas had accepted that the prediction that regional organizations such as the EU would develop incrementally, propelled forward by various dynamics such as spillover, failed to encapsulate the reality of European cooperation (Haas 1975, 1976). He recommended a different approach to regional integration, based on theories of interdependence which were being developed in the mid-1970s by Keohane and Nye (1975, 1976), amongst others. This approach argues that institutions such as the EC/EU should be analysed against the background of the growth in international interdependence, rather than as regional political organizations (Haas 1976: 208). Referring to European integration, Haas wrote that 'What once appeared to be a distinctive "supranational" style now looks more like a huge regional bureaucratic appendage to an intergovernmental conference in permanent session' (Haas 1975: 6). In so arguing, Haas himself abandoned the theory he had been so instrumental in developing.

Haas had argued that one of the factors reducing the level of predictability or inevitability of integration was the replacement of traditional forms of functional policy links (that is, functional spillover) by what he referred to as 'deliberated linkage'. In essence, what Haas was saying was that political forms of spillover were replacing the original functional logic. This meant that over time the political linkage of package deals became more and more central and more and more complex, increasing the uncertainty surrounding the integration process both for the researcher and for the participant (Haas 1976: 209). Haas emphasized another, and possibly more important, deficiency – that the theory of regional integration had focused too narrowly on the region as an isolated entity, ignoring the impact of external factors.

In the third group of objections to the theory, it was argued that neo-functionalism had placed undue emphasis on the supranational component in regional integration. Critics suggested that greater importance should be attached to the nation state, and that regional forms of cooperation should be analysed as intergovernmental organizations. This line of attack was adopted by Moravcsik (1993, 1998, 2005) amongst others, under the rubric of liberal intergovernmentalism (see Chapter 7): 'Whereas neo-functionalism stresses the autonomy of supranational officials, liberal intergovernmentalism stresses the autonomy of national leaders' (Moravcsik 1993: 491). This can be read as a claim that the nation state remains the core element in an understanding of international relations, including interpretations of the development of cooperation within the EU framework. If we accept this thesis, it obviously imposes limits on opportunities for political integration. The assumption appears to be that political integration is based exclusively on the aggregate interests of the single nation state and on its determination to survive. Nation states are thus prepared to cede formal competence to supranational institutions only if by so doing they ensure, or possibly regain, control of specific areas of policy.

Finally, there is also a different type of criticism, which relates to what we might call the elitist nature of neo-functionalism. This criticism attacks the prescriptive implications of the approach, rather than the theory itself and so is of a different nature to the critiques already outlined. The argument here is that neo-functionalism not merely is a scientific and objective theory of regional integration, but also has become an essential part of a model of European integration. It is this model, which some call the **Monnet method** or the **Community method**, that is subject to the criticism that it does not involve European citizens in this momentous process of change, and that it is therefore undemocratic. Neo-functionalism sees integration primarily as a process of functional or technocratic change, with experts largely running the show. As pointed out by Risse: 'Haas was not that much concerned about mass public opinion and the loyalties of the ordinary citizens, as he regarded European integration as an elite affair' (Risse 2005: 297). This has led to accusations that neo-functionalist integration implies 'integration by stealth'. Not only is this not an appropriate model for European integration in the early twenty-first century, it also is no longer an accurate depiction of the process itself though, as we shall see in Chapter 22 on the democratic deficit, not everyone would agree that things have changed very much from the early days of the Community.

Neo-functionalism first and foremost focused on political and administrative elites and on the processes that developed the cooperation between different national elites. The assumption was that if the elites started to cooperate then the populations would follow their line of policy. The experience related to different national referenda about EU treaties points to the fact that the unilateral focusing on political elites is a major weakness in neo-functionalist theory. Although the political and administrative elites at the national and European level, for example, agreed upon the new Constitution, this did not mean that the voters followed the elites. In this respect one could say that neo-functionalism as a theoretical tradition has a blind spot in the lack of understanding of the need for the EU to establish legitimacy among the peoples of Europe.

As the above suggests, the original neo-functionalist project has been subjected – from many different angles – to critical reappraisal at both the theoretical and empirical levels. Yet this did not mean that neo-functionalism died as a theoretical project. As we shall see in the next section, neo-functionalist theory experienced a sort of renaissance in the late 1980s and 1990s, as neo-functionalist concepts such as 'spillover' were once again used to explain contemporary developments in European integration.

KEY POINTS

- Neo-functionalism is criticized on both empirical and theoretical grounds.
- On empirical grounds it was argued that neo-functionalism no longer fitted with the reality of the EC in the 1970s.
- On theoretical grounds, critics denied the importance of elite socialization, stressed the importance of the international dimension of integration, and sought to reposition the nation state at the heart of the study of the EC.

The revival of neo-functionalism

After years of obsolescence, there was a revival in interest in neo-functionalism at the beginning of the 1990s. There are a number of reasons for the theory's renewed popularity. The first has to do with general developments in the European Community. The Single European Act (see Chapter 16) and the creation of the Single Market marked a new phase of economic and political cooperation in Western Europe in the mid-1980s. And the processes of integration associated with these developments seemed very much in line with the sort of spillover predicted by neo-functionalist theory (Tranholm-Mikkelsen 1991).

However, this renewed interest in neo-functionalism involved much more than just a step back to the 1960s. Rather than simply adopting the traditional or classical model, many of those who sought to reuse neo-functionalist theory accepted it as a partial theory, that is, as a theory which would explain some but not all of the European integration process. This contrasts with the earlier ambition of the neo-functionalists – to create a grand theory of European integration.

An important contribution to this new approach was made by Stone Sweet and Sandholtz (1998; see also Stone Sweet and Brunell 1998 and Stone Sweet 2004). Although not neo-functionalists in any traditional sense, Stone Sweet and Sandholtz do claim that their theoretical considerations have 'important affinities with neo-functionalism' (Stone Sweet and Sandholtz 1998: 5). They argue that the traditional distinction made in the theoretical study of European integration – that it is either supranational or intergovernmental – is no longer sufficient. While both tendencies are represented in the real world of European politics, they appear differently in different policy areas within the Union, so that some are characterized by more intergovernmentalism, others by more supranationalism (Stone Sweet and Sandholtz 1998: 9). However, Stone Sweet and Sandholtz do not use the spillover concept when they seek to explain processes of political integration and the formation of supranational institutions. Instead they develop what they call a 'transaction-based' theory of integration. This draws attention to the increasing levels of transactions (such as in the fields of trade, communications, and travel) across EU borders, which in turn increase demands for European-level regulation (Stone Sweet and Sandholtz 1998: 11). In time, these demands generate a process of institutionalization leading to the establishment of what the authors call 'supranational governance'.

One of the supranational institutions analysed using this approach was the European Court of Justice (Stone Sweet and Caporaso 1998; Stone Sweet 2004; see also Chapter 12). Stone Sweet and Caporaso observe how the Court interprets the Treaty expansively within its rulings. In doing so, they confirm their theses about the autonomy of the EU's supranational institutions and about supranational governance and their theoretical relation to neo-functionalism. And elsewhere, Stone Sweet and Brunell explain the extent to which their analysis is similar to that formulated by Haas:

> Our results provide broad support for some of the core claims of 'neo-functionalist' theory, first developed by Ernst Haas . . . Haas . . . tried to show that market expansion and political development could be connected to one another through positive feedback loops that would push steadily for more of both. We formalized these insights as hypotheses, gathered data on the processes commonly associated with European integration, and tested our hypotheses in different ways. The evidence support Haas' basic intuitions
>
> (Stone Sweet and Brunell 2004: 52).

Others have also used the European Court to provide evidence of the existence of neo-functionalist dynamics in the EC. Burley and Mattli (1993) argue that the European Court has been a very important institution in the building of a supranational community as it has played an active role in the creation of Community authority in legal matters. They stress that the founding member states of the Community had no intention of giving the court supremacy over national legal systems. However the European Court was able to develop its doctrine over the course of the 1960s and 1970s. According to Burley and Mattli, the Court has also been able to advance political integration by using technical and apolitical arguments in the legal arena, a process which is close to the type of integration mechanisms proposed by neo-functionalist theory.

Along similar lines, references to neo-functionalist theory have increased dramatically since the beginning of the 1990s. And in policy areas such as defence (Guay 1996), social policy (Jensen 2000), and telecommunications (Sandholtz 1998), and on the question of attitudes among European civil servants (Hooghe 1999; Risse 2005), authors have discussed neo-functionalism as a possible frame for explaining specific forms of integration – even if they have refrained from 'buying into' all aspects of the 'classical' theory of the 1950s and 1960s.

Conclusion

Since the first writings of E. B. Haas in the 1950s, theories of regional integration, or neo-functionalism as it is more popularly called, have had their ups and downs. As a means of explaining cooperation between states in the 1960s, neo-functionalism became very popular. The new types of cooperation that developed after the Second World War, especially in Europe, demanded new research perspectives. Neo-functionalism was able to describe and explain these developments in a way that was novel and of its time. In the period after the war, the fashion was for grand theorizing, the construction of scientific theories that would explain the 'big picture'. Nowadays, theorists (and particularly those working on the EU) are content to devote their energies to the generation of less ambitious, middle-range theories (see Chapter 8) that explain only part of the process.

Focusing on the supranational aspects of the new international organizations, neo-functionalism explained cooperation using concepts like spillover and loyalty transfer. States were expected to cooperate on economic matters in order to realize the economic advantages that come with increased levels of trade. This would lead to demands for political coordination across state borders, and in some cases to the establishment of supranational institutions. Cooperation in one policy area would involve cooperation in new areas, thereby initiating an incremental process of political integration. Over time, the supranational institutions would become more and more independent and able to formulate their own agendas, forcing the national states to delegate further competences to the supranational level.

Yet by the mid-1970s neo-functionalism was no longer a credible position to hold. Even traditional proponents of the theory, like Haas, argued that it could not fully explain European developments in regional cooperation. Indeed, he accepted that the European Community did not develop in the way that neo-functionalists had predicted. States remained key actors and it became hard to distinguish supranational institutions from more traditional international organizations.

Supranationalism did experience a revival at the beginning of the 1990s, however. The establishment of the Single European Market and the creation of the EU at Maastricht opened the door to new interest in supranational developments and institutions. The EU suddenly began to look much more like the kind of institution that Haas and others predicted would emerge as a result of regional economic and political integration. But although there was some interest in neo-functionalism at this time, most of the 'new' neo-functionalists felt free to pick and choose from those elements of the theory that best suited their research agendas. Finally, despite the renaissance of the theory in the 1980s and 1990s, neo-functionalism is still rarely considered as at the forefront cutting-edge of research on European integration and EU politics. It seems that the mainstream now belongs more to variants of intergovernmentalism and other newer competing theories of the EU (see Chapters 7 and 8).

QUESTIONS

1. What do neo-functionalists mean by political integration?
2. How helpful is the spillover concept in explaining the development of European integration since the 1950s?
3. How can private interest groups influence the processes of political integration?
4. How convincing is Moravcsik's critique of neo-functionalism?
5. According to neo-functionalist theory, what role do the supranational institutions play in the European integration process?
6. What evidence is there that 'loyalty transfer' among the civil servants in the supranational institutions actually occurs?
7. Does the conduct of the European Court support the neo-functionalist thesis?
8. Why is it very difficult for neo-functionalism to analyse and explain the rejection of the Constitution by the French and Dutch voters at the referendum in 2005?

GUIDE TO FURTHER READING

■ *Journal of European Public Policy*, **'The Disparity of European Integration: Revisiting Neo-functionalism in Honour of Ernst Haas', 12(2), 2005.** A Special Issue of this journal with contributions from Phillip C. Schmitter, Andrew Moravcsik, Ben Rosamond, Thomas Risse, and others. This is the latest up-to-date evaluation of neo-functionalism and its contribution to the study of European integration.

■ **Moravcsik, A.** ***The Choice for Europe: Social Purpose and State Power from Messina to Maastricht*** **(London: UCL Press, 1998).** The seminal text on liberal intergovernmentalism by its key proponent. It includes a very useful critique of neo-functionalism.

■ **Pentland, C.** ***International Theory and European Integration*** **(New York: The Free Press, 1973).** A classic study of European integration theory, which though dated still provides a helpful introduction to neo-functionalism.

■ **Sandholtz, W., and Stone Sweet, A. (eds)** ***European Integration and Supranational Governance*** **(Oxford: Oxford University Press, 1998).** An edited volume which develops the notion of supranational governance, drawing on aspects of neo-functionalist theory.

■ **Tranholm-Mikkelsen, J. 'Neo-functionalism: Obstinate or Obsolete? A Reappraisal in the Light of the New Dynamism of the EC',** ***Millennium: Journal of International Studies*****, 20(1), 1991, 1–22.** The key reference for examining the application of neo-functionalism to the post-1985 period.

IMPORTANT WEBSITES

● **http://globetrotter.berkeley.edu/people/Haas/haas-com0.htm** An interview with Ernst Haas, a few years before his death.

Visit the Online Resource Centre that accompanies this book for lots of interesting additional material. http://www.oxfordtextbooks.co.uk/orc/cini2e/

7

Intergovernmentalism

MICHELLE CINI

Chapter Contents

Reader's Guide

This chapter provides an overview of intergovernmentalist integration theory, focusing particularly on the works of Stanley Hoffmann and Andrew Moravcsik. It first introduces the basic premises and assumptions of intergovernmentalism, identifying its realist underpinnings and the state-centrism which provides the core of the approach, before examining in more detail the specific characteristics of Hoffmann's work. The subsequent section examines some of the ways in which intergovernmentalist thinking has contributed to new research into European integration. The topics covered in this section are confederalism; the domestic politics approach; and analyses that stress the 'locked-in' nature of nation states within the integration process. The chapter concludes by focusing on Moravcsik's liberal intergovernmentalism, which since the mid-1990s has become the main focal point for intergovernmentalist research.

Introduction

From the mid-1960s to the present day, intergovernmentalism – in one form or another – has comprised the heart of European integration theory. For decades, students of European integration learnt about the two competing approaches which explained (and in some cases predicted the course of) European integration: neo-functionalism (covered in Chapter 6) and intergovernmentalism. Although this dichotomy was supplemented by a new division, in response to the 'governance turn' addressed in Chapter 8 below, intergovernmentalism, or at least a contemporary variant of it, continues to dominate much of the academic discourse on European integration. It is in this sense that one might see it as the dominant paradigm for explaining European integration at the start of the twenty-first century, even if many researchers into EU politics would rather this were not the case.

This chapter provides a general introduction to the arguments and critiques of intergovernmentalist theory. It does so by focusing on the works of Stanley Hoffmann (particularly in the 1960s), and Andrew Moravcsik (from the early 1990s). It also unpacks some of the premises and assumptions underpinning intergovernmentalist thinking. The chapter begins by addressing the question 'What is intergovernmentalism?' In this section, the general characteristics of the approach are outlined. In the section that follows, Hoffmann's writings in the 1960s are summarized, and criticisms of his particular brand of intergovernmentalism are addressed. Hoffmann's ground-breaking insights into the phenomenon of European integration, together with critiques of his work, led to new developments in theories of European integration from the 1970s on. Although these might not always be termed 'intergovernmentalist' in any narrow sense, they are premised upon a 'state-centrism' which owes much to Hoffmann's work. Important examples of these 'variants' of intergovernmentalism are dealt with in the remainder of the chapter. The first highlights the confederal characteristics of the European Union. The second draws attention to the importance of domestic politics; while the third brings together examples of research that has considered how states, still central actors, become 'locked into' the European integration process. The final section looks at the work of Andrew Moravcsik and more specifically at his 'liberal intergovernmentalist' (LI) theory of European integration. Although this is an extremely rich and influential theory, LI has been subjected to many criticisms. Some of these are addressed at the end of the chapter.

What is intergovernmentalism?

Intergovernmentalism is a theory of European integration, or perhaps more accurately a conceptual approach which seeks to explain the European integration process (see Box 7.1). It is characterized by its **state-centrism**. In other words, intergovernmentalism privileges the role of (national) states within European integration. It sees integration as a **zero-sum game**, claims that it is limited to policy areas that do not touch on fundamental issues of national sovereignty, and argues that 'European integration is driven by the interests and actions of nation states' (Hix 1999: 15).

Intergovernmentalism is drawn, whether explicitly or implicitly, from classical theories of International Relations, and, most notably, from realist or neo-realist analyses of interstate bargaining. **Realism** incorporates the claim that international politics is about the interaction of self-interested states in an anarchic environment, where there is no global authority capable of securing

 KEY CONCEPTS AND TERMS 7.1

Intergovernmentalism as theory and method

In this chapter, intergovernmentalism is defined as a theory of European integration. This implies that intergovernmentalism is an approach which explains what European integration (or European cooperation) is. Intergovernmentalism may also serve as a model of European integration. This is something rather different. This sort of intergovernmentalism is prescriptive in the sense that it is likely to advocate reducing the role of the supranational institutions (Commission, Parliament, and Courts) in favour of a greater role for the European Council and EU Council, representing national governments. It might also imply a reinstatement of unanimous voting in the Council and the repatriation of European policies to the national level.

order (Morganthau 1985). From this perspective, states are rational, unitary actors that define their interests based on an evaluation of their position in the system of states (Rosamond 2000: 131). State interest is, therefore, primarily about survival, with other concerns, such as economic growth, of secondary importance. Thus, the theory 'is centred on the view that nation states are the key actors in international affairs and the key political relations between states are channelled primarily via national governments' (Nugent 1999: 509).

Neo-realism (Waltz 1979), like realism, sees states as self-regarding actors coexisting in an anarchical system. However, it also understands that there is some potential for order, on the basis of international cooperation (see Axelrod 1984; Keohane 1988) if only as a rational means to state survival. According to neo-realists, regimes are arenas for the negotiation of zero-sum agreements, with the outcomes of those negotiations shaped by the distribution of state power within the regime. Yet, despite the promise of international cooperation, neo-realism is underpinned by the assumption that states have their own distinctive problems and concerns, and that they face very different internal circumstances. This means that their policy preferences (or interests) will often fail to converge. As a consequence, any attempt to build a community *beyond the state* will be fraught with difficulties, and may even intensify the sense of difference felt across state borders. Neo-realists accept that international institutions of all kinds are established to reduce the level of anarchy within the states system, and see the European Union as just another of these institutions, albeit within a highly institutionalized setting. While neo-realists have not been particularly interested in any explicit way in European integration (but see de Grieco 1995, 1996), their influence on intergovernmentalism is clear (Rosamond 2000: 132). It should be stressed however, that intergovernmentalism and (neo-)realism are not synonymous (Church 1996: 25).

'Intergovernmentalism' is not just associated with EU politics. It also refers to a type of decision-making that occurs within all international organizations. International organizations are intergovernmental bodies, in that they serve as forums in which states meet to discuss common issues, to share ideas, and to negotiate agreements. They are usually based on international treaties, and membership is voluntary. They tend not to have powers of taxation, and rely therefore on member state contributions for their operation. Generally, they do not have independent powers, and usually find it difficult to enforce decisions where individual members are recalcitrant (McCormick 2002: 4). While some international organizations stray from this model, intergovernmentalists (in the EU sense) apply this kind of framework to their understanding of the European Union.

According to intergovernmentalists, there are costs and benefits attached to involvement in European integration. (Note, however, that intergovernmentalists may prefer to talk of European *cooperation*, rather than of integration.) Participation in cooperation of this kind will rest on a weighing up of the pros and cons of membership and on the extent to which European integration improves the efficiency of bargains struck among its member states. The main aim in engaging in this qualitative cost–benefit analysis is that of protecting their national interests.

Cooperation within the EU, then, is essentially conservative and pragmatic. It rests on the premise that common solutions are often needed to resolve common problems. To put it another way, cooperation has nothing to do with ideology or idealism, but is founded on the rational conduct of governments as they seek to deal with the policy issues that confront them in the modern world. For intergovernmentalists, European integration is normal or even 'mundane' (O'Neill 1996: 57) behaviour on the part of state actors. There is nothing particularly special about it, other than it has taken a highly institutionalized form in Western Europe since the 1950s. As international cooperation always occurs simultaneously on a variety of levels and taking many different forms, cooperation within the European Union is deemed to be only one example of a more general phenomenon. This is why intergovernmentalists are reluctant to admit that there is a European integration *process*, as such. Rather, they see cooperation occurring in fits and starts, and not as a trend heading inexorably in one direction, towards some sort of European political community or federal state.

As an institutionalized form of interstate cooperation, the argument goes, European integration facilitated the survival of the West European state in the bipolar context of the post-1945 period (see Box 7.2). It is perhaps not so surprising to find, then, that in the early 1990s it was argued that European integration would probably not survive the end of the Cold War (Mearsheimer 1990). Yet even if this prediction has proved inaccurate (though some might say that it is too early to be sure of this), there is no disputing the fact that the nation state has survived (O'Neill 1996: 54), despite the post-1945 sentiment that nationalism ought to be constrained.

At the heart of the intergovernmental thesis lies a particular conception of the sovereignty of national states. Sovereignty remains a very emotive word, particularly when raised in the context of European Union politics. It has various meanings, holding associations with 'notions of power, authority, independence, and the exercise of will' (Nugent 1999: 502). One useful definition states that sovereignty implies 'the legal capacity of national decision-makers to take decisions without being subject to external restraints' (Nugent 1999: 502); another claims that sovereignty is 'the right to hold and exercise authority' (McCormick 2002: 10). However, many use the word sovereignty as little more than a synonym for 'independence', particularly in public discourse (for example, in the media).

According to intergovernmentalists, not only are the member states deemed to be the most important actors by far, they also manage to involve themselves in European integration without ceding sovereignty. This implies that states remain very much in control of the process. According to intergovernmentalists, European cooperation implies at most a *pooling* or sharing of sovereignty, rather than any *transfer* of sovereignty from national to supranational level (Keohane and Hoffmann 1991: 277).

CASE STUDY 7.2

The European rescue of the nation state

In his book, *The European Rescue of the Nation State* (1992), the economic historian Alan Milward analysed European integration in the 1940s and 1950s. He argued that the European integration process in the post-1945 period 'saved' rather than undermined the nation state. Governments at this time had a number of difficult problems to resolve, arising out of increasing interdependence and increased disaffection from social actors. The successful delivery of policy programmes was a matter of survival for the states of Western Europe (Rosamond 2000: 138). European integration become a means to this end. As Rosamond (2000: 139) notes, 'The idea of integration as a progressive transfer of power away from the state managed by emerging supranational elites is given little credence by this hypothesis'. Rather, the key actors are governmental elites.

However, read in a particular way, Milward's work can be seen as challenging the standard polarization of intergovernmentalism and supranationalism. Integration does not necessarily entail the drift toward supranational statehood and states can be seen as controlling agents with an interest in the promotion of degrees of integration (Rosamond 2000: 139).

Intergovernmental cooperation might also involve a delegation of sovereignty. Indeed, intergovernmentalists accept that European integration involves the delegation of functions from state executives and, to a lesser extent parliaments of the member states, to the European institutions – the Commission and the Court of Justice in particular. The argument is that national governments find it in their interest to hand over certain regulatory functions in order to make cooperation work more effectively (to make commitments more credible). This emphasis on delegation colours how intergovernmentalists understand the role of the EU's supranational institutions. Rather than assuming that these institutions are capable of playing an independent or autonomous role within the European integration process, intergovernmentalists stress that supranational actors, such as the Commission, are little more than the servants of the member states. While the supranational institutions are permitted a more important role in less controversial areas of policy, the functions they perform in more sensitive policy domains are severely curtailed. The European institutions that really matter are the EU Council (of national ministers) and the European Council (of Heads of State and Government), while the role of the other European institutions is considered somewhat marginal.

KEY POINTS

- Intergovernmentalism has been influenced by realist assumptions. It privileges the role of the state within European integration.
- Intergovernmentalists believe that sovereignty rests with the EU's member states, although it may be in states' interests to share/pool sovereignty and to delegate it to European institutions.

Hoffmann and his critics

Intergovernmentalism, as a theory of European integration, emerged in the mid-1960s, out of a critique of neo-functionalist theory (see Chapter 6) and as a reaction to federalist assumptions (see Chapter 5) that the European Community would eventually transform itself into a fully fledged state. By the end of the 1960s it had become the dominant paradigm used to explain European integration, replacing the earlier neo-functionalist orthodoxy and reflecting more accurately, it seemed, the practice of European integration by that time. After French President General de Gaulle's 'boycott' of the European institutions in mid-1965, his 'empty chair policy', and the signing of the accord which came to be known as the Luxembourg Compromise in early 1966 (see Chapter 2), a tide turned in the history of European integration. The persistence of the national veto post-1966, instability in the international political economy, and institutional changes which privileged the Council of Ministers and institutionalized the European Council as key decision-makers within the Community (O'Neill 1996: 57–9) all pointed to the limits of supranationalism and to the continued primacy of state actors in European politics. That the Commission began to play a more cautious role post-1966 than it had done in the early years of the EC was also an important factor supporting the intergovernmental thesis.

It was Stanley Hoffmann who laid the foundations of the intergovernmentalist approach to European integration upon which most of the state-centric variants of the 1970s and after drew. His intergovernmentalism rejected neo-functionalist theory, claiming that in concentrating on the *process* of European integration, neo-functionalists had forgotten the *context* within which it takes place (Rosamond 2000: 76). More specifically, Hoffmann rejected neo-functionalist claims that European integration was driven by a sort of snowball effect known as spillover (see Chapter 6), arguing that this was more an 'act of faith' than a proven fact. He stressed that international politics remained characterized by a perpetual conflict over interests (O'Neill 1996: 61).

According to Hoffmann, there was nothing inevitable about the path of European integration, nor was there evidence of any political will to create a federal state in Europe (O'Neill 1996: 63). If anything, the federalist rhetoric did little more than highlight the enduring qualities of the nation state – in that it sought to replicate it on a European scale. As for neo-functionalism, not only did it ignore the global context within which European integration was taking place, he argued, it also missed the importance of cultural differences that were continuing to influence how states perceived their interests. Thus Hoffmann contrasted the idea of 'the logic of integration' against his own preferred 'logic of diversity', reiterating the point by stating that European integration involved a dialectic of fragmentation and unity (Hoffmann 1966). This diversity was a consequence of the unique context of internal domestic politics, and of global factors (that is, the situation of the state in the international system), both of which contributed to inexorable centrifugal forces placing limits on European integration (Rosamond 2000: 76).

Hoffmann's intergovernmentalism offered a 'systematic contextualization' (Rosamond 2000: 75) of the events of the mid-1960s, drawing on empirical studies of French presidential politics under President Charles de Gaulle. In this sense it was much more than just an application of realist theory to the European Community case. Indeed, Hoffmann's view was that, in the post-1945 period, nation states were dealing with regional issues in very different ways than had earlier been the case. While he accepted that traditional, exclusive notions of sovereignty were now obsolete, and that there was a blurring of the boundaries between the national state and international organizations (Hoffmann 1966: 908), this did not mean that nation states and national governments had lost their significance. National sovereignty and the nation state were being tamed and altered, he argued, but they were not being superseded (Hoffmann 1966: 910–11); and while the national dimension may well have seemed less important in the immediate post-1945 period than it had in earlier times, it had not taken long for states to reassert themselves (Hoffmann 1966: 867–9). Indeed, national states had proven extremely resilient actors in international politics (O'Neill 1996: 60). 'The nation-state is still here, and the new Jerusalem has been postponed because the nations in Western Europe have not been able to stop time and to fragment space' (Hoffmann 1966: 863). Thus, from the title of one of his best known articles, he claimed the nation state to be 'obstinate' not 'obsolete' (Hoffmann 1966). Despite the fact that societal changes posed real challenges for the nation state, state governments remained powerful for two reasons: first, because they held legal sovereignty over their own territory; and secondly, because they possessed political legitimacy, as they were democratically elected (George and Bache 2001: 13).

Although he recognized the successes of European cooperation, its distinctive characteristics, and the possibility that it may well produce more than zero-sum outcomes (Hoffmann 1995: 4), Hoffmann argued that the events of the 1960s highlighted the differences between member states as much as it pointed to common interests. This was an important point, since 'preference convergence' was deemed a prerequisite for European integration. Thus where states met with uncertainty, and as supranational institutions began to develop agendas of their own, national governments would respond by going their own way (Rosamond 2000: 78).

Hoffmann's starting point was the political rather than the technocratic (Rosamond 2000: 78). Crucial in this account was the distinction that he made between high and low politics. Whereas high politics (and the political sphere) was said to touch on national sovereignty and issues of national identity, low politics (the economic sphere) tended to be more technocratic, and much less controversial. According to Hoffmann, there were clear boundaries between more dramatic economic integration possible in areas of low politics, and the 'impermeable' and very 'political' domain of high politics (O'Neill 1996: 61), where integration would not occur. While functional spillover might occur in the former, there could be no assumption that states would allow it to be transferred to the latter.

Although Hoffmann's analysis was based very generally upon realist assumptions, he differed from realists in his approach to the concept of the state. Indeed we might say that 'Hoffmann's intergovernmental position was more sophisticated than that of realists . . . and his political awareness was also greater than that of the neo-functionalist writers who tended to adopt a rather simplified pluralist view of political processes' (George and Bache 2001: 13). To Hoffmann states were more than just 'black boxes'; they represented communities of identity and belonging. '[T]hey are constructs in which ideas and ideals, precedents and political experiences and domestic forces and rulers all play a role' (Hoffmann 1995: 5). Hoffmann was particularly critical of the earlier theorists of European integration who had adopted a simplistic and unrealistic view of how governments defined their interests. He argued that these interests were not reducible to power and place alone (Hoffmann 1995: 5), but were calculated on the basis of various historical, cultural, and indeed political concerns.

However, Hoffmann's intergovernmentalism has been subject to a number of critiques. Many of these rejected his rigid demarcation between high and low politics (O'Neill 1996: 65). Even in the 1970s, there were claims that the existence of European Political Cooperation (EPC), the forerunner to today's European foreign policy (see Chapter 15), and an area of 'high politics', seemed to disprove this particular aspect of his theory. This seems be have been borne out by recent events, most notably since the establishment of the single currency and the common foreign and security policy. Indeed, since the 1960s, Hoffmann has softened his line on this issue.

Hoffmann was also criticized for playing down the constraints imposed on states as a consequence of their increasing interdependence (O'Neill 1996: 65; see Box 7.3). Moreover, it was argued that he failed to take into consideration, within his analysis, the novelty and the complexity of the European integration project. The EC, it was claimed, was about more than just the creation of a regional regime, and bargains struck at European level could not simply be reduced to a set of national interests (Rosamond 2000: 79).

While Hoffmann's intergovernmentalism was not a theory in any systematic sense (Church 1996: 26), but was, rather, part of an approach which dealt with the wider phenomenon of regional cooperation, it was extremely influential in shaping the way scholars of European integration thought about the (then) European Community. As such it set the agenda for future research undertaken in the field of integration theory from the 1970s on.

KEY CONCEPTS AND TERMS 7.3

Interdependence and intergovernmentalism

Interdependence theory emerged in the 1970s, its key proponents being Robert Keohane and Joseph Nye (1975). Its main influence on intergovernmentalism was to set it in a broader context than had earlier been the case. It was argued that 'Many of the factors that have influenced . . . [the] development [of the EC] have applied to it alone, but many have not' (Nugent 1999: 511). In other words, in many instances what we might consider to be the effects of European integration are really effects of a much wider phenomenon. Changes to the international political economy – international modernization in particular – have led to greater and greater levels of interdependence, and these have changed the way in which states and other non-state actors relate to each other in the international sphere (Nugent 1999: 511).

While interdependence theory cannot really be considered a discrete theory of European integration, it does add to our understanding of the background conditions, and helps to make the point that the EC might not be quite as unique as some (such as the neo-functionalists) claimed. While it highlights the fact that states may not always be able to act unconstrained within the international system, it is best viewed as a response to a rather specific weakness in intergovernmentalism, rectified by an increasing emphasis on the global dimension.

Thus, accepting the limits of Hoffmann's approach as it was constructed in the 1960s did not mean opting for a supranational theory of integration. Rather, it allowed the door to be opened to new variants of intergovernmentalism, some of which are dealt with in the section that follows.

KEY POINTS

- Stanley Hoffmann was the key proponent of intergovernmentalism in the mid-1960s. His work on French, European, and international politics led him to critique the work of the neo-functionalists.
- Hoffmann distinguished between high and low politics, arguing that while functional integration might be possible in less controversial areas (the economic sphere), states would resist any incursion into areas of high politics (the political sphere).
- Critics have questioned Hoffmann's use of the high/low politics distinction, based on empirical evidence (such as recent moves towards foreign policy integration). However, his approach has been extremely influential.

Beyond classical intergovernmentalism

This section presents some examples of how Hoffmann's intergovernmentalism has been supplemented and adapted since the 1960s. While setting aside for the moment the most important example of this adaptation (liberal intergovernmentalism), which is dealt with later in the chapter, this section first deals with confederalism; secondly, with the 'domestic politics approach' to European integration; and finally with a number of analyses that have sought to explain how states become locked into the European integration process.

Confederalism

As a model or framework for European integration the idea of confederation (Forsyth 1981) seems closely allied to intergovernmentalism. Confederation may be viewed as a particular type of intergovernmental arrangement, in which national sovereignty remains intact despite the establishment of a common institutional framework (O'Neill 1996: 71). O'Neill calls it the antithesis of federalism, a concert of sovereign states. Wallace stresses that there must be no assumption that confederation will lead ultimately to unity. Rather, it implies that the 'Community is stuck, between sovereignty and integration (Wallace 1982: 65).

Confederal approaches draw attention to the institutionalized nature of the European integration process, recognizing (in contrast to intergovernmentalism) its distinctiveness. Along similar lines, Paul Taylor (1975) has argued that confederation (or confederalism) is a helpful supplement to intergovernmentalism, allowing us to move beyond its inherent constraints, while retaining its state-centric core. In this respect, Wallace points to the importance of supranational/international law in differentiating confederalism from intergovernmentalism. Taylor puts it rather differently. He suggests that '[t]he salient feature of confederal Europe is that the scope of integration is extensive . . . but the level of integration is low' (Taylor 1975: 343). Moreover '[t]he Europe of this Confederal phase of integration is . . . decentralized but highly interdependent, potentially autarchic but in practice united by intense practices of consultation' (Taylor 1975: 343). It is also characterized, he claims, by the defensive posture of national governments against the further extension of the powers of supranational actors, by an interpenetration of European politics into the domestic sphere, and by an oscillation between advanced proposals for integration and retreats into national independence. Much of this argument is state-centric, with Taylor arguing that the nation state is likely to be strengthened through confederation. The state-centric nature of the argument adds to intergovernmentalist understandings of European integration by characterizing the framework within which cooperation and integration take place.

The domestic politics approach

In the 1970s and 1980s, an approach which focused on domestic politics and policy-making became fashionable in the field of European integration studies. Although not a theory of European integration per se, the approach was critical of intergovernmentalism's failure to capture the transnational nature of the EC policy process (Church 1996: 26) and sought, as a consequence, to focus attention on the impact of domestic politics on EC policy-making (Bulmer 1983). In this, we can identify the origins of what today would be called the 'Europeanization' literature (see Chapter 25). We might also see this approach as one which links Hoffmann's intergovernmentalism to later state-centric research projects – and particularly to liberal intergovernmentalism (see below) (Rosamond 2000: 76).

The idea behind the domestic politics approach was that it was said to be impossible to understand the European Community without taking domestic politics into consideration (Bulmer 1983). Thus Bulmer, a key proponent of this approach, sought to identify the domestic determinants of preference formation (Rosamond 2000: 80). One way of doing this was to undertake in-depth case studies of the European policy process, which allowed researchers to identify variations in patterns of policy-making, emphasizing the linkages between the national and supranational dimensions of European politics. Bulmer was particularly interested in two dimensions of domestic politics: policy-making structures, and attitudes towards the EC (Bulmer 1983).

There are a number of elements involved in this approach, which when taken together provide a framework for analysing the behaviour of member states. First, the national polity was considered the basic unit of the EC/EU. Secondly, each national polity was acknowledged to be different, in terms of its unique socio-economic characteristics; and it was these differences that shaped national interests. Thirdly, European policy was deemed to be only one facet of national political activity. Fourthly, the national polity lay at the juncture of national and European politics. And finally, an important lens through which one might understand these elements was that of the policy style concept (Bulmer 1983: 360).

The importance of the domestic politics approach is that it demonstrated how intergovernmentalists had failed to look in any coherent way within the member states when analysing the European integration process (Bulmer 1983). Although it was stated earlier in this chapter that intergovernmentalism is closely related to (neo-)realism in International Relations, newer variants of intergovernmentalism have also been greatly influenced by neo-liberal ideas. **Neo-liberalism**, as an approach to the study of International Relations, is concerned with the *formation* of state preferences (Rosamond 2000: 135) or 'national interests'. Whereas neo-realism is focused exclusively on politics between nations, neo-liberalism draws attention to the content of the 'black box' of domestic politics and tries to address from where national interests originate. It therefore places the national polity, rather than just national executives, or governments, at the heart of the European integration project. Although the influence of neo-liberal ideas in the domestic politics approach may not be explicit, the concerns are very much the same. This is a point which will be picked up on again when we come to look at the work of Andrew Moravcsik.

The 'locking in' of states

As a more recent example of how intergovernmentalism has evolved, a number of analyses explain how states have become *locked into* the European integration process. These draw heavily on a particularly German approach to the study of federalism, in which 'interlocking politics' (*Politikverflectung*), characterizes interactions between different levels of government (Risse-Kappen 1996: 60–1). While these approaches rest on state-centric premises, they move quite far beyond classical intergovernmentalism and show how European integration is about much more than interstate bargains. In the process, they emphasize the importance of institutional factors (see Chapter 8) and show how intergovernmentalist ideas may provide a starting point from which new arguments about and analyses of the European integration process develop.

Wolfgang Wessels (1997) has advanced an argument about European integration which rests soundly on state-centric premises in that it sees national interests as the primary driving force of integration. It also, however, links 'integration processes to the evolution of the state' (Wessels 1997: 274–5). He called this his 'fusion thesis'. In this approach, Wessels argues that after 1945, West European states became increasingly responsible for the welfare of their citizens, enhancing their legitimacy as a consequence. But for the welfare state to persist, national economies needed to be strong. In order to maintain economic growth to this end, states recognized the need to open up their markets, which led governments to rely more and more on the joint management of shared policy problems. This is what Wessels means when he talks of the 'fusion' of the West European states (1997: 273) – in essence a 'merger of public resources located at several state levels whereby steering instruments are increasingly used in concert' (Wessels 1997: 274). This amounts to much more than a pooling of sovereignties. As states have become more interdependent, they have lost the ability to act autonomously, blurring the lines of accountability and responsibility that connect citizens to the state. He claims that it is increasingly difficult to reverse these trends without drastic action being taken.

Also grounded in state-centrism, Fritz Scharpf (1988) drew an analogy between German federalism and the European Community. He did this to explain how European integration has become almost irreversible, because of the intense institutionalization to which it has been subject. Like Wessels, Scharpf focuses on how EC decision-making offered states the ability to solve problems jointly. He argues, however, that the outcomes of these decisions are likely to be suboptimal, in that they do not emerge from any assessment of the best available solutions, but are reached through a process of bargaining which inevitably leads to compromises being struck. In other words, as national interests determine policy positions, creative (and rational) problem-solving is not possible (Scharpf 1988: 255). Therefore no member state is likely to be entirely satisfied by what the process of integration has to offer. This is something that will contribute over time to the slowing down of European integration. Yet the institutionalization of the decision-making process means that retreating from integration is not an option. States are trapped in a Community from which they cannot escape, in a paradox characterized by Scharpf as 'frustration without disintegration and resilience without progress' (Scharpf 1988: 256), which he labels a joint-decision trap.

More recently, historical institutionalists have sought to explain how states become locked into the European integration process through a process of path dependence. The argument, advocated by Paul Pierson (1998) amongst others, is that the more states integrate, the more future options become constrained (see Chapter 8). While this does not imply an inevitability about the 'process' of integration, it does mean that the only way of escaping from further integration is by provoking a dramatic break with past practice, a so-called 'critical juncture'.

KEY POINTS

- Confederalism complements intergovernmentalism, by acknowledging the institutionalized character of the European Community.
- The domestic politics approach claimed that it is impossible to study European integration without looking at policy-making within the member states.
- Wessels' fusion thesis, Scharpf's joint decision trap, and Pierson's path dependence explain how states have, over time, become locked into the European integration process.

Liberal intergovernmentalism and its critics

In 1988, Robert Putnam published an influential article in which he explored the dynamics of domestic and international politics using the metaphor of 'two-level games' (Putnam 1988). To explain this concept we need to understand that two-level games are played by states. The first game deals with how states define their policy preferences (or national interest) at home within the domestic environment. The second game is played on the international stage and involves interstate bargains being struck.

> "Putnam's core point is that national executives play games in two arenas more or less simultaneously. At the domestic level, power-seeking/enhancing office holders aim to build coalitions of support among domestic groups. At the international level, the same actors seek to bargain in ways that enhance their positions domestically by meeting the demands of key domestic constituents"
>
> (Rosamond 2000: 136).

Putnam's main aim was that of providing a framework for analysing the myriad entanglements involved in domestic–international interactions (Putnam 1988: 433). This image of the two-level game is helpful in that it provides a starting point for understanding Moravcsik's theory of liberal intergovernmentalism (LI).

Moravcsik's liberal intergovernmentalism

Since the early 1990s, Andrew Moravcsik's theory of liberal intergovernmentalism (LI) has become one of the – if not *the* – most influential accounts of the European integration process. It has become a touchstone against which all integration theory is now judged, 'a model of parsimony and clarity' (Risse-Kappen 1996: 63), even for those who do not agree with its assumptions or its conclusions. Drawing on and developing earlier intergovernmentalist insights, it offers a theoretical approach which is much more rigorous than its antecedents (George and Bache 2001: 13), incorporating within it both realist and neo-liberal elements (Rosamond 2000: 136) and dealing explicitly with the interface between domestic and international politics. It was 'initially presented as a framework for synthesizing theories into a coherent account of large EU decisions taken under unanimity, though it can be applied to other types of decisions as well' (Dinan 2000: 280).

The European Union is identified as a successful intergovernmental regime designed to manage economic interdependence through negotiated policy coordination. The theory is based on assumptions drawn from the 'rational actor model', in that it

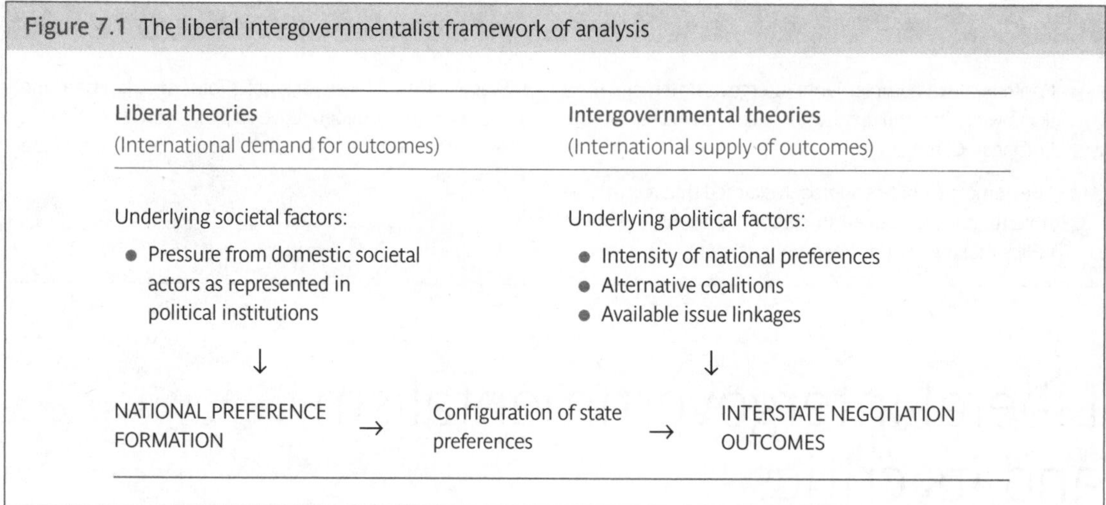

Figure 7.1 The liberal intergovernmentalist framework of analysis

assumes that states behave rationally, 'which means that the actions of states are assumed to be based on utilizing what are judged to be the most appropriate means of achieving their goals' (Nugent 1999: 509). In true intergovernmentalist fashion, LI emphasizes the importance of the *preferences* and *power* of states. While national politicians embody state interests that reflect domestic policy preferences, all decisions made by the EU are ultimately the result of bargaining amongst states. Agreements are (usually) reached on a lowest common denominator basis, with clear limits placed on the transfer of sovereignty to supranational agents. Thus, according to Moravcsik, 'The broad lines of European integration since 1955 reflect three factors: patterns of commercial advantage, the relative bargaining power of important governments, and the incentives to enhance the credibility of inter-state commitment' (Moravcsik 1998: 3). When economic or commercial concerns converge, integration takes place.

There are two separate dimensions to LI: the supply and the demand side. The argument is that both the *demand* for cooperation which derives from the national polity, and the *supply* of integration, arising out of interstate negotiations, are important in understanding European integration outcomes. To explain the link between the demand and supply sides, the theory is divided into three steps, each of which is explained by a different set of factors (and drawing on different theories): economic interest; relative power; and credible commitments (Moravcsik 1998: 4) (see Figure 7.1).

First, drawing on liberal theories of *national preference formation*, and applying a domestic politics approach, Moravcsik shows how 'state goals can be shaped by domestic pressures and interactions which in turn are often conditioned by the constraints and opportunities that derive from economic interdependence' (Nugent 1999: 509). Thus he identifies underlying societal factors that provoke an international demand for cooperation. National political institutions are subject to myriad pressures from nationally based interests, provoking a process of preference formation. State preferences are formed, and these feed into interstate negotiations, as groups compete with each other for the attention of government elites. To put it another way, policy preferences at national level are constrained by the interests of dominant, usually economic, groups within society. Resting on a very pluralistic understanding of state–society relations, national governments end up representing these interests in international forums. Thus Moravcsik sees national interests as derived from the domestic politics of the member states and not the 'sovereign state's perception of its relative position in the states system' (Rosamond 2000: 137), that is, from geo-political concerns. As Moravcsik has stated: 'the vital interest behind General de Gaulle's opposition to British membership in the EC . . . was not the pursuit of French *grandeur* but the price of French wheat' (Moravcsik 1998: 7).

The second and supply-side strand of LI is based on *intergovernmentalist theories of interstate relations*, with European integration supplied by intergovernmental bargains (such as treaty reforms) (Moravcsik 1998: 7). This part of LI 'draws on general theories of bargaining and negotiation to argue that relative power among states is shaped above all by asymmetrical interdependence, which dictates the relative value of agreement to different governments' (Moravcsik 1998: 7). Thus, this second element in the theory emphasizes the centrality of strategic bargaining among states and the importance of governmental elites in shaping interstate relations. At this point, states are considered as unitary actors, and supranational institutions are deemed to have a very limited impact on outcomes. In other words, the theory focuses mainly on the European and EU Councils. This generally involves a two-stage process of negotiation. First, governments must resolve the policy problems that confront them, taking decisions to that effect; and only after that do they try to reach agreement on institutional mechanisms which would allow them to implement those decisions. Important is the process by which states engage in interstate bargaining. Various strategies and techniques, such as 'coalitional alternatives to agreement', the linking of issues, and threats of exclusion and inclusion, shape outcomes. A bargaining space (a sort of window of opportunity) is formed out of the amalgamation of national interests, with the final agreement determining the distribution of gains and losses. This points to the restrictive range of possible integration outcomes. Yet Moravcsik accepts that interstate bargains can lead on occasion to positive-sum outcomes (Hix 1999: 15). As a consequence, governments will bargain hard to gain the upper hand. Not surprisingly, the power of individual states is very important in determining whose interests matter. And because this is so, Moravcsik focuses his attention largely on the preferences of the largest EU states: UK, France, and Germany. In stressing the point that integration *benefits* states, that states face few constraints in the Council, and that interstate negotiations enhance their domestic autonomy, the issue of why governments engage in European integration when it might otherwise seem like an irrational thing to do is addressed by this part of the theory (Rosamond 2000: 138).

The third element within LI is *institutional delegation*. The argument here is that international (European) institutions are set up to improve the efficiency of interstate bargaining. 'To secure the substantive bargains they had made . . . governments delegated and pooled sovereignty in international institutions for the express purpose of committing one another to cooperate' (Moravcsik 1998: 3–4). Thus, the European institutions create linkages and compromises across issues, where decisions have been made under conditions of uncertainty, and where non-compliance would be a temptation. In other words, institutional delegation reflects the desire for 'credible commitments'.

In this respect Moravcsik's work has been influenced by the liberal institutionalism of Robert Keohane (1989). Keohane views institutions as ways of facilitating positive-sum bargaining ('upgrading the common interest') among states, but claims that there is no evidence that supranational institutions bias the outcomes of decisions away from the longer-term self-interest of the member states (Rosamond 2000: 143). In line with this sort of thinking, according to Moravcsik, 'The entrepreneurship of supranational officials . . . tends to be futile and redundant, even sometimes counterproductive (Moravcsik 1998: 8).

Together, these three elements result in integration outcomes (treaty change, for example). Applying the theory to actual cases in the history of European integration, Moravcsik came to the following conclusions. First, he concluded that the major choices made in favour of European integration were a reflection of the preferences of national

BOX 7.4

Moravcsik's five case studies

In his book, *The Choice for Europe* (1998), Andrew Moravcsik applies his theory of liberal intergovernmentalism to five cases in the history of the European integration process. These are:

1. The negotiation of the Treaty of Rome (1955–8).
2. The consolidation of the Common Market and the Common Agricultural Policy (CAP) (1958–83).
3. Monetary Cooperation and the setting up of the European Monetary System (EMS) (1969–83).
4. The negotiation of the Single European Act (SEA) (1984–5).
5. The negotiation of the Treaty on European Union (TEU) (1988–91).

governments and not of supranational organizations. Secondly, he stressed that these national preferences reflected a balance of domestic economic interests, rather than any political bias of politicians or national strategic security concerns. Finally, he stressed that the outcomes of the negotiations reflected the relative bargaining power of the states, and that the delegation of decision-making authority to supranational institutions reflected the wishes of governments to ensure that commitments made were adhered to (George and Bache 2001: 14). In short, Moravcsik is arguing that 'European integration can best be explained as a series of rational choices made by national leaders' (Moravcsik 1998: 18; see also Box 7.4).

Critiques of liberal intergovernmentalism

Although Moravcsik's theory of liberal intergovernmentalism (LI) has been subject to a great deal of criticism it remains an extremely useful instrument for organizing data and constructing empirical studies. At the same time, it presents a serious challenge for competing models that seek to explain the European integration process (Rosamond 2000: 145). This is largely because liberal intergovernmentalism has been said to offer an 'almost uncompromising framework' (Nugent 1999: 510), which can be hard, if not impossible, to reconcile with alternative interpretations of European integration and EU politics.

Perhaps the most often repeated criticism of LI is that it simply does not fit the facts. This tends to be argued on the basis of empirical analyses and specific case studies of EU politics. This is, however, part of a related criticism, which is that Moravcsik's work has too narrow a focus to be called a theory of European integration, as it is 'too selective with his empirical references when seeking to demonstrate the validity of . . . [the] framework in the EU context' (Nugent 1999: 510). In other words, thus far liberal intergovernmentalism has been applied only to those cases that will (almost inevitably) result in proving that the theory is correct. It has been claimed by Scharpf (1999: 165), for example, that applying the theory to cases of *intergovernmental negotiation*, where economic integration is the main concern and where decisions were taken on the basis of unanimous voting in the Council, will invariably lead to the conclusions that Moravcsik reaches. 'Given this focus for his attention, it is hardly surprising that Moravcsik comes to the view that the EC is primarily motivated by the aggregation and conciliation of national interests (Wincott 1995: 602). However, in 'harder' cases, where international negotiations are not the primary form of decision-taking, and where majority voting applies, LI may not produce such clear-cut results.

The critique is often set out in the following way: that Moravcsik's theory may well apply for the majority of 'history-making' decisions (Peterson 1995) which deal with the future of European integration, that is, those high-profile policy steps of major constitutional significance, which often involve treaty change and occur through interstate negotiations (Wincott 1995: 602). LI is much less able to explain the way in which the EU works in matters of day-to-day politics, however.

The second criticism that is often raised with regard to Moravcsik's work is that his conception of the state is a rather narrow one. LI pays little attention to the way in which the 'state' may be broken down into its component parts. Critics argue that in order to understanding fully how governmental positions (or preferences) are determined (Nugent 1999: 510), a more subtle analysis of domestic politics is required. Indeed, as George and Bache (2001: 14) claim: 'in some ways it [LI] was less sophisticated in its account of domestic politics than was that suggested by Hoffmann'. In Moravcsik's pluralist or liberal view, the primary determinant of government preferences is the balance between *economic* interests (George and Bache 2001: 14). But in practice, there is a huge range of diverse influences that are likely to impinge on national preference formation. Risse-Kappen (1996: 63) points, for example, to the potential importance of the impact of domestic structures. On this basis, Moravcsik's account is too simplistic when it focuses solely on economic and (to a lesser extent on) geo-political concerns (Wincott 1995: 600–1). Moreover, it is argued that the two-level game metaphor does not depict the reality of EU politics today – and that the EU is now much more of a multi-level than a two-level polity (see Chapter 8).

Thirdly and highly important as a critique of LI, is the point that the theory understates the constraints faced by key policy-makers. The case of the Single Market programme is often used to back up this argument. There are, however, a number of dimensions to this general critique. First, it is frequently argued that Moravcsik plays down to too great an extent the role of supranational actors within the European integration process. In other words, he does not provide a full enough account of the supply side of his model, when focusing solely on interstate negotiations. As the roles of the European Commission and the European Court of Justice are deemed relatively unimportant, if not entirely irrelevant in terms of policy outcomes, their interests and strategies do not figure particularly strongly in Moravcsik's work. This assumption about the supranational institutions' potential influence over integration outcomes (even at times in history-making decisions) has been contested by many academics.

> Moravcsik's portrayal of the Commission as exercising a role of little more than a facilitator in respect of significant decision-making has attracted particular criticism, with numerous empirically-based studies claiming to show that the Commission does exercise an independent and influential decision-making role, be it as . . . an *animateur*, a policy entrepreneur, or a motor force
>
> (Nugent 1999: 510–11).

There is empirical evidence of how the Commission has been able to influence policy outcomes, by means of its policy entrepreneurship. Wincott (1994) and Burley and Mattli (1993) have highlighted the European Court's impact on European integration, through its innovative legal rulings in cases such as those pertaining to human rights. Pollack's analysis (1997) has shown how despite the fact that supranational institutions tend to operate within the boundaries set by member-state preferences, they are able to exploit the differences between these preferences in order to promote their own independent agendas. As Rosamond (2000: 143) points out, this adds a layer of institutionalism to intergovernmentalism, whilst retaining many of its core characteristics.

A similar point also applies to non-state 'transnational' actors, such as European firms and European interest groups. Cowles (1995) has demonstrated, for example, how important business groups were in influencing the Single Market project in the 1980s. While she accepts that business groups were not the sole cause of the '1992' programme:

> Intergovernmental theory cannot explain the activities of the key non-state actors in the 1992 process. The single market programme was not merely the result of conventional statecraft. Nor were Member States' actions predicated solely on the basis of domestically defined interest group activity, as suggested by a recent version of intergovernmentalism [LI] . . . Indeed, the story of the ERT [European Round Table of Industrialists] points to the fact that non-state actors – and in

particular, multinational enterprises – also play two-level games in EC policy-making ”

(Cowles 1995: 521–2).

This point is not just about which actors and institutions matter in the process of European decision-making. It also reflects Moravcsik's emphasis on the more formal aspects of that process, at the expense of the informal, 'behind-the-scenes' dimension. If informal politics matter in shaping policy outcomes, this may mean that actors who appear on the surface to be responsible for decision-taking may not really be in control of the process. As Wincott has stated – again of the Single Market case – 'the basic, innovative policy techniques required for the internal market programme had been fashioned in the daily work of the supranational institutions long before the Member States considered these issues' (1995: 606). The substance of interstate negotiations had therefore already been framed well before intergovernmental conferences and European summits met to take their formal decisions.

Finally, Wincott has criticized LI for not being a theory, at least in his understanding of the term. He makes this claim, as he believes that a rigorous theory ought to spell out the conditions under which the theory might be refuted or disproved. Wincott argues that LI does not do this, but engages in an act of closure on certain types of argument about European integration. He claims that LI should therefore be considered an 'approach' rather than a theory – one which brings together three existing theories (preference formation, intergovernmental bargaining, and institutional delegation) to provide a 'pre-theory' or 'analytical framework' (Forster 1998: 365) which can be applied to the European integration process. Not surprisingly, these points, along with all the others mentioned above, are vehemently rejected by Moravcsik.

KEY POINTS

- LI provides a tripartite explanation of integrative outcomes: as national preference formation; interstate bargaining; and institutional delegation.
- The theory supplements a rich account of bargaining inside the Council, with a concern for how national interests (or preferences) are formed. Moravcsik argues that it is mainly powerful domestic economic interests that determine national interest.
- Moravcsik is criticized for focusing only on 'history-making decisions' (treaty change, in particular) and for ignoring day-to-day politics and the multi-level character of the European Union.

Conclusion: the future of intergovernmentalism

This chapter has reviewed the general approach to European integration known as 'intergovernmentalism', which is associated in its classical form with the work of Stanley Hoffmann. The chapter has shown how intergovernmentalist premises (and, more specifically, state-centrism) have provided the foundations for a range of theories and models, which have sought to specify the structure of the EC, the nature of decision-making, and the 'locking in' of states within the European integration process. Andrew Moravcsik's work now provides the core intergovernmentalist thesis. Even if one is not convinced by all of his arguments, his liberal intergovernmentalism provides a theoretically rigorous and rich point of departure for critiques.

But what future might we imagine for intergovernmentalism? While it continues to provide inspiration for scholars of European integration, new developments within the study of the European Union have tested the resilience of intergovernmentalist arguments. Yet, intergovernmentalism has been flexible enough to adapt to new conditions and new theories which appear to resonate with today's European integration process, and to cope with the empirical evidence provided by recent treaty change, as well as by less high-profile policy developments. As we shall see in the next chapter, there are many who contest the (liberal) intergovernmentalist account of European integration. But for all of us researching and studying the European Union, it makes an important contribution to our understanding of what European integration is or might be.

? QUESTIONS

1. How plausible are intergovernmentalist accounts of European integration?
2. Why do you think Andrew Moravcsik's theory of liberal intergovernmentalism has been so influential?
3. What are the main critiques of liberal intergovernmentalism?
4. How useful a model for explaining the EU is confederalism?
5. What are the main elements of Stanley Hoffmann's intergovernmentalism?
6. How central is the nation state within the process of European integration?
7. In what sense and to what extent is European integration a 'mundane' affair?
8. How might Moravcsik respond to recent critiques of his liberal intergovernmentalism?

GUIDE TO FURTHER READING

- Hoffmann, S. *The European Sisyphus: Essays on Europe 1964–1994* (Oxford: Westview Press, 1995). An excellent collection of Stanley Hoffmann's work, showing how his ideas have changed (or not) over the years. Includes seminal articles published in the 1960s which set the scene for future intergovernmentalist writings.

- Moravcsik, A. *The Choice for Europe: Social Purpose and State Power from Messina to Maastricht* (London: UCL Press, 1998). The seminal liberal intergovernmentalist book. Chapter 1, 'Theorizing European Integration', both provides a critique of neo-functionalism and sets out the characteristics of LI in some detail.

- O'Neill, M. *The Politics of European Integration: A Reader* (London: Routledge, 1996), chapter 4. Ostensibly a 'reader', but also includes a useful chapter on state-centric approaches to European integration.

- Rosamond, B. *Theories of European Integration* (Basingstoke: Macmillan, 2000), chapter 6. The most recent, overarching text on European integration theory, with numerous references to intergovernmentalism, and a specific chapter devoted to 'Intergovernmental Europe'.

IMPORTANT WEBSITES

- www.princeton.edu/~amoravcs Andrew Moravcsik's homepage. Includes access to published and forthcoming papers.

Visit the Online Resource Centre that accompanies this book for lots of interesting additional material. http://www.oxfordtextbooks.co.uk/orc/cini2e/

8 New Theories of European Integration

BEN ROSAMOND

Chapter Contents

Reader's Guide

This chapter deals with recent theoretical work on the European Union. It concentrates upon approaches, which, in various ways, seek to depart from the established theoretical positions established by neo-functionalism (see Chapter 6) and intergovernmentalism (see Chapter 7). This chapter commences with a discussion of how 'newer' approaches identify the limitations of the 'classical' debate. Much of this discussion hinges on how analysts characterize the EU. For many the EU is best conceived of as a political system, which suggests that the theoretical tools of conventional political science and policy analysis might have greater explanatory power than approaches from the discipline of International Relations (IR). To explore the plausibility of this proposition, this chapter discusses in turn the contribution to EU studies of new institutionalist political science (see new institutionalism), approaches from policy analysis, the idea of multi-level governance and constructivism. The chapter also explores how International Relations theories might be brought back into EU studies. The purpose of the chapter, aside from introducing the contemporary theoretical repertoire in EU studies, is to show how the EU raises significant questions about the nature of authority, statehood, and the organization of the international system in the contemporary period.

Introduction

Much of the academic work on the European Union remains under the spell of the 'classical' debate between neo-functionalism and intergovernmentalism (see Chapters 6 and 7). There is a rationale for continuing to explore the opposition between these two schools. Thinking in this way forces us to address key issues of continuity versus change in European politics. Does the growth of the EU imply the transcendence of the European nation-state system? If so, does this bring to the fore a new group of activist supranational institutions and confirm the rise to prominence of powerful non-state actors?

Alternatively, are the member states the key actors in this process and are the EU's key dynamics intergovernmental? These rival academic discourses have their equivalents in the policy world. The strategy of the founding fathers of integration (such as Jean Monnet and Robert Schuman) has often been thought of as 'neo-functionalist', while politicians still tend to use a vocabulary that is underwritten by statist and intergovernmentalist assumptions.

However, recent years have witnessed concerted attempts to 'think otherwise' about the EU. This chapter deals with these 'new' theoretical approaches. It is worth pausing to consider what 'new' might mean in this context. The term implies, after all, that some theories are 'old' or perhaps redundant. In particular, many academics who offer new theoretical prospectuses tend to begin with the proposition that the 'classical' terms of debate – as represented by the rivalry between neo-functionalism and intergovernmentalism – fail to capture adequately what is going on in the contemporary European Union. This chapter is attentive to this premise and begins with a deeper discussion of its soundness as a proposition for theoretical departure.

This discussion alerts us to the importance of thinking carefully about theoretical work. Theory is not simply a self-indulgent exercise. Nor can it be side-stepped by any serious student of the EU. Rather, being conscious of the theoretical propositions chosen by authors is vital because alternative 'readings' of the EU and European integration follow from alternative theoretical premises. That said, writers rarely (these days at least) attempt to construct 'grand theories' of integration. Instead, since the 1970s, they have tended to build theories to aid understanding and explanation of *elements* of (a) the integration process and (b) EU governance. Even the direct descendants of neo-functionalism and intergovernmentalism (discussed in the previous two chapters) have limited ambitions. For example, Sandholtz and Stone Sweet's theory (1998) of supranational governance explicitly 'brackets' (that is, sets aside) the origins of the EU, because the theory has no way of explaining this. Moreover, Moravcsik (2001) has emphasized that his liberal intergovernmentalism is not intended to be a comprehensive theory of European integration, but rather a theory of intergovernmental bargaining only.

These caveats still do not bypass the objection that the old neo-functionalist–intergovernmentalist debate fails to capture highly significant attributes of the present EU. The principal objection, explored in the first substantive section of this chapter, is that 'old' theories are rooted in an outdated conception of what the EU is. However, we need to be aware that the study of the EU is not something that simply ebbs and flows with the 'real-world' development of European integration and the evolution of the European Union. It is also – and perhaps more predominantly – bound up with the developments in social scientific fashion. Many scholars think about this in terms of theoretical 'progress' – that is, as social science in general and political science in particular 'improves' its techniques, so we can expect objects of study such as the European Union to be treated more rigorously than hitherto. The alleged consequence is that theoretical advancement delivers more robust and reliable results, thereby advancing our empirical knowledge of the EU.

The limits of the classical debate

As the previous two chapters have indicated, the legacies of neo-functionalism and intergovernmentalism remain intact in much current writing about integration and the EU. Moreover, even when analysts of the EU attempt to offer an alternative point of theoretical departure, they invariably set their coordinates with reference to the established neo-functionalist and intergovernmentalist positions. There is always a danger that the histories and trajectories of neo-functionalism and intergovernmentalism can end up being caricatured in such accounts. It is not the job of this chapter to offer a revisionist reading of the 'classical' theoretical literature; suffice to say that the early texts of integration theory repay careful reading by present-day students. This is not just because of the obviously useful legacies of ideas such as **spillover**. It is also true to say that the ways in which these 'old' theories are criticized is open to contest. Indeed the idea that there is a convenient and rigid division between 'new' and 'old' theories is open to considerable critical scrutiny (see Haas 2001, 2004; Rosamond 2005a).

The 'old' debate has been criticized on at least three interrelated counts: its alleged inability to capture the reality of integration and the EU; its supposed entrapment in the disciplinary wilderness of International Relations; and its so-called 'scientific' limitations.

On the first of these, neo-functionalists – in particular – were heavily criticized for the lack of correspondence between their theory of integration and the unfolding reality of European integration. The assertion of intergovernmental politics from the mid-1960s, the obstinacy of nationalist sentiment within the member states, and the peculiarity and non-replicability of the European experience all provided serious body blows to neo-functionalist discourse by the mid-1970s (see Chapter 6). Similarly, intergovernmentalism is open to the charge that it offers only a partial representation of both integration and EU governance. The focus on politics between member state executives and the claim that substantive change in European integration is traceable only to intergovernmental bargains stands at variance with a lot of the empirical evidence gathered by those at the 'coal face' of EU studies (see Chapter 7). However, while much of what goes on within the EU – in terms of day-to-day legislative and regulatory activity – is bound up with the actions of 'non-state actors', this does not mean that neo-functionalism is necessarily best placed to make a comeback.

To take an example, one of the big debates to emerge in the literature of the late 1980s and early 1990s concerned the origins of the Single Market programme as codified in the **Single European Act** (SEA) (1987) (see also Chapters 3 and 16). Intergovernmentalists honed in on the SEA as an obvious case of treaty reform initiated by an intergovernmental bargain. It was argued that change became possible because of the convergent interests of the three most powerful member states (France, Germany, and the UK). Moreover, these national preferences emerged out of processes of domestic political exchange in all three countries (Moravcsik 1991). Against this it was claimed that the SEA represented the formal consolidation of practices that had emerged in recent years. This in turn reflected acts of institutional creativity by the Commission, the jurisprudence of the Court of Justice, and processes of institutional interaction (Wincott 1995). At the same time, neo-functionalists found some evidence of spillover as initiatives to create the Single Market prompted calls for incursions into the realms of social policy and monetary union (Tranholm-Mikkelsen 1991). But while the evidence for this spillover was impressive, it was also true that there was a lot more going on in the Communities besides progression to the Single Market and beyond. In any case, other (newer) theoretical perspectives had developed strong explanations of how and why the Single Market and subsequent progress to monetary union came about.

The next criticism of 'old' theories builds on the allegation that they emerge from the disciplinary homeland of International Relations (IR). From this vantage point, IR is claimed to be a discipline preoccupied with two core themes: questions of war and peace and relations between *states*. European integration was originally of interest to IR scholars because European states seemed to be embarking on a project that sought to undermine and eliminate the recurrent causes of war on the continent. This led IR-derived theories into two ways of thinking. Neo-functionalists became concerned with the progressive mechanics of the integration process, while intergovernmentalists developed an interest in the ways in which diplomacy between national governments either survived or became institutionalized in the context of European integration.

This in turn sparks two types of complaint. The first is that the EU is about a lot more than the 'integration question'. Simon Hix (1994, 2005) makes the point that the question of whether there should be more or less *integration* does not motivate the behaviour of most of the actors involved in the business of the EU. Rather, he argues, these are individuals and groups pursuing their interests within a complex political system. As analysts of the EU, we are in fact confronted with the evergreen political science question of 'who gets what, when, how?', to use Harold Lasswell's classic formulation (Lasswell 1950). If we think that the 'integration question' is all that the EU is about, then we fall into the same trap as those politicians who conceptualize the EU in terms of the simple zero-sum opposition between 'nation-state' and federal 'superstate'. This leads to the second type of complaint. This maintains that we need to break out of the 'state fixation' that characterizes so much of the routine academic and political discourse about the EU. For one thing, many – perhaps most – students of the EU would want to argue that the EU has evolved into a peculiar form of polity or political system that does not really fit into any established template for understanding the state. On the other hand, the EU is a system that delivers coherent and binding policy outputs. The allegation is that IR perspectives fail to deal with these criticisms.

The third criticism of the classical debate brings together a number of concerns about the type of theory involved. Neo-functionalism in particular has been criticized as a **grand theory** – an attempt to develop a set of general 'laws' about the dynamics of regional integration across the world. Such attempts at overarching theory came under intense scrutiny in the early 1970s and it is no coincidence that this was the period in which neo-functionalism was abandoned by its foremost practitioners (Moravcsik 1998: 11; Rosamond 2000: 190). In place of grand, universal theories, social scientists became more interested in developing **middle-range theories**. As the name suggests, middle-range theories do not have totalizing ambitions; they seek to explain aspects of a phenomenon rather than its whole. As we will see below, most contemporary theoretical work is concerned with explaining aspects of the policy process and regulatory fabric of the EU. Theories of European *integration* are by and large obsolescent (though see Haas 2004).

Of course, this criticism often merges with the critique of IR to suggest that the problem of International Relations is that it continues to trade in the currency of grand theory. Another way of thinking about this problem is to identify 'old' theory as concentrating on the *form* that integration would take. For many contemporary scholars of the EU, this is simply an irrelevant question. What merits attention and explanation are the processes through which the EU delivers authoritative outputs and not the 'big picture' question of what the EU is becoming.

It would be a mistake to think that these criticisms have been completely decisive and have ushered EU studies into a new theoretical age. Each is contested and, even where scholars agree that there is some substance in the above, many argue that the theoretical landscape is more nuanced and complex than many of the critics of classical theory suggest. Some of these points will be elaborated more fully in the conclusion to this chapter. For now it is worth recognizing that not all critiques would take the failures of neo-functionalism and intergovernmentalism to match 'reality' as a legitimate starting point.

Theorists working in what is sometimes called the **constitutive tradition** regard the relationship between theory and reality as intimate and problematic and would choose altogether different criteria for evaluating theories than their ability to correspond to and/or predict the 'real' world.

Moreover, those who dismiss International Relations as a parent discipline have been taken to task by those who suggest that what goes on within IR departments and journals bears little resemblance to the grand theorizing and state-fixated area of study depicted by the critics (Rosamond 2000, although for a clear critique of IR's continuing fixations in this area, see Sørensen 2004). In any case, it is a bold claim that overstates the extent to which the study of European integration was ever cordoned off as a subfield of IR. The likes of Ernst Haas, Karl Deutsch, Leon Lindberg, and Philippe Schmitter studied the early communities as self-conscious (and often pioneering) exponents of the latest political science (Haas 2001, 2004; Ruggie *et al.* 2005). Integration theory's most obvious connection to IR was its contribution to the emergence of International Political Economy (IPE), a sub-area that explicitly emphasizes the fuzziness of the boundaries between domestic politics and international relations (Katzenstein, Keohane, and Krasner 1998). Others suggest that IR theories retain a significant place in EU studies because they act as valuable tools for understanding the global environment within which the EU operates (Hurrell and Menon 1996; and Peterson and Bomberg 1999).

The third point – the type of theorizing involved in the 'old' debate – is less a criticism than an observation about how the study of a phenomenon (in our case the EU) is bound up with the ebbs and flows of social science, as much as it is related to the context supplied by that phenomenon.

Another way of thinking about this shift from the 'old' to the 'new' is supplied by Markus Jachtenfuchs (2001). He draws a distinction between a classical phase of integration theory where the 'Euro-polity' was the **dependent variable** and the contemporary 'governance' phase in which the 'Euro-polity' becomes the **independent variable**. In other words, the EU has shifted from being a phenomenon that analysts seek to explain to becoming a factor that contributes to the explanation of other phenomena. This amounts to moving from asking 'Why does integration occur?' to posing the question 'What effect does integration have?' While the evolution of the European Union may explain why the nature of EU studies (and the theoretical work that informs it) has shifted in this way, it is clearly not the only reason. It is important to remember that the preoccupations and fashions of the political sciences also change over time. For example, the growth of policy analysis as a key component of EU studies reflects an explosion (in political science more generally) of policy analytic work. In particular this has concentrated upon less formal, 'softer' forms of governance, thereby exposing a dense array of informal institutional mechanisms and non-hierarchical policy methodologies within the EU system (Jachtenfuchs and Kohler-Koch 2004). Theoretical development (or, for some, progress) in a particular field is about assimilating the currently predominant conceptual toolkit and the preoccupations of social science. Some would say that this delivers progress in a field in the form of better explanations of the reality of the object of enquiry (in our case the EU) and more rigorous forms of social science. Others would argue that our knowledge of the social world is governed by prevailing conceptions of what counts as valid knowledge, thereby skewing the game in favour of some forms of theory over others.

KEY POINTS

- Recent years have seen renewed interest in theorizing the EU. Most scholars accept that there has been a significant shift towards newer styles of theoretical work.
- Critics of the classical debate regard neo-functionalism and intergovernmentalism as theories that ask the wrong sorts of question about the EU.
- Discussions about the obsolescence of 'old' theories raise some interesting questions about the nature and purpose of theory.

Institutionalism and the EU

By the standards of regional integration schemes worldwide, the EU is heavily institutionalized. It possesses a distinctive set of supranational institutions such as the Commission, the Parliament, and the Court of Justice (see Chapters 9–12). In addition, the EU features a number of intergovernmental bodies, not to mention several smaller bodies, such as the Economic and Social Committee (see Chapter 1), that wield less in the way of formal power yet form distinct cogs in the European policy-making machinery. The treaties define the roles of these various institutions as well as the ways in which they are supposed to interact.

Four points are worthy of note. First, the founders of the European Communities sought to capture their desired balance between national and supranational forces through careful institutional design. Most accept that the balance has altered over time (Wallace 1996), but the formal institutional structure of European integration has remained remarkably resilient for half a century. Secondly, close observers of the EU often note the growth of distinct cultures within the various institutions. It is not just that there is a particular modus operandi within the Commission, but that individual Directorates-General (DGs) of the Commission possess distinct institutional cultures. The same is true of different Councils. Thirdly, scholarship has revealed the existence of various informalities within the formal institutional shape of the EU. This work suggests that much that is decisive within the policy process is the consequence of regularized practices that do not have formal status within the treaties. In spite of that, these established routines are frequently thought of as institutions. Fourthly, much recent scholarly effort has been directed at understanding the *multi-level* character of the EU's institutionalized polity. Thus EU institutions (whether formal or informal) are constituted not simply by the world of Brussels and Strasbourg, but by a dense network of institutions that extend into the fabric of domestic and local polities (see Box 8.1).

So much of the corpus of EU studies involves the analysis of formal and informal institutions and the impact that institutionalized practices have upon policy outcomes. As Mark Pollack has noted, '[t]he European Union is without question the most

 KEY CONCEPTS AND TERMS 8.1

Institutions and the new institutionalism

For most students of politics, 'institution' brings to mind phenomena such as the legislative, executive, and judicial branches of government – what we might think of as ongoing or embedded sets of formalities, often underwritten or codified by constitutional prescription. Early political science dealt with the study of this sort of institution. Scholars explored how such bodies operated, how they interacted, and how they supplied sets of rules that helped to account for the ways in which political systems operated. Often such studies concluded that institutional patterns reflected the character of a country's politics. This 'old' institutionalism was criticized – especially by behaviouralists – for an overemphasis on the formal, codified aspects of politics at the expense of looking at the nitty-gritty of politics: the interaction of groups in pursuit of their interest and the basis, form, and consequences of individual and collective political behaviour. However, classical institutional studies did bequeath a concern with the impact of rules upon the behaviour of actors and thus upon political outcomes more generally. 'New' institutionalism proceeds from the axiom that 'institutions matter' as shapers of and influences upon actor behaviour (rather than as mere expressions of political culture). This is combined with a broader definition of 'institution' to embrace not only formal rules, but also forms of ongoing social interaction that form the 'compliance procedures and standard operating practices' in the political economy, to borrow Peter Hall's well-established definition (Hall 1986: 19). Thus, from the new institutionalist vantage point, we may be talking about anything from written constitutional rules through to norms or even collectively recognized symbols when we speak of institutions. With this in mind, it is hardly surprising that the EU has become a favoured venue for the practice of new institutionalist political science.

densely institutionalized international organization in the world' (Pollack 2004: 137). At the same time, as studies of the EU have multiplied in recent years, so the wider world of political science has become infused with the so-called 'new institutionalism' (Hall and Taylor 1996).

It would be a mistake to regard the new institutionalism as a single theoretical perspective. Institutionalists agree, more or less, that institutions matter. As Aspinwall and Schneider note:

> "Institutions contain the bias individual agents have built into their society over time, which in turn leads to important distributional consequences. They structure political actions and outcomes rather than simply mirroring social activity and rational competition among disaggregated units."
>
> (Aspinwall and Schneider 2001a: 2).

Importantly, institutionalists of different hues have alternative accounts of just *how much* institutions matter. Aspinwall and Schneider think about institutional political science as a spectrum. At one end of this spectrum sits an economistic-rationalist position which sees institutions as the consequence of long-run patterns of behaviour by self-seeking agents. Institutions, in this account, are both modifiers of the pursuit of self-interest and a medium through which actors may conduct their transactions with greater efficiency. At the opposite end of the spectrum is a sociological position where actors' interests are actually constructed through processes of institutional interaction. The landmark discussion of Hall and Taylor (1996) identifies three sub-species of institutionalism: rational choice, historical, and sociological. Each of these has a presence in EU studies (see Table 8.1).

Rational choice institutionalism is the most obvious – and, for some, the most successful – way in which rational choice approaches to politics have infiltrated EU studies (Dowding 2000). Rational choice institutionalism is, as Roger Scully (2006) notes, a close relative – in terms of foundational theoretical premises – of Moravcsik's liberal intergovernmentalism. Rational choice theory – perhaps the dominant (though much criticized) strand in contemporary American political science – is based on the idea that human beings are self-seeking and behave rationally and strategically. The goals of political actors are organized hierarchically. They form their preferences on the basis of their interests. Institutions are important because they act as intervening variables. This means that institutions do not alter preference functions, but will have an impact upon the ways in which actors pursue those preferences. Consequently, changes in the institutional rules of the game, such as the introduction of the **codecision procedure** (which, following the Maastricht and Amsterdam treaties, gave the Council and the European Parliament co-legislative power in certain areas) or alterations to the voting rules within the Council (say from unanimity to qualified majority), will induce actors to recalculate the ways in which they need to behave in order to realize their preferences.

Table 8.1 The 'new institutionalisms'

TYPE OF INSTITUTIONALISM	Rational Choice Institutionalism	Historical Institutionalism	Sociological Institutionalism
RESEARCH OBJECTIVE	The changing relative power of institutions	The long-term effects of institutions	The role of culture OR persuasion and communicative action

Source: Hall and Taylor (1996).

By and large, rational choice institutionalists have been interested in how their theory develops propositions about the changing relative power of institutional actors in the policy process (see Box 8.2). As Crombez (2001) shows, scholars of this persuasion assume that institutional actors seek policy outcomes that correspond as closely as possible to their preferences. This is why institutions are created in the first place (the so-called functionalist theory of institutional design). The construction of formal models, often deploying the type of reasoning found in formal economic analysis, allows for the empirical research on specific cases to be mapped against the formal decision rules that apply. Thus EU studies has developed lively debate about matters such as the agenda-setting power of the various institutions. Another key component of the rationalist argument has been the application of 'principal-agent analysis' to EU politics. Here self-regarding actors ('principals') find that their preferences are best served by the delegation of certain authoritative tasks to common institutions ('agents'). In the EU case, this approach provides powerful explanations for member states' decisions to create and assign tasks to supranational institutions such as the Commission and the European Court of Justice (Pollack 2002).

For their proponents (such as Dowding 2000), such rational choice perspectives offer rigorous foundations for the development and testing of falsifiable hypotheses around a series of core shared propositions. This improves knowledge in a progressive and cumulative way. Scholars work from a set of (admittedly stylized) assumptions to produce progressively better understandings of how the EU works. For their opponents, rational choice institutionalists miss the point. Their focus on formal rules leads them to ignore the various informal processes that grow up around the codified practices. It is these informalities that better explain policy outcomes. Moreover, rational choice accounts of actor preferences tend to leave these fixed rather than recognizing the ways in which processes of socialization can mould interests and identities (Hooghe 2001).

BOX 8.2

Rational choice and the science of EU studies

Supporters of rational choice institutionalism believe that this approach to the EU is able to build knowledge in a systematic way. Scholars working under the auspices of rational choice subscribe to particular methods of theory building. This usually involves the development of models capable of generating hypotheses, which can then be subjected to confirmation or disconfirmation through exposure to hard empirical evidence. Such work relies on the deployment of (often quite stylized) assumptions and the use of game theory as a tool of analysis. The substantial work of Geoffrey Garrett and George Tsebelis (for example Tsebelis 1994; Garrett and Tsebelis 1996) yields the counter-intuitive claim that the codecision procedure has strengthened the Council at the expense of the Commission and the European Parliament. The analysis is sophisticated, but relies on the assumption that institutions' preferences are arranged along a continuum according to the amount of integration that they favour. For critics, this type of work may produce intriguing results, but it relies too much on unrealistic assumptions and describes games that bear no relation to the complex interactions that take place between EU institutions on a day-to-day basis. Another dimension to this debate is that rational choice institutionalists often advance the view that theirs is a more rigorous form of political science than that offered by either EU studies 'traditionalists' or those of a more constructivist persuasion.

Historical institutionalists are interested in how institutional choices have long-term effects. Institutions are designed for particular purposes in particular sets of circumstances. They are assigned tasks and in this process acquire interests and ongoing agendas. If institutions interact with one another in a decision-making process then patterns that are constitutionally prescribed or evolve in the early lifetime of the institutions concerned may 'lock in' and also become ongoing. This 'lock-in' means that a 'path-dependent' logic may set in. The ongoing nature of institutional interests (their continuing bureau-shaping agendas and their preference for self-preservation) means that institutions become robust and may well outlive their creators. This also means that institutions may have an impact that their creators could not have foreseen, not least because they survive to confront new circumstances and new challenges. But these new challenges are met through the prism provided by pre-existing institutions. Thus the range of possible action and policy choice is constrained. Policy entrepreneurs may attempt to redesign institutions to meet current needs, but they do so in the face of institutional agendas that are locked in and which are, therefore, potentially difficult to reform.

Like the other two variants of institutionalism, historical institutionalism is not exclusive to EU studies. But its applications are obvious. That said, scholars use this basic template in various ways. Paul Pierson's well-known discussion of path dependency (Pierson 1998) looks at the problem of unintended consequences. He argues that the immediate concerns of the architects of the European Communities (EC) led them, at a critical juncture, into acts of institutional design that ultimately helped to erode the capacity of national governments to control the governance of their economies. So while the intention of West European governments of the 1950s may have been to rescue the nation state, Pierson's work suggests that the long-term consequence of their deliberations may have been to engineer precisely the obverse. The implications for research from this theoretical insight are quite interesting. It pushes students of the EU to think about policy pathways – how particular EU-level competencies emerge over time as a result of specific decisions. We are asked to think about how rational acts at one point in time influence rational action in the future.

Less wedded to rational actor assumptions is other historical institutionalist work such as that of Kenneth Armstrong and Simon Bulmer (1998) in their extensive study of the Single Market. Armstrong and Bulmer are more interested in the way that institutions can become carriers of certain ideas, values, and norms over time. Once again we are directed towards thinking about how such normative and ideational 'matter' is loaded into institutions at their inception. But students of the EU are also invited to explore how institutional cultures (say of the Commission generally or of specific Directorates-General) impact upon all stages of the policy process, influence action and policy choice, and (perhaps) assist in the conditioning of the interests of actors.

This last comment provides a link to sociological institutionalism, a strand of literature that is closely bound up with the constructivist 'turn' in international and European studies (see Risse 2004; Wiener 2006 for comprehensive overviews). This is discussed later in the chapter, so the exposition in this section will be relatively brief. It is important to note that sociological institutionalists tend to reject the other institutionalisms because of their inherent 'rationalism'. The meaning of this term is again discussed below, but for now it is worth remembering that sociological institutionalists/constructivists operate with a quite distinct **ontology** (an underlying conception of the world). This boils down to a very particular take on the nature of actors' interests. While rational choice and (most) historical institutionalists see interests as exogenous (external to) interaction, so sociological institutionalists see them as endogenous (internal). That is to say that interests are not pre-set, but rather the product of interaction between actors.

This leads sociological institutionalists towards a concern with two broad issues: the 'culture' of institutions and the role of persuasion and communicative action within institutional settings (Börzel and Risse 2000). By 'culture' is meant the emergence of common frames of reference, norms governing behaviour, and 'cognitive filters'. As Hall and Taylor note, in this account 'institutions do not simply affect the strategic calculations of individuals, as rational choice institutionalists contend, but also their most basic preferences and very identity' (Hall and Taylor 1996: 948). With this in mind, sociological institutionalist analysis of the EU looks at the ways in which ongoing patterns of interaction and 'normal' forms of behaviour emerge within institutional settings. As one writer puts it, 'institutions have theories about themselves'

(Jachtenfuchs 1997: 47). Thus institutions contribute to actors' understandings of who they are, what their context is, and what might be the motivations of other actors. This sort of work aims to add substance to often heard claims such as the idea that different Directorates-General (DGs) of the European Commission function in quite distinct ways. Another area in which the application of this sort of thinking seems appropriate is the investigation of whether formally intergovernmental processes such as those associated with the Common Foreign and Security Policy (CFSP) conform to established patterns of interstate interaction, or whether they bring about new norms of exchange between the envoys of member states, thereby transforming long-established norms of interstate politics.

The roles of communication, argument, and persuasion are seen as particularly important in these contexts. This is likely to occur in settings where norms have been established, but these deliberative processes also contribute to the establishment of common understandings. Thus, sociological institutionalists often embark upon empirical quests for so-called 'norm entrepreneurs' – 'well placed individual actors . . . [who] . . . can often turn their individual beliefs into broader, shared understandings' (Checkel 2001: 31). Sociological institutionalism is not simply interested in the EU level of analysis. A lot of work is being done on the interaction of national and European-level norms and in particular the ways in which 'European' norms filter into the existing political cultures of the member states (Börzel 2002).

KEY POINTS

- The EU has become a major venue for the application of 'new institutionalist' political science and for debates between its main strands.
- Rational choice institutionalists are interested in how the relative power of actors shifts in accordance with changes in institutional rules.
- Historical institutionalists focus on the long-term implications of institutional choices made at specific points in time.
- Sociological institutionalists pay attention to the 'culture' of institutions and the ways in which patterns of communication and persuasion operate in institutional settings.

Theories of policy-making and the EU

One of the major features of EU studies in recent years has been the growth of work that draws on theories of public policy-making. This is barely surprising. The EU is a major source of authoritative policy outputs in Europe. Moreover, most observers agree that there has been a substantial 'drift' of policy-making competence from member states to the European level since the initiation of the Communities in the 1950s. Consequently, there is an obvious and increasing need to make sense of how policy is made in this context. This confirms the idea, discussed above, that the EU is about rather more than 'integration'. If we think of the EU as a policy system, then it follows that scholarship needs to explore the ways in which policy agendas are set, policies are formulated, decisions are made, and legislation is implemented.

This also constitutes a move away from the idea that the key EU outputs are 'big' history-making decisions such as treaty revisions. Much of what the EU does is in the area of technical regulation and the finer points of economic governance. Others – such as those scholars associated with the **multi-level governance** school discussed below – note that different patterns of policy-making occur in different areas of EU activity. Thus, the politics of agricultural regulation might be quite dissimilar to the politics of merger control. This suggests that detailed empirical scholarship is needed on a sector-by-sector basis if we are to properly comprehend the complexity of EU governance. However, this does not mean that theory is irrelevant or marginal to this enterprise. All political science – however empirical – is informed by theory.

The EU has always been a port of call for theoretical work constructed elsewhere in the social sciences and the concern with the minutiae of policy-making suggests an important role for theories of policy analysis. In their discussion of EU decision-making, John Peterson and Elizabeth Bomberg (1999) suggest that different levels of action in the EU require different sorts of theory. They identify three levels of action: super-systemic, systemic, and meso (sectoral). At each level analysts are interested in different variables – respectively, changes in the wider environment of the EU, institutional change, and resource dependencies. Thus, each level requires different theoretical tools. IR theories work well at the super-systemic level, while new institutionalist theories suit the systemic level of analysis.

At the sectoral level, where regulatory complexity prevails and where 'stakeholders' in the policy process exchange information and resources, Peterson and Bomberg recommend the deployment of policy network analysis (see also Peterson 2004b). The concept of policy networks provides a way of thinking about complex decision-making situations characterized by ongoing relations between multiple 'stakeholding' actors. They are situations where ideology is largely secondary and expertise is at a premium. This is not to say that politics is absent. On the contrary, policy network analysis deals with the politics of influence and mutual dependency in situations where power is dispersed. The actors involved in policy networks have, by definition, an interest in policy outcomes. In national contexts – where the policy network approach was first developed – emphasis was placed upon the relationships between government departments, pressure groups, and various agencies and organizations. The main insight of such work was that networks often involved the ongoing exchange of resources between its component members. The impact of such work is that it guides us away from thinking about policy-making in terms of rule-bound interactions between (constitutionally defined) institutions that are organized hierarchically. It emphasizes the need to understand the specific relations of mutual dependency that obtain in different sectors.

Opinion is divided as to whether policy network analysis has a place in the study of the EU. Kassim (1994), for example, criticizes policy network approaches for neglecting the interaction of institutions that is so central to a proper understanding of the EU policy process. Peterson, on the other hand, points to the regulatory, uneven, fluid, and multi-actor character of the EU policy game as ample justification for the application of the policy network template to the EU. Also, as Richardson (2001) reminds us, the concept of policy networks (as opposed to the rather more rigid idea of 'policy communities') is fluid and adaptable and thus well suited to the fact that EU policy-making is segmented, complex, and populated by multiple stakeholders.

The take-up of this approach by students of the EU begs the interesting question of whether the tools used to study national governance and policy-making can be applied straightforwardly to the European level. This takes us back to some of the fundamental issues discussed at the beginning of this chapter. But policy network analysis is not alone in making this assumption.

Another good example emerges from the work of Giandomenico Majone (1994, 2005) who has been a central figure in the development of idea of the 'regulatory state'. The regulatory state literature offers a view of how the management of advanced capitalist economies has shifted in recent times in the face of challenges posed by changes in the global economy. In Majone's terms, the EU has many of the key features of a regulatory state, the paradigm example of which is the USA. Regulatory states are distinct from positive interventionist states. Whereas the latter involved government intervention to engineer the redistribution of resources (usually through the mechanism of the welfare state), so the former busies itself only with the rectification of market failure. Much of what the EU does is bound up with the regulation of the Single Market. It – pretty much – lacks the welfare function associated most with the post-war (West) European state. The EU's relatively modest resources are best targeted at regulatory forms of policy-making. But Majone's point is that regulation is a form of governance that is becoming widespread across the Western world. It is not a development unique to the EU. However, the EU can be thought of as a set of regulatory institutions created by the member states to solve problems of market imperfection. In this respect Majone's analysis shares a lot with principal-agent analysis (see above).

Not everyone would agree that the EU is solely a regulatory state, but the model of negative market integration/regulation is increasingly seen as one important dimension of the way in which governance in Europe is delivered (Wallace 2005; Jørgensen and Rosamond 2002). The regulatory mode of governance proceeds from quite distinct logics when compared to the classic **Community method**. It is worth noting that much of the earlier theoretical work in EU studies was concerned with exploring the dynamics of the Community method. The growth of regulation within the EU policy process thus – arguably – has forced a corresponding recalibration of theory. One thing that would appear to unite political scientists working on the EU with, on the one hand, scholars of International Political Economy and, on the other, analysts of national and subnational policy-making is an interest in *governance* (Pierre 2000). The term is usually defined in terms of the range of actions and institutions that supply order. What we conventionally understand as *government* is one way in which order is delivered, but the literature on governance suggests that the traditional methods of public regulation, intervention, and legislation are being displaced and that authority is becoming dispersed amongst a variety of actors. The state retains a key role in governance, but its role is being reformulated and, arguably, residualized. The EU is thought of as a very interesting and pertinent laboratory for the exploration of these trends, a point taken up by the literature on multi-level governance.

KEY POINTS

- The status of the EU as a polity that is responsible for the delivery of coherent and meaningful policy outputs challenges us to think about it in terms other than the classical theoretical discourse of integration.
- With this in mind many have sought to treat the EU as a policy system. This requires the application of the tools of policy analysis. Many of these approaches, such as policy network analysis, originally emerged in the study of national political systems.
- A slightly different take on this question is to think about the EU in terms of trends that are shaping the ways in which governance is delivered in modern complex societies.

Multi-level governance

Much of the work introduced in the previous section builds on the claim that policy-making within both nation states and the EU is a complex affair that cannot be captured by static models of the decision-making process focusing on formal legislative institutions. Analysts who adopt the theoretical language of policy networks and the regulatory state force us to question whether there is any meaningful distinction between policy-making at different levels of governance. Perhaps the crucial changes are taking place in terms of policy-making styles rather than policy-making levels. We can take this a little further to say that the character of governance in Europe has changed significantly over the past 50 years. If we adopt this position, then we might suggest that the boundaries between national policy-making and European policy-making have been blurred to the point of insignificance. The EU policy process is not something that simply happens at the European level. It penetrates into national political and legal systems in complex ways. So while there has been an undoubted 'drift' of authority in various policy areas to the European level (Hooghe and Marks 2001; Schmitter 1996), we need to move away from the image of there being two distinct domains of politics in Europe – the national and the supranational/European level.

This claim represents a direct challenge to theories such as Moravscik's liberal intergovernmentalism (LI) (see Chapter 7). LI relies on the idea of a two-level game to describe how governments' preferences emerge in the context of domestic politics and are then the foundations for intergovernmental bargaining within European-level institutions. Such a picture is directly challenged by the idea of multi-level governance.

The term multi-level governance (MLG) has become commonplace in EU studies in recent years and the term is usually used to capture the peculiar qualities of the EU's political system. As with most of the literature discussed in this chapter, the growth of MLG language in EU studies is an echo of work within several fields including IR, local government, and policy analysis (Hooghe and Marks 2003). The two leading proponents of the idea define MLG as 'the dispersion of authoritative decision-making across multiple territorial levels' (Hooghe and Marks 2001: xi). Rather than thinking about the extent to which Europe has become 'integrated', it is helpful to explore how *loci* of authority have shifted over the past half-century. Hooghe and Marks find that authority has become more dispersed since the late 1950s. So while there has been a drift of authority from the national to the European level, there has also been a general devolution of decision-making competence in most West European countries. At the same time, however, national governments remain important sites of authority.

So we have a picture of the EU policy process consisting a several tiers of authority (the European, the national, and the subnational). But the idea of MLG goes beyond this. It also emphasizes fluidity between these tiers, so that policy actors may move between different levels of action. Moreover, dispersion of authority is uneven across policy areas.

At present MLG remains more of an organizing metaphor than a theory (for a cogent discussion, see Warleigh 2006). It is within this metaphor that particular approaches – such as policy network analysis – can sit comfortably. But it does rest on some fundamental theoretical preconceptions that differentiate it squarely from LI (Marks, Hooghe, and Blank 1996). We have already noted the departure from the conceptions of political space offered by two-level game theorists. It is also worth saying that MLG proceeds from a more pluralistic and organizational conception of the state than the likes of LI. This means that analysts beginning with an MLG frame of reference dispute quite fundamentally the intergovernmentalist account of what the EU is. The MLG version of the EU is a 'set of overarching, multi-level policy networks [where] . . . [t]he structure of political control is variable, not constant across policy space' (Marks *et al.* 1996: 41). In many ways MLG represents an attempt to capture the complexity of the EU, but it also represents a clear denial of the idea that there can be a single all-encompassing theory of the EU.

KEY POINTS

- The literature on multi-level governance (MLG) encourages us to think about the EU as a political system across multiple levels including national and subnational arenas of action as well the institutional environment of Brussels.
- MLG is premised on the idea that authority has gradually moved away from national governments over the past half-century. But authority has not simply shifted upwards to state-like European institutions; it has become dispersed among a variety of private and public agents.
- This yields a picture of complex, variable, and uneven patterns of policy-making in contemporary Europe.

Social constructivist approaches to the EU

Constructivism has been the big news in International Relations theory over the past few years. The work of constructivist scholars like Alexander Wendt (1999) has come to pose a serious challenge to the established schools of IR theory. Until recently, the main debate in mainstream IR was between forms of realism and liberalism. While realists offer a state-centric view of the world that emphasizes the primacy of self-help and power, liberals contemplate the ways in which international cooperation, commerce, and institutionalization are able to temper tendencies towards war in the international system. Constructivists note that both of these approaches emerge from similar foundations. They are both *rationalist* theories. Defining rationalism takes us into the complex realm of metatheory, and we cannot do justice to it here (see S. Smith 2001 for a deeper discussion). They tend to operate with a view of the world (an ontology) that sees interests as materially given. They also adhere to a positivistic conception of how knowledge should be gathered. This involves a commitment to 'scientific' method, the neutrality of facts, and the existence of observable realities (S. Smith 2001: 227). While such sentiments characterize much social science, they are not shared universally. Ranged against rationalism is a range of *reflectivist* approaches – such as postmodernism, forms of feminism, and varieties of critical theory – that begin from wholly different premises (Keohane 1988 discusses this distinction).

The appeal of constructivism – or at least the type of constructivism that has entered the IR mainstream in the last decade – is that it claims to offer a middle way between rationalism and reflectivism. Constructivists such as Wendt see interests as socially constructed rather than pre-given, which means that regularities in the international system are the consequence of collective (or 'intersubjective') meanings. So the challenge to rationalism is primarily ontological. Constructivists, as we have seen with the discussion of sociological institutionalism earlier in this chapter, are interested in how collective understandings emerge and how institutions constitute the interests and identities of actors. However, writers like Wendt (1999) and Jeffrey Checkel (2001), who has written extensively about Europe, insist that constructivism can and should share the rationalist commitment to developing knowledge through clear research programmes, refutable hypotheses, and the specification of causal mechanisms that produce regularities.

This is undoubtedly what most IR constructivists aspire to. However, not all of those working within a broadly constructivist tradition accept that a constructivist ontology is compatible with a rationalist **epistemology** (i.e. the way in which knowledge is acquired). There is no need to pursue this debate here beyond acknowledging its existence and pointing out that it raises some fundamental questions about what amounts to 'proper' or 'good' social science (Risse 2004). This has obvious implications for a subdiscipline such as EU studies because contests over these questions will affect what is published in academic journals and books about European integration and, by extension, will influence how the subject is taught in universities.

The editors of the first collection of constructivist essays on the EU accept that the various authors occupy different positions along the continuum between rationalism and reflectivism (Christiansen, Jørgensen, and Wiener 2001). Moreover the commitment to 'break bread' with rationalist theories such as liberal intergovernmentalism varies from author to author. That said, constructivists argue that they are best placed to study integration as a *process*. While intergovernmentalists recommend that the EU be studied as an instance of interstate bargaining and comparativists think about the EU as a political system, constructivists purport to investigate the character of the move from a bargaining regime to a polity (Christiansen, Jørgensen, and Wiener 2001: 11). Thus if we think about European integration as a process bound up with change, then it makes sense to draw on a metatheoretical position that treats reality as contested and problematic. This means that constructivist-inspired work should focus on 'social ontologies and social institutions, directing research at the origin and reconstruction of identities, the impact of rules and norms, the role of language and political discourse' (Christiansen, Jørgensen, and Wiener 2001: 12).

More concretely, as Risse (2004) notes, constructivists are predisposed to think about how human agents interact in ways that produce structures (be they norms, institutions, shared cultural understandings, or discourses) that simultaneously shape and influence social interaction and the possibilities for action that follow. Constructivists endeavour to understand the constitution of interests and (thus) identities. Moreover, they are interested in the ways in which institutions act as arenas for communication, deliberation, argumentation, persuasion, and socialization. Constructivists also touch base with discourse analysts (Wæver 2004) to emphasize the power resident in the capacity to create meaning and so frame policy choices in often non-negotiable ways.

Perhaps the best way to unravel constructivism in EU studies is to mention a few examples of what constructivists actually work on. Many are interested in how European identities emerge. So the idea of a 'European economy', a 'European security community', or 'European citizenship' should not be read as a consequence of actors' interests changing rationally in response to external material changes such as the onset of globalization or the end of the Cold War. Rather, constructivists insist that we need to investigate the ways in which these identities are constructed through the use of language, the deployment of ideas, and the establishment of norms. We also need to pay attention to the ways in which these norms and ideas are communicated and to the processes of learning of socialization that take place among actors. 'Norms' are particularly important in the constructivist vocabulary. These are defined as 'collective expectations for the proper behaviour of actors with a given identity' (Katzenstein 1996: 5). It is through the internalization of norms that actors acquire their identities and establish what their interests are. This is what constructivists mean when they talk about the 'constitutive effects' of norms.

The emerging constructivist research agenda in EU studies (which has much in common with that of sociological institutionalism outlined earlier in this chapter) also pays attention to the ways in which European-level norms, ideas, and discourses penetrate into the various national polities that make up the EU (Börzel 2002).

KEY POINTS

- Constructivism is a recent import to EU studies, having taken on a particular character in debates in international theory.
- Constructivism is not a theory of integration, but a position on the nature of social reality (an ontology). It follows that there are many constructivist approaches and significant disagreement about the compatibility of constructivism with rationalist theories.
- Constructivists are interested in European integration as a process. They focus in particular on questions of identity and the ways in which European norms are established and play out within the EU institutions and the member states.

International Relations and International Political Economy revisited

We saw earlier in this chapter that the discipline of International Relations (IR) has been thought of by some as an inappropriate disciplinary homeland for students of the EU. If the EU is about much more than 'integration', runs the argument, then we need to break away from a discipline that is really only capable of asking questions about whether there is more or less integration and which actors influence the integration process. One counter-argument, as we have seen, is to challenge this image of what IR is all about. For example, there are plenty of scholars working in IR departments, attending IR conferences, and writing in IR journals who see the discipline as at the forefront of thinking about emergent transnational economic and social spaces and the forms of governance that arise in such circumstances. Another is to question the notion of a hard boundary between 'political science' and IR and to point out that integration theory was founded by figures – like Karl Deutsch and Ernst Haas – who were engaged in the explicit application of the newest political science ideas to the study of a very interesting new phenomenon (regional integration in Europe) (Haas 2001, 2004; Ruggie *et al.* 2005).

This is a debate worth having, but in recent years there have emerged other reasons for 'bringing IR back in'. Two, in particular, stand out: (a) the possibility that the EU can be studied as an instance of the so-called 'new regionalism' that has emerged in recent years across the world as (perhaps) a response to globalization; and (b) the growing significance of the EU as an actor on the world stage.

The EU and the 'new' regionalism

Regional integration – especially in the form of free trade areas and customs unions – is not a new phenomenon. However, the period since the mid-1980s has been characterized by the growth of many regional economic blocs in the global political economy. Among the most conspicuous are the North American Free Trade Agreement (NAFTA), Asia Pacific Economic Co-operation (APEC), and Mercosur in South America. Not surprisingly, these cases of 'regionalism' have generated considerable scholarly interest and analysts have been keen to explore the possibility that their more or less simultaneous emergence has something to do with exposure to common stimuli.

The most obvious explanation for the revival of regional integration is the development of **globalization**. Globalization is a deeply contentious topic, but is usually though of as a combination of things like heightened capital mobility, intensified cross-border transactions, the multinationalization of production, and the spread of neo-liberal economic policy norms – in short, the growth of market authority at the expense of formal political authority. This debate is very complex, but one line of argument is that regionalism (as represented by NAFTA, Mercosur, and so on) is the primary way in which states have responded to globalization. The move to regionalism suggests that states have seen fit to pool resources in order to recapture some of the authority that globalization has taken away – a type of collective insurance against globalization.

Debate exists over the extent to which states actually and effectively lead the creation of regional integration schemes. This is where a distinction between regionalism and regionalization is important in the literature. While regionalism describes state-led projects of institution-building among groups of countries, regionalization is a term used to capture the emergence of a de facto regional economy, propelled by the cross-border activities of economic actors, particularly firms. The question here is whether the formal institutions of regional integration are created to deal with and regulate this emergent transnational economic space, or whether the growth of cross-border activity is stimulated by the decisions of governments. These are empirical questions at one level, but the two positions in this particular debate emerge from two different theoretical accounts of the world – one largely state-centric and one not.

There is also a debate in international economics about the impact of regional agreements on the global economy. All of the instances mentioned above are actual or aspirant free trade areas. The question is whether the creation of regional free trade zones creates or diverts trade on a global scale. Put another way, it asks whether we are heading for a regionalized world (of competing regional blocs) or a globalized world. Again, such matters can be measured empirically, but theoretical intervention is needed if we are fully to understand the meaning of a term like 'globalization'. Notice, also, how much of the foregoing implies a particular type of relationship between globalization and statehood and, it should be said, between structure and agency. Alternative accounts place differential emphasis upon the structural qualities of globalization – its ability to set imperatives and shape the behaviour of actors.

The theoretical relevance of the questions raised in the preceding paragraphs becomes especially apparent when we think about their application to the EU. Thinking theoretically, as James Rosenau and Mary Durfee (1995) point out, involves asking the 'of what is this an instance?' question. The 'new regionalism' literature forces us to ask whether the EU is a comparable case to, say, NAFTA. If the answer is yes, then the study of comparative regional *integration* is brought back in with the EU as one of the primary cases.

Of course, the EU is at best a deviant case of regionalism. Its longevity rules out any claim that the EU was *created* as a response to global economic upheavals in the late 1970s and early 1980s. Moreover, compared to other cases of regionalism the EU is considerably more institutionalized and much more deeply integrated. To use the EU as a benchmark case against which other regional projects should be measured is clearly a fallacy. Yet at the same time the acceleration of economic integration through the Single Market programme and progress towards monetary union has coincided with the growth of regional projects elsewhere.

The problem is not a new one for theoreticians of European integration. In many ways, the problem defined the project of the first generation of integration theorists. For neo-functionalists (as we have seen in Chapter 6), comparison was a 'must' because only then might a generalizable theory of regional integration emerge from the case study supplied by the European Communities. Integration theorists and their critics have long grappled with the so-called $n = 1$ problem, that is, the uncomfortable possibility that the European Union may be nothing other than an instance of itself.

There are two suggestions as to how the field of EU studies might be reunited with the study of comparative regional integration without the EU becoming the paradigm case. The first follows Warleigh's (2006) argument that EU studies itself – thanks to many of the theoretical developments discussed in this chapter – offers a rich and fertile range of ideas for scholars interested in questions of governance beyond the nation state, the interplay between domestic politics and collective institutions, and the possibilities for post-nation democracy and legitimacy. The second suggested strategy involves the rediscovery of some of the neglected themes of classical integration theory, particularly neo-functionalism (see Chapter 6), where there was an overt emphasis on the study of the requisite material and cognitive background conditions for the formation and consolidation of regional projects (Rosamond 2005a; 2005b).

The EU as an actor

The external policy of the EU is discussed at length elsewhere in this book (see Chapters 14 and 15). The task here is to concentrate on what this might mean for the ways in which we might conceptualize and theorize the EU's role in the global political economy.

The question that first emerges is whether we can conceptualize the EU as an *actor*. That is to say, is the EU a discernible entity with its own capacity to act on the basis of its own interests? To be sure, the EU possesses certain formal roles in world politics and in the management of the global economy. It speaks with a common voice in international trade negotiations and has the makings of an embryonic foreign and security policy (M. Smith 2001a). On the other hand it consists of 25 member states, all of which operate as actors within the current international system (note how the very phrase 'inter-national system' connotes an order founded on the interaction of authoritative national states).

That the EU is not a state (at least in the conventional modern sense of the term) is not really in dispute (see Box 8.3). But is it becoming one? If this is the case, then we might want to argue that the EU is an embryonic state writ large, formed through the gradual merger of its component member states. This might then allow us to slot the EU – as a constituent unit of the international system – into long-established theories of IR, such as realism. This would construe the EU as an entity seeking to advance its own interests and, particularly, to render itself secure from external threat.

However, we might be reluctant to arrive at this conclusion. The EU might appear to be a rather unique entity, lacking those decisive authoritative attributes normally associated with modern (supposedly sovereign) nation states. If we think about the image of the EU that is described by the literature on multi-level governance (discussed earlier in this chapter) and then project outwards, then students of integration are confronted with something that seems to fit very badly with conventional theories of IR (Ruggie 1998: 173–4). Indeed, rather than trying to fit the EU into IR theory, perhaps IR theorists need to look carefully at their established theoretical toolkits if they are properly to comprehend the EU. Theories such as neo-realism and neo-liberal institutionalism (which dominate theoretical discourse in IR, especially in the USA) are built around the idea of states as the dominant units of analysis in the world system. The EU might be a freak occurrence, specific to the peculiarities of Western Europe, but the ways in which the boundaries between domestic and international politics have become blurred along with the styles of governance that have evolved may well have a much wider application (see also Tonra 2006).

One rider to this is that the EU's external action takes place, whether in terms of foreign policy or commercial (trade) policy, in conditions that still respond to the rules of state-centred inter-national politics. Thus, for the EU to acquire legitimacy and recognition as a valid actor in the system, we might hypothesize that it has to conform to the rules of that system. This in turn would create pressures for the EU to become state-like. Therefore, the paradox is that while the EU may appear to transcend the international system, it is still in meaningful ways constituted (as constructivists would put it) by the norms of that very system.

BOX 8.3

The EU and statehood

Much of the routine political discourse surrounding European integration bothers itself with the question of whether the EU is becoming a 'federal superstate', which, by definition, is supplanting the powers of its constituent member states. While such debates will seem simplistic to close students of the EU, they open up interesting avenues for theorists. Without doubt, the EU lacks some of the classical indices of 'statehood' as it has come to be understood (not least in Europe) over the past three and a half centuries. For example, the EU lacks fixed territorial boundaries and it does not possess monopolistic control over the legitimate means of violence. It does not engage in extensive programmes of redistribution, yet it does exercise meaningful and emphatic authority over the governance of its constituent economies, and by extension over the lives of hundreds of millions of Europeans. Moreover, the presumption of many current theorists is that the EU is sufficiently similar to national political systems to allow the deployment of the tools of normal political science and policy analysis. But statehood also has external dimensions. Thus world politics has developed into a game played between states with the notion of 'sovereignty' as the ultimate rule. Much contemporary International Relations literature debates the extent to which processes such as globalization have begun to transform this system. Yet the language of statehood, international politics, sovereignty, and diplomacy remains central to world politics. We might argue that the condition for admission to the world polity remains the achievement of statehood. So the question becomes whether the EU is being constituted and shaped by the existing world system or whether it is contributing to a radical reshaping of world politics.

KEY POINTS

- The dismissal of International Relations as a suitable (co-)parent discipline for EU studies may be somewhat premature.
- Much recent conceptual thinking in IR has been directed towards the analysis of the growth of regionalism in the global political economy, of which the EU may be a (peculiar) instance.
- Also important is recent thinking that challenges the state-centric vision of the world that has characterized much mainstream IR theory. The particular character of the EU as a presence in the global system confronts this traditional imagery by pointing to a number of ways in which structures of authority and patterns of politics may be changing.

Conclusion

The revival of interest in theory in EU studies has occurred within the context of some serious thinking about the role of theory in political science. Some of the 'new' theories discussed in this chapter have emerged from a concern to render theoretical work more rigorously 'scientific'. Other newer approaches have emerged from positions that explicitly challenge the rationalist mainstream in social science. Others still – notably certain constructivists – try to occupy a middle position between rationalism and reflectivism. These debates have begun to intrude into EU studies (Christiansen, Jørgensen and Wiener 2001) and have been played out more extensively in the broader International Relations literature (Baylis and Smith 2005). To the newcomer, this might seem like complex academic navel-gazing and thus divorced from the real business of studying the EU.

But theoretical reflection and debate simply bring out into the open assumptions that reside in any empirical discussion of the EU. Alternative theories have different accounts of social reality and sometimes lead to quite different strategies for acquiring valid knowledge about that world. This translates eventually into a set of disagreements about matters fundamental to this book. What sort of entity is the EU and how should it be studied?

Much of the 'new' theoretical work introduced above represents a self-conscious departure from thinking about the EU in terms of 'integration'. Its status as a supplier of authoritative policy outputs suggest that the toolkit of political science and policy analysis might be useful. At the same time, however, the fact that the EU is not a state as conventionally understood poses all sorts of challenges to those seeking to understand not only European integration, but also the nature of world order in the early twenty-first century. The EU may offer a clear indication of what a 'denationalized' world order might look like (Kohler-Koch and Eising 1999). It sits between nation states and the international system and arguably transforms both through its very existence.

The facts that the EU is multidimensional, that integration is uneven, and that EU governance is composed of multiple, coexisting policy modes all force us to think carefully about how the nature of authority is changing. The trick – as employers of the 'multi-level governance' metaphor remind us – is to think about the EU as part and parcel of this changing pattern of governance. To treat the EU as a political system 'above' national political systems ignores the complex interpenetration of the domestic and the supranational in contemporary Europe. The task of theories – whether drawn from the formal disciplinary domains of 'International Relations' or 'political science' – is to offer ways of organizing our thoughts about what is going on in this context. We might continue to be confused about the complexity of the EU, but the present vibrant theoretical culture in EU studies at least gives us a chance of being confused in a reasonably sophisticated way.

QUESTIONS

1. Is it fair to say that Comparative Politics provides a better disciplinary homeland for EU studies than International Relations?
2. Can there be a single institutionalist research agenda in EU studies?
3. How helpful is the idea of 'multi-level governance' for organizing the way we think about the EU?
4. How might one study the EU from a policy networks perspective?
5. What added value do social constructivists bring to the study of the EU?
6. How might we go about theorizing the EU's role in the world?
7. To what extent is it possible to compare the EU with other instances of 'regionalism' in the global political economy?
8. Why is it important to theorize European integration and the European Union?

GUIDE TO FURTHER READING

■ Aspinwall, M., and Schneider, G. (eds) *The Rules of Integration: Institutionalist Approaches to the Study of Europe* (Manchester: Manchester University Press, 2001). A rigorous set of essays exploring the contributions made by the various forms of institutional analysis to the study of the EU.

■ Christiansen, T., Jørgensen, K. E., and Wiener, A. (eds) *The Social Construction of Europe* (London: Sage, 2001). A collection of constructivist-inspired readings of aspects of European integration. Contains critical responses and a notable new essay by Ernst Haas, the founder of neo-functionalism.

■ Cini, M., and Bourne, A. K (eds) *Palgrave Advances in European Union Studies* (Basingstoke: Palgrave Macmillan, 2006). A collection on the state of the art in EU studies with numerous theoretical insights.

■ Hix, S. *The Political System of the European Union*, 2nd edn (Basingstoke: Macmillan, 2005). A landmark text on the EU that begins from the claim that the EU is best studied through the lens of comparative politics.

■ Hooghe, L., and Marks, G. *Multi-level Governance and European Integration* (Boulder, CO: Rowman & Littlefield, 2001). The first book-length discussion of the theory and practice of multi-level governance

■ Rosamond, B. *Theories of European Integration* (Basingstoke: Palgrave, 2000). A critical discussion of past and present theories of integration.

■ Wiener, A., and Diez, T. (eds) *European Integration Theory* (Oxford: Oxford University Press, 2004). Practitioners of a wide variety of theoretical perspectives discuss and apply their approaches to the EU.

IMPORTANT WEBSITES

● http://eiop.or.at/erpa/erpaframe.html European Research Papers Archive. A collection of online working papers relating to EU studies, where much innovative theoretical work is showcased for the first time.

Visit the Online Resource Centre that accompanies this book for lots of interesting additional material. http://www.oxfordtextbooks.co.uk/orc/cini2e/

PART THREE

Institutions and Actors

9 The European Commission

MORTEN EGEBERG

Chapter Contents

- Introduction
- The functions of the Commission
- Commission influence
- The President and the commissioners
- Commissioners' *cabinets*
- The Commission services
- Connecting to national administrations: committees and networks
- Conclusion

Reader's Guide

This chapter provides a general introduction to the European Commission. It argues that it is more productive to compare the Commission to national executives or to a government than to a secretariat of a traditional international organization. It begins with a summary of the Commission's functions within the EU's policy process. It then considers the question of Commission influence and autonomy, before moving on to look at the structure and demography of the organization, that is, at the role of the President of the Commission and the commissioners, at the commissioners' personal staffs, at the Commission administration, and at the committees and administrative networks that link the Commission to national administrations and interest groups. The chapter concludes by emphasizing that the Commission is moving away from its intergovernmentalist roots towards becoming much more of a European(ized) institution than it was at its inception.

Introduction

To many observers, the Commission is a unique institution. It is much more than an international secretariat, but not quite a government, though it has many governmental characteristics, as we shall see. The Commission encompasses elements of both intergovernmentalism (a national dimension) and supranationalism (a European dimension). It is the opposing pull of these two elements that forms the focal point of this chapter. By exploring the national and supranational features of the Commission's organization, the chapter reopens the question: what sort of institution is the European Commission?

The chapter begins with a brief review of the Commission's main functions, which revolve around its role in the EU policy process. These involve the Commission in agenda-setting, and more specifically in the drafting of legislation, in the implementation of policies (albeit at arm's length) and the management of programmes, and in the formulation and negotiation of certain aspects of the EU's external relations. Moreover the Commission also has a role to play in mediating between the Parliament and Council and amongst national government and non-state actors involved in European policy-making, and in presenting its own, or a European, perspective on issues and events. The second section focuses on the question of Commission influence and autonomy, viewing this matter through the lens of European integration theories (see Chapters 5–8). In the sections that follow, attention turns to organizational features and to their behavioural consequences, with the focus first on the Commission President and College of Commissioners; second, on the commissioners' *cabinets* (their personal staffs); third on the Commission administration; and finally on the role of committees and external administrative networks. In perusing these sections, however, readers should be aware that the Commission is undergoing continuous organizational reform, which may well alter some of its structure and processes. However, the conclusions to the chapter are likely to hold true all the same – that the Commission is becoming a more European institution than it ever was in the past.

The functions of the Commission

The European Commission is, like governments, composed of a political executive wing (the commissioners and their staffs) and an administrative wing (the 'services'). It has a wide range of functions within the EU system – policy initiation, the monitoring of policy implementation, the management of European programmes, an important external relations role, and other functions which involve it as a mediator amongst the 25 member states and between the EU Council and the European Parliament (EP), as well as asserting its own European identity. The Commission is clearly involved in the EU's policy process from start to finish. In much the same way as are national executives, the Commission is responsible for the initiation and formulation of policies, usually in the form of legislative, budgetary, or programme proposals. To put it bluntly, the Commission drafts the legislation. It is in this sense that in the majority of policy areas – that is, in those policies falling under the first or EC pillar of the EU, such as the Single Market (see Chapter 16) – the Commission performs an exclusive agenda-setting role. Other actors, such as the European Council (the heads of state/government), the EP, national officials, and interest groups, may also take initiatives and advance policy proposals. But it is generally up to the Commission to decide how these ideas will be picked up and subsequently passed on to the legislature in the form of a formal legislative proposal, even if in practice these sorts of policy initiative quite often originate from outside the Commission.

By contrast, under the two more intergovernmental pillars – the Common Foreign and Security Policy (CFSP) or second pillar and the third pillar covering Police and Judicial Cooperation in Criminal Matters (formerly within Justice and Home Affairs) – the Commission does not have an exclusive agenda-setting role, although it may still be active in developing policy programmes. However, the executive tasks of the Justice and Home Affairs area have gradually been transferred to the Commission. Under the EU's foreign and security policy, the Secretary-General of the Council has also been appointed as the High Representative for the Union's CFSP. The strengthening of the Council's General Secretariat in this respect presents a direct challenge to the Commission's executive role, and illustrates the considerable tension between intergovernmentalism and supranationalism in this particular policy arena.

Also very much in line with the functions performed by national executives, the Commission has an important role to play in the implementation of European policies. What this means in an EU context is that the Commission is responsible for the *monitoring* of implementation within the EU's member states. In much the same way as occurs in Germany, the execution or putting into effect of policy remains largely the responsibility of the member state governments. However, before implementation can occur at the national or subnational level it may be necessary for secondary (or administrative) legislation to be agreed. This is because laws made by the Council, usually together with the EP, tend to take the form of broad policy guidelines or frameworks, rather than detailed steering instruments. Thus it is up to the Commission, in close cooperation with the member states, to detail and fill in EP/Council legislation by agreeing more specific rules, often in the form of *Commission* directives or regulations, in what is called delegated legislation. Only in very few policy areas, such as competition policy, is the Commission responsible for implementation in the sense of handling individual cases.

Finally, the Commission's external representation role has become increasingly important, particularly since the early 1990s. Just like national governments, the Commission staffs and runs delegations (in effect, EU embassies) around the world. There are no fewer than 130 offices in non-member countries. Also under the rubric of external representation the Commission acts as the main negotiator for the Union in trade and cooperation negotiations and within international bodies such as the World Trade Organization (WTO) (see Chapter 14).

The Commission also performs other less tangible and more diffuse functions within the EU. Important amongst these is its role as a mediator amongst the EU's 25 member states, and between the EP and the Council. Thus, the Commission does its best, once it has produced a proposal, to ensure that agreement is reached within the Union's legislative bodies. After having agreed a policy proposal internally (see below for more on the internal functioning of the Commission), the officials who drafted the proposal may attend meetings of the relevant EP committee and plenary sessions (see Chapter 11), the relevant Council working party, the Council Committee of Permanent Representatives (COREPER), and the relevant Council ministerial meeting (see Chapter 10) in order to defend their line, and, if necessary, to mediate between conflicting parties. The Commission also presents policy documents to heads of state/government at European Council (summit) meetings and at Intergovernmental Conferences (IGCs). The Commission not only is helping in the process of achieving a final agreement, but also has its own institutional position to advance, one which may involve the presentation of a more European picture of events than emerges from national quarters (or even the EP).

KEY POINTS

- The European Commission has a variety of functions to perform in the EU system, including policy initiation, implementation, management, external relations.
- The Commission is involved in almost all stages of the European policy process.
- The Commission plays a reduced role in Pillars 2 and 3 of the EU (those dealing with foreign policy, and police and judicial cooperation).

Commission influence

It is all very well to state that the Commission is involved at almost all stages of the EU policy process (at least in the first pillar, Pillar 1), but to what extent does the Commission have any real influence? In studies of the European Commission, there is a great deal of dispute over whether Commission initiatives make a significant difference or not to EU outcomes.

On the one hand, intergovernmentalists believe national governments are the real driving forces in the European project. In the *liberal* intergovernmentalist version of this theoretical stance (see Chapter 7), it is accepted that the Commission has an important role to play in first-pillar policies (such as the internal market, agricultural policy, and regional policy). However, they claim that the authority it exercises as an agenda-setter and overseer of implementation at the national level is merely a derived and delegated authority (Moravcsik 1998). According to this view, the Commission may facilitate intergovernmental cooperation, but it has no real power basis of its own, as the Commission's powers are decided upon and framed by the member states within treaty negotiations.

Intergovernmentalist thinking on the role of the Commission is countered by those whose approach might be labelled as 'supranationalist' or 'institutionalist'. Most of these institutionalists would argue that there is ample evidence that the Commission has displayed strong leadership and has even had a profound effect on the outcomes of 'history-shaping' and frame-setting IGCs and European Council meetings, on a number of occasions. For example, Armstrong and Bulmer (1998) assign a highly significant role to the Commission (and indeed to other EU institutions) in the process that led to the creation of the Single Market. The Single Market programme is one of the important frameworks within which the Commission operates under the first (EC) pillar. Institutionalists argue that treaty-based frameworks, which are the main focus of intergovernmentalists, are quite often vague and ambiguous constructions that need to be translated into practical politics through day-to-day policy-making. And when it comes to this sort of crucial follow-up work the Commission is one of the key actors.

Another, but related, scholarly dispute questions the extent to which the Commission is able to affect significantly decisions even within its own organizational boundaries. Not surprisingly perhaps, to many intergovernmentalists the Commission appears very much as an arena permeated by national interests. From this perspective, commissioners, their personal staffs (*cabinets*), as well as officials in the Commission's departments (services), are primarily pursuing the interests of their respective nation states. By contrast institutionalists tend to emphasize that the Commission, like other institutions, furnishes individual actors with particular interests and beliefs, and that it may even be able to resocialize participants so that they gradually come to assume supranational identities.

KEY POINTS

- Intergovernmentalists see the Commission as relatively insignificant.
- By contrast institutionalists (supranationalists) view the Commission as having an independent impact on policy outcomes.

The President and the commissioners

The European Commission has both a political and an administrative dimension. While there is no doubt that the actions of the administrative branch also have political significance, there is still a useful distinction to be made between the Commission's political leaders – the 'College of Commissioners' – and the officials who sit in the Commission's services (or departments).

The 'College' consists of 25 commissioners, including the President of the Commission. Within the Commission's internal decision-making process contentious issues that have not been resolved at the lower echelons of the Commission are lifted to this highest political level in the last instance. The College strives to achieve consensus through arguing and bargaining. If this does not result in a consensus, voting may take place, although this seems to be relatively rare. When it does happen, all commissioners, including the President, carry the same weight – one vote each and an absolute majority is necessary for a final decision to be reached. Since the College operates on the basis of the principle of collegiality, in other words since all commissioners are collectively responsible for all decisions taken, it would be reasonable to assume that a relatively large proportion of all decisions are referred to the College. Although a minister in a national government is usually granted greater room for manoeuvre than a commissioner, the principle of collegiality may also be found at the national level, as it is in the Swedish Council of Ministers.

The President of the Commission, who chairs the meetings of the College, used to be thought of as *primus inter pares* (first among equals) as he (there has so far been no female President) had no more powers than any other member of the College. Since the early 1990s, however, the role of the President has become more important, so that it is now accepted that the work of the College is subject to the President's political leadership (see below). And like a national prime minister, the President also has at his disposal a permanent secretariat, the Secretariat-General (or General Secretariat as it is sometimes called).

Commissioners have policy responsibilities (portfolios) which normally involve oversight of one Commission department. These departments are known as Directorates-General or simply as DGs. As DGs tend to be organized sectorally (according to purpose) or functionally (according to process), one might expect this to provide a particular source of conflict among commissioners. This expectation is explained in Box 9.1.

Although commissioners are supposed not to take instruction from outside the Commission, and do not represent national governments in any formal sense, they are, nevertheless, nominated by them. Previously, larger countries had two commissioners each, while the other member states had to make do with one each. From 2004 on, with 25 member states, all governments nominate only one commissioner each. A major concern has been avoiding the College becoming too large since this could threaten its decision-making capacity.

Before appointing commissioners, however, the national governments must first agree on a candidate for the Commission Presidency. This is necessary if the new President is to be given an opportunity to influence the composition of the

CASE STUDY 9.1

Politics in the Commission

This case study explains how politics within the Commission may reflect the sectoral and functional specialization of its organizational structure and related interest groups.

The weekly newspaper, *European Voice* (31 May–6 June 2001) reported that the Transport Commissioner Loyola de Palacio was set for a clash with the Environment Commissioner Margot Wallström over the future direction of EU transport policy. 'Officials from Wallström's services have only just begun studying de Palacio's White Paper on transport after it was released for consultation between Union executive departments. But already they say there are "things missing" from the 120-page document that are likely to prompt criticism from Wallström.' The newspaper reported that Wallström was likely to intervene with some concerns raised by environmental interest groups over the policy proposal, which seeks to freeze road traffic at its current 44 per cent share of all transport, but makes no attempt to reduce its overall growth. 'Green groups say the White Paper fails to live up to the Amsterdam Treaty obligation to bring environmental objectives into all policy areas. . . . Environmentalists insist the proposal will make it harder for the EU to comply with its Kyoto obligations to reduce greenhouse gas emissions.'

College. Over time the President's role in selecting his/her colleagues has grown. In the revisions to the Treaty, agreed at Amsterdam in 1997, the President is able, for the first time, to reject candidates nominated by member governments. The President will also have the final say in how portfolios are allocated and will even have the right to reshuffle the team during the Commission's five-year term of office by redistributing dossiers (portfolios).

National governments have increasingly seen their role in the make-up of the College of Commissioners diminish. By contrast, the European Parliament (EP) has gradually gained more of a stake in the process in a number of different ways, indicating that the EU has taken some steps in the direction of a parliamentary system. First, from the very start, the EP has been able to dismiss the entire College by taking a vote of no confidence. Secondly, the term of office of the commissioners has been extended from four to five years, so as to bring it into close alignment with the term of the EP. This means that the appointment of a new College takes place after the EP elections to allow MEPs to have a say on the matter. Not only is the EP consulted on the choice of President, it also has the right to approve the nominee's appointment. In fact, the outcome of the 2004 European elections was probably decisive for the choice of a candidate close to the European People's Party (EPP), since this party formed the largest group in the EP. Moreover, the EPP got a say as regards the person nominated as Commission President. The former Prime Minister of Portugal, Mr Barroso, had been a Vice-President of the EPP and was this party's candidate. Steps have also been taken to render the Commission more directly accountable to the Parliament, as illustrated by the fact that the EP committees now scrutinize nominated commissioners and the political programme of the Commission.

What kind of College **demography** does this inspire? First, it means that the political leadership of the Commission always has a fixed mix of nationals. Secondly, it tends to bring people into the College who have the same political party background as the national government nominating them. Over time, nominations to Commission posts have included people with impressive political experience, and it is now quite usual to see prominent national ministers in the list of nominees. Such a recruitment pattern obviously furnishes the College with political capital, though probably not in a strict party-political sense. A coherent party platform for the College is almost unthinkable under the current appointment procedure. Instead, a commissioner's nationality is likely to be a more crucial background factor to take into account in explaining their conduct. This is so since national governments, lobbyists, and the like tend to contact 'their' commissioner as a first port of call, when they want to obtain information or have a say at the very highest level of the Commission structure. And commissioners may also become involved in social networks with their compatriots – for example, in gatherings at their respective Permanent Representations (their national embassies to the EU) in Brussels.

It should not be concluded from this, however, that commissioners act primarily as agents of the national government that nominated them. In fact, it is the commissioner's portfolio which is more likely to explain their behaviour with regard to a particular decision. However, like national ministers, commissioners see multiple and often conflicting role expectations imposed upon them: at one and the same time they are supposed to feel some allegiance, albeit informal, to the geographical area from which they originate, to champion Commission interests, to advance their own portfolio, and to assume a party-political role. Balancing these diverse pressures is not always an easy task.

KEY POINTS

- The European Commission is composed of a political leadership in the form of the College of Commissioners.
- Commissioners are nominated by national governments, but they are expected to act independently and seem to do so to a considerable extent.
- Steps in the direction of a parliamentary system have been taken.

Commissioners' *cabinets*

Like many national ministers in Europe, commissioners have their own political secretariat or private office. The commissioner's *cabinet* (note that the French pronunciation is often used), as it is called, is organizationally separate from the administrative services of the Commission. It is composed of people trusted by the commissioner in question, and who may be hired and fired at their discretion. Consequently, their tenure can last only as long as their commissioner's. A *cabinet* consists of five to seven advisers, plus a number of clerical staff. Their role is to help push a commissioner's ideas down to the services, on the one hand, and on the other, to edit and filter policy proposals coming up from the DGs before they are referred to the commissioner and the College. As an integral part of this 'editorial work' a commissioner's *cabinet* frequently interacts with other *cabinets* in order to register disagreements and pre-empt objections that might be raised at the level of the College. Due to the principle of collegiality, in essence a form of mutual responsibility, each of the 25 *cabinets* covers all Commission portfolios. Thus, a commissioner's *cabinet* is vital as a source of information about issues beyond their own remit. Ahead of the weekly meeting of the College, the *chefs de cabinet* (*cabinet* heads) convene to ensure that the Commission acts as coherently and cohesively as possible. At these inter-*cabinet* gatherings the head of the President's *cabinet*, as chair, naturally assumes the role as mediator and broker, as necessary.

In addition to the role played by *cabinets* in coordinating, both vertically and horizontally, the flow of information within the Commission, they also have important functions at the interface between the Commission and the outside world. *Cabinets* are crucial points of access for governments, lobbyists, and other actors and institutions keen to influence the Commission. Their role is to assist commissioners in this respect, with *cabinet* members responsible, amongst other things, for writing commissioners' speeches, standing in for them, and representing them at conferences and meetings. *Cabinets* have also acted as a kind of liaison office between the commissioners and 'their' respective governments, particularly via 'their' Permanent Representations. Thus, they are able to inform the national governments about forthcoming Commission proposals that might become politically interesting from a national point of view, whilst at the same time acting as a conduit for information about national positions on policy initiatives under consideration in the Commission.

Cabinets have often been portrayed as national enclaves. This description was appropriate given that (in the past) the nationality of *cabinet* personnel almost directly reflected the nationality of the lead commissioner. From the Prodi Commission on, however, at least three different nationalities should be represented in each *cabinet*, and the head or the deputy head of the *cabinet* should be of a different nationality from that of the commissioner. Moreover, at least half of *cabinet* members should now be recruited from within the Commission services. This may also have interesting implications for the role of nationality in the *cabinets* since those coming from the Commission administration may have weaker ties to any particular national constituency. Those who have come to the *cabinets* from outside the Commission have for the most part served in national administrations, but some have also come from other kinds of organizations, for example from the political party to which the commissioner belongs.

Before the Prodi Commission's reforms of the *cabinet* system one would probably have concluded that the structure as well as the demography of these internal bodies would tend to foster highly intergovernmental patterns of behaviour. However, the structure and demography of the *cabinets* have changed. Thus, multinational staffing and an increased emphasis on internal recruitment seems to fit better with institutionalist explanations. As a consequence of these reforms, it would seem very likely that the role of *cabinets* as the interface between national governments and the Commission will be profoundly redefined.

KEY POINTS

- Each commissioner is supported by a personal staff, known as a *cabinet*.
- The *cabinet*, traditionally a 'national enclave' within the Commission, has become more multinational in recent years.

The Commission services

As is the case in national executives, the political leadership of the Commission is served by an administrative staff. In the Commission this administration is often referred to as the Commission 'services' (see Box 9.2). Key components of the Commission's administration are the 22 Directorates-General (DGs) that are roughly equivalent to the administrative components of national government departments, and which now cover almost all possible policy fields. The basic principles of organizational specialization are also quite similar to those of national ministries. While DG Agriculture and DG Justice, Freedom and Security reflect a sectoral organization, DG Budget and DG Personnel and Administration are organized around the functions they perform. Precisely because they are functionally orientated, DG Budget and DG Personnel and Administration are also said to be the Commission's horizontal services, that is, the administrative units that are assigned coordination tasks or that deal with issues cutting across sectoral departments. The Secretariat-General is the most important of these horizontal services. As the permanent office of the Commission President it plays an important role in shaping a coherent policy profile for the Commission as a whole, and also has a crucial part to play in managing relationships between the Commission and other key institutions inside and

BOX 9.2

Commission services

General services

- European Anti-Fraud Office
- Press and Communication
- Publications Office
- Secretariat-General
- Statistical Office (Eurostat)

Policies

- Agriculture and Rural Development
- Competition
- Economic and Financial Affairs
- Education and Culture
- Employment, Social Affairs and Equal Opportuinities
- Enterprise and Industry
- Environment
- Fisheries and Maritime Affairs
- Health and Consumer Protection
- Information Society and Media
- Internal Market and Services
- Joint Research Centre
- Justice, Freedom and Security
- Regional Policy
- Research
- Taxation and Customs Union
- Transport and Energy

External relations

- Development
- Enlargement
- EuropeAid Co-operation Office
- External Relations
- Humanitarian Aid Office (ECHO)
- Trade

Internal services

- Budget
- Bureau of European Policy Advisers
- Informatics
- Infrastructures and Logistics
- Internal Audit
- Interpretation
- Legal
- Personnel and Administration
- Translation

outside the Union. The role of Secretary-General, the head of the secretariat, very much parallels that of a permanent secretary within national prime ministers' offices. In other words, he or she may be identified as the first among equals, of the administration. Examples of the other horizontal services are the Press and Communication Service, the Statistical Office (Eurostat), the Translation Service, and the Legal Service. The Legal Service provides much of the Commission's legal expertise, though lawyers are also found in large numbers in other parts of the Commission. Thus, the Legal Service primarily serves as an expert body which other departments consult. It makes sure that legislative proposals drafted within the DGs comply with the technical and linguistic standards that are deemed appropriate for EU legislation, thereby pre-empting future challenges to European legislation in the European or domestic courts (see Chapter 12).

Headed by a director-general, DGs usually consists of several Directorates, with each of these headed by a director. Each Directorate is usually further split into units. Obviously, some tasks and new policy initiatives do not fit well into this strictly specialized hierarchical structure. To meet such needs, special task forces or interdepartmental working groups are created. Sometimes these temporary or ad hoc bodies become institutionalized and end up as new DGs or departments. The DGs usually have a total permanent and full-time staff of about 300–600 each, but their size varies considerably. The largest DG, DG Personnel and Administration, has around 3,000 employees, while another big player, DG Agriculture, has 1,000. Together the DGs and the horizontal services employ approximately 22,000 people. Of these about 1,000 are temporary posts. The most prestigious posts belong to the so-called A-grade, which consists of around 7,000 officials engaged in policy-making and policy management. When the scholarly literature deals with 'Commission officials' it is referring to staff in this category (rather than those in the executive, clerical, and manual grades).

In addition to staff paid by the Commission, the services also include between 700 and 800 Category A officials seconded from the member governments. These seconded officials, or 'detached national experts', have their salaries paid by their national employer. In the early days of the High Authority of the European Coal and Steel Community, the forerunner of the Commission (see Chapter 2), most officials were appointed on temporary contracts or seconded from the member states. Over time this has changed. As we have seen, an overwhelming majority of the posts are now permanent, while temporary jobs are used for hiring personnel who might provide additional expertise on particular policy issues that are under consideration in the services.

Recruitment of new A-grade candidates for a career in the Commission services is based largely on the meritocratic principle. What this means is that appointments should be made on what a person has achieved in their educational and professional career so far, rather than on any other criteria, such as a candidate's social or geographical background, or gender, or the extent to which an applicant has 'good contacts'. This principle is inherently linked to an understanding of what a modern and well-functioning bureaucracy should look like if it is to avoid nepotism, favouritism, and corruption. Thus, in accordance with this principle, those who want to embark on a Commission career are normally required to hold a university degree. Subsequently, they have to pass a competitive exam called the *concours*. The *concours* is modelled on the French standard entry route into the higher civil service which means in practice that all applicants have to pass written as well as oral tests. These tests are arranged in the member states on a regular basis and may involve as many as 50,000 applicants. However, no more than 150–700 reach what is called the 'reserve list', and even these lucky few are still not guaranteed a job; rather they have to wait for a vacancy and hope that they will be contacted about it. At this stage visibility is likely to be crucial, so that those with good networking skills are likely to be at an advantage.

A quota system regulates the intake of new recruits on a geographical basis. As a result, those hired should be drawn proportionately from all member states, so that larger countries provide more candidates than smaller ones. In a way this sort of quota arrangement is at odds with the meritocratic principle outlined above, however, the huge number of qualified applicants should nevertheless provide for a highly professional staff. This system does ensure that the Commission – or rather, the A-grade – is not over-populated by staff from only a few of the EU's member states (see Box 9.3).

Once officials are in post, seniority matters for promotion at the lower levels of the A-grade. In addition to an official's immediate superior, the staff unions also play a significant role in decisions about promotion at this level. For appointments as head of unit and above, achievements in earlier positions matter more than seniority as a criterion for promotion. The role of staff unions is also considerably reduced at these senior levels. Instead, nationality reappears as a crucial factor, and increasingly so the more senior the level of the appointment. Obviously, the narrower the pyramid, the more complicated it becomes to manage the national quota system in a fair manner, while at the same time paying heed to merit as the basic norm for promotion. In these cases, national governments are often keen to look after 'their share' of jobs, and it has conventionally been up to commissioners and their *cabinets* to intervene if the 'balance' is deemed

CASE STUDY 9.3

Personnel policies

This case study shows how personnel policies in the Commission are increasingly 'normalized' or 'domesticated'.

The weekly *European Voice* (21–7 February 2002) published a small notice that neatly illustrates how personnel management in the Commission has become more multifaceted than we expect to find it in international institutions. While balancing meritocracy and a proper national balance has been the dominant concern, gender equality has also become an issue in the Commission. In the notice, the European Ombudsman calls for urgent action over *ethnic* imbalance. He says the Commission does not take possible racism in recruitment seriously enough. 'When I look around the various institutions – the Commission, Parliament and Council – the only staff I see from ethnic groups are security guards and cleaners. Given that an estimated 30 million people of ethnic minority origin live in the EU, I wonder why so few appear to be in more senior posts.'

to be threatened. These concerns about proportionality are supplemented by the requirements that a top official's immediate subordinate and superior should be of a different nationality. The argument goes that a multinational chain of command will prevent policy proposals from reflecting only narrow national concerns.

It would seem that while the services should continue to maintain a broad geographical balance, nationality will, following the Prodi Commission reforms, no longer be allowed to be the determining factor in appointing a new person to a particular post. The aim was clearly to abolish the convention of attaching national flags to senior positions. New and strict procedures seem in fact to have effectively encapsulated processes in which top officials are appointed: senior Commission officials themselves seem to orchestrate such processes, and commissioners, who take the final decision, usually adhere to the 'shortlist' of candidates presented to them (Egeberg 2006). New member states may claim a reasonable share of posts at all levels of the hierarchy, and this has meant that highly experienced national officials have had to be brought into the senior ranks of the Commission administration. However, also these officials have to compete for vacant jobs and are subject to the same strict appointment procedures.

In accounting for the behaviour of Commission officials, how important is their national background? Given the enduring interest that national governments have shown towards recruitment and appointments we are led to think that nationality matters very much indeed (see Box 9.3). However, the attention devoted to the issue does not necessarily correspond to the impact that national origins might have. There is no doubt that officials bring to the Commission administrative styles and general attitudes that can be linked to their country of origin. For example, officials stemming from federal states like Germany or Belgium seem to view the prospect of a federal Europe more favourably than do those from unitary states, probably because the former are already familiar with that kind of a system (Hooghe 2001). However, the extent to which experience of national administration affects the Commission must depend on the career patterns of the officials involved. In the early years of the Commission, when many officials were on temporary contracts or secondments from their national governments, more Commission officials were imbued with national styles and attitudes. Under the current staffing regime, though, relatively few officials have in fact had the opportunity to acquire much administrative experience back home. Thus, they are arriving at the Commission without much 'baggage' in this respect.

Although a considerable number of Commission officials are without administrative experience in their home country, they may still make interesting interlocutors for their compatriots. A common language and nationality facilitate interaction so that Commission officials become points of access for those keen to know what is going on in the Commission. Moreover, officials of the same nationality often socialize together in Brussels and this may be enough to sustain a sense of national belonging. However, there is virtually no evidence of a direct link between an official's administrative style, personal attitudes, or informal contact patterns, and their decision behaviour in the Commission, as organizational roles, decision-making procedures, and the eyes and ears of colleagues and bosses tend to diminish this sort of variation in conduct. In fact, the attachment of officials to their DGs seems far more important than their national background as an explanation for the preferences and for the choices they make in their daily work (Egeberg 1996; Trondal 2005).

Certain organizational characteristics suggest that the conduct of Commission officials is intergovernmentally driven in the sense that it reflects national interests and influence. These include the national quota and the temporary contracts systems. Quotas might serve to legitimate national identities and, consequently, national policy orientations, while those on temporary contracts may have an incentive to pursue the interests of their current employer back home – usually their national government. However, there are also a number of organizational features that suggest that the institutionalist perspective is more accurate. Examples include the fact that specialization in the Commission occurs according to sector or function rather than geography; that there is a clear majority of permanent posts; that recruitment is basically on merit; that the Commission comprises multinational units and chains of command; and that there are life-long career patterns, which facilitate the resocialization of personnel. Over time these institutional factors have gained in importance: the proportion of officials on temporary contracts or secondments has been constantly declining; and recruitment on merit and internal promotion to senior levels in the Commission has gained ever-increasing support, particularly from the European courts, the staff unions, and, indeed, the College of Commissioners. However, the current practice of allowing new member states to have a share of the senior jobs in the Commission immediately after accession probably represents the most serious challenge to further development in this direction.

KEY POINTS

- The Commission's administrative services comprise sectoral and functional (horizontal) departments, called Directorates-General (DGs).
- Officials' actual decision behaviour is probably best explained by their DG affiliation.
- Officials within the services are recruited on a merit basis with a view to an appropriate geographical balance among member countries.

Connecting to national administrations: committees and networks

In order to assist the Commission in its preparatory work on new legislation and in other forms of policy-making, between 300 and 400 temporary expert committees and about 150 standing advisory groups have been established. The practical work on a policy initiative often starts in such a committee, which is usually composed of national officials and other experts. Committees of this sort are supposed to provide additional expertise on a particular subject and thus complement the work of the Commission's permanent staff. They may also serve as an arena for floating policy ideas and anticipating future reactions to them. Involving interest organizations that might ultimately be affected by a new proposal might make political support and legitimacy more likely. The Commission particularly welcomes European-level interest groups (see Chapter 13). In policy areas where these sorts of interest organizations have been lacking, the Commission has actively tried to encourage their formation. This is understandable since it is far more convenient to communicate with one group than with 25 or more, all representing different national, sectional interests. Encouraging the establishment of transnational interest groups may serve other purposes as well, though. Like the Commission itself, interest group systems structure themselves primarily along functional and sectoral lines, rather than territorially. Thus, the Commission may see transnational interest groups as future partners in an evolving EU polity.

Commission officials chair expert committees and advisory groups, calling officials from member governments to participate. The Commission covers their travel expenses, and they are expected to behave like independent experts and not as government representatives. In general, national officials participating in Commission committees assign considerably less weight to the role as government representative than those attending Union Council committee meetings (Egeberg, Schaefer, and Trondal 2003).

When committee work comes to an end, the policy proposal is processed in the administrative and political ranks of the Commission before it is submitted to the Council and the EP. When a final decision has been reached in the Council, the issue is again handed over to the Commission for implementation. As mentioned earlier, some Council directives may need to be supplemented by rules of a more technical nature. This kind of legislative work is delegated to the Commission in the same way as national legislatures may let governments hammer out specific regulations. In order to monitor the Commission's legislative activity, however, the Council has set up so-called **comitology** committees (also sometimes known as 'implementation committees'). The memberships of these committees are formal representatives of national governments, though it is the Commission which calls and chairs the meetings, sets the agenda, submits the proposals requiring discussion, and writes the protocols. Some comitology committees are only entitled to advise the Commission (advisory committees). Others have competence to overrule the Commission's proposals under certain conditions (management committees and regulatory committees). In practice, however, the Commission usually gets its own way, though this is not to say that national representatives have no influence. It is, of course, also quite possible that the Commission deliberately chooses proposals that national governments are likely to endorse (see Schaefer *et al.* 2000).

When it comes to the implementation of EU policies at the national level, the Commission has to rely on member state administrations since the Commission does not itself possess agencies at this level. This may result in considerable variation in administrative practices across countries. However, there are signs that national regulatory authorities that often work at arm's length from ministries become a kind of 'partner' of the Commission in implementation as well as in policy preparation processes. Due to these authorities' 'semi-detached' status, they seem to be in a position in which they might be able to serve two masters simultaneously: both the national ministry *and* the Commission. Within a range of policy sectors (like competition, telecommunications, environment, food safety) we observe transnational networks of national agencies in which the Commission constitutes the hub (Egeberg 2006). Do we see a multi-level genuine *Union* administration emerging?

KEY POINTS

- Expert committees have an important role to play in the preparatory work of the Commission.
- Comitology committees monitor the Commission when it is issuing delegated legislation.
- National officials behave less 'intergovernmentally' in Commission committees than in Council committees and comitology.
- Issue-specific networks are emerging among the Commission and semi-detached national agencies.

Conclusion

The Commission has often been portrayed as a hybrid and unique organization because of its mix of political and administrative functions. This is understandable if the Commission is compared to the secretariat of a traditional international organization, since such secretariats are not expected to have a political will of their own. However, the Commission is probably better compared to a national executive. Like governments, the Commission is headed by executive politicians who are responsible for various administrative services. In a fashion similar to national executives the Commission is authorized to initiate and formulate policy proposals, and to monitor the implementation of policies. The Commission has not, however, achieved full control of all executive tasks at the EU level, sharing its executive function in some respects with the EU Council. Most importantly, perhaps, the Union's Common Foreign and Security Policy (CFSP) is largely the executive responsibility of a strengthened Council Secretariat.

This chapter has focused on how the various parts of the Commission are organized and staffed, and how these structural and demographic features might be related to the way decision-makers actually behave. Are these features mainly conducive to intergovernmental ways of behaving, or do they instead evoke patterns of decision-making that are more in line with what institutionalists would predict? At all levels – the College, the *cabinets*, the services, and the committees – there are components that are certainly more in line with intergovernmental decision processes than with other kinds of processes. However, those organizational components that work in the opposite direction are becoming more and more important. These components tend to focus attention along sectoral, functional, partisan, or institutional cleavages, that is, on lines of conflict and cooperation that cut *across* national boundaries, and that evoke non-territorial feelings of belonging among commissioners and their officials. If these trends persist, the Commission is set to become much more of a European institution than in the past, though one which will inevitably continue to exhibit a mix (albeit a different mix) of both intergovernmental and supranational characteristics.

QUESTIONS

1. To what extent is the Commission comparable to a national government/executive?
2. How influential is the Commission within the EU policy process?
3. How important is the national background of commissioners in shaping their preferences and decisions?
4. What is the role of the commissioners' *cabinets*?
5. How are the Commission services organized, and what are the possible implications for patterns of conflict within the Commission?
6. How might nationality affect decision-making within the services?
7. What is comitology?
8. Which roles do national officials evoke in EU committees?

GUIDE TO FURTHER READING

- Cini, M. *The European Commission: Leadership, Organisation and Culture in the EU Administration* (Manchester: Manchester University Press, 1996). This is a broad introductory text that covers most aspects, including the historical roots of the Commission.
- Coombes, D. *Politics and Bureaucracy in the European Community: A Portrait of the Commission of the E.E.C.* (London: George Allen & Unwin, 1970). The 'classic' academic text on the Commission in its early period. It is empirically rich and firmly anchored in administrative and political theory.
- Dimitrakopoulos, D. G. (ed.) *The Changing European Commission* (Manchester: Manchester University Press, 2004). This book focuses in particular on the Prodi Commission: the College, the administrative reforms, and relationships to member states and the Council.
- Edwards, G., and Spence, D. (eds) *The European Commission*, 2nd edn (London: Cartermill, 1997). This anthology also covers most topics, and is particularly detailed and informative on the structure and personnel of the Commission.
- Egeberg, M. (ed.) *Multilevel Union Administration: The Transformation of Executive Politics in Europe* (Basingstoke: Palgrave, 2006). This book deals with politics within the Commission as well as between the Commission and other institutions, in particular national administrations, from an organization theory perspective.
- Hooghe, L. *The European Commission and the Integration of Europe: Images of Governance* (Cambridge: Cambridge University Press, 2001). The author maps officials' attitudes on topics like intergovernmentalism and supranationalism, regulated capitalism and liberalism, and tries to explain them by using survey and interview techniques.
- Nugent, N. *The European Commission* (Basingstoke: Palgrave, 2000). This is probably the most empirically rich and balanced textbook on the Commission.
- Page, E. C. *People Who Run Europe* (Oxford: Clarendon Press, 1997). The author presents the Commission with a view to administrative traditions and practices in national bureaucracies.
- Smith, A. (ed.) *Politics and the European Commission. Actors, Interdependence, Legitimacy* (London: Routledge, 2004). This book deals both with the political and administrative level, and with the Commission's relationships to the media.
- Stevens, A., with Stevens, H. *Brussels Bureaucrats? The Administration of the European Union* (Basingstoke: Palgrave, 2001). The book contains much detailed information on administrative life and practices in Brussels.

IMPORTANT WEBSITES

- http://europa.eu.int/comm This is the official website of the European Commission. It has links to its work programme, documents, calendar, the commissioners, the services, and the delegations.
- www.eurunion.org The European Union in the USA. The website of the EU delegation of the European Commission, based in the USA.
- www.cec.org.uk The European Commission Representation in the UK.

Visit the Online Resource Centre that accompanies this book for lots of interesting additional material. http://www.oxfordtextbooks.co.uk/orc/cini2e/

10 The Council of the European Union

JEFFREY LEWIS

Chapter Contents

Reader's Guide

This chapter looks at the heart of decision-making in the EU, the Council of the European Union (or EU Council). The Council is the EU institution which unabashedly represents national interests in the European integration process and is therefore a site of intense negotiation, compromise building, and at times acrimonious disagreement between the member states. The Council is not a single body however, more a composite of national officials working at different levels of specialization and political seniority – think of it as a system of decision-making machinery. From the heads of state and government to the ministers, and all the way down the ladder to the expert-level *fonctionnaires* (bureaucrats), the Council embeds governments of the EU into a complex collective decision-making system which deeply penetrates into the national capitals and domestic politics of the member states. The result, as this chapter explains, is the most advanced and intensive forum of international cooperation between sovereign nation states in the modern world. This chapter looks at the organization and functioning of the Council, at its component parts (the European Council, the EU Council, the Committee of Permanent Representatives (COREPER), working groups, the Secretariat), and at how it has evolved as an institution over time.

Introduction

The focus of this chapter is the Council of the European Union, also known as the EU Council and the more outdated 'Council of Ministers'. The Council is the epicentre of EU decision-making and plays a pivotal role in the making of European policy. Although ostensibly representing the interests of the EU's 25 member states, the Council is also a European institution; and though formally one the EU's legislative bodies, it is also an important arena for interstate diplomacy and negotiation.

To explore these seemingly paradoxical traits of the EU Council, this chapter begins by outlining the way in which the institution is structured. The first section also emphasizes the difference between the EU Council and the European Council (the latter involving heads of state and government, rather than just national ministers). In the second section, the operation of the Council comes under scrutiny. Here, the focus is on the Presidency, which rotates from member state to member state, as well as on the relationship between the Council, the Commission, and the Parliament. In the third section, the layers of Council decision-making are peeled away, and we focus, from the top down, on European Council summits, on Council meetings themselves, on the work of COREPER (involving senior national civil servants), and on that of the more technical working groups. This section also considers the increasingly important role of the Council's own officials in the Council General Secretariat (CGS). Finally, the chapter turns to consider some of the challenges facing the Council – the institutional challenges, the democratic deficit, and the wider implications of enlargement.

The heart of EU decision-making

The Council of the European Union is the institutional heart of decision-making in the EU. It is the institution designed to represent the member states and, as the creation of sovereign nation states, it was unsurprisingly endowed with extensive legislative and executive functions. The central legislative function is that all EU proposals (originating from the Commission) must be approved by the Council before becoming EU law. Despite newer decision-making procedures granting the European Parliament a more coequal status (called codecision), the Council remains at the core of the EU's legislative process. The Council has a central executive function as well: to provide leadership and steer the pace and direction of European integration, seen especially in areas of diplomacy and foreign affairs.

Legally speaking, there is only one Council, but this is misleading since in reality there are numerous formations organized by policy specialization (see Box 10.1). Each formation of the Council manages a specialized policy sector, and the participants authorized to adopt legislative acts are the national ministers from each of the member states who hold domestic responsibility for that sector. Hence, the 25 EU ministers of agriculture preside over the Agricultural and Fisheries Council, the environmental ministers over the Environment Council and so on.

Historically, the 'senior' Council formation with general institutional responsibilities and charged with overall EU policy coordination has been the foreign affairs ministers who meet as the General Affairs and External Relations Council (GAERC) (see Box 10.2).

Since the dawn of the euro, and some argue earlier, the finance and economics ministers have increased in stature through their work on the

BOX 10.1

Formations of the Council

General Affairs and External Relations (GAERC)

Economic and Financial Affairs (ECOFIN)

Justice and Home Affairs (JHA)

Employment, Social Policy, Health and Consumer Affairs

Competitiveness

Transport, Telecommunications, and Energy

Agriculture and Fisheries

Environment

Education, Youth, Culture

Source: Council's website.

CASE STUDY 10.2

From GAC to GAERC – the 'new' General Affairs Council

Following widespread agreement in the latter half of the 1990s that the Council's premier ministerial body – the General Affairs Council – was impossibly over-burdened and increasingly dysfunctional, the European Council decided at the 2002 Seville meeting to formally bifurcate the GAC's work into two tracks:

- General Affairs
- External Relations

Since 2002, the GAC has been reforged as the GAERC, or General Affairs and External Relations – although the cast of characters remains largely identical.

The 'new' General Affairs portion is tasked with 'preparation for and follow-up to the European Council (including the coordination of activities to that end), institutional and administrative questions, horizontal dossiers which affect several of the Union's policies and any dossier entrusted to it by the European Council, having regard to EMU operating rules'.

The External Relations (or Foreign Policy) portion is assigned 'the whole of the Union's external action, namely common foreign and security policy, European security and defence policy, foreign trade, development cooperation and humanitarian aid'.

Technically, the two strands now operate independently, with their own meetings and agendas, but in practice, the GAERC tends to meet on the same day(s) back-to-back with the foreign affairs ministers at both. One big difference, if the Constitutional Treaty (CT) ever enters into force, would be who runs each grouping: the new Union Foreign Minister would chair the External Relations portion and the member state holding the rotating Presidency would chair the General Affairs portion. Whether this new arrangement imparts greater coherence to the work of the foreign ministers and renews the leadership role of 'General Affairs' is an open question.

Sources: Presidency Conclusions, Seville European Council, 21–2 June 2002; Treaty Establishing a Constitution for Europe, OJ C310, 16.12.2004.

Economic and Financial Affairs Council, otherwise known as ECOFIN. The newest Council additions include the interior ministers who meet in the Justice and Home Affairs Council, and the defence ministers who meet in a 'jumbo' Council format with the foreign ministers to discuss European Security and Defence Policy (ESDP).

The policy segmentation of the Council's work into distinct, separate formations is a hallmark of how the EU works. Each formation has its own pace and legislative agenda, with some meeting monthly (GAERC, ECOFIN, Agriculture) and others meeting maybe twice per year (Education, Youth, Culture). Each Council also has its own organizational culture, often including a set of informal (unwritten) rules and distinctive working habits. For example, some, such as the GAERC, rely on highly restricted lunchtime sessions to discuss issues of particular importance or sensitivity. And the GAERC has institutionalized the right to meet on the day before all European Council summits to conduct final preparatory negotiations and adopt a definitive agenda for the heads of state and government (see Box 10.2). Taken together, 'the Council' is a multifaceted decision-making structure across a wide range of policy domains, with negotiations going on concurrently. In one guise or another, the Council is almost continually in session.

But the ministers are only the tip of the iceberg. If it were only the ministers meeting at most a few days per month in Brussels, the EU would be an inchoate and chaotic system of decision-making. The work of the Council involves a much larger contingent of national officials. First, there are the EU permanent representatives who staff the Committee of Permanent Representatives (COREPER). COREPER is responsible for preparing forthcoming Council meetings which often involves intensive discussions to pave the way for agreement by the ministers. The EU permanent representatives (two per member state: each appoints their own EU ambassador and a deputy) live in Brussels, meet weekly, and literally 'eat, drink, and breathe EU issues seven days a week' (Barber 1995). Each member state also maintains a permanent representation in Brussels run by the EU ambassador and deputy and staffed by policy specialists from different national ministries. But that is still not all. The bulk of day-to-day Council activity takes place at the expert working group level. At any point in time, the Council has around 250 working groups in existence. Even assuming one expert per group, that's 6,250 national officials. Working groups examine proposals in the early stages of negotiation and serve as a clearing house for non-controversial and technical issues to be settled and as an early warning system for complications or political issues that will need to be addressed at the level of COREPER or the ministers. In total, the Council involves thousands of national officials meeting in dozens of working group, COREPER, or ministerial settings each week to negotiate and decide on EU proposals. If you add up all of the national civil servants and policy specialists involved, estimates place the total number who work on EU affairs at around 25,000 (Wessels and Rometsch 1996: 331). Taking into account the 10 newcomers, and the growth of policy activity in the foreign, security, military, and justice fields, this number today must be closer to 35,000–40,000!

In terms of how it operates, the Council is perhaps the least documented of all the EU institutions. Part of this stems from inaccessibility, but more important is the Council's enigmatic appearance. It is the 'chameleon' of EU institutions (Wallace 2002) because it blurs intergovernmental and supranational organizational traits and behaviourisms. The standard, glossary image of the Council is one of a stronghold of individualistically oriented national actors who focus more or less exclusively on their own self-interests rather than on the welfare of others or the group as a whole. This interpretation of the Council also forms a basic theoretical foundation for intergovernmentalist approaches. But the Council is a more complex and variegated institutional construct. The Council, as an institution, equals more than the sum of its parts (the member states). National actors in the Council also act collectively, and many develop a shared sense of responsibility that the work of the Council should move forward and the legislative output of the Council (even if in only one specialized policy area) should be a success. Working in this chamber of continuous negotiation across a wide range of issues, national actors often develop long-term relations of trust, mutual understanding, and obligations to try to help out colleagues with domestic political difficulties or requests for special consideration. Council participants can also develop collective interests in the process of joint decision-making itself. This can become a kind of 'global, permanent interest' in addition to the specific national interest on a given subject or proposal. In short, the member states who participate in the system also become socialized into a collective decision-making system. As one leading scholar on the Council has summarized the enigma, 'The Council of the EU is both an institution with collective EU functions and the creature of member governments' (Wallace 2000: 16).

The Council and the European Council: not the same thing

No portrait of the Council would be complete without including the role of the European Council. The European Council is the pre-eminent political authority for the EU because it brings together the 25 heads of state and government (and the President of the European Commission). Overall strategic guidance for the EU is supplied by the European Council, and the Prime Ministers, Chancellors, and Presidents meeting in the high-profile summits have assumed extensive responsibility for such key subjects as institutional reform, the budget, enlargement, and foreign, security, and defence policy. Issues such as future national budgetary contributions, relative voting weights, or how to finance new foreign policy missions have proven too politically charged for the ministers to settle and they have relied on the European Council to break deadlocks, overcome interministerial discord (especially between finance and foreign affairs), and broker the big, interlocking package deals for which the history-making 'constitutional' turning points in the EU are famous. The European Council meets formally at least twice a year (June and December), and at least twice more as 'informal' gatherings organized around a specific topic or theme (such as the 2005 'globalization' summit at Hampton Court outside London). European Council summits attract intense public scrutiny, covered by some 1,200 journalists, and increasingly, accompanied by large turnouts of protesters (ranging from farmers to anti-globalization groups) which have led to violent clashes with police (such as at the 2001 Gothenburg summit in Sweden).

The European Council was innovated in the early 1970s, and by 1974 was informally institutionalized. Many EU scholars credit the European Council with holding the Union together during the nearly two decades of Eurosclerosis. For the first dozen years or so, the European Council was not a legally recognized part of the Community's institutional system, and was not acknowledged in the Treaties until the Single European Act of 1986. Thus, the European Council was considered an extra-legal institution of the EU, and though it receives mention in the 'common provisions' section of the TEU, it is still separate from the original European Community institutions to defray the image of becoming too closely controlled by the member states and avoid upsetting the delicate institutional balance between intergovernmentalism and supranationalism. While the European Council rarely ever makes a decision on a specific proposal (though there is nothing legally preventing it from doing so), the summits supply the EU with critical navigation and the usual output for a meeting is a 30+ page *communiqué* (known as the 'Presidency conclusions') which summarizes positions on issues and sets priorities for future EU policy-making. The as yet unratified Constitutional Treaty (CT) contains a big innovation for the European Council's leadership (see Box 10.7 for a summary) by removing the grouping from the regular rotating Presidency (see below) and creating a new semi-permanent President who would chair all summits and provide a single face for the Union externally. While a number of members, particularly smaller states who harbour suspicions about the EU developing along the lines of a 'big state' *directoire*, view any change to the equalizing role of the rotating Presidency as undesirable, this was seen as a necessary risk to instil greater coherence and intangible leadership in the Union's most politically potent and visible forum.

KEY POINTS

- The Council was designed to represent the member states, and has both executive and legislative functions in the EU system of governance.
- The work of the Council is compartmentalized into nine sectoral formations.
- The Council involves a tremendous number of national officials (25,000+) who meet at the ministerial, COREPER, and working group levels.
- The European Council is a distinct component of the Council, which brings the heads of state and government together in multiannual summits to discuss the most pressing business and provide strategic guidance.
- As an institution, the Council is enigmatic: it is both defender of the national interest and a collective system of decision-making, blurring the theoretical distinctions between intergovernmentalism and supranationality.

How does the Council work?

The most common way to portray the Council is as a hierarchy of levels. The European Council forms the top level, followed by the ministerial level (with the GAERC and ECOFIN as *primus inter pares*). Below them is the COREPER level which serves as a process-manager between the ministers and the working groups who form the base of the hierarchy. This portrayal is not wrong, but it is distorted. The reality is a more labyrinthine and nuanced decision-making system, with significant variation by issue area. In some policy areas and with issues that are of a highly technical nature, the specialists in the working group may forge substantive agreement on important issues. In other cases, the permanent representatives who meet in COREPER conduct the detailed negotiations over substance, perhaps because of their legal expertise in applying Treaty articles, or institutional memory in a specific policy area, or sometimes to 'keep the lid' on a controversial subject that risks becoming hamstrung by the ministers. It is also not uncommon, particularly when a Presidency is not run efficiently (see below), for a ministerial meeting or even a European Council summit to have the detailed, technical minutiae of a proposal on its agenda for discussion. In organizational imagery, the actual operation of the Council is perhaps closer to a network relationship of interorganizational authority than a corporate hierarchy which is the typical portrayal.

The role of the rotating Presidency

The Council Presidency rotates between member states every six months. The Presidency is responsible for planning, scheduling, and chairing meetings of the Council and European Council. The same goes for all meetings of COREPER and the working groups. The Presidency also represents the EU internationally by acting as a spokesperson in EU external affairs. The true genius of the rotating Presidency is that it acts as a great equalizer between big and small states, giving tiny Luxembourg the same chance to run things as, say, Germany, France, or Britain. The rotation is set to give variation between big and small, newer and older member states. The order also alternates so that no member state becomes permanently fixed in either the 1 January or 1 July slot, since that would entail always handling the same fixed aspects of the legislative agenda (such as setting annual fisheries quotas in the autumn or agricultural prices in the spring).

Holding the chair carries formidable logistical duties, as the Council's work is organized into a six-month calendar. Planning for the Presidency usually begins 18 months prior to the start date. Despite the workload, the Presidency is highly coveted by member states as a chance to run things, since that member state not only organizes meetings but has a close involvement in setting the agenda – what issues are covered and in what order, and in finding solutions – brokering deals, suggesting compromises, drafting conclusions. The EU Presidency involves much quiet diplomacy, behind the scenes and often in bilateral conversations at the margins of meetings (known as 'confessionals') in order to make progress on new proposals as well as deal with the inevitable unexpected developments and crises as they arise. Running the Presidency is a real art form, and involves subtle diplomatic skills such as knowing what order to call on member states during discussions to ensure the best chances of success (or failure), when to call for coffee breaks, and how to time the right moment for suggesting a 'Presidency compromise'. The Presidency can be an important source of leadership in the EU, and member states see their turn at the helm as a chance to leave their imprint on the integration process.

The Presidency is a great example of the Council's enigmatic identity, since the country holding the position must simultaneously work to advance collective European solutions and be on the lookout for a particular set of national interests. This can be a delicate balancing act, especially in policy areas where there are highly mobilized domestic constituencies and costly economic issues at stake. Member states that handle this balancing act with a deft touch can accumulate a great deal of political capital and respect. The Finnish Presidency of 1999 helped earn that country a reputation for being very communitarian and skilful at compromise-building despite being relative newcomers to the EU game. Likewise, it is possible to be seen as using the Presidency to pursue a more narrow national agenda or to push through new policies without widespread support, as the French found out during their rotation in 2000 when smaller states accused the Presidency of trying to force through new voting weights which advantaged the big states.

Relations with other EU institutions

From the earliest days of the Union, interactions between the Council and Commission constitute the main pulse and dynamic of European integration. But as the two institutions were created with a certain degree of inbuilt tension, with the Council representing individual member states and the Commission representing the 'European' interest, relations have at times been quite strained. The worst crisis in the history of the Union, the empty chair crisis of 1965, was prompted when French President de Gaulle felt the Commission had overstepped its authority in seeking to obtain its own sources of revenue (see Chapter 2). During other periods, relations between the Council and the Commission have been smoother, such as the period in the late 1980s when the bulk of legislation to create the Single Market was adopted in a steady stream by the Council. More recently, signs of strains have shown up again in areas of foreign policy, between the External Affairs Commissioner and the Council's Secretary-General and High Representative of CFSP over who should represent the EU internationally. The Constitutional Treaty attempts to resolve this problem with a very hybrid institutional solution – should the CT ever enter into force, the EU will have a dedicated Minister of Foreign Affairs who would at the same time be a central Council actor *and* a Vice-President of the Commission in charge of the external relations budget and policy field (see Box 10.7).

In contrast to the Commission, relations with the European Parliament for most of the Union's history were fairly much at arm's length and mostly one-sided. Prior to the Maastricht Treaty, the Council merely had to consult the EP before adopting legislation and proposed EP amendments were not binding (see Chapter 11). This all changed when the codecision procedure was introduced to selected issue areas, the essential feature of this procedure being that the EP is a coequal legislator with the Council, and it is now much more difficult for the Council to ignore or overrule EP amendments.

Since the 1990s, with each new Treaty (Maastricht, Amsterdam, Nice), codecision has been introduced or extended to more issue areas. The Constitutional Treaty goes even further, codifying codecision as the EU's 'ordinary legislative procedure' rather than something exceptional or allowed under certain circumstances (Article I-34). Under codecision rules, where the Council disagrees with EP amendments there is a procedure known as 'conciliation' where the two sides meet to reach compromise on a final text. Conciliation meetings have dramatically intensified Council–EP relations over the last decade. Working relations between the Council and EP have improved to the point where the number of codecision files that are concluded by compromise (during the first or second reading) without the need for lengthy conciliation negotiations has steadily increased. Today, 85 per cent of codecision files are concluded by Council–EP compromise without the need for conciliation. The growth of codecision represents a new dynamic of interinstitutional networking in the EU and shows how the legislative process has evolved to become more like that of other bicameral federal political systems (Lewis 2005).

KEY POINTS

- The Council has a clear hierarchical structure from the heads of state and government down to the experts, but in practice the lines of authority and decision-making are more akin to a complex network relationship.
- Leadership of the Council is supplied by a rotating Presidency which alternates every six months.
- The Council Presidency is both a huge job of planning and chairing meetings and a huge reward for all member states to have an equal chance at running things.
- Relations with the Commission are an integral part of the EU's federal-like system of overlapping powers, and the Commission's right of initiative gives it the 'twenty-sixth' seat at the table.
- Relations with the European Parliament have become more intense as the codecision procedure has grown and the EP is treated more like a co-legislator in key areas of EU policy-making.

The layers of Council decision-making

The following section looks at the Council hierarchy from the top down, moving from the European Council to the Council of the EU, then to COREPER and the Council's working groups. The section also considers the growing range of functions performed by the Council's own bureaucracy, the General Secretariat.

European Council summitry

Over the last 30 years, the European Council has been at the heart of the major 'history-making' moments of European integration. This includes the creation of the European Monetary System in the late 1970s, the resolution of major budgetary disputes in the early 1980s, launching new intergovernmental conferences that would lead to new Treaty agreements (SEA, TEU, Amsterdam, Nice), and so on. As the grouping that brings together the heads of government and state (in the case of France and Finland), no other EU body can match the political authority of the European Council. As a result, the summit conclusions pack tremendous legitimation for daily decision-making at the ministerial, COREPER, and working group levels. For instance, following the European Council's special meeting in October 1999 in Tampere, Finland, to discuss the creation of a 'common area of freedom, security, and justice' the policy area of Justice and Home Affairs received a great burst of activism, including a new influx of Commission proposals and the adoption of several new directives by the JHA Council in areas covering immigration, asylum policy, and cross-border crime (see Chapter 19).

The Ministers' Council(s)

In terms of formal decision-making authority, the ministers are the national representatives empowered to vote and commit member states to new EU legislation (Article 203). As we shall see, a lot of informal decision-making takes place in COREPER and the working groups, but the distinction between formal (juridical) and informal (de facto) decision-making authority is important to understand since the ministers are the elected officials who are accountable to their domestic constituencies for the policies adopted in Brussels.

Three Council formations have more work and meet more frequently than the others: GAERC, ECOFIN, and Agriculture. These three meet each month, usually for one or two days. The workload is particularly intense during certain periods, such as the end of a Presidency when there is a final push to complete a legislative calendar.

The types of legislative acts adopted by the ministers vary by policy area. In traditional 'Community pillar' (first pillar) affairs, legislation is typically in the form of directives, regulations, or decisions (see Figures 3.1 and 3.2 for the three pillars). For Justice and Home Affairs (third pillar) and Common Foreign and Security Policy (second pillar), most legislative acts are made in the form of a joint action or a common position (see Box 10.3). Depending on the issue area, there are a number of different decision-making procedures which generally dictate what type of legislative act will be used. The number of decision-making procedures is extensive (determining the level of involvement by the EP under consultation, cooperation, codecision, assent, and so on); depending on how you count them, there are close to 30 in all! See Box 10.3 for definitions.

There are also rules for voting. Voting rules divide into two main categories: unanimity and qualified majority voting (QMV), though some procedural issues are passed by a simple majority vote. The key to understand how the Council reaches decisions is to understand the different dynamics between unanimity and QMV. Under the unanimity decision-rule, any member state can block a proposal with a 'No' vote. If a delegation wants to signal disagreement with some aspect of a proposal, but not block adoption by the others, it can abstain. Abstentions do not count as 'No' votes. Since the 1986 Single European Act (SEA), many areas of policy are no longer subject to unanimity, though key areas which still are include CFSP, JHA, taxation, and institutional reform.

QMV now applies to most areas under the first ('Community') pillar and its reintroduction with the SEA was considered a crucial precondition for establishing a Single Market by the 1992 deadline. Under QMV rules, each member state has a 'weighted' vote based crudely on size. In anticipation of future enlargement(s) to Central and Eastern Europe, the voting weights were reconfigured at the Treaty of Nice creating a new controversial

KEY CONCEPTS AND TERMS 10.3

Types of Council act

Regulation: is binding in its entirety and directly applicable in all member states.

Directive: is binding as to the result to be achieved, but leaves to the national authorities the choice of form and methods.

Decision: is binding in its entirety upon those (and only those) to whom it is addressed.

Recommendations and opinions: have no binding force.

Joint action: addresses specific situations where operational action by the EU is deemed to be required; covers objectives, scope, the means to be made available to the EU, if necessary their duration, and the conditions for their implementation.

Common position: defines the approach of the EU to a particular matter of a geopolitical or thematic nature; member states shall ensure that their national policies conform.

Source: Adapted from the Treaty on European Union, Articles 14, 15, and 249.

reweighting and a complicated triple-majority system of adopting legislation (see Table 10.1). QMV weights became politicized during the Nice Treaty negotiations and several member states' behaviour reaffirmed that national power and influence on the Council is highly coveted and carefully guarded. The French, for example, insisted on keeping a parity weighting with Germany despite having 23 million or so fewer national citizens. Spain and Poland also came out disproportionately ahead in the weightings, while Belgium actually gave up some relative voting power. Under the new QMV rules (which will be replaced by an entirely new system if the CT is ever put into force – see Box 10.7 below), the three steps to pass legislation require:

- a majority of member-states,
- who represent at least 63 per cent of the EU population,
- and a minimum of 232 votes in favour (representing 72.3 per cent of the total votes).

But even where QMV applies, voting is a relatively uncommon occurrence. Rarely is there ever a 'show of hands'; typically, the Presidency summarizes discussion and announces that a sufficient majority has been reached, or asks if anyone remains opposed, and, if not, notes the matter is closed. Voting is also unpopular in the EU because there is a highly ingrained culture of consensus, and it is simply considered inappropriate to 'push for a vote' where there is one or more delegation with remaining objections or difficulties. But the potential recourse to the vote (the so-called 'shadow of the vote') is a powerful reminder to delegations to avoid becoming isolated by simply saying 'No' and being unopen to compromise. For this reason, Council participants claim that the fastest way to reach consensus is with the QMV decision rule.

A feature common to all formations of the Council is how the agenda is structured. The agenda has two parts: Part A contains issues that need no further discussion and are approved in a single block by the ministers at the beginning of each meeting. This can be quite a long list of 20–30 items, known as 'A points', and not necessarily in the ministers' areas of expertise. Part B is the portion of the agenda which does require discussion by the ministers. These issues, known as 'B points', are the focus of the ministers' discussions. Because of time constraints and the size of the EU – a single *tour de table* where each of the 25 delegations (and the Commission and Presidency) state their position or note problems can take hours – the number of substantive B points which can be covered in any detail is limited.

The meetings themselves take place in Brussels (except during April, June, and October when they are held in Luxembourg as part of an agreement

Table 10.1 Current qualified majority voting weights

	Weighted votes
Germany, France, Italy, United Kingdom	29
Spain, Poland	27
Netherlands	13
Belgium, Czech Republic, Greece, Hungary, Portugal	12
Austria, Sweden	10
Denmark, Ireland, Lithuania, Slovakia, Finland	7
Cyprus, Estonia, Latvia, Luxembourg, Slovenia	4
Malta	3
EU25 Total	*321*
Romania*	14
Bulgaria*	10
EU27 Total	*345*
Turkey*	?
Croatia*	?
EU29 Total	?

*EU applicant countries.

Source: Treaty of Nice (2001/C 80/82); no decisions have been made for Turkey or Croatia.

from the 1960s over how to divide where the EC institutions would be located). The official residence of the Council is the Justus Lipsius building, inaugurated in 1995 and named after the sixteenth-century philosopher. The meetings take place in large rooms equipped with rectangular tables and surrounded by interpreters' booths to provide simultaneous translation into the official EU languages. The meetings are far from intimate; typically, each delegation (and the Commission) will have three seats at the table (minister, permanent representative, assistant) and up to another half-dozen who are waiting in the margins for a specific agenda point to be discussed. Normally, there are more than 100 people in the room at any one point, with lots of bilateral conversations, note-passing, and strategizing going on while the individual who has the floor is speaking.

BOX 10.4

Division of labour between COREPER I and COREPER II

COREPER II

- General Affairs and External Relations Council
- Justice and Home Affairs
- multiannual budget negotiations
- structural and cohesion funds
- institutional and horizontal questions
- development and association agreements
- accession
- IGC personal representatives (varies by member state and IGC)

COREPER I

- Single European Market (Internal Market, Competitiveness)
- Conciliation in areas of codecision
- Environment
- Employment, Social Policy, Health and Consumer Affairs
- Transport, Telecommunications, and Energy
- Fisheries
- Agriculture (veterinary and plant-health questions)
- Education, Youth, and Culture

COREPER

COREPER is the preparatory body of the Council, making it one of the most intense sites of negotiation in the EU. Whereas the ministers meet monthly at best, COREPER meets weekly. Officially, COREPER is charged with 'preparing the work of the Council', wording which reveals remarkably little about how important the committee has become in making the Council run smoothly. Whereas any particular ministerial Council will be focused on a particular sectoral issue or set of policies, the members of COREPER negotiate across the entire gamut of EU affairs and thus hold the unique responsibility for maintaining the performance of the Council as a whole. In short, COREPER acts as a process manager in the Council system between the ministers and the experts in the working groups. As an institution, COREPER has a unique vantage point because it is vertically placed between the experts and the ministers and horizontally situated with cross-sectoral and interpillar policy responsibilities.

Because of the heavy workload in preparing forthcoming Councils, since 1962 COREPER has split into two groups: I and II (see Box 10.4). COREPER I is made up of the deputy permanent representatives and they are responsible for preparing the so-called 'technical' Councils (Competitiveness, Environment, Transport, and so on). The ambassadors (who hold the title of 'EU permanent representative') preside over COREPER II and primarily work to prepare the monthly GAERC meetings as well as issues with horizontal, institutional, or financial implications.

COREPER I and II are functionally independent bodies (responsible for different formations of the Council) though the EU ambassadors and COREPER II have a more senior status in Brussels and the national capitals. The permanent representatives live in Brussels and hold their positions for several years; some stay for a decade or longer, often outliving their political masters (ministers, prime ministers) and providing crucial continuity in the representation of national interests. The selection of an EU ambassador and deputy is considered a top appointment by member states, and some argue this may be the single most important posting that a member state will make.

The most critical feature of COREPER is nowhere discernible in the Treaties, namely the intensity of the negotiations that take place to prepare the ministers' meetings. Aside from the weekly meetings, COREPER also holds restricted lunch sessions (not even the translators are allowed in the room) to sort out the most sensitive and tricky problems. The permanent representatives also sit beside the minister at Council meetings, and attend European Council summits. But putting a finger on the precise value added by COREPER is difficult since the permanent representatives have no formal decision-making authority. It is clear however that COREPER is an important de facto decision-making body, seen by the steady stream of 'A points' which are sent to the ministers for formal adoption. Over the years, COREPER has functioned under a fairly heavy cloak of confidentiality and insulation from domestic politics and domestic constituent pressures. This insulation enables a level of frankness in COREPER discussions that is essential to reaching compromise across so many different subject areas.

Because of the intensity of negotiations and the long periods of tenure, COREPER officials often develop close personal relations with one another, based on mutual trust and a willingness to try to help each other. In this kind of normative environment and under the pressures to keep the Council moving forward, the permanent representatives are always on the lookout for ways to reach compromise. At times, the search for collective solutions can border on collusion, and the permanent representatives will at times 'go out on a limb' to sell the results of an agreement back home to the relevant authorities. The permanent representatives also exemplify the enigmatic identity of the Council – in order to succeed, they must at the same time represent a national set of interests and share a responsibility to finding collective solutions. COREPER illustrates how the Council is more than just defending national interests, it is also a collective decision-making process embedded in social relations and informal norms of mutual responsiveness, empathy, and self-restraint.

Working groups

The expert group is the workhorse of the Council. Currently numbering over 250, the working group level is a vast network of national officials who specialize in specific areas (such as food safety, the Middle East, olive oil, financial services) and form the initial starting point for negotiations on any new proposal or issue. The working group is also used in the later stages of negotiation to contemplate specific points of disagreement, and can serve as a convenient way to place a proposal in 'cold storage' until the political climate is more favourable for an agreement. Some working groups are permanent, while others are ad hoc and disappear after tackling a specific question or issue. The working groups are staffed with officials travelling from the capitals or from the Brussels-based permanent representations, depending on the issue area involved. The purpose of the working group is to pre-solve as much technical and fine detail as possible, while leaving areas where there is disagreement or the need for political consideration to the permanent representatives or the ministers who have neither the time, or in many cases, the substantive knowledge to hold such finely grained discussions.

It is easy to assume the working group level is well catalogued, orderly, and coherent, but the reality is much the opposite. The working group level suffers from bureaucratic sprawl in the Council system, and because it covers such a wide range of issues and policy sectors, it is very difficult to monitor on the whole. For example, in 2005, over 50 groups were linked to the GAERC alone – 19 covering horizontal questions (for example, enlargement, legislative codification) and 36 dealing with external relations (for example, Africa, sanctions, terrorism, the Middle East peace process).

The working group 'expert', though a vital part of the Council's performance, is not always appreciated at other levels of the Council. The permanent representatives meeting in COREPER, for example, can view their own national experts with some disdain for what one described as their 'bloody single-mindedness' over technical merits without an appreciation of political realities or the broader picture. Likewise, an expert will sometimes feel undermined when a permanent representative or a minister concedes a point that they spent five months defending as absolutely essential at the working group level.

BOX 10.5

Organization of the Council General Secretariat

Office of the Secretary-General and High Representative of CFSP

Office of the Deputy Secretary-General

Private Office (top advisers to the Secretary-General and the Deputy Secretary-General)

Legal Service

Directorate-General A: Personnel and Administration

Directorate-General B: Agriculture, Fisheries

Directorate-General C: Internal Market, Competitiveness, Industry, Research, Energy, Transport, Information Society

Directorate-General E: External Economic Relations, Common Foreign and Security Policy

Directorate-General F: Press, Communication, Protocol

Directorate-General G: Economic and Social Affairs

Directorate-General H: Justice and Home Affairs

Directorate-General I: Protection of the environment and of consumers, Civil protection, Health, Foodstuffs, Education, Youth, Culture, Audiovisual

Source: Council's website.

The Council General Secretariat

The Council employs a bureaucracy of approximately 2,500 officials known as the Council General Secretariat (CGS). Jobs are carefully allotted to all 25 member states, with the majority being linguistic and clerical positions. The top jobs are the 'A-grade' (policy-making) positions which number about 300 in total. At the very top are the highly prestigious Secretary-General and Deputy Secretary-General positions which are filled only after an agreement is made by the heads of state and government. The CGS is the administrative backbone and institutional memory of the Council. Organizationally, the CGS is divided into the Private Offices of the Secretary-General and the Deputy Secretary-General, a Legal Service, a Press Office, and eight Directorates-General for different policy areas (see Box 10.5).

The CGS is officially charged with keeping record of all meetings, including note-taking (and producing the minutes of the meeting), and translating all documents into the EU's 20 official languages. The CGS is also an important asset and ally of the Presidency, by providing logistical assistance, offering advice, and helping to find constructive solutions (the famous 'Presidency compromise'). Over the years, the CGS has earned the reputation of being a dedicated, highly professional team. The commitment of the CGS personnel to the Council's work has also earned them the reputation of being 'honest brokers' and of helping the Presidency find solutions acceptable to all (see Box 10.6).

Perhaps the key factor in the ascendance of the CGS in EU politics is the office of the Council Secretary-General. In the history of the EU, the position has changed hands only five times. There

CASE STUDY 10.6

The Council General Secretariat as an honest broker

The Council General Secretariat (CGS) has earned a reputation for finding creative EU solutions to deadlocked negotiations and helping defuse potential political crises. In particular, the CGS legal staff, who are well versed in the intricacies of the Treaties, are a team of committed Europeanists and an important source of supranational entrepreneurship in the EU. At the time of writing (early 2006) the head of the Council's Legal Service is Director-General Jean-Claude Piris, and he is legendary for his ability to innovate new legal solutions to seemingly intractable problems. The most famous is his work on devising a Danish 'opt-out' to the Maastricht provisions on joining the Single Currency and foreign policy cooperation with defence implications (following Denmark's 'No' vote). The opt-outs were a creative way to make the TEU palatable to Danish voters yet avoided renegotiating the entire Treaty. Some point out that the Danish opt-outs also had the unintended consequence of creating a precedent for other member states to use in the future when they disagreed with new EU policies, creating new momentum for an *à la carte* EU (pick-and-choose).

Another example, again involving Denmark, was the 1998 EU blocking regulation of the US law (known as the Helms–Burton Act) extending the embargo on Cuba to include the right to sue overseas companies who had invested in expropriated property (the EU argued that this amounted to an extraterritorial US law regulating EU companies). The legal basis for the proposed EU blocking regulation included Article 308 (ex-Art 235) which is the so-called implied powers provision enabling EU actions in new areas when deemed necessary to attain Treaty objectives. But the use of Article 308 had become extremely politicized in Denmark where a pending court case involved a citizens group arguing that Article 308 resulted in an unconstitutional surrender of national sovereignty. This was a proposal which all EU member states supported as a strong and coordinated 'antidote' to the US law, but it was impossible for Denmark to accept the legal formulation because of domestic political opposition. Once again, the crack legal staff of the CGS, under the direction of Jean-Claude Piris, helped come up with a novel solution: they drew a legal reference to an obscure 1968 Brussels Convention on judicial cooperation and argued that under these circumstances the EU blocking regulation did not create any *new* EU competencies, and hence, there was no need for the Article 308 formulation. Described by participants at the time as a 'creative legal gimmick', this allowed the EU foreign ministers to adopt the new EU law without appearing to create any new EU competencies.

Finally, the CGS has become such a skilful adviser to the presidency that some member states have started to ask the CGS for help with domestic coordination meetings on EU policy. During the 1998 Austrian Presidency, members of the GCS were asked to travel to Vienna and brief the cabinet ministers on the state of the *Agenda 2000* negotiations, which covered reform of EU spending policies and the 2000–6 budget. As one adviser in the secretary-general's office recalls, the trip to Vienna was designed so that the CGS would 'orchestrate an internal coordination meeting' among the Austrian ministries to help produce a set of presidency conclusions (interview, Brussels, May 2000). This case nicely illustrates how the CGS is trusted as an honest broker.

is no official rule about how long a Secretary-General serves for, but the long tenure of the position gives the Council an important element of continuity and leadership. Under Niels Ersbøll, the long-serving Secretary-General (1980–94) from Denmark, the CGS was transformed from relative obscurity to a central position in Council negotiations, albeit with a behind-the-scenes role that is not often credited in public (Hayes-Renshaw and Wallace 1997: 108–9). The position of Secretary-General has been granted new authority following the decision by the heads of state and government at the 1999 Cologne summit to upgrade the office to include the title of High Representative of Common Foreign and Security Policy (unofficially dubbed 'Mr CFSP') and to appoint the then Secretary-General of NATO, Javier Solana, to the position (see Box 10.7 for more). The Deputy Secretary-General is now entrusted with the task of overseeing the day-to-day operations of the Council, and participates in the weekly COREPER II meetings.

KEY POINTS

- European Council summits are the source of most 'history-making' decisions in the history of European integration.
- The European Council is under great demand to provide leadership and overall guidance in setting the pace and direction of the integration process.
- The ministerial Councils are divided by policy sector, and three (the GAERC, ECOFIN, Agriculture) stand out for the level of work and frequency of meetings.
- COREPER is the official preparatory body for the Council which gives the EU ambassadors and deputies the primary responsibility of pre-negotiating and discussing the agendas of every forthcoming Council session.
- The working groups are the biggest single dimension of the Council's work, involving thousands of national experts and handling the technical and finely grained detail of specific proposals.
- The Council has a permanent secretariat, the CGS, which helps facilitate meetings, takes notes, translates documents, and serves as an adviser to the Presidency.

Institutional evolution over time and current challenges

Of all the accolades that one can find written about the Council's ability to forge compromise among sovereign states with divergent interests, few claim that the Council is an efficient decision-making system. It takes about 18 months on average for a new proposal to undergo the stages of negotiation in the Council and with the EP, though there are some cases that take much longer. A few notorious examples include the directive on lawnmower noise (84/538/EEC) negotiated over a dozen years to harmonize the maximum decibel level mowers can make, or the chocolate directive (2000/36/EC) which took 26 years to reach agreement on a common definition for 'chocolate products'! In short, EU decision-making is a 'gas-guzzling' form of governance (Hayes-Renshaw and Wallace 1997: 284).

The ministers' meetings in particular show signs of strain. Never known for their punctuality and often the brunt of jokes for their lack of preparedness, the ministers do not always hold highly productive meetings. One former British minister, Alan Clark (1993: 139), recalls his fondness of Council meetings in his memoirs : 'The ministers arrive on the scene at the last minute, hot, tired, ill or drunk (sometimes all of these together), read out their piece and depart.' This has become more problematic as the competencies of the EU have evolved and agendas have grown more extensive, even overloaded. For example, GAERC agendas grew from an average of 8.4 agenda items per meeting in 1990 to 36.2 in 2000 (Gomez and Peterson 2001: 7–8). One implication is that as agendas continue to swell, the actual discussions over substance are taking place at the level of COREPER, seen by the growth of 'A points' which are merely rubber-stamped by the ministers. In 1995, the number of items on the GAERC agenda that were passed without debate was 34 per cent of the total agenda; in 2000, that figure had increased to 54 per cent (Gomez and Peterson 2001: 9). Another implication of this overload is that overall coordination gets increasingly left to the European Council. In light of these dysfunctions and in anticipation of adding new members from the East, the CT devised a number of important institutional revisions for the Council (see Box 10.7). Whether the CT is eventually

BOX 10.7

Constitutional Treaty reforms that would impact the Council's new qualified majority voting system (Article I-25)

Possibly the single most contentious item debated during the IGC was how to reform the system of qualified majority voting. The new design is a double-majority system that scraps the controversial voting weights reset during the Nice Treaty in anticipation of future enlargements. The new system has two threshold requirements:

- support of at least 55 per cent of the member states (that is, at least 15 in an EU25),
- who represent at least 65 per cent of the total EU population.

An additional clause requires at least four member states to form a 'blocking minority'. This safeguards against hypothetical big state coalitions blocking legislation (any three of the big four – Germany, France, Britain, Italy – represent more than 35 per cent of the EU's population).

European Council President (Article I-22)

Part effort to improve coherence and part effort to leverage Europe's ability to speak with a single voice, the idea of a senior statesperson to represent the Union and chair the summits of the heads of state and government was an institutional innovation widely hailed in national capitals. The European Council appoints the president by qualified majority for a term of 2.5 years (renewable once). The Council president cannot wear a 'double hat' – they must not simultaneously hold a national office (Article I-22.3). The European Council President is expected to:

- Chair meetings of the European Council and 'drive forward its work';
- 'Ensure the preparation and continuity of the work of the European Council';
- 'Endeavour to facilitate cohesion and consensus';
- Issue a report to the EP after each summit.

European Union Minister for Foreign Affairs (Article I-28)

Upgrading the 'Mr CFSP' post to a Minister for Foreign Affairs (MFA) was an early consensus of the Convention. It is the area where, practically speaking, the EU gains the most visible international legal personality, for a hypothetical Union MFA will be able to stand next to the foreign ministers and Secretaries of State of other nation states with the same diplomatic status and protocol. For those who predict the CT is dead, the EU MFA job is usually cited as one of the top pieces to salvage from the wreckage. The political significance of a Union foreign minister, landed as Europe's answer to Henry Kissinger's famous quip, 'I wouldn't know who to call if I wanted to talk to Europe', was that the position was viewed as a way to upgrade CFSP and ESDP.

For scholars of the EU, the MFA post is intriguing because it explicitly blurs the institutional boundaries between the Council and Commission in ways previously unheard of. To avoid organizational chaos in EU external relations, the new MFA is not only a top Council actor, but a vice-president of the Commission in charge of the sizeable external relations budget. Duties would include:

- chairing the External Relations portion of the GAERC;
- attending European Council meetings;
- serving as a vice-president of the Commission and running the External Relations DG;
- representing the EU externally and conducting high-level diplomacy.

The Union MFA is appointed by the European Council. There is no fixed term or term limit; the European Council may simply 'end his or her term of office' by qualified majority. Last, it is worth noting that there is wide agreement that the current EU foreign policy 'supremo', Javier Solana, would become the inaugural Union MFA.

Enhanced cooperation (Article I-44)

Seen by many as the formalization and legitimation of an *à la carte* ('pick-and-choose') Europe, this was packaged as a way to 'further the objectives of the Union, protect its interests and reinforce its integration process' but a more cynical way of putting it is that vanguard or core members can be held back longer in policy areas by the most reluctant integrationists. Enhanced cooperation is however considered 'a last resort' when 'cooperation cannot be attained . . . by the Union as a whole'. Outsiders may still participate in deliberations but they will have no voting rights. Adopted acts will only bind participating member states and do not become part of the EU *acquis*.

Source: Treaty Establishing a Constitution for Europe, OJ C310, 16.12.2004.

adopted in full or in part remains to be seen, but few Council participants believe the current system can continue for much longer without fundamental reform.

If, internally, the Council shows signs of strain and overload, the external problem of credibility with EU citizens is equally a concern. Since the 1990s, the issue of the 'democratic deficit' has been at the top of the EU's agenda. But the inner workings of the Council have so far avoided scrutiny. Reducing the democratic deficit has centred on reforming the EU's decision-making procedures, increasing involvement by the European Parliament, and introducing the subsidiarity principle to keep decisional authority as close to the citizens as possible. But addressing the democratic deficit inside the Council remains controversial. Every member government pays lip-service to the need for the Union to be more transparent, more accessible, and more connected to EU citizens but there is less agreement among them on how best to accomplish this task in Council deliberations. One innovation was to hold 'public debates' by broadcasting select Council meetings on television, but this has had the perverse effect of stifling real dialogue since the ministers simply began reading from set speeches. Instead of increasing the transparency of the Council's work, public debates merely promote the reading of 'successive monologues' (Galloway 1999). According the to Council's rules of procedure, every six months the GAERC and the ECOFIN should hold a public debate on the work programme of the current Presidency as well as at least one public debate on important new legislative proposals (Article 8).

While the EU doggedly remains hard to predict, there are two areas that show signs of posing future challenges with potentially unsettling implications. The first issue is enlargement (see Chapter 26). Can the Council continue to operate in the same way in an EU of 27 or more member states? Some believe that the Council will become such an unwieldy and heterogeneous body that it will become little more than a 'talking shop' of ministers reading from set speeches. An EU of 27 will place new strains on the Council's decision-making structures – originally built for six members – and is likely to slow down the pace and output of new legislation even further. Enlargement is also likely to increase the workload of COREPER and the expert groups which will hold greater responsibilities for discussing substantive issues and finding agreements at their levels. Finally, how easily the Council's decision-making system can consolidate its new members will depend on how quickly and extensively they become socialized to the EU's normative environment. If, for example, the new members are slow to absorb the established norms of compromise and accommodation, the Council may develop a more rigid 'veto culture' or even divide into different voting blocks along geographic or GDP lines. Of particular concern is the future admission of Turkey, which could alter the balance of national voting power in the Council in dramatic and unpredictable ways (see Box 10.8).

The second issue is differentiation and variable geometry. How will the Council change as the EU becomes more polycentric and differentiated? 'Enhanced' forms of cooperation, which were for the first time incorporated into the Treaties with Nice, pose certain risks in altering the very finely tuned mechanisms of exchange and consensus-seeking which have become reflexive habits among Council participants. While many view differentiation as a method of promoting diversity and preventing the blockage of integration by reluctant or recalcitrant members, others see differentiation as setting a dangerous precedent for different 'classes' of membership which challenge the principle of equality.

CASE STUDY 10.8

How Turkey might unbalance the 'big state' club of voting power in the Council

The eventual membership of Turkey in the EU 'club' is one of Europe's most highly politicized issues. In the media, the issue is often posed as whether Turkey is part of 'Europe', and there is discussion of the identity politics of Islam and Christianity stretching back over the centuries. Academics tend to focus more on the high hurdles Turkey faces in meeting the *acquis communautaire* or passing the constitutionally required referendum of support in France. Less attention is paid to how radically Turkey could shake up the delicate balancing of national power within the Council. Assuming the CT is eventually adopted (see Box 10.7), the problem, in a nutshell, is this – overnight Turkey would become the first or second most powerful vote on the Council, leapfrogging the French, the British, the Italians, the Spanish, the Polish, and eventually overtaking the Germans. By current demographic projections, Turkey would be the most populous state in a future hypothetical EU some time after 2020 and, hence, the most powerful vote on the Council. Thus, it is likely that behind the more vocal worries of smaller members such as Austria and Greece lie deep reservations by many of the founding and big state members who are concerned about the institutional and decision-making implications of adding such a large and heterogeneous newcomer.

Population/ Projections (in millions)	Year			
	2005	2020	2030	2050
Turkey	69.7	79.7	84.2	86.5
Germany	82.4	81.4	79.6	73.6
France	60.7	62.8	63.2	61.0
United Kingdom	60.4	63.1	64.3	64.0
Italy	58.1	57.0	55.4	50.4
Spain	40.3	40.1	39.0	35.6
Poland	38.6	38.0	36.5	32.1

Source: Summary Demographic Data, US Census Bureau, International Data Base, April 2005 version.

KEY POINTS

- The Council has grown in membership and scope to the point where decision-making structures are under strain, ministerial discussions are limited to a few substantive issues, and agendas are overcrowded. Many believe the Council needs serious institutional reform, but there is little agreement on what to change.
- Council decision-making remains remote, opaque, and mysterious to EU citizens.
- Efforts to 'democratize' Council negotiations, by holding public debates on television, has resulted largely in staged performances for the cameras while the substantive discussions have taken place elsewhere (restricted sessions, COREPER, working groups).
- Enlargement to 27 or more members will result in new voting weights in the Council and presents certain challenges to prevent negotiations from becoming too unwieldy, depersonalized, and unreceptive to compromise-building.

Conclusion: national, supranational, or both?

The Council is the main decision-making body of the EU. It is the premier EU institution for representing national interests and power. But it is also a collective system of governance which locks member states into permanent negotiations with one another. National officials who participate in this system have developed their own 'rules of the game' which include a culture of behaving consensually through compromise and mutual accommodation. Thus, strictly speaking, the Council is both an institution that represents national interests and a body at the supranational level that makes collective decisions. When examined closely, researchers often find evidence that the Council blurs the traditional distinctions between the national and European levels, between intergovernmentalism and supranationality. As a leading study of the Council concludes, national officials who participate in this system face a 'continuous tension between the home affiliation and the pull of the collective forum' (Hayes-Renshaw and Wallace 1997: 279). It is this feature more than any other that really distinguishes the Council of the European Union from other international institutions and forums of interstate cooperation.

But whether the Council can continue to operate as it has for the last 50 years remains open to debate. There are signs of strain on decision-makers, as agendas continue to balloon and the lines of coordination and coherence between Councils continue to atrophy. Enlargement of the EU to 27 or more members risks stretching the system to the point of paralysis. Even at 15, following the 'Nordic round' of enlargement in 1995, many Brussels insiders characterized the Council as operating 'over capacity'. In pragmatic terms, the decision-making system originally made for six cannot function in the same way when there are nearly 30; Council participants claim that such a large table is now needed for meetings that many rely on small-screen televisions strategically placed in front of each delegation to see the face of whoever is talking.

There are also serious questions of democratic accountability which remain unanswered, as Council deliberations continue to be obscure and mysterious to EU citizens. Reshuffling the formations of the ministers' meetings or splitting the work of 'general affairs' into an internal institutional and external foreign policy format is more a shell game (confidence trick) than substantive remedy. Council reform faces sharp trade-offs between greater transparency which is ineffective (public debates leading to set speeches) and more effective decision-making which takes place behind closed doors and out of the public spotlight (lunches, restricted sessions).

Finally, the new focus on differentiated integration could have perverse effects on Council decision-making as some member states may find themselves excluded from certain discussions altogether, as we already see in areas of eurozone policy-making (see Chapter 20). This would have the unprecedented effect of creating different tiers or classes of membership. On the other hand, the EU has shown a remarkable capacity over the years to cope with crises and innovate new governance solutions. The current halfway house status of the CT is only the most recent illustration of this. The issue of 'institutional reform' is thus likely to be unresolved for some time, and, in a governance system as advanced as this, may even be an endemic feature of the EU's agenda.

? QUESTIONS

1. In what manner does the Council perform both legislative and executive functions in the European Union?
2. What kind of institution is the Council? Is it intergovernmental or supranational?
3. Do big states outweigh smaller states in power resources and influence in the Council? If so, how? If not, why?

4. How do the member states coordinate the representation of national interests in Council negotiations?
5. What are the differences between regulations, directives, and decisions?
6. What role does the rotating Presidency play in EU governance?
7. How does the Council General Secretariat act as a 'neutral umpire' and facilitator of meetings?
8. How and why have European Council summits increased in importance over time?

GUIDE TO FURTHER READING

- Bulmer, S., and Wessels, W. *The Council: Decision-making in the European Community* (London: Macmillan, 1987). A detailed analytical and historical overview of EU Council summitry.

- de Bassompierre, G. *Changing the Guard in Brussels: An Insider's View of the EC Presidency* (New York: Praeger, 1988). A candid, highly readable account of the role of the Presidency in running the Council.

- Hayes-Renshaw, F., and Wallace, H. *The Council of Ministers*, 2nd edn (New York: St Martin's Press, 2006). The definitive study of the Council as a decision-making institution, newly updated to reflect changes since the mid-1990s.

- Noël, E. 'The Committee of Permanent Representatives', *Journal of Common Market Studies*, 5(3), March 1967, pp. 219–51. The best early examination of COREPER – a classic.

- Peterson, J., and Bomberg, E. *Decision-making in the European Union* (Basingstoke: Macmillan, 1999). An impressive research design that uses extensive interview data and case study analysis to provide an overview of the dynamics of Council decision-making.

- Westlake, M., and Galloway, D. *The Council of the European Union*, 3rd edn (London: Cartermill, 2004). A comprehensive study, including a useful comparison of the working methods of different formations of the Council.

IMPORTANT WEBSITES

- http://ue.eu.int/en/summ.htm The Council's official homepage. The website includes links to specific policy areas such as Common Foreign and Security Policy, Justice and Home Affairs, Economic and Monetary Union, etc. There is also a link to the EU Presidency which offers basic information about meetings such as dates and agendas as well as the 'Presidency conclusions' of recent European Council summits. Access to documentation (including the minutes of Council meetings since 1999) continues to improve, and it is quite easy to locate recent Council acts though the archives remain patchy in many areas.

Visit the Online Resource Centre that accompanies this book for lots of interesting additional material. http://www.oxfordtextbooks.co.uk/orc/cini2e/

11 The European Parliament

ROGER SCULLY

Chapter Contents

Reader's Guide

This chapter examines the European Parliament (EP), and its role within the institutional system of the European Union. Unlike the bodies covered in the previous two chapters, the Commission and the EU Council, the EP has only recently assumed prominence in the EU's governing structures. The first section of the chapter outlines the origins of the Parliament as an essentially marginal institution within the developing structures of European cooperation. The following section then reviews in detail the significant increases in powers experienced by the EP in recent times, and discusses how these have transformed the importance of the chamber. After that, the chapter goes on to examine the complex internal politics of the EP – its membership, organization, and working practices. Finally, the chapter considers the 'electoral connection': the links between the EP and the European public. The general conclusion is that the European Parliament has been strikingly successful in gaining more powers, but far less successful in linking the EU to the peoples of Europe.

Introduction

Compared to many national and even subnational legislatures, the European Parliament (EP) enjoys a relatively low public profile. Scholars of the European Union, too, have not traditionally devoted substantial attention to the EP, judging it less important than other governing institutions of the Union. However, since the mid-1980s, the EP has undergone probably more substantial changes than any other major EU body. And the cumulative effect of many of these changes has been to enhance greatly the importance of the Parliament within the Union's governing structures. For much of its life, the EP could have justly been labelled a 'multilingual talking shop'. This is no longer the case.

This chapter examines the development of the EP, and its role within the EU's political system. As with parliamentary institutions in other systems, to understand the role of the European Parliament adequately we must consider three major topics. These are:

- The *legislative work* of the Parliament: its role in developing and shaping policies and laws.
- The *internal politics* of the Parliament: the organizational structures of the chamber, and the competition within it between different political parties and ideologies.
- The *representative* role of the Parliament: as a chamber comprised of elected representatives, its role as 'voice of the people' in linking the political system to the public.

As we shall see, while the EP has developed considerably as an institution, it still faces significant challenges with regard to the representation dimension – challenges that matter not just for the Parliament, but potentially for the EU as a whole. Before examining all this, however, it is necessary to give a brief overview of the origins and development of the EP.

The origins and development of the European Parliament

For much of its life, the European Parliament has been fairly marginal to the development of European integration and to the politics of the EU. To understand that, and to appreciate how much has changed since the mid-1980s, we must be aware of the EP's rather modest origins.

What is now the European Parliament began life as the Common Assembly of the nascent European Coal and Steel Community (ECSC) in 1952. This new assembly was not central to the plans of the 'founding fathers' of integration. 'In Jean Monnet's vision, it was, together with the European Court of Justice, an institution of control and scrutiny, not of decision-making' (Neunreither 2000: 133). Thus, the new chamber was given limited and specific responsibilities. It could discuss policies, and scrutinize their execution. And it could, in principle, dismiss the High Authority (forerunner to today's European Commission – see Chapter 9) for gross mismanagement. But over new policies and laws it could only issue opinions to which other institutions were not compelled to respond. A further source of weakness was that the Assembly's membership was not directly elected by voters, but drawn from member states' national parliaments. This provided a direct link between the ECSC and national political systems, but it also ensured that the Common Assembly, as well as having restricted powers, could only ever be a part-time institution, as its members still had national parliamentary responsibilities to fulfil.

The Assembly met, originally, in Strasbourg. Among the many reasons for this was the symbolism of a parliamentary chamber meeting to discuss European cooperation in a city that had long been disputed territory between France and Germany. Support staff for the Assembly were originally based in Luxembourg, alongside the ECSC High Authority. As what became the EU has increasingly centred its operations in Brussels, the EP has come to conduct more of its operations and base more staff in the Belgian and EU capital. However, rather than locate all EP activities there, national governments have continued to insist (against the wishes of most EP members) that the Parliament hold regular plenary sessions in Strasbourg, and maintain some staff in Luxembourg. This situation hampers the work of the EP, requires costly duplication of buildings and other facilities, and generates some understandable ridicule.

The original Common Assembly consisted of 78 nominated national parliamentarians from the then six ECSC member states. By the time of the 2004 elections, the European Parliament (as it had renamed itself in 1962) comprised 732 elected representatives from 25 states. (See Table 11.1 for a description of how the EP has enlarged over time.) The Rome Treaty in the late 1950s had called for the chamber to become an elected institution. Yet the first European Parliament elections did not take place until 1979. A central reason for this delay was that governments and parties hostile to the development of stronger European-level institutions foresaw an elected European Parliament being in a powerful position to argue for greater powers: after all, the EP would be (indeed, it remains to this day) the only directly elected European institution, and it could use this democratic status to argue for enhanced powers. Such fears proved well founded and, whatever wider concerns remain regarding EP elections (see below), the elected Parliament has proven a strong

Table 11.1 The growth of the EP

Year	No. of MEPs	No. of member states	Status of MEPs	Title of chamber
1952	78	6	Nominated	ECSC Common Assembly
1958	142	6	Nominated	EC Common Assembly
1973	198	9[a]	Nominated	European Parliament
1979	410	9	Elected	European Parliament
1981	434	10[b]	Elected	European Parliament
1986	518	12[c]	Elected	European Parliament
1994	567	12[d]	Elected	European Parliament
1995	626	15[e]	Elected	European Parliament
2005	732	25[f]	Elected	European Parliament

[a] Enlargement to Denmark, Ireland, and the UK.
[b] Enlargement to Greece.
[c] Enlargement to Spain and Portugal.
[d] German enlargement and seat redistribution.
[e] Enlargement to Austria, Finland, and Sweden.
[f] Enlargement to Cyprus, Czech Republic, Estonia, Hungary, Latvia, Lithuania, Malta, Poland, Slovakia, and Slovenia.

advocate both of closer European integration generally, and more powers for itself in particular (Corbett 1998; Rittberger 2005). By the mid-1990s, the EP was no longer a marginal institution, but a central, 'mainstream' part of the Union's governing system.

KEY POINTS

- The European Parliament originated as an unelected, part-time institution with limited powers.
- The EP's powers were originally restricted to the supervision and scrutiny of other institutions, apart from the ability to remove the High Authority/Commission in exceptional circumstances.
- Over time, the chamber has changed its name (to the European Parliament), grown substantially in size, and become an elected institution.

The powers and influence of the European Parliament

Since the 1970s, Treaty amendments and institutional agreements have greatly enhanced the European Parliament's powers. (Box 11.1 summarizes the major changes described below.) The first major advance for the Parliament came in the realm of the community budget. Two treaties in the 1970s granted the EP the right to propose modifications to planned 'compulsory' spending (mainly on agriculture), to insist on amendments to 'non-compulsory' spending, and the right (if supported by an absolute majority of all MEPs, and two-thirds of those voting) to reject the budget outright. This

CHRONOLOGY 11.1

The development of the European Parliament's powers

Year	*Event*	*Impact on EP powers*
1970	Treaty changes on budget	Greater budgetary powers for EP
1975	Treaty changes on budget	More budgetary powers for EP; EP given considerable influence over non-CAP spending
1980	Isoglucose judgment of ECJ	Right of consultation for EP reinforced
1987	Entry into force of Single European Act	Cooperation procedure introduced for some legislation, giving EP greater scope for delay, amendment, and blocking laws; assent powers to EP on some matters
1993	Maastricht Treaty enters into force	Codecision procedure introduced for some legislation; EP given approval power over nominated Commission
1999	Amsterdam Treaty enters into force	Codecision procedure altered in EP's favour, and extended in scope; EP given formal right to veto nominee for post of Commission President
2003	Nice Treaty enters into force	Codecision procedure further extended in scope

power has been exercised twice, in 1979 and 1984. The Parliament's budgetary role was further enhanced from the late 1980s on by a series of 'Inter-Institutional Agreements' between the Council, Commission, and Parliament, which meant that parliamentary approval was henceforth needed for increases in most areas of EU spending; these agreements ran parallel to multiyear budgetary deals that, by fixing for several years ahead broad spending priorities, allowed the Parliament to give greater attention to monitoring EU expenditure.

The Parliament has made more limited progress in terms of 'executive oversight' – in part because the EU political system lacks a clear 'executive branch' to oversee. Many executive functions, notably in foreign affairs, remain in the hands of national governments who yield only reluctantly, and to a limited extent, to scrutiny from the EP. Nonetheless, the Parliament can dismiss the Commission and would have used this power in March 1999, in response to evidence of Commission mismanagement, had it not been pre-empted by the Commission's resignation. The EP's powers over the Commission were enhanced by the Maastricht and Amsterdam Treaties, which first gave the chamber veto power over the new Commission nominated by national governments, and then separate vetoes over both the Commission President-designate and the entire team of commissioners. In 2004, these powers gave the Parliament sufficient political leverage to require changes to the team under the new Commission President, José Manuel Barroso, before parliamentary approval could be obtained (see Box 11.2). In addition, day-to-day scrutiny of the Commission is increasingly pursued by EP committees.

The greatest advances made by the EP, however, have been in the area of EU law-making. Prior to the Single European Act, the EP's role here was very limited. EU laws (other than Commission legislation) were processed via 'consultation'. Under this legislative procedure, the Parliament could offer opinions, but could not force the Commission or Council to respond to them. Aside from using delaying tactics (such as postponing the formal presentation of its opinion), the EP had no mechanism by which to influence legislation.

Strong lobbying of national governments for greater parliamentary powers bore some fruit in the Single European Act. Consultation was retained

CASE STUDY 11.2

Appointing the Barroso Commission

The appointment of the European Commission in 2004, under new President (and former Portuguese Prime Minister) José Manuel Barroso, illustrated the powers that the EP now possesses here, and also the willingness of MEPs to use these powers.

Mr Barroso, the centre-right Portuguese Prime Minister at the time, was nominated by national governments of the EU member states in June 2004, shortly after the 2004 EP elections. The following month, he appeared before the European Parliament to seek endorsement for his nomination. Although this was forthcoming, Barroso received opposition from a significant number of MEPs; the final vote (413: 251, with 44 abstentions) saw him winning significantly less than two-thirds support.

However, Mr Barroso's problems became more serious when he sought to win approval for the team of commissioners to work under him as President. Several of the nominees (agreed between Mr Barroso and the respective national governments of each nominee) did not impress EP committees when forced to undergo 'confirmation hearings' by those committees. Opposition was particularly strong to the Italian nominee, Rocco Buttiglione. Mr Buttiglione was the prospective commissioner on Justice, Freedom and Security; but when appearing before the EP's Civil Liberties Committee he made disparaging comments regarding homosexuals and women that rendered him unacceptable to many MEPs, particularly on the left.

Mr Barroso, along with the Italian Prime Minister, initially refused to withdraw Mr Buttiglione from the list of Commission nominees. However, on the day (27 October) that the approval vote was due to occur, Mr Barroso was forced to postpone the vote when informed that he was likely to be defeated. A delay of some weeks occurred before agreement was reached on an alternative Italian commissioner (Franco Frattini), and the Commission team won a comfortable majority in the EP in November.

for most laws. But for much legislation related to the Single Market Initiative, the 'cooperation' procedure was introduced. This allowed Parliament to propose amendments to draft legislation (which, if supported by the Commission, could be overturned only by a unanimous Council but accepted by a qualified majority of states), or to issue a veto on pieces of legislation that could be overturned only by a unanimous Council of Ministers. This was undoubtedly a significant advance for the EP. The Single European Act also gave the EP 'assent' power (that is, a simple yes/no vote) over matters like association agreements with non-EU states, and the accession of new member states to the Union.

The Maastricht Treaty produced a further significant change; after Maastricht, around one-quarter of laws were processed under another new procedure, 'codecision'. Codecision laws were designated as joint Acts of the Parliament and Council (rather than the Council alone), and the Parliament was granted the ability to exercise an irrevocable veto over legislative proposals. Most observers saw this as a considerable step forward. As Duff has noted: 'Maastricht marks the point in the Community's development at which the Parliament became the first chamber of a real legislature . . . The codecision procedure means that it has now come of age as a law-making body' (Duff 1994: 31). The 1997 Amsterdam Treaty revised codecision slightly, in a manner somewhat beneficial to the Parliament, and also extended it to further areas of EU law. The procedure is now used for around half of EU laws, with most of the rest processed under consultation.

The precise degree to which these various changes have boosted the EP's role within the institutional structures of the EU, and how, has been a matter of some debate by scholars. Any formal power granted to an institution only becomes relevant if there is a willingness to use that power. And in the complex world of European law-making, where the EP has to interact with the Council and Commission, some scholars argued that a veto power would be of little practical benefit to the Parliament, as it would be available for use only in circumstances where vetoing proposed laws would mean, for most MEPs, losing more than they would gain. A strong 'revisionist' perspective suggested that the cooperation procedure had actually given the EP greater scope to set the legislative agenda (see Garrett and Tsebelis 1996; Tsebelis and Garrett 1997). However, this argument, developed through abstract theoretical models of legislative bargaining, was subject to theoretical criticism (Scully 1997a, 1997b; Moser 1996; Rittberger 2000) and appears not to be supported by empirical evidence that the Parliament's success in advancing legislative amendments increased significantly under codecision compared to the cooperation procedure (Kreppel 1999; Shackleton 2000; Tsebelis *et al.* 2001).

It is clear that the EP has become a much more powerful institution than it used to be. But how does the contemporary EP compare to other parliaments, like those in EU member states, in terms of power and influence? Such comparisons are difficult to make with great precision. But two things are fairly clear. The first is that even after the expansion of codecision, the EP's formal powers are still more limited than those of many national parliaments, most of which have formal approval power over all pieces of legislation. But the second, and possibly more important, point is that the EP actually *uses* its powers to a greater extent than do most national legislatures. Parliamentarians in most national chambers are bound by strong ties of party loyalty to support or oppose a government, and most governments have secure majorities that allow them effective control over parliaments. In the EP, with no clear government to either support or oppose, and with party loyalties also rather more diffuse, one sees a much greater willingness to exploit available powers to the full. Those who have attempted to evaluate the European Parliament's influence in comparative perspective thus tend to conclude that the EP actually ranks higher in this respect than many of its national counterparts (Scully 2000; Bergman and Raunio 2001).

KEY POINTS

- The EP gained significant powers over the European budget in the 1970s.
- In the 1990s, the Parliament gained an enhanced role in the appointment and supervision of the Commission.
- The EP gained significant powers over EU legislation in the 1980s and 1990s through new legislative procedures introduced in several treaties; the Parliament is now more influential over policy than many national parliaments.

The internal politics of the European Parliament

Life inside the European Parliament is complex. This complexity arises not only from the detailed and technical nature of the EU policies that the Parliament spends much of its time dealing with. Complexity is virtually inherent in the multinational, multilingual and multiparty political environment that the EP constitutes. This section of the chapter highlights some of the major features of politics within the Parliament.

MEPs in the 2004–9 Parliament represent well over 100 separate national parties from the 25 member states. The Parliament thus encompasses a huge diversity of political viewpoints and previous political experiences. Although turnover at each election tends to be high (more than 50 per cent of members elected in June 2004 had not previously been MEPs), there are also many who have built long-term political careers at the European level. To an increasing extent, MEPs are professional politicians for whom being in the EP is a full-time job. Although some parties have been known to use the EP as a sort of 'political retirement home' – the current EP contains several former national Prime Ministers among its membership – most members work hard. The EP was once known for high levels of absenteeism amongst members compared to national parliaments; this is no longer the case. The EP also used to be known as a bastion of pro-integrationist opinion: in part because those less interested in the EU were more reluctant to stand as candidates for the EP. However, recent parliaments have included greater numbers of Eurosceptic and anti-EU figures.

Individual national party delegations to the EP join together in multinational party groups, based broadly around political ideology. Being members of both national parties and European party groups, nationally elected yet working in a European institution, makes the task of the individual MEP as a representative potentially quite complicated. Most MEPs recognize the importance of balancing the interests of the several different 'constituencies' that they represent. The party groups seek to bring together like-minded members from different states, yet they must always remain aware of differing national traditions and interests. Recent research has shown that in parliamentary votes the groups attain levels of intraparty unity that are, given the diversity of membership of the larger groups in particular, very high. Differences within the Parliament are structured far more frequently along party lines than national ones, and the voting unity of the party groups in the EP is much higher than that of the two parties in the US Congress (Raunio 1997; Hix *et al.* 2006). Yet this unity must often be built on the basis of substantial 'give and take' between national delegations within the group, with agreement often following the lowest common denominator; even so, dissent from party group positions most often occurs when large numbers of MEPs from one or more national delegation refuse to support a group line (Hix 2002).

Although the party groups are ideologically based, intergroup relations in the Parliament have traditionally rested on cooperation rather than confrontation. The largest groups in the chamber have always been from the centre-right (the European People's Party (EPP) group of Christian Democrats and some Conservatives) and the centre-left (the Party of European Socialists (PES) group representing moderate social democrats and socialists). For many years, these two blocs cooperated in sharing out most of the senior posts in the EP, as well as seeking consensus in most other matters before the Parliament. The 1999–2004 chamber saw increasing conflict between the major groups, however, and growing levels of voting division along left/right lines in the chamber. A prime example has been the election of the Parliament's President: for some years, the two leading groups had shared this job (which is held by each incumbent for two-and-a-half years, half of a five-year EP term) between them and supported each other's candidates when the other group's 'turn' came around. In both July 1999 and January 2002, however, a PES candidate sought (unsuccessfully) the presidency in opposition to candidates endorsed by the EPP.

Party interests play an important part in the organization of business in the EP. The parliamentary hierarchy is headed by the Conference of Presidents, comprising the President (Speaker) of the EP, 14 Vice-Presidents, and the Presidents of the party groups. This body handles much of the scheduling of parliamentary business, and the allocation of things like committee chairships. The business of the Parliament itself is organized very tightly. The parliamentary timetable defines specific weeks as set aside for plenary sessions (usually one four-day session per month in Strasbourg, with a few additional 'mini-sessions' of two days in Brussels), other weeks being for committee work (usually two weeks in a month), with the balance of time reserved for 'party group weeks' and 'constituency weeks'. This 'hyperorganization' of the parliamentary timetable extends also into the conduct of plenary sessions. Largely because of the need for extensive translation facilities, time for debates and individual contributions is organized very closely – literally almost down to the second.

The EP has a now well-established system of permanent committees (20 in the 2004–9 parliament – see Box 11.3). These committees cover most areas of EU policy, and individual committees undertake both legislative work (scrutinizing draft legislation and drawing up amendments) and oversight activity (looking into the conduct of policy) in their area of responsibility. Some committees have also taken on a broader role: the Institutional Affairs Committee in previous parliaments (now the Constitutional Affairs Committee) sought to

BOX 11.3

The committees of the 2004 – 9 European Parliament

- Foreign Affairs
- Development
- International Trade
- Budgets
- Budgetary Control
- Economic and Monetary Affairs
- Employment and Social Affairs
- Environment, Public Health and Food Safety
- Industry, Research and Energy
- Internal Market and Consumer Protection
- Transport and Tourism
- Regional Development
- Agriculture and Rural Development
- Fisheries
- Culture and Education
- Legal Affairs
- Civil Liberties, Justice and Home Affairs
- Constitutional Affairs
- Women's Rights and Gender Equality
- Petitions

develop visionary proposals for deepening integration; the Women's Rights and Gender Equality Committee has often sought to broaden the degree to which gender-related considerations are incorporated into the EU; and the Foreign Affairs Committee has rarely felt itself restricted to discussing matters fitting directly within the Union's Common Foreign and Security Policy. Many committees contain considerable expertise on their subject matter within their membership, and the committee system as a whole is widely regarded as the place where the bulk of the serious work of the Parliament is done. That work can sometimes be shaped by the influence of strong committee chairs. But, at least as often, committee work is led by the 'group coordinators' appointed by the major party groups to each committee. And, on particular matters of policy, there is considerable scope for individual MEPs to have an impact, particularly if they are appointed *rapporteur*: the person delegated by a committee to prepare its report on a specific topic.

Plenary sessions include the great set-piece occasions of the EP's business. MEPs are frequently addressed by Prime Ministers and Foreign Ministers of member states, and sometimes of third countries. And on some occasions, as with the debates held over the nominations of new Commission Presidents, or that over the possible resignation of the Santer Commission in 1999, these can be genuinely dramatic events. Far more commonly, however, plenary sessions are tedious in the extreme: speeches tend to be more about putting certain views 'on the record' than trying to persuade people, while Voting Time witnesses large numbers of votes, often on unrelated topics, being held one after the other. The problems of a multilingual institution also hamper plenary debates, making it often boring at best, confusing and even farcical at worst (see Box 11.4).

Where does power ultimately lie in the EP? Compared to the executive-dominated parliaments of many countries in Europe, power in the EP is much more widely diffused. The lack of a controlling government party in the chamber, the importance of committees, and the multiparty and multinational nature of the institution all make the EP a highly complex and relatively 'de-centred' institution. This complexity, and the fact that some of the EP's major powers require the mobilization of 'super-majorities' before they can be deployed (an absolute majority of all MEPs, not simply a majority of those participating in a particular vote) makes compromise and coalition-building a necessity and places a premium on subtle political skills. But this sort of environment also grants individual parliamentarians who possess such political skills greater scope to achieve substantive policy objectives in the EP than their national counterparts can achieve in most other parliamentary institutions.

CASE STUDY 11.4

The problems of multilingual parliamentary plenary sessions

The 25 member states of the EU produce, collectively, 20 official languages for the Union (to say nothing of other 'minority' languages like Catalan and Welsh). MEPs are permitted – indeed, expected – to make plenary speeches in their 'native' language. Even with excellent translation facilities, the resulting 'Tower of Babel' effect can often hamper the cut and thrust of debate when the EP is in plenary session.

At a minimum, debate becomes more cumbersome. When speakers are using some of the less common languages (say, Portuguese or Finnish) their words are translated into certain 'core' languages (usually English and French) before being retranslated into other tongues (like Danish and Italian). Even when translation is entirely successful this can produce bizarre consequences: a joke can potentially produce three waves of laughter!

Often the effect of translation is to lose subtleties of meaning, the passion of speeches, and even to produce total misunderstandings. The classic case occurred in the late 1990s. A French MEP was lamenting that discussion of an issue was not employing the common sense of the country people of Normandy, from where he hailed. Those hearing the English translation, however, were told that to solve this problem, we need Norman wisdom. To a large section of his audience – those familiar with the British comedian called Norman Wisdom – the serious point this MEP was seeking to make was thus entirely lost.

KEY POINTS

- The membership of the EP comes from many different national political parties, is increasingly dominated by full-time MEPs, and now includes a significant number of 'Eurosceptics' as well as integration enthusiasts.
- Party groups draw together individual national party delegations into broadly ideological collectives. The groups often have to compromise among different national viewpoints. The groups organize much of the work of the EP.
- Committees are where much of the detailed work of the EP is done. They provide opportunities for individual MEPs to make an impact on policy.
- EP plenary sessions are hampered by translation problems, and, with rare exceptions, tend to be dull and undramatic.

Elections, the people, and the European Parliament

Elected parliaments are a central, defining feature of democratic political systems. Their importance is more than simply symbolic. That institutions comprising the chosen representatives of the people are able to debate and give assent to major items of public policy, to voice public grievances, and to hold the executive to account, plays an important practical role in the legitimation of public authority. Put more simply, elected parliaments connect the people to the political system, and make legitimate the things done in the name of that political system. As the elected institution in the EU, how well does the European Parliament connect the people to the Union, and help legitimate the exercise of public authority at a European level?

EP elections are, in many respects, quite extraordinary exercises in democratic politics. In June 2004, many millions of people across 25 different countries voted (or at least were able to vote if they so wished) for a common legislative institution. (Table 11.2 summarizes the number of MEPs elected in each country and how.) This is an event that has no close equivalent anywhere in the world, and to many people has had a powerful symbolism. But when one examines the elections more closely it becomes more difficult to sustain one's enthusiasm. EP elections are generally characterized by low turnouts, campaigns that fail to address seriously major issues facing the EU, and little popular interest or engagement.

Public participation in European elections is almost invariably at much lower levels than in national parliamentary elections. Moreover, as Figure 11.1 shows, average turnout levels across the Union have fallen in each of the last five elections, even as the EP has seen its powers rise. Research on EP elections has suggested that one major reason for low (and declining) turnout is the widespread public perception that the elections are relatively unimportant. Such perceptions are in turn facilitated by the behaviour of political parties: in most member states, the major parties tend to focus their campaigns for EP elections on familiar national issues. While the behaviour of parties is quite rational (emphasizing the themes most salient to voters), the outcome is election campaigns that do little to educate voters about the EU, or persuade them that there is much substantively at stake when they go to the polls. Rather, EP elections are treated by most parties and the vast majority of voters as 'second-order national elections', rather than contests where alternative visions of 'Europe' might be offered, debated about, and decided upon by voters (van der Eijk and Franklin 1996). Given that the elections are

Table 11.2 Representation in the European Parliament

Country	No. of MEPs	Population (millions)	Constituency type	People per constituency (average, millions)
Austria	18	8.1	National	8.1
Belgium	24	10.2	Regional	3.4
Cyprus	6	0.8	National	0.8
Czech Rep.	24	10.3	National	10.3
Denmark	14	5.3	National	5.3
Estonia	6	1.4	National	1.4
Finland	14	5.1	National	5.1
France	78	60.4	Regional	7.6
Germany	99	82.0	National	82.0
Greece	24	10.5	National	10.5
Hungary	24	10.2	National	10.2
Ireland	13	3.7	Regional	0.9
Italy	78	57.6	National	57.6
Latvia	9	2.4	National	2.4
Lithuania	13	3.5	National	3.5
Lux.	6	0.4	National	0.4
Malta	5	0.4	National	0.4
Netherlands	27	15.8	National	15.8
Poland	54	38.6	National	38.6
Portugal	24	10.8	National	10.8
Slovakia	14	5.4	National	5.4
Slovenia	7	2.0	National	2.0
Spain	54	39.4	National	39.4
Sweden	19	8.9	National	8.9
UK	78	58.6	Regional	4.9

widely perceived as not mattering much, many voters take the opportunity to deliver a 'protest vote' against government parties, who tend to do worse than opposition parties. But recent elections have also witnessed growing support for explicitly Eurosceptic or anti-EU parties, who now have significant representation in the EP (see Table 11.3).

Direct measures of public attitudes indicate very limited public awareness of the European Parliament. Though political elites now recognize the growing importance of the chamber, there is little or no evidence of this translating into public perceptions of a similar nature. The *Eurobarometer* survey of public opinion across the EU conducted in summer 2005 found 90 per cent of citizens claiming to have heard of the EP. However, merely one year after the previous set of elections to the institution, only 50 per cent of the sample knew that the Parliament was directly elected by EU citizens (*Eurobarometer* 63)! The survey evidence does not suggest public hostility to the EP; more simply that the majority of the public neither know nor care enough to develop anything as active as hostility. Answers to survey questions about the Parliament by most citizens almost certainly embody a high degree of what public opinion specialists term 'non-attitudes': in short, voters may be able to answer a question on the EP, but such answers draw on little more than a general attitude towards the EU as a whole. Overall, it is difficult to dissent from the view that the Parliament suffers from a 'failure to even begin to penetrate the consciousness of so many of its electors' (Blondel *et al.* 1998: 242).

Figure 11.1 Turnout levels in six EP elections

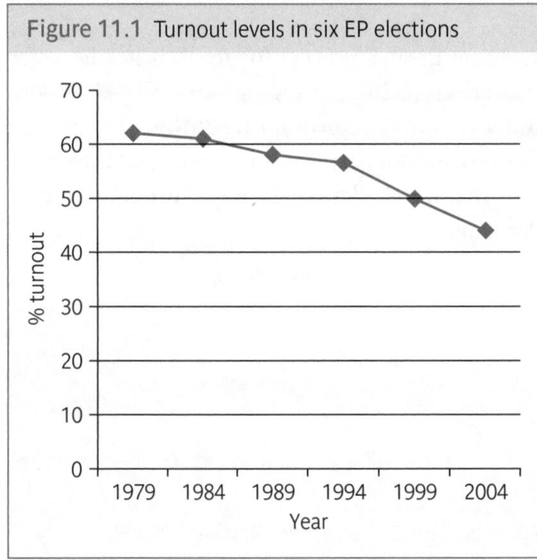

Does this matter? Probably so, in two respects. It matters in an immediate sense for the EU as a whole. As stated earlier, elected parliaments are normally vital for the legitimation of the wider political system of which they are a part. Some in the EU have hoped that enhancing the powers of the elected institution might enhance the wider public legitimacy of European-level governance. Thus far, there is no sign that this strategy has worked or will work – the public popularity of the EU has generally declined as the EP has grown in powers. And, in addition to this general implication for the EU, there is a specific implication for the EP itself. The Parliament has used its status as an elected body as an effective lever with which to gain its own empowerment. The EP's failure to build strong public support, either for itself or for the wider Union, may well lead in time to a fundamental questioning of the EP's role. As one sympathetic observer has suggested, 'it risks . . . [an] insidious withering away of its basis of legitimacy because of voter disinterest' (Neunreither 2000: 135; see also Scully 2000).

Table 11.3 The European Parliament after the 2004 elections

Party group	Political orientation	No. of MEPs (% of total)
European People's Party/ European Democrats	Centre-right (Christian Democrats & Conservatives)	268 (36.6%)
Party of European Socialists	Centre-left	200 (27.3%)
Alliance of Liberals and Democrats	Liberal	88 (12.0%)
European United Left/Nordic Green Left	Left-wing	42 (5.7%)
Greens/European Free Alliance	Environmentalist & some Regionalists	41 (5.6%)
Independence/Democracy	Eurosceptic/anti-EU	37 (5.1%)
Europe of Nations	Eurosceptic and generally right-wing	27 (3.7%)
Non-attached	Various	29 (4.0%)

KEY POINTS

- As the elected institution, the EP ought to link the people and the EU, and thus build legitimacy for the Union.
- EP elections see low (and falling) turnout levels, and little debate about Europe featuring in the campaigns.
- Public knowledge of the EP is very limited, and this lack of public awareness and interest may bring the role of an elected EP into question.

Conclusion

The European Parliament is no longer a marginal part of the European Union's political system. It is a significant player in making EU policy, and it is thus important that students of the Union understand how the EP works. However, while the Parliament has been strikingly successful in accruing greater powers for itself, it has been far less effective in developing a profile with and support from the peoples of Europe. Addressing this task, rather than gaining powers, is surely now the major challenge facing Europe's elected Parliament.

QUESTIONS

1. If the EP had been a powerful institution right from the beginning, how might the EU have developed differently?
2. Why did national governments increase the powers of the EP during the 1980s and 1990s?
3. Are there further powers that the EP ought to seek, in addition to those it now has?
4. Some people have suggested that the European Commission be elected from among the membership of the EP, rather than being separate from the Parliament and nominated by national governments. How might this innovation alter the internal politics of the EP if it were ever implemented?
5. Are MEPs European politicians, national ones, both, or neither?
6. Are European Parliament elections a waste of time?
7. What practical steps could the EP take to build awareness of and support for the institution among the European public?

GUIDE TO FURTHER READING

■ Corbett, R. *The European Parliament's Role in Closer EU Integration* (London: Macmillan, 1998). A detailed historical study of the EP's efforts to promote European integration and enhance its own role, written by someone heavily involved in the process.

■ Hix, S., and Scully, R. *The European Parliament at Fifty: Special Issue of the Journal of Common Market Studies*, 41(2), 2003. An important collection of articles, focused around the fiftieth anniversary of the EP's creation.

■ Jacobs, F., Corbett, R., and Shackleton, M. *The European Parliament*, 5th edn (London: John Harper, 2005). A superb introduction to the ins-and-outs of the EP, written by two long-time parliamentary officials and one MEP.

■ Kreppel, A. *The European Parliament and the Supranational Party System: A Study in Institutional Development* (Cambridge: Cambridge University Press, 2002). An excellent study of the development of the EP's party group system.

■ Rittberger, B. *Building Europe's Parliament: Democratic Representation Beyond the Nation State* (Oxford: Oxford University Press, 2005). By far the best scholarly study of the historical development of the EP.

■ Scully, R. *Becoming Europeans? Attitudes, Behaviour and Socialisation in the European Parliament* (Oxford: Oxford University Press, 2005). A study refuting widespread conjectures about MEPs 'going native' in Europe, and drawing some important implications from this finding for how we understand and study the EP.

■ Steunenberg, B., and Thomassen, J. (eds) *The European Parliament on the Move: Towards Parliamentary Democracy in Europe?* (London: Rowman & Littlefield, 2005). A collection of interesting articles about many aspects of the EP.

■ van der Eijk, C., and Franklin, M. (eds) *Choosing Europe? The European Electorate and National Politics in the Face of Union* (Ann Arbor, MI: University of Michigan Press, 1996). The classic – though pessimistic – study of European Parliament elections and all their faults.

IMPORTANT WEBSITES

● www.europarl.eu.int This is the homepage for the EP's own multilingual website, with considerable information on the members and activities of the Parliament, and links to official documents.

● www.lse.ac.uk/Depts/eprg This is the homepage for the European Parliament Research Group, a multinational team of researchers who study the EP. The page includes contact details of leading scholars, details of published work and ongoing research, and a series of working papers.

● www.elections2004.eu.int This link contains detailed election results for EP elections, analysed by party group and by member state.

Visit the Online Resource Centre that accompanies this book for lots of interesting additional material. http://www.oxfordtextbooks.co.uk/orc/cini2e/

12 The Courts of the European Union

ILIAS KAPSIS

Chapter Contents

Reader's Guide

This chapter examines the organization, jurisdiction, procedure, and role of the courts of the European Union. These consist of the Court of Justice (ECJ), the Court of First Instance (CFI), and the European Civil Service Tribunal, which was created in 2004 as a result of the judicial reform introduced by the Treaty of Nice. The chapter focuses on the courts' jurisdiction under the first, supranational pillar of the EU, the European Community (see Figures 3.1 and 3.2 on the EU pillars). The chapter looks to the powers conferred on the courts by the Community Treaties and to the way in which the courts have exercised these powers. Jurisdictional issues, such as infringement proceedings, judicial review, and preliminary rulings, are considered in this context. The chapter also looks at the criticism the ECJ has attracted because of the way in which it has exercised its powers. Lastly, the chapter examines the judicial reform which was introduced by the Treaty of Nice in order to improve the efficiency of the Community Courts.

Introduction

The judicial branch of the European Union comprises the Court of Justice (ECJ), the Court of First Instance (CFI) and, after the entry into force of the Treaty of Nice in 2003, the 'judicial panels'. Together, these courts have the task of ensuring that the law is observed in the interpretation and application of the Treaties constituting the European Union. In addition to these courts, there is a Court of Auditors (CoA) whose function it is to 'examine the accounts of all revenue and expenditure of the Community'. However, the roles of the ECJ and the CFI are more important for the EU citizens and therefore this chapter will focus on these two courts and on the judicial panels, which are attached to the CFI (but on the CoA see Laffan 1999).

The Court of Justice is a creature of the Treaty establishing the European Coal and Steel Community (ECSC), which was signed by six European states (Belgium, France, Germany, Italy, Luxemburg, and the Netherlands) in 1951. The signing of the ECSC Treaty constituted the first step towards the unification of Europe. The Court was one of the institutions created to serve the new European Community and it was given the task of ensuring that 'in the interpretation and application of this Treaty and of rules laid down for the interpretation thereof, the law is observed'. The Court's powers were further expanded in 1957 when the same states signed two new Treaties in Rome: the Treaty establishing the European Economic Community (EEC), later renamed the European Community (EC), and the Treaty establishing the European Atomic Energy Community (Euratom). The Court was given the task of serving all three Communities. Thus, the Court emerged as a supranational court, which had compulsory jurisdiction covering all areas falling within the scope of the three Treaties. The Court's jurisdiction covered such issues as interpretation of Community law and determination of rights and obligations. Its decisions were binding on Community institutions, member states, and individuals.

In 1986, as the number of member states of the Communities had significantly grown, the Single European Act (SEA), which amended the three Treaties (ECSC, EEC, and Euratom), introduced the notion of a single European Community consisting of all three Communities. Amongst other issues, the SEA provided for the establishment of a court of first instance to be attached to the Court of Justice. The Court of First Instance commenced operations in 1989. The SEA also excluded from the jurisdiction of the ECJ matters relating to foreign policy.

The establishment of a new structure, the European Union (EU), by the Maastricht Treaty (officially known as the Treaty on the European Union), in 1992, constituted a big step forward for European integration, but had initially, at least, little impact on the powers of the ECJ. In particular, the new entity had broader scope than the European Community, which was oriented mostly towards economic integration, and established two new areas of integration: Common Foreign and Security Policy (CFSP); and Justice and Home Affairs (JHA). In the three-pillared structure of the EU, the European Community formed the first and most important pillar, with CFSP and JHA forming the second and third pillars respectively. The first pillar, whose scope was expanded with provisions for the establishment of a European Monetary Union (EMU) and a so-called 'Social Charter' intended to give a social dimension to the Community, remained 'supranational' in nature, with the Community institutions and legal structures playing a central role in policy and law-making. The first pillar remained under the jurisdiction of the ECJ. In respect of the second and third pillars, they were kept at a distance from the Community institutional and legal structures and largely beyond the jurisdiction of the ECJ. The new pillars concerned sensitive areas of policy touching upon core issues of national sovereignty, and therefore the governments considered it more appropriate that the new pillars should remain intergovernmental and outside the institutional and legal structure of the Community. As regards the Court, an additional reason for its exclusion was related to concerns raised by some governments over the Court's 'judicial activism', a term used to describe practices of the Court aimed at strengthening its powers and role in the Community and promoting European integration. Certain aspects of this activism, which are examined later in the chapter, were seen by opponents to run counter to national interests, and this played a role in its exclusion.

The Treaty of Amsterdam, which in 1997 amended the Maastricht Treaty, gave new powers to the Court, particularly with regard to the third pillar. Furthermore, the Treaty of Nice, which entered into force in 2003, introduced further amendments, bringing about a judicial reform. Under the new provisions, the CFI is no longer attached to the ECJ but is a court in its own right. The Treaty of Nice also provided for the establishment of specialized 'judicial panels' attached to the CFI. The first such judicial panel, the Civil Service Tribunal, was established in 2004. Lastly, the Constitutional Treaty confirmed the new structure and gave additional powers to the Court of Justice, though this treaty has not entered into force (see Chapter 4).

Since the Community pillar of the Union is the most developed and significant, and the European Courts' jurisdiction and role in this area are crucial for European integration and have therefore had the greatest practical importance, this chapter will focus on the developments in this area. The term 'Community Courts' will be used to describe the jurisdiction and the role of the ECJ, the CFI, and the judicial panels in the legal order of the European Community (the first pillar).

Composition, structure, and procedure

The ECJ is based in Luxembourg. It is the Court of the EU and has no relationship with two other European courts: the European Court of Human Rights, based in Strasbourg, which was established under the European Convention on Human Rights, and the International Court of Justice, based in The Hague (Netherlands), which is attached to the United Nations.

The ECJ is made up of 25 judges (one judge per member state) whose duty it is to perform the tasks assigned to the Court by the Treaties. Eight Advocates-General (AGs) assist the Court by delivering opinions in open court on cases brought before the ECJ. AGs give a second opinion on the case (though the opinion is published prior to the judges' decision). They have the same status as judges, act with 'complete impartiality and independence', and their opinions, even if not binding on the Court, have a real impact on its decisions. The Court also appoints a registrar for six years who is responsible for procedural and administrative matters.

The judges and AGs of the ECJ are selected from persons 'whose independence is beyond doubt and who possess the qualifications required for appointment to the highest judicial offices in their respective countries or who are jurisconsults of recognised competence'. The appointment of female judges is very rare and for many decades there was no female judge in the ECJ. The first, Fidelma Mackem, was appointed by Ireland in 1999. The member states nominate judges in accordance with their national traditions. They are usually academics, law practitioners, or domestic judges. Nationality is not a criterion of selection. However, as regards the AGs, each of the five largest member states appoints one AG and the remaining member states appoint on a rotational basis the other three.

The appointment of all judges must be 'by common accord of the governments of the member states'. The process is private, taking the form of a diplomatic meeting, which has given rise to criticism that it does not meet democratic standards. The judges are appointed for staggered terms of six years, which allows for a partial replacement of either 13 or 12 judges every three years. They are eligible for reappointment and there is no retirement date. The British Advocate-General, Francis Jacobs, has been at the Court since 1988. The judges and AGs cannot be removed during their term in office and their duties end on their death or resignation. A judge or AG can be dismissed by a unanimous decision of the other judges and AGs if he or she no longer fulfils the requisite conditions or meets the obligations arising from the office.

The judges elect the President by a secret ballot for a renewable three-year term. The President's main duties are to direct the judicial and administrative activities of the Court and preside over sessions of the Grand Chamber. Following the same method of election as the judges, the AGs elect the First Advocate-General for a one-year term.

The ECJ sits in chambers of three or five judges or in a Grand Chamber consisting of 13 judges. In exceptional cases the Court sits as a full court. The Chambers are presided over by their respective President of Chamber who is elected by the same process used to elect the President of the Court.

The procedure before the ECJ has a written and an oral stage. The written stage involves the submission to the Court and the communication to the parties of the application, and of all the relevant documents of the case (statements, defences, and so on). In the oral stage, the *judge-rapporteur*, the judge assigned to the case, issues a report for the hearing, which sets out the facts of the case and summarizes the legal arguments put forward by the parties to the dispute. Following oral submissions by the parties and the AG, and the hearing of any witnesses or experts, the Court will put some questions to the parties and will then decide the case by issuing its judgment. This is signed by all of the judges, and there are no dissenting opinions. The judgment, which is delivered in open court, is then published, with a summary provided in the EU's Official Journal (OJ) and a more detailed version in the official law report.

The Court of First Instance consists of 'at least' one judge per member state and currently has 25 judges. It commenced operations in 1989, and was created to lessen the workload of the ECJ, relieving it of less important cases (Hartley 2003: 60). The CFI was initially 'attached' to the ECJ, meaning that it was not strictly a separate body. However, following the Treaty of Nice amendments, the CFI no longer has this relationship with the ECJ, and more cases have been transferred to it.

The rules for the appointment of judges of the CFI and their terms of office are the same as those for the ECJ judges. The CFI judges are selected from persons whose independence is beyond doubt and who possess the 'ability required for appointment to high judicial office'. It has no AGs but, when necessary, one of its judges will be appointed to perform the task of an AG. The judges of the CFI elect a President for a renewable three-year term, and appoint a Registrar.

The CFI sits in Chambers of three or five judges. It may sit in a Grand Chamber of 13 judges, and may also be constituted by a single judge. In special cases it sits as a full court. The judgments of the CFI are subject to appeal to the ECJ. Like the ECJ, the CFI delivers its judgments in open court following written and oral proceedings. There are no dissenting opinions.

Finally, the European Civil Service Tribunal was created in 2005 as a result of the entry into force of the Treaty of Nice. This provides for the establishment of specialized 'judicial panels' attached to the CFI. These panels are intended to reduce the workload of the CFI by relieving it of cases in specific areas. The European Union Civil Service Tribunal is intended to deal with disputes involving the Communities and their servants. This Tribunal consists of seven judges appointed for a six-year term. The judges are selected from former members of the ECJ and the CFI and lawyers of recognized competence. They must be persons whose independence is beyond doubt and must possess the ability required for appointment to judicial office. The Tribunal, which elects its own President, sits in Chambers of three judges. In certain cases it may also sit in a Chamber of five judges or of a single judge or in full Court. The procedure before the Tribunal has a written and an oral stage. The oral stage may be cancelled in cases where in the written stage a need arises for a second exchange of written pleadings. The decisions of the Tribunal can be appealed on points of law to the CFI.

KEY POINTS

- The ECJ is composed of 25 judges and eight Advocates-General (AGs) whose duty is to perform the tasks assigned to the Court by the Treaties.
- The CFI was created to lessen the workload of the European Court. It consists of 25 judges. There are no permanent AGs.
- The European Civil Service Tribunal is attached to the CFI and consists of seven judges.

Jurisdiction

The EC Treaty requires the Community Courts to ensure the enforcement of Community law. To achieve this objective the Treaty confers on them specific powers, which include: the power to ensure the compliance of the member states with the provisions of the Community law; the power to ensure that the institutions of the Community act within their powers under Community law; the power to assist national courts with the application of Community law; the power to review the legality of Community legislation; and to fill existing gaps in legislation.

As far as judgments are concerned, the distinction is often made between direct actions and references for preliminary rulings. Both have played a crucial role in the establishment of the Community's legal order and have shaped the relationship between the Community law and the national law of the member states.

Direct actions

Direct actions begin and end in the Community Courts. The Community Courts also examine appeals against these decisions. The ECJ examines appeals against decisions of the CFI, while the CFI examines appeals against decisions of the European Civil Service Tribunal. The decisions of the ECJ are not subject to appeal, however. In exceptional cases the ECJ also reviews the CFI's appeal decisions against decisions of the Tribunal. The scope of the appeals is limited to points of law and factual issues are not examined.

Direct actions can be brought by individuals and 'legal persons', such as companies and organizations, and by member states or Community institutions. Actions brought by individuals and legal persons are dealt with by the CFI and on appeal by the ECJ. In 2004 and in accordance with the Treaty of Nice amendments, the ECJ transferred to the CFI jurisdiction over certain direct actions brought by member states against Community institutions. The transferred cases were previously reviewed by the ECJ. Also, the establishment of the European Civil Service Tribunal resulted in the transfer of certain specific categories of cases from the CFI to the jurisdiction of this Tribunal, namely those involving disputes between the Community and its civil servants. The CFI examines appeals against decisions of the Tribunal.

There are two main types of direct action: infringement proceedings against member states and actions for judicial review seeking either to annul an unlawful Community measure or to force a Community institution to adopt a Community measure which it had previously wrongfully failed to adopt.

The EC Treaty provides the Commission with power to bring proceedings before the ECJ against member states that have failed to fulfil their obligations under the Treaty. Such a situation may arise, for instance, if a provision of national law is inconsistent with Community law. The Commission has made frequent use of infringement proceedings because they are an 'important weapon for ensuring compliance by the member states with their Treaty obligations' (Arnull 1999: 23). The Treaty grants the same power as that of the Commission to the member states but the latter use it rarely. The Commission regularly monitors member state compliance with Community law and this has helped to detect infringements. Complaints from citizens have also been a crucial way of detecting infringements, and the Commission has worked with the European Ombudsman to create a formalized system for processing them.

The infringement procedure has an administrative stage, during which most cases are solved, and a judicial stage, which follows the failure of the administrative procedure. The purpose of the administrative stage is to give the member state an opportunity to justify its position and, as the case may be, to enable the Commission to persuade the member state to comply of its own accord with the requirements of the Treaty. At this stage the Commission informs the member state of the alleged infringement and invites it to submit its observations on the issue. If the member state's response and subsequent discussions with the Commission fail to solve the problem, the Commission will issue a ***reasoned opinion***, which will state the factual and legal grounds on which the alleged infringement is based, setting a deadline for the state's compliance. If the state fails to comply with the opinion within the time period laid down by the Commission, the Commission may bring the case to the Court.

The judicial stage begins at this point. The ECJ, which enjoys full jurisdiction, examines all issues, seeking to determine whether the alleged infringement has actually occurred. If the Court concludes that infringement has occurred, it will declare that the member state has failed to fulfil an obligation under the Treaty. However, the Court has no power to *order* the member state to do anything (or desist from doing something), even if the state is obliged by the Treaty to comply with the Court's judgment. If it does not comply it will have committed *another* Treaty infringement, for which a new action before the Court may be taken. Although member states generally comply with the Court's judgments, there have been some cases where compliance has not occurred. Therefore the Maastricht Treaty, which amended the EC Treaty, gave the Court power to impose fines on disobedient member states.

The Court also found another way to increase pressure on member states to comply with Community law. In the famous *Francovich* case (1991), examined under the preliminary rulings procedures (see below), the ECJ ruled that a member state is liable to compensate individuals in this way for the loss they suffered as a result of a breach of Community law for which it is responsible (see Box 12.1). The possibility of compensation to individuals reduced the significance of the rule on fines, though this is still useful where the application of the *Francovich* principle cannot be effective.

Judicial review of Community acts by the ECJ is intended to ensure that Community institutions act within the powers given to them by the Treaties. In democratic states the constitution normally sets limits to the powers exercisable by governmental bodies, and the role of the courts is to ensure that these bodies act only within prescribed limits. In the Community, where there is no formal constitution, the Treaties perform this function and give specific powers to the Community institutions. The role of Community Courts is to ensure, through the process of judicial review, that the institutions act within these powers.

The EC Treaty gives the ECJ power to review the legality of acts adopted jointly by the European Parliament and the Council, acts of the Council, the Commission, and the Central Bank, other than recommendations or opinions, and acts of the European Parliament intended to produce legal effects vis-à-vis third parties. The Court's powers

 CASE STUDY 12.1

State liability for breach of Community law – *Francovich and Bonifaci vs. Italy* (1991)

The applicants in this case brought proceedings against Italy before the ECJ for failure to implement EC Directive 80/987, which provided employees with a minimum level of protection in the event of their employers' insolvency. The Directive provided that the member states should give specific guarantees of payment of unpaid wage claims. The applicants, who were owed wages from their insolvent employers, sued the Italian government claiming that the latter had to pay them either the sums payable under the Directive or compensation for the damages suffered due to the non-implementation of the Directive.

The ECJ rejected the first argument but accepted the second, concerning the right to compensation. The Court stated that the EC Treaty had created its own legal system which was an integral part of the legal systems of the member states and which their courts were obliged to apply. The system created by the Treaty was affecting both the member states and individuals by imposing on them obligations or giving them rights. The national courts when applying Community law had to ensure that the rights conferred on individuals by the Treaty were adequately protected. The full effectiveness of Community law would be impaired and the protection of rights which it grants would be weakened if individuals were unable to obtain compensation when their rights were infringed by a breach of Community law for which a member state was responsible. As a result, the principle of state liability for breaches of Community law is inherent in the system.

The Court found further support for its argument in Article 5 (now 10) EC, which provides that member states are required to take all appropriate measures to ensure fulfilment of their obligations under Community law, including the obligation to nullify the unlawful consequences of a breach of Community law.

The importance of the Court's ruling in *Francovich* is that by establishing for the first time state liability for breaches of Community law, it opened the way for individuals of the Community to claim compensation for the damages suffered as a result of the breach. The principle of state liability was further explained and developed in subsequent Court decisions.

cover not only binding Community acts (see Box 12.2), but also any other act which has binding force or which produces legal effects. If the action taken is successful, the Court will declare void the act concerned.

The grounds on which an action of annulment can be based are: lack of competence (for example, where a Community institution adopts an act which it has no power to adopt under the Treaty); infringement of an essential procedural requirement (for example, where the institution fails to comply with a requirement to give reasons for its decision); infringement of the Treaty or of any rule of law relating to its application (for example, where the institution's act violates an express prohibition stated in a Treaty provision); and misuse of powers (for example, where the institution exercises its powers for a purpose other than that for which these powers were provided by the Treaty).

There are three categories of applicant that can bring annulment procedures: the member states, the Council, the Commission and, following the Treaty of Nice amendments, the European Parliament. These are considered 'privileged applicants' who are presumed to have interest in the legality of all types of Community act and therefore always have the right to bring procedures. The European Central Bank and the Court of Auditors have 'semi-privileged' status, meaning that they can bring procedures only to protect their prerogatives. Natural and legal persons (for example, companies), the so-called 'non-privileged' applicants, can bring procedures only if the Community act in question is addressed to them or is of direct and individual concern to them.

Individuals are included in the 'non-privileged' category, because there is a real risk that a huge number of individual applications could disrupt the normal operations of the Court and the Community. However, individuals seeking to challenge Community acts not addressed to them can bring procedures before their national court where

KEY CONCEPTS AND TERMS 12.2

Types of binding Community act

Article 249 EC provides for three main types of binding acts:

- *Regulations*: have general application and are binding and directly applicable in all member states. Directly applicable means that they do not normally require the adoption of measures for their implementation by member states.
- *Directives*: are addressed to all or some of the member states. They are binding as to the result to be achieved, but leave to the national authorities the choice of form and methods. This means that directives lay down specific objectives which have to be achieved by specific dates and leave to the discretion of the member states the decision on the best way to achieve these objectives.
- *Decisions*: are addressed to individuals and are binding in their entirety.

The ECJ has ruled that the list of Community acts in Article 249 is not exhaustive and therefore it is possible that an act has a legally binding character even if it does not fall into any of the three categories mentioned above.

they can contest the validity of the Community act. In such cases the national court may, and in some cases *must*, refer a question on the validity of the Community act in question to the ECJ, through the preliminary ruling procedure,.

Apart from the annulment of unlawful Community acts, the EC Treaty also provides for action in cases where a Community institution has failed to act in an infringement of the Treaty. This procedure can be brought against the European Parliament, the Council, and the Commission only in situations where the failure of the institution concerns acts producing legal effects (see Box 12.2). Non-privileged applicants can apply only if the act is addressed to them. If the application is successful, the infringement will be established and the institution is required to take action. The Court's judgment has only a declaratory character, however, and the institution retains discretion over the content and form of the act as is conferred on it by the provision requiring the act to be performed.

References for preliminary rulings

Community Courts share responsibility for applying Community law with the courts of member states. Community law may arise in national courts through its directly applicable provisions (for example, regulations) or through its application by national agencies (for example, measures of implementation of directives taken by a member state).

The increasing number of matters covered by Community law due to the deepening of European integration and the need to achieve uniform interpretation and application of Community law in the territory of member states have made necessary the development of a cooperative relationship between the Community Courts and the national courts. This cooperative relationship is based on a system of references according to which national courts can, and in some cases must, refer to the ECJ issues of Community law arising in cases examined by them. The ECJ will rule on these issues and then will send the cases back to the national courts, which will apply the Community law, as proposed by the ECJ, to the facts of the cases at hand. The ECJ's rulings are **interlocutory**, meaning that they constitute only intermediate stages in the proceedings, which begin and end in the national courts. The national courts are under no obligation to apply Community law in the cases for which references to the ECJ were made, but if they do apply it, they are bound by the Court's rulings.

The EC Treaty provides the ECJ with jurisdiction to give preliminary rulings on the interpretation of the Treaty; the validity and interpretation of acts of the institutions of the Community and of the European Central Bank; and the interpretation of the statutes of bodies established by an act of the Council, where those statutes so provide. In addition the Treaty of Amsterdam extended, in a modified form, the ECJ's jurisdiction regarding preliminary rulings to cases related to the new Title IV of the EC Treaty which deals with 'Visas, Asylum, Immigration, and other Policies related to the free movement of persons'. Also, in accordance with Article 35 of the Treaty on the European Union, which deals with 'Police and Judicial co-operation in Criminal matters' in the context of remodelled Pillar 3, the ECJ is provided with jurisdiction to give preliminary rulings only in cases referred to it from courts in the member states which have accepted the Court's jurisdiction by making a declaration. Prior to the Treaty of Nice, only the ECJ could give preliminary rulings. The Treaty of Nice conferred on the CFI powers to give such rulings in specific cases.

The preliminary rulings procedure has been used to serve several Community objectives, such as to achieve uniform interpretation and application of Community law by member states, to establish a supranational Community legal order, to familiarize national courts with the Community legal order, to determine the situations in which Community law is directly applicable in the territory of member states, and to shape the relationship between national and Community law.

From the numerous decisions adopted under the procedure particular emphasis should be given to the ECJ's rulings on the direct effect of Community law, which opened the way for the establishment of the Community as a new supranational legal order independent of the legal orders of the member states. Regarding relations between Community law and national law for which the EC Treaty does not provide any guidance, the ECJ decided in favour of Community law, holding that national courts should give primacy to Community law over incompatible national law.

In more detail, in the *Van Gend en Loos* case (see Box 12.3), which constitutes one of the most important judgments ever handed down by the ECJ, the Court held that the Community constitutes a new legal order which not only imposes obligations, but also confers rights on individuals independently of the legislation of the member states. This is known as the principle of direct effect. The EC Treaty is therefore capable of creating individual rights, which national courts must then protect.

CASE STUDY 12.3

The establishment of a Community legal order – *Van Gend en Loos vs. Nederlandse Administratie der Belastingen* (1963)

The Van Gend en Loos Company imported from Germany into the Netherlands a chemical substance. The Dutch authorities charged the company an import duty, which Van Gend en Loos claimed had been increased since the entry into force of the EEC Treaty, contrary to Article 12 (now 25) of that Treaty. The Dutch court, which examined the dispute, referred two questions to the ECJ, one of which was whether Article 12 conferred individual rights which the national courts were bound to protect.

The ECJ responded as follows:

The Community constitutes a new legal order of international law for the benefit of which the states have limited their sovereign rights, albeit within limited fields, and the subjects of which comprise not only member states but also their nationals. Independently of the legislation of the member states, Community law therefore not only imposes obligations on individuals but is also intended to confer upon them rights which become part of their legal heritage. These rights arise not only where they are expressly granted by the Treaty, but also by reason of obligations which the Treaty imposes in a clearly defined way upon individuals as well as upon the member states and upon institutions of the Community.

The Court concluded that according to the spirit, the general scheme, and the wording of the Treaty, Article 12 must be interpreted as producing *direct effects* and creating *individual rights* which national courts must protect.

The importance of *Van Gend en Loos* lies in the fact that it confirmed the binding nature of Community law for member states and required that member states should internalize it – often without the need for any national implementing measures – within their domestic legal system. Without such a ruling, the uniform application of Community law by member states could have been difficult to ensure, since some member states follow a 'dualist' approach to international law, according to which the domestic effect of international Treaties, such as the EC Treaty, is determined in accordance with the constitutional law of each of the states that are parties to the Treaty. In countries following a dualist approach, for example the United Kingdom, international agreements do not have direct effect, meaning that they do not confer any rights on their citizens unless these countries take domestic measures, for example through legislation, to implement them. However, in other countries, which follow a 'monist' approach, the automatic application of international agreements in their territory (direct effect) is possible.

Where some member states follow the dualist approach and others the monist one, the absence of a Court ruling like that in *Van Gend en Loos* could have resulted in a situation where the EC Treaty would have conferred individual rights on the citizens of some member states but not on the citizens of others. This could have undermined the creation of a common market.

The ECJ, in subsequent decisions, further developed the concept of direct effect. A provision of Community law can be **directly effective** if it is sufficiently clear, precise, and unconditional. Both EC Treaty provisions and regulations can be enforced not only against member states (so-called vertical direct effect), but also against individuals (so-called horizontal direct effect). Directives can produce vertical direct effect but, unlike regulations and Treaty provisions, they cannot produce horizontal direct effect.

The relationship between Community law and national law was examined by the ECJ in the *Costa vs. ENEL* (1964) case, which concerned a reference from an Italian court. In its *Costa vs. ENEL* decision, the ECJ built on *Van Gend en Loos*. It held that Community law irrespective of its nature (for example whether it is a Treaty provision, or the provision of a Directive), due to its special and original character, could not be overridden by domestic law, irrespective of the nature of national law (for example whether it is a constitutional provision or a statutory provision). Otherwise the special character of Community law would be undermined and the existence of a Community legal order called into question.

A reference for preliminary ruling may be made by any court or tribunal of the member states. This includes any national institution exercising judicial functions in accordance with Community law, even if it does not constitute a court or tribunal in accordance with national law. The EC Treaty distinguishes between national courts whose decisions are subject to a judicial remedy (for example appeal) under national law, and national courts whose decisions are final. The former are given discretion to refer to the European Court, while the latter are under obligation to refer.

Following the submission of a reference for a preliminary ruling to the ECJ the referring court has to suspend the proceedings before it and await the ECJ's ruling. Subsequently the ECJ's ruling is binding on the referring court, which has to apply it to the case in which the reference was made.

KEY POINTS

- Direct actions begin and end in the Community Courts. They can be brought by individuals and 'legal persons', such as companies and organizations, and by member states or Community institutions.
- There are two main types of direct action: infringement proceedings against member states, and actions for judicial review.

The 'judicial activism' debate

The Community Courts have played a crucial role in the process of European integration. The ECJ, in particular, has persistently pursued legal integration in the territory of the Community by 'giving flesh and substance to an outline Treaty' (Craig and De Búrca 2002: 87), filling in gaps in the European legislation, and enhancing the effective application of Community law in the territory of the member states.

The text of the Treaties often uses language which is extremely vague, and does not define crucial terms. In such cases the ECJ has had to use its creative capabilities in order to achieve a satisfactory interpretation and application of Community law. Moreover, the Treaties provide the Community Courts with only limited jurisdiction by requiring these Courts to perform only specific tasks. Over the years, however, the ECJ has used the gaps and vagueness in areas of Community law to remove the barrier of limited jurisdiction and thus to expand its powers and role. The Court has also persistently sought to use its expanded powers to promote European integration.

This ECJ activism has been criticized as disregarding the Treaties and promoting the Court's own political agenda of European integration. Hjalte Rasmussen (1986), one of the most vocal critics of the Court, argued that this was 'a dangerous social evil' and that the Court's excessive activism was threatening to undermine its authority and legitimacy. A few years later Sir Patrick Neill (1995) contended that the Court was uncontrollable and dangerous, as its decisions were 'logically flawed or skewed by doctrinal or idiosyncratic policy considerations', that the Court was seeking to take 'more power into its own hands', and that it was driven by a special elite mission. In 1998, Rasmussen further accused the Court of 'federalizing' the Treaties in disrespect of the 'legal commands of the treaties texts' (Douglas-Scott 2002: 211). Some critics were particularly concerned that the ECJ's policy to strengthen the role of the Community was at the expense of the interests of the member states.

The decisions that attracted the most criticism were those establishing and strengthening the Community as a legal order, independent of the legal orders of the member states, and those giving precedence to Community law and institutions over national law and institutions. The relevant ECJ decisions included those establishing the doctrine of direct effect (*Van Gend en Loos*); prohibiting national courts from declaring the invalidity of Community legislation (the *Foto-Frost* case where the ECJ held that it alone, and not the national courts, could invalidate Community acts); declaring the supremacy of Community law over national law (*Costa vs. ENEL*); expanding the Court's powers in disregard of Treaty provisions (*Les Verts* case, where the ECJ brought the European Parliament within the scope of its judicial review, though the EC Treaty mentioned only the Council and the Commission); and establishing state liability for breaches of Community law (*Francovich*). In general, the Court's methods of interpretation of Community law have been considered as 'purposive or teleological, although not in the sense of seeking the purpose or aim of the author of a text' (Craig and De Búrca 2002: 98), while the Court's reasoning in many cases has been considered as inadequate.

This criticism of the Court for excessive activism is not very convincing, however. The Court has been called upon to interpret Treaty provisions whose content is often general, containing no precise definitions. These general rules mean that is often impossible to predict the issues that will arise in a process of Community development which is complex and dynamic. The Court is obliged to take initiatives to fill existing gaps in the Community legislation, and it tries to do this without damaging the spirit of the Treaties or undermining the Treaties' aims and objectives. The central objective of the Treaties, which were signed by all member states, is the promotion of European integration, and the Court's decisions such as those in *Van Gend en Loos*, *Costa v. ENEL*, *Les Verts*, and *Francovich* are not inconsistent with this objective.

Furthermore, the Court, without always having adequate support from the Treaties or the member states, has had to strike and maintain a difficult balance between the Community and the member states, and to ensure the uniform interpretation and application of Community law in the national territory of member states that demonstrate varying political and legal traditions and varying objectives regarding the form and pace of European integration. Moreover, there is no proper legislature in the Community and often the legislation passed is the result of tough negotiations and compromises. The task of the Court becomes even more difficult in light of conflicting political, economic, or other national interests. In this complex environment, the development of judicial activism is inevitable, and indeed potentially desirable, provided that the spirit and the objectives of the Treaties are not harmed.

However, more recent ECJ decisions have demonstrated that the Court also possesses a capacity for restraint. The decision in *Facini Dori* (1994), where the ECJ refused to give horizontal direct effect to directives and thus to expand further the scope of Community law and its powers at the expense of national law, constitutes an example of this. The Court's self-restraint can also be seen with respect to certain politically sensitive issues touching upon the economic and social policies of the member states, where the Court has been less willing to interfere (Arnull 1999: 564).

KEY POINTS

- 'Judicial activism' is used to describe the practice of the ECJ to exploit the gaps and vagueness existing in areas of Community law so as to expand the Court's powers and role in the Community.
- Critics say that the Court's activism exceeds its judicial powers and falls into the area of policy-making.
- The criticism is not convincing. The Court's activism has not damaged the aims and spirit of the Treaties. In certain cases the Court has even demonstrated a capacity for restraint.

Reforming the Union's judicial system

One of the most pressing problems currently facing the European Courts concerns their ever growing workload, which is the result of the deepening of European integration and the expansion of the law of the European Union and the jurisdiction of the European Courts into new areas. The establishment of the Court of First Instance in 1989 helped to relieve the ECJ of part of its workload, by transferring to it certain categories of cases. However, the solution proved only temporary because soon the workload started to rise again, this time not only in the ECJ but also in the CFI. The problem is not insignificant since the large volume of cases threatens the efficient operation of the EU's judicial system and the proper and timely award of justice.

The Treaty of Nice contained certain provisions seeking to reform the Union's judicial system to make it more efficient. The most important changes imported by the Treaty of Nice are the following.

- The role of the CFI was strengthened. The CFI was no longer attached to the ECJ.
- For the first time the CFI was given jurisdiction to give preliminary rulings in specific cases.
- The CFI was given jurisdiction over some direct actions previously under the jurisdiction of the ECJ.
- The CFI shall consist of 'at least' one judge per member state, thus leaving open the possibility of the appointment of additional judges.

- Judicial panels attached to the CFI were created to deal in the first instance with cases in specific areas. The CFI examines the appeals against the decisions of these panels. The European Civil Service Tribunal was the first panel created in 2004 to deal with disputes between the Community and its civil servants.
- A distinction was made between decisions of the CFI subject to appeal and those subject to review by the ECJ. The review procedure will apply to decisions given by the CFI against decisions of the judicial panels and on questions referred for a preliminary ruling.

Conclusion

The process of European integration, which began more than 50 years ago, is still evolving. The establishment of the EU in 1993 and of a common currency in 2002 were major breakthroughs, but there are still many unsolved problems. In this ever changing environment, the Courts of the EU are playing a considerable role in European integration. Even if granted only limited jurisdiction and at times facing negative responses to their decisions by national courts and governments, the Courts of the EU, and particularly the ECJ, have succeeded not only in expanding their powers and role in the Community, but also in establishing a Community legal order independent of the legal orders of the member states, an achievement largely facilitating the process of European integration. In respect of European integration, one further contribution of the ECJ is that it successfully fulfilled the task of ensuring the uniform interpretation and application of Community law by removing the barriers to integration posed by varying national political and legal traditions.

Even if certain ECJ practices have not escaped criticism, it is clear that the overall impression of the Court in Europe is a positive one. There can be no more clear proof of this than the compliance with the ECJ's decisions demonstrated by all the national courts and political institutions. Thus far, there have been no major objections raised against the Court's jurisdiction by member states and this adds value to the ECJ's achievements. Moreover, since its establishment in 1951, the ECJ has seen its powers increase, which is another positive sign.

However, the process of integration within the EU is still developing and so is its judicial system, which needs to improve its efficiency if it is to confront current and future challenges. The Treaty of Nice adopted certain measures to improve the efficiency of the Courts of the Union, but it is too soon to judge the effects of these measures as yet. What is certain is that Nice was not the end of the road and that efforts to establish a more efficient and reliable judicial system in the EU will continue in the future.

QUESTIONS

1. What is the role of the Community Courts in the process of European integration?
2. Why were the judicial panels established? What role does the European Civil Service Tribunal play?
3. What legal and political consequences ensue if a member state fails to comply with its Treaty obligations?

4. Under what circumstances can an action for annulment be brought?
5. Why is the system of preliminary rulings important for European integration?
6. What is the significance of the ECJ's ruling in *Van Gend en Loos?*
7. Do you agree with the view that the ECJ has demonstrated excessive activism?
8. What were the main changes made by the Treaty of Nice to the judicial architecture of the EU?

GUIDE TO FURTHER READING

■ Arnull, A. *The European Union and its Court of Justice* (Oxford: Oxford University Press, 1999). This book records and analyses the contribution the Court has made to shaping the legal framework within which the Community operates.

■ Arnull, A., and Wincott, D. (eds) *Accountability and Legitimacy in the European Union* (Oxford: Oxford University Press, 2002). This contains an interdisciplinary collection of essays on various aspects of accountability and legitimacy in the EU. Two of the essays examine the judicial architecture of the EU after Nice and the rule of law in the EU.

■ Brown, L., and Kennedy T. *The Court of Justice of the European Communities*, 5th edn (London: Sweet & Maxwell, 2000). This work covers the organization and composition of the ECJ and the CFI, their respective jurisdictions, and their procedure and practice.

■ Craig, P., and De Búrca, G. *EU Law: Texts, Cases and Materials*, 3rd edn (Oxford: Oxford University Press, 2002). An exhaustive analysis of the role of the Court and the relationship between Community Courts and national courts.

■ Douglas-Scott, S. *Constitutional Law of the European Union* (London: Longman, 2002). This study offers comprehensive coverage of the constitutional and institutional structures of the EU. One of its chapters discusses the judicial activism of the Court of Justice.

■ Hartley, T. *The Foundations of European Community Law*, 5th edn (Oxford: Oxford University Press, 2003). A detailed analysis and assessment of the powers of the Court and the relationship of Community law to national law.

■ Lasok, K. P. E., and Millett, T. *Judicial Control in the EU: Procedures and Principles* (Richmond: Richmond Law & Tax, 2004). An exhaustive analysis of the Court's composition, jurisdiction, procedure, and practice.

■ Lenaerts, K., and Van Nuffel, P. *Constitutional Law of the European Union* (London: Sweet & Maxwell, 2004). This book examines the position of the Court following the drafting of the Constitutional Treaty.

IMPORTANT WEBSITES

- http://www.curia.eu.int The official website of the Community Courts.

Visit the Online Resource Centre that accompanies this book for lots of interesting additional material. http://www.oxfordtextbooks.co.uk/orc/cini2e/

13 Interest Groups and the European Union

RAINER EISING

Chapter Contents

Reader's Guide

This chapter examines the role of interest groups in the European Union in the context of the broader system of **interest intermediation** that now exists at European level. It also considers the way in which the EU as a political institution influences interest group structure and activity in both European and domestic political arenas. The chapter begins with a brief overview of the relationship between the EU institutions and interest organizations, and examines the steps taken thus far to regulate that relationship. It then looks at the structure of the system, focusing in particular on two salient aspects: the difference between national and EU organizations; and the difference between business and non-business interests. Finally, the chapter addresses the **Europeanization** of interest intermediation (see also Chapter 25) to question how EU membership may have altered the structure and activities of domestic interest groups.

Introduction

The EU institutions do not make policy in a vacuum and the links that they have with civil society take many different forms. Interest groups have a particularly important role to play in connecting European-level institutions to the citizens of the European Union. Indeed, the European Commission recently counted over 900 EU-level interest organizations operating in Brussels. Given the extent of this activity, the organization and function of these groups would seem to be worth analysing.

Interest groups have always been regarded as 'Janus-faced' creatures, in that they look towards both state and society. They may even be regarded as 'factions' that serve to undermine the general interest, pursued by elected representatives of the people. But interest groups are also indispensable, not only because they give a voice to citizens between elections, but also because they can serve as 'schools for democracy', socializing citizens as political beings, and contributing to the formation of a general will out of the specific concerns of groups. Perspectives such as these are important markers in the study of interest organization in the EU as well as in the way the EU institutions incorporate them in EU policy-making. Early on, Caporaso (1974) criticized European interest organizations for pursuing only very narrowly defined interests and thereby undermining the legitimacy and accountability of the European institutions. By contrast, other authors have suggested that interest organizations offer European civil society the potential to participate in EU policy-making and institution-building (Heinelt 1998). In recent years, the EU institutions have also stressed civil society participation in EU policy-making as a way of enhancing the democratic quality of the European Union (European Commission 2001a, 2002b).

Before evaluating these views on the role of interest groups, the following sections set out the broad terrain of EU interest intermediation. The first section highlights the institutional setting, and the second the efforts that the EU institutions have made to regulate access by interest organizations and incorporate civil society into EU policy-making. The third section summarizes the structure of the EU interest group system, while the fourth discusses how the EU may have affected the structure and functions of domestic interest groups, through a process which is now referred to as Europeanization.

The EU institutions and interest groups

According to institutional theory, political institutions, such as the EU, have important effects on interest organizations. They can shape the formation, the role, and the functions of interest groups as well as the strategies they use to exert influence on political decisions. The EU institutions are important to interest groups because they influence their environment and activities, or those of their members, through the formulation and implementation of European public policy (see Mazey and Richardson 2001). Thus, although EU institutions do not *determine* political action, they are important, and for this reason this chapter begins by considering interest groups from the perspective of the EU's institutional setting. This setting forms a political opportunity structure – it shapes the political opportunities that are available to interest groups (see Marks and McAdam 1996). Four characteristics of the EU are particularly relevant in this context. First, the EU is a highly dynamic system; secondly, the EU is a complex system that is horizontally and vertically differentiated; thirdly, the EU is a system that privileges consensus-building; and finally, the legitimacy of the EU is considered to be fragile. All

KEY CONCEPTS AND TERMS 13.1

Lobbies and interest groups

The literature on the European Union's interest groups rests on a body of research in the field of Comparative Politics. In this literature, non-governmental organizations (NGOs) have been labelled and defined in very different ways. Lobbies, pressure groups, interest groups, and interest organizations are the most common terms used.

The term 'lobbyist' originates in the nineteenth century, when individuals waiting in the parliamentary lobby exerted influence on members of legislatures to pass bills on behalf of unknown customers. Lobbying was then almost exclusively regarded as a commercial activity. Later, attempts by organizations to influence public bodies were also included in this narrow definition. Since the 1920s, the term 'pressure group' has increasingly been used in the political science literature, on the understanding that it is a familiar term needing little explanation. Its meaning comes close to that of a lobby group in that it centres on the functions of these groups to influence – or put pressure on – Congress/Parliament or Government. The term 'interest group', its primary contender, refers to the underlying rationale of these groups and has less negative connotations. Members join groups as they share common attitudes, or interests (Truman 1951: 34). These interests include 'frames of reference for interpreting and evaluating' as well as 'attitudes toward what is needed or wanted in a given situation, observable as demands or claims upon other groups in the society' (Truman 1951: 33–9). While reserving the term 'political interest group' for those groups that place demands on public bodies, Truman often uses the term interchangeably with 'interest groups'. In several accounts, individual actors, such as large firms, are also regarded as interest groups, even though, strictly speaking, the term does not apply because they do not have members. 'Interest organizations' refers to interest groups that are highly formalized. It highlights the fact that organizations make for continuity, they cope with complexity by means of differentiation. It also draws attention away from particular leaders and members, and towards the effects of organizational form.

of these characteristics affect how interest groups have sought to influence the European institutions and how they incorporate interest groups into EU policy-making.

Since the mid-1980s, the EC (and after 1993, the EU) has extended its competences far beyond market integration, to include areas such as environmental policy, justice and home affairs, and foreign and security policy. This steady accretion of powers gives some indication of the dynamism that characterizes the European political agenda. This dynamism has had two important consequences for interest groups. On the one hand, in a short-term perspective, the dynamic political agenda makes it difficult for interest organizations to forecast short-term political developments in the European Union. Therefore, they are quite often uncertain about political options and stakes, particularly in the early phases of the policy process. Accordingly, they have no option but to devote considerable resources to monitoring EU developments.

On the other hand, in a long-term perspective, the number of groups operating at European level has steadily increased and so has the number of interests that are present in the European arena (Figure 13.1). The most dynamic phases of group formation have been the foundation years of the European Communities up until the early 1960s and the period from the formulation of the Single European Act until the enactment of the Maastricht Treaty. Many of the groups were set up as a direct response to or in anticipation of European institution-building and regulation. In several cases, the formation of European interest groups triggered responses from competing interests, which led to even more groups being established. As a result, the interest group landscape in the EU has become much more diverse over time. Initially, the interest group system consisted mostly of economic groups. Groups representing diffuse interests, such as environmental groups or development NGOs, have become more vocal only since the 1970s and 1980s. And while there were only a limited number of national groups from the six founding member states, EU policies nowadays attract the attention of organizations from all 25 member states, as well as from other affected interests such as multinational firms. With the Eastern enlargement of 2004, the membership of EU-level interests has

Figure 13.1 The evolution of European associations from 1843 to 2001

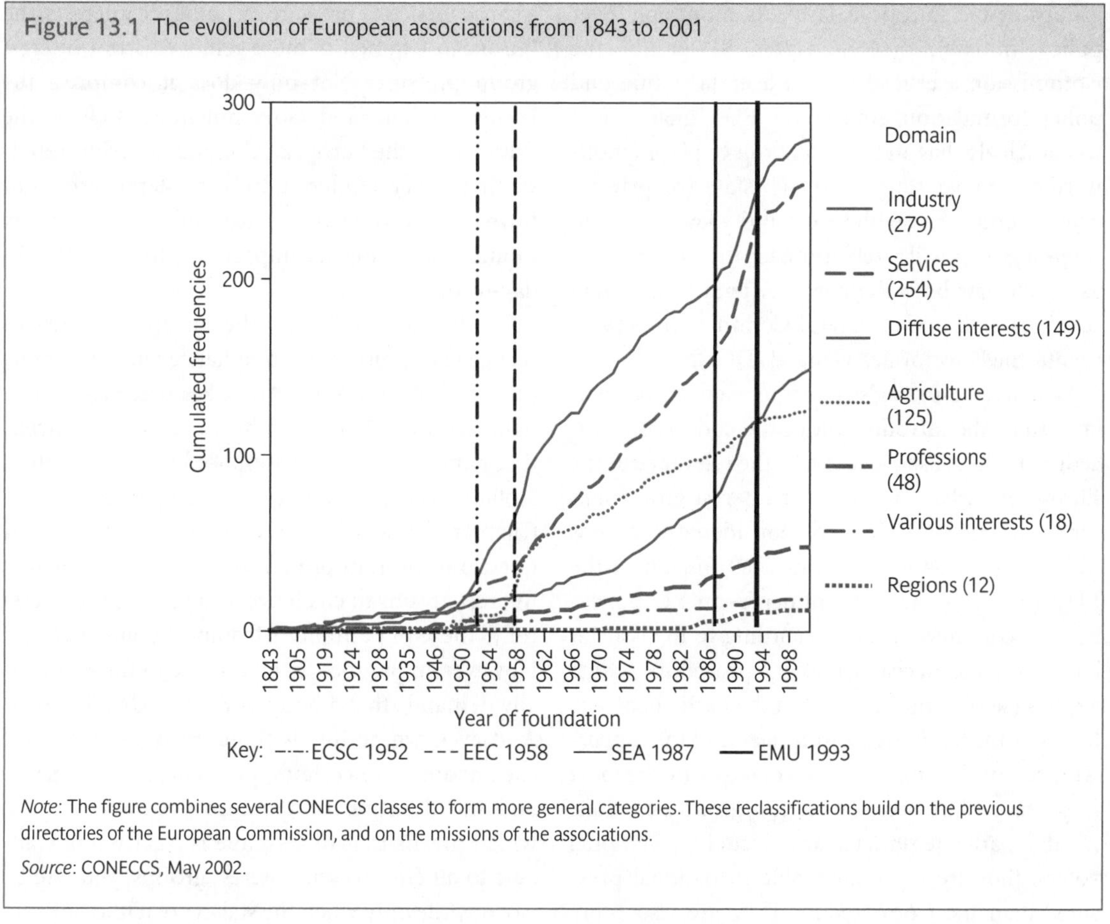

Note: The figure combines several CONECCS classes to form more general categories. These reclassifications build on the previous directories of the European Commission, and on the missions of the associations.

Source: CONECCS, May 2002.

widened considerably, making for greater internal heterogeneity.

The EU is also a complex polity that is horizontally differentiated. This means that the importance of interest groups varies substantially across policy areas. In the first pillar of the European Union, the European Community (EC) pillar (see Chapter 3), interest groups have relatively good access to the European institutions. This is much less the case in the EU's other two pillars, which cover common foreign and security policy (CFSP) and police and judicial cooperation in criminal matters (formerly justice and home affairs). These second and third pillars operate more intergovernmentally, allowing member governments quite easily to prevent interest groups from gaining access to the EU policy process. By way of an example, during the development of the EU's refugee and asylum policy in the early 1990s, Amnesty International complained that it was shut out of EU decision-making to the extent that 'virtually all agreements and policy proposals . . . [were] drafted behind closed doors in meetings of government officials' (van der Klaauw 1994: 279). Since then, important elements of the third pillar have been transferred to the European Community pillar (Pillar 1), thus allowing for greater political participation and judicial review.

For most interest groups, then, the EC pillar provides the greatest potential for access to the EU institutions, not least because it comprises the vast majority of the Union's regulatory and distributive policies. In this pillar, the European Commission is the most important point of contact for interest groups at the European level. Its monopoly over policy initiation (see Chapter 9) grants the Commission a crucial role in agenda-setting and policy formulation. And as the EU's 'guardian of treaties', it also has an important role to play in monitoring member states' and non-state (or private) actors' compliance with Community law. However, interest groups will rarely approach the Commission as a collegiate body. Rather, they tend to maintain relations with one or several Commission departments, the Directorates-General (DGs).

With its growing legislative competencies, particularly since the introduction of the codecision procedure in the Maastricht Treaty, the relevance of the European Parliament (EP) for interest groups has increased. However, it is still considered to be less important than the European Commission or the EU Council, because its influence on EU policy-making continues to vary according to the issue at hand and the decision-making procedure which applies (see Chapter 1). Within the Parliament, the heads of the Standing Committees and the *rapporteurs* responsible for particular dossiers are the most important addressees for interest group demands. As the parliamentarians are elected by national voters, they are more amenable to national pressures than the Commission. They are also more open to protectionist demands than the Commission and the EU Council as the debate on the service liberalization directive has indicated (Eising 2005), and they are more responsive to 'weak' (or what are often called 'diffuse') interests, including those representing the environment, consumers, or large groups such as the unemployed and pensioners (Kohler-Koch 1997: 6–7; Pollack 1997).

Owing to its pivotal position, the EU Council is a highly relevant contact for interest groups. However, the Council and its administrative machinery, the Committee of Permanent Representatives (Coreper) and the Council Working Groups (see Chapter 10), are rarely lobbied directly. Rather, domestic interest groups tend to address their concerns to particular government departments, representing specific interests at national level. While the Council's policy positions evolve often along national lines, in part as a consequence of pressure by domestic interests, the European Council is more removed from interest group pressure. Not only does it comprise the Heads of State and Government as well as the President of the European Commission, thus representing general interest to a greater degree, but formally it also needs to meet only once every six months, lessening its impact on the minutiae of day-to-day politics.

As the EU's judiciary, the European Court of Justice (ECJ) monitors compliance with and interprets EU law. European law takes precedence over national law and grants rights to individual citizens that national courts must uphold (Hix 1999: 108). Notably, the preliminary rulings procedure (see Chapter 12), which allows national courts to refer questions of European law to the ECJ, enables interest groups to challenge, in some cases successfully, the compatibility of domestic and EU law. However, in practice, to take a case to the ECJ usually demands that a body of EU law already exists. And even where this is the case, the outcome of such action is uncertain, the financial costs heavy, and the duration of the case generally lengthy, which means that this avenue is clearly not available to all citizens and interest groups, and will be worthwhile only when the stakes are felt to be especially high.

Finally, the Economic and Social Committee (ESC) was set up to channel the opinions of organized interests into the European policy process. The ESC is a tripartite body composed of individual members who are nominated by the EU member states and represent employers, workers, and other interests. It is generally considered to be of minor importance for the representation of interests within the EU. Direct contacts between the EU institutions and interest organizations are now much more important than this institutionalized forum for interest intermediation. Nonetheless, during the debate about the role of civil society in European democracy (see below) the ESC has sought to establish itself (see ESC 2004) as an important voice of European civil society and had developed several proposals for strengthening its participation in EU policy formation and institution building (Smismans 2003).

Policy-making in the EU is not confined to the European institutions, however. Individually, the 25 member states also have an important say in decisions taken by the Union. The European Union is vertically differentiated and increasingly regarded as a multi-level system (Hooghe and Marks 2001; see also Chapter 8), implying that many different public actors located at different territorial levels within the EU share political authority. Hence, multiple points of access are open to interest organizations (Pollack 1997). Groups must take heed of political developments at both the European and national levels and need to be present at both levels (as well as in any relevant regional and local political arenas) if they hope to see their interests well represented and defended. They also need to ensure that their strategies are coordinated across each level. But only a minority of the interest groups can pursue multi-level strategies in the sense of establishing direct contacts with political institutions at each level. This is because they are tied to their local, regional, national, or European memberships in one form or another, and must also make sure that they use their resources as efficiently as they can. As we might expect, EU interest groups are much more involved than national groups in policy-making at the EU level, while national groups dominate in the domestic political arena. Whereas large firms can easily afford to be present in both the domestic and the European arenas (see Coen 1997, 1998), this holds only for a minority of national interest organizations (Eising 2004).

Owing to the complexity of the EU's political system with its emphasis on power-sharing, as well as a consequence of the unpredictability of the EU policy agenda, EU institutions and member states prefer to strive for consensus over European political decisions (see Katzenstein 1997; Kohler-Koch 1999). For member states, consensual decision-making guarantees some protection against being outvoted in the EU Council when vital interests are at stake. However, even though it may increase the legitimacy of EU policy, consensual decision-making may ultimately result in suboptimal policy outcomes, outcomes that satisfy no one fully. Decision-making by consensus, rather than on the basis of a majority, implies that EU institutions and the national governments need to take the opinions of all relevant interest groups into account to prevent groups opposed to the legislation ultimately blocking the agreement. Yet, despite the norm of consensus, national groups can no longer rely on the national veto in the EU Council.

KEY POINTS

- Political institutions such as the EU influence the formation and behaviour of interest groups.
- The EU's institutional setting – its dynamic political agenda; its complexity; its multi-level character; and its reliance on consensus – shapes the interest group system and interest intermediation within the EU.
- There are multiple points of access to the EU policy process, including the Commission, the Parliament, the Council and the Court, as well as national political institutions.

EU democracy and civil society

The fragile legitimacy of the European Union has also important consequences for the involvement of interest groups in EU policy-making. Following the referenda on the Maastricht Treaty, the debate about the democratic deficit of the European Union intensified in the 1990s (see Chapter 22). While interest groups have always been important to the EU institutions, the institutions have come to emphasize the contribution interest organizations can make to European democracy.

Interest groups are important to the EU institutions for a number of reasons. They define, aggregate, and articulate the interests of their members or their constituencies, making it easier for the European institutions to monitor social change and consider new political concerns. Moreover, the EU institutions (and especially the Commission) rely on the special expertise of interest groups in the design of public policy. The Commission consults groups because it has only limited in-house resources and needs to draw on external sources of information in order to perform its policy functions effectively. In these consultations, the Commission also learns about support for and the resistance to its proposals.

In the context of the debate on the EU's democratic deficit, both the Commission and the Economic and Social Committee have highlighted the virtues of civil society participation in policy consultations. In the words of the Commission: 'By fulfilling its duty to consult, the Commission ensures that its proposals are technically viable, practically workable and based on a bottom-up approach. In other words, good consultation serves a dual purpose by helping to improve the quality of the policy outcome and at the same time enhancing the involvement of interested parties and the public at large' (2002b: 5). According to this reasoning, involving interest groups adds an element of functional representation to the imperfect dual legitimacy of EU policies provided for by the representation of citizen interests through the European Parliament and of territorial interests through the EU Council (see European Commission 1992b, 1999, 2001a, 2002b). As a result of the changed discourse on interest groups, various efforts have been made to institutionalize and regularize consultations with civil society.

The contacts that the EU institutions have with interest groups range from a variety of informal ad hoc meetings to more formal arrangements in EU committees. These practices differ greatly across the EU institutions. The Commission has long preferred not to regulate these practices but to apply existing administrative rules to the consultation of interest groups, and to operate on the basis of self-regulatory principles. Thus, it has encouraged professional consultancies to develop codes of conduct that satisfy some minimum standards (European Commission 1992b). At present, two such codes are in force.

Unlike the United Nations, the Commission does not approve of the accreditation of interest groups, as it feels that this would impede open access to EU policy-makers. However, in 2002, it adopted general principles and minimum standards for consulting interest groups even though it does not consider them to be legally binding (European Commission 2002b: 15). On the input side of the political process, the principles and standards are supposed to enhance the transparency and accountability of consultations. They are also meant to ensure that all interested parties are properly consulted so that they contribute to political participation. On the output side, the standards are aimed at enhancing the effectiveness and coherence of EU policies. According to the Commission, they are applicable whenever an extended impact assessment of EU policies is required. This leaves out a range of EU policy measures in which no such assessment is deemed to be necessary and omits issue areas in which other modes of consultation have already been established – such as for the conclusion of international treaties and agreements. According to some critics, therefore, the standards are clearly insufficient to streamline the Commission's consultation patterns (Obradovic 2005: 35). According to other critics, building linkages with public interests is also an inept strategy for coping with the democratic deficit because EU-level interest groups are rather removed from domestic constituencies (Warleigh 2001). In sum, these standards establish a Commission obligation:

- to ensure clear and concise communication;
- to announce open public consultations at a single access point on the Internet;
- to ensure adequate coverage of target groups (those with a direct interest in the policy; those who are important for its implementation; and those who are affected by the policy);

- to introduce a time limit for consultations (at least eight weeks for receiving replies to written consultations and 20 working days' notice for meetings);
- to acknowledge the receipt of comments and to report on the results of open public consultations on the Internet (European Commission 2002b: 19–22).

In its White Paper on European Governance, the Commission (2001a: 17, 21) also envisaged more extensive partnership arrangement with interest groups. In 2001, it also signed protocols with the Economic and Social Committee and the Committee of the Regions to involve these bodies much earlier in the EU policy-making process and to strengthen their function as intermediaries between the EU, on the one hand, and civil society and the regions, on the other. However, thus far, it is unclear how these consultations relate to the direct consultation of civil society by the Commission. Finally, as a preliminary effort at strengthening and institutionalising civil society participation in 2004, the draft Constitutional Treaty gave political participation constitutional status by including a new title VI on democratic life in the European Union. Under this title, Article I-47 acknowledges the principle of participatory democracy and Article I-48, the importance of the social partners (see below).

Owing to its functions, the European Parliament (EP) has different perspectives on civil society participation from that of the Commission and the Economic and Social Committee. Its members have certainly established wide-ranging contacts with interest groups but, as elected representatives of the European citizens and subject to public scrutiny, members of the EP regard interest group influence as potentially problematic in two respects. First, in their response to the White Paper on European Governance, they maintained that 'European and national parliaments' rather than civil society groups 'constitute the basis for a European system with democratic legitimacy'. They consider organized civil society as important but also as 'inevitably sectoral' so that it 'cannot be considered as having its own democratic legitimacy' (European Parliament 2001: points 8, 11a). In other words, the parliamentarians do not consider functional representation by interest groups as equivalent to electoral representation by parliaments. Secondly, concerns about the lack of transparency involved in interest group influence, and about the 'misbehaviour' of interest groups, led to calls for their regulation. In 1996, the EP decided to establish a register of interest groups. After registration and on acceptance of a code of conduct, interest representatives receive a pass that eases access to the EP and is valid for a year. Currently, about 3,400 of these are issued annually (Greenwood 2003: 71), though they do not really grant any more rights than a normal citizen of the EU might get. Under the rules of parliamentary procedure, the Members of the European Parliament (MEPs) and their assistants are also obliged to indicate their paid activities and the donations they receive, clarifying any relationship they might have with groups outside the Parliament.

KEY POINTS

- In recent years, the EU institutions – notably the European Commission and the Economic and Social Committee – have emphasized the importance of civil society consultations for enhancing the legitimacy of EU policies; and they have taken measures to institutionalize political participation.
- Despite these measures, the EU institutions do not regulate interest group activity in any comprehensive way.
- Owing to its different status in the EU political system, the European Parliament takes a different stance on interest group participation from that of the Commission and the Economic and Social Committee.

European interest groups

There are a huge number of interest organizations operating at the level of the EU institutions. At the turn of the millennium, 250 large companies, 170 national interest groups, 171 regional bodies, 143 commercial public affairs firms, and 125 law firms had set up offices in Brussels (Greenwood 2003: 9). In its CONECCS (Consultation, the European Commission, and Civil Society) database, the Secretariat-General of the EC listed over 900 European interest organizations in May 2002 (see Figure 13.1). Subsequently, this number dropped to some 700 associations as several of these groups no longer provided sufficient information to be included in the database.

As indicated, most of these groups are only consulted on EU policy. They provide technical information, indicate the position of their members, or suggest alternative courses of action. In a few cases, however, interest groups are allowed to formulate or implement policy themselves. As social partners, the European Trade Union Congress (ETUC), the Federation of European Industry (UNICE), and the federation representing European public-sector firms (CEEP) have been given this right in the field of EU social policy; and their national members are entitled to implement these measures falling under the Social Dialogue. But even where the formal role of interest organizations is less substantial, interest groups can be important implementers of European public policy. In this respect, they are sometimes considered as more democratic, more decentralized, more effective, and less bureaucratic instruments of policy implementation than public administration. However, stressing the need for a uniform implementation of EU law in all EU member states, emphasizing the lack of governance capacities of many groups, and highlighting potentially negative external effects on third parties, both the Commission (2001a) and the ECJ are hesitant to devolve policy implementation to interest organizations.

There are various ways of classifying interest groups, such as according to type, number, or the homogeneity of their members. Here, two criteria are considered in greater detail because they have particularly important implications for the EU policy process. In the first section, the differences and similarities between EU and national groups are discussed; while in the second and third sections, business and non-business interest groups are compared.

EU and national groups

It is important to distinguish national from EU-level interest groups (the latter are sometimes called 'Euro-groups'), first, because their organizations and constituencies differ and secondly, because they pursue different strategies when representing their interests. EU interest groups provide expertise and arguments which they use to persuade the EU institutions of the merits of their cases. National associations tend to represent their interests to national members of the EU institutions as well as to their national administrations and governments, and in so doing tend to emphasize the *national* character of their interests. Typically, EU interest groups are composed of national associations, rather than having a direct membership of individuals. According to a survey conducted in the late 1990s, about two-thirds of EU interest organizations are in fact federations of national interest groups, with the remainder either having a direct membership of other organizations (such as firms), or combining these two elements (Aspinwall and Greenwood 1998). An example of the latter is the European Chemical Association (CEFIC), which brings together both national associations and individual firms.

Generally, EU associations have fewer functions than their national members, and as a consequence their resources are much smaller. To different degrees, they serve to create links among their memberships, to provide and distribute information on EU activities, to develop common positions, and to promote the interests of their members (Lindberg 1963: 98). Compared to national associations they concentrate to a greater extent on the *representation of interests* rather than on the *provision of services* for their members. Moreover, owing to the multinational make-up of their membership and the heterogeneity of the national settings covered by these bodies, EU groups often have real difficulty in reaching agreement internally on important policy questions and in controlling their members' compliance with the agreements that were struck with the EU institutions (see Haas 1958). As in the EU institutions, unanimity rules or qualified majority thresholds guarantee that national interests are taken into account as groups seek to establish common positions.

Despite these differences, a fairly elaborate division of labour has evolved between the EU associations and their national counterparts. European interest groups are far more visible at the level of the European Union than are national associations (Eising 2004) and have increasingly become important intermediaries between their national members and the EU institutions. This holds particularly when the EU political agenda is set and when policies are being formulated by the EU institutions. National associations are more vocal than

CASE STUDY 13.2

EU electricity liberalization and the organization of interests

EU electricity liberalization illustrates the extent of changes that EU policies can trigger in the organization of interests (see Eising 1999). In 1996, after lengthy negotiations, the EU institutions agreed on a partial liberalization of electricity markets. The liberalization directive demanded not only the opening of the market but also the so-called unbundling of firms, namely the separation of electricity generation, transport, and distribution to consumers.

This reform triggered major changes in the organization of sectoral interests. In the early 1990s, smaller regional suppliers formed European interest organizations, either to seek special exemptions from competition as public sector utilities (CEDEC – European Federation of Local Public Energy Distribution Companies) or to support liberalization in an effort to reduce their dependence on the large electricity providers (GEODE – Groupement Européen de Sociétés et Organismes de Distribution d'Energie). Large industrial energy consumers supported the liberalization plans mostly through the established associations (IFIEC – International Federation of Industrial Energy Consumers), as well as through major European industry associations such as CEFIC (European Chemicals Industry Federation). A few large companies such as Bayer, ICI, Mercedes Benz, and Akzo Nobel went so far as to form ENERG8 in 1992, to underline their demands for lower energy prices.

In their unsuccessful attempt to forestall this directive, major European utilities and national associations that were members of the long-standing international association of the sector, UNIPEDE (International Union of Producers and Distributors of Electrical Energy), formed the European interest group EURELECTRIC (Union of the Electricity Industry) which became fully operational in 1990. In 1999, then, UNIPEDE was dissolved and merged with EURELECTRIC to save overhead costs and provide for better sectoral coordination. Recently, EURELECTRIC has limited full membership to national associations thus excluding individual utilities. Thus, EURELECTRIC seeks to avoid discrimination among different companies in the liberalized market and necessitates the establishment of national associations even in countries such as France that are still characterized by a dominant national supplier (Electricité de France).

After the liberalization of the sector and as a consequence of the demand to separate the transmission of electricity from its generation and distribution, ETSO (European Association of Transmission Systems Operators) was formed to represent the interests of the transmission system operators. In sum, EU electricity liberalization had wide-ranging effects on the interest groups in the sector. It led to the build-up of a European layer of associations, provoked the realignment of international associations, institutionalized new structural interests in the sector, and also had major repercussions on the interest group systems in the member states.

EU associations when EU policies are being transposed into domestic law or implemented by the public administration.

Business interests

At first sight, the EU interest group system looks broadly pluralist (see Streeck and Schmitter 1991). Both the number of groups and their huge variety suggest that a great many interests are represented in the EU institutions. Usually, no interest group enjoys a clear monopoly of representation in any one policy area. Of the EU groups present in the agricultural sector, for example, many reflect particular product specializations. Some of these compete and bargain not only with groups across policy areas, such as with environmental or consumer groups, but also with groups within the agricultural domain. Coalitions are generally fluid and depend on shared interests. However, as is usual in advanced industrial countries, business interest organizations outnumber non-business interests (see Figure 13.1). About 80 per cent of the EU organizations listed on the Commission database can be categorized as producer or employer interest organizations. The extent of bias in the interest group system has reduced over time because, in the 1990s, the growth rate of diffuse interest groups in the EU has been higher than that of interest groups in several other domains (see Figure 13.1). Note, however, that the extent of change has not equalled that in some countries such as the USA (Baumgartner and Leech 1998: 102–6) where citizen groups constitute a much larger proportion of the interest group population.

Business interests responded quickly to European integration. UNICE, the Union of Industrial and Employers' Confederations of Europe, which is the top-level European association of national producers' and employers' associations for private firms, was set up as early as 1958. The equivalent public-sector association, the CEEP (Centre Européen des Entreprises Publics), followed soon after in 1961. Both of these bodies have been accorded the privileged status of a social partner in the EU. A third body, EUROCHAMBRES, the federation of the chambers of commerce in the European Union, representing small and medium-sized enterprises (SMEs), was founded in 1958, and eight other cross-sectoral associations also draw their membership from small and medium-sized firms. Beside these EU federations, there are a number of cross-sectoral associations that have a direct membership of firms. For example, the American Chamber of Commerce (AMCHAM) represents the European Council of American Chambers of Commerce and has a total of 900 European and American corporate members. The European Round Table of Industrialists is composed of around 50 executives of leading European firms. The Round Table was particularly influential in pushing for acceptance of the Single Market Programme in the mid-1980s (Cowles 1997; see also Chapter 16).

The involvement of large firms in direct membership organizations (rather than in federations) may undermine the ability of associations to aggregate interests along national lines and discipline their members' behaviour. However, the EU institutions prefer to cooperate with these kinds of organizations as they are able to agree more easily than the EU federations on common positions. Indeed, large firms have become increasingly important in the interest group landscape, as is clear when we look at the restructuring of associations since the 1980s. Within UNICE, for example, large firms were able to secure top positions in the standing committees, giving them a key role in the formulation of joint positions (Cowles 1997). Moreover, in several sectors, such as automobiles, chemicals, and biotechnology, large firms, acting independently, outside the framework of interest organizations, or forming direct membership organizations, seem to have acquired greater influence than either the national or the EU federations. Individual lobbying by large firms is commonplace nowadays, with these firms often having better access than the EU and national associations to both EU and domestic political institutions. This has led scholars to characterize EU interest intermediation as a form of 'elite pluralism' (Coen 1997, 1998; Cowles 2001).

BOX 13.3

Business interest groups: some examples

The Union of Industrial and Employers' Confederations of Europe (UNICE)

UNICE was set up in 1958 to promote the common professional interests of firms in both EU decision-making and the dialogue of the social partners (employers and labour). It encompasses 39 national member associations from 33 European countries. Five other national associations have observer status. UNICE claims to represent more than 20 million firms in all. It has around 45 full-time members of staff, and 90 per cent of its funding is covered by membership fees.

The European Centre for Enterprises with Public Participation and of Enterprises of General Economic Interest (CEEP)

CEEP was founded in 1961. As a cross-sectoral employer and producer association, it represents the interests of its members (mainly public-sector firms) in the EU decision-making process and also in the social dialogue. CEEP brings together 20 national sections and one additional section for Benelux (Belgium, Luxembourg, and the Netherlands). These have several hundred members – public firms, associations, and other organizations – that are supportive of the aims of the CEEP. It also has two associated sections from Romania and Turkey. It claims to represent the interests of about 14 per cent of the non-agricultural trading economy. It has a staff of 14 that work at least part-time and membership fees covering nearly 100 per cent of its funding.

The American Chamber of Commerce, Belgium (AMCHAM)

Set up in 1948, AMCHAM represents the interests of around 900 American and European firms in Belgium and at the EU level, with the aim of improving business and investment opportunities for US firms. AMCHAM has a staff of six members and is financed by membership and user fees.

The European Round Table of Industrialists (ERT)

The ERT was set up in 1983 in order to contribute to an improved dialogue between industry and governments both at the national and EU levels. It is composed of 47 leaders of large firms from 18 countries, all with their headquarters in Europe, and all engaged in substantial multinational activities. Membership is personal (not corporate) and at the invitation of existing members. However, the ERT is funded by multinational firms and has a staff of seven members.

The Association of the European Chambers of Commerce (EUROCHAMBRES)

Founded in 1958, EUROCHAMBRES represents the interests of members of the chambers of commerce and industry (small and medium-sized enterprises – SMEs) to the EU institutions. It incorporates 44 national associations of the chambers of commerce and industry, one per country, and claims to represent more than 18 million firms. It employs a staff of 32, and is largely funded by membership fees.

The European Association of Craft, Small and Medium-sized Enterprises (UEAPME)

UEAPME was established in 1979 to defend the interests of crafts, trades, and small and medium-sized enterprises in the EU and the candidate states. It brings together 37 national member associations from the 25 EU member states, a merger group of three associations, 11 associated members from non-EU states, 19 European and international sectoral associations, and nine other associate members. It claims to represent 11 million firms in the EU. It has a staff of 19, and is financed by membership fees.

Sources: European Commission CONECCS Database and the websites of the above-mentioned organizations (accessed in April 2006).

Yet, the extent to which the business community is able to pursue its interests effectively varies enormously across time and across issues. Moreover, business is far from being a unitary actor. For example, within the Single Market Programme of the late 1980s, many economic sectors such as transport, electricity and gas, and telecommunications were liberalized in the face of strong resistance from the incumbent firms. In the case of electricity liberalization, even Europe's largest utility, Electricité de France (EdF), had to accept the loss of its monopoly position in the French market, which it had done its best to defend.

Yet, it is still relevant to ask whether the strong presence of the business community results from the greater variety of interests that need to be represented, or whether it has more to do with firms being better able to form interest groups and pursue their interests than is the case for more diffuse, non-economic interests. Interest group theories have predominantly focused on the latter reason, raising important questions about the democratic implications of interest group activity.

Diffuse interests

There are fewer religious, social, human rights, consumer, and environmental groups than business interest organizations in the European Union. Only around 20 per cent of EU-level interest organizations can be categorized as 'diffuse', reflecting the fact that these groups represent societal groups that are not necessarily (well) organized or cohesive. This reflects a relative lack of activity on the part of the EU institutions. Only intense regulatory activity has provoked the mobilization of socially orientated interest groups at the EU level. The only exceptions have been the domestic consumer organizations that formed the BEUC (Bureau Européen des Unions des Consommateurs), the European consumer association, in 1962. They did this with the support of the European Commission, as a response to market integration (Young 1997: 157–8), ultimately bringing together (by 2006) 40 member organizations from 29 countries.

In the early years of the European integration process, non-governmental organizations (NGOs) did not generally focus their activities on the European Community. Even well into the 1970s, welfare and social policy groups were conspicuously absent from Brussels (Harvey 1993: 189–90). The foundation of the European Environmental Bureau (EEB) came about as a consequence of the EC's first environmental programme in 1974. Today, the EEB is the most comprehensive European environmental organization, bringing together more than 140 national associations. By the mid-1990s, some 13 European environmental associations and networks were present at the EU level (Hey and Brendle 1994: 389), a reflection of new regulatory powers in this policy area. Four of them dominate the

CASE STUDY 13.4

The initiative against animal testing for cosmetics

At the end of the 1980s, the Commission intended to amend the EU cosmetics directive to improve product information and to implement single market goals. But its draft proposals had the potential to increase animal testing for cosmetics. The British Union for the Abolition of Vivisection (BUAV), acting as a political entrepreneur, organized a coalition at the EU level against certain aspects of the proposal. The coalition initiated an EU-wide public campaign and collected more than 2.5 million signatures in support of a ban on the testing of cosmetics on animals. Lobbying at the EU level concentrated mainly on the European Parliament and on the Commission. The public campaign and a demonstration by 4,000 supporters in Brussels led to the full endorsement of these demands by the EP. In negotiations with the EP, the Commission was also prepared to accept the idea of an animal test ban, subject to certain conditions. But the '[c]oalition's armoury was . . . depleted and it began to lose momentum' when negotiations shifted to the Council and into the member states' (Fisher 1994: 236). This was likely to weaken the animal protection character of the Commission proposal. In late 1992, the Council agreed on a substantially weakened animal test ban from 1998 onwards and rejected any further amendment by the EP to its position without further discussion.

However, the difficulties BUAV had in exerting influence must be seen in light of national practices. At the national level, it had little access to the British government. It 'had been unsuccessful in securing the support of the UK government on this issue and was also at loggerheads with the UK trade association' for cosmetics. BUAV was therefore 'struck by the accessibility of the European Parliament and Commission and the openness of its officials compared to the UK' (Fisher 1994: 231 – 2). The EU institutions can be an important alternative channel of access for those organizations that find it difficult to access national political institutions. Nonetheless, it is important to bear in mind that empirical analyses across a large number of national associations demonstrate that this is only rarely the case (Eising 2004).

representation of interests for this area: the EEB, the World Wide Fund for Nature, Greenpeace, and Friends of the Earth, with the others having a more specialized focus. For the vast majority of non-business interests, however, it was only in the 1980s that their numbers began to increase. This came as a response to new European programmes. For example, the growth of anti-poverty groups in the second half of the 1980s was a direct consequence of new EU programmes in this policy area (Harvey 1993: 190).

In general, diffuse interests are characterized by their absence of clear purpose and membership and, aside from a small number of European federations, they also tend to lack a high degree of organization. Moreover, with increasing group size and a lack of social control, potential members have strong incentives to freeride on the provision of collective goods. As a consequence of ideological differences, differential linkages to national member organizations, overlapping responsibilities, and scarce EU funds, organizations of this kind sometimes end up competing with each another. When this happens it can limit their effectiveness as intermediary organizations for their domain (on consumer associations, see Young 1997: 66).

The Commission and the Parliament have sought to improve the organizational capacities of diffuse interest groups so as to enhance their standing in the policy process, and have offered financial support for that purpose. These grants amount only to a small proportion of the EU budget. However, to the interest groups concerned, EU sources of funding can be of major importance (see Pollack 1997: 581). The supranational institutions also support the activities of various social groups by providing project funds within EU programmes, as in the area of women and poverty. According to a survey conducted in the late 1990s, 59 per cent of EU associations representing diffuse interests received funds from the EU (Aspinwall and Greenwood 1998). Initially, the European Environmental Bureau received an overwhelming proportion of its budget from such sources (Hey and Brendle 1994). In 2004, it still received 52 per cent of its financial resources from the Commission and 24 per cent from other public authorities. Only 8 per cent of its resources were member contributions. Table 13.1 presents the sources of revenue of major environmental interest groups. In other areas, the European consumers association, BEUC, received about 50 per cent of its financial resources

Table 13.1 The sources of revenue of major EU environmental interest groups

	Source of revenue (per cent of total revenue)				
	EU	Other public authorities	Members	NGOs	Other
Birdlife International	13	16	2	18	52
Climate Action Network Europe	61	28	1	–	10
European Environmental Bureau	52	24	8	4	18
Word Wide Fund for Nature – Europe	20	–	50	20	10
Greenpeace – Europe	–	–	–	100	–
Friends of the Earth – Europe	47	38	15	–	–

Source: CONECCS database, April 2006.

from the EU institutions in 2005. In 2004, these financed 80 per cent of the funds of the European Women's Lobby (CONECCS data, April 2006). Not only does this financial support improve the organizational capacity and facilitate the staffing of these associations, it also improves their access to relevant expertise. For example, part of the EU's financial support granted to the European Trade Union Confederation (ETUC) goes to its college, which trains unionists for EU-level activities (Martin and Ross 1999: 325).

However, there are no clear-cut criteria for the funding of some of these organizations. Some EU budget lines grant interest groups mid-term financial security, while others provide financial means on a year-by-year basis, endangering the continuity of the organizations' work and even their survival. After a legal battle (Case C–106/96) with a few member states on the legal basis of budget lines for interest group funding to overcome social exclusion, in which the ECJ ruled against Commission practices, the EU bureaucracy introduced a set of guidelines for the management of grants, in order to establish uniform practices across its services and to provide for more transparency. However, the funding of NGOs, which has grown up in a piecemeal fashion, remains bound up with complicated budget procedures in need of further revision.

Some members of social policy interest groups also fear that the support given by EU institutions is little more than a convenient way for the EU to give a human face to the Single Market. Moreover, there is a risk that interest organizations might become too dependent on the EU institutions, influencing their political positions and activities. Financial support might allow the EU institutions to co-opt interest organizations, limiting their opposition to European initiatives. Some associations, such as Greenpeace, do not accept EU funding

BOX 13.5

Diffuse interest groups: some examples

The European Trade Union Confederation (ETUC)

Formed in 1973, the ETUC seeks to represent its members' interests in EU decision-making and has the aim of establishing a Europe-wide system of industrial relations. It has a membership of 79 trade union confederations from 35 European countries. Two national confederations from Macedonia and Serbia have observer status. Eleven European industry federations are also affiliated to the ETUC, which claims to represent 60 million individual members of these confederations. The ETUC employs a staff of 60 and, according to its constitution, is mainly financed from contributions by the affiliated national confederations that pay fees proportional to the size of their memberships.

The European Consumers Organization (BEUC)

BEUC was founded in 1962 and is an advocate for the interests of European consumers in the EU policy process. It has a membership of 40 national consumer organizations from 29 countries and has a staff of 25. Half of its financial means are provided by the European Commission and the other half by membership fees.

The European Environmental Bureau (EEB)

The EEB was founded in 1974 to promote the protection of the environment. It is the most comprehensive of all EU environmental organizations, having 131 full members and 12 associate member organizations from 31 countries. It has a staff of 14. In 2006, funds from the European Commission amounted to 52 per cent of its financial resources.

The European Womens' Lobby (EWL)

The EWL's goal is to eliminate discrimination against women and to serve as a link between the EU institutions and womens' organizations. It encompasses 28 national bodies from 25 countries. It also organizes 18 European or international member organizations that operate in at least half of the EU member states. It claims to represent more than 4,000 women's organizations in all. It has a staff of 10 and, in 2004, it received 80 per cent of its funds from the European Commission on the basis of an operating grant.

Sources: European Commission CONECCS database; websites of the above-mentioned organizations (accessed in April 2006).

for that reason. Yet there is 'no ready evidence of attempts by the Commission to steer networks towards, or for that matter away from, particular policy positions' (Harvey 1993: 191). Nonetheless, little is known about the extent to which EU programmes draw the attention of these groups away from areas in which no such public funding is available. In sum, financial support enables 'weak' interest organizations to participate in decision-making and allows the Commission to broaden its support base, to improve its expertise on the divergent arguments of different groups, and to claim that the legitimacy of EU policies has increased.

The Europeanization of domestic interests

There is no doubt that the European integration process has provoked an increase in interest group activity at the European level. But the EU may also have important consequences for *national* interest groups. These may take a number of different forms.

First, the growing importance of EU policy may lead national interest groups to redefine their interests. In the short term, new opportunities and risks posed by EU policies may trigger a process of reassessment within domestic organizations (Eising and Jabko 2001). In the longer term, the presence of the European institutions and the importance of their policies may mean that national groups begin to look at issues from a European perspective, rather than continuing to define problems in purely national terms (Katzenstein 1997). If this were to happen, interests would become Europeanized.

Secondly, as a consequence of the European integration process, domestic interests will increasingly have to coordinate interest representation at a variety of different levels of governance. As the EU extends its remit, more and more issues of concern to interest groups are likely to involve the European institutions. As the level of negotiation shifts to the supranational level, ordinary members of national groups may feel that they are losing out. To cope with these changes, national groups may use a variety of strategies to retain control of their role in the decision-making process, for example by making sure a consensus is reached before negotiations begin, and by confining the negotiation to the broad outline of that consensus. In sum, the Europeanization process would seem to involve a need for domestic interest groups to *adapt* to new circumstances, so as to allow them to retain some control over their involvement in the policy process. This 'need' may ultimately lead to organizational changes within the interest groups concerned. Hence, the logic of multi-level policy-making not only impinges upon interorganizational relations, but also affects the intraorganizational mode of operation (see Lehmkuhl 2000; Grote and Lang 2003).

Thirdly, the impact of the EU on domestic patterns of interest intermediation is yet unclear, even if this is a recurrent theme in the literature on interest groups. For example, despite the emergence of new European policies, the majority of German, British, and French trade associations continue to lobby domestic political institutions rather than the EU institutions when seeking to represent their interests. Indeed, only a minority of national interest organizations routinely maintain contacts with both EU and national institutions (Eising 2004). It is clear then that relations with domestic institutions do not necessarily weaken because of European integration. In fact, European integration may even contribute to a strengthening of existing ties (Benz 1998: 583) in cases, for example, where there is some uncertainty over new EU legislation which prompts national actors to exchange information. Shared concerns over the impact of EU directives and regulations may lead to new or may reinforce existing domestic alliances among groups and national political institutions. In short, even if many national associations now take an interest in both the European and national levels of governance, and even if the changes in the institutional environment lead to some kind of adaptation, the majority of national groups still remain rooted in their domestic contexts.

How then does the EU affect the influence of interest organizations and state institutions? It is debatable whether European integration strengthens the influence of state institutions or that of interest organizations on public policy. On the one hand, three factors are enlisted to support the hypothesis that multi-level policy-making strengthens state actors. Andrew Moravcsik (1998) has emphasized that European integration strengthens national executives because the latter act as gatekeepers between the national and the European arenas and obtain more resources from European integration than other actors. It appears that European integration strengthens their capacity to set the domestic political agenda, control policy information, legitimize their political actions, and contain the ability of opposing actors to veto their political initiatives. Secondly, domestic interest organizations may also lose ground due to the 'paradox of weakness': the very loss of autonomy incurred by public actors in the horizontal and vertical negotiations that are characteristic of EU decision-making may, at the same time, allow them to gain autonomy vis-à-vis private actors (Grande 1994). The strategy of 'self-binding' themselves to certain policy stances and the reference to negotiation pressures in the EU are supposed to be suitable means for public actors to turn down unwarranted interest group demands. Finally, the complexity of the EU multi-level system and the allocation of competencies to a multitude of public actors is said to make it impossible for interest organizations to identify 'the' decisive locus of political authority in the EU (Grande 1994).

On the other hand, several authors doubt that European integration generally strengthens state actors vis-à-vis interest organizations. They highlight various aspects of the EU institutional setting or emphasize the cooperation of public and private actors in EU policy networks. Some authors argue that the EU multi-level system increases the influence of interest organizations because it grants them many points of access for voicing their political demands (Pollack 1997). Such studies pay greater attention to the total number of access points in the multi-level setting than to the negotiation logic that may arise from its interlocking structure of political authority. In this view, easy access to and the resource dependencies of the EU institutions may tip the balance in favour of private players. Other institutionalist arguments emphasize the legal opportunities of the EU system. EU law can enable interest organizations and their constituencies to proceed against established domestic rules and practices.

Finally, studies drawing on the policy networks or advocacy coalitions literature pose a conceptual challenge to the claim that private interests lose out to public institutions. They emphasize that European policies are predominantly made in constellations that consist of both private and public actors and that may stretch from the EU-level into the member states. From this perspective, it is necessary to disaggregate the public and the private sectors, rather than to refer to the 'public sphere' or the 'private sphere' in order to identify in detail the winners and the losers. Thus the internal negotiations among the state institutions are embedded in the constitutive policy networks of private and public actors so that, at best, specific coalitions made up of private *and* public 'win' (or 'lose'). In sum, good reasons are given to back up the view that the EU *strengthens* the state, and that private actors are empowered, so that the evidence on this question remains inconclusive.

KEY POINTS

- The increase in European regulation may cause domestic interest groups to redefine or 'Europeanize' their interests.
- Interest groups may change in order to retain some control over public policy as it becomes more Europeanized.
- European integration may strengthen the ties between domestic institutions and interest groups.
- It is unclear whether European integration strengthens national governments at the expense of interest groups or vice versa.

Conclusion

European integration has left its mark on patterns of interest intermediation in the European Union. A new multilayered interest group system has emerged to reflect the multi-level institutional set-up of the EU. While the EU is characterized by numerous points of access for interests, which is a potential source of confusion, it also – because of its preference for consensual decision-making – grants interest groups an important say in the European policy process. Moreover, the EU institutions actively promote the formation of European-level groups, by providing funds for weaker, more diffuse interests and supporting those involved in implementing European policy.

Compared to national groups, those operating at the EU level tend to perform a narrower set of functions, acting as information brokers, representing the interests of their affiliates, and providing linkages to other interest organizations and to the EU institutions. Some even argue that interest groups have the potential to remedy the EU's democratic deficit (see Chapter 22), as they allow for greater political participation. However, this kind of argument has to recognize that there is a potential bias built into the system of EU interest organization. The system is highly asymmetric, with four-fifths of all groups representing business interests, and only one-fifth more diffuse social interests. Lacking in organizational capacity, the latter are highly dependent on support from the European institutions. Moreover, interest groups provide for a different sort of representation than bodies such as national parliaments or subnational regional authorities. It is therefore questionable whether the institutionalization of civil society participation in which the European Commission and the Economic and Social Committee have engaged offers an appropriate remedy to the problems of democracy and accountability from which the European Union is currently suffering.

? QUESTIONS

1. How have the European institutions sought to institutionalize, regulate, and structure interest group activity?
2. In what way and to what extent does the EU support interest groups? Why does it do this?
3. How do interest organizations benefit the European Union?

4. How does the institutional setting of the EU impact upon interest intermediation?
5. How important is each of the European institutions as an addressee of interest group demands?
6. What are the similarities and differences between national and EU groups?
7. Why are there more business than non-business interests present in the EU?
8. In what sense has there been a Europeanization of interest intermediation?

GUIDE TO FURTHER READING

■ Balme, R., Chabanet, D., and Wright, V. (eds) *L'Action Collective en Europe/Collective Action in Europe* (Paris: Presses de Sciences Po, 2002). This Franco-British co-production is a very comprehensive and informative compilation of articles on the theme of 'collective action'. About half the contributions are in English, the remainders in French.

■ Greenwood, J. *Interest Representation in the European Union* (New York: St Martin's Press, 2003). This textbook provides a useful introduction to the role of interest groups in the European Union.

■ Imig, D., and Tarrow, S. (eds) *Contentious Europeans: Protest and Politics in an Emerging Polity* (Lanham, MD: Rowman & Littlefield, 2001). This volume merges the social movement literature with that of European Union studies. Drawing on a quantitative analysis of protest events in the EU, as well as on case studies in different issue areas, the book illustrates the extent to which EU policies have been contentious and have been the source of political protest.

■ Smismans, S. (ed.) *Civil Society and Legitimate European Governance* (Cheltenham UK/Northampton, MA: Edward Elgar, 2006 forthcoming). This edited volume presents a variety of theoretical perspectives and empirical analyses that centre on the role of civil society in EU democracy.

■ Streeck, W., Grote, J., Schneider, V., and Visser, J. (eds) *Governing Interests: Business Associations Facing Internationalism* (London: Routledge, 2005). The contributions to this volume explore how business interest groups try to cope with the internationalization of markets, both in the EU member states and outside the EU.

IMPORTANT WEBSITES

● http://europa.eu.int/comm/civil_society/coneccs/index_en.htm The database for Consultation, the European Commission and Civil Society (CONECCS) on this website is maintained by the Secretariat-General of the European Commission. It includes a list of EU-level interest organizations, some basic data on these groups, useful links to these organizations as well as a directory of the Commission's consultation bodies.

● www.euractiv.com This Internet newsletter, as well as being of general interest, provides a listing of EU-level interest organizations, structured according to categories of interest. The section on opinion and governance provides useful dossiers about the governance reforms of the European Union. The section on public affairs provides more specific information on lobbying and NGOs. The website also provides useful links to the official EU documents on these issues and to position papers of private actors and member states.

● http://europa.eu.int/comm/governance/index_en.htm The Commission website on the governance debate, which includes contributions on political consultation, co-regulation by interest groups, and political participation.

Individual interest organizations usually also have their own websites. Here are some examples:

- www.unice.org The Union of Industrial and Employers' Federations.
- www.beuc.org The European Consumers Association.
- www.eeb.org The European Environmental Bureau.
- www.etuc.org The European Trade Union Confederation.
- www.socialplatform.org The Platform of European Social NGOs.

Visit the Online Resource Centre that accompanies this book for lots of interesting additional material. http://www.oxfordtextbooks.co.uk/orc/cini2e/

PART FOUR

Policies and Policy-Making

14 European Union External Relations

MICHAEL SMITH

Chapter Contents

Reader's Guide

This chapter focuses on the external economic relations of the EU – the longest-established area of EU international policy-making and action. The chapter begins by examining institutions and policy-making in the 'Community pillar' (Pillar 1), where the Commission plays a central role in initiating and conducting policy, and looks especially at the Common Commercial Policy. It goes on to look at two areas of 'mixed competence', where policy responsibility is shared between the EU institutions and national governments: development assistance policy and international monetary policy. The chapter then proceeds to explore the substance and impact of EU external economic policies, and to assess the role of the EU as a global 'economic power'. The conclusions draw attention to a number of tensions and contradictions in EU external economic policies.

Introduction

The European Union is unquestionably one of the largest concentrations of economic power in the global arena. As can be seen from Table 14.1, the Union possesses 'assets' in the form of economic resources, human resources, and territory that put it at least on a par with the USA, Japan, China, Russia, and other leading economic actors, and well ahead of several of them. Equally, in trade, investment, and other forms of international production and exchange, the EU can be seen as a potential economic 'superpower', not least because it constitutes the largest integrated market in the world. It is rich, it is stable, and it is skilled, and thus it inevitably occupies a prominent position in the handling of global economic issues. This fact of international economic life has only been underlined by the accession of the 10 new member states in 2004 (see Chapter 26).

Basic to the conversion of this economic potential into economic power and influence, as in so many other areas of EU policy-making, is the institutional context for the conduct of external economic policy. From the very outset in the 1950s, with the establishment of the Customs Union, the EEC had to develop a Common Commercial Policy to handle its relations with partners and rivals in the world economy. During the 1960s, the Community also initiated what was to become a wide-ranging and complex development assistance policy, primarily to manage relations with the ex-colonies of Community members. As early as the 1970s, there was a proposal also to establish a Monetary Union, with an external monetary policy, but this did not finally become established (and then only for some EU member states) until the twenty-first century. Each of these key areas of external economic policy presents the EU with distinct institutional problems, and with distinct opportunities for the exertion of international influence.

The purpose of this chapter is to explore these areas of external economic policy, to link them with the institutions and policy-making processes that they generate within the EU, and to explore the ways in which these create challenges and opportunities for the EU in the global arena. By doing this, the chapter will expose a number of areas in which there are tensions and contradictions within EU policies, as well as linkages between them; it will also enable us to evaluate EU policies towards major partners and rivals in the global arena and the extent to which the EU has been able to establish itself as a global 'economic power' by converting its potential into action.

Table 14.1 The European Union and its major rivals in the global political economy*

	Population (m)	Area (million sq km)	GDP (€bn)	Share of world trade (%)
China	1,300	9.6	1,326	Imports 7.2 Exports 9.1
India	1,087	3.3	531	Imports 1.3 Exports 1.2
Japan	128	0.4	3,753	Imports 6.2 Exports 7.9
Russia	142	17.1	468	Imports 1.2 Exports 2.6
USA	294	9.8	9,433	Imports 20.1 Exports 11.9
EU25 (2003)	457	3.9	9,727	Imports 14.0 Exports 13.0

*All figures for 2004 except where noted.

Sources: http://www.europa.eu.int/Comm/trade/en/; http://www.eurunion.org/profile/EUUSStats.htm.

The Common Commercial Policy (CCP)

The core of the EU's external economic relations is the Common Commercial Policy (CCP). Established by the Treaty of Rome, but not fully implemented until the late 1960s, the CCP is the means by which the EU manages the complex range of partnerships, negotiations, agreements, and disputes that emerge through the operation of the Customs Union (on the Customs Union, see Chapter 16). As we shall see later, the definition of 'commercial policy' has broadened considerably since the initiation of the EEC, but it is important to understand the core principles and policy-making procedures of the CCP as the basis for understanding the whole of the Union's external economic policies.

As established in the Treaty of Rome, the CCP was based on Article 113 of the Treaty – since amended to become Article 133 of the consolidated treaties in the late 1990s. Article 133 sets out not only the principles on which the CCP is to be pursued, but also the policy-making processes through which it is to be implemented. In terms of principles, as set out in Box 14.1, the CCP embodies not only a set of aims for the external policies of the Union, but also a set of far broader aims in relation to the operation of the world trade system. This key tension is at the heart of the successes registered and the difficulties encountered by the CCP, since it sets up a series of contradictions. Is the EC to achieve the aim of prosperity and stability for Europeans at the cost of international stability and development? Or is it to privilege the aim of global prosperity and development at the expense of the EU's citizens and their welfare? The reality of course is that there is a complex balancing process for EC policy-makers as they utilize the instruments of the CCP.

What are those instruments? Essentially, they fall into two broad areas. The first deals with what might be called trade promotion: the activities that develop the EC's international activities and organize them around certain core practices. These instruments fall partly within the control of the EC itself, but are also to be found in the broader global institutions and rules established in the world arena. Thus, the EC has developed a complex range of trade and commercial agreements, covering almost every corner of the globe. Some of these are bilateral, with individual countries such as Russia; others are interregional, covering relations with groupings such as ASEAN (the Association of Southeast Asian Nations); others still are multilateral, with the prime example being the World Trade Organization (WTO). In all of these areas of trade promotion, the EC aims to

BOX 14.1

The Common Commercial Policy

Article 131

By establishing a customs union between themselves Member States aim to contribute, in the common interest, to the harmonious development of world trade, the progressive abolition of restrictions on international trade and the lowering of customs barriers . . .

Article 133

1. The Common Commercial Policy shall be based on uniform principles, particularly in regard to changes in tariff rates, the conclusion of tariff and trade agreements, the achievement of uniformity in measures of liberalisation, export policy and measures to protect trade such as those to be taken in the event of dumping or subsidies.

2. The Commission shall submit proposals to the Council for implementing the Common Commercial Policy.

3. Where agreements with one or more states or international organisations need to be negotiated, the Commission shall make recommendations to the Council, which shall authorise the Commission to open the necessary negotiations . . . The Commission shall conduct these negotiations in consultation with a special committee appointed by the Council to assist the Commission in this task and within the framework of such directives as the Council may issue to it.

Source: These extracts are taken from the Consolidated Version of the Treaty establishing the European Community, 2002.

establish stable partnerships and relationships, often with a set of formal rules, which enable trade to develop and diversify.

A second set of CCP instruments are those of trade defence. Here, the EC is concerned to counter perceived unfair trade practices by its key partners, such as the dumping of goods at unrealistically low prices on the EU market, the subsidization of goods, or the creation of barriers to EC exports. To support it in these areas, the Community has developed a battery of trade tools: anti-dumping and anti-subsidy measures, rules of origin, sanctions, and other punishments. But it does not exercise these powers in isolation; frequently, the Community works through the WTO to counter what are seen as unfair practices, using the WTO dispute settlement procedures to defend itself at the global level. Trade and partnership agreements also include procedures for dealing with trade disputes, as a matter of routine, and sometimes linkages are made with other areas of external policy such as those on human rights and development assistance (see below).

The policy processes through which the CCP is implemented are those of the 'Community pillar', making use of the Community method. This is why in this section we talk of the EC and not the EU (see Chapter 1 for further explanation of the distinction between the two). In practical terms, this means that the Commission has the power of initiative, not so much on legislation as on the initiation, conduct, and implementation of commercial policy agreements. In many cases, the Commission will propose 'negotiating directives' in which its negotiating mandate is set out; where this is the case, the Council has to approve the mandate as well as any changes in it, and the Commission is monitored by a special Council committee, the so-called '133 Committee' of member state representatives. In other areas, the Commission has delegated powers to apply regulations (for example, on anti-dumping cases) subject to monitoring and approval by the Council. The Commission has developed a sophisticated apparatus for the conduct of trade negotiations and the conduct of 'commercial diplomacy' through its delegations and specialist missions such as that to the WTO in Geneva. It might be argued on this basis that in this area the EC has effectively displaced the national trade policies of the member states (in contrast to the position on foreign and security policy, where the member states remain supreme).

As time has passed, the Community has had to respond to the changing nature of world trade and exchange, and the CCP has been reshaped to reflect the key trends. In a number of instances, this has exposed the continuing tension between the national preferences of the member states and the 'European' perspective of the Commission, thus raising questions about the extent to which the EC has really undermined the independence of national commercial policies. A key issue here is that of competence: in the Treaty of Rome and for a long time afterwards, the CCP was assumed to be about trade in manufactured goods, but the changing world economy has given a much more prominent role to trade in services (for example, aviation services or financial services) and to related questions such as that of 'intellectual property' (the trade in ideas, such as those embodied in computer software). In order to cater for these changes, the scope of Article 113 and then 133 has had to be expanded, and this has not always been a simple process, as member states have found reasons to resist the expansion of the Commission's role.

Another area of tension, which has existed from the earliest days of the Community, reflects the linkage (or the gap) between 'internal' EC policies and the Community's external relations. As internal integration reaches new areas, it is inevitably found that these have external policy consequences. Thus, in the early days of the Community, the Common Agricultural Policy (CAP) was recognized to be not only a policy about what went on within the Community, but also a policy about the regulation of food imports, and so it has remained ever since. More recently, the completion of the 'single European airline market' during the late 1990s raised questions about who was to negotiate with countries such as the USA about the regulation of international air routes. Only after a prolonged struggle was it agreed that the Community (and thus the Commission) could exercise this power. A large number of other 'internal' policy areas, such as competition policy, environmental policy, and industrial policy are inevitably linked to the global economy, and this will continue to be an issue for the conduct of the CCP and related policies.

As a result of these trends and processes, the CCP has in a sense 'spread' to encompass new areas of external commercial policy, especially in the area of regulatory policy. The EU has become engaged with a very large number of international institutions in the conduct of these policies, and has developed a complex web of agreements with which to manage them. Not all of the EU's international economic policies fall into this framework, however, and we will now turn to look at two of the most important of these.

Development assistance policy and monetary policy

From the very earliest days of the EEC, there has been pressure for the Community and now the Union to expand the scope of its international economic policies. Thus from the 1960s onwards there has been a continuing concern with development assistance policy, stimulated originally by the process of decolonization in the French empire, and since the 1970s there has been a realization that the process of monetary integration in Europe must be accompanied by some form of international monetary policy. In contrast to the trade and commercial policy area, though, these areas have never been subject to the full Community method and thus to the leading role of the Commission. As a result, they demonstrate distinctive patterns of institutions and policy-making.

Let us first look at Community policies on development assistance. Starting in the early 1960s, a series of increasingly ambitious agreements between the EEC, its member states, and a growing range of ex-colonies created a unique system for the multilateral management of development assistance issues. Box 14.2 summarizes the key phases in this process, especially the progression from the 'Yaoundé system' to the 'Lomé system' and then to the present 'Cotonou system' (each taking its name from the place in which the agreements were finalized). It can be seen from this summary that the successive conventions have set progressively larger ambitions for the scope of the activities they cover, and also that they have covered an increasing number of partners from less developed countries (as well as a growing EC and then EU). As a result, the Cotonou system now covers well over half of all countries in the international system, including some of the very richest and a large number of the very poorest.

The initiation of the Lomé system in the 1970s was widely felt (especially by EC member states) to herald a revolution in development assistance policy by setting up an institutionalized partnership between the EEC and the African, Caribbean, and Pacific (ACP) countries. Processes were established to create and maintain a stable partnership, in which the ACP group would have its own collective voice, and to underpin the development of the poorest economies in the face of an unstable world economy. As time passed, however, there was criticism that the Lomé framework was increasingly irrelevant to the development of a global economy, and as a result the Cotonou system places a much greater emphasis on what might be called 'bottom-up' processes of development, in which individual ACP countries or groups of them produced their own plans for sustainable development to be negotiated with the EU. The Cotonou system also contains markedly more in the way of what has come to be called conditionality; in other words, provisions that make the granting of EU aid conditional on good governance, observance of human rights, and the introduction of market economics. In this way, it parallels broader developments in the provision of aid on a global scale.

The EU's development assistance policies have thus had to respond to the changing nature of the

CHRONOLOGY 14.2

Key stages in the evolution of the EU's relations with African, Caribbean, and Pacific (ACP) countries

1963: First Yaoundé Agreement (renewed 1969)

- Reciprocal preferential trade access between EEC member states and associated states (former colonies of member states)
- European Development Fund
- Joint Council of Ministers, Joint Parliamentary Assembly, and Committee of Ambassadors

1974: Lomé Convention (renewed 1979, 1984, 1990, 1995)

- Includes former British colonies. ACP Group established with Secretariat in Brussels
- ACP partners increase from 46 (1974) to 68 (1995)
- Non-reciprocal trade preferences
- Schemes to support ACP agricultural prices (STABEX, 1979) and mineral export prices (MINEX, 1984)

2000: Cotonou Agreement

- Twenty-year agreement (entered into force April 2003)
- ACP partners 78 (2006)
- Multilateral agreement to be supplemented by bilateral or minilateral Economic Partnership Agreements (EPAs) by December 2007
- Conditionality: aid payments linked to democratic government and human rights provisions

Source: European Commission at http://www.europa.eu.int/comm/development/en.

world economy. Not only the Lomé and Cotonou frameworks have felt this pressure: over a wide range of other development assistance activities, the EC and then the EU have had to adjust, to take account of new linkages (for example between trade and development, environment and development, and so on) and to balance the needs of the developing countries against those of the EU and its member states. The most acute tensions come in the area of agricultural policy: the CAP does demonstrable damage to the economies of some of the poorest countries, by depressing commodity prices, preventing free access to the European market, and subsidizing EU exports. Here again, we can see that external economic policy is closely connected to internal policy processes, and it is not always a profitable linkage.

Central to the problems encountered by the EU's development assistance policies are two factors. The first is an 'internal' institutional problem: the mixture of policy competences between the EU and its member states. The second is an external factor: the ways in which development assistance policies have become increasingly politicized in the contemporary world arena. In terms of the EU's institutional make-up, development assistance policy is an area of 'mixed competence', in which policies proposed and implemented at the EU level coexist with national policies for international development. Thus, although the EU claims to be the world's largest donor of development aid (see Table 14.2), the majority of the aid figure consists of aid given by member states as part of their national programmes. The complex programmes that have evolved at the European level are also, unlike the CCP, the result of a complex division of powers between the European institutions and the national governments represented in the Council. As a result, the Commission and the Community cannot claim to speak for Europe in this area, although their policies and initiatives have had considerable influence on the ways in which development assistance is targeted and allocated. Agreements such as the Lomé and Cotonou conventions are mixed agreements, and the Council collectively and the member states individually have the power to ratify or not to ratify them.

In addition to the problems created by internal institutional factors, EU development assistance policies have to contend with the fact that issues of economic and social development have become intensely politicized within the global arena. This means that aid is not simply an economic matter; it has become linked to problems of human rights, of 'good governance', and of statehood in the less developed countries, and the EU has had to develop mechanisms to deal with this. There has been an increasing tendency to concentrate the EU's development assistance policies, especially through the EuropeAid

Table 14.2 EU net bilateral and multilateral overseas development assistance (ODA), 2004

Country	Amount (US$, millions)
France	8,473
United Kingdom	7,883
Germany	7,534
Netherlands	4,204
Sweden	2,722
Italy	2,462
Spain	2,437
Denmark	2,037
Belgium	1,463
Portugal	1,031
Austria	678
Finland	665
Ireland	607
Greece	465
Luxembourg	236
Poland	118
Czech Republic	108
Hungary	55
Slovenia	31
Slovak Republic	28
Malta	10
Lithuania	9
Latvia	8
Estonia	5
Cyprus	5
EU25 Total (bilateral and multilateral)	*43,274*
USA	19,705
Japan	8,906

Source: *EU Donor Atlas 2006, Vol. 1* (European Commission/Organization for Economic Cooperation and Development, February 2006) found at http://www.europa.eu.int/comm/development/en.

development office, and to link them with the operation of agencies such as the European Community Humanitarian Office (ECHO). Since the end of the Cold War, there has also been a series of conflicts, for example in the former Yugoslavia and in Afghanistan, in which the EU has played a key role in coordinating reconstruction and post-conflict economic assistance. As a result, the EU's development assistance policies have moved away from their primary focus on the ACP countries, and a far wider range of recipient has been identified. Among these, post-Communist regimes and those involved in conflict form a key focus, as do the poorest countries, who are granted additional concessions in terms of free access to the European market for their goods.

Development assistance policy thus represents a long-established yet continually changing focus in the EU's external economic relations. Far less well established is the management of the international monetary relations that are an inevitable consequence of the adoption of the euro by 12 of the EU's member states. It has long been the ambition of enthusiasts for European integration to see the establishment of a 'real' European currency that might rival the US dollar on the world stage. Although there was significant European monetary coordination during the 1980s and 1990s, it was only with the adoption on the euro in 2000 that this became a political and economic reality (and then only for a certain number of EU member states, now in a minority since the enlargement of 2004). The euro experienced a harsh baptism, declining against the dollar continually for two years or more, but then recovered during the period 2003–5 as the dollar itself came under pressure. This is not the place to discuss the internal workings of the euro, but it is important to note that the launching of the euro has created at least a partial alternative to the dollar; it has become part of the currency reserves of a wide variety of countries, and it has become a target for those concerned at their overwhelming reliance on the US currency.

The euro is managed through a complex institutional process in which the European Central Bank (ECB) plays a key role. Because it has not been adopted by all of the EU member states, it exists alongside the remaining national currencies such as the pound sterling, the Danish krone, and the Polish zloty; whilst the governments of the non-euro countries are represented in a number of the bodies overseeing the euro and responsible for economic performance in the EU as a whole, there is differential membership, which gives rise to a number of frictions and tensions. The result is a complex picture of overlapping institutions, and this has its implications for international monetary management. The euro is a common currency among a number of countries, but it is not managed by a single government: the ECB does not report to a European Finance Minister, and there is no EU system of taxation or macroeconomic management. Yet the establishment of the euro has led to calls for adjustment of membership in international financial institutions such as the International Monetary Fund (IMF) to reflect the fact that 12 governments have merged their currencies into one. Not surprisingly, the USA has been prominent among those who note that 'Euroland' should have only one voice in such bodies as the IMF or the World Bank, and that the persistence of the national representations is an anomaly.

External policy objectives

As noted above, the EU is nothing if not explicit about many of its external economic policy objectives. The tone is set by the provisions of Article 113 (133) of the Treaties, in which the Common Commercial Policy (CCP) is established according to explicit principles, applying not only to the EEC and then to the EU but also to the broader management of international commercial relations. This has been backed up over the years by an extremely wide-ranging and sophisticated series of trade agreements with a wide range of partners, which go into great detail about the privileges and concessions to be given to specific partners. This can be seen as establishing an elaborate hierarchy or 'pyramid of privilege' in which the EU manages and adjusts its relations with individual partners (or groups of partners as in the ACP case). From time to time, this set of arrangements raises questions about exactly how particular partners should be dealt with: for example, in the case of China, the EU has had to change its approach as the country has developed economically, and as it has increasingly become integrated into the world economy through membership of the WTO and other international bodies.

At the same time, the EU has to balance its external obligations against the internal needs of the member states and of European producers and consumers. We have already noted that the CAP provides extensive safeguards (often said to be discriminatory) for EU farmers, but this is often at the expense of consumers whose food bills are higher because of the protectionism built into the CAP. During 2005, there was a major crisis in trade between the EU and China because of a surge of Chinese textile and clothing exports; this led to the imposition of quotas on Chinese products, but this in turn brought howls of anguish from EU retailers who had ordered products from China only to see them prevented from entering the European market. A large number of the disputes between the EU and the USA (who between them account for the majority of disputes brought before the WTO) have been exacerbated by the lobbying of producer groups in both the EU and the USA, which has created political problems around disputes that might in earlier times have been managed in a technocratic manner by officials and experts.

The net result of these cross-cutting tensions and pressures is a complicated picture in which the EU professes its commitment to the global management of trade issues but often acts as if it wishes to pursue its own interests in a unilateral manner. Some of the same sorts of tensions emerge in relation to development assistance, as has already been noted: the EU trumpets its commitment to international development and claims to be a pioneer of new types of development assistance policies, but there is always a balance to be struck between the broader international aims, those of the EU as a collective, and those of individual member states. This is institutionalized in the EU, thanks to the mixed nature of the institutional framework and the need to get agreement from the member states on major policy initiatives, and also reflects a number of powerful historical and cultural forces arising from the history of the European empires.

In international monetary policy, we have also noted the tensions between the requirements of internal management of the euro and the pressures of the global economy. The ECB has as almost its only major policy objective the achievement of monetary stability and the reduction of inflation, but this has been held responsible for some of the problems experienced by EU economies during the early 2000s, and thus for their inability to compete on a global level. Whatever the truth or the final conclusion of that argument, there is no doubt that the major economies of 'Euroland' have generally underperformed against their major global rivals, and that the need to bed down the eurozone system has contributed to this problem. It can also be argued that the primacy of monetary stability in the eurozone has made it more difficult for the eurozone countries and the ECB to respond rapidly to international financial crises such as those in the late 1990s, where unfavourable contrasts were drawn between the speed of movement of the US system and the lack of movement from Europe.

The EU thus has to face up to a number of tensions emerging from its pursuit of external economic policies. These have become more significant as the EU (either as a whole or through major subgroups such as the eurozone countries) has expanded its role in the world economy, and as the linkages between economic, political, and security activities have become more pronounced. One way of stating these tensions is in terms of the competing demands of multilateralism, interregionalism, bilateralism, and unilateralism in EU external economic policies. Each of these patterns can be seen in current EU policies, and they have to be held in a complex and fluctuating balance by a set of collective institutions and individual member states with competing interests.

Obstacles and opportunities: the EU as a power in the world economy

As noted earlier, the EU has enormous potential for influence and activity in the world economy, but it is equally clear from the argument here that it faces a number of important constraints on its capacity to turn potential into reality. We has already noted that a series of complex balances have to be struck in the making and implementation of EU external economic policies:

- Between the collective interests of the EU as a whole and those of individual member states or groups of member states.
- Between the claims and competencies of specific institutions and the pressures generated by different sectors of external economic policy.
- Between the claims of different partners and rivals in the world arena, which demand different patterns of incentives and resources from the EU.
- Between the economic dimension of the EU's involvement in the world arena and the increasing levels of politicization that accompany international economic transactions.
- Between the competing claims of multilateralism, interregionalism, bilateralism, and unilateralism in the pursuit of EU policies, often within cross-cutting institutional frameworks with complex patterns of demands.

In some ways, of course, these are no more demanding than the problems confronting any national government in the globalizing world economy. All governments and international institutions are subject to at least some if not all of these dilemmas. In the case of the EU, though, they are compounded by the fact that the EU itself is founded on a series of institutional compromises and a process of continuous negotiation. This makes the competing claims more obvious and in some ways less manageable than they might be for a national government, no matter what its size or complexity.

Against this, the EU has considerable assets and opportunities in the world economy. We have already noted that the EU is the world's 'champion trader' with a key position in the exchange of goods, services, and ideas, and its position as manager of the world's largest integrated market provides it with opportunities as well as with challenges. In recent years, the Community through the Commission has sought to exploit a number of these opportunities and to establish itself as a key player in the emerging global economy. Thus, it has become increasingly active in leading global trade negotiations, with varying levels of success; it has taken a leading role in the handling of international environmental issues such as those dealt with by the Kyoto Protocol on global warming; it has pursued its claim to be a leader in the provision of international development assistance and increasingly of humanitarian aid and disaster relief; and it has begun to exercise material influence, albeit often indirectly and haltingly, on the conduct of international monetary policy.

This means that the EU has increasingly become acknowledged as a 'power' in the world economy. It has acquired the legal and institutional apparatus with which to pursue this ambition, and as we have seen that legal and institutional framework gives it the capacity to carry out a number of important 'state functions' to preserve and enhance the prosperity of its citizens in a changing world economy. It has been able to establish itself as a key participant in global economic processes, both in formal institutional terms and in less formal terms of engagement in fundamental processes of trade, production, and exchange. In this, it has had to cope with challenges created by a number of other international economic 'powers' such as the USA, Japan, and (increasingly) China and India. It has created an impressive network of international economic partnerships, and has in many cases been able to link these with increasingly political conditions or requirements, for example through the use of economic sanctions. It has also taken an increasing role in global governance through its support for the regulation of international economic conditions through multilateral action.

It remains unclear in some respects what the EU as a global economic 'power' is for or against. As we have seen, this is a reflection of the complex institutional and other forces operating on its external economic policies, and the cross-cutting pressures to which its policy-making processes are subject. The result is a constant disparity between the EU's claims to global economic distinctiveness and the reality of its untidy policy-making processes. One thing that is clear, however, is that the enlarged EU of 25 members will continue to pursue an ambitious external economic policy and will continue to have a significant global economic impact.

Conclusion

This chapter has dealt with the core elements of the EU's external economic policies: institutions and policy-making, aims and objectives, constraints and opportunities, and the impact of the EU's activities. It has done so by focusing especially on three areas of policy: external trade and commercial policy, development assistance policy, and monetary policy. Each of these areas of policy has its own characteristic 'history' in terms of the evolution of institutions, and in terms of the EU's international engagement. We have seen that the Common Commercial Policy was almost built into the foundations of the EEC because of the need to manage the customs union, whilst the development assistance policy responded to the need to deal with the ex-colonies of the EU's member states, and the EU's international monetary policy emerged directly from the internal integration process expressed in the establishment of the euro. In each of these cases, the history matters, because it situates the external policy in a certain framework of institutional development and also because it locates the policy in terms of the development of the global economy.

It is also clear that in each of the policy areas we have explored, there is a complex and shifting array of pressures and demands, to which the EU has more or less successfully responded. The 'internal' pressures from member state governments, from producer or consumer groups, and from competition between the institutions, intersect with the external pressures created by globalization, by competition from major established and emerging economies, and by the pursuit of the EU's sizeable ambitions in a changing world. In these areas, the EU has for a long time had to deal with real and pressing policy dilemmas, which are a natural product of its assumption of major 'state functions'.

Despite these contradictory pressures and the difficulties of constructing policy in a global economy, the EU can claim in its external economic relations to have gone some distance 'beyond the nation state'. This does not mean that the member states are redundant: far from it, they are a major source of policy pressures and challenges for the Union's institutions, and they are a key source of the legitimacy which has been acquired by those institutions in the context of global governance; but there is also the legitimacy that has been acquired by decades of steadily deepening involvement in the global economy, and the acquisition of the knowledge and skills that go with it. This is what gives the EU's external economic relations a distinctive significance and impact and makes them a key subject for study.

? QUESTIONS

1. What are the key sources of the EU's power in the global economy, and how have they changed in importance during the course of European integration?
2. What are the key features of the distribution of power between the EU institutions in issues of trade and commercial policy? Has the balance of power between the institutions changed, and if so how and why?
3. How has the changing nature of world trade affected the EU's Common Commercial Policy?
4. What does it mean to say that development policy and monetary relations are areas of 'mixed competence' in the EU, and how does that affect processes of policy-making?
5. Why is it appropriate to describe the EU's development policies in terms of a 'pyramid of privilege'?
6. What are the key differences between the Lomé and Cotonou systems of EU development policy?
7. Why has the EU not become a 'monetary superpower' since the establishment of the euro? What developments might enable it to become one?
8. What contribution does the EU make to the governance of the global economy? Does this contribution match its potential?

GUIDE TO FURTHER READING

■ Eeckhout, P. *External Relations of the European Union: Legal and Constitutional Foundations* (Oxford: Oxford University Press, 2004). This is a detailed legal analysis, which is best used when you already know something about the legal and institutional frameworks.

- Guay, T. R. *The European Union and the United States: The Political Economy of a Relationship* (Sheffield: Sheffield Academic Press, 1999). A good general survey of the evolution and functioning of EU–US economic relations up to the end of the 1990s.
- Hill, C., and Smith, M. (eds) *International Relations and the European Union* (Oxford: Oxford University Press, 2005). Chapters 4, 8, 11, 12, and 14 deal with various aspects of policy-making and implementation in the EU's external economic relations.
- Holland, M. *The European Union and the Third World* (Basingstoke: Palgrave/Macmillan, 2002). The best general review of the EU's relations with developing countries, including the negotiation of the Lomé and Cotonou agreements.
- Verdun, A. (ed.) *The Euro: European Integration Theory and Economic and Monetary Union* (Lanham, MD: Rowman & Littlefield, 2002). Analysis of the political economy of the euro which includes discussion of its international role.
- Young, A. *Extending European Cooperation: The European Union and the 'New' International Trade Agenda* (Manchester: Manchester University Press, 2002). Detailed analysis of the changing nature of trade policy and the ways in which it relates to changes in EU policy-making.

IMPORTANT WEBSITES

- www.europa.eu.int The Commission's web portal guides you to separate websites for trade, monetary relations, and development policies.
- www.eurunion.org This is the website of the European Commission delegation in Washington, DC, which contains analysis of EU–US economic relations as well as links to a large number of other related sites.
- www.wto.org The website of the World Trade Organization, which contains analysis and commentary on current trade issues and trade disputes, as well as large amounts of detailed information about trade negotiations.
- www.oecd.org The website of the Organization for Economic Cooperation and Development, which includes analysis of EU trade and economic policies among a large range of other studies.
- www.apcsec.org The website of the Secretariat for the African, Caribbean, and Pacific (ACP) states, which are the EU's partners in the Cotonou Convention.
- www.ecb.int The website of the European Central Bank which includes studies on the international role and impact of the euro.

Visit the Online Resource Centre that accompanies this book for lots of interesting additional material. http://www.oxfordtextbooks.co.uk/orc/cini2e/

15 The EU's Foreign, Security, and Defence Policies

ROBERT DOVER

Chapter Contents

Reader's Guide

This chapter outlines key historical, institutional, and thematic developments within the EU's foreign, security, and defence policies. It argues that the EU has been an awkward foreign and security policy actor, unable to formulate a cohesive identity or credible capabilities with which to project itself on the world stage. This situation has arisen because of the post-Second World War pre-eminence of NATO (the North Atlantic Treaty Organization) as a security actor, binding US political, economic, and military capabilities into the Western European area, allowing, as a consequence, European governments to freeride on the USA. Since 1991 and the end of the Cold War both the EU and NATO have been seeking to position themselves in the spheres of foreign and security policy; the dawn of a new age of asymmetric military threats – currently terrorist attacks on public transport – is refocusing the EU's security efforts on 'homeland security' whilst simultaneously trying to promote stability in the world and assist in post-conflict reconstruction efforts where necessary. This dualism with NATO is a recent development and looks likely to shape the EU's security agenda until 2020.

Introduction

A decade and a half after the negotiators at the Maastricht Intergovernmental Conference (IGC) of 1992 confirmed that 'a common foreign and security policy is hereby established' (Article J, Treaty on European Union), the EU has not moved very much closer towards a supranational foreign policy. With the EU being a Union of 25 countries and 456 million people, and having an economy now broadly comparable to that of the USA, the absence of a functioning EU foreign policy

 CHRONOLOGY 15.1

Common Foreign and Security Policy

1947 Dunkirk Treaty – an Anglo-French agreement on mutual defence

1948 Brussels Treaty Organization (BTO) – promoting joint security between the UK, France, Belgium, the Netherlands, and Luxembourg

1949 North Atlantic Treaty Organization (NATO) founded

1954 West Germany and Italy join the BTO; it is is renamed the Western European Union (WEU)

1962 Failure of a French attempt, the Fouchet Plan, to develop closer political and military cooperation through an intergovernmental framework

1970 European Political Cooperation (EPC) instituted

1986 Single European Act (SEA) codifies the status of the EPC as part of the EC

1992 Maastricht Treaty establishes that CFSP is the successor to EPC

1993 The Eurocorps created: a small European army inaugurated by President Mitterrand and Chancellor Kohl

1996 The Amsterdam Treaty reinforces the Maastricht proposals in more specific terms and strengthens the position of the Commission in foreign and defence policy formation but without moving significantly from an intergovernmental framework

1998 (October) the Pörtschach informal ministerial summit sees UK Prime Minister Blair outlining a general desire to be more positive on EU defence

(December) Anglo-French summit at Saint Malo, PM Blair and President Chirac agree to take positive and concrete steps to support the formulation of a common European defence initiative

1999 The Cologne European Council puts capabilities at the heart of the ESDP. The Capabilities Catalogue is created

2001 The Nice Treaty provides for the development of an EU military capacity, the creation of permanent political and military structures, and the incorporation into the Union of the crisis management functions of the WEU (enters into force on 1 February 2003)

2002 (February) An EC delegation begins work in Afghanistan to support post-conflict reconstruction

(May) The EU carries out the first ever practice crisis management exercise under the ESDP banner

(December) The EU and NATO formalize the Berlin Plus arrangements that provide the EU with access to NATO assets

2003 (January) EU ministers approve the first action under ESDP, sending assistance to Former Yugoslav Republic of Macedonia (FYROM)

(March) US and UK forces invade Iraq against the wishes of the French and German governments who say they will block a second UN Resolution

(April) France, Belgium, Germany, and Luxembourg call for deeper cooperation on ESDP

2004 (March) Terrorists attacked commuter trains entering Madrid

(June) The EU pledge €200m to support the reconstruction of Afghanistan

2005 – (May) German and French governments affirm that the Constitutional Treaty is an important milestone for the development of the EU's external identity

(7 July) The London public transport system attacked by four bombers

(September) The EU states decide by a qualified majority to retain email and mobile phone communications for two years

2006 (January) The EU3 (UK, France, Germany) decide to end negotiations with Iran over its attempts to acquire advanced nuclear technologies

confirms that while the EU is a 'civilian superpower', it is not a military one. However, whilst the Maastricht, Amsterdam, and Nice Treaties failed to reduce intergovernmentalism in foreign policy cooperation, governments have begun to bring the policy to Brussels to a greater extent than in the past. Yet the move towards a 'Brusselized' Common Foreign and Security Policy (CFSP) has been a slow and piecemeal process, one that is largely taking place outside of treaty-making IGCs.

This chapter presents an overview of historical and institutional developments in the fields of foreign policy, security, and defence. The chapter also analyses some of the main contemporary debates within the Common Foreign and Security Policy (CFSP) and the European Security and Defence Policy (ESDP), as well as issues that are relevant to the medium and long-term future of the policies.

Some history: European Political Cooperation (EPC)

The EU has a well-established reputation as a 'civilian superpower' (see Chapter 4). The first attempt at extending this responsibility to foreign affairs came with the establishment of European Political Cooperation (EPC). This was a product of the Luxembourg Report of 1970, later to be incorporated into the European Community (EC) by the 1987 Single European Act (SEA). Even within the 1987 regime, however, EPC was distinct from regular Community procedures. Bringing EPC within the Treaty did indicate a willingness in the Union to draw external political relations closer to the activities of the Community.

EPC was principally a means of coordinating meetings between foreign ministers. Until 1987 it did not have its own institutions and it was managed by a *troika*, led by the country holding the EU Presidency. This was problematic as the Presidency (and the *troika*) changed every six months, with the result that there was limited scope for continuity and long-term planning, hindering EU efforts to formulate common positions (Fraser 1999).

The pre-and post-1987 EPC regimes were quite similar in that the Commission and the European Parliament remained subservient to the member states. The role of the Commission, which was more extensive in economic negotiations, was also more substantial where its competence over trade matters impinged on the external relations function of EPC. Yet EPC was often criticized for being weak and lacking in substance (Nuttall 1992; Allen 2002), even if it did generate joint positions during the 1980s that gave some sense of a European world view. EPC's light-touch approach and its loose framing made it ill equipped to project a common European vision at the end of the Cold War and this led to criticism that it was reactive. The absence of a common European response to the collapse of the Soviet Union was at least in part due to a lack of European foreign policy identity.

KEY POINTS

- EPC was a forerunner to the Common Foreign and Security Policy.
- Although EPC was able to secure opportunities for dialogue amongst the EC's members, it was frequently criticized for being reactive.
- EPC was unable to forge a common response to the end of communism and the collapse of the Soviet Union in the late 1980s and early 1990s.

The changing context of European foreign policy

By the 1990s the EU was well placed to play a leading role in the new economic world order. Although the Cold War organizations had lost their *raison d'être* with the fall of communism, they had kept the USA politically engaged in Europe. This was especially important because of the support that the USA could give to the newly independent states of Central and Eastern Europe as they began to reconstruct.

The collapse of the Soviet Union removed some significant barriers to the EU's eastern enlargement. It also allowed members of the European Free Trade Association (EFTA) (Sweden, Finland, Austria, Norway) to submit applications to join the EU as the need for a 'buffer zone' between Russia and 'the West' had been greatly reduced. The debate over whether to enlarge the Community immediately or to add first to the Community's competencies was resolved with a very European compromise which involved the extension of competencies, the reform of the EU institutions, a codification of foreign and security policy, *and*, in a much more measured way, preparations for enlargement.

A more developed form of foreign policy cooperation was made possible at this point because of the end of the Cold War. The USA saw in the demise of Soviet Union an opportunity to reap a peace dividend, to be achieved by limiting US involvement in mainland Europe. This would be possible, however, only if European governments were able to shoulder more of their own security burden. A European foreign policy would assist in this process.

KEY POINTS

- The EC was well placed to benefit from the end of the Cold War.
- The end of the Cold War opened the door to new opportunities for Europeans to develop their own foreign policy.

Common Foreign and Security Policy (CFSP)

The Maastricht European Council agreed a Common Foreign and Security Policy (CFSP), which was to form the second pillar (Pillar 2) of the new European Union. Pillar 2 was to be intergovernmental, involving very little input from the European Commission and European Parliament. Moreover, the CFSP's decision-making framework was to rest on a unanimous voting system in the EU Council, giving each government the ability to veto any policy initiative or operation. This was to be a lowest common denominator policy, leading to policy outputs that were extremely conservative.

The CFSP sought to assist EU governments in formulating common foreign policy positions. However, problems arose as the policy was positioned outside of the Community pillar (Pillar 1), which dealt with external economic policy (see Chapter 14); and it was also divorced from immigration, asylum, terrorism, and trafficking issues dealt with in Pillar 3 (see Chapter 19). Some

KEY CONCEPTS AND TERMS 15.2

The intergovernmental institutional framework

The European Council

The European Council (heads of government) meets at least once every six months to set priorities and agree on the big issues of the day, including CFSP and other external relations issues. The European Council lays down the guidelines for CFSP and adopts Common Strategies. *The EU Council (of Foreign Ministers)* meets at least monthly under the banner of the General Affairs Council. It makes decisions on external relations issues, including CFSP, possibly leading to Joint Actions and Common Positions.

The Council is supported by the Committee of Permanent Representatives (COREPER), composed of member states. These are ambassadors to the EU who meet at least once a week to prepare Council meetings and decisions, including those related to the General Affairs Council and CFSP. Anecdotal evidence from senior officials shows that COREPER plays a crucial role in organizing the work of CFSP and smoothing over policy disagreements. *Relex Counsellors* analyse the institutional, legal, and financial aspects of proposals made under the CFSP umbrella. The Counsellors prepare COREPER'S work on Joint Actions and try to ensure consistency across the three EU pillars. The *CFSP Working Groups* are staffed by experts from the member states and the Commission. They examine policy documents and options for the consideration of the various CFSP institutional bodies.

The Presidency

The Presidency is held by EU countries on a six-monthly basis and plays an important role within CFSP, as it sets the agenda for the political decision-making process. It provides the background administration for meetings and is responsible for trying to resolve disagreements and difficulties on all policy issues. This is particularly important in relation to CFSP, as decisions are made unanimously and disagreements result in vetoes. The Presidency is assisted in its work by the Council Secretariat and, since the Amsterdam Treaty, by the Secretary-General/High Representative for CFSP.

The Policy Planning and Early Warning Unit

The Policy Planning and Early Warning Unit is based within the Council Secretariat and has a responsibility for monitoring and assessing international developments, as well as analysing emerging threats and crises. The Early Warning Unit's analytical role is important in so far as it provides the member states with the information they require to formulate a common foreign policy.

The Political and Security Committee

The Political and Security Committee (PSC or COPS) is central to CFSP and ESDP. It is the hub in organizing the EU's response to any crisis, and is composed of national representatives. The PSC prepares recommendations on how CFSP (and ESDP) should develop and also deals with the routine elements of these policies. In the event of a crisis, the PSC is the body that analyses the options open to members and manages the EU's approach to the crisis. A group of *European Correspondents* in all EU member states and within the Commission coordinates the day-to-day business of the CFSP and prepares the PSC meetings. The correspondents are also responsible for ensuring that CFSP business is included on the agendas of the General Affairs Council and European Councils. They liaise via the encrypted telex network known as Coreu (Correspondance européenne) which connects member states and the Commission.

coordination of European external policy across the three pillars was achieved by giving the Commission and the Parliament formal roles, later expanded upon. In Pillar 2, the Commission is '*associated with* all aspects of the CFSP', and has an equal right of initiative with member governments. In Pillar 1, by contrast, the Commission has sole right of initiative. The European Parliament has to be 'kept informed' of policies and initiatives conducted under CFSP; and the European Court of Justice has no role at all. These latter two institutions have been kept out of CFSP policy-making to ensure the preeminence of the member states in this policy area.

The enactment of the Treaty on European Union (TEU) at Maastricht provided three identifiable sources of external relations policy for the EU, binding the states and supranational institutions together. First are the member states, with their own foreign, defence, and security policies pursued independently of CFSP. Second is the coordinating

CFSP framework which places a responsibility on member states to 'inform and consult each other [on] matters of foreign and security policy', with the aim of increasing the international leverage they can exert by working together.

The EU Council is able to establish Common Positions (see below), as it has done in the case of the eradication of landmines. Joint Actions are a second instrument. These require a unanimous vote if they are to be approved; and a further unanimous vote to decide whether issues of implementation can be decided by a qualified majority vote. Joint Actions allow the EU to go beyond merely consulting on issues (as had been the case under the EPC framework), obliging member states to conform to the positions they adopt. The Commission's extensive responsibilities over trade policy, and its large number of overseas representations, provide a third source of foreign policy stimuli in the EU.

The Maastricht Treaty also stated that the EU should work towards creating a common defence policy and eventually a common defence. This would later be used as the basis for developing a European Security and Defence Policy. In the meantime, the Treaty established a review procedure for CFSP. This began with the setting up of a reflection group of civil servants in 1996, and culminated in a new IGC, and another treaty revision which was approved at the Amsterdam European Council in June 1997.

At Amsterdam, the British and French governments disagreed over how the policy should develop. The British felt that the Yugoslav experience (see Box

BOX 15.3

The supranational institutions in CFSP and ESDP

The European Commission

The strengthening of the Council with regard to CFSP has implications for the role of the Commission. A Declaration added to the Amsterdam Treaty outlined how the Commission proposed to reorganize its Directorates-General to bring external relations under the remit of one Vice-President, rather than four commissioners, as was earlier the case. However, the Commission President, Romano Prodi, appointed in 1999, did not observe the Declaration and appointed four external relations commissioners with functional rather than geographic responsibilities. Prodi did appoint Chris Patten to a post responsible for coordinating external relations policy. Whilst Patten was not formally a Vice-President his role was intended to be of equivalent stature – that of a kind of Foreign Minister for the EU. The other three external relations portfolios covered trade, enlargement, and development. Since 2004 Commission President Barroso has held a generic foreign policy role as the lead official for the Commission.

Over the years there have been many criticisms of the Commission's role in CFSP, focusing particularly on the transparent nature of their procedures. There have been doubts about the quality of internal security in the Commission, with leaked information potentially endangering the safety of officials in the field (Dassu and Missoroli 2002). As a result of these criticisms, Javier Solana has tried to shield the policy formulation apparatus of his section from the rest of the Commission, causing frictions in the EU's institutions.

In the Prodi Commission, Chris Patten was vocal in his complaint that the Council made foreign policy without reference to the bodies that would implement it (notably the Commission). He recognized an important gap in responsibility between the decision-makers and the implementers. Prodi's solution was to suggest that the High Representative be made Permanent Chair of the PSC (see Box 15.2) *and* a member of the Commission, to make the Commission's stakeholder role more prominent. Whilst the vast majority of EU 'business' impacts on the world outside of the EU and therefore has foreign and, tangentially, security implications, only those activities requiring the application of military force are generally included in the CFSP and ESDP frameworks. The crossover between these two types of activities is confusing and often paradoxical, making it look as though the EU's external relations are inconsistent or even incoherent.

The European Parliament

The European Parliament has no formal CFSP/ESDP role, but is regularly kept informed and is consulted on issues within these areas. Members of the European Parliament (MEPs) have been very active arranging debates, tabling questions, and putting pressure on national governments. Not surprisingly, perhaps, the Parliament is keen to have more foreign and security policy competencies.

15.4) confirmed that the EU was incapable of formulating a common foreign policy, whereas the French government argued that this demonstrated why such policy was necessary (Howarth 2000). Neither argued with the proposition that CFSP had achieved remarkably little in its first few years, however.

The Amsterdam Treaty was negotiated as the UK government changed hands in May 1997. While the new Labour government was elected on a pro-European platform (Forster 2002), the changeover came too late for the CFSP. Of the changes introduced, the introduction of constructive abstention was notable. This provision enabled fewer than one-third of member states to opt out of a Joint Action without vetoing it for the others.

Two further significant measures were agreed at Amsterdam. The first was the creation of the High Representative for the CFSP, a post which was combined with that of Secretary-General of the EU Council. The second was the creation of the Policy Planning and Early Warning Unit in the Council Secretariat (the 'Policy Unit'). When the ESDP was established by the Treaty of Nice (see below), the unit was expanded to incorporate officials from the newly created Military Staff (EUMS). These initiatives brought external foreign relations closer to Brussels, even if the member states were able to guarantee the use of intergovernmentalist working methods and, as a consequence, their continued pre-eminence over this policy field.

CASE STUDY 15.4

The EU and the Balkans

The Yugoslav civil war was an enormous wake-up call and a profound embarrassment for the EU. After Jacques Poos' rather optimistic statement that 'now is the hour of Europe', and the negotiations to codify CFSP, the EU's response to Yugoslavia in the peried 1991–5 highlighted weaknesses within the EU foreign and security policies. In unilaterally recognizing Slovenian independence in June 1991, the German government hastened the crisis in the Balkans. This in turn led to the recognition of independence of Croatia and Macedonia (June 1991 and September 1991 respectively) and political moves to establish a sovereign Bosnia. These attempts to fracture the federation of Yugoslavia prompted a military response from the predominantly Serb Yugoslav National Army (JNA) under the civilian control of Slobodan Milosevic.

The EU's response to the genocide, displacement of populations, and imperial conquests has been widely condemned as inadequate (Bellamy 2002). The institutional historical memory of the First and Second World Wars and country allegiances to Croatia and Serbia partially guided EU governments in the early stages of the conflict. There was strong evidence that Croatian forces had been armed by Germany, and a great deal of captured Croatian material had been manufactured in Germany; whilst the French and British governments held historical allegiances with Serbia. This created problems early on in formulating a 'European' response. The need for unanimity in EU foreign policy meant that statements and policies that blamed one side or the other in the conflict were politically untenable. These allegiances were less prominent after events such as the siege of Sarajevo in 1994 where a prevailing international norm of revulsion at the military action led to a more universal approach.

The USA played a very low-key role in the early stages of the civil war (1992–4), which further exposed the EU's inability to formulate a credible policy towards the conflict. For example, without being able to deploy a credible threat of military force, international agreements brokered with Milosevic were breached with impunity by the Serbs. It was only when the USA began to take an active role in brokering peace between the warring factions that the implied threat of the use of military force saw these agreements honoured.

Furthermore, the EU seemed obsessed with trying to deploy the levers of economic foreign policy to bring the conflict to a close. Economic sanctions on the one hand and infrastructural aid on the other were policies that the EU governments were able to agree on. However, both the sanctions regime, and the distribution of aid and infrastructural support were strongly criticized by practitioners and academics alike as having been ineffective (Keane 2004). However, economic foreign policy was a policy area where the EU was more confident and experienced, and in particular regarding economic aid, which had already been committed by the member states.

Finally, the Amsterdam Treaty also introduced a new instrument, the Common Strategy. This is decided unanimously by the European Council on the basis of a recommendation by the EU Council (of foreign ministers). Strategies are implemented by adopting Joint Actions and Common Positions which can be achieved through qualified majority votes in the Council, unless a member argues that the measure runs contrary to its core national interest – in which case it can exercise a veto. Thus far only one Strategy, on Russia, has been agreed.

KEY POINTS

- Maastricht established a Common Foreign and Security Policy, which was largely intergovernmental in character.
- The first tests of CFSP were far from impressive. The Amsterdam Treaty revisions sought to rectify some of the institutional problems, but failed to address the question of a European defence policy

European Security and Defence Policy (ESDP)

As already noted, the Maastricht Treaty did more than just set up the CFSP. It also foresaw EU cooperation in matters of defence. However, it was not until 1998 that an opportunity arose for pursuing further convergence in this area.

The St Malo process

The process which began at the port of St Malo in France in December 1998 opened the way for a new phase in European foreign policy cooperation, one which would involve the emergence of a defence policy, and the gradual militarization of the European Union. 'The Saint Malo process' was led by the UK and French governments. For the newly elected UK government, the initiative was to bring defence cooperation into the heart of their European programme, making it a symbol of the government's pro-European leanings. From the UK perspective it was also an initiative which was designed to prevent the French, Italian, and Spanish governments from forcing military and security policy on to the agenda in a way that disadvantaged British interests (Dover 2005).

But St Malo also has to be seen in a more general political context. The main 'European' issue of the day was the development of the single currency, which the UK government found impossible to support. Blair put out a call to his cabinet ministers to find policy areas in which the UK could further advance integration (Dover 2005). The Ministry of Defence (MoD) was the only department to reply to this call with a proposal for deepening European defence integration without undermining NATO's role. The MoD proposal resulted in the Pörtschach Declaration of October 1998, in which Blair stated his desire to see closer European defence cooperation, and the St Malo Declaration of December 1998, which pledged Anglo-French cooperation on defence issues within an EU framework.

As the least transatlantic of any of the EU governments, and the keenest to see NATO scrapped at the end of the Cold War, the French were surprised to be approached by British officials seeking to advance an EU-based security solution (Howarth 2000). Getting the French government on board with plans for Europeanizing security was seen as crucial by the British, as the agreement at St Malo had to bring together both ends of the security spectrum – the proactive (French) and highly reactive (British).

The St Malo meeting and the texts it produced were the high-water mark of Anglo-French cooperation. The agreements also demonstrated the influence of the 'Big Three', the UK, France, and

Germany, over large initiatives of this kind. The German government was seen as America's closest European ally in the late 1990s and it also had a post-war allegiance to NATO as it was on the front line of any potential clash between NATO and the Warsaw Pact countries. Convinced that ESDP was not intended to undermine the transatlantic alliance, the German government was happy to lend its support to the initiative. Agreement among these governments ensured that the policy would be successful.

After St Malo

Through several European Council meetings in Cologne (1999), Helsinki (1999), and Sintra (2000), the ESDP proposals were amended and adapted. Of particular note was the inclusion of what would become the Petersberg tasks and a Headline Goal for the EU – to be able to deploy 60,000 troops, in 60 days, sustainable for up to one year (Rutten 2002). Proposals such as these were transformed into a Capabilities Catalogue, a pool of personnel, expertise, and military equipment pledged by member governments, which could be used in EU-sponsored military actions. In explicitly connecting capabilities to the St Malo process, its British and French government sponsors aimed to make ESDP more than just a paper policy.

The ESDP is composed of three elements: military crisis management, civilian crisis management, and conflict prevention. In June 1999, the Cologne European Council placed crisis management and the capabilities required to deliver it at the heart of renewed efforts to strengthen the CFSP. Subsequent European Councils refocused efforts on the assets available to the EU, which would allow it to conduct autonomous actions, ranging from advanced policing, through conflict prevent, right up to peace enforcement operations.

British and French government negotiators expected the policy to be fully functioning by 2003. However, governments have been unable to meet the relatively modest targets set out within the Capabilities Catalogue. This has been in part due to internal pressures to spend money on more electorally attractive areas such as health and education, whilst foreign and security budgets have been consumed by

CASE STUDY 15.5

ESDP – the military and civilian dimensions

The military dimension

The military side of ESDP was introduced at Helsinki in 1999, and developed at the Nice 2001 European Council. Helsinki resulted in the so-called Headline Goal, whilst Nice provided the institutional structures that supported the policy, namely the Political and Security Committee (PSC), which is assisted by a politico-military working group, a committee for civilian aspects of crisis management, as well as the Military Committee (EUMC) and the Military Staff (EUMS).

The civilian dimension

The Feira (1999) and Gothenburg (2001) Councils developed the civilian element of ESDP, which aimed to fill the 'soft' security gaps left open by the international community. The Nice Council provided four institutional arrangements to fill these gaps, supplemented by a civil–military relations committee to ensure that these interventions ran smoothly:

- Police cooperation: creating a capability to deploy 5,000 police, including 1,000 within 30 days, for tasks ranging from the training of local police to assisting military forces in restoring order.
- Rule of law: an ambition to be able to provide up to 200 judges, prosecutors, and other legal experts to areas in crisis.
- Civilian administration: providing officials to assist in the basic tasks of government administration, like establishing education, infrastructure, and elections.
- Civil protection: the ability to assist in humanitarian assistance at short notice – the EU to be capable, within three to seven hours, of providing two to three assessment teams as well as intervention teams consisting of up to 2,000 people.

the conflicts in Afghanistan and Iraq and by the implementation of anti-terrorist measures.

The emphasis on Petersberg-style military tasks has reinforced the EU's self-constructed soft-security identity, and has acted as a barrier to the formulation of EU responses that include the full range of military equipment – for example expeditionary warfare as in the US–UK invasion of Iraq in 2003. The inclusion of the Petersberg tasks in ESDP supports the view that ESDP is a product of the EU's inability to deal with peacekeeping and peace-enforcement operations like those presented by the Yugoslav civil war, and a realization that the threats to the EU will come from non-state military actors in the medium to long term (Dover 2004; M. Smith 2001b). The EU's experience in Yugoslavia demonstrated that it had neither adequate policy tools to deal with this kind of conflict, nor pan-European agreement on how it should act should similar circumstances present themselves again. Positively, the Yugoslav experience also showed the UK and France that they could work closely together without diplomatic conflict, something that was particularly important in the run-up to St Malo.

Civil wars and the consequences of failing states demand the sort of response the Petersberg tasks aim to deliver – humanitarian and rescue tasks; peacekeeping tasks; peacemaking; and crisis management. To give the EU an opportunity to address these scenarios effectively it was necessary to ensure that it had access to NATO assets. The negotiations to secure this access was one of the most important tasks at the periphery of the Nice European Council meeting in December 2001. The so-called 'Berlin Plus' arrangements were a key marker of whether the ESDP might function as an independent policy area, avoiding duplication with the institutions and assets of NATO and the UN. In this matter Turkey proved to be a considerable stumbling block to the EU being able to secure rights to these assets, as the Turkish government was keen to veto access to NATO equipment unless Turkey was allowed to join the EU. Turkish opposition was removed through intensive diplomacy by NATO and the British and US governments in December 2000.

KEY POINTS

- The agreement of the British and French governments at St Malo in December 1998 created an overwhelming momentum towards a common European security and defence policy.
- Some of the key negotiations that took place over ESDP concerned the relationship between the EU and NATO. A deal was finally secured in 2002.
- The negotiations resulted in the production of a Capabilities Catalogue. As of early 2006 the Capabilities Catalogue had still to be fully 'populated'.

The Nice Treaty

The negotiations for ESDP were largely conducted outside formal EU negotiating frameworks so as to avoid the input of Commission officials and Members of the European Parliament (MEPs). They were bilaterally agreed between governments before the final signatures at the Nice European Council. The Cologne, Helsinki, and Sintra Councils had provided the opportunities, between St Malo in December 1998 and the Nice Treaty negotiations in December 2000, to conclude much of the detail of ESDP before it was codified at Nice. Therefore, the final negotiations were concluded quickly.

The Nice Treaty empowers the Commission to ensure that the EU's actions are consistent, and designed to meet the objectives laid down by national governments. This strategy aims to provide stability and to restore a political and economic environment conducive to peace in the affected region. It also brings EU foreign and security policy closer to Brussels, albeit within the very strict parameters of oversight and sequencing roles, reaffirming once again the primacy of the member governments.

The Nice Treaty also allowed the Council to use qualified majority voting (QMV) for decisions relating to internal matters, that is, institutional design or the adoption of Joint Actions. QMV was also to be used where the Council was to appoint a

Special Representative to a region in crisis. The Political Committee was replaced by a Political and Security Committee (PSC), with the High Representative chairing the PSC in place of a representative from the Presidency, once again suggesting a drift away from the national capitals to Brussels. Further evidence of this drift can be found in the role of the so-called CFSP 'ambassadors' who had previously travelled from capital to capital, but who after Nice were to be based in Brussels in semi-permanent session.

Despite these changes, the 'Brusselsization' of foreign and security policy has been taking place at an incredibly slow pace, with the majority of foreign and security activity in the Union controlled, as ever, by national governments. The Constitutional Treaty (see Chapter 4) sought to bring ESDP and CFSP even closer to Brussels within a 'new' policy named 'Common Security and Defence Policy'. It demanded that all member governments improve their military capabilities to meet the demands of the Capabilities Catalogue and the Union's international commitments. It reaffirmed the EU's commitment to a common European defence, although the right of individual governments to veto this and retain independent defence policies remained. An enhanced level of cooperation was established to improve pan-European defence procurement, with this being tied to the Lisbon Agenda, which is a strategy for growth and employment. New provisions were also established to encourage solidarity between the member states in the event of crises. A cohesive European defence identity was also to have been assisted by the establishment of a Union Minister for Foreign Affairs, an individual responsible for ensuring the consistency of EU foreign policy. Unfortunately for those who drafted these provisions, the Constitutional Treaty stood and fell as a complete document, once the French and Dutch voted against the Treaty in their referenda in May/June 2005. However, the consensus seems to be that the foreign and security policy measures are likely to be resurrected outside of these moves to codify this constitutional framework.

Financing operational expenditure

Budgetary problems have long plagued the operation of foreign policy cooperation in the EU. The CFSP's overall budget for 2005 was estimated at €62.6 million or 1 per cent of the entire budget for external relations. This is a small amount considering the potential costs of crisis management. On the civilian side of CFSP pre-accession aid, cooperation, and humanitarian aid have eaten into the budget. One of the largest commitments in a Joint Action was for a policing presence in the Former Yugoslav Republic of Macedonia (FYROM) which ran to a cost of €15.9 million (December 2005).

The Maastricht Treaty stipulated that CFSP operations should be financed either from the Community budget or by the member states, depending on a complicated scale that is decided on a case-by-case basis. The Amsterdam Treaty changed this system to one where expenditure was routed from the Community budget – with the exceptions of military and defence operations, or if the Council unanimously decided otherwise. In these cases, member states can abstain, issue a formal declaration, and will not be obliged to contribute to this financing. These arrangements are still problematic because most operations cut across crisis management (EU) and military (member state) obligations, pulling finance from different sources, and further complicating the lines of financial responsibility.

The Global War on Terror (GWOT)

The 'Global War on Terror' (GWOT), as US President George W. Bush described his quest to eradicate people, groups, and governments whom his administration designated as presenting a threat to liberty and the 'Western way of life', has presented the EU with a new set of security and justice issues. The GWOT is likely to remain the largest foreign and security challenge for the EU in the medium and long term. It raises issues that cut across foreign and security policy as well as for the justice and home affairs sphere (see Chapter 19).

The GWOT has generated new domestic and external agendas. The domestic agenda has centred on immigration, policing, and intelligence, whilst the external agenda has focused on the expeditionary warfare efforts of the USA and its allies in Afghanistan and Iraq, and since 2003 the prospect of military action against North Korea and Iran, a situation which escalated significantly in 2005. The policy outputs generated as a result of the GWOT have caused lengthy political debate in the EU and amongst the Union's member governments. There are those who see pre-emptive military activity against states that sponsor terrorist organizations as imperative, whilst others argue that such action is highly problematic both legally and with regard to the quality of intelligence available to policy-makers. These debates have had serious implications for internal political harmony within the EU, with mistrust and rankling over security policy spilling over into ostensibly unconnected issues like agricultural reform and the Community budget.

The USA invaded Afghanistan after '9/11' following the Taliban government's refusal to hand Osama Bin Laden over for trial. The USA declared war on Afghanistan on the basis of Article 51 of the UN Charter: that of self-defence. Whilst the UN Security Council did not authorize the invasion, neither did it censure the USA or its allies for the attack, named Operation Enduring Freedom. After the removal of the Taliban from power nearly all the EU's member states provided military and logistical support to the UN and the NATO-controlled International Security Action Force (ISAF) efforts. This was an important show of solidarity with the USA, demonstrating the EU's keenness to move into an international niche which involves it acting to support high-end military operations financially, providing some military capabilities, and offering post-conflict reconstruction support (Den Boer and Monar 2002).

The invasion of Iraq and the subsequent removal of Saddam Hussein from power caused a significant strain in relations between the EU member states and also between the EU and the USA. A war against Iraq had long been mooted by the so-called 'neo-conservatives' in the US Republican Party after the first Gulf War in 1991, which had left Saddam Hussein in power. The 9/11 attacks provided a backdrop to a fresh attempt to remove Saddam, using the rationale that Iraq had supported terrorist groups financially and in terms of military equipment and training, with intent to attack Western interests. These claims, fleshed out by the then US Secretary of State, Colin Powell, before the UN on 5 February 2003, and supported by the UK government, were contested and were later shown to be inaccurate.

Within the EU, the French and German governments were strongly opposed to military action against Iraq (Gaffney 2004). The French government, with its Permanent Membership of the UN Security Council, threatened to veto the US–UK attempt to secure a UN mandate for an invasion, because the action was premised on Iraq holding weapons of mass destruction, a claim the French government rejected and which has subsequently been proved to be correct. This meant that the military action was conducted without a second UN resolution. Moreover, the German Chancellor Gerhard Schröder made his anti-war stance a central plank of his re-election campaign in 2002, which some commentators argued helped him secure a further term in office (Peterson 2004a). The anti-war stance of Belgium, France, and Germany brought them into public disagreement with the USA, with the Secretary of State for Defence, Donald Rumsfeld, describing them as 'old' Europe (with overtones of defeatism), implying that the UK and the EU candidate states in Eastern and Central Europe were clearly 'new' Europe. French President Chirac further inflamed this situation by suggesting to 'new' Europe that they should remember their junior position within the Union and remain quiet, a suggestion that was greeted with dismay across Europe.

The effects of this diplomatic schism were seen almost immediately. The French and British governments who had worked very closely together on EU security and defence matters between 1998 and 2000 immediately saw a dramatic deterioration in relations. President Chirac is even said to have ordered his staff not to assist UK diplomats in the further development of the ESDP.

Subsequently the EU has attempted to respond to threats to its security by constructing a European Security Strategy (December 2003), widely seen as a reply to the USA's National Security Strategy of 2002. This identifies key threats to the EU: terrorism; the proliferation of weapons of mass destruction; regional conflict; failed states; and organized crime, all of which fit into the general thrust of ESDP and its formulation between 1998 and 2000. Similarly the Commission tabled a proposal that there would be compulsory sharing of intelligence between national intelligence agencies. The latter was strongly rejected by the head of the UK's domestic secret service (MI5) in September 2005. The Commission also proposed the mandatory logging of emails and mobile phone records to assist in policing terrorist threats. This was accepted by member states (on a qualified majority vote) in the same month, but may be subject to legal challenge.

The terrorist attacks in Madrid, which killed 176 people on 11 March 2004, and the coordinated bombings on three underground trains and a bus in London on 7 July 2005, with a follow-up attempt on 21 July 2005, have brought into sharp focus the threats that the EU faces in the post-Cold War era. The pre-eminent militarized threat facing the EU and its member states is not from territorial attack – in the style of a classic Cold War confrontation on the German plains – but in the form of well-coordinated and planned multiple explosions, by small teams, using small devices placed in key locations. An interesting side-effect of the pan-European attempts to confront terrorism is that it has produced a deepening of European integration on areas beyond traditional conceptions of security. These have been pragmatic responses to the terrorist outrages. The ad hoc provision of intelligence-sharing rules, and closer police cooperation, have brought a greater number of security competencies under European scrutiny and have produced a greater day-to-day understanding between the police and justice officials of the different member states.

KEY POINTS

- The GWOT has refocused EU security efforts on to 'homeland security' and the efficacy of expeditionary warfare and 'regime change'.
- This has witnessed a large pan-European investment in technology-led measures, such as electronic intelligence (emails, phone calls, global positioning technology) and broader surveillance and control measures like improved identity cards and CCTV.
- These issues have had a dire effect on the internal harmony and political cohesion amongst the member states and the transatlantic alliance, spilling over into unrelated policy spheres like agriculture and finance.

Conclusion

The predominant role of the EU in trade is not matched by its role in foreign, security, and defence policies. Although these policies have developed substantially since the early 1990s, they are still very much under the control of national governments. The EU still conducts its foreign and security policy as extensions of national foreign policy. However, there has been a substantial shift from national capitals to Brussels, a process known as 'Brusselsization'.

Despite some reluctance from certain governments, there has been a high demand for collective EU action in foreign and security policy since 1991 from both governments and groups within the member states and from the Parliament and Commission. A common criticism of the EU is that it has not been able to generate sufficient capabilities to meet these demands and therefore has been an ineffective foreign policy actor. The key success of European policy has been the formulation of Joint Actions and Common Positions. However, neither of these produce radical or ambitious policies, but have been subject to the telltale EU traits of lowest common denominator policy-making.

Less successful have been Common Strategies that were introduced in 2000 and 2001 with papers on Russia, Ukraine, and the Mediterranean. These have achieved little and were criticized by Javier Solana (Norman 2001: 9), the EU's High Representative for Foreign Policy, as being a distraction from well-established policies on these countries and regions (Spencer 2001). Solana's complaints – particularly given that the Common Strategy towards Russia had failed to give the EU any leverage over Chechnya – resulted in the abandonment of the plan to draft a Common Strategy towards the Balkans. Solana's critique of these instruments was that as they are publicly available they have hamstrung Presidencies. He suggested that if the documents were not open to public scrutiny it would give member states greater leverage to act.

Since 1998 the EU's foreign and security policy agenda has been dominated by ESDP. This domination has caused the Commission to commit time and resources to prevent itself from being overwhelmed by a failing militarized external relations agenda. If a balance was restored between the ESDP agenda and the 'civilian' foreign external relations agendas then the Commission could play a larger working role in the EU's foreign and security policy profile.

Theoretically, the development of ESDP and CFSP has conformed closely to intergovernmentalist explanations of integration. The dominance of member states in the negotiation of these policies, and in their operational execution to the exclusion of the EU's central institutions, places foreign and security policy outside of 'functionalist' explanations of institutional spillover. For the most part ESDP provisions have been developed bi- or tri-laterally between the British, French, and German governments and in the 1999–2000 period between the French and British governments negotiating with individual governments outside of any formal EU structure, thus keeping EU officials away from these negotiations (Dover 2004). This form of negotiation is particularly stark in foreign and security policy.

In sum, EU foreign, security, and defence policies have been a mixed bag of successes and failures. The notable successes have occurred through Joint Actions that have covered issues from landmines to marshalling accession countries through the enlargement process. The failures have been more notable: the response to the Yugoslav civil war has been widely analysed as a collective humiliation for the EU; attempts to draw up Common Strategies have been less than successful; and cohesion on the big security issues of the day, namely Iraq and GWOT, have also been lacking. Greater levels of cooperation between member states is likely to come with greater exposure to collective foreign policy responses and through a shared foreign policy vision, which can only come through greater levels of dialogue.

The EU is edging very slowly and incrementally towards a fully working set of foreign and security policies and associated instruments. The adaptations and amendments to the CFSP have not produced much useful output. The Commission still feels sidelined and unaccountable, the Council retains all foreign policy positions with a veto, and the utility of Common Strategies and Joint Actions is open to serious question. However, outside of issues of core sovereignty, including defence, the EU and its member states are showing a clear commitment to foreign and security policy and are doing good work with regard to development policy. In the context of the GWOT they are showing a willingness to work on Common Positions and Joint Actions inside and outside formal EU routes, with the working practices of the being CFSP and EU security policy in general directed increasingly towards Europeanized solutions to problems that affect all EU states.

QUESTIONS

1. To what extent does the EU's CFSP and/or ESDP threaten to undermine NATO?
2. Is a Europeanized foreign and security policy likely to strengthen the position of the member states in international affairs?
3. What are the main hindrances to a fully functional Common Foreign and Security Policy?
4. Has NATO found a post-Cold War security role and made CFSP and ESDP obsolete?
5. Is the EU destined to remain a 'soft-security' actor?
6. Did the terrorist attacks on Madrid in 2004 and London in 2005 change the European security environment? Should the EU's security efforts now be focused on 'homeland' security?
7. To what extent do the 'Big Three' (France, Germany, and the United Kingdom) dominate CFSP and ESDP, both in Treaty negotiations and in the everyday operation of policy?
8. Is it desirable for the European Commission and European Parliament to have greater powers over foreign, security, and defence policy?

GUIDE TO FURTHER READING

- Howarth J., and Keeler, J. T. S. *Defending Europe: The EU, NATO and the Quest for European Autonomy*, (Palgrave MacMillan: New York, 2003). Notable for its two concluding chapters – one sceptical, one positive – by Jolyon Howarth and Anand Menon, this book pulls together some very strong thinkers analysing EU defence policy and the relationship between the EU and NATO.

- Kagan, R. *Paradise and Power: America and Europe in the New World Order* (Atlantic Books: New York, 2004). This book has generated a great deal of academic commentary about the nature of the existing transatlantic alliance and the prospects for the future alliance. It provides a key to understanding how US – EU military efforts coexist.

- Keohane, D., and Brady, H., *Fighting Terrorism: The EU Needs a Strategy Not a Shopping List* (London: Centre for European Reform, 2005), October, http://www.cer.org.uk/pdf/briefing_terrorism_11oct05. pdf. One in a series of intelligent think-tank publications that demonstrate the sorts of debates currently taking place between government, practitioners, and think-tanks.

- Rees, W., and Aldrich, R. J. 'Contending Cultures of Counterterrorism: Transatlantic Divergence or Convergence?', *International Affairs*, 81(5), 2005, pp. 905 – 23. An important work that analyses the different approaches taken by American and European governments to twenty-first-century terrorist atrocities.

- Smith, H. *European Union Foreign Policy: What It Is and What It Does* (Pluto Press: London, 2002). An excellent, comprehensive analysis of the EU's foreign policy, written from a unique perspective and including an analysis of the relationship between the global north and south.

IMPORTANT WEBSITES

- http://europa.eu.int/comm/external_relations/ The EU's official external relations website.
- http://www.osce.org/ The official website of the Organization for Security and Cooperation in Europe.

- http://www.nato.int The North Atlantic Treaty Organization (NATO).
- http://www.cer.org.uk/ The Centre for European Reform, based in London, publishes useful briefing papers, often on CFSP and ESDP-related issues.
- http://www.eri.bham.ac.uk/ The European Research Institute – one of the UK's leading research centres on the European Union, which has a particular focus on European foreign policy research.

Visit the Online Resource Centre that accompanies this book for lots of interesting additional material. http://www.oxfordtextbooks.co.uk/orc/cini2e/

16 The Single Market

MICHELLE EGAN

Chapter Contents

Reader's Guide

This chapter charts the evolution of the Single Market project, from its original conception in the 1950s to its realization in the 1990s. Although much works remains to be done in the forging of a Single Market in Europe, large steps were taken in this direction after 1985. This required new principles and approaches to economic or market integration at the time without which the Single Market ambition would have remained little more than an ideal. The chapter begins with the Treaty of Rome, and focuses first on the association between a Single Market and the harmonization of national laws at European level. It explores the role of the European Court in promoting market access; the balance between different economic ideals; and the regulatory strategies used to foster market integration. The chapter concludes with a brief look at how theories of European integration have explained the advent of the Single Market.

Introduction

This chapter discusses the creation of the single European market, and pays particular attention to the integration of national economies and the removal of **barriers to trade** that impede cross-border transactions. Charting the integration process from its beginnings in the 1950s, the chapter looks at the different strategies used to foster **market integration**; at the role of the European Court of Justice in tackling trade barriers; and at how private firms participated in these developments. A further section looks at the origins and content of the '1992' Single Market programme, and at the efforts to make the Single Market work effectively. The final section draws on traditional International Relations theories of European integration as well as on more recent theories of regulation and governance in order to explain the dynamics of market integration.

Market integration in historical perspective

In the space of one year, from the Messina Conference in June 1955 to the Venice Conference in May 1956, the idea of economic unification among six West European states had taken root. Detailed objectives and timetables were hammered out throughout months of lengthy discussion. In what became known as the Spaak Report, after its principal author, the idea of an entirely new kind of interstate economic relationship was taken as the basis for treaty negotiations (Bertrand 1956: 569). The Spaak Report provided a blueprint for a single market in Western Europe, with three main elements: (a) the establishment of normal standards of competition through the elimination of protective barriers; (b) the curtailing of state intervention and monopolistic conditions; and (c) measures to prevent distortions of competition, including the possible harmonization of legislation at the European level. The economic intent of such proposals dovetailed with the **federalist** agenda (Laurent 1970; see also Chapter 5). Yet turning the single market idea into a political reality has been extremely contentious and protracted.

The Treaty of Rome (1957) follows the Spaak Report in many respects. Its immediate objectives were to establish a **common market** by promoting and coordinating economic activities, ensuring stability and economic development, and raising standards of living. At the core of the proposed European common market was the creation of a **customs union** (see Box 16.1). This meant that member states would not only abolish all their customs duties on mutual trade, but also apply a uniform tariff on trade with non-EC countries. The other measures proposed to promote internal trade liberalization, including free movement of labour, services, and capital, and a limited number of sectoral policies (agriculture, transport, and

BOX 16.1

Stages in economic integration

Free trade area – reduces tariffs to zero between members.

Customs union – reduces tariffs to zero between members and establishes a common external tariff.

Single market – establishes a free flow of factors of production (labour and capital, as well as goods and services).

Economic union – involves an agreement to harmonize economic policies.

competition), were to be regulated and managed at the European level.

The transformation of the Community into a common market was to take place over a period of 12 to 15 years. It began with efforts to create a single market by addressing traditional tariffs, starting with the elimination of customs duties and quantitative restrictions in 1958, and by introducing a common external tariff in 1968. Internal tariff reductions were also frequently extended to third countries (non-member states). This limited the discriminatory effects of the customs union to non-members, which was politically important in the formative period of the EC (Egan 2001: 41).

Membership of the European Community meant more than simply a customs union, however. There was also a commitment to 'free movement'. The Treaty established the 'four freedoms' – the free movement of goods, services, capital, and labour, as central features of the Single Market. However, the requirements for each freedom varied according to the political exigencies at the time the Treaty was drafted. The removal of trade barriers for *goods* focused on the removal of tariffs and quantitative restrictions, and then on the removal of non-tariff barriers. This meant dismantling quotas, subsidies, and voluntary export restraints, and measures such as national product regulations and standards, public purchasing, and licensing practices which sometimes reflected legitimate public policy concerns, but were often a thinly disguised form of protectionism designed to suppress foreign competition (Egan 2001: 42). For the free movement of *capital*, the goal was freedom of investment to enable capital to go where it would be most productive. Yet vivid memories of currency speculation in the interwar period meant that liberalization was subject to particular conditions or 'safeguard clauses', frequently used during recessions. With regard to free movement of *services*, it meant the freedom of establishment for industrial and commercial activity, that is, the right to set up in business anywhere in the Community. However, the Treaty provisions on services contained virtually no detail on what should be liberalized (Pelkmans 1997). For *labour*, the provisions for free movement meant the abolition of restrictions on labour mobility, allowing workers to get jobs anywhere in the EC.

National governments were receptive to early efforts to eliminate trade barriers and create a customs union because they were able to use social policies to compensate for the increased competition stemming from market integration. Favourable starting conditions for the European trade liberalization effort were thus due to the fact that it occurred against the backdrop of the mixed economy and welfare state, which were central components of the postwar settlement (Tsoukalis 1997). Yet even with these national policies, it was still felt politically necessary to provide some sort of financial aid at the European level to ease the effects of competition through basic investment in underdeveloped regions, suppression of large-scale unemployment, and the coordination of economic policies (see Spaak 1956; Bertrand 1956).

But while the Community experienced substantial economic growth and increased trade among member states, the transition to a common market did not remove all obstacles to the expansion of trade. The prevalence of domestic barriers to trade and the pervasive role of nation states as regulators of economic activity across all four freedoms signalled the enormity of the task (Tsoukalis 1997: 78).

A major characteristic of Western Europe has been its historical and national variation in areas such as industrial relations, social welfare, and financial systems (Zysman 1994; Berger and Dore 1996; Rhodes and van Apeldoorn 1998). There are systematic differences in how national economies are organized, and member states have chosen ways of regulating production, investment, and exchange that constitute different varieties of capitalism (Hall and Soskice 2001: 15). Thus, efforts to create a single market in Europe have sought to unify disparate interests and market ideologies, and the process of market integration has often been deeply contested.

The clash between laissez-faire and interventionist ideologies began in the earliest years of the European Community. The implied commitment to a free market economy, stressing the virtues of competition and greater efficiencies through specialization and economies of scale, was balanced by a widespread acceptance of *dirigisme* and intervention by state agencies and nationalized monopolies. More recently, this tension has been further refined as a distinction between 'regulated capitalism' and 'neo-liberalism' (Hooghe and Marks 1997; see Box 16.2). Different and sometimes competing strategies contributed to the fragmentation of the European market, preventing new firms from entering the market and taking advantage of new commercial opportunities. How, then, did the Community tackle such deep-seated differences in rules, standards, and practices as it sought to create a single European market?

 KEY CONCEPTS AND TERMS 16.2

The characteristics of capitalism

Neo-liberalism

- Market liberalization: remove restrictions to trade, provide regulatory climate attractive to business; laissez-faire approach.
- Regulatory competition among member states: competition among different national regulatory policies rather than harmonization.
- Rejection of greater regulatory power for institutions at EU level: insulation of market from political interference; and retention of political authority at national level.
- Supporters include conservative political parties, multinationals, and industry associations and financial institutions.

Regulated capitalism

- Market intervention: government intervention in market.
- Social market economy and social solidarity: emphasis on welfare state and distributive politics.
- Increased capacity to regulate at European level: mobilize particular social groups; and reform institutions to generate greater use of qualified majority voting; enhance legislative legitimacy.
- Supporters include Jacques Delors, Social Democrat and Christian Democrat parties.

Source: Adapted from Hooghe and Marks (1997).

KEY POINTS

- The objective of creating a single European market can be traced to the Spaak Report of 1956 and the Treaty of Rome in 1957.
- The aim of the Treaty was to liberalize trade by dismantling barriers to trade among the six EEC members.
- Difficulties arose as a consequence of the variety of economic interests and ideologies across Western Europe.

Harmonization: the politics of intervention

In order to tackle those domestic regulations that thwarted the creation of a common or single market, the European Community promoted a policy of harmonization (or standardization) that was to provide a lightning rod for criticisms of the integration process (see Box 16.3). The harmonization of policies was a means of reconciling differences in national regulatory practices and creating common rules (Cosgrove Twitchett 1981).

CASE STUDY 16.3

The politics of harmonization

The Dutch spread jam on their bread for breakfast. They like it smooth and sugary. Most French people would not touch smooth jam with a butter knife. They commonly eat jam straight from the jar with a spoon. Negotiations meant getting the Dutch who wanted more sugar in their jam and the French who wanted more fruit to compromise. Just as that happened Britain, the largest jam consumer, joined the EC, and a further problem emerged: marmalade. It seems that the low-quality jam in much of Europe was called marmalade, a confusion Britons refuse to tolerate. In the end, after further negotiations, low-grade jam simply became jam.

After two decades of haggling, the European Commission unveiled a jam standard in 1979 only to find the French still unwilling to accept the resulting compromise. By 1984, everyone was on board. This illustrates the seemingly endless years of negotiations required for the many thousands of other products involved in cross-border trade in Europe.

Source: Adapted from Egan (2001).

Public opposition mounted over efforts to regulate what many felt were long-standing national customs, traditions, and practices (Dashwood 1983; see Box 16.3). Although the Commission drew attention to the benefits of harmonization in creating a large 'barrier-free' single market, this was met with criticisms from member states about the years of fruitless arguments harmonizing noise limits on lawnmowers, the composition of bread and beer, and tractor rear-view mirrors. Overall results were minimal.

However, the reasons for such limited results stem from a number of factors. First, the decision rule of unanimity on single market issues made it extremely difficult to get agreement amongst member states, and allowed individual governments to exercise their veto on specific legislative proposals. Secondly, harmonization was a complex technical process, and efforts to address non-tariff barriers were hampered by rapid changes in production and technology that often made agreements obsolete by the time they were adopted. The relative lack of political interest in the process of harmonization was understandable, as there was little to be gained by explaining the importance of technical issues to the wider public (Puchala 1971).

The inappropriateness of harmonization in addressing barriers to trade reflected a *regulatory mismatch* where the instruments chosen were ill suited to the problem (Breyer 1982). With a new strategy called 'reference to standards' the European Commission set out broad regulatory guidelines, leaving the private sector or non-governmental bodies (NGOs) to provide the necessary standards. This meant that the European Commission shifted more responsibility and delegated more tasks to the private sector. While two organizations, CEN and CENELEC, brought together firms and trade associations to set standards, along with a limited number of consumer groups and trade unions, their efforts to get collective agreement among diverse interests are often difficult. The main policy aim of such co-regulation is the creation of a level playing field and the correction of any market failures. The resulting effect is one of both deregulation and re-regulation in the creation of a single market. Mutual recognition and harmonization reduce the barriers created by national regulations but provide the necessary equal basis without which the absence of regulations for product and process standards might lead to a 'race to the bottom' in social and environment standards, if states sought to reduce their domestic measures to attract foreign direct investment.

KEY POINTS

- Harmonization was the main strategy used to integrate national markets in the 1960s and 1970s.
- Harmonization achieved limited success due to a number of factors, including: unanimous decision-making; rising protectionism; the sheer number of non-tariff barriers; and the lack of political will. This necessitated a new regulatory framework for delegating responsibility and functions to the private sector.

The free trade umpire: the European Court of Justice and judicial activism

The problems associated with addressing trade restrictions through harmonization did not go unnoticed by the European Court of Justice (ECJ), which has often used its judicial power for the purposes of fostering an integrated economy (see Chapter 12). Indeed, a large measure of the credit for creating a single market belongs to the judicial activism of the ECJ. Confronted by restrictions on their ability to operate across national borders, firms began to seek redress through the Community legal system. The Court was asked to determine whether the restrictions on imports imposed by member states were legitimate under the Treaty.

Examples of member states' restrictions included Italy's prohibition on the sale of pasta not made with durum wheat, Germany's 'beer purity' regulations prohibiting the sale of any product as 'beer' that was not brewed with specific ingredients, and Belgian regulations that required margarine only to be sold in cube-shaped containers to prevent confusion with butter which was sold in round-shaped containers. As many of its decisions illustrate, the Court had the task of reconciling the demands of market integration with the pursuit of legitimate regulatory objectives and policy goals advanced by member states.

Several landmark cases limited the scope and applicability of national legislation. One of the most important in this regard came in the *Dassonville* case in 1974. Dassonville imported whisky into Belgium purchased from a French supplier. The firm was prosecuted by Belgian authorities for violating national customs rules that prohibited importation from a third country without the correct documentation. Dassonville argued that the whisky had entered the French market legally, that it must therefore be allowed to circulate freely, and that restrictions on imports within the EC were illegal. In a sweeping judgment, the Court argued that 'all trading rules that hinder trade, whether directly or indirectly, actually or potentially, were inadmissible'.

National measures that negatively impact trade were therefore prohibited (Stone Sweet and Caporaso 1998: 118). This was softened by the recognition that reasonable regulations made by member states for legitimate public interests such as health, safety, and environment policies were acceptable if there were no European rules in place. The judgment was predicated on the belief that the European Commission should adopt harmonized standards to allow free movement across markets, while at the same time giving the ECJ the opportunity to monitor member states' behaviour and scrutinize permissible exceptions.

In what is probably its best known case, *Cassis de Dijon*, the Court, in 1979, ruled on a German ban on the sale of a French blackcurrant liqueur because it did not conform to German standards in terms of alcoholic content (see Egan 2001: 95). The Court rejected German arguments that Cassis, with its lower alcoholic content, posed health risks, but noted that the protection of the consumer could be aided by the labelling of alcoholic content. Most importantly, it clearly defined what national measures were deemed permissible. The most cited part of the ruling suggested that 'there was no valid reason why products produced and marketed in one member state could not be introduced into another member state'.

The notion of equivalence of national regulations, which this ruling introduced, opened up the possibility that harmonization would not always be necessary for the construction of a single market. This was the crucial step in launching a new regulatory strategy, **mutual recognition**, which would make for an easier circulation of trade and commerce in the Community. Mutual recognition implies that it is only in areas that are not mutually equivalent that member states can invoke national restrictions, practices, and traditions and restrict free trade in the Community.

The Court argued that derogations from (or exceptions to) the free trade rule for the purposes of public health, fair competition, and consumer protection were possible, but that they had to be based upon reasonable grounds. Governments, whether national, local, or subnational, must demonstrate that any measure restricting trade was not simply disguised protectionism. Anxious to safeguard the Community-wide market, the Court has continued to determine on a case-by-case basis whether specific laws are valid under the Treaty. However, faced with a growing number of cases, the Court in the *Keck* case (1993) reduced the scope of judicial scrutiny where cases applied to all traders operating in specific national territory, under certain conditions. Thus, the Court would not examine issues such as Sunday trading, mandatory closing hours, or other issues that had a limited effect on cross-border trade and that reflected national moral, social, and cultural norms.

The creative and constitutive role of law is crucial in understanding the consolidation of markets in Europe. Market integration involves a substantive legal project that shapes public and private policies. The ECJ has placed state and local laws under its purview, and also determined the economic relationship between public intervention and the market, and the political relationship between member states and the Union. European case law opened up opportunities by reducing much of the cost of innovation and entrepreneurship by shifting the focus towards creating the context for open markets and competition.

KEY POINTS

- Legal rulings by the ECJ in cases such as *Dassonville* and *Cassis de Dijon* have played a key role in addressing non-tariff barriers to trade.
- Mutual recognition is a key concept in trade liberalization, promoting mutual reciprocity of standards rather than harmonization.

Market-making: the politics of neo-liberalism

Throughout the 1970s and early 1980s, member states' efforts to maintain import restrictions and discriminatory trade practices thwarted efforts to create a single market. Growing recognition of a competitiveness gap vis-à-vis the USA and Japan, on the one hand, and newly industrializing countries, on the other, led to strenuous efforts to maintain overall levels of market activity and provide conditions for viable markets (Pelkmans and Winters 1988: 6). While past economic policies had succeeded in promoting national economic growth, the tools of national politics were no longer able to cope with changes in the international economy. Neo-corporatist class compromises and consensual incomes policies, which underpinned Keynesian economic policy, were under immense pressure as government capacity to manage the economy failed. As trade deficits soared, attention focused on the strengthening of European strategies in areas such as research and development as a way to improve the environment in which companies operate.

Assessments were so bleak that, on the twenty-fifth anniversary of the Treaty of Rome, *The Economist* put a tombstone on its cover to proclaim the EC dead and buried. These assessments contributed to a growing consensus among business and political leaders that a collective strategy was needed to stop an 'escalating trade war' (*Financial Times*, 25 July 1980). Business interests were promoted through the establishment of a European

Roundtable of Industrialists. Through the European Roundtable, heads of European companies put forward numerous proposals to improve European competitiveness. Their influence on the European agenda was accomplished largely through a campaign of proactive lobbying, ambitious proposals, and visible political engagement (*Financial Times*, 20 March 2001).

In addition, the American Chamber of Commerce (AMCHAM) noted problems of industry standards, border formalities, and export licences, identifying France and Italy as the worst offenders. The European Confederation of National Employers' Associations (UNICE) also articulated the concerns of many trade associations about the effects of non-tariff barriers. Responding to this groundswell, the European Commission produced numerous studies and resolution, and forwarded a list of the most problematic barriers existing in the member states. More than 800 national measures were viewed as causing significant problems in preventing cross-border trade (*Financial Times*, 23 September 1980; *The Economist*, 22 October 1983).

Governments, well aware that their efforts to create national champions, protect labour markets, and maintain public spending were not stemming rising trade imbalances and deficits, sought new solutions. Efforts to contain import competition and stabilize industries had failed. Disenchantment with Keynesian tax-and-spend policies led to a shift towards market liberalization. This did not mean a common consensus around **neo-liberalism**, however, since different conceptions of the operation of the market economy and the agenda for European integration continued.

While the British government advocated a genuine common market in goods and services, and promoted a radically neo-liberal agenda, the French government argued for the creation of a common industrial space in which trade barriers could be reduced internally, provided that external trade *protection* would compensate for increased internal competition (Pearce and Sutton 1983). Though some political opposition to the Single Market continued, major steps taken at the European Council meeting in Fontainebleau in 1984 broke the immobility that had stifled progress. Key was agreement over long-running disputes over Britain's contribution to the Community budget and the pending Iberian enlargement. The meeting also established the Dooge Committee to focus on the reform of the institutional and decision-making structure of the Community.

Further agreement at the 1985 **intergovernmental conference** in Milan to 'study the institutional conditions under which the internal market could be achieved within a time limit' proved critical for the market integration process. This built on several earlier developments including the Spinelli Report which focused on the need to link national regulations and institutional reform, and the Parliamentary Draft Treaty on European Union on institutional reform, which included increased parliamentary powers and greater use of qualified majority voting in the Council. At the subsequent intergovernmental conference, the proposed Treaty reforms were brought together to become the Single European Act (SEA) (see Chapter 3).

Historically significant as the first substantial treaty reform undertaken by member states, the SEA endorsed the single market and altered the decision-making rules for single market measures (with exceptions such as taxation and rights of workers) from unanimity to qualified majority voting (QMV). This linked institutional reforms to substantive goals, and made it more difficult for recalcitrant member states simply to veto legislative action, as had been the case under harmonization. The SEA also strengthened the powers of the European Parliament with respect to single market measures by allowing for the rejection or amendment of proposals under the **cooperation procedure**.

KEY POINTS

- The tools of domestic policy no longer seemed able to solve the problems of international competitiveness for member states.
- Business engaged in extensive lobbying for the Single Market. It supported measures to improve European competitiveness.

The 1992 Programme: a blueprint for action

By early 1985 the stage was set for an ambitious initiative. The newly appointed Commission President, Jacques Delors, and Internal Market Commissioner Lord Cockfield, a British neo-liberal and former Secretary of State for Industry, put together a package of proposals that aimed to achieve completion of the Single Market by 1992. The 300 proposals – subsequently modified and amended to become 283 proposals – became a Commission White Paper entitled *Completing the Internal Market* (European Commission 1985). The final product became known as the '1992 Programme'.

The White Paper contained a comprehensive assessment of the remaining obstacles to trade, grouped together in three major categories: physical, technical, and fiscal barriers (see Box 16.4). Lord Cockfield used this very simple and deceptive categorization to introduce a series of measures across goods, services, capital, and labour markets to improve market access, prevent distortions to competition and restrictive business practices, and coordinate policies to prevent market failure. The European Commission bolstered support by commissioning a series of economic evaluations on the 'costs of non-Europe'. Although overly optimistic, the estimated trade and welfare gains from removing barriers to trade were compelling. Not only would there be lower trade costs and greater economies of scale, as firms exploited increased opportunities, but it was expected that there would also be greater production efficiency achieved through market enlargement, intensified competition, and industrial restructuring.

At the core of the Single Market project was the concept of mutual recognition, the consequence of which would be increased competition not only among firms within the EU, but also among different national regulatory systems (see Sun and Pelkmans 1995). Governments sponsoring regulations that restricted market access would be under pressure since firms from other EU member states would not be required to abide by them, putting

 KEY CONCEPTS AND TERMS 16.4

The Single Market programme

The Single Market programme involved the removal of three kinds of trade barriers: physical barriers to trade; technical barriers to trade; fiscal barriers to trade.

- *Physical barriers*: the removal of internal barriers and frontiers for goods and people; the simplification of border controls (including the creation of a single administrative document for border entry).
- *Technical barriers*: coordinating product standards, testing, and certification (under the 'new approach'); liberalization of public procurement; free movement of capital (by reducing capital exchange controls); free movement of services (covering financial services, such as banking and insurance, to operate under home country control); liberalization of the transport sector (rail, road, and air); rights of 'cabotage'; the liberalization of markets and removal of monopolies, state subsidies, and quotas or market-sharing arrangements; free movement of labour and the mutual recognition of professional qualifications (including non-discrimination in employment); Europeanization of company law, intellectual property, and company taxation (including the freedom of establishment for enterprises; the agreement of a European Company Statute; new rules of trade marks, copyright, and legal protection).
- *Fiscal barriers*: the harmonization of divergent tax regimes, including value added or sales tax; the agreement of standard rates and special exemptions from sales tax and other indirect taxes with the aim of reducing restrictions on cross-border sales.

their own local firms at a disadvantage. The European Commission sought to apply this innovative strategy to the service sector as well. The concept of 'home country control' was to allow banks, insurance companies, and dealers in securities to offer the same services elsewhere in the Community that they offered at home. A single licence would operate, so that these sectors would be licensed, regulated, and supervised for the most part by their home country.

A policy framework for action on the legislative proposals contained in the White Paper was also required. Building on the legal decisions outlining the doctrine of mutual recognition as a broad free trade principle, and reference to standards as a more flexible regulatory strategy, the Commission drafted a proposal on harmonization and standards in 1985 (Pelkmans 1987). This 'new approach', as it was called, reflected a critical effort to address barriers to trade by sharing regulatory functions between the public and private sector. Where possible, there was to be mutual recognition of regulations and standards and Community-level regulation was to be restricted to essential health and safety requirements. The necessary standards to meet them would be set by the European standards bodies, CEN, CENELEC, and European Telecommunications Standards Institute (ETSI) (Egan 2001).

Despite being a rather dry bureaucratic document, the White Paper gained widespread political support by providing a target date for the completion of the Single Market. Though the Single Market 'is not something you can fall in love with', noted Delors, the White Paper constitutes a radical break with Europe's interventionist tradition, emphasizing the merits of economic liberalism. Tapping into these sentiments, the White Paper included a diversity of measures across the four freedoms, such as the abolition of frontier controls, mutual recognition of goods and services, rights of establishment for professional workers, and the abolition of capital-exchange controls. While the bulk of the measures outlined in the White Paper focused on market access or **negative integration** measures, such as removing technical barriers to trade, dismantling quotas, and removing licensing restrictions for cross-border banking and insurance services, they were complemented by a series of market-correcting or **positive integration** measures such as health and safety standards, rules for trade marks and deposit insurance, and solvency ratios for banks and insurance.

While most attention focused on the political deadline of 1992, continued obstacles to cross-border movements were indications of the complexities involved. The resistance to tax harmonization was predictable, since the issue of distortions created by differential tax regimes has been problematic since the early days of the Common Market. The White Paper also conspicuously avoided a number of issues including a strong social dimension, as well as other politically sensitive areas such as textiles, clothing, and taxation of savings and investment income, despite the evident distortions and restrictions in these areas.

Completion of the Single Market meant tackling politically difficult dossiers and ensuring that the legislation was put into effect in all member states; otherwise the confidence of consumers and producers in realizing economic benefits would be undermined. Nationally important sectors such as utilities (gas and postal services, for example) were given special exemptions in the Single Market on the basis of social and economic arguments that 'universal services' must be provided, resulting in natural monopolies and limited competition. With rapid liberalization and technological pressures that enabled new entrants to bypass public networks, however, the traditional economic rationale for such ***dirigiste*** policies was being undermined. Pressure to open up telecommunications, electricity, and gas markets resulted in the Commission forcing the liberalization of these basic services through its competition powers. Yet resistance towards service liberalization has continued, in part due to concerns about the effects on employment in these heavily protected sectors (see Box 16.5).

European integration has focused its community-building process in terms of the creation of a competitive market economy. While further changes are required as the Single Market deepens,

CASE STUDY 16.5

Frayed edges of the Single Market – the case of services

While the Single Market in goods is largely complete, the rise of national self-interest has thwarted attempts to open up the Single Market in services. While services represent 70 per cent of the European economy and liberalization is expected to generate significant gains, there are low levels of intra-EU trade in services (only 20 per cent are cross-border). Yet the so-called 'Bolkstein Directive', which aims to do for services trade what the '1992' agenda did for internal market activity in goods has sparked fierce criticism and protest across Europe. Although a key ambition of the directive is to extend the well understood EU principle of 'mutual recognition' to the service sector, it has stoked fears of a flood of cheap labour from new member states under the so-called 'country of origin principle'. Under this principle a firm would be able to operate in a foreign country according to the rules and regulations of its home country, leading to concerns that an influx of cheap labour from Central and Eastern Europe would undercut working conditions, wage levels, and welfare benefits in Western Europe. Such 'social dumping' became an issue in the campaign for the French referendum on the EU Constitutional Treaty in 2005, when President Chirac expressed concerns about the influx of cheap 'Polish plumbers' into an economy suffering from high unemployment and job insecurity. The 'Polish plumber' as an emblematic job snatcher has come to symbolize concerns about opening of borders to trade and workers from new EU member states. Never mind the fact that Poland is constrained by the restrictions on labour market access for a transition period of up to seven years and only Britain, Ireland, and Sweden have eased rules on labour mobility from the new member states. The prospect of unfettered labour immigration touched a nerve. Never mind that France suffers a chronic shortage of plumbers – the tactic worked (*Chicago Tribune*, 14 August 2005). This hotly debated directive has seen sharp disagreements about its impact on regulatory standards and basic employment protections, with disagreements being waged in both the Parliament and Council on how far liberalization should proceed.

more recent policy reforms and structural adjustments have been the product of new modes of governance. In the post-war period, the basic European model was one of growth promotion through lowering barriers to trade and increasing competition (Hamilton and Quinlan 2005: 255). While closer economic cooperation has challenged the sovereign capacity of states in terms of their capacity for autonomous action within their own borders, further integration has run into resistance as the irreversible pressures of market liberalization and economic globalization have challenged the European social model. Although high unemployment, low economic growth, and the resulting sense of insecurity in many European states have fuelled pressure for economic reform, there has been strong resistance as states have sought to protect certain strategic sectors from the competitive effects of market integration. Although Europe has experienced a remarkable expansion of free markets and trade going beyond eliminating tariffs and non-tariff barriers to regulate and harmonize a range of policies in many sectors, this expansion has also triggered a reaction as anxieties are stoked, and reaction intensifies towards the costs of further integration. A key issue remains the continued existence of service barriers within the EU itself in areas such as finance, transportation, and telecommunications (*Financial Times*, 15 March 2005; Hamilton and Quinlan 2005). Often forgotten is that the internal market agenda is unfinished (see Box 16.5) as a large amount of work remains to be done in the area of financial services, customs, company law, and taxation.

KEY POINTS

- The 1992 Programme provided a clear outline for a legislative agenda laid down in the White Paper on the internal market.
- The 1992 Programme was a package of measures to liberalize trade. The Single Market project is still a work-in-progress. Efforts continue to remove barriers to trade.

Maintaining and correcting the market

The Single Market programme turned out to be about much more than free movement and the removal of trade barriers among the Community's member states. As we shall see, it also involved a number of interventionist policy measures and institutional steps to ensure the implementation and effectiveness of the new legislation.

Market correcting: the politics of regulated capitalism

The renewed emphasis on market integration through the '1992 Programme' also brought pressures for ancillary policies along social democratic lines (Scharpf 1999). Dealing with the pressures from increased competition led to policy proposals reflecting the ideological cleavages that had always underpinned the Community project. Fearful that excessive competition would increase social conflict, proponents of a regulated capitalism approach (see Box 16.2) proposed a variety of inclusive mechanisms to generate broad-based support for the Single Market. These included structural policy for poorer regions to promote economic and social cohesion, consumer and environmental protection, and rural development (see Chapters 17, 18, and 21). Fiscal transfers spread the burden of adjustment and assisted the adversely affected countries.

Labour representatives also sought to address the impact of market integration through the creation of an ongoing social dialogue (see Chapter 17). These initiatives were narrower than the traditional social market philosophy and distinct from *dirigiste* policies of state ownership and control, but they complemented efforts to shift regulation to the European level. The effort to promote a European social dimension also acknowledged that the domestic political pressures on national welfare states meant that they could no longer compensate for the effects of integration as they had done in the past (Scharpf 1999).

The goal of regulating markets, redistributing resources, and shaping partnership among public and private actors led advocates of regulated capitalism to propose provisions for transport and communications infrastructure, information networks, workforce skills, and research and development (Hooghe and Marks 1997). The progressive expansion of activities at the European level brought into focus two long-standing opposing views about the economic role of governments.

Despite the neo-liberal rhetoric, some have argued that the Single Market has progressively increased the level of statism or interventionism in Western Europe (Messerlin 2001). The economic consensus in favour of market forces and neo-liberalism under the Single Market programme in the 1980s have been offset by increased intervention or regulated capitalism in labour markets (minimum wage and working time), and new provisions for culture (broadcast quotas), industry (shipbuilding, textiles, and clothing), and technology (new energy resources, biotechnology, and broadband networks) in the 1990s. The market-orientated policies underpinning the Single Market have been balanced by a number of market-interventionist measures.

Market maintenance: the politics of efficiency and effectiveness

The credibility of the Single Market process is dependent on its living up to the spirit, as well as the letter, of a 'barrier-free' market (*The Economist*, 26 September 1992). Facing the challenges of constructing a single market, the EU was forced to tackle not only the design and passage of legislation but also its implementation and evaluation (Radaelli 1998; Chatham House 2004). Since the Community level of governance does not derive its authority and legitimacy from direct electoral support, the effectiveness and credibility of the Single Market has meant that market management issues are increasingly salient, and efforts to make the Single Market work in practice have risen on the political agenda (Metcalfe 1996).

The rather anticlimactic arrival of the Single Market on 1 January 1993 did not signal an end to the Single Market project. The poor performance of member states in terms of implementation has been a particularly crucial shortcoming. As the adoption of legislation requires implementation at the national level, the success of the Single Market project depends on the transposition of directives into national law. In some instances, poor preparation and lack of commitment by national administrations and legislators have accounted for some of these problems. In other cases badly drafted rules were also to blame (Radaelli 1998). To tackle such problems, and to ensure that implementation problems did not cause further trade barriers, all of the European institutions have sought to promote regulatory reform and enhance the governance of the market. Ease of market entry needs to be reinforced across Europe, and measures to improve efficiency, competition, and openness are necessary to enhance the potential benefits from market consolidation.

The aim of improving the functioning of the Single Market has resulted in an internal review and evaluation of the European Commission's own organizational structure and effectiveness (see Chapter 9). Initially the European Commission produced the 1992 Sutherland Report on the internal market, which emphasized the need for administrative partnerships between the Commission and public administrations at the national level (European Commission 1992a). However, the push for administrative and organizational reform has been motivated by business requests for easing regulatory burdens. For the past decade, the European Commission along with other European institutions has responded to criticisms on the need to improve rule-making in terms of the quantity and quality of legislation as a prerequisite for the achievement of a European-wide single market (Molitor *et al.* 1995; Mandelkern Group Report 2001). This has led to specific simplification initiatives, including SLIM (Simpler Legislation for a Single Market) in 1996, which recognized that complicated regulations may reduce the competitiveness of business. Likewise, the Action Plan for the Single Market (1997) has sought to increase transparency and access as part of a larger effort to improve governance. It has also introduced a scoreboard to generate adverse publicity for those member states that were lagging behind (European Report, 28 November 1997). The results of such peer pressure have in fact improved compliance. National governments are finally implementing EU internal market laws, with good results for both the new member states and old member states (European Report, 20 July 2005). Yet there remain problems of infringement of European law, and the different challenge of ensuring actual compliance with single market obligations (Falkner *et al.* 2004). While the Commission has actively pursued infringement proceedings (under Article 226 of the Treaty) whereby it formally notifies member states of their legal obligations, and then proceeds to take legal action if non-compliance continues, it is more difficult to police the Single Market to ensure that common rules for industrial and consumer products are respected, and that the application of mutual recognition is correctly applied. The slow pace of standardization has led to continued pressure on the European standards bodies to improve their overall output and performance so that firms have common standards and legal certainty in producing and marketing for a single Europe-wide market.

Although sporadic attention is given to 'completing' the Single Market, many areas remain fragmented and shielded from competition (see Box 16.5). Surveys indicate that firms still believe they face serious obstacles which prevent them from realizing the full benefits of the Single Market. Differences in national tax systems and differences in national regulations remain, along with other barriers that hinder overall growth and competitiveness (European Commission 1997; Chatham

House 2004). Despite recent efforts in areas such as financial services, the overall potential of services as an engine of growth in Europe has not yet materialized. In economic terms, the Single Market has promoted the liberalization of trade and restructuring and consolidation in numerous industrial sectors. In political terms, as efforts to deepen market integration continue, it has triggered a reaction from inefficient producers or unions worried about the impact of increased competition. Such market liberalization presents opportunities for mobilization and provides a new context in which opposition can be expressed (Imig and Tarrow 2001). Yet the Single Market has also enabled the EU to exercise its authority in multilateral trade negotiations, and use market access as an instrument of 'soft power' to promote economic and political reform in Central and Eastern Europe and the Balkans through stabilization and association agreements to eventual membership and accession.

Even though the Single Market is now well entrenched, its feasibility and effectiveness are dependent on two conditions. First, it requires well-defined legal and judicial mechanisms to enforce the rights and obligations of a single market to ensure enforcement and compliance. A second factor in generating political support and legitimacy for economic integration is the pursuit of an acceptable distribution of tangible benefits. In this respect, the relationship between economic rights and social rights needs to be considered since viable and sustainable integration is likely to be more successful if economic growth is fairly distributed.

KEY POINTS

- The market-orientated policies of the 1980s were balanced by a number of market-interventionist measures in the 1990s.
- The operation of the Single Market is under tremendous political scrutiny to ensure correct implementation and compliance, adequate standards, and improved internal coordination and management within the institutions.
- Emphasis has been given to designing better regulatory policies to ease burdens on business and promote competitiveness.

Theorizing the Single Market

Although the Single Market has evolved over time, many studies focus primarily on the 1980s to explain the causes, consequences, and content of the Single Market programme. Some scholars highlight the economic factors driving the 1992 project, whereas others emphasize the political origins of the Single European Act to explain this resurgence of activity. These studies fall squarely within the major theoretical debates in the field of integration studies (see Chapters 5–8), and draw on different factors to explain the *relance européen* (the relaunch of the European project).

Intergovernmentalists (see Chapter 7) claim that the institutional dynamics that underpin the Single Market project were the result of a convergence of policy preferences in the early 1980s (Moravcsik 1991). Parties that advocated neo-liberal market reforms came to power in a number of states such as Britain, Denmark, and Belgium. Their emergence, coupled with developments in France, where failed efforts to pursue a Keynesian fiscal policy to counter economic recession forced the post-1981 Socialist government to reverse its policies in 1983, meant that the resulting Single European Act represented a familiar pattern of bargaining and negotiation between Britain, Germany, and France to reach a common solution.

For intergovernmentalists, national interests and policies are thus expected to continue to constrain integrationist impulses. Garrett (1992) adds an important nuance to the intergovernmentalist position, arguing that in important areas of legal activity, the Court was constrained by member states' governments. According to Garrett, the Court anticipates reactions from member states, and serves their interests (especially those of the most powerful member states) in rendering its judgments.

By comparison, the neo-functionalist account stresses the importance of supranational actors in shaping the Single Market agenda. Sandholtz and Zysman (1989) stress the importance of the Commission as an innovative policy entrepreneur in shaping the European agenda, supported by big business interests seeking to reap the benefits of an enlarged market. Burley and Mattli (1993) add to the neo-functionalist argument by claiming that Court rulings have resulted in interactions between national and European courts, creating a distinctive legal regime that shapes rules and procedures governing markets. When political attempts to create a common market stalled, the Court advanced its supranational authority over national courts, expanding its jurisdictional authority in order to make a pivotal contribution to the promotion of free trade (see Egan 2001; Shapiro 1992). Cameron (1992) seeks to blend these different theoretical perspectives by arguing that the 1992 initiative was the result of the complex interaction of different actors and institutions, simultaneously accelerating economic integration and supranational institution building, while also representing intergovernmental bargaining among states.

While International Relations theories have focused on the impact of market integration on the member state's capacity to act, and the degree to which the emerging European political system has strengthened or weakened the state, or embedded it in a system of multi-level governance, an emphasis on state resources, power, and bargaining to understand the driving factors of economic integration remains the dominant approach. More recently, the Single Market process has been examined through the lens of comparative policy analysis. Empirical studies have shown that European policies are a patchwork of different policy styles, instruments, and institutional arrangements (Héritier 1996).

One crucial element of this debate is the argument that the EU as a political system specializes in regulation (Majone 1996). With limited fiscal resources at its control, the EU has sought to expand its influence through the supply of regulations where the costs are borne by the firms and states responsible for complying with them. Thus, the Single Market is an effort to reduce transaction costs and resolve problems of heterogeneity through collective action and coordination. Majone (1995) argues that non-majoritarian institutions (such as courts or regulatory agencies) can better achieve a credible commitment towards maintaining a single market than traditional political interests such as parties, legislatures, and interest groups.

Focusing on issues of governance, other scholars have stressed the impact of the Single Market on regions, sectors, and classes by looking at the relationship between economic development and democratic conditions, seeking to demonstrate that the Single Market may not be entirely benign in its consequences (Scharpf 1999; Hirst and Thompson 1996; Amin and Tomaney 1995). Few subjects have generated more debate than the effects of economic integration and globalization on the policy autonomy of governments. Opponents argue that the increasing constraints on national policy choices, especially the pressures on the welfare states and government-owned monopolies, have in fact contributed to the growing opposition among the populace about further European integration. Proponents of market integration underscore the central role of governments in shaping EU policies and outcomes, and in so far as Europe can focus its energies and resources on market-creating and market-facilitating activities, the historical record suggests a capacity to achieve sustained, significant economic growth.

Yet as important as economic imperatives are, market integration is also the product of politics, most notably, but not exclusively, tensions and conflicts about sovereignty and governance. There is a strong relationship between economic and political developments, as the Single Market and its ancillary policies require political support and legitimacy on the one hand, and institutional capabilities and effectiveness on the other. Market integration has revealed that there are disparate ideas about how to stabilize and regulate markets, conflict and bargaining over institutional power and authority, and continual pressure from interests to shape the evolving polity.

KEY POINTS

- Two main approaches, intergovernmentalism and neo-functionalism, have been used to account for the resurgence of European integration in the mid-1980s.
- Other approaches have focused on the implications of the Single Market programme. Majone's regulatory approach focuses on the supply and demand factors driving economic integration, and the growth of non-majoritarian institutions that depoliticize decision-making, reduce transaction costs, and promote efficient outcomes.
- Scharpf stresses the impact, upon democratic legitimacy, of shifting economic policies to the European level, and the limited role of national welfare and distributive policies to compensate for increased competition due to welfare state retrenchment.

Conclusion

Though it is not yet complete, the single European market has achieved an impressive amount in a remarkably compressed period of time. Ranging across a number of policy areas, European efforts to remove obstacles and distortions in goods, services, capital, and labour have transformed the European economic landscape. Over the past four decades, the process of integrating divergent national markets, based on different models of capitalism, has meant balancing different ideological and economic perspectives.

The pressures for neo-liberal market reforms, with their emphasis on liberalization and competition, have been offset by new demands for regulated capitalism, with their emphasis on social solidarity and economic intervention. The process has been shaped by a mix of regulatory styles, instruments, and philosophies that reflect the policy styles and traditions of different member states.

Thus, various strategies and policies have been tried and tested to see how best to synthesize 25 different sets of rules, regulations, and practices into a workable functioning internal market. Each strategy seems to reflect the dominant mode of governance at the time. Efforts at harmonization in the 1950s and 1960s reflect the corresponding practices of ***dirigisme*** and interventionism, whereas later efforts at mutual recognition and standardization reflect the changing emphasis in the 1980s and 1990s towards the dynamics of regulatory competition and private sector governance. The Single Market is one of the most noteworthy accomplishments of the European integration project. Yet we need to recognize that there is more to the functioning of the Single Market than the passage of legislation. The politics of bargaining and negotiation need to be balanced by the politics of rule enforcement and compliance.

Understanding the Single Market requires more than just an analysis of its origins; it is also important to look at matters of implementation and effectiveness. This also requires us to link economic performance and political development to an understanding of how political processes and institutions evolve to support the growth of a single market and its ancillary policies. While no region in the world today comes as close as the European Union to a 'single market' within its territory, it is important to remember that those originally involved in the project believed that 'it is not just a movement for free trade between separate economies. It is a movement to fuse markets and economies into one' (Walter Hallstein, Harvard University, 22 May 1961).

QUESTIONS

1. What are the main barriers to trade in the EU?
2. What type of policy instruments has the EU used to integrate national markets?
3. How successful has the EU been in establishing a single market free of restrictions to trade and commerce?
4. What were the driving forces behind the 'relaunch' of the Single Market project in the 1980s?
5. How have different theories and approaches been used to explain the Single Market programme?
6. What role has the ECJ played in addressing barriers to trade?
7. Explain the different types of regulatory strategy used to tackle barriers to trade in Europe. What accounts for their success or failure?
8. What are the main challenges the EU faces in making the Single Market operate efficiently and effectively?

GUIDE TO FURTHER READING

- Armstrong, K., and Bulmer, S. (eds) *The Governance of the Single European Market* (Manchester: Manchester University Press, 1998). A new institutionalist approach to the study of the political and economic dynamics of the Single Market.

- Camps, M. *The European Common Market and American Policy* (Princeton, NJ: Center for International Studies, 1956). A short and informative discussion of early developments in the common market.

- Egan, M. *Constructing a European Market: Standards, Regulation and Governance* (Oxford: Oxford University Press, 2001). A comprehensive account of the regulatory strategies and institutional arrangement adopted by the EU in promoting the Single Market.

- Grin, G. *Battle of the Single European Market: Achievements and Economic Thought 1985–2000* (London: Kegan Paul, 2003). A study of the Single Market from its early origins to 2000.

- Pelkmans, J., and Winters, A. *Europe's Domestic Market* (London: Royal Institute for International Affairs/Chatham House, 1988). A critical analysis of the '1992' commitment.

IMPORTANT WEBSITES

- www.eurunion.org/infores/standard.htm This provides information and sources on standards.

- www.europa.eu.int/comm/internal_market/index_en.htm The official website of the European Union on the Single Market.

- http://europa.eu.int/comm/internal_market/score/index_en.htm The Single Market Scoreboard. The official website of the European Commission that documents implementation statistics.
- www.newapproach.org European standards activities under the 'new approach' directives representing the standardization organizations: CEN, CENELEC, and ETSI.
- http://www.accenture.com/NR/rdonlyres/FAD399B3-1856-4356-95C9-7C9D4CA5B060/0/unfinished_business.pdf *Unfinished Business: Making Europe's Single Market a Reality*. Survey on European business environment with recommendations.

Visit the Online Resource Centre that accompanies this book for lots of interesting additional material. http://www.oxfordtextbooks.co.uk/orc/cini2e/

17

The EU's Social Dimension

GERDA FALKNER

Chapter Contents

Reader's Guide

This chapter looks at the way in which European social policy has evolved since the late 1950s. It begins by reflecting on the intergovernmental character of the policy in the early days, and on how the gradual introduction of qualified majority voting and the widening scope of the policy allowed the European institutions and European-level interest groups much more of a say in the European social dimension. The chapter also looks at the work of the European Social Fund. Focusing on newer developments, later sections chart the arrival of the open method of coordination, a non-regulatory approach to European policy-making in this field, and the growing importance of social partnership, the involvement of the social partners (employers and labour representatives) in making European-level social policy. The chapter concludes by arguing that social regulation will become even more difficult now that the EU is enlarging to incorporate ever more of the Central and East European (CEE) states.

Introduction

What is social policy? In a famous definition, T. H. Marshall (1975) talked of the use of political power to supersede, supplement, or modify operations of the economic system in order to achieve results which the economic system would not achieve on its own. Such a wide definition would include, for example, redistributive EU actions, which provide funding through the EU's structural funds (that is, the social, agricultural, cohesion, and regional funds) (see Chapter 18). This would go far beyond what is usually understood as European social policy and would introduce too vast an array of topics to be covered in this brief chapter. It seems, therefore, more useful to apply a pragmatic understanding of social policy. This involves actions which fall under the so-called 'social dimension of European integration': that is, any acts carried out under the social policy chapter of the EC Treaty; policies targeted at facilitating the freedom of movement of workers in the social realm; and last, but not least, action to harmonize the quite diverse social or labour law standards of the member states, whatever the relevant Treaty base may be. It should be added that most writers on EC social policy have chosen a similar approach to this.

This chapter will first outline the division of social policy competences between the European Union and its member states; the interpretation of these Treaty provisions in the day-to-day policy process over time; and the latest formal reforms at Amsterdam and Nice. It will then analyse the incremental development of EC/EU social regulation and activities, including the European Social Fund and the so-called open method of coordination. Since patterns of decision-making are quite distinctive in the social, as opposed to the other, fields of EU politics, this chapter will also outline how the EU-level interest groups participate therein (see also Chapter 13). The conclusion not only summarizes the contents the chapter, but also discusses the performance of European integration within its 'social dimension'.

The EEC and its member states

Under the Treaty of Rome (1957), social policy competences were to remain a largely national affair. It did not provide for the Europeanization of social policies, as too many delegations had opposed this at the negotiations leading up to the Treaty. Some governments (especially the German government) pleaded for a neo-liberal, free-market approach to social affairs, even in the realm of labour and social security; others opted for a limited process of harmonization. The French delegation, notably, argued that its comparatively high social charges and its constitutional principle of equal pay for men and women might constitute a competitive disadvantage within the newly formed European market, while Italy feared that the opening up of Community borders might prove costly for the southern part of the country, which was already economically disadvantaged. In the end, a compromise was found, but this did not include explicit EEC competences for active social policy harmonization at the European level. The dominant philosophy of the 1957 Treaty was that improvements in welfare would be provided by the economic growth that arose as a consequence of the liberalization of the European market, and not from the regulatory and distributive form of public policy (see Barnard 2000; Leibfried and Pierson 1995).

Nevertheless, the Treaty contained a small number of concessions for the more interventionist delegations. These were the provisions on equal pay for both sexes (Article 119); the maintenance of 'existing equivalence between paid holiday schemes' (Article 120); and the establishment of a European Social Fund (Articles 123–8). Two of the three above-mentioned concessions (that is, equal pay and the Social Fund) increased in importance as the European integration process progressed. There was to be no follow-up, however, on the equivalence of paid holiday schemes.

While other provisions of the Treaty's Title III on 'social policy' included some solemn social policy declarations, they failed to empower the EEC to act. 'Underwriting this arrangement was the relative feasibility of nation state strategies for economic development in the first decades after World War II. The common market, as it was constructed, was designed to aid and abet such national strategies, not transcend them' (Ross 1995: 360). Yet in other areas of activity the Commission was empowered to present legislative proposals to the Council, proposals that would ultimately become binding law. For social policy, however, the Commission was permitted to act only by undertaking relevant studies, delivering opinions, and arranging consultations both on problems arising at national level and on problems of concern to international organizations. In legal terms, then, Article 118 reflected a confirmation of national (as opposed to European) responsibility for social policy.

Paradoxically, the sole explicit Community competence for social policy regulation under the original EEC Treaty was not in the part of the Treaty that dealt explicitly with social policy. It belonged, rather, to Part II, on the Foundations of the Community, which contained provisions on the free movement of goods, labour, services, and capital. Articles 48–51 thus provided for the establishment of the freedom of movement for workers, as part of the Treaty's market-making activities. This implied the abolition of all discrimination based on the nationality of workers in the member states in the areas of employment, remuneration, and other conditions of work and employment (Article 48). In order to 'adopt such measures in the field of social security as are necessary to provide freedom of movement for workers' (Article 51), the Council was mandated to aggregate the laws of the several EEC countries, so as to establish Community-wide rights to benefits and a way of calculating the amount of those benefits for migrant workers and their dependants.

Yet although there were almost no explicit social policy competences in the original EEC Treaty, an extensive interpretation of the Treaty basis provided, in practice, some room for manoeuvre. This was possible because, where necessary or useful for market integration, intervention in the social policy field was *implicitly* allowed in the 1957 Treaty, through the so-called 'subsidiary competence' provisions. In other words, laws in the member states which 'directly affect the establishment or functioning of the common market', could be approximated by unanimous Council 'decision on the basis of a Commission proposal (Article 100). Moreover, if action by the Community should prove necessary to attain, in the course of the operation of the common market, one of the objectives of the Community, and this Treaty had not provided the necessary powers, the Council should, acting unanimously on a proposal from the Commission and after consulting the European Parliament, take the appropriate measures (Article 235).

These provisions provided, from the 1970s on, a loophole for social policy harmonization at EC level. However, the unanimous Council vote necessary for this to happen constituted a high threshold for joint action. Each government could veto social measures and as a result the EEC found itself in what Scharpf (1988) has called a **joint-decision trap**.

In 1987, the Single European Act came into force as the first major Community Treaty revision (see Chapter 3). As in the 1950s, an economic enterprise was at the heart of this fresh impetus in favour of European integration. But, despite the member states' commitment to a single market programme, the Europeanization of social policy remained controversial, for example, over how much social regulation was needed. In various so-called 'flanking' (supporting) policy areas, notably environmental and research policy, Community competence was formally extended (see Articles 130r–t and 130f–q). But this was not so for social policy: the delegations representing the EC's national governments seemed unwilling to give the Community a broader role in this field.

However, one important exception was made. Article 118a on minimum harmonization concerning health and safety of workers provided an escape route out of the unanimity requirement. For the first time in European social policy, it allowed directives to be agreed on the basis of a qualified majority of the Council members. The standards adopted following this Article were minimum regulations only. Nevertheless, under this provision reluctant member states could be forced to align their social legislation with that of the majority of member states, even against their will. It should be stressed that agreement on this article was only possible because occupational health and safety issues were closely connected to the Single Market.

Governments did not expect this 'technical' matter to facilitate social policy integration in the significant way that it would in the decade to follow. An extensive use of this provision was possible mainly because the wording and the definition of key terms in Article 118a were somewhat vague:

> "Member States shall pay particular attention to encouraging improvements, especially in the working environment, as regards the health and safety of workers, and shall set as their objective the harmonization of conditions in this area, while maintaining the improvements made. In order to help achieve the objective laid down in the first paragraph, the Council, acting by a qualified majority on a proposal from the Commission, . . . shall adopt, by means of directives, minimum requirements for gradual implementation . . ."

This formulation made it easy to play what has since been called the **treaty base game** (Rhodes 1995). It allowed the governments to adopt not only measures improving the working environment (for example, a directive on the maximum concentration of air-borne pollutants), but also measures which ensured the health and safety of workers by improving working conditions in a more general sense (for example, limiting working time). It was clear that the reason why this Treaty base was frequently chosen was the fact that only this Article allowed for majority voting at the time.

KEY POINTS

- The 1957 EEC Treaty meant that social policy remained largely a national affair. The coordination of social security systems for migrant workers was an exception to this rule in the legislative field.
- The Single European Act introduced qualified majority voting to a limited area of social policy, though at the time governments did not realize its implications.

The Treaty reforms from Maastricht to the Draft Constitutional Treaty

The Intergovernmental Conference (IGC) preceding the Maastricht Treaty negotiated a reform of the social policy provisions. However, under the requirement of unanimous approval by all (then) 12 member states, the social provisions could not be significantly altered because of the strong opposition from the UK government. At the end of extremely difficult negotiations which threatened existing compromises achieved within the IGC, the UK was granted an opt-out from the social policy measures agreed by the rest of the member states. In *The Protocol on Social Policy* annexed to the EC Treaty, the 11 (and after 1995, the 14 – in other words all members except the UK) were authorized to use the institutions, procedures, and mechanisms of the Treaty for the purpose of implementing their 'Agreement on Social Policy' (sometimes called the Social Chapter).

Because of the UK opt-out (or the 'opt-in' of the other member states), the European Union after Maastricht (from November 1993) had two different legal bases for the adoption of social policy measures. The EC Treaty's social provisions remained valid for all member states. As introduced in the 1986 Single European Act, it allowed for minimum harmonization as well as for qualified majority voting in the area of worker health and safety provisions only. By contrast, the innovative social policy provisions of the Social Agreement, applicable to all but the UK, comprised what had been perceived during the IGC as an amendment to the social provisions of the Treaty. These constituted an extension of Community competence into a wide range of social policy issues, including working conditions; the information and consultation of workers; equality between men and women with regard to labour market opportunities and treatment at work (as opposed to only equal pay before); and the integration of persons excluded from the labour market (Article 2.1, Social Agreement). Some issues were, however, explicitly excluded from the scope of minimum harmonization under the Maastricht social policy provisions: namely, pay; the right of association; the right to strike; and the right to impose lock-outs (Article 2.6.).

Additionally, qualified majority voting was extended to many more issue areas than before, including the information and consultation of workers. Unanimous decisions remained, however, for social security matters and the social protection of workers; the protection of those whose employment contract is terminated; representation and collective defence of interests of workers and employers, including codetermination; conditions of employment for third-country nationals legally residing in Community territory; and financial contributions for promotion of employment and job creation (see Article 3, Social Agreement).

In contrast to the Maastricht negotiations, in the 1996–7 IGC preceding the Amsterdam Treaty, social policy reform was not a major issue (except for, assuming one chooses a wide notion of social policy, employment promotion). Because of the fierce resistance to social policy reforms in the UK's Conservative government (in office until May 1997), the IGC decided to postpone the topic until the very end of negotiation period, awaiting the result of the 1997 general election. Under the new Labour government, which came into office at this point, the UK's opt-out from the Social Agreement came to an end with the Amsterdam Treaty. Apart from this, the only significant innovation (compared to the provisions of the Social Agreement) was the new employment policy chapter (now in Articles 125–130). While excluding any harmonization of domestic laws, it provides for the coordination of national employment policies on the basis of annual guidelines and national follow-up reports. Furthermore, a new Article 13 on Community action against discrimination was inserted. On this legal basis, a couple of important new directives on fighting discrimination based on grounds of sex, race, ethnic origin, belief, disability, age, and sexual orientation have been adopted in recent years.

Finally, the Nice Treaty of 2001 was not particularly innovative in social policy matters. In some fields, the Council is now allowed to decide unanimously upon the use of the codecision procedure (see Chapter 1). This applies to worker protection where employment contracts have been terminated; to the representation and collective defence of collective interests; and to the interests of third-country nationals (non-EU nationals) (see Article 137.2). Furthermore, measures can now be adopted on all social issues, not just those concerning social exclusion and equal opportunities, as was the case after Amsterdam.

It should be mentioned here that the Draft Constitutional Treaty, which failed to be ratified both in France and the Netherlands in 2005, did not suggest any really major changes in the social policy realm. Social security provisions for migrant workers was the only new issue area to fall within qualified majority voting in the Council (to the great disappointment of the European Trade Union Confederation). Additionally, the 2000 Charter of Fundamental Rights of the Union would have been inserted into the Treaty, which would have finally given it legal status.

KEY POINTS

- On the basis of the Maastricht Social Protocol (Social Chapter), the UK had an opt-out that ended only after the Labour government took office in 1997.
- The Agreement on Social Policy gave the Union more competences and allowed for more majority voting.
- The Amsterdam Treaty transferred the Social Agreement's innovations into the main Treaty which is now binding for all.
- Although the recent Nice Treaty changed only a few aspects of EU social policy, it is clear that formal competences have been extended over time to a significant extent.

The development and scope of European social policy

There are a number of important subfields of social legislation, the most important of which are labour law; health and safety in the workplace; and gender equality. The following sections outline when and how they were developed. During the early years of European integration, social policy consisted almost exclusively of efforts to secure the free movement of workers and in that sense was rather non-controversial. In a number of EC regulations, national social security systems were coordinated with a view to improving the status of internationally mobile workers and their families.

During the late 1960s, however, the political climate gradually became more favourable to a wider range of European social policy measures. At their 1972 Paris summit, the Community heads of state and government declared that economic expansion should not be an end in itself but should lead to improvements in more general living and working conditions. With relevant Community action in mind, they agreed a catalogue of social policy measures that were to be elaborated by the Commission. In the resulting Social Action Programme (that is, a list of intended legislative initiatives, covering a number of years) of 1974 (OJ 74/C 13/1), the Council expressed its intention to adopt a series of social policy measures within two years.

That the Council stated that Community social policy should furthermore be conducted under Article 235, which goes beyond purely economic considerations, was a major development. This was confirmation that governments now perceived social policy intervention as an integral part of European integration. As a consequence, the Treaty's subsidiary competence provisions were increasingly interpreted in a regulation-friendly manner in day-to-day policy-making. Originally, only issues which directly restricted the Single Market had qualified for harmonization (or 'approximation') under Article 100. During the 1970s, a shift occurred. Henceforth, regulation was considered legitimate if it facilitated the practice of the free movement of production factors, that is, goods, services, labour, or capital. Several of the legislative measures proposed in the 1974 Social Action Programme were adopted by the Council in the years that followed, and further Social Action Programmes followed the first one.

Figure 17.1 shows the growth in social policy directives from 1974 on. By the end of 2003, 59 social directives, 19 reforms of existing directives, and seven geographical extensions of directives (to the former East Germany, to new member states, and to the UK after Amsterdam) had been adopted. The total number of decisions on social directives was 85. These directives typically fall within what at the national level is called labour law, and not within the field of social security. There are three

Figure 17.1 The increase in EC social directives

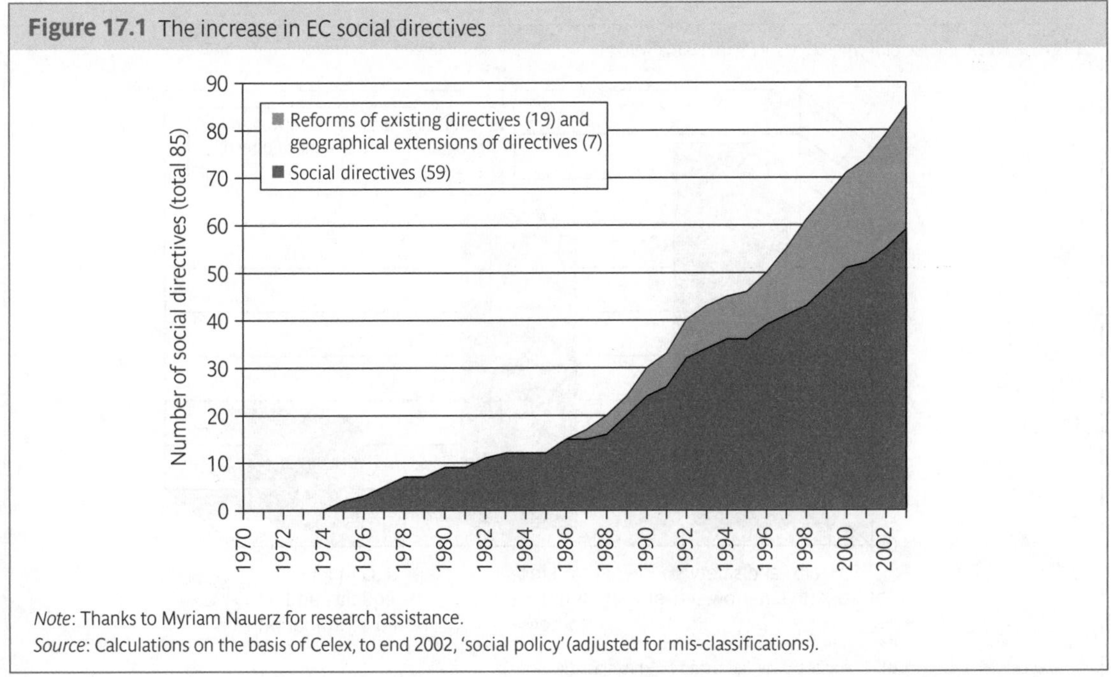

Note: Thanks to Myriam Nauerz for research assistance.
Source: Calculations on the basis of Celex, to end 2002, 'social policy' (adjusted for mis-classifications).

main fields: health and safety; other working conditions; and equality between women and men in the workplace.

With regard to *gender equality*, the European Court of Justice (ECJ) had become a major actor ever since it had provided a broad interpretation of Article 119 on domestic measures to ensure equal pay, opening the way for action on the basis of the subsidiary competence provisions (as outlined above). Matters such as equal pay for work of equal value, the equal treatment of men and women regarding working conditions and social security, and even the issue of burden of proof in discrimination lawsuits were finally regulated at EU level (Hoskyns 1996; Mazey 1998).

In the field of *working conditions*, a number of directives were adopted during the late 1970s, for example on protection of workers in cases of collective redundancy, the transfer of undertakings, or employer insolvency. Many more directives followed during the 1990s, including those on worker information, on conditions of work contracts, on the equal treatment of atypical (such as shift or part-time) workers, and on parental leave.

With regard to *health and safety at work*, regulation was based on a number of specific action programmes. Directives include those on the protection of workers exposed to emissions (or pollutants) and responsible for heavy loads, as well as protection against risks of chemical, physical, and biological agents at work (such as lead or asbestos). Figure 17.2 indicates the number of directives in these three subfields.

KEY POINTS

- The development of EC social legislation has increased since the late 1950s, with the 1990s being the most active period.
- In addition to the issue of the free movement of workers and equal treatment in national social security systems, the main areas of regulatory European social policy are working conditions, gender equality, and health and safety in the workplace.

Figure 17.2 EC social directives in three subfields

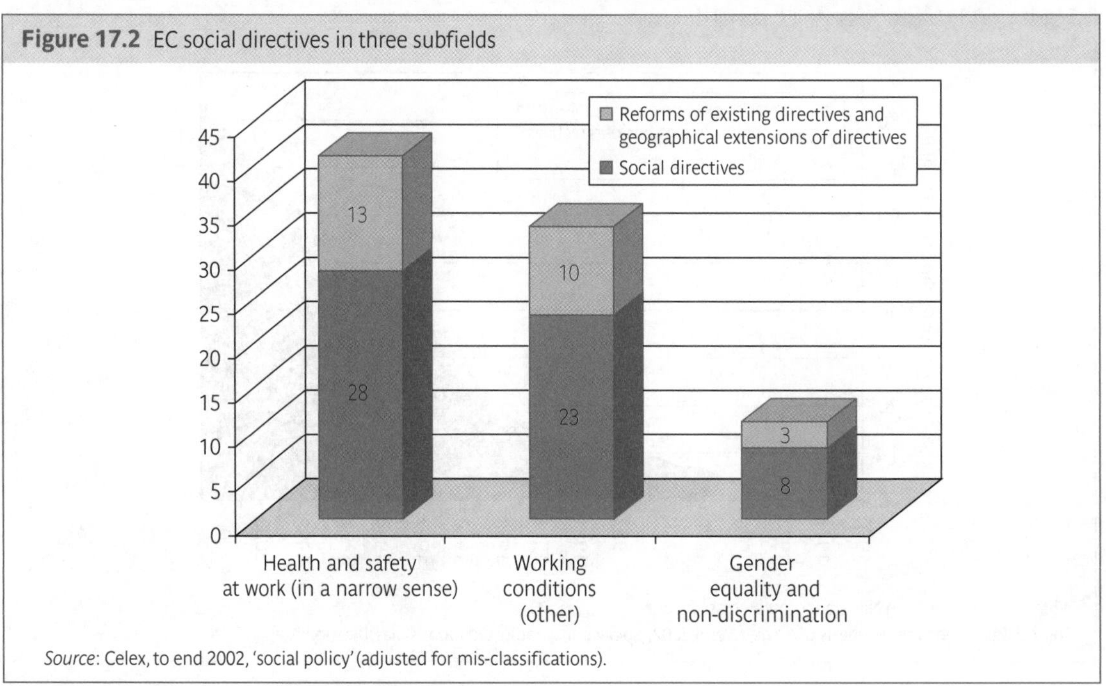

Source: Celex, to end 2002, 'social policy' (adjusted for mis-classifications).

The European Social Fund

European Community policy is largely regulatory, and this is particularly the case in the social field. However, as this and the following section will outline, the relative importance of regulation has declined in recent years, as both funding opportunities and 'soft' forms of governance have increased. In the case of funding, the 1957 Treaty provided for a European Social Fund (ESF). Its goal was to simplify the employment of workers, to increase their geographical and occupational mobility within the Community, and to facilitate their adaptation to change, particularly through vocational training and retraining. Initially, the ESF reimbursed member states for some of the costs involved in introducing and implementing such measures. The Fund did not have any controlling function, however, as the transfer of money to the member states' employment services was quasi-automatic. And, in contrast to its original objective of rectifying specifically Italian problems after the opening up of market borders, it tended to be the best-funded and best-organized domestic labour market administrations who received most of the money (Germany, for example). It was this anomaly in the system which prompted the first major reform of the ESF in 1971. This involved an agreement on the definition of target groups, and the co-funding of only those domestic projects considered appropriate from a Community perspective. After a number of further reforms, the ESF now co-finances projects for young people seeking employment, for the long-term unemployed, for disadvantaged groups, and for promoting gender equality in the labour market. The aim is to improve people's 'employability' through strategic long-term programmes (particularly in regions lagging behind), to upgrade and modernize workforce skills, and to foster entrepreneurial initiative.

In addition to the Social Fund, other EU Funds also seek to combat regional and social disparities (see Chapter 18). These are the European Regional Development Fund (ERDF), the European Agricultural Guidance and Guarantee Fund (EAGGF) (Guarantee Section) (see Chapter 21), and the Financial Instrument for Fisheries Guidance. Finally, the Cohesion Fund finances environmental projects and trans-European infrastructure networks in member states whose gross domestic product (GDP) is less than 90 per cent of the EU average. In sum, the EU's social dimension is less regulatory than is often assumed. As Figure 17.3 highlights, the funding distributed by the ESF has grown steadily, both in relative and in absolute terms.

The Social Fund's share of total EC spending was 1.1 per cent in 1970; 4.4 per cent by 1980; 7.3 per cent by 1990; 8.6 per cent in 2000; and 9.4 per cent by 2002. The share of all Structural Funds has grown even more quickly – from 2.8 per cent in 1970 to 35.4 per cent in 2002 (that is €33,838 million). This increase cannot hide the fact, however, that the Guarantee Section of the Agricultural Fund is very much larger – €44, 255 million.

Finally, the steering effect of the EU's labour market policy is much stronger than the ESF figures indicate. The ESF figures display only the EU's part of the overall project budgets. The impact of the EU's criteria for project selection is greater than this, since national authorities also apply these criteria, with the prospect of European co-funding in mind (in order to get national contributions back from Brussels). Moreover, the relative importance of EU funding has increased at a time of national spending cuts.

Figure 17.3 European Social Fund and Structural Funds as percentages of total EC budget

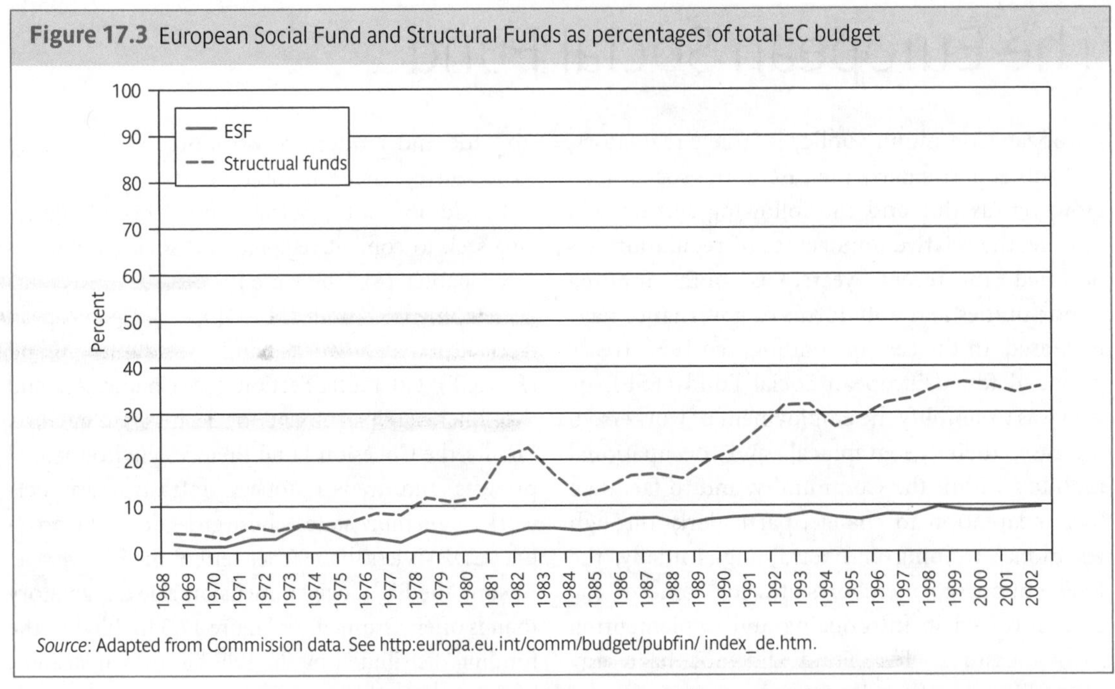

Source: Adapted from Commission data. See http:europa.eu.int/comm/budget/pubfin/ index_de.htm.

KEY POINTS

- The 1957 Treaty established a European Social Fund. Its aims are narrower than its name suggests as they concern only labour market policy and mostly target specific regions.
- The ESF co-funds projects and programmes in the member states. It has had, since 1971, its own priorities for funding, with a certain steering effect on national policies, as national governments want a share of the EU budget to flow back into their country.
- As of 2002, ESF expenditure had grown to 9.4 per cent of the EU budget.

New developments: the open method of coordination

If the legislative (or regulatory) track of EU social policy seems to have comparatively less importance at the turn of the millennium, this is not due to any significant slowdown in legislative proposals, but because of a new (often called a 'softer') style of intervention known as the **open method of coordination** (see de la Porte and Pochet 2002). Thus, the EU has a novel role as both driver and constraint on national, social, and structural reform (see Goetschy 2001).

The main features of the open method of coordination were developed (initially with no

Treaty basis) in the field of employment policy, as a follow-up to the Essen European Council of 1994. The Amsterdam Treaty's employment chapter later formalized the method. Every year since, the EU has adopted employment policy guidelines. Specification and implementation of these is left, however, to the national level so that the domestic situation and party political preferences can be taken into consideration. All the same, member states must present annual reports on how they have dealt with the guidelines, and why they have chosen particular strategies in their 'National Action Plans'. They have to defend their decisions at the European level in regular debates on national employment policies, so that peer pressure comes into play and has, at least potentially, a harmonizing effect on social policies in Europe.

The open method of coordination has recently been extended to new fields, including pension reform, social inclusion, and education. To date, its success is hard to judge, as the lack of reliable data on its practical effects in the member states is only slowly being rectified (but see Zeitlin and Pochet 2005). In any case, the net effect of this strategy will always be difficult to measure since there is no counter-factual basis of comparison available (Pochet and de la Porte 2004). It is plausible to expect that the joint policy learning (Sabatier and Jenkins-Smith 1993) and mutual adaptation (DiMaggio and Powell 1991) that results from this approach will have some beneficial effects, and that EU-level obligations, however loosely defined, will help governments to justify reforms domestically that they might otherwise not have dared to enforce for fear of electoral losses. Where national governments are not ready for policy change, however, the national action plans may do no more than either restate pre-existing domestic policies or perform a symbolic function (Scharpf 2002). In such cases the EU is helpless, since EU-level harmonization by means of more formal regulation (new laws) is explicitly ruled out under the open method of coordination.

KEY POINTS

- The open method of coordination is a new EU-level approach that is gaining in importance as an alternative to regulation.
- It is based on European guidelines, national action plans, and national reports using common indicators, and uses EU-level evaluations that feed into new policy guidelines.
- The practical effects of the open method have not yet been sufficiently and systematically evaluated.

Social partnership at the European level

Contemporary Community social policy-making is characterized by a style that some call 'Euro-corporatism' (Gorges 1996). This involves intense cooperation between public and private actors in the EU's social dimension. Corporatism is a way of making policy that includes not only public actors, but also interest groups as decisive co-actors (Streeck and Schmitter 1991; see also Chapter 13). All agree that EU social policy since Maastricht has been characterized by the complexity of government negotiations in the Council and collective bargaining between the major economic interest groupings. As a consequence, the rather particular, closed, and stable policy network in EU social policy may be defined as a 'corporatist policy community' (Falkner 1998).

The legislative procedure in EU social policy now works as follows: when the Commission consults on any planned social policy measure, European-level employer and labour groups may inform the

Commission of their wish to initiate negotiations on the matter under discussion in order to reach a collective agreement. This process brings standard EC decision-making (see Chapter 1) to a standstill for nine months. If a collective agreement is signed, it can, at the joint request of the signatories, be incorporated in a 'Council decision' on the basis of a prior Commission proposal.

In recent years, bargaining on social policy issues has therefore been pursued in two quite distinctive (but interdependent) arenas. The traditional pattern of social policy-making is dominated by the Council and its working groups (see Chapter 10), although the adoption of a directive demands a Commission proposal and action by the European Parliament (EP), depending on the specific procedure at stake. The interests represented by politicians (and bureaucrats) involved are predominantly territorial (in the Council) and party political (in the EP). In this 'intergovernmental arena' for EU social policy, negotiations proceed according to the detailed rules about decision-taking that are specified in the EC Treaty. These are complemented by informal rules which have resulted from decades of EC negotiation practice.

A second, quite different arena now surrounds negotiations between management and labour. Here, procedures are not prescribed in the Treaties, which only contain provisions about 'interface situations' where the intergovernmental procedure and collective bargaining meet, notably specifying the rules on bringing standard decision processes to a standstill, or initiating Council negotiations on implementation. Since the Treaties did not even specify who 'labour and management' should be, this was decided informally. Moreover, the Commission and the Council did not designate the European interest groups as being responsible for carrying out the collective negotiations, even if in practice they approved the special status of the Union of Industrial and Employers' Confederations of Europe (UNICE), the European Association for Public Sector Firms (CEEP), and the European Trade Union Congress (ETUC) as the responsible cross-sectoral **social partners**. These three groups, who wanted and received the leading role in 'negotiated legislation' (Dølvik 1997) on European social policy, had already participated in a **social dialogue** with the Commission since the mid-1980s. When parental leave, the first issue to be discussed under the Social Agreement, was under consideration, the Commission stopped the standard legislative processes at the request of these groups and considered it appropriate to implement the agreement that resulted in a binding directive. Smaller interest groups excluded from this process complained about this, but the legal action taken by the Union of Craft, Small and Medium-sized Enterprises (UEAPME) was rejected by the European Court. Recently, both UNICE and ETUC have concluded cooperation agreements with smaller groups on the European social dialogue, while ultimately keeping their negotiation prerogatives intact.

Yet it is important to underline the point that the social partner negotiations on EC social policy issues are entirely independent of the intergovernmental arena. There is intense contact and a large degree of interdependence amongst all relevant actors in EC social policy, that is amongst the Council, the social partners, the Commission, and, to a lesser extent, the EP. To date, three legally binding, cross-sectoral collective agreements on labour law issues have been signed and implemented in EC directives (Falkner 2000a): on parental leave (December 1995); on part-time work (June 1997); and on fixed-term work (March 1999).

A number of other negotiations failed to reach agreement, for example on the issue of temporary agency work, or were not initiated, such as those on fighting sexual harassment, and on information and consultation of employees in national enterprises. Recently, further agreements were concluded or are being negotiated that the social partners (above all, industry) want to be non-binding and/or implemented in accordance with specific national procedures and practices, rather than by a directive (for example, the agreements on telework, 2002; and on work-related stress, 2004). This can be interpreted as a move away from social partner agreements on effective minimum standards that are applicable throughout the EU. At the sectoral level, however, there are a couple of recent agreements with subsequent binding directives (for example, on working time in various industries).

KEY POINTS

- Since Maastricht, EU social policy has involved a 'corporatist policy community'.
- The organized interests of labour and industry are free collectively to agree social standards that are later made binding in Council directives.
- They have done so in three cases, but have failed or have settled for less binding recommendations in others.

Conclusion

The preceding sections have indicated that European social policy has been considerably extended and differentiated over time. Treaty bases have been revised several times to extend the range of competences. The European Social Fund has increased its resources, and has had a practical impact on national employment promotion projects. The number of social directives has also increased over time, with the 1990s being by far the most active decade so far. It should also be mentioned that the European Court of Justice in Luxembourg has been influential on a number of social policy issues and, as a consequence, has significantly increased the practical impact of EU social law. The equal treatment of women in the workplace and the protection of workers' interests when enterprises change hands are two important examples (Leibfried and Pierson 2000).

If we look at social policy developments at the EU level, at least four different evaluation criteria seem worth considering (Falkner 2000b). First, the closing of a number of gaps in labour law, introduced or widened by the Single Market Programme, was a major task for EU social policy (Barnard 2000: 62). According to this indicator, the EU performed much better than most experts expected during the early 1990s and all important gaps are now closed. A somewhat more far-reaching criterion for judging EU social law is the differential between Commission proposals and Council legislation. There was a huge gap during the late 1980s and early 1990s which has been almost completely filled. Even some of the most controversial projects, on sexual harassment in the workplace and on employee consultation in the European Company Statute, have been adopted.

A third indicator of the scope of the EU's social dimension is action taken to prevent reductions in national social standards, potentially induced by the increased competitive pressures of the Single Market and the Economic and Monetary Union (EMU) (sometimes called **social dumping**). One possible means of avoiding the need for such action would have been to agree on fluctuation margins, which would have prevented one country from gaining competitive advantages through lowering social standards. However, such proposals were only thought realistic in a small number of member states, notably Belgium, France, and Germany (Busch 1988; Dispersyn *et al.* 1990). At the level of the Social Affairs Council there was little support. Finally, a fourth evaluation criterion might be the rather small extent to which the EU has forged a truly supranational social order.

In any case, a full evaluation of the success of existing European social law is restricted by lack of knowledge about its practical effects in the member states. One comparative study of 90 case studies of domestic adaptation performance across a range of EU social directives (see Falkner *et al.* 2005) has recently revealed that there are major implementation failures and that, to date, the European Commission has not been able to perform its control function adequately. While all countries occasionally fail to implement social directives, some usually take their EU-related duties seriously. Others frequently privilege their domestic political concerns over the requirements of EU law. A further group of countries neglects these EU obligations almost as a matter of course.

In any case, the enlargement of the European Union makes the adoption of common standards more difficult, as social standards differ even more widely in an enlarged EU. Although agreement on legislation was already impossible in a number of social fields, it seems fair to conclude that, in the future, common social standards will be of rather more importance. At the same time, agreement on binding standards (in particular, costly ones) will be even more difficult to achieve.

? QUESTIONS

1. Why did the evolution of a 'social dimension' lag behind the market integration aspects of European integration?
2. Why is the Treaty base so important for EC social law?
3. What are the main areas of EU social law?
4. To what extent is EU social policy a regulatory policy, and how has social policy regulation developed over time?
5. How does the European Social Fund influence national policy?
6. What is the method of open coordination and what are its merits?
7. To what extent is EU social policy corporatist?
8. Which criteria are best used for evaluating the development of the EU's social dimension?

GUIDE TO FURTHER READING

- Falkner, G. *EU Social Policy in the 1990s: Towards a Corporatist Policy Community* (London: Routledge, 1998). The social dialogue between EU-level organized interests of labour and management is analysed from both the theoretical and the practical angles.

■ Falkner, G., Treib, O., Hartlapp, M., Leiber, S. *Complying with Europe: EU Minimum Harmonization and Soft Law in the Member States* (Cambridge: Cambridge University Press, 2005). This book examines the implementation of six social directives (on working time, parental leave, part-time work, etc. in 15 member states.

■ Hoskyns, C. *Integrating Gender* (London: Verso, 1996). This is still the most comprehensive book by a political scientist on the EU's equal treatment and gender equality policy.

■ Leibfried, S., and Pierson, P. (eds) *European Social Policy: Between Fragmentation and Integration* (Washington/DC: The Brookings Institution, 1995). This is a classic which is still a very rewarding collection of essays on EU-level social law and policy.

■ Scharpf, F. W. *Governing in Europe: Effective and Democratic?* (Oxford: Oxford University Press, 1999). This book puts EU social policy in a wider perspective of governance in the multi-level system.

■ Shaw, J. (ed.) *Social Law and Policy in an Evolving European Union*. (Oxford: Hart, 2000). An excellent collection of essays on EU social policy.

■ Zeitlin, J., and Pochet, P. (eds) (with Lars Magnusson) *The Open Method of Coordination in Action: The European Employment and Social Inclusion Strategies* (Brussels: PIE-Peter Lang, 2005). This edited book provides the most up-to-date information on the various fields of open coordination.

IMPORTANT WEBSITES

● http://europa.eu.int/comm/employment_social/index_en.htm The homepage of the European Commission's Directorate-General for Employment and Social Affairs provides up-to-date information on all fields of European social law and policy.

● http://europeangovernance.livingreviews.org/ *Living Reviews in European Governance* (LREG) is an innovative e-journal, publishing solicited state-of-the-art articles in the field of European governance research that will always be kept up to date by their authors.

● http://www.eiro.eurofound.ie/ 'European industrial relations observatory on-line' is an excellent source of information on all social dialogue issues, whether national or at EU level.

● http://eiop.or.at/euroint/ 'EuroInternet' is the most comprehensive collection of information resources on the Internet relating to European integration. It contains relevant publications, and details of institutions (both EU and national), associations, databases, people, topics, etc. A special 'subject section' is devoted to social policy.

● http://eiop.or.at/erpa/ The European Research Papers Archive (ERPA) is a common access point for high-quality online working paper series (currently nine) in the field of European integration research (including, for example, that of the European University Institute). Hundreds of articles can be searched and the full text read, at no cost. 'Social policy' is one of the key areas covered.

● http://eiop.or.at/eiop/ *European Integration online Papers* (EIoP) is a free, but fully reviewed, interdisciplinary e-journal on European integration issues. Since 1997, scholars from all over the world have published more than 80 articles there for over 1,300 subscribers. Social policy is covered in a number of articles.

Visit the Online Resource Centre that accompanies this book for lots of interesting additional material. http://www.oxfordtextbooks.co.uk/orc/cini2e/

18 Regional Europe

ANGELA K. BOURNE

Chapter Contents

- Introduction
- Regions in EU decision-making
- Origins and development of EU regional policy
- Building EU regional policy: from the Treaty of Rome to the present
- The implementation of EU regional policy
- Conclusion: implications of regional Europe

Reader's Guide

This chapter examines two main dimensions of regional Europe. The constitutional dimension relates to the impact of the EU on member states' subnational authorities and their role in EU decision-making. Both of these issues were highly relevant for regions in recent EU constitutional debates. The policy dimension of regional Europe relates to the evolution of, and rationale behind, EU regional, or **cohesion**, policy. Both of these facets of regional Europe raise pertinent questions for theoretical accounts about the nature of the contemporary EU.

Introduction

European integration has long affected regions within member states, as indeed it has affected many aspects of member states' domestic politics. However, since the mid-1980s, the impact of the EU on regions has become much more significant. EU powers conferred by the Single European Act (SEA) and the Maastricht Treaty impinge upon many more regional decision powers than in the past. Additionally, the Single Market programme, Economic and Monetary Union (EMU), and the increase in regional disparities within the EU following successive enlargements has encouraged the EU to take regional economic development more seriously. Member states have agreed new rules to strengthen EU regional policy on a number of occasions and substantially increased contributions to 'Structural Funds', the Community funds for poorer regions. Developments such as these not only made EU policies more relevant to regions, but also turned many regional actors into lobbyists and stakeholders in the EU decision process. The active participation of many regions in recent EU constitutional debates shows that EU politics continues to be relevant for the regions.

This chapter explores these developments by examining two aspects of regional Europe. In the first part, it analyses the Europeanization of regional activism and the growing presence of regions in the EU's policy process. In this section the participation and demands of regions in recent EU constitutional debates receives particular attention. The second and third sections examine EU regional policy, starting with a review of its principal rationales. This is followed by analysis of how policy deepening and enlargement affect the development of regional policy. The chapter finishes with an outline of how the policy is implemented. The conclusion considers some of the broader implications of regional Europe for EU politics.

Regions in EU decision-making

In this chapter, 'region' is used to describe segments of divided territorial space situated immediately below the level of the state. The simplest way of identifying regions is by their formal institutions, or the presence of parliaments and/or executive or administrative bodies. A region may be more, or it may be less, than a political space, however. For instance, a region may be a functional space, with institutions responsible for planning and the implementation of regional policies but lacking directly elected bodies. A region can also be a cultural space, especially in so far as it is inhabited by an ethnically or linguistically distinguishable group like the Basques, Catalans, Scots, Welsh, Bretons, or the Flemish.

In recent decades, the region has become a more important feature of the domestic political landscape in Europe. Immediately after the Second World War, there were only a handful of European states with regions exercising significant political powers, notably West Germany, Austria, and Switzerland. Since then, devolutionary reforms began to unravel the political centralization of many European states. New regional institutions were set up in countries like Belgium from the 1960s, in France, Spain, and Italy from the 1970s, and in the United Kingdom since the late 1990s. Since the fall of communism, regional-level authorities have also been established in some Central and Eastern European (CEE) member states, such as the Czech Republic, Poland, and Slovakia. Decentralization takes many forms, with some regions enjoying very significant powers, others mostly administrative powers.

One important impact that the EU has had on this decentralizing process has been the Europeanization of regions' experience of political autonomy. EU decisions affect regions in a range of policy areas and many regions now regularly take an active interest in EU decisions (see Box 18.1). In order to aid lobbying and information gathering, many regions have established regional information offices. The number of such offices has grown significantly. From just a handful in the mid-1980s, a list of sub-national authority offices in Brussels in 2005 includes well over 200 entries, with regional authorities taking up a large share of these. (For a list of links see Brussels in Europe, www.blbe.irisnet.be.) Furthermore, many regional (and indeed local) governments are involved in international regional associations, the number of which also bloomed from the mid-1980s. From this time, many new associations were set up to provide a collective regional lobby and to facilitate cooperation between regions from different parts of Europe. The Assembly of European Regions is the largest of these, comprising more than 300 members from all over Europe. The Conference of European Regional Legislative Parliaments (CALRE) and the Conference of European Regions with Legislative Powers (REGLEG) are among the most recently established interregional associations. Both conferences developed lists of common demands on EU constitutional matters and presented them to heads of state and government and the Convention on the Future of Europe. There are many other regional associations, with activities covering a range of functional, political, and cultural activities.

CASE STUDY 18.1

The Basque government's European policy

The Basque government is the executive institution of the Basque Autonomous Community, one of the 17 regional entities established in Spain from the 1970s. *Partido Nacionalista Vasco* (PNV, the Basque Nationalist Party) has always been dominant in the Basque government. It is a moderate, Christian democratic, Basque nationalist party with a long tradition of supporting European unity. From its position at the helm of the Basque government's European policy machinery, the PNV has been able to pursue the Basque nationalist agenda abroad by presenting itself as a foreign policy player or by pursuing policies popular in the Basque Country but not necessarily finding Spanish central government support. Not surprisingly, this tactic has often caused tensions between Basque and Spanish central governments.

However, like other Spanish autonomous communities and indeed, many other regional governments in the EU, the Basque government pursues many interests at the EU level (Bourne 2002 and 2003). The Basque government has paid close attention to each major round of structural fund reforms, including the recent *Agenda 2000* round where it battled against the odds (and without success) to get part of its territory declared an 'Objective 1' area. The Basque government has had an interest in the progress of EU legislation in many other fields, including agriculture, fishing, transport, and competition policy, and it routinely lobbies EU decision-makers – at both national and supranational levels – to try to influence EU laws. The Basque government also has a strong interest in the development of a more powerful institutionalized role for regions in EU decision-making. To this end the Basque government was involved in activities with other EU regions to influence the content of the Constitutional Treaty.

Regional authorities have become a more important part of EU politics thanks in large part to the achievements of successive campaigns to increase their say in EU decision-making. As the process of policy deepening instigated by the SEA and Maastricht Treaty began to bite, a new regions lobby demanded recompense for the fact that the political costs of European integration were intrinsically higher for regional than for central governments. Powers transferred to the EU level in the course of integration came from competencies allocated to both regional and central governments in domestic constitutional arrangements. However, central governments received forms of 'compensation' for those transferred competencies, while regional governments did not. For example, central governments were compensated because their representatives were, until recently, the only officials able to vote in the powerful EU Council. This meant that central governments participated in decisions made in the EU Council, even if the policy matter in question was formally allocated to, or shared with, regions in domestic constitutions. Not surprisingly, regional governments demanded – and continue to demand – EU-level change to ensure that they do not 'lose' powers in the process of European integration.

In the last few decades, and more recently during EU constitutional debates, some regions (especially German regions) called for increasing protection against EU incursions into their decision powers (Jeffrey 2004). One suggestion considered during these debates was to establish a 'competence catalogue' more clearly delimiting EU, member state, and regional competencies. A form of competence catalogue was eventually incorporated in Title III of the Constitutional Treaty (CT). EU regions have also called for a more inclusive definition and better enforcement of the subsidiarity principle. 'Subsidiarity', currently encoded in Article 5 (ex 3b) of the EC Treaty but amended by the CT, seeks to limit the scope of Community action to areas where Community action is most effective. In accordance with the wishes of EU regions, the CT amended the text of the EC treaty to include reference to subnational authorities. CT amendments to Article 5 of the current EC treaty are indicated in italics of the text below:

> " In areas which do not fall within its exclusive competence, the Community shall take action, in accordance with the principle of subsidiarity, only if and in so far as the objectives of the proposed action cannot be sufficiently achieved by the Member States, *either at central or at regional and local level*, and can therefore, by reason of the scale or effects of the proposed action, be better achieved by the Community. "

CT provisions to improve the enforcement of subsidiarity also included a regional dimension. For instance, regions represented in chambers of state-level parliaments would have a say in whether that chamber issued a 'vote' against an EU legislative proposal considered in violation of subsidiarity. If sufficient votes were issued from parliaments across the EU, the legislative proposal would be reconsidered.

Regions have also made demands for a greater role in EU decision-making, which has led to further changes in the EU's institutional architecture. The Committee of the Regions (CoR), established by the Maastricht Treaty, is the most visible of these changes. The CoR began work in 1994 as a body of 222 representatives of EU member states' local and regional authorities. After the 2004 enlargement, the size of the CoR increased to 317 members. The Commission and the EU Council are obliged to consult the CoR in a range of policy areas that directly affect local and regional authorities. These areas, expanded in successive treaty reforms, now include economic and social cohesion, trans-European infrastructure networks, health, education, and culture (included in the Maastricht Treaty); employment, social policy, environment, vocational training, and transport (added by the Amsterdam Treaty).

Formally the CoR is weak. It is a purely advisory body whose opinions can be ignored by other institutions in the legislative process. The CoR faces certain internal tensions, including differences between typically much weaker local governments and more powerful regional governments (Christiansen 1996: 96; McCarthy 1997: 440). It has faced criticisms over the blandness of its opinions. Regions have also been critical of the CoR, stating in a 2002 Declaration agreed in Florence that the CoR 'did not correspond to the expectations of regions with legislative powers' (www.regleg.org). Nevertheless, there is evidence to suggest that the Commission in particular, an institution that played an important role in setting up the CoR in the first place, does take the CoR's opinions seriously (Loughlin 1997: 160). Another source of strength is that some of the CoR's members are powerful and experienced politicians at home, a factor that adds political weight to CoR opinions (Loughlin 1997: 160). Six representatives of the CoR were given formal observer status in the Convention on the Future of Europe although they participated on a similar basis to full members. The CT increased CoR powers by allowing it to take actions to the European Court of Justice to defend CoR prerogatives or if the CoR considered EU actions an infringement of the subsidiarity principle.

Another amendment agreed at Maastricht (Article 203) opened up the possibility that regional ministers could represent their state – in some cases with voice and vote – in the EU Council and its working groups. The details were left to each individual state to decide and there are, as a consequence, important differences in arrangements for each state's regions to participate in the Council. Regional ministers from Germany, Austria, Belgium, the UK, and, after many years of domestic debates, Spain have attended Council meetings. Importantly, regional ministers are not allowed to participate merely as representatives of their own region's interests. Regional ministers, like central government ministers, represent and must vote for their state as a whole. Interestingly, one of the suggestions made to the Convention on the Future of the EU was that states be allowed to split their vote in the Council and in so doing allow regional and central government representatives in member state delegations to vote differently on a single piece of EU legislation. Not surprisingly, this proposal did not prosper. Nevertheless, the importance of regional participation in the Council is often the opportunities it provides for regional ministers to steer negotiations in a direction that may correspond to regional interests and to provide insider information and contacts which regions can use to their advantage in both domestic and EU decision processes.

From the foregoing, it is clear that the EU has made – or contemplated – many changes to respond to the demands of EU regions. However, it must be acknowledged that many regions consider reforms taken so far to be insufficient. It must also be recognized that there is no such thing as a coherent 'regions agenda' on EU constitutional issues more generally or on specific EU policies. Regions (and local authorities) may have quite different policy competencies and political powers, economic interests, and ideological preferences. At times regions may even compete with each other over resources and for influence. Nevertheless, the experience of the past 20 years or so shows that when goals and interests coincide, regional authorities from different member states may find it useful to join forces.

KEY POINTS

- Since the mid-1980s, regional governments' experience of political autonomy has acquired more of a European dimension. Many regional governments have offices in Brussels, participate in regional associations, and lobby EU decision-makers.
- European integration can be costly for regions, particularly those with legislative powers. The EU's institutional arrangements tend to favour full involvement of central over regional authorities.
- Since the Maastricht Treaty, institutional changes have helped address such problems, but they have yet to fully solve them. The CoR and provisions allowing regional governments to participate in the EU Council are two key reforms that sought to enhance regional influence in the EU.
- Regions' representatives participated in the Convention on the Future of Europe and associations of regions like REGLEG and CALRE developed joint positions on constitutional issues. CT responses to regions' demands included new provisions on subsidiarity and new powers for the CoR.

Origins and development of EU regional policy

This section examines the origins and development of EU regional policy. Before doing so, it is necessary to examine briefly the general objectives of regional policy and why an organization like the EU might develop such a policy.

In general terms, regional policy seeks to reduce regional economic disparities. It aims to ameliorate conditions within regions with lower economic growth, employment, or per capital income levels than other regions. It may be employed to address specific economic problems, such as industrial decline or a region's geographic isolation. There are often important economic disparities among regions within a state, so it is not surprising that there are also significant disparities among regions in the EU more generally. Before the 2004 enlargement, there were already significant disparities among regions in the EU15. However, disparities are now much larger (see Box 18.2).

Many EU member states already conduct their own regional policies. Why, then, do they also need a supranational regional policy? This question can be examined from an economic, political, and social perspective. In the first place, the integration of markets may exacerbate regional economic disparities (Armstrong and Taylor 2000). Economic integration does not affect all regions in the same way. It generally favours regions located geographically at the centre of the Single Market. This is where economic activity, populations (and thus consumers and workers), transport, and other infrastructure already tend to be concentrated. Deepening economic integration, as undertaken in the Single Market programme and EMU, may further exacerbate regional economic disparities between centre and periphery. At the same time, the process of creating a single market has obliged member states to give up some important policy instruments that could have been used to improve regional economic disparities at home. Those taking part in EMU, for example, can no longer manipulate their exchange rates to assist poorer regions and there are limits placed, in the context of EU competition policy, on the amount of subsidies member governments can spend on their regions (George 1996: 231).

BOX 18.2

Regional disparities in the EU

Gross domestic product (GDP) per capita

- Disparities in member states' GDP per capita (measured in purchasing power parities) are large. In 2003, levels ranged from 41 per cent of the EU average in Latvia to 214 per cent in Luxembourg. Ireland is the second most prosperous country in these terms with a GDP of 132 per cent of the EU average.
- Disparities are also large among EU regions. In 2002, levels of GDP per head ranged from 189 per cent of the EU25 average in the 10 most prosperous regions to 35 per cent of that average in the 10 least prosperous ones.
- In new member states 90 per cent of the total population live in a region with GDP levels at below 75 per cent of the EU average. Among EU15 the regions with the lowest incomes are concentrated in southern parts of Greece, Portugal, Italy, and Spain as well as Germany's formerly communist regions.

Employment rates

- In 2003 the average rate of employment for EU25 was 62.9 per cent. This is below the target of 70 per cent set by member states in the Lisbon strategy. Only four member states – Denmark, Sweden, the Netherlands, and the United Kingdom – reach the 70 per cent rate, although employment rates fall to as low as 51.2 per cent for Poland.
- Disparities are reflected at the regional level. Only a quarter of the EU population live in a region where the 70 per cent employment rate target has been met. In contrast, almost 15 per cent of the population live in a region where the rate of employment is below 55 per cent. The latter are predominantly located in new member states and in southern parts of Spain and Italy.

Source: Commission of the European Communities, *Third Progress Report on Cohesion: Towards a New Partnership for Growth, Jobs and Cohesion*, COM (2005) 192 final, Brussels, 17 May 2005

Presented in this manner, the justification for creating EU-level regional policy appears to lend weight to the neo-functionalist 'spillover' thesis (see Chapter 6). Functional spillover describes the process whereby integration in some sectors requires integration in others, a process that sets in motion an incremental movement towards closer union. Applied to the case of EU regional policy, it could be argued that the problems market integration and EMU may create – that is, the marginalization of peripheral regions and the removal of regional policy instruments – produce a situation in which EU regional policy becomes more necessary. But there is also a case for arguing that the rationale behind EU regional policy is largely political and that factors other than spillover account for its development. As the following section will show in more detail, there is evidence that the exigencies of intergovernmental bargaining have been important for understanding the development of EU regional policy. Many authors emphasize, for example, the importance of EU regional policy as a form of compensation or 'side payment' necessary to get agreements on contentious issues (Moravcsik 1993; Allen 2005). Some authors also argue that the ambitions of supranational actors like the Commission and changing policy-making fashions played an important part in the development of EU regional policy (Marks 1992; Kohler-Koch 1996; Tömmel 1998).

Finally, for the last 20 years, EU regional policy has been associated with the term 'cohesion' and indeed, 'regional policy' and 'cohesion policy' are often used interchangeably. Since the SEA, regional policy measures have been grouped under a title of the EC Treaty called 'Economic and social cohesion', a heading which the CT amends to 'Economic, social and territorial cohesion'. Since Maastricht, there has also been a special 'Cohesion Fund' for the poorer member states (see Box 18.3). 'Cohesion', particularly 'economic and social cohesion' is an imprecise, but suggestive term, evoking social goals like the equalization of living standards and access to employment and other social goods. However, it is important to acknowledge that EU regional policy is not, on its own, well placed to achieve such ambitious goals, despite the rhetoric. In the first place, its budgetary resources are limited. Furthermore, as Barry and Begg point out, EU regional policy focuses on the long-term competitiveness of regions, which contrasts with the range of instruments member states possess (for example, social security payments or central government grants) to address social cohesion through income redistribution (2003: 782–3).

Building EU regional policy: from the Treaty of Rome to the present

The Treaty of Rome provided the seeds for EU regional policy. In the Treaty's preamble, member states noted their desire to 'ensure their harmonious development by reducing differences existing between the various regions and the backwardness of the less-favoured regions'. However, it was not until 1975 that the Community established the European Regional Development Fund (ERDF), the Community's first policy instrument specifically dedicated to the problem of unequal development between EU regions. With the creation of this fund, the first of a series of phases in the development of EU regional policy commenced. The creation of the ERDF would be followed in the second phase (1985–97) by the implementation of reforms creating a more substantial regional policy and in a third phase (1997–2006) by the implementation of further major reforms to prepare for eastward enlargement. EU regional policy is currently undergoing a further round of reform designed to meet the problems of regional economic development now that enlargement has taken place.

The first moves to create the ERDF were made by the Commission, which produced the first legislative proposal for a Community regional policy in 1969. While the Commission's proposal originally found little support from most member states, other key decisions taken at that time soon helped produce a new coalition favourable to the creation of an ERDF (George 1996: 231–2). At the 1969 summit in The Hague, member state leaders decided to pursue EMU and to open accession negotiations with the UK, Ireland, Denmark, and Norway. The entry of the UK and Ireland in particular – both of which had regional problems more serious than those of most member states (with the notable exception of Italy) – increased the number of potential beneficiaries of a regional fund. Furthermore, their insistence that an ERDF was a necessary condition for their participation in EMU went a long way towards winning over the previously reluctant **net contributors** to such a fund, especially what was then West Germany (George 1996: 233). The fact that the final decision to set up the fund was eventually made at the 1972 and 1974 Paris summits rather than on the basis of the Commission's proposal indicated that the regional policy ball was firmly in the member governments' court. So too was the merely token figure of around 5 per cent of the Community budget they allocated to the fund. There was no real likelihood that such a small figure would significantly reduce regional disparities in the Community.

The Single European Act laid the basis for a more substantial EU regional policy. A new 'Social and economic cohesion' title (Title XVII, Articles 158–62, formerly Title XIV, Articles 130a–e) was inserted into the Treaty of Rome entrenching a commitment to reduce regional economic disparities and the 'backwardness' of the Community's 'least favoured regions'. Three financial instruments – the ERDF, the European Social Fund (ESF), and the 'Guidance' section of the European Agricultural Guidance and Guarantee fund, collectively denominated the 'Structural Funds' – were to be the principal mechanism for achieving these objectives (see Box 18.3). Another crucial change following from the SEA was the first of a series of massive increases in the money allocated to structural funding in the Community budget. In 1988, member states sanctioned the Delors I financial perspective and doubled Structural Fund commitments for the period 1989–93. Then, in the 1992 Delors II package they doubled it again for the 1993–9 period. These represented increases from around 5 per cent of the Community budget in 1975 to just under 40 per cent by 1999 (see Figure 18.1).

KEY CONCEPTS AND TERMS 18.3

EU funds for regional development

The Structural Funds

European Regional Development Fund (ERDF): finances infrastructure, job-creating investments, local development projects, and aid for small firms.

European Social Fund (ESF): promotes the return of the unemployed and disadvantaged groups to the workforce, mainly by financing training and systems of recruitment aid.

'Guidance' section of the European Agricultural Guidance and Guarantee Fund: finances rural development measures and aid for farmers, mainly in regions lagging in development. The 'Guarantee' section of this Fund also supports rural development under the Common Agricultural Policy in all other areas of the EU.

Financial Instrument for Fisheries Guidance: helps adapt and modernize the fishing industry.

The Cohesion Fund

Set up in 1993, this fund provides assistance to the poorest EU member states – with a GNP per capita of below 90 per cent of the EU average – to finance major projects in the field of environment and transport.

More changes were just around the corner. At Maastricht, member states also established a new, generously resourced financial instrument known as the Cohesion Fund. The Cohesion Fund was set up to assist those states – *not* regions within them – expected to find meeting the convergence criteria for EMU difficult. Nevertheless, it could be considered regional policy in the sense that it sought to deal with economic disparities between richer and poorer areas of the EU. The Cohesion Fund would provide financial contributions to projects in the field of environment and transport infrastructure networks for those states with a per capita GDP of less than 90 per cent of the EU average. Spain, Portugal, Greece, and Ireland have been the principal recipients of this funding, but since May 2004 recipients are Greece, Portugal, Spain, Cyprus, the Czech Republic, Estonia, Hungary, Latvia, Lithuania, Malta, Poland, Slovakia, and Slovenia. The Cohesion Fund was allocated €25.5 billion for 2000–6 (in 1999 prices).

Policy changes since the SEA were an integral part of the relaunch of the Community. They were intimately linked to the desire to complete the common market and later to support EMU and to combat some of the likely problems these might bring. But, as in the previous stage, enlargement and policy deepening were also triggers for change. In the 1980s, Community membership expanded to include Greece (1981) and Portugal and Spain (1986). These states had far lower GDP per capita levels than all other member states (except Ireland) at the time of joining and included regions with extremely low levels of GDP per capita. As in the previous enlargement which brought in the UK and Ireland, this increased the coalition of states pushing for a more generous regional policy fund. And again, as in the EMU negotiations of the 1970s, this coalition of potential net recipients made regional funding a condition of their participation and consent to this second attempt at EMU (George 1996: 237). In other words, EU regional policy funds served as a 'side payment', a form of 'compensation' effectively used by richer EU member states to 'buy' the consent of poorer ones to facilitate bargains over other non-regional policy related issues (Allen 2000: 245). After a decade of policy expansion, however, the challenge of enlargement meant member states would have to rethink regional policy.

The influx of applications from Central and Eastern European (CEE) states to join the EU meant that enlargement would once again bring a case for regional policy reforms. The CEE states emerged from the communist era with a series of structural problems and were, collectively, a great deal worse off economically than existing member states. Together, the 10 CEE states who applied in the 1990s had an average GDP per capita of around one-third that of existing member states (Baun 1999: 271) (see also Box 18.2). These differences presented very important implications for many EU policies and especially fundamental budget implications for Community structural and agricultural policies (see Chapters 17 and 21). Virtually all the CEE applicant states would be eligible for the highest structural funding contributions and under existing rules many would qualify for similarly high Common Agricultural Policy (CAP) subsidies (Armstrong and Taylor 2000: 315). Given that, together, structural and agricultural spending consume most of the EU budget, significant budgetary increases would be needed to meet such demands. At the same time, enlargement was likely to bring further challenges for existing EU regions. Research published by the Commission suggested that the CEE enlargement would be more beneficial for regions in the UK, France, and especially those in Germany than for already poorer peripheral regions and Southern Europe (European Commission 1996). Member states had good reasons to support the structural adjustment of future member states, but the economic disparities and new problems facing regions in existing member states meant a new balance had to be struck between the demands of enlargement and existing regional problems.

In July 1997, the Commission presented its comprehensive *Agenda 2000* document which included, among other things, proposals to reform EU regional policy to make way for enlargement

(European Commission 1997). In the document, the Commission argued that economic and social cohesion should remain one of the basic pillars of EU action. However, taking note of the critical mood in many member states towards the idea of budgetary expansion, the Commission recommended that structural and cohesion spending should be stabilized. Negotiations leading up to the deal eventually made at the Berlin European Council in March 1999 brought out the old cleavages between net contributors – now including Germany, the Netherlands, Austria, and Sweden – and the net recipients, enthusiastically led by Spain (Laffan and Shackleton 2000: 231–6). In the end a deal was struck and Structural Funds were allocated €258 billion (at 1999 prices) between 2000 and 2006: €213 billion for needy regions within existing member states; €45 billion for CEE applicant states before and after accession; and €18 billion for the Cohesion Fund. The growth and decline of structural funding between 1988 and 2006 is shown in Figure 18.1.

EU pre-accession instruments finance similar objectives to those covered by the Structural and Cohesion Funds (Bailey and de Propris 2004: 83). In addition, these instruments seek to prepare applicant states for working within the strictures of EU regional and cohesion policy regimes. The PHARE programme (Poland and Hungary Aid for Economic Restructuring), which has existed since 1989, was modified in the late 1990s to focus on helping the CEE states to better meet the requirements of accession. This included preparing applicants for receipt of the Structural Funds and financing projects in areas covered by the Structural Funds. Two new programmes were also introduced. The Pre-accession Structural Instrument (ISPA) was established to fund transport and environmental schemes in applicant states along the same lines as the Cohesion Fund. The Special Accession Programme for Agriculture and Rural Development (SAPARD) was set up to help applicants prepare for the CAP, including the agricultural and rural development measures provided under the 'Guidance' section of the European Agricultural Guidance and Guarantee Fund.

At the end of 2005, EU regional policy was partway through further reforms. The centrepiece of this reform process was the negotiation of a new 'Financial Perspective' for 2007–13, which determined, among other things, how much the EU allocated to structural and cohesion spending during this period. In February 2004 the Commission published its proposals for budget reform and, after many months of difficult negotiations, agreement was finally reached following a European Council

Figure 18.1 Annual resources of the Structural Funds and the Cohesion Fund, 1988 – 2006*

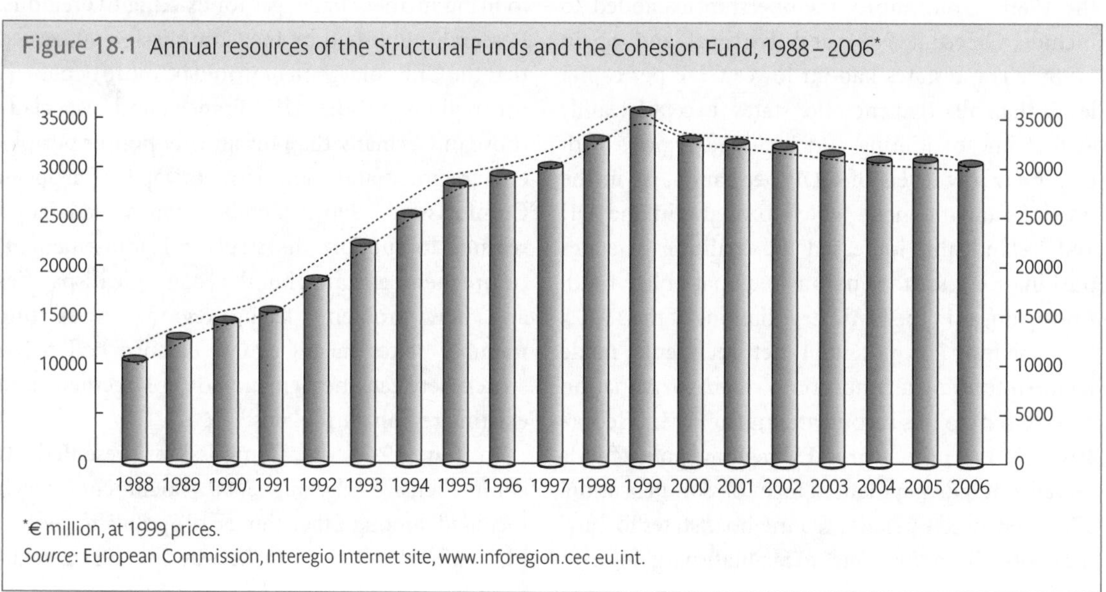

*€ million, at 1999 prices.
Source: European Commission, Interegio Internet site, www.inforegion.cec.eu.int.

Summit in December 2005. Member states agreed to allocate €303.6 billion (in 2004 prices) for structural and cohesion fund spending for 2007–13. This represents 35.7 per cent of overall EU spending for the budget period. The next step was negotiation of new regulations, based on Commission proposals put forward in July 2004.

Both the budget and legislative negotiations are complex but a number of key issues dominate the reform process (Bachtler and Wishlade 2005; Barry and Begg 2003: 788–92; Allen 2005: 235–8):

- How to provide for the needs of new, poorer member states while also satisfying the needs of member states and regions that currently receive support.
- How to reconcile the interests of net contributors to the EU budget and those of net recipients.
- Should all member states receive some EU funding (as at present), or should all structural and cohesion funding go to those states and regions lagging behind? Closely associated with this question is the issue of whether regional policy should be repatriated, or undertaken solely in the domestic arena, for the richer member states.
- How to accommodate the Lisbon Agenda in EU regional policy. The Lisbon Agenda, agreed by EU heads of state and government at a summit in Lisbon in March 2000, sought to make the EU 'the most competitive and dynamic knowledge-based economy in the world, capable of sustainable growth with more and better jobs and greater social cohesion' within a decade.
- How to ensure that new member states have the administrative capacity and ability to absorb structural and cohesion funding allocated to them.
- How to make structural and cohesion policy simpler, more effective, and more decentralized.

KEY POINTS

- EU regional policy developments may be divided into three main phases: an early phase inaugurated by the creation of the ERDF; an expansive phase corresponding to the SEA and Maastricht Treaty reforms; and a final phase characterized by the pressures of enlargement.
- Further reforms are currently under way to balance the needs of new and existing regions, adapt EU regional policy to Lisbon goals, and improve its effectiveness. The 2007–13 'Financial Perspective' allocates some 35.7 per cent of the EU budget for structural and cohesion funding.
- Part of the explanation for EU regional policy lies in the functional imperatives captured by the metaphor of functional spillover. Justifications include the negative effects of market integration on peripheral regions and states and the fact that European integration restricts the range of policy instruments that member states can use to combat regional differences.
- There are also political explanations for regional policy expansion. Progressive enlargements helped build a coalition of potential net contributors, and policy deepening provided an opportunity for them to link demands for funds to issues like EMU.

The implementation of EU regional policy

This section is about how the Community manages its regional policy and more specifically the operation of the Structural Funds. Post-SEA reforms established the basic systems and ground rules for the implementation of EU regional policy that continue to be used today. So far, reforms have taken place in three rounds. The first were set out in a series of 1988 regulations; the second in regulations in force in 1993; and the third, post-*Agenda 2000* reforms, were in force in 1999 regulations. In 2004 the Commission inaugurated a fourth round by publishing a new set of proposals. As of early 2006, these were still to be agreed by the Council and Parliament. They will need to be agreed before the end of 2006, when current Structural Fund programmes and instruments are completed. (For updates see http://www.europa.eu.int/comm/regional_policy/index_en.htm.)

In 1988, Structural Fund spending was directed towards achieving six basic objectives. Three of these were limited in their geographical scope to disadvantaged regions. These were:

- Objective 1: development and structural adjustment of least-developed regions.
- Objective 2: conversion of regions facing industrial decline.
- Objective 5b: development of rural areas.

The remaining priorities were focused on the whole EU:

- Objective 3: combating long-term unemployment.
- Objective 4: combating youth unemployment.
- Objective 5a: adjustment of agricultural structures.

The accession of Sweden and Finland in 1995 brought with it a new objective:

- Objective 6: help low-population-density regions.

The *Agenda 2000* round of Structural Fund reforms cut the number of objectives from seven to three: a new Objective 1 remained unchanged in its focus on the regions whose development is lagging behind, although it did come to incorporate the aims of the old Objective 6. A new Objective 2 brought together the old Objective 2 (industrial decline) and 5b (rural development) and became broader in scope, aiming 'to support the economic and social conversion of areas facing structural difficulties'. A new Objective 3, a horizontal objective focusing on all the EU and not just disadvantaged regions, brought together the social aims of the old Objectives 3 and 4 to focus on 'supporting the adaptation and modernization of policies and systems of education, training and employment'.

For 2007–13, it looks likely that a new system will be adopted based, again, on three objectives – a 'convergence objective' mainly for less-developed regions, a 'regional competitiveness and employment objective' for the rest of the EU, and a new 'territorial cooperation objective'. Aspects of the reform agreed by the member states in December 2005, based on Commission proposals, are summarized in Table 18.1.

Five main principles currently govern the Structural Funds and these are likely to be maintained (with some modification) in the future. The five principles are: coordination, concentration, programming, additionality, and partnership.

Coordination involves the integration of all the three structural funds (ERDF, ESF, and the Guidance section of the EAGGF, see Box 18.3) into a single framework centred on the achievement of the sets of core objectives outlined above (Objective 1, Objective 2, and so on). The Commission proposed maintaining something similar for the three new objectives identified in Table 18.1. The convergence objective will be funded by ERDF, ESF, and the Cohesion Fund. The regional competitiveness and employment objective will be funded by ERDF and ESF, and the territorial cohesion objective will be funded by the ERDF.

The *concentration* principle requires that Structural Fund spending goes to regions in greatest need. So far, this has meant that Objective 1 regions, defined as the EU's least developed areas, have received about two-thirds of all Structural Funds. For the 2007–13 budget period, member states agreed to continue prioritizing development of the poorest regions and member states. As Table 18.1 shows, a total of 81 per cent of structural and cohesion funding will be allocated to the new convergence objective. The concentration of Structural Funds on the least developed regions (previously 'Objective 1' regions) has prompted many regional bodies, including the Basque government (see Box 18.1) and the

Table 18.1 New regional and cohesion policy objectives and financial perspective, 2007–13*

Aim	Objective	Eligibility	Funding for 2007–13 (€m, 2004 prices)
Convergence	Speed up convergence of less developed regions and member states	Regions whose GDP per capita (measured in purchasing power parities) is less than 75 per cent of the EU25 average. Cohesion Fund will be available for member states whose per capita gross national income (measured in purchasing power parities) is less than 90 per cent of the EU25 average and which have a programme for meeting EMU economic convergence criteria.	251, 330 (81.7 per cent), of which 61,518 (25 per cent) will be for the Cohesion Fund
Regional competitiveness and employment objective	Strengthen regions' 'competitiveness', 'attractiveness', and 'employment'	Entire territory of the EU except those obtaining structural funding under convergence objective (above)	48,789 (21.3 per cent)
Territorial cooperation	Strengthening territorial cooperation at cross-border, transnational, and interregional levels.	Internal, external, and maritime border regions for cross-border cooperation financing.	7,500 (2.4 per cent)
	Establishing cooperation networks. Furthering exchange of experience at the appropriate territorial level	Entire territory of the EU for interregional cooperation, cooperation networks, and exchange of experience.	

*Approved by member states, December 2005.

Source: European Commission, 'Financial Perspective 2007–13', Brussels, 19 December 2005, 15915/05.

Welsh National Assembly (see Box 18.4), to clamour for the ignominious title of a 'backward' or 'underdeveloped' EU region.

Programming requires that Structural Fund expenditure be distributed in accordance with preplanned, multiannual programmes, bringing together a range of projects designed to improve economic conditions in individual regions, rather than be distributed on an ad hoc, project-by-project basis. From 1988 a small amount of the Structural Fund budget was set aside for Community Initiatives. Compared to other Structural Fund spending, which involves a great deal of input from member states, Community Initiatives are predominantly governed by the Commission. For 2000–6 there are four Community Initiatives, consuming 5.35 per cent of the Structural Funds and directed towards cross-border cooperation, sustainable development in cities, rural development, and labour market inequality. While Commission proposals for future reforms retain multiannual programmes, they do away with Community Initiatives.

The *additionality* principle requires that Structural Fund spending must not substitute for member state regional policy expenditure but should complement, or be 'additional' to, that expenditure. Implementing additionality has been one of the hardest principles to put into operation. From the outset, as Joanne Scott observed, 'member state governments have tended to regard ERDF commitments as a welcome but unexpected windfall' which could be used as a 'reimbursement of their own regional aid expenditure' (1995: 17). The Commission, has, nevertheless, doggedly pursued additionality and has even used its powers to withhold Structural Fund payments when there was a strong case that additionality had been violated (John 1996; Allen 2005).

The 1988 Structural Fund Regulations entrenched the *partnership* principle into the Community's regional policy regime. Partnership required that in addition to member state central governments, the regions and the Commission should have a role in the preparation of programmes and in the assessment and monitoring of those programmes as they were put into practice. When it was introduced, partnership excited a great deal of academic interest. Partnership brought together actors from multiple levels of government into new transnational policy networks and in so doing seemed to empower both regional and EU-level institutions (Marks 1992). Since the 1988 reforms, however, there have been important changes significantly diluting the potential of partnership as a source for regional influence. In the 1993 round of Structural Fund reforms, 'partnership' was extended to include 'economic and social partners', and after 1999 it was extended again to include 'any other relevant competent body', such as environmental and social equality groups. Moreover, at the planning or programming stages, procedures were soon 'streamlined' and 'simplified', changes that effectively meant the exclusion of partners and central government domination of the process (Allen 2000: 254).

KEY POINTS

- EU Structural and Cohesion Funds concentrate on addressing the problems of the least developed EU regions and states. Structural Funds have also been used to tackle industrial decline, rural development, and social issues like unemployment.
- EU regional policy is governed by principles that seek to ensure coordination of spending across different funds; concentration of spending on the poorest regions and states; multiannual programmes rather than ad hoc interventions; that EU funding is additional to state spending; and that regional and other social partners have some role in decision-making.

CASE STUDY 18.4

West Wales and the Valleys 'Objective 1' funding

After an intensive campaign by Welsh authorities, West Wales and the Valleys became an Objective 1 region for 2000–6. Acquiring this status meant this part of Wales officially became one of the poorest and least-developed areas of the EU. But this ignominious title came with a healthy reward of €1,853.4 million for 2000–6. The money will go towards projects designed, among other things, to increase the competitiveness of the region by improving economic conditions for small and medium-sized enterprises and the use of new technologies. Additionally, funding will be spent on combating social exclusion and helping the unemployed by increasing their access to business opportunities, education, and training. Further support is targeted to help rural development, the sustainable use of natural resources, and infrastructure development, including transportation.

Conclusion: implications of regional Europe

This chapter explored two aspects of regional Europe. It described the Europeanization of regional activism and the presence of regions in EU policy-making. It also examined the origins, development, and operation of the EU's regional policy. What are the implications of these developments for understanding the nature of the EU?

The emergence of a regional dimension in EU politics challenged some old ideas about the EU and gave birth to some new ones. As we have seen in earlier sections of this chapter, regional policy provided a new case for examining the dynamics of European integration. It provided an opportunity to consider questions about why the decision was made to expand regional policy. Was it evidence of 'spillover'? Was it the result of intergovernmental bargaining? Furthermore, regional policy development provided an opportunity to consider the role of ideas in EU policy-making. According to Kohler-Koch (1996), for instance, innovations such as the 'partnership' principle can be traced to new regional policy ideas favouring endogenous economic development of regions, decentralized decision-making, and involvement of public and private actors from multiple levels of government. In addition to regional policy provides a fruitful area for examining the impact of enlargement not just on the EU itself, but on applicant states too. A good example of this is the research of Hughes, Sasse, and Gordon (2004) on implementation of the regional policy *acquis* in applicant member states, which provides important insights on the limits of the EU's ability to drive policy change and institution building in applicant states.

Additionally, the presence of a new set of policy participants – regional actors – in EU decisions invited academics to move beyond 'classical' integration theorists' concerns with challenges to the state from above, to consider whether there was a simultaneous challenge 'from below' as well. Concepts like 'Europe of the Regions' and 'multi-level governance' launched a lively debate about how regional activism and EU regional policy reforms – particularly the partnership principle in EU regional policy – might transform the EU polity (see, for instance, Marks, Hooghe, and Blank 1996; Hooghe 2001; Hooghe and Marks 2001; John 1996; Loughlin 1996). These ideas have been conceptualized in a variety of different ways, but all hint at the need to conceive of the EU not as a two-level game, but as a multi-level one involving EU, state, *and* regional actors. In this work, attention has been dedicated to the possibility that the Commission has been an agent promoting the role of regions in order to increase its influence (Marks 1992; Tömmel 1998). Critiques of this approach caution against assuming the increased presence of regions equates with increased power of regions (Le Galès and Lequèsne 1998). Others critics point to central government 'gatekeeping' powers (J. Anderson 1990; Bache 1999a and 1999b), which allow them to block unwelcome changes, and the ability of central governments to 'establish the institutional context in which both the Commission and regional governments act' (Pollack 1995). If nothing else, the Europeanization of regionalism and the recent evolution of EU regional policy did force many to rethink, or at least defend once more, some long-standing ideas about European integration and the nature of the EU.

QUESTIONS

1. How does the EU affect regional governance?
2. Should EU regions be satisfied with reforms enhancing their participation in EU decision-making? Or are further changes needed?
3. Does European integration present more costs than opportunities for EU regions?
4. Does the EU need a regional policy?
5. Why have enlargement and Economic and Monetary Union been such important triggers in EU regional policy development?
6. Does the neo-functionalist 'spillover' thesis of European integration explain the development of EU regional policy?
7. What is the significance of EU regional policy's 'partnership' principle?
8. Is governance in Europe becoming multi-level governance?

GUIDE TO FURTHER READING

■ Bache, I. *The Politics of European Union Regional Policy: Multi-level Governance or Flexible Gatekeeping* (Sheffield: Sheffield Academic Press, 1999). This book provides a theoretically informed account of EU regional policy development.

■ Hooghe, L. (ed.) *Cohesion Policy and European Integration: Building Multi-level Governance* (Oxford: Oxford University Press, 1996). Through a series of country-by-country case studies, this book applies the ideas of multi-level governance in the area of EU regional policy.

■ Hooghe, L., and Marks, G. *Multilevel Governance and European Integration* (Lanham, MD: Rowman & Littlefield, 2001). This books presents an updated reflection on multi-level governance.

■ Keating, M. *New Regionalism in Western Europe* (Cheltenham: Edward Elgar, 2000). This book provides an insightful analysis of European regionalism by one of the most authoritative authors on this topic.

■ Keating, M. 'Regions and the Convention on the Future of Europe', *South European Society and Politics*, 9(1), 2004, pp. 192–207 and Jeffrey, C. 'Regions and the EU: Letting Them In and Leaving Them Alone', *Federal Trust Online Paper*, XX04, 2004. These two articles provide analysis of regional dimensions of EU constitutional debates.

■ Scott, J. *Development Dilemmas in the European Community* (Buckingham: Open University Press, 1995). This book provides another good analysis of the origins and development of EU regional policy.

IMPORTANT WEBSITES

● http://www.cor.eu/int/ The Committee of the Regions (CoR) is a consultative organ of the EU composed of 317 representatives of regional and local bodies. The website contains up-to-date information on CoR activities and research resources like CoR opinions and declarations.

● http://www.inforegio.cec.eu.int/ This is a European Commission website on EU regional policy. It contains detailed but accessible information on the operation of EU regional policy, country-by-country profiles of fund spending and programmes, as well as access to in-depth analysis, reports, and relevant official documents.

- http://www.are-regions-europe.org/ The Assembly of European Regions (AER) is a political organization bringing together around 300 European regions. The website contains information on AER activities, a comprehensive database on constitutional, political, and socio-economic characteristics of its members, and an extensive list of other region-orientated weblinks.

- http://www.calre.be.

- http://www.regleg.org The Conference of the European Legislative Parliaments and Conference of European Regions with Legislative Power are two relatively new interregional associations. These weblinks provide information about the structure and organization of the Conferences and access to documents outlining common positions on issues dealt with in recent EU constitutional debates.

Visit the Online Resource Centre that accompanies this book for lots of interesting additional material. http://www.oxfordtextbooks.co.uk/orc/cini2e/

19 Justice and Home Affairs

EMEK M. UÇARER

Chapter Contents

- Introduction
- Preludes to cooperation
- The Schengen experiment
- Maastricht and the 'third pillar'
- Fixing the third pillar: the Amsterdam and Nice Treaties
- Policy output: baby steps to bold agendas
- Extending JHA cooperation outwards
- Conclusion

Reader's Guide

This chapter looks at one of the most recent European policies, Justice and Home Affairs (JHA). JHA comprises policy areas such as immigration and asylum, and police and judicial cooperation, some elements of which are found in the EU's third pillar (see Figures 3.1 and 3.2 on the EU's pillars). The chapter focuses first on the early years of cooperation in this policy area, and includes an introduction to the Schengen Agreement. It then reviews the procedural steps taken first by the Maastricht Treaty (1993) and then at Amsterdam (1999). The second half of the chapter concentrates on policy output, again looking at steps taken at Maastricht and Amsterdam, but also in the landmark Tampere European Council meeting and the Hague Programme. It argues that although steps have already been taken to Europeanize JHA policy, this field continues to be characterized by intergovernmentalism. Moreover, given the inherent tensions in the policy, numerous challenges remain to be resolved.

Introduction

Justice and Home Affairs (JHA) cooperation has undergone a remarkable ascent – from humble beginnings to a fully fledged and vibrant EU policy. JHA is one of the newest additions to the EU mandate and seeks to engage the EU in the fields of immigration and asylum policy, and police judicial cooperation. Because of the sensitive nature of the issues involved, cooperation has been slow and difficult. However it has resulted in a body of policies that apply across the EU's internal and external borders, and which have locked previously inward-looking national authorities into a multilateral process. This has involved significant political compromise, which has led to the introduction of a complicated mix of communitarized and intergovernmental institutional procedures peculiar to this field. The EU is now well on its way to developing a complex immigration and asylum regime, and is also making some progress on police and judicial cooperation. Particularly after the conclusion of the Amsterdam Treaty, the EU's capacity to reach collective and binding decisions in the JHA field has improved considerably. This has created momentum towards further cooperation and has increased concerns about the creation of a Fortress Europe into which access is increasingly restricted.

Preludes to cooperation

If, in the late 1960s, government ministers responsible for home affairs and justice had been told that they would soon need to consult with fellow European ministers while formulating policies regarding immigration, asylum, judicial, and police matters, they would no doubt have found this a very unlikely, and undesirable, prospect. Yet, during the last two decades of the twentieth century, issues falling within the mandate of interior and justice ministries increasingly became of collective EU concern, provoking efforts to deal with them at the European, rather than exclusively at the national level. Beginning in the mid-1970s and gathering momentum in the 1980s, immigration, asylum, police, and judicial cooperation increasingly appeared on the collective political agenda. This led to the creation of new, overlapping fora within which these issues could be discussed (see Box 19.1).

There were two broad sets of catalysts that drove this development. The first was the consequences of increased cross-border movements into and across Europe. After the Second World War, Western

BOX 19.1

Catalysts for early cooperation in justice and home affairs matters

Linked to immigration

- Increase in cross-border movements between West European countries.
- Increase in labour and family unification migration into West European countries.
- Increase in applications for asylum.
- Concerns about cross-border organized crime.

Linked to the European integration project

- Undesirable impacts of delays at borders on economic activities.
- Desire to complete the Single Market by gradually removing controls at the Union's internal borders.
- Recognition of the necessity to develop common measures to apply to external borders before doing away with controls at the internal borders.

Europe became an area of immigration. Cross-border movements increased, straining border patrols, and causing delays at points of entry. With the rise in cross-border movements came growing concerns about transnational crime, which could proliferate because of weak border controls and a lack of effective communication among European national law enforcement agencies. The second catalyst was the revitalization of the European integration agenda after the signing of the Single European Act (SEA) in 1986 (see Chapter 16). The removal of internal EU border controls had been written into the 1957 Treaty of Rome, even though this had not been fully realized by the early 1980s. With this goal back on the agenda in the 1980s, attention turned to the need to create external Community borders and to develop common and coherent rules on access. Early efforts targeted three groups: the citizens of the EC/EU (whose freedom of movement within the Community was to be secured); long-term EU residents of third countries (non-EU citizens who had relocated to the EU and who held residence and work permits); and third-country nationals (TCNs), including labour migrants and refugees seeking to enter the collective territory of the EC/EU (see Box 19.1). Early efforts to tackle this field were launched by the Council of Europe (CoE), a regional international organization distinct from the European Community (EC), whose membership comprised both East and West European countries. Judicial matters were raised often at CoE meetings, leading to binding treaties that would subsequently be incorporated into EU law. The CoE regularly brought together officials from its member states, which got them used to cooperating. But, while the CoE's work was path-breaking, the drawbacks of its processes were also clear. Because of the need to reconcile a wide variety of divergent interests and opinions, policy-making was slow and the output modest, reflecting little more than the lowest common denominator.

With the shortcomings of the CoE in mind, member states set up the 'Trevi Group' in 1975 as an informal assembly to deal with cross-border terrorism through closer cooperation among EC law enforcement authorities. Trevi was really a loose network rather than an institution, and the meetings concluded in non-binding consultations on organized international crime, including drug and arms trafficking. Subsequently, several other groups were established, including the Judicial Cooperation Group, the Customs Mutual Assistance Group, and the Ad Hoc Groups on Immigration and Organized Crime. These groups spanned the four policy clusters that were gradually becoming Europeanized: immigration policy, asylum policy, police cooperation, and judicial cooperation.

KEY POINTS

- Cooperation in the field of Justice and Home Affairs (JHA) was not foreseen in the Treaty of Rome.
- The Council of Europe (not an EC institution) was the main forum for the discussion of JHA issues, but it worked slowly and its output was meagre.
- The Trevi Group was set up in 1975 as a loose network within which terrorism might be discussed at European level. It led to the setting up of similar groups in related areas.

The Schengen experiment

Aside from these developments, perhaps the most ambitious project of these early years was what became known as Schengen. In 1985, a number of EC member states decided to do away with border controls. This was formalized in the 1985 Schengen Agreement and later the 1990 Schengen Implementation Convention. Belgium, the Netherlands, Luxembourg, Germany, France, and

Italy thus created a new system which would connect their police forces and customs authorities. They also created the Schengen Information System (SIS), an innovative, shared database that stored important information (such as criminal records and asylum applications), and which was accessible by national law enforcement authorities.

Schengen's primary objective was to develop policies that would apply to the Community's external borders and which would eventually remove the EC's internal borders. This was a very ambitious goal, and some EC member states, namely the United Kingdom, Ireland, and Denmark, remained extremely sceptical. Given this opposition, Schengen was a compromise. However, despite the fact that only some member states were involved, it became a model for the EC (and later the Union) as a whole.

Within the Schengen framework, significant progress was made in each of the four emergent areas of cooperation. With respect to asylum, Schengen instituted a new system for determining the state responsible for reviewing asylum claims in individual cases. Signatory states agreed to assign responsibility to one state in order to stop multiple asylum applications. Member states thus hoped to reduce the administrative costs of processing duplicate asylum claims. Schengen also provided the groundwork for an EU-wide visa policy by negotiating a common list of countries whose citizens would need an entry visa. Member states also agreed to issue uniform Schengen visas for the Schengen territory. There was a more modest start in judicial cooperation which involved work on easing extradition procedures between member states. Finally, Schengen involved cooperation on law enforcement matters, particularly those involving drug trafficking. However, since most of this work fell outside the framework of the EC decision-making structure, it was conducted away from the scrutiny of the general public and their elected representatives (see Box 19.2).

KEY POINTS

- The 1985 Schengen Agreement was a commitment by a subset of EC member states to remove controls at their internal borders.
- Steps were taken by the Schengen members to agree common rules on their external borders with regard to visa policy, for example.
- For those countries involved, Schengen allowed national civil servants in these fields to become accustomed to European-level cooperation.

KEY CONCEPTS AND TERMS 19.2

What is Schengen?

Named after the small Luxembourg border town where a subset of the member states of the EU resolved to lift border controls, the Schengen system is considered a path-breaking initiative to provide for ease of travel between its member states. In 1985, France, Germany, and the Benelux states signed the first Schengen Agreement and were later joined by nine other EU members, bringing the total number of participating states to 15. The Schengen accords sought to remove controls on persons, including TCNs, at their internal borders while allowing member states to reintroduce them only under limited circumstances. Member states agreed to develop common entry policies for their collective territory, issue common entry visas to entrants, designate a responsible state for reviewing asylum claims, and jointly combat transnational crime. They also created a novel database – the Schengen Information System, or SIS – to exchange information between the member states on certain categories of individuals and property. As the original SIS was designed to interlink at most 18 countries, a new version, SIS II, is being developed, made necessary by the May 2004 enlargement of the EU. Current Schengen countries are Austria, Belgium, Denmark, Finland, France, Germany, Iceland, Italy, Greece, Luxembourg, the Netherlands, Norway, Portugal, Spain, Sweden, and Switzerland. Three of these countries (Norway, Iceland, and Switzerland) are not members of the European Union. Two European Union countries (the United Kingdom and Ireland) are not part of the Schengen system, though they have recently chosen to opt in on an issue-by-issue basis. The 10 member states that joined the EU in 2004 have signed the agreement and are expected to implement Schengen in 2007.

Maastricht and the 'third pillar'

If the 1970s and early 1980s saw increasing, if sporadic, consultation between some West European states on immigration, asylum, judicial, and police matters, the early 1990s represented an intensification of these efforts and a shift in the locus of decision-making towards the European institutions. This involved the consolidation of existing groupings as well as the creation of a new institutional framework within which JHA matters could be discussed. This proved to be a challenge.

With the coming into force of the Treaty on European Union in 1993, JHA was brought under the auspices of the EU, forming the 'third pillar' of the Union. The Maastricht Treaty identified nine areas of 'common interest': asylum policy rules applicable to the crossing of the Union's external borders; immigration policy and the handling of TCNs; combating drug addiction and drug trafficking; tackling international fraud; judicial cooperation in civil and criminal matters; customs cooperation; police cooperation to combat and prevent terrorism; and police cooperation in tackling international organized crime.

The Treaty also created a new institutional home for the plethora of groups that had been set up in earlier decades, and created a decision-making framework. However, this new JHA pillar was the product of a rather awkward interstate compromise. In the run-up to Maastricht, while a majority of member states supported bringing JHA matters into the Union, they remained divided over how this should be done. Some argued that JHA should be handled within the EC (in what became the 'first' or EC pillar), as a supranational policy. Others were uncomfortable with handing control over to the European institutions in such a sensitive field and preferred to keep JHA as a largely intergovernmental dialogue.

Title VI of the Maastricht Treaty reflected the institutional consequences of this political compromise. In creating a third pillar of the European Union, the Treaty established an intergovernmental negotiating sphere which marginalized the Community institutions, particularly the European Commission, within the JHA decision-making process. This third pillar set-up diverged significantly from standard decision-making in the EC (see Chapter 1). For one thing, JHA cooperation was placed within a five-tier negotiation framework, compared to the three-tier structure of the first pillar (or the EC pillar). Accordingly, the key decision-taking body became the JHA Council. The European Commission's usual function as the initiator of European legislation (see Chapter 9) was diminished by its shared right of initiative in JHA, so that it was only one of 16 possible points of origin for JHA policies (the other 15 being the member states themselves) (Uçarer 2001a). The role of the European Parliament (EP) did not extend beyond consultation, a situation that led to accusations that JHA exacerbated the Union's democratic deficit (see Chapter 22). Moreover, the European Court of Justice (ECJ), the body that might have enhanced the accountability and judicial oversight of policy, was excluded from JHA matters.

Although bringing JHA into the EU was an important step, critics of the 'third pillar' abounded. Two sets of interrelated criticisms were advanced. Critics lamented the lack of policy progress in the post-Maastricht period. Indeed, what little was accomplished after 1993 seemed to relate to policies that had already been in progress before Maastricht. While some of this apparent inertia was due to a lingering reluctance by member states to yield to the Union on JHA matters, it was also regarded as a consequence of a much larger set of problems that were institutional in nature.

The problem was that the post-Maastricht institutional arrangements were ill equipped to handle the projected or indeed the existing workload falling under JHA. The decision-making framework was cumbersome, with the often non-binding policy instruments necessitating long drawn-out (and potentially inconclusive) negotiations. All decisions in the third pillar had to be reached unanimously and often this led to deadlock. And when unanimity was reached, the result was often a lowest common denominator compromise that pleased few. Negotiations continued to be secretive and the EP remained marginalized. This was particularly problematic at a time when the Union was trying hard to improve its image vis-à-vis its citizens.

KEY POINTS

- The Maastricht Treaty (Treaty on European Union or TEU) which came into effect in 1993 created a 'third pillar' for Justice and Home Affairs.
- The institutional framework put in place was intergovernmental and cumbersome and was subject to much criticism.

Fixing the third pillar: the Amsterdam and Nice Treaties

In the run-up to the 1999 Amsterdam Treaty, proposals for reforming JHA included enhanced roles for the Commission, Parliament, and Court; the elimination of the unanimity rule; and the incorporation of the Schengen system into the EU. As with Maastricht, there was a fierce political debate over these issues.

The challenge facing those drafting the Amsterdam Treaty was to make the Union 'more relevant to its citizens and more responsive to their concerns', by creating 'an area of freedom, security and justice (AFSJ)' (European Council 1996). Within such an area, barriers to the free movement of people across borders would be minimized without jeopardizing the safety, security, and human rights of EU citizens. The compromise reached at Amsterdam led to three important changes. First, parts of the Maastricht third pillar were transferred to the first (or EC) pillar, or 'communitarized'. Secondly, the institutional framework for issues that remained within the third pillar was streamlined. And thirdly, the Schengen framework was incorporated into the Union's acquis.

New first pillar issues under Amsterdam

The insertion of Title IV into the Treaty was the most significant development at Amsterdam with respect to JHA matters. This brought a number of third pillar issues into the first or EC pillar for the first time. These provisions, captured in Articles 61–4 of the Amsterdam Treaty, called for the Council to adopt policies (within five years of the entry into force of the treaty, by 1 May 2004) which would ensure the free movement of persons within the Union, whilst at the same time putting in place security measures with respect to immigration, asylum, and external border controls. Article 67 specified new decision-making rules. For the first five years after the entry into force of the Amsterdam Treaty, a transition period was foreseen, during which time unanimity was required in the JHA Council following consultations with the EP. The Council would act on a proposal from the Commission or a member state, the latter retaining their shared right of initiative. In other words, the Maastricht decision rules were to remain in place. After five years, however, the Commission would gain an exclusive right of initiative. And, while the Parliament's access to the decision-making procedure would still be limited to consultation in most cases, an automatic shift to the codecision procedure, which would give the EP much more of a say, was foreseen in the area of uniform visa rules and the procedures for issuing visas. The ECJ would receive a mandate for the first time, allowing it to interpret Title IV and to undertake preliminary rulings in policy areas falling within the first pillar, in response to requests by national courts (see Chapter 12). Despite these improvements, however, the new Amsterdam architecture turned out to be a formidable maze created through masterful 'legal engineering' for political ends, opaque for even seasoned experts (European Parliament 1997).

The left-over third pillar: cooperation in criminal matters

The Amsterdam reforms left criminal matters in the third pillar. The amended Title VI included combating crime, terrorism, trafficking in persons and offences against children, illicit drugs and arms trafficking, corruption, and fraud (European Union 1997). The Treaty envisaged closer cooperation between police forces, customs and judicial authorities, and with Europol (see below), seeking an approximation of the criminal justice systems of the member states as necessary. Also envisaged were common positions defining the Union's policy on particular questions, framework decisions, and intergovernmentally negotiated and legally binding conventions.

While the new Title VI essentially retained the intergovernmental framework created at Maastricht, the Commission obtained a shared right of initiative for the first time, an improvement over its pre-Amsterdam position. The Parliament gained the right to be consulted, but that was all. The Treaty constrained the ECJ in a similar fashion in that it recognized the jurisdiction of the Court to issue preliminary rulings (that is, to comment on relevant cases before domestic courts) on the instruments adopted under Title VI, but importantly it made this dependent on the assent of the member states. While the Commission, Parliament, and Court were to continue to struggle to play an active role in the third pillar, the Council retained its dominant decision-making function, and unanimity remained the decision rule used in third pillar legislation. Table 19.1 summarizes the institutional development of JHA from its early origins to its post-Amsterdam state.

Absorbing Schengen

After much debate, Schengen was incorporated into the EU by means of a protocol appended to the Amsterdam Treaty. The Protocol provided for the closer cooperation of the Schengen 13 (that is, the EU15 minus Ireland and the United Kingdom) within the EU framework. With this development, cooperation on JHA matters became even more complicated, involving various overlapping groupings. There were those EU members that agreed to be bound by the Amsterdam changes (EU12): Denmark chose to opt out, and the UK and Ireland would remain outside unless they chose to opt in. Moreover, there were actually 15 signatories to the Schengen agreement (the Schengen 15), of which 13 were EU members and two were not (Iceland and Norway). The two members of the EU that remained outside the Schengen system, the UK and Ireland, decided to take part in some elements of Schengen, including police and judicial cooperation. Non-EU member Switzerland would eventually join and the 10 countries that joined the EU in 2004 were expected to implement Schengen in 2007. In essence, the incorporation of Schengen into the EU *acquis* did not result in the simplification hoped for, but rather maintained, if not augmented, the convoluted system that emerged in the early 1990s. Not surprisingly, some now regard JHA as the ultimate example of a multi-speed or à la carte Europe (see Chapter 24 for a full discussion).

The Treaty of Nice made few substantial changes to the institutional developments highlighted above. Perhaps the biggest change was the extension of a shared right of initiative for the Commission in the otherwise intergovernmental left-over third pillar.

Table 19.1 Justice and home affairs cooperation: from Trevi to the Hague

	Pre-Maastricht JHA	Post-Maastricht Third Pillar Title VI TEU, Article K	Post-Amsterdam First Pillar (*Communitarized* areas of former Third Pillar): Immigration, Asylum,Police and Judicial Cooperation in Civil Matters Title IV TEC, Articles 61 – 9		Post-Amsterdam Third Pillar (Non-*Communitarized* areas of former Third Pillar): Police and Judicial Cooperation in Criminal Matters Title VI TEU, Articles 29 – 42
			1999 – 2004	Post-2004	
European Parliament	No role	Limited role, restricted to consultation	Consultation	Codecision	Consultation
European Court of Justice	No jurisdiction	No jurisdiction	Referral for an obligatory first ruling for national last-instance courts		Preliminary rulings on the validity and interpretation of framework decisions and decisions on the interpretation of conventions established under Title VI and on the validity and interpretation of the measures implementing them
Council	No direct role	Dominant actor	Dominant actor but Commission and Parliament increasingly empowered	Shared power position in decision-making	Dominant actor
Commission	Consultative Occasional observer status at intergovernmental meetings	Shared right of initiative for the Commission and member states except for judicial and police cooperation matters in which there is no right of initiative	Commission has shared right of initiative (member states have encouraged the Commission to assume an exclusive right for asylum issues)	Commission has exclusive right of initiative	Shared right of initiative (previously not possible)
Decision-making mechanisms	Intergovernmental negotiations Non-binding decisions in the form of resolutions Binding decisions in the form of treaties	Unanimity rule on all issues	Council acts unanimously on proposals from Commission and member states *for the first five years* UK,Ireland,and Denmark not bound unless they choose to opt in	Council will act unanimously on proposals from the Commission A move towards QMV (except legal migration) UK and Ireland retain opt-in, Denmark retains opt-out	Council acts unanimously on proposals from Commission and member states

Note: This covers asylum policy, the crossing of the external borders of the Union, immigration policy and the handling of third-country nationals, combating drug addiction and trafficking, tackling international fraud, judicial cooperation in civil and criminal matters, customs cooperation, and police cooperation to combat and prevent terrorism and organized international crime.

Source: Adapted and expanded from Uçarer (2001a).

KEY POINTS

- The Amsterdam Treaty sought to address the shortcomings of the third pillar by bringing immigration and asylum as well as judicial and police cooperation in civil matters into the first pillar.
- The third pillar, cooperation in criminal matters (police and judicial cooperation), remained intergovernmental.
- Schengen was incorporated into the Treaty, but this did not result in simplification given the overlapping memberships involved in this Agreement.
- The Nice Treaty added few changes to the Amsterdam set-up and extended a right of shared initiative to the Commission in the third pillar.

Policy output: baby steps to bold agendas

There have been several spurts of policy since the humble beginnings of JHA cooperation, building on the early pre-Maastricht efforts, but gathering momentum after Maastricht and Amsterdam. More recently, in addition to making progress on the four main dossiers (immigration, asylum, police cooperation, and judicial cooperation), the EU has acknowledged the importance of the external dimension of JHA, and has embarked on attempts to export its emergent policies beyond the Union.

Post-Maastricht developments in policy

After Maastricht, member states first focused on rules to apply to TCNs entering the Union territory. The Council formulated common rules in this area for employment and education, and recommended common rules for the expulsion of TCNs. It also suggested a common format for 'bilateral readmission agreements' (which would allow for the return of TCNs) between Union members and third countries. In 1997, an extradition convention was concluded among the EU member states. Agreement was also reached on the format of a uniform visa as well as on a list of countries whose nationals required a visa to enter EU territory. These agreements, which were relatively unambitious, sought to develop comparable procedural steps for the entry, sojourn, and expulsion of TCNs.

Asylum policies were also disappointing for some. The most notable development was the conclusion of the 1990 Dublin Convention, an instrument of binding regional international law, which designated one member state to be responsible for the handling of each asylum claim. The politically significant London Resolutions introduced the concepts of safe countries of origin and transit into the EU, rejecting applications lodged by the nationals of countries deemed safe or by those who had passed through safe countries en route to Union territory. Refugee rights activists frowned upon these policies as excessively restrictive, and warned that such rules could potentially weaken refugee protection.

Subsequent JHA Councils adopted resolutions on the definition of a refugee, minimum guarantees for asylum procedures, and a common format to help determine the state responsible for reviewing an asylum claim. During this period, work began on the EURODAC fingerprinting system, which would allow member states to keep track of asylum seekers, as well as on the negotiation of a common framework for the reception of individuals seeking temporary protection status in Union territory.

The Maastricht Treaty also took earlier efforts to cooperate in customs, public safety, and cross-border matters further by embarking on the ambitious agenda to create a European Police Office (Europol), a project that was initiated by Germany in 1991 to enhance police cooperation and information exchange in combating terrorism and the illicit trafficking of drugs and human beings. Based in The Hague, Europol was formally created in 1995 and became operational in October 1998. Two new bodies – the Centre for Information, Discussion, and Exchange on the Crossing of Frontiers and Immigration (CIREFI) and the Centre for Information, Discussion, and Exchange on Asylum (CIREA) – were approved in 1994 to facilitate cooperation between practitioners in the field. Ministers of the member states also signed an agreement in 1993 to create a European Drugs Unit (EDU) to assist in criminal investigations. Through the EDU, the Union sought to enlist the help of countries that the EU considered to be suppliers contributing to the drugs problem, particularly in the Caribbean and in Latin America.

Amsterdam and Tampere

Following the signing of the Amsterdam Treaty and its relatively rapid entry into force in 1999, progress in JHA cooperation accelerated substantially, aided by a special European Council dedicated exclusively to JHA. The goal of this summit, which was convened in Tampere, Finland, in October 1999, was to take stock of developments to date, evaluate the impact of Amsterdam, and discuss the future direction of JHA cooperation. There, policy steps were outlined towards creating an Area of Freedom, Security, and Justice (AFSJ). Included in the 'Tampere milestones' were a reiterated commitment to a common market complete with freedom of movement; the development of common rules for the fair treatment of TCNs, including guidelines for dealing with racism and xenophobia; the convergence of judicial systems; and the fostering of transparency and democratic control. Among the more far-reaching goals were better controls on and management of migration and the deterrence of trafficking in human beings. Importantly, the member states asked the Commission to keep track of and report on the progress made in all of the relevant dossiers.

On matters of immigration and asylum, Tampere advocated a 'comprehensive approach', closely linked to the combating of poverty and the removal of the political and economic conditions that compel individuals to leave their homes. A High-Level Working Group on Asylum and Immigration (HLWG) was created to study such linkages (van Selm 2002). At Tampere, basing its argument on case studies done on Albania/Kosovo, Afghanistan, Iraq, Morocco, Somalia, and Sri Lanka, the HLWG advocated actively linking JHA policies to tools of foreign policy, including development cooperation, and economic relations, rather than imagining JHA solely as 'domestic' EU policy. Predictably, the HLWG called for intensified cooperation between countries of origin and transit to address the causes of flight, empowering neighbouring countries to offer adequate protection to those in flight, and speeding up the removal of illegal immigrants from Union territory.

EU member states further committed themselves to creating a Common European Asylum System (CEAS), including common standards for reviewing claims and caring for asylum applicants, and comparable rules for refugee recognition. The Commission was asked to act as the coordinator of policy proposals dealing with asylum. With this new charge, the Commission soon introduced numerous proposals relating to asylum, including policies on reception conditions for refugees, a common set of minimum standards for the review of asylum claims, as well as common family reunification schemes for refugees. The Union also approved the creation of the European Refugee Fund, designed to aid EU recipient states during massive refugee influxes, such as those recently experienced during the fallout from Bosnia and Kosovo. By this point, the Dublin Convention had taken effect, and the EURODAC fingerprinting system was now functioning. The creation of the CEAS was in progress.

In matters of judicial and police cooperation, still third pillar matters, the ambition to create a

European Judicial Area (EJA) occupied a prominent place at Tampere. The proposed EJA would target the mutual recognition of judicial decisions and cross-border information exchange for prosecutions, as well as minimum standards for civil procedural law. With respect to criminal matters, the Council was required to expedite the ratification of the EU Conventions on extradition.

Tampere also created 'Eurojust'. Composed of national prosecutors, magistrates, and police officers, Eurojust would aid national prosecuting authorities in their criminal investigations of organized crime. A European Police College (CEPOL), which would also admit officers from the candidate countries, and a European Police Chiefs Task Force were also planned. Priorities were established for the approximation of judicial and police practices in the member states, with particular regard to money laundering, corruption, euro counterfeiting, drug trafficking, trafficking in human beings, the exploitation of women, the sexual exploitation of children, and high-tech and environmental crime. Europol was designated as the lead agency in these efforts. Importantly, Tampere also established benchmarks and set deadlines for the accomplishment of its goals, which enlivened the policy process. In the following months the draft EU Charter of Fundamental Rights was completed (December 2000), and there was progress in the mutual recognition of judicial decisions. The Commission developed a framework decision, under the new Title VI, on combating terrorism, and this was adopted on 13 June 2002.

Nonetheless, debate on the numerous items on the agenda after Tampere proved to be protracted. Blame for the delays was variously attributed. While the member states (operating through the Council) blamed the Commission, critics noted that the Council itself was in no particular hurry to press forward with the adoption of these measures. There was some progress in 2002 on immigration and asylum, through the adoption of a comprehensive plan to combat illegal immigration and to regulate the management of external borders. The Commission tabled new and revised initiatives relating to asylum procedures, on reception conditions for asylum seekers, on the definition and status of refugees, and on a first pillar instrument to replace the Dublin Convention. Still, the Presidency Conclusions issued at the end of the June 2002 Seville European Council called emphatically for a 'speeding up' of work, suggesting continued frustration with the progress made since Tampere.

KEY POINTS

- Since Maastricht, significant policy progress has been made in the fields of immigration, asylum, police, and judicial cooperation, even though policy output has fallen short of initial expectations.
- Policy-making focused on developing common rules for travel within and entry into the Union, harmonizing policies offering protection to asylum seekers and refugees, creating better information exchange and cooperation between law enforcement officials, and developing mutual recognition of judicial decisions within the EU.

The Hague Programme and the Constitutional Treaty

In June 2004, the Commission published an assessment of the Tampere Programme, characterizing the previous five years as a time of progress hampered by the drawbacks of the decision-making rules (European Commission 2004). The next phase in JHA cooperation, the Commission argued, would involve creating an integrated border management system and visa policy, complete with a Visa Information System (VIS) database to store biometric data of visa applicants, a common policy on the management of migration flows to meet economic and demographic needs, and the creation of the EJA. The Hague Programme that was subsequently adopted at the Brussels European Council of 4–5 November 2004 reiterated the call for the abolition of internal border controls soon after the projected launch of SIS II in 2007 (European Council 2004a). To compensate for the abolition of internal border controls, a recurring theme since the 1970s, the European Council called for the strengthening of external borders to be set forth through the Hague Programme. Of note in the Programme was the affirmation of the move to qualified majority voting (QMV) (except for measures involving legal migration where unanimity continues to apply) and codecision. The Hague Programme called for (among other things) the implementation of a common asylum system by the year 2010 and the gradual expansion of the European Refugee Fund to €150 million per year by 2008. The Hague Programme endorsed the Council Secretariat's SitCen, the situation centre which would provide strategic analyses of terrorist threats, and called for the creation of a European Border Management Agency by 1 May 2005, with the possible creation of a European System of Border Guards. It invited greater coordination on the integration of existing migrants. As for the external dimension of JHA cooperation (see below), the Hague Programme stressed partnership with countries of origin and/or transit and the conclusion of further readmission agreements as necessary.

Of additional importance was the Convention on the Future of Europe and the Intergovernmental Conference of 2003–4, culminating in the October 2004 signing of the Constitutional Treaty. Leading up to this, a far-reaching overhaul of the JHA field was recommended by the Convention's working party on JHA, which proposed the 'normalization' of JHA by abolishing the pillar structure. Greater use of QMV was proposed to overcome problems in decision-making, although unanimity would still need to be retained for judicial and police cooperation in criminal matters. The final text of the Constitution reflected many of these proposals and eliminated the pillar structure. It retained the shared right of initiative for the Commission and the member states in judicial cooperation in criminal matters but foresaw proposals coming from coalitions of at least 25 per cent of the membership of the Union. While the Convention proposed an extension of the use of QMV in judicial cooperation, it qualified this with an additional mechanism through which a member state in significant opposition to the Council could suspend negotiations. These were all efforts to streamline the decision-making process whilst preserving a diminished capacity for member states to block decisions. The Constitutional Treaty further provided for a role for national parliaments to monitor the implementation of JHA policies and for a judicial review of compliance by the ECJ. Finally, the Constitution retained the UK and Irish opt-ins, and the Danish opt-out (European Council 2004b). However, the Constitution, which would have meant another reform of JHA, was stalled as it ran into ratification problems when it was rejected in referenda in France and the Netherlands on 29 May and 1 June 2005 respectively.

Extending JHA cooperation outwards

During the initial phases of JHA cooperation, the immediate goal was to lift barriers to the free movement of persons within the EU. As the 1990s progressed, the planned enlargements of the Union projected the collective territory outwards, making it necessary to discuss JHA matters with the Union's *future* borders in mind. Member states began, early on, to involve certain third countries in some of their initiatives, attempting to solidify EU border controls by recruiting other countries to tighten their own border controls (Lavenex and Uçarer 2002, 2004). This involved entering into collective agreements with countries of origin and transit. These attempts to recruit neighbouring countries to adopt close variations of the EU's emergent border management regime were particularly pronounced in Central and Eastern Europe (CEE), the Maghreb, and the Mediterranean basin because of the proximity of these areas to the EU.

EU policies began to radiate out to neighbouring countries, particularly those applying for membership. Schengen countries collectively signed agreements with Poland, Hungary, and the Czech Republic, in which the latter agreed to readmit individuals returned from EU territory. Most CEE countries were declared safe countries of origin and transit, compelling them to accept asylum seekers who had travelled through their territory to get to the EU. At the 1993 Copenhagen European Council, future membership was made conditional upon the rapid incorporation of the EU's JHA *acquis* which, after Amsterdam, also included the Schengen *acquis*. The accession partnerships included an aid component, some of which was tied to the improvement of border controls. The EU assumed an advisory role for policy-making in CEE countries with the aim of helping them develop policies in line with those of the EU (Grabbe 2000). Applicant countries began adopting the EU's JHA policies even if that meant implementing, often at the risk of souring relations, restrictive policies vis-à-vis countries whose citizens previously enjoyed, for example, visa-free access into their own territories. The 2004 enlargement included the majority of these accession countries. Romania and Bulgaria, which did not make the 2004 enlargement but are set to join in January 2007, and Turkey and Croatia, which commenced accession negotiations on 3 October 2005, are required to make similar changes in preparation for membership.

JHA's external dimension extends further than would-be member countries, however. The EU expects similar adjustments of countries that are not part of the enlargement process. These expectations are situated in the broader setting of the Union's external relations (see Chapters 14 and 15), and, more specifically, have become part of its aid and trade policies. Thus, North African, non-enlargement Mediterranean, and African, Caribbean, and Pacific countries are steered towards adopting some of the Union's deflective immigration and asylum policies to ease migratory pressures into the Union by including sending and transit countries in the screening process. To these ends, the EU is in the process of negotiating readmission agreements with Morocco, Sri Lanka, Russia, Pakistan, Hong Kong, Macao, and Ukraine, while working on obtaining a mandate to start negotiations with Albania, Algeria, China, and Turkey. On 27 November 2002, the EU signed a readmission agreement with Hong Kong, which is the first of its kind signed between the EU and a third country. Soon after, two more were signed with Sri Lanka and Macao. The Hague Programme further charged the EU to develop EU Regional Protection Programmes in partnership with the third countries concerned. It further asked for a new European Neighbourhood and Partnership Instrument to create a strategic framework for furthering cooperation and dialogue on asylum and migration with neighbouring countries and for initiating new measures. One of the newest initiatives in this vein is the development of the EU Returns Directive (dubbed the Expulsion Directive by its critics) which seeks to lay down common procedures for returning illegally resident individuals to third countries. Developments in October 2005 in the Spanish enclaves of Ceuta and Melilla, where hundreds of sub-Saharan Africans attempted to jump razor-wire fences to gain access to Spanish territory, and were subsequently expelled to Morocco, intensified calls to cooperate with third countries to secure Europe's borders.

The external dimension of JHA is firmly rooted in the effort to develop compensatory measures, as the EU seeks to manage its collective borders. Yet the EU's efforts to extend its strict border controls outwards, by assisting (and in some cases demanding) the adoption of stricter border control measures elsewhere, involves an irony. While the EU attempts to liberalize the freedom of movement within its territory, it does so by applying potentially illiberal policies at its borders and by advocating such policies in its relations with third countries (Uçarer 2001b) (see Box 19.3).

CASE STUDY 19.3

Fighting terrorism in the European Union

JHA cooperation owes its genesis partly to the efforts of the Trevi Group, whose main goal was to establish cross-border cooperation in the fight against organized crime and terrorism. These matters were subsequently incorporated into the Union under Title VI of the Maastricht Treaty and revised by the Amsterdam Treaty. EU members authorized the creation of Europol to facilitate the tracking down and prosecution of transborder criminals and established jointly accessible databases to enhance police cooperation. Noting that terrorism 'constitutes one of the most serious threats to democracy, to the free exercise of human rights and to economic and social development', the Commission began work in late 1999 to develop an instrument that would outline the Union's position on terrorism. The instrument was to address not only terrorist acts directed against member states and the Union itself, but also international terrorism.

Following the 11 September 2001 attacks on the twin towers of the World Trade Center in New York and the Pentagon in Washington, DC, JHA ministers were called to an Extraordinary EU Council on Justice and Home Affairs, held on 21 September 2001. During this and following meetings, EU politicians expressed solidarity with the USA and confirmed their support for the military operations launched in Afghanistan. The events in the USA gave impetus to the EU's efforts to move speedily towards adopting anti-terrorist policies that were already in preparation. Terrorism was defined as 'offences intentionally committed by an individual or a group against one or more countries, their institutions or people, with the aim of intimidating them and seriously altering or destroying the political, economic, or social structures of a country' (European Commission 2001b). In October 2001, the Council expressed its intention to 'fast-track' the Framework Decisions on Terrorism and the European Arrest Warrant and committed the Union to adopting a common definition of terrorist offences, a common decision on the freezing of assets with links to suspected terrorists, and to establishing the European Arrest Warrant which was designed to replace the protracted extradition procedures between EU member states with an automatic transfer of suspected persons from one EU country to another. It urged better coordination between Europol, Eurojust, intelligence units, police corps, and judicial authorities and announced work on a list of terrorist organizations that would be jointly drawn up by the end of 2001. Such a list was adopted in 2001 and was updated in March 2005. The Framework Decision called for increased vigilance with regard to possible biological and chemical attacks, even though such attacks had never previously occurred in the EU. Finally, linking the fight against terrorism to effective border controls, the Council insisted on the intensification of efforts to combat falsified and forged travel documents and visas (European Council 2001). The Framework Decision on combating terrorism and the Framework Decision for the European Arrest Warrant (which included a list of 32 Euro-crimes) were adopted in June 2002.

The attention on anti-terrorism intensified yet further after the 11 March 2004 subway attacks in Madrid. Though no stranger to terrorist attacks from separatist Basque militants, Spain's trauma sharpened its attention to terrorism, which quickly became the primary preoccupation in the JHA field. The possibility that violent acts could be perpetrated by ill-integrated migrants – highlighted by the widely publicized murder of a prominent Dutch film director allegedly at the hands of a Muslim who held dual Dutch and Moroccon citizenship – rekindled the integration debate. Fears about 'home-grown' terrorism hit another peak with the 7 July 2005 London (Underground and bus) bombings, prompting swift condemnation from JHA ministers at an extraordinary ministerial meeting on 13 July 2005.

The Union is also working on improving its information exchange infrastructure to help with its anti-terrorism efforts. Along with a second generation Schengen Information System (SIS II), a new EU Visa Information System (VIS) is in preparation. Envisaged as having interactive capabilities, these databases will collect and compare information on persons, also targeting anti-terrorism work. SIS II will include additional information to be entered on 'violent troublemakers' (including football hooligans but potentially also political protesters) and suspected terrorists and would also store biometric information (digital pictures and fingerprints). In turn, the VIS will collect and store data from all visa applications in all member states, including biometric data in the form of digital photos and all 10 fingerprints, something that is criticized for potentially running afoul of data protection measures. SIS II and VIS are expected to become operational in 2006.

While the urgent attention directed towards anti-terrorist measures is certainly warranted, the EU's efforts in this field have already attracted criticism from civil liberties and migrants' rights advocates (Statewatch 2001). Activists caution against a possible backlash against migrants of Arab descent and argue against fastening the Union's outer doors even more firmly. As in the USA since 11 September 2001, European anti-trafficking measures have attracted sharp criticism from civil libertarians in Europe. The challenge in Europe is similar to that in the USA: developing policy instruments that meet security needs while protecting the civil liberties of individuals resident in the EU territory. Criticism aside, the events of 11 September, 11 March, and 7 July seem to have brought JHA cooperation full circle to its Trevi origins. It is certain that this dossier will remain very lively, if controversial, in the future.

KEY POINTS

- JHA cooperation has developed a significant external dimension, particularly vis-à-vis the Union's neighbours.
- The enlargement of the Union not only pushes its borders (and therefore the Area of Freedom, Security and Justice (AFSJ)) eastward, but also commits applicant countries to adopt JHA rules before their accession.
- JHA policy output also has an impact on countries that are not part of the enlargement process.

Conclusion

JHA cooperation has come a long way since its obscure beginnings in the 1970s. It currently occupies a prominent and permanent position in EU governance. The European Commission now has a more active role in JHA, facilitated by the creation within it of a new Directorate-General. The status of the EP and the ECJ has also improved since Amsterdam and they remain hopeful about the prospects for further institutional gains in the future. However, the Council remains the key actor, and decision-making is still hamstrung by the unanimity rule. Matters discussed within the JHA framework continue to strain the sovereign sensibilities of the EU's member states, and the policy remains intrinsically intergovernmental. However, few believe that the Union can achieve its common market goals without making significant progress in JHA. As the fallout in the USA of the events of 11 September 2001 and the attacks in Madrid and London clearly demonstrate, the tackling of transborder issues so typical of the JHA dossier demands coordination and cooperation beyond the state.

JHA is a young field compared to the other more established competences of the EU. Its birth pangs, as well as the continuing difficulties it faces, are comparable to the state of affairs in, say, environmental policy some decades ago. But the EU must contend with a number of important, and sometimes conflicting, challenges specific to JHA cooperation. In order to lift internal border controls on people moving within the EU, the Union must articulate and implement policies to manage its *external* borders. These policies should foster the freedom of movement of EU citizens and TCNs within the EU. They should also spell out common rules on the entry of TCNs into the Union. To demonstrate its commitment to basic human rights and democratic principles, the EU must protect TCNs against arbitrary actions, uphold their civil liberties, and deter acts of violence against them. To maintain the rule of law, the EU must press forward with judicial and police cooperation, while ensuring the privacy and civil liberties of those living in the EU. To live up to its international obligations, the EU must keep its policies in line with its pre-existing treaty obligations, particularly in the field of refugee protection. To protect its legitimacy and improve its public image, the EU must take pains to address issues of transparency and democratic deficit. And finally, it must undertake these endeavours without raising the spectre of an impenetrable 'Fortress Europe', which some argue already exists. The challenges facing the policy field remain substantial.

QUESTIONS

1. What are the catalysts that have led to the Europeanization of JHA policy?
2. Fostering cooperation in JHA matters has not been a straightforward process. What have been the impediments to effective cooperation in this field?
3. The issues dealt with in JHA can also be addressed through unilateral decisions by individual countries, or by bilateral agreements concluded with interested parties. Why, then, is there such an effort to develop multilateral and collective responses in this field?
4. What are some of the lingering shortcomings of post-Amsterdam JHA cooperation?
5. How might the EU improve transparency and close the democratic deficit in JHA?
6. What are the negative consequences of closer cooperation in JHA matters?
7. How is the EU extending the impact of its JHA policies beyond its borders?
8. To what extent was the European Council meeting held at Tampere a watershed in the evolution of JHA policy?

GUIDE TO FURTHER READING

■ Bieber, R. and Monar, J. (eds) *Justice and Home Affairs in the European Union: The Development of the Third Pillar* (Brussels: European Interuniversity Press, 1995). Covers the third pillar after Maastricht, focusing on the institutional framework and on early policy developments, particularly in the fields of immigration and asylum.

■ Geddes, A. *Immigration and European Integration: Towards Fortress Europe?* (Manchester: Manchester University Press, 2000). One of the first single-authored studies of the EU's immigration regime. Very accessible and well informed.

■ Geddes, A. *The Politics of Migration and Immigration in Europe* (London: Sage, 2003). A very useful comparative look at European migration policies which also takes stock of EU-level developments.

■ Lavenex, S., and Uçarer, E. (eds) *Migration and the Externalities of European Integration* (Lanham, MD: Lexington Books, 2002). An edited volume that focuses on the external dimension of EU's migration policies.

■ Lavenex, S., and Wallace, W. 'Justice and Home Affairs: Towards a "European Public Order"?', in H. Wallace, W. Wallace, and M. Pollack (eds), *Policy-making in the European Union*, 5th edn (Oxford: Oxford University Press, 2005). A very helpful textbook treatment of JHA to supplement the present chapter.

■ Monar, J., 'The Dynamics of Justice and Home Affairs: Laboratories, Driving Factors and Costs', *Journal of Common Market Studies*, 39(4) (2001), pp. 747 – 64. A useful article which seeks to explain the rapid development of JHA policy, by looking at early 'laboratories' (such as the Trevi Group) and at driving factors (such as challenges to internal security). It also points to the costs of this rapid evolution, in terms of the democratic deficit and other problems with the policy.

IMPORTANT WEBSITES

- http://ec.europa.eu/justice_home/index_en.htm
- http://www.consilium.europa.eu/cms3_applications/applications/newsroom/loadBookasp?BID=86&LANG=1&amsid=352
- http://www.europarl.europa.eu.int/committees/libe_home.htm
- http://www.europol.eu.int
- http://www.europarl.europa.eu/comparl/libe/elsj/news/default_en.htm
- http://www.cepol.net
- http://www.eurojust.eu.int The EU's websites are the best source of information on JHA matters. To foster transparency in this field, the Commission, Council, and Parliament have each created websites which highlight policy initiatives.
- www.statewatch.org Statewatch website. This provides a more critical approach to the JHA role of the EU than you will find on the EU websites.
- www.migpolgroup.com Migration Policy Group website, including the monthly *Migration News Sheet*.

Visit the Online Resource Centre that accompanies this book for lots of interesting additional material. http://www.oxfordtextbooks.co.uk/orc/cini2e/

20 Economic and Monetary Union

AMY VERDUN

Chapter Contents

Reader's Guide

This chapter provides an introduction to Economic and Monetary Union (EMU). It describes the key components of EMU and what happens when countries join. It argues that EMU was not an overnight event but rather one that was carefully prepared and based on collaboration and learning over a period of three decades. It discusses the period from 1969 (when the European Council first agreed to EMU), through to 1991 when, at the Maastricht summit, the European Council agreed to include EMU in the Treaty on European Union); 1992–2002 (the period in which EMU was being prepared and in the latter part of which exchange rates became irrevocably fixed); and briefly discusses the period since EMU started. It also reviews various economic and political theoretical explanations of why EMU was created and looks at some criticisms of the EMU project. The chapter discusses why a majority of the population in some EU countries is against EMU and it examines the criticisms of EMU's institutional design. Finally it looks to the future, and discusses what we can expect of EMU in the years to come.

Introduction

The introduction of the euro banknotes and coins on 1 January 2002 was a major happening. From one day to the next more than 300 million people in 12 European Union (EU) member states converted from their national currencies to the euro. All EU member states except Denmark, Sweden, and the United Kingdom (UK) participated. It was without doubt the biggest logistical operation in contemporary Europe during peace time. It also signalled the start of a new era in the history of the European Union. The majority of EU citizens are now confronted daily with a concrete symbol of European integration. What can be more prominent than a shared common currency?

Although it may seem obvious and logical to have a single currency in light of progress in European integration, the preparations for the introduction of the euro were by no means easy; nor were they uncontested. In order to appreciate this historical moment, we need to look behind the big eye-catching event of 1 January 2002 and examine the path that led to the euro.

Economic and Monetary Union (EMU) has been an integral part of the European integration process since the early 1970s, but did not always find the necessary support. Once it was firmly back on the agenda in the late 1980s and 1990s, supporters wanted to make sure that European monetary unification was done properly. Member states agreed that there should be sufficient economic and monetary convergence prior to starting EMU. They also agreed that there must be criteria that each country had to meet before it could join. At the same time, there were member states (such as the UK) that did not want to join EMU because they disliked the idea of giving up their own currency in favour of a common European one. Today there are still those who are highly sceptical about the whole EMU project.

What is EMU?

Having a common currency is not unique to the EU. Various countries have introduced a common currency at certain points in history. For example, the Romans had a single currency which was used throughout their empire. Belgium, France, Italy, Switzerland, and others were part of a Latin Monetary Union (LMU) from 1865 to 1927. They minted francs that were of equal value across their union. In 1872 the Danes, Norwegians, and Swedes launched a single currency, the Scandinavian krone that lasted until the outbreak of the First World War in 1914. Although the nineteenth-century European monetary unions were significant, the scale and scope of EMU in the EU is farther reaching, as these earlier unions harmonized coinage, but did not introduce a single monetary policy or a central bank. Thus, EMU is without doubt the most spectacular and ambitious monetary union of all times.

The component parts of EMU

EMU, as we know it in the EU, refers to a union in which participating countries have agreed to a single monetary policy, a single monetary authority, a single currency, and coordinated **macroeconomic policies**. Let us clarify these features.

First of all, what is monetary policy? **Central banks** conduct monetary policy (in some cases in collaboration with the government, that is, the ministry of finance and sometimes also the ministry of economics). Monetary policy aims at influencing the **money supply** and **credit conditions**. Central banks set a key (short-term) interest rate (often termed a policy rate), which through its influence over other interest rates is capable of changing the financial climate in a way conducive to the control of inflation. But what does it mean to have a single monetary policy, and no longer a national monetary policy? It means that participating countries no longer conduct monetary policy at the national level. Instead of having the national central bank conduct this policy, it is now formulated at the European level by a single monetary authority, the European Central Bank (ECB). The ECB sets a unified short-term interest rate for the euro area, also known as the EONIA – European Overnight Index Average. Long-term interest rates have converged, but they can still differ for a variety of reasons, such as the risk premium attached to member states with high national debt.

In December 1991, at the Maastricht summit, the heads of state and government of the European Community (EC) member states agreed to create this new European institution to conduct the single monetary policy in EMU. The formal name of the new institution is the European System of Central Banks (ESCB). Besides the ECB, the ESCB consists of the already existing national central banks. Under EMU, however, the latter are just 'branches' of the new ECB. The ECB is responsible for formulation of the monetary policy for the participating countries – the Eurozone or euro area. In EMU, the ECB conducts monetary policy for all EMU countries. It is responsible for the new single currency, sets interest rates, and monitors the money supply. To facilitate coordination of economic and financial policies, an informal group has been set up. The so-called eurogroup consists of the ministers of finance (and sometimes economics) who get together to seek to coordinate policies. The group typically meets before the Council of Ministers of Economic and Financial Affairs (ECOFIN).

EMU is famous for having introduced a single currency – the euro – in the EU. Nevertheless, as was mentioned above, EMU could have been introduced without there being a single currency. There were two alternatives. Participating countries could have kept their national currencies, and just agreed to fix their exchange rates irrevocably; or they could have introduced a common currency in parallel to the national currencies already circulating in the member states. In fact, the British government made such a proposal in 1990 – the 'hard ecu proposal'. But that plan was not adopted. While a parallel currency is introduced *alongside* existing national currencies, a single currency *replaces* them. The European heads of state and government preferred to have a single currency rather than fixed exchange rates or a parallel currency. A single currency would be beneficial economically, as it would reduce transactions costs that banks charge when currencies are exchanged. But, more importantly, it was considered to be politically more attractive, as it would signal a full commitment to EMU.

Finally, in order to have a successful policy mix between fiscal and monetary policies, EMU envisages the coordination of economic policies Article 99 of the Treaty Establishing the European Community (TEC). This implies that member states need to pursue economic policies in such a way that they do not undermine the aims of EMU. For example, when EMU was reconceptualized in the late 1980s and early 1990s, it was felt that the single currency should be a low-inflation currency. Also, member states' governments should not have excessive debts and deficits. Thus, it was decided that there should be rules on public debts and budgetary deficits (Article 104 TEC). The Article states that member states must avoid budget deficits in excess of a reference value (set at 3 per cent of gross domestic product (GDP), in a protocol annexed to the Treaty) and general government debt should be below a reference value (that is, should aim to be at or below 60 per cent of GDP).

Furthermore it was agreed that monetary financing of the debts and deficits would not be permitted. This meant that countries could no longer use the printing press to print more money to service their debt. Some countries had done this in the past, thereby enabling governments gradually to reduce their public debts but at the expense of increased inflation. This arrangement can be seen as a way of reducing the need for the ECB to bail out member states should they run into difficulties (this so-called 'no bail-out clause' is also stipulated explicitly in the Treaty in Article 103). A failure by one member state to service its debt could provoke a financial crisis in the euro area. These provisions were also intended to protect member states from excessive borrowing by member states. Prior to EMU, a member state that ran high budget deficits with inflationary consequences would be punished in the form of higher short-term interest rates. Under EMU, all euro area member states would be asked to share this burden. Coordination of economic policies can include much more than is currently envisaged. In fact, if one looks at the acronym, EMU, one sees a union with two components: 'economic' and 'monetary'.

The term 'Economic' and 'Monetary' Union is a little awkward. In fact, most newspaper commentators erroneously refer to the acronym EMU as 'European' Monetary Union. This is not very surprising as the most prominent feature of EMU is indeed the 'monetary' component. The reason EMU is called '*Economic and* Monetary Union' can be traced back to the discussions about EMU in the late 1960s and early 1970s. The policy-makers at the time were not sure how best to create the end result. To have fixed exchange rates – and ultimately a single currency – required some coordination of economic policies. But some countries – Belgium, Luxembourg, and France – thought that one could fix the exchange rate, and that the necessary cooperation between the related economic policies would naturally start to occur. The proponents of this strategy towards EMU became known as the 'Monetarists'. The then Federal Republic of Germany and the Netherlands on the other hand held the opposite position. In their view, economic policies needed to be coordinated *before* one fixed exchange rates or introduced a single currency. The proponents of this strategy towards EMU became known as the 'Economists'. This debate is referred to as the debate between the 'Monetarists and the Economists'. (Note that the term 'Monetarists', used in this context, does not have the same meaning as the term 'Monetarists' that refers to the followers of the ideas of Milton Friedman.)

The question of how to reach EMU had already been discussed in some detail by the economic thinkers of the 1960s such as Bela Balassa and Jan Tinbergen. According to these and other thinkers economic integration can be subdivided into a number of stages (see also Chapter 16).

The least far-reaching form of integration is a free trade area (FTA). In an FTA, participating members remove barriers to trade amongst themselves but maintain the right to levy tariffs on third countries. The next stage of integration is a customs union (CU). In addition to the free trade amongst members, a CU has common external tariffs on goods and services from third countries. A common market (CM) is characterized by free movement of goods, services, labour, and capital among the participating states and common rules, tariffs, and so on, vis-à-vis third countries. An *Economic Union* implies not only a CM but also a high degree of coordination of the most important areas of economic policy and market regulation, as well as monetary policies and income redistribution policies. A *Monetary Union* contains a CM but also further integration in the area of currency cooperation. (This is not *always* the case: the Scandinavian Monetary Union did not contain a customs union.) It has either irrevocably fixed exchange rates and full convertibility of currencies, or a common or single currency circulating within the monetary union. It also requires integration of budgetary and monetary policies. An *Economic and Monetary Union* (EMU) combines the features of the economic union and the monetary union. This combination is what European leaders had in mind when they discussed EMU in 1969 and again in 1988. A *Full Economic Union* (FEU) implies the complete unification of the economies of the participating member states and common policies for most economic matters. A *Full Political Union* (FPU) is the term used when, in addition to the FEU, political governance and policy-making have moved to the supranational level. Effectively political unification occurs when the final stage of integration has taken place and a new confederation or federation has been created. Note that the exact meaning of FEU is rather vague, which is why it is unclear what should be expected to be 'the next stage' after EMU has been created.

The eventual institutional design of EMU in the 1980s and 1990s was an asymmetrical one (Verdun 1996, 2000). It featured a relatively well-developed monetary union, but a much less developed economic union. In the sphere of monetary policy a complete transfer of policy-making to a new European supranational institution was envisaged, whereas in the area of economic policy-making, decisions remained to be made by the national governments. One may see here the difference between positive and negative integration. Positive integration refers to the creation of common rules, norms, and policies. Negative integration is all about taking away obstacles, eliminating rules and procedures that are an obstruction to integration. As regards EMU we find that in the area of monetary policy a new institution and a common policy are created. By contrast, in the area of economic union one may see mainly negative integration: the completion of the single market (that is, removing barriers to trade), and accepting only numerical ceilings on budgetary policies – which should have the effect of coordinating policies. Neither a common institution nor a common policy was created in this area of policy-making. As we shall see in the next section, the reason this asymmetry existed was that in the area of monetary policy a convergence of policy-making had occurred, whereas in the area of economic policy there was still a great deal of divergence.

KEY POINTS

- Before EMU there were other monetary unions, such as the Latin Monetary Union and the Scandinavian Monetary Union.
- EMU consists of a single monetary policy, a single monetary authority, a single currency, and coordinated macroeconomic policies.
- There were differences in opinion as to how to obtain EMU. The debate was between the 'Monetarists' and the 'Economists'.
- One can distinguish various stages of integration: from a free trade area to a full political union.

From The Hague to Maastricht (1969–91)

At the 1969 summit in The Hague, the heads of state and government decided to explore a possible path to EMU. A group of experts, headed by Pierre Werner, Prime Minister and Finance Minister of Luxembourg, drafted the blueprint. The 1970 Werner Plan proposed three stages to reach EMU by 1980. On the institutional side it recommended setting up two supranational bodies: a 'Community System for the Central Banks' and a 'Centre of Decision for Economic Policy'. The former would pursue monetary policies, whereas the latter would coordinate macroeconomic policies (including some tax policies). Although the Council took over most of the recommendations of the Werner Plan, EMU did not take off in subsequent years.

There were two reasons for this. First, there were substantial differences among the member states about how to get to EMU (the difference of opinion between the 'Monetarists and the Economists'). Secondly, the international economic and monetary situation changed rapidly in the early 1970s, making for a totally different climate for cooperation. During the post-Second World War era the so-called Bretton Woods agreement had made possible stable exchange rates in Western Europe. This came to an end in August 1971. West European countries responded by setting up their own exchange rate mechanism, the so-called snake, which functioned with moderate success throughout the 1970s. Not all member states were part of it. Some member states' currencies dropped out, whereas the currencies of several non-members participated in it.

Developments leading to the relaunch of EMU in the late 1980s

In 1979 a truly European Community (EC) Exchange Rate Mechanism (ERM) was developed as part of the European Monetary System (EMS). All EC member states participated in the EMS, though not all were immediately part of its most important feature, the ERM – a system of fixed but adjustable exchange rates. For example, the UK was not part of the ERM throughout the entire 1980s but its currency was part of the European Currency Unit (ECU) – the unit of account at the heart of the EMS. In 1991 the British pound did join the ERM, however. Other countries, such as Italy, participated in the ERM from the outset but were initially given more leeway. Throughout the 1980s the Italian lira was permitted to fluctuate more than other currencies within the ERM. The rules stipulated that most currencies could not fluctuate more than ±2.25 per cent from an agreed parity, whereas the bandwidth for those who needed more leeway was set at ±6 per cent from the parity. If a currency threatened to move outside the agreed band, central banks would intervene by buying or selling currencies in order to keep the currency from leaving the band. If an imbalance was persistent the so-called EC Monetary Committee would decide whether or not to adjust the parities. The Monetary Committee had been created by the Rome Treaty and at the start of EMU was renamed the Economic and Financial Committee. It is an informal advisory body that discusses monetary policy and exchange rate matters.

The ERM took some time to become successful. The first four years (1979–83) were learning years. This period was characterized by numerous parity adjustments and exchange rate fluctuations. Between 1983 and 1987 the participating currencies became more stable, and between 1987 and 1992 the ERM witnessed no realignments. It had become an important 'symbol' of successful European integration.

As a result of the exchange rate cooperation of the 1980s, the German currency, the Deutschmark or D-mark, became the 'anchor currency'. Because it had been such a strong currency, monetary authorities in ERM countries took German monetary policies as their point of reference. Most EC central banks followed the decisions of the German central bank (the Bundesbank) quite closely. By doing so, these countries imported some of the Bundesbank's and the D-mark's reputation, low inflation rates, interest rates, and stable exchange rates.

During the 1980s a few other important developments took place that eventually helped relaunch the EMU process. In the mid-1980s the Single European Act (SEA) facilitated completing the single internal market and the SEA mentioned the need to relaunch EMU. EMU was given new life at the Hanover Council meeting in 1988. The Council asked Jacques Delors to head a committee that would study how to obtain EMU. The committee was composed of the 12 central bank presidents, another EC commissioner, and a few experts. Like the earlier Werner Report, the Delors Report (issued in April 1989) proposed a road to EMU in three stages (see Box 20.1). It also envisaged the need for a European System of Central Banks. In contrast to the Werner Report, it did not find it necessary to set up a similar supranational institution in the economic sphere. But the end aim was the same: full freedom of goods, services, capital, and labour, and, if possible and if the political will was there, to introduce a single currency. On the basis of the Delors Report the European Council in Madrid in June 1989 adopted EMU and agreed to the start of the first stage to EMU (the liberalization of capital markets) on

CHRONOLOGY 20.1

Three stages to Economic and Monetary Union

First stage	1 July 1990 to 31 December 1993	• Free movement of capital between member states • Closer coordination of economic policies • Closer cooperation among central banks
Second stage	1 January 1994 to 31 December 1998	• Convergence of the economic and monetary policies of the member states (to ensure stability of prices and sound public finances)
Third stage	From 1 January 1999	• Establishment of a European Central Bank • Fixing of exchange rates • Introduction of the single currency

1 July 1990. To discuss the details of the next stages an **intergovernmental conference** (IGC) was held that started in Rome in October 1990 and closed in Maastricht in 1991 (see Chapter 3). Strictly speaking there were two IGCs, one on EMU and another on political union. One of the decisions taken during the IGC negotiations was that, in order to safeguard a successful EMU with low inflation and a stable currency, countries would have to meet certain criteria, which were dubbed 'convergence criteria'.

The **convergence criteria** (see Box 20.2) referred to good performance in the area of inflation rates, interest rates, and exchange rates. Moreover participating countries should not have excessive budgetary deficits or public debts. Finally, the national central bank needed to be made independent from political influence, and national monetary authorities could no longer use the printing press (monetary financing) to deal with public debts and budgetary deficits. It is important to note that right from the outset there were 'escape clauses' built into the wording of the Maastricht Treaty. It was generally thought they would be applied generously in relation to the debt criterion as it was clear that some countries, such as Belgium and Italy, would never be able to meet the **reference value** in less than a decade. As for the budgetary criteria, however, they *had* to be met.

It has been suggested that the creation of EMU was assisted by the coincidence that the autumn of 1989 also witnessed the end of communist regimes in Central and Eastern Europe and that 1990 saw the fall of the Berlin wall. The observant reader will have noted, however, that the Delors Report had already been completed by April 1989, and therefore preceded these turbulent political developments. Nevertheless, the political determination of the German Chancellor, Helmut Kohl, to secure EMU was connected to his eagerness to move ahead quickly with German reunification. In any event, the IGCs were completed in December 1991 in Maastricht with a summit meeting that agreed to revise the Treaty of Rome, and accept a new Treaty on European Union. It was signed on 7 February 1992, and eventually came into force on 1 November 1993 after the national parliaments of all of the then 12 member states ratified it. As we shall see below, not all member states' parliaments and citizens were immediately very happy with the new Treaty.

BOX 20.2

The Maastricht convergence criteria

- Budget deficits should be no more than 3 per cent of gross domestic product (GDP).
- Accumulated public debt should be no more than 60 per cent of GDP.
- Exchange rates should have stayed within the normal margins set by the exchange rate mechanism for at least the previous two years.
- Inflation should not exceed by more than one-and-a half points the average of the three best performers.
- Long-term interest rates should be no more than two points above the average of the lowest three.

Source: Consolidated Version of the Treaty Establishing the European Community, Article 121 and Protocols.

Debt and deficit escape clauses

- As regards the deficit criteria, the Treaty stipulated that the reference value had to be met or else the deficit needed to have 'declined substantially and continuously and reached a level that comes close to the reference value', or that the situation was only 'exceptional and temporary' and that the deficit 'stayed close to the reference value'.
- As regards the debt criteria the Treaty stated that an exception was acceptable if 'the ratio is sufficiently diminishing and approaching the reference value at a satisfactory pace'.

Source: Consolidated Version of the Treaty Establishing the European Community, Article 104.

KEY POINTS

- In the 1970s, EMU stalled because of differences of opinion among the member states and because of changing international circumstances
- Various developments – such as the 'snake', the EMS, and the SEA – contributed to the relaunch of EMU in the late 1980s
- The Delors Report offered a blueprint for EMU.
- The Treaty changes necessary for acceptance and implementation of EMU were negotiated in an intergovernmental conference which was completed in Maastricht in 1991.
- To join EMU, member states needed to meet the 'convergence criteria'.

From treaty to reality (1992–2002)

This section examines how the EMU project almost died before being brought back to life by a combination of time, bureaucratic perseverance, elite political support, and institutional **path dependence**.

Ratification problems

Though signed in 1992 by the heads of state and government, the Maastricht Treaty still had to be ratified by the parliaments of all 12 EC member states before it could enter into force. This ratification process turned out to be very tricky. Only months after the Treaty was signed, on 2 June 1992, Danish citizens voted against the Treaty in a referendum. Even though the outcome of the referendum was very close (50.7 per cent against versus 49.3 per cent in favour) the Treaty was rejected. In a reaction to the Danish referendum, the French President François Mitterrand also decided to hold a referendum in France on the acceptability of the Treaty on 20 September 1992.

Against the background of major speculation in the financial markets, which resulted in the British pound and the Italian lira leaving the Exchange Rate Mechanism days before the referendum, the French result came out with only a very slim majority of 51.05 per cent in favour and 48.95 per cent against accepting the Treaty. The result had surprised most observers as the French had until then typically been supporters of the European integration process. This period put an important mark on the run-up to EMU. The aftermath of the events of late 1992 was a period of continued turbulence in the ERM which, in the months following, came under further pressure. It resulted eventually in a broadening of the bands from ±2.25 per cent to ±15 per cent. After the introduction of the euro, a new system, the ERM II, was set up. It maintained the ±15 per cent bands.

The birth of the Stability and Growth Pact

In the mid-1990s the German finance minister, Theo Waigel, suggested that there should be arrangements beyond the convergence criteria. He wanted to formulate rules that countries had to obey once in EMU. These rules took the form of the Stability and Growth Pact (SGP). The SGP was put in place to ensure that no single member state, once a member of EMU, could freeride on the system, for example by incurring high debts and deficits. Under the SGP, member states that violate the rules requiring them to keep their public debt and budgetary deficit low can be penalized and may have to pay a fine. Understandably, the SGP was not without its critics. The rules can be seen as artificial. Furthermore, imposing a fine on a member state is politically difficult. Indeed, the SGP was designed to work as a deterrent, and offered a political symbol important for countries, such as Germany, that felt worried at the time about the behaviour of high debt countries (such as Belgium and in particular Italy) once they became members of EMU. It is ironic that Germany has since been one of the countries to have problems meeting the rules and objectives of the SGP (see Box 20.3 and further discussion below).

At the start of the 1990s it seemed that many countries could easily meet the convergence criteria. However, as time went on, it became clear that even the largest country (and in the monetary sense the most important country), Germany, was unable to do so. At some point only Luxembourg, a country with less than half a million inhabitants, met the criteria. Thus, throughout the 1990s it was unclear what the politicians would do with this lack of adequate performance.

Who should join the euro area?

Eventually the 1998 deadline approached in which the European Council had to decide which countries were ready to join EMU. During the 1990s the European Monetary Institute (set up in 1994, and the forerunner of the ECB) had already designated some countries as being ready to join EMU. Many were surprised to discover that Austria, Denmark, Portugal, the Netherlands, and Spain were among the first judged by the EMI to have fulfilled the convergence criteria. By contrast, France and Germany, traditionally the lead countries on EMU, were *not* part of this first group. France and Germany were having problems in particular with the debt and deficit criteria. It is not fair to say, however, that these countries were doing very much worse than the other countries. Rather, the Treaty stipulated that countries needed to meet the convergence criteria or should be moving continuously and steadily in the right direction. France and Germany were both countries that had performed well on these criteria in the early 1990s. In fact, when the criteria were determined they either met or almost met them, but moved away from them as the 1990s progressed. Thus, ironically, it looked as though EMU might happen with a group of countries some of which traditionally had been considered second-tier countries, while the participation of France and Germany – traditionally the leaders of the European

BOX 20.3

The Stability and Growth Pact

The Stability and Growth Pact aims to ensure that member states continue to practise budgetary discipline after the introduction of the euro. The examples of Portugal and Germany illustrate the implementation of the excessive debt procedure (EDP).

Dates	Decisions
The *Stability and Growth Pact* was a European Council resolution (adopted at Amsterdam on 17 June 1997) and two Council regulations of 7 July 1997 (revised on 27 June 2005).	• Surveillance of budgetary positions and coordination of economic policies. • Implementing the EDP.
Annually since 1 March 1999	• Member states have undertaken to pursue the objective of a balanced or nearly balanced budget and to present the Council and the Commission with a stability programme. • Member states not taking part in the third stage of EMU are also required to submit a convergence programme. • Opening and closing (where appropriate) of an EDP for EU member states.

Portugal:
November 2002: Council decides on the basis of a Commission proposal that an excessive deficit exists (Council recommendation Art 104(7)). By April 2004 Commission decides that an excessive deficit no longer exists; a recommendation adopted by the Council (Art 104 (12)). By May 2004, EDP effectively closed.

Germany:
21 January 2003: Council decides on the basis of a Commission proposal that an excessive deficit exists (Council decision Art 104(6); and Council recommendation (Art 104(7)).

25 November 2003: Commission recommendation for a Council decision to give notice (Art 104(9)) not adopted at the Council of 25 November 2003.

1 March 2006: Commission recommendation for a Council decision to give notice (Art 104(9)).

The Stability and Growth Pact enables the Council to penalize any participating member state which fails to take appropriate measures to end an excessive deficit. Initially, the penalty would take the form of a non-interest-bearing deposit with the Community, but it could be converted into a fine if the excessive deficit is not corrected within two years.

The legal text of the SGP consists of: (1) Resolution of the European Council on the Stability and Growth Pact, [1997] OJ C236/1; (2) Council Regulation No. 1466/97 of 7 July 1997 on the strengthening of the surveillance of budgetary positions and the surveillance and coordination of economic policies, [1997] OJ L209/1 as amended by Council Regulation 1055/105 of 27 June 2005; and (3) Council Regulation No. 1467/97 on speeding up and clarifying the implementation of the excessive deficit procedure, [1997] OJ L209/6 as amended by Council Regulation 1056/2005.

Source: http://europa.eu.int/comm/economy_finance/about/activities/sgp/sgp_en.htm.

integration process – was not yet formally approved. Reports in the media in 1997 and 1998 even suggested that France and Germany were 'cooking the books', and there was talk of 'creative accounting'. Yet everyone realized that EMU would be unthinkable without France and Germany. Finally, in May 1998, the European Council decided that 11 countries would participate in EMU from 1 January 1999 – the day when exchange rates would be irrevocably fixed between the participating member states. However, Denmark, Sweden, and the UK did not want to join at that point, whereas Greece took until June 2000 to be considered ready (the latter joining the euro area as the twelfth member as of 1 January 2001).

When eight Central and Eastern European countries (CEECs) and two very small Mediterranean countries joined the EU on 1 May 2004 the arrangement was that these countries would eventually have to join EMU. However, they would have to wait at least two years, fulfil the convergence criteria before they could join the last stage of EMU, and thereafter adopt the euro. Though the timetable is still subject to change, it is clear that the new member states will not all join EMU at the same time. Some countries, such as Slovenia, might be keen and ready to join in 2007. Two Baltic states (Estonia and Lithuania) are also very keen but might have to wait until 2008 due to the inflationary pressures these countries have been witnessing. Cyprus, Latvia, and Malta are also seeking to join in 2008, whereas Slovakia is on track for 2009. The Czech Republic and Hungary are due to join in 2010, whereas there is no clear timetable for Poland. Some speculate that Poland might not be so keen to join EMU in the foreseeable future (European Commission 2005c).

Managing EMU: difficulties with the Stability and Growth Pact (SGP)

As we saw above, the SGP was created in the mid-1990s to ensure that member states kept their budgetary deficits under control. The SGP regulates multilateral budgetary surveillance (a 'preventive arm') and specifies a deficit limit and the Excessive Deficit Procedure (EDP) (a 'corrective arm'). When – on the basis of a Commission recommendation – the Council decides that an excessive deficit indeed exists, the member state concerned is obliged to reduce its deficit below the Treaty's reference value of 3 per cent of GDP; otherwise, in theory, after a series of steps financial sanctions can be levied against the member state in question.

In 2002, France, Germany, and Portugal were each at different times given an early warning in keeping within the EDP. Portugal made the necessary corrections and hence the EDP was abrogated in 2004. But France and Germany continually failed to make the necessary adjustments to correct the budgetary deficits. By November 2003 both France and Germany were heading for the next step in the excessive deficit procedure (Art. 104 (9) TEC), and thus were coming closer to the financial sanctions set out in the SGP. Neither country was keen to move to the next step, and thus sought to get support from other member states to avoid that situation. At a meeting of the Council of Ministers of Economic and Financial Affairs (the ECOFIN Council), on 25 November 2003 a proposal by the Commission to move France and Germany closer to the sanctions was defeated. The result was that the SGP was interrupted in the cases of France and Germany. Other member states, notably Austria, Finland, the Netherlands, and Spain, were outraged at the situation. Their judgement was that France and Germany had been exempted from the process because they were large enough to rally other member states around their cause. The four were particularly upset because they were convinced that if a smaller member state had faced the same situation, it would not have been able to obtain the same amount of support for its cause. The resulting crisis atmosphere prompted the European Commission to ask the European Court of Justice (ECJ) whether this Council decision was legal. In July 2004 the ECJ ruled that it was in fact *illegal* as the Council had adopted its own text outside the context of the Treaty. But the ECJ did confirm that the Council has the right not to adopt the recommendations of the

Commission. The result of all these developments was that the SGP was undermined, and thus the SGP rules needed to be adjusted. By the spring of 2005 the SGP was revised so that there is now more flexibility regarding the circumstances under which member states may temporarily run deficits in excess of the 3 per cent reference value, and small adjustments were made to the time schedule. It remains to be seen, therefore, how 'successful' the SGP will be in ensuring that deficits be kept under the 3 per cent reference value.

The preventive arm of the SGP has been strengthened by a stronger and more differentiated medium-term orientation of the rules. The new provisions ensure that due attention is given to the fundamentals of fiscal sustainability when setting budgetary objectives. In future, the medium-term budgetary objective of a country will be based on its debt ratio and potential growth. In practice, this will mean that countries with a combination of low debt and high potential growth will be able to run a small deficit over the medium term, whereas a balanced budget or a surplus will be required for countries with a combination of high debt and low potential growth. The preventive arm of the SGP is strengthened because member states have committed to consolidate further public finances, when they face favourable economic conditions, and have accepted that the Commission will be giving 'policy advice' if this consolidation fails to occur under these circumstances. The new agreement also is more sensitive to the effects of member states' efforts to make structural reforms. The SGP's corrective arm has also been adjusted; leaving more room for economic judgement, and leaving open the possibility that the one-year deadline for the correction of an excessive deficit could be increased to two years.

KEY POINTS

- The period following the signing of the Maastricht Treaty posed challenges to the EMU project. The challenges included difficulties with the ratification of the Treaty; the ERM crises; countries encountered difficulties meeting the convergence criteria.
- Since the start of EMU member states have had difficulties avoiding excessive deficits.
- There have been difficulties with the implementation of the SGP.

Explaining EMU

Let us now turn to a few explanations of why EMU happened, examining explanations from economics and political science.

Explaining EMU from an economics perspective

In the field of economics, discussions of EMU place the main emphasis on the question of whether it would make economic sense to create an EMU in the EU. There are two schools of thought. The first school argues that EU member states should move forward to the next stage of integration (that is, from a common market to an economic and monetary union) only if they constitute a so-called optimum currency area (OCA).

According to OCA theory, countries should adopt a single currency when they are sufficiently integrated economically; when they have mechanisms in place that can deal with transfer payments if one part of the country is affected by an economic downturn; and when they no longer need the exchange rate instrument to make those adjustments. Most analysts claim that the EU is *not* an OCA, though a few think that a small number of its countries come close to being one. OCA theory states that if countries do not fulfil the conditions of constituting an OCA they should not give up the exchange rate instrument, but use it to make adjustments as the economic situation dictates. Those analysts argue that the EU should not have moved to EMU. Others who have observed that the EU does indeed constitute an OCA are less critical of this situation. They use a broader definition of an OCA claiming that the original OCA theory is too rigid. They point out that according to the original definition none of the current federations (such as Canada, Germany, and the USA) would constitute an OCA. Hence, they argue that the EU can introduce a single currency just as has happened in any other monetary union or federal state. In their view it does not 'cost' too much to give up the exchange rate instrument. Other developments that have influenced the thinking about the role of exchange rates in recent years are the effects of financial markets on exchange rate policies – particularly those of smaller open economies. Foreign exchange markets can create their own disturbances that can be irrational. This effect is worse for smaller open economies than for larger established countries. The original OCA theorists did not take the destabilizing effects of exchange rate freedom into consideration (Buiter 2000).

Another school of thought focuses on central banks and the importance of credibility. It argues that over the past two decades the EU has witnessed long periods of collaboration in central banking. From this perspective, central banks can be effective only if financial markets have confidence in their policies. In the case of the ERM, participating countries had to keep their exchange rates stable. In order to do that, they focused on the monetary policy of the strongest currency, the D-mark. Individual central banks followed the policies of the leader (the Bundesbank), and hence in practice had no opportunity to pursue alternative policies. The most credible way to secure monetary policies is to commit firmly to them in a treaty. That is in fact what happened with the Maastricht Treaty. A regime was set up that envisaged full central bank independence, and gave the ECB a clear single mandate, namely to maintain price stability.

Explaining EMU from a political science perspective

Political science has drawn on European integration theories (see Chapters 5–8) to explain EMU. It is noteworthy that scholars from opposing schools of thought have more or less convincingly argued that EMU can be explained using different theoretical approaches. For reasons of simplicity we shall focus on the two best-known opposing schools in order to capture a larger set of arguments.

A neo-functionalist explanation (see Chapter 6) claims that EMU can be best explained by considering it to be the result of spillover and incremental policy-making. The success of the ERM and the completion of the Single Market necessitated further collaboration in the area of monetary integration. To maximize the benefits of these developments, EMU was needed. Furthermore, significant monetary policy convergence had occurred, arising out of the collaboration within the framework of the ERM and the tracking of German policies by other member states. Hence, EMU could be seen as a natural step forward. Moreover, it is argued that supranational actors were instrumental in creating EMU – which is another characteristic of the neo-functionalist explanation of European integration. The supranational actors involved were not only the Commission President and the services of the Commission (in particular the Directorate-General for Economic and Financial Affairs), but also various EC committees – such as the Monetary Committee. Each of these supranational actors and institutions proved to be influential.

An intergovernmentalist explanation (see Chapter 7) argues that EMU can best be understood by examining the interests and bargaining behaviour of the largest member states. This approach sees the European Council meetings as crucial for decisions such as the creation of EMU. Thus, by examining the interests of the largest member states, one is able to see why EMU happened. From this point of view EMU was in the interests of France, Germany, and the UK, and this made it acceptable. France was in favour of EMU because it was a way to contain German hegemony. Germany, in turn, was able to secure a monetary policy regime that was sufficiently close to its domestic regime. Some argue that the reason that Germany was in favour of EMU in the early 1990s was that it wanted to signal its full commitment to the European integration project, having just completed German unification. The UK was not so much in favour of EMU, but rather was aware that EMU was likely to happen. Thus, the UK aimed to take part in the process and to be involved in the agenda-setting and the determination of the process. It has also been argued that EMU served the economic interests of the business communities within these countries, which subsequently led to the governments being more supportive of the project.

Although some authors have argued that the above-mentioned approaches are mutually exclusive, and that one should be 'more correct' than the other, both approaches have something to offer. It may be, then, that only when they are taken together is one able to fully appreciate why EMU happened.

KEY POINTS

- OCA theory is often used as a point of departure for an economic critique of EMU.
- Theories of European integration offer a political science perspective on EMU.

Criticisms of EMU

This section discusses various criticisms of EMU. These are quite diverse, ranging from popular opposition to the whole project, to elite criticism of its institutional design.

Countries opposing EMU

Denmark and Sweden are very proud of their own political, social, and economic achievements and doubt that joining EMU will benefit their respective countries. Their populations have been relatively sceptical about the EU, and see EMU as yet another example of unnecessary or undesirable European integration. In both countries a referendum was held (in Denmark in 2000; in Sweden in 2003) and in both cases the majority of those who voted were against joining EMU. Denmark has an opt-out and thus can choose to stay outside the euro area; the Swedish government does not have an opt-out, but 'just' pursues policies so that Sweden does not qualify for EMU.

The case of the UK reflects an even more Eurosceptic population. A large segment of the UK population has had doubts about aspects of European integration ever since the UK first joined the EC in 1973. British citizens, the media, and the Conservative Party seem deeply suspicious about policy-making in the rest of Europe and fear they will have to make too many changes if they follow the lead of other European states. Another argument often heard in the UK is that since there is no strong economic rationale to create a single currency, there is no real need to do so. The benefits of the euro have been calculated to be around 1 per cent of GDP.

The main benefits of EMU are the elimination of transactions costs (costs related to the exchange of money), a strong monetary policy, the fact that a single currency further strengthens the single or 'internal' market, and dynamic effects that come about as a result of clarity about prices once they are all denominated in the same currency. Yet these benefits are not guaranteed. It is likely for example that the monetary policy pursued by the ECB may not benefit each country equally. Some have argued that the case of the UK is different from all others because the UK's business cycle and the financial structure of business are not fully in line with those of the rest of Europe (and are closer to those of the USA). Hence, they argue that a common monetary policy might do more harm than good. Others state that the City of London is a special feature of the UK economy which puts the UK in a unique position.

However, it is not entirely clear whether these issues really make very much difference. In recent years, the UK business cycle has become somewhat more aligned with that of the rest of Europe, as a result of the larger share of total trade going there. Thus, regardless of the importance of these concerns originally, they now carry less weight. But more important than whether the UK is ready economically, the core question is whether it is ready politically. In his first election campaign in 1997, the Labour leader, Tony Blair, first rejected the idea that the UK might join EMU during his first term of office. However, after he entered his second term, he kept the door open for possible entry. Blair announced that a referendum would be held on EMU, and it was agreed by his Chancellor (finance minister), Gordon Brown, that the UK might join if it met five 'economic tests'. These tests are considered to contain an important degree of political judgement. The UK Treasury assessed the situation in June 2003 and determined that not all five tests were met, though many feel that this decision was as much a political as an economic one. Chancellor Gordon Brown was typically sceptical of joining the euro, whereas Blair was much more keen. However, many have pointed to the fact that Blair lost his political opportunity to take the UK into EMU when he took the UK into the war in Iraq in March 2003 – a decision that was not in line with the wishes of British citizens at the time. As public opinion in the UK is largely sceptical of joining EMU, and as Blair has lost considerable credibility over the Iraq war, it is extremely unlikely that Blair could mobilize sufficient public support to win a referendum on the euro, especially as Gordon Brown is so sceptical. As the UK Conservative Party is also against joining EMU, most observers do not expect the UK to join in the next few years.

Elsewhere in the EU citizens have generally been supportive of the introduction of the euro. Based on current *Eurobarometer* data, the populations of some countries are outright enthusiastic (Luxembourg, Ireland, Belgium, and France with three-quarters or more in favour) or strongly in favour (such as Italy, Austria, Portugal, Hungary, the Czech Republic, and Lithuania where a two-thirds majority is in favour); whereas others have been more subdued (as is the case in Germany and Spain where there is still a majority supporting the single currency). The three countries where popular support for the euro at this time dropped below 50 per cent are Greece (49 per cent); Sweden (48 per cent); and the UK (28 per cent). Figure 20.1 illustrates aggregate support by EU citizens for the euro from 1999 to 2005.

Criticism of the institutional design of EMU

Aside from popular opposition to the introduction of the euro, EMU has been criticized for its poor institutional design. The scholarly literature, in particular, has picked up on this issue. It argues, for instance, that the extreme independence of the ECB may lead to problems of legitimacy and accountability. The argument is developed in three steps. First, the ECB is more independent than any other central bank in the world. Its independence and its primary mandate (to secure price stability – in effect low inflation) are firmly anchored in the Treaty on European Union. The Treaty also stipulates that no one is allowed to give instructions to the ECB; nor should it take instructions from anyone. Secondly, it is close to impossible to change the ECB mandate. A change to the ECB statute demands a Treaty change which requires unanimity from the heads of state and government of all EU member states, as well as ratification by all EU

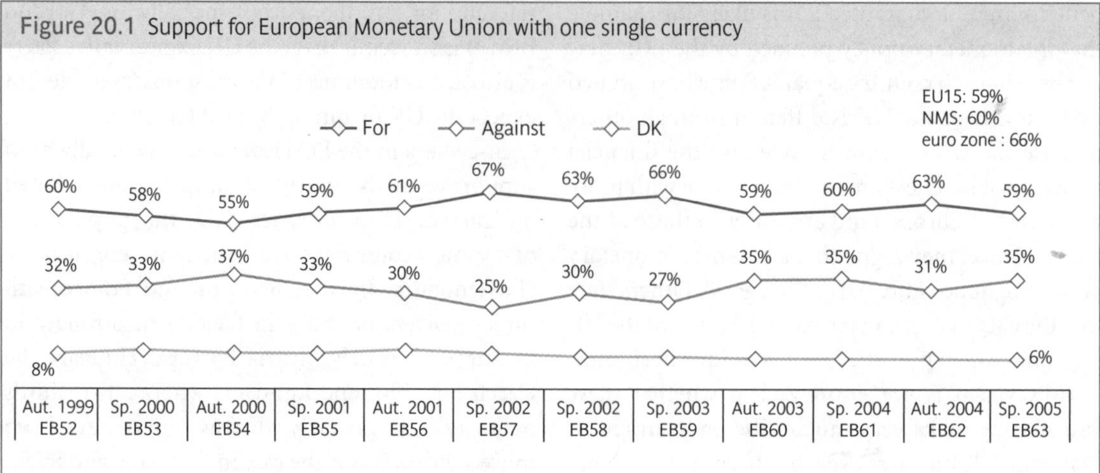

Figure 20.1 Support for European Monetary Union with one single currency

From a socio-demographic point of view, the main supporters of the euro are:

- Men;
- Citizens aged under 55;
- Citizens having a higher level of education;
- Citizens who place themselves on the left of the political spectrum;
- 'Leaders of opinion';
- Citizens who are well informed about the European Union.

Note: EU15, European Union – 15 Member States before most recent enlargement (1 May 2004); NMS, New Member States – 10 Member States which joined the EU during the last enlargement; DK, 'Don't know'

Source: *Standard Eurobarometer Report*, No. 63, p. 163. http://europa.eu.int/comm/public_opinion/archives/eb/eb63/eb63_en.htm.

national parliaments (and possibly referenda too). Thirdly, there are very few checks and balances in place to ensure that policies are pursued that the member states want – except for the one clear one, namely to secure price stability (low inflation). And even on that issue there is not too much control. The ECB president gives quarterly reports to the European Parliament (EP), but the EP cannot give instructions to the ECB. Thus, one must simply trust that the ECB will pursue policies in accordance with its mandate and that the policy outcome will benefit the EU as a whole. Fourthly, no supranational institution can pursue flanking policies that may correct imbalances occurring as a result of the policies pursued by the ECB. Let us clarify this issue a little further.

Compared to mature federations the institutional design of EMU is incomplete. On the one hand there is a strong ECB that decides monetary policies for the entire euro area. Yet, there is no equivalent economic institution that sets economic policies for that same area. Thus, budgetary and fiscal policies are set by the governments of national states. Though countries such as France argued strongly in favour of creating such an 'economic government' (*gouvernement économique*), the choice was made not to go down that route. What are the advantages and disadvantages of having a European 'economic government'? The advantage would be that policies could then be pursued to correct imbalances that result from a strict monetary policy (one that focuses on combating inflation). An example may serve to clarify this point.

Let us imagine a situation in which the ECB is pursuing restrictive monetary policies (that is, interest rates are set fairly high so that the supply of money in the economy is restricted). The result is that the average inflation rate in the whole euro area stays at 2 per cent or below. Let us also assume that there is divergence in growth throughout the euro area. For example, in Ireland the economy is growing at 8 per cent, whereas there is a recession in Germany. Hence a good monetary policy for Ireland might be an even more restrictive monetary policy (higher interest rates), whereas in Germany the economy would benefit from a more relaxed monetary policy (lower interest rates). If the euro area was governed by an economic government, that body would examine what it would need to do to alleviate the negative effects of the monetary policy for parts of the euro area and make or recommend necessary adjustments (for example, it could suggest transfer payments to the regions or sectors that are not benefiting from the set monetary policy).

The disadvantage of an economic government is that such a body would make sense only if a majority of the citizens of the euro area felt comfortable with it. If it did not have that support, then a decision by such a body would be illegitimate. The current situation in Europe is that most citizens feel most comfortable with their national government setting budgetary and fiscal policies. Thus even though there may be good economic and political reasons to flank a monetary institution with an economic government, if there is insufficient support for it the time is not right to create such a body. Maybe in the future it will appear to be necessary, if an EMU *without* an economic government becomes too costly an experiment for particular sectors, regions, or countries.

KEY POINTS

- In some countries a majority of the population is against joining EMU (Denmark, Sweden, the UK).
- There has been criticism of the institutional design of EMU.

Conclusion

Euro banknotes and coins were introduced overnight, but it has taken more than 30 years to create Economic and Monetary Union (EMU). It was a long, slow process that ultimately led to the creation of a single monetary policy, a new European Central Bank (ECB), and rules on budgetary policies and public debts. Behind the fanfare and festivities of the introduction of the new currency lay a lengthy and gradual process of learning about economic and monetary cooperation. Not only was it necessary for countries to have met the convergence criteria, it was also crucial that member states had practised maintaining stable exchange rates stable during the 1970s and 1980s, and that they had agreed on the common goals for EMU.

We have seen that there were economic and political motivations underlying the plan to move to EMU. Though one can make a case for a purely economic rationale for EMU, its ultimate creation cannot be understood without appreciation of the political dimension. EMU is seen as a new step in European integration. It signals the capability of EU member states to take firm action together. It also places the EU more firmly on the international map. Yet, a number of issues remain unresolved. The discussion of an asymmetrical EMU indicated how fragile the balance is between 'economic' and 'monetary' union. It is not unthinkable that in the future further integration might be needed in the area of 'economic union' or indeed that steps will have to be taken towards further political unification, if only to redistribute more evenly the costs and benefits of EMU. At the same time, we have seen that European integration is a gradual process that if pushed ahead too quickly will lack legitimacy.

What will the future of the EU be with EMU in place? The euro is a currency that has been introduced in an area which contains more than 300 million citizens. The continuing presence of the euro may well give the EU a stronger position in world politics, if only because it might offer an alternative to the US dollar. Moreover, the euro contributes to the symbolism of European integration. It offers a concrete token indicating the rapid and far-reaching process of integration taking place in the EU.

As for the regional use of the euro, politicians and citizens can be pleased with the result. The euro is legal tender in the 12 members of the euro area. It is not unthinkable that some of the EU member states still outside the euro area (such as Denmark and Sweden, and, perhaps later, the UK) may want to join in the not so distant future, thereby adding more credibility and, strength to the euro. Furthermore, the member states that joined the EU in 2004 may also join in the years to come, once they have met the convergence criteria. Yet, not all monetary unions in the past have lasted. EMU will survive only if it continues to be supported by the citizens and the national and European politicians. Leaders will have to keep listening to the needs of their citizens. If they are able to do this satisfactorily, the euro may well have a very promising future.

? QUESTIONS

1. Why was the term 'economic' and 'monetary' union used? What, in this regard, is an 'asymmetrical EMU'?
2. What was the argument between the 'Monetarists' and the 'Economists'?
3. Name and describe the various stages of economic integration from a free trade area to full political unification.
4. What are the convergence criteria, and why were they invented?
5. Why is the Stability and Growth Pact difficult to implement?
6. Two political science theories were discussed in this chapter. What are they? Are they opposing or complementary theories?
7. What are the main criticisms of EMU?
8. Discuss how the creation of EMU was both an economic and politically driven process.

GUIDE TO FURTHER READING

■ De Grauwe, P. *The Economics of Monetary Union*, 6th edn (Oxford: Oxford University Press, 2005). An economics textbook on monetary integration that adopts various models and economics tools.

■ Dyson, K., and Featherstone, K. *The Road to Maastricht: Negotiating Economic and Monetary Union* (Oxford: Oxford University Press, 1999). A very influential political science volume which looks at the steps leading to the agreement on EMU at Maastricht, based on hundreds of interviews with key informants.

■ Gros, D., and Thygesen, N. *European Monetary Integration: From the European Monetary System to Economic and Monetary Union*, 2nd edn (Harlow: Longman, 1998). A very good economics textbook on EMU.

■ Hosli, M. O. *The Euro: A Concise Introduction to European Monetary Integration* (Boulder CO: Lynne Rienner, 2005). As the title suggests, a wonderful short introduction to EMU written in language accessible to the non-specialist.

■ Tsoukalis, L. *The Politics and Economics of European Monetary Integration* (London: George Allen & Unwin, 1977). A seminal book on the history of EMU.

■ Verdun, A. *European Responses to Globalization and Financial Market Integration: Perceptions of Economic and Monetary Union in Britain, France and Germany* (Basingstoke: Palgrave-Macmillan, 2000). A volume on EMU, based on original research, examining perceptions of EMU from the perspective of the member states and which considers how actors use EMU to serve their own interests or frustrate those of other members.

■ Verdun, A. (ed.) *The Euro: European Integration Theory and Economic and Monetary Union* (Lanham MD: Rowman & Littlefield, 2002). This book focuses on EMU as part of a wider process of European integration. It examines how various theoretical approaches assist us to understand better the process that led to the introduction of the euro.

IMPORTANT WEBSITES

- http://www.ecb.int The official website of the European Central Bank. The ECB website features exchange rates, speeches by the ECB president, monetary reports, and useful statistics.
- http://www.europa.eu.int/pol/emu/overview_en.htm The website of the European Commission that deals with EMU and the euro. This website offers an introduction in simple language to EMU and the euro.
- http://europa.eu.int/comm/economy_finance/euro/our_currency_en.htm This is the European Commission's website on the euro, Europe's single currency.
- http://europa.eu.int/comm/economy_finance/about/activities/sgp/sgp_en.htm This site offers useful links and information about the Stability and Growth Pact.

Visit the Online Resource Centre that accompanies this book for lots of interesting additional material. http://www.oxfordtextbooks.co.uk/orc/cini2e/

21 The Common Agricultural Policy

EVE FOUILLEUX

Chapter Contents

Reader's Guide

This chapter examines one of the first European policies, the Common Agricultural Policy (CAP). It does so by focusing on the policy's objectives, instruments, actors, and debates. It looks at the way in which the CAP has evolved since the 1960s, and attempts to explain this evolution by asking and answering a number of important questions. Why has the CAP been so problematic for European policy-makers? Why has it proven so resistant to change? Given the constraints identified, how has reform come about? This chapter also looks at some of the challenges facing agricultural policy, as new debates take place among citizens on the social, cultural, and environmental roles performed by agriculture.

Introduction

The Common Agricultural Policy (CAP) has long been of symbolic importance to the European integration process, and has been subject to calls for reform ever since the 1960s. This chapter focuses on this reform process as a way of exploring not only the character of the 'old' CAP, but also the form that this controversial policy might take in the future. It begins with a brief introduction to the principles underpinning the CAP, and then provides an explanation of why it has taken (or is taking) so long to reform this policy. The CAP reform of 1992 is the focus of the second section, after which attention turns to the subsequent reforms of 1999 and 2003. The fourth section presents some of the new thinking in the agricultural policy domain, involving the integration of environmental and social concerns into the policy, rural development, and the introduction of the concept of **multifunctionality**. Throughout the chapter, emphasis is placed on the role of the international context in providing incentives for reform, and on the national context which, more often than not, acts as a constraint.

The early days of the CAP and the issue of CAP reform

This section presents the main principles and instruments of the CAP and an overview of the CAP's brake mechanisms at national and European levels.

The early days of the Common Agricultural Policy

The objectives of the CAP were laid down in the Treaty of Rome in 1957 (Article 39) and subsequently at the Stresa Conference in July 1958, which came into force from 1962. Three general principles underpinned the policy: **market unity**; **Community preference**; and financial solidarity. The initial move in establishing a European agricultural market (applying the market unity principle) was the setting up of **Common Market Organizations** (CMOs) for all agricultural products, and most notably for wheat, barley, rye, corn, rice, sugar, dairy products, bovine meat, pork, lamb, wine, and some fruits and vegetables. The idea was to allow free trade internally within the Community, but also to erect barriers to the outside world, to protect European farmers' revenues. The CMOs usually operated on the basis of three complementary policy tools: a **guaranteed price**, a public intervention system, and some variable levies at the Community's border.

First, the notion of a guaranteed price is crucial to understanding how the CAP operated. The idea was that the specificities of the farming sector (dependence on climatic conditions and vulnerability to natural disasters), and the consequent structural instabilities of agricultural markets, made some public intervention necessary to guarantee decent living conditions for farmers. This is why, instead of allowing the market to determine price levels, the prices farmers received for their produce were institutional prices, that is, they were fixed centrally by Community civil servants and politicians. Such a system had the objective of both supporting farmers' incomes and boosting agricultural production; the more farmers produced, the more money they earned. Indeed, with the food shortages of the post-1945 period and the security concerns of the Cold War in mind, the aim of self-sufficiency in foodstuffs was presented as one of the major objectives of the policy. In practice, the level of guaranteed prices was initially set on the basis of a political compromise between France and Germany. In the early 1960s the Germans had a very inefficient cereal sector, but very politically powerful farmers, and asked for a high level of support for cereals. Though the French were more efficient in this field, and had a lower national price for cereals, they did not mind setting guaranteed prices higher under the CAP, as long as they did not have to pay for them. It is for this reason that Germany has ended up as the primary contributor to the CAP since 1962, while France has always been among the main financial beneficiaries.

Secondly, if the price began to fall due to an excessive internal supply for example (which would have had the effect of depressing farmers' incomes), intervention agencies would step in when the price reached a certain level (the **intervention price**) to buy up the surplus and store it until the market was balanced again, thus keeping prices high. This was clearly an extremely interventionist system.

Thirdly, if the price fixed inside the EC was to be high enough to support farmers' incomes, it was imperative to prevent cheap imports from flooding the common market. Therefore, to achieve the second CAP principle, Community preference, a system of variable levies was set up for each product. Produce could generally enter the common market only if it was priced at or above the internal price; if not, the importer had to pay a tariff equalling the difference to the European budget. Moreover, a system of 'reimbursements' (refunds), similar to export subsidies, was also put in place, enabling European producers to sell their products on the world market at world prices without losing income. These subsidies covered the difference in cost between the world and the higher European prices.

Finally, so as to promote the CAP's third principle, that of financial solidarity, a common fund was set up, to cover the financing of the CAP. This fund is known as the European Agricultural Guidance and Guarantee Fund (EAGGF). EAGGF comprised two parts – guidance and guarantee. While the guarantee section covered costs involved with the market system, such as the costs of intervention and export refunds, the much smaller guidance section was responsible for funding structural policies. The EAGGF originally represented almost all of the general budget of the European Community. However, the proportion of the budget spent on agriculture has decreased substantially since the early 1980s, falling from 65.1 per cent of the total EC budget in 1986 to 53.8 per cent in 2000, and 42.3 percent in 2004. Moreover, despite the principle of financial 'solidarity' among member states, the issue of who gets what, as a consequence of the funding mechanisms at the heart of the CAP, has monopolized many agricultural negotiations in the EU Council, with important consequences for the pace of reform – as we shall see.

Reforming the CAP?

Initially the policy was very successful in that it very quickly met its initial objective of increasing productivity and of achieving European self-sufficiency. But, by the 1970s, overproduction had become a more important political issue, with the first surpluses having appeared in the form of the famous 'butter mountains' and 'wine lakes' of this period. These problems of overproduction, caused when the supply of agricultural produce outstrips demand, increased throughout the 1980s. And with an ever increasing volume of products surplus to internal requirements being paid for at the guaranteed price, being stored at high cost, and finally being exported out of the Community, with support again from the agricultural budget to compensate for lower prices on the world market, the CAP was becoming more and more costly to operate. It is far from surprising, then, that the CAP was frequently denounced during this time for being too expensive and for taking up too many EC resources, thereby preventing the development of other potentially important political priorities. As a consequence, agricultural policy began to be a major concern for European policy-makers, and the issue of CAP reform appeared on the European political agenda.

The policy has proven very resistant to change, however. Some reforms took place from the late 1970s to the end of the 1980s, but these are generally understood to be marginal and incremental. The economic policy tools that were used during this first period of reform were mainly orientated towards controlling the supply of produce, by imposing quantitative restrictions on production (see Box 21.1). These took the form of 'guaranteed ceilings' for crops in 1981, milk quotas in 1984, and a regime imposing maximum guaranteed quantities (MGQ) for cereals in 1987–8, generalized to other commodities in 1988–9. Despite these changes, the principle of guaranteed prices for agricultural products remained the core element of the CAP.

This incrementalism can be explained by institutional factors rooted in the workings of CAP decision-taking. Beyond the formal rules of the process (see Box 21.2), decision-taking in this policy area is based on what might be termed an 'inflationist bargaining dynamic'. As the CAP is a redistributive policy, each member state's minister of agriculture is under pressure to bring home the maximum possible from that part of the European budget dedicated to agriculture. As a consequence of the number of member states involved in the negotiations (all of them trying to increase their CAP budgetary return), the range of products involved, and the rules that govern the CAP (such as unanimity), there is an inbuilt inflationary tendency. A typical example of this is in the annual 'price package' review, where each minister in the Council agrees to price increases in their neighbour's favoured products in order to get the increases that they themselves want. As a consequence, decisions that would lead to a reduction in agricultural costs, or that would change the redistributive effects of the policy, are more than likely to be rejected by the Agricultural Council. This makes it very difficult for a body such as the Commission to propose reforms that cut costs. The CAP is also an excellent example of what happens when there is no real link between the EU institutions and the EU's citizens. In such circumstances it is easy for governments to use the

BOX 21.1

Quotas or price cuts? Two options for CAP reform

From an economic point of view, with the CAP guaranteeing high prices to farmers, there were two ways of dealing with the overproduction of foodstuffs (that is, when the supply of food exceeds demand). The first option was to impose production quotas: this aimed at limiting the supply of food (the amount produced by farmers) by imposing limits on the quantities produced, without touching the guaranteed price. This was the solution chosen by European policy-makers during the 1980s. This can be seen as a compromise, allowing EC policy-makers to cope temporarily with the CAP budget explosion whilst placating, for electoral purposes, their agricultural constituencies by keeping the guaranteed price intact.

However, since the 1970s, most agricultural economists have opposed production quotas because they tend to freeze production capacity, limiting the competitive advantage of individual producers, and constructing entry barriers for the sector. The second option available, which was implemented in CAP reforms after 1992, was to cut institutional prices in order to restore the role of market forces in adjusting supply and demand. As prices fall, farmers have less of an incentive to produce more food. Most economists promote the price decrease solution because it gives regulatory powers back to the market and allows distortions between producing countries and individual farmers to be done away with. From a social perspective, it also allows farmers' revenues to be supported by the state via direct payments, but decouples those payments from the act of production. For economists, direct payments also have the advantage that they can be more precisely targeted at certain categories of farmers or in rewarding specific practices (environmentally friendly, for example). They also allow for more transparency.

EC as a scapegoat for decisions that they really do not want to take. The Commission is restricted in what it can do when this happens, and often ends up taking the blame for a policy it would like to see reformed.

In addition to these European brake mechanisms, the incrementalism of CAP reform can also be explained by national political pressures, which are exported to the EC level through the agriculture ministers of each member state in the Agricultural Council. Due to their ability to mobilize support in many European countries, farmers' organizations are able to exert pressure on governments to support their line on the CAP. Political influence of this kind was particularly intense in France and Germany in the 1970s and 1980s. In both countries, farmers were important in electoral terms, as public opinion, influenced by a deep-rooted affinity for rural life, viewed farmers' interests favourably. In the French case, close links were established from the late 1950s between the government and the main farmers' representative organizations, the FNSEA (Fédération Nationale des Syndicats d'Exploitants Agricoles) and the CNJA (Centre National des Jeunes Agriculteurs). Thanks to their capacity of collective action, these organizations were able to impose their views on both right-wing governments (their traditional allies) and successive Socialist ones after 1981. Although the left-supporting farmers did manage to organize themselves during the 1980s, with the establishment of the Confédération Paysanne in 1987, which had a rather different position, they were still too weak to challenge the power of the right-leaning FNSEA. Consequently, over the course of the 1980s, the French position on the CAP remained very close to that of the FNSEA.

Farmers' opposition to CAP reform is usually explained by simply referring to their will to protect their economic interests. However, there is an additional factor to be taken into account. The conservatism of farmers' associations has much to do with deep-rooted symbolic issues linked to the identity of the farming community. In the French case, for example, the FNSEA has vehemently refused to replace the guaranteed price system with direct payments, even if the latter were calculated to

CASE STUDY 21.2

The formal CAP decision-making process

The main actors in the CAP decision-making process are the European Commission and the Agricultural Council. The Commission is responsible for drafting legislation, as well as having an important managerial role within the policy, while it is the EU Council that takes decisions. The European Parliament (EP), which in many policy areas now shares decision-making responsibility with the Council, has only a very limited role, amounting to consultation, in agricultural policy. The only exception to this rule is where money is concerned, as the Parliament has a critical role in the EU's budgetary decision-making mechanisms.

CAP decision-making usually begins with a proposal from the Commission that may be made either on the basis of a broadly defined request from the European Council (the heads of government), or on a voluntary basis by the Commission. Once formulated, the Commission's proposal is then submitted to the EP for consultation and the Agricultural Council for decision. It is also transmitted to the Committee of Agricultural Organizations in the EC (COPA), the main interest group representing European farmers, and to other institutions as appropriate, such as the Committee of the Regions (representing regional interests) for consultation. The Agricultural Council may reject the Commission's proposal or ask for modifications. Alternatively it may begin to negotiate on the basis of what the Commission has proposed, resulting ultimately in a decision. Within the Agricultural Council, the unanimity rule has applied until very recently (on an informal basis, as a consequence of the 'empty chair crisis' in the late 1960s (see Chapter 2) because the formal rule is in fact qualified majority voting). This has meant that each member has had the right to veto any decision. Decision rules such as this have had important consequences for the CAP, especially regarding the pace of reform. The Agricultural Council meets monthly, more frequently than most of the EU Councils. One of these meetings was usually set aside to discuss what was called the 'price package' for the following year, at which the member states decided on such issues as the level of guaranteed prices for each product and the amount of quota by country.

provide a higher income for farmers than the former. Such a position can be explained by certain ethical and professional values that have been inherited by CNJA and FNSEA leaders, arising out of their early experiences in the 1950s with the Young Christian Movement, the JAC (Jeunesse Agricole Chrétienne). Farmers were considered to be individual entrepreneurs, actively working the land and selling the products they had grown in order to earn their living. It is for this reason that they could not tolerate the idea of living and supporting their families on the back of direct income payments, which were viewed either as salaries or, even worse, as a form of social security/welfare payment.

But a second explanation relates directly to the nature of the CAP itself. In upholding the idea that all farmers should get the same rewards, guaranteed prices symbolically feed the myth of farmer unity. This is something of a paradox, as in practice such tools provide very different levels of support across the EU, across farmers, and across products. For example, the bigger you are as a farmer, the more financial support you get. In fact, guaranteed prices have always been used as a political tool by farming elites and, as such, can even be viewed as fundamental to the FNSEA's monopoly in representing French farmers. Thus, by mobilizing support to defend and promote the level of agricultural prices, particularly when the 'price package' event was taking place in Brussels, they were able to consolidate their own dominant position within the farming community.

KEY POINTS

- The CAP was based on three fundamental principles: market unity; Community preference; and financial solidarity.
- The original CAP comprised the institutional guaranteed price, a system of variable levies at borders, and public intervention (storage).
- The CAP began to pose problems in the 1970s: agricultural surpluses soon began to accumulate, and the cost of the CAP increased dramatically, but an inflationary bias in decision-making prevented reform.

A dramatic shift in 1992

Despite these brake mechanisms, a first radical reform took place in 1992, which cast aside the original rationale for the CAP. To examine this 'U-turn', we must consider international factors beyond the EU.

Increasing external pressures on the CAP in the 1980s

World agricultural markets in the early 1980s were affected by massive instabilities. In 1982, member countries invited the OECD Secretariat-General to undertake a review of agricultural policies to analyse their effects on international trade, so as to seek recommendations which would lead to balanced reductions in agricultural protection, to better integrate agriculture into the multilateral trading system – in other words to liberalize agriculture.

The officials in charge asked a number of academics, mainly agricultural economists, for advice. These economists provided them with both theoretical and technical tools to construct an economic model which enabled estimates to be made of the impact of domestic policies on world prices and trade. These studies were initially used to classify the distorting effects of national policies, and later to rank policies, demonstrating which of them was in most serious need of reform. This process engendered a learning process within the international agricultural policy community, and induced a profound change in the way agricultural policy issues were defined. Most notably, it was concluded that to be less distorting, instruments used within an agricultural policy had to be 'decoupled' from agricultural production, so that they would have no direct impact on the type and quantity of commodity produced by the farmer. This conclusion spoke directly to the CAP's price support system(see Box 21.1).

The process transformed the ideas and beliefs dominating the agricultural policy community towards more 'liberal' approaches, and led to concrete decisions – ultimately to the end of the so-called 'agricultural exception' in international trade negotiations. In 1986, the GATT (the General Agreement on Tariffs and Trade) 'Uruguay Round' opened. For the first time the negotiations included agriculture. As is often the case in GATT Rounds, the main players were the USA and its allies, the Cairns Group, a group of 14 net exporters of agricultural produce, notably Argentina, Australia, New Zealand, Uruguay, and Thailand. This group was on the offensive from the start, arguing strongly for a radical liberalization of international agricultural markets. The USA denounced the CAP as a system which allowed European farmers to eschew competition with the rest of the world, thereby generating trade distortions for producers in third (or non-EU) countries. They called for an end to all trade-distorting domestic subsidies and tariff barriers on agricultural products. The EU, with traditionally more protectionist countries like Norway and Japan, found themselves on the defensive.

At the Heysel Ministerial Conference in December 1990, US and EU positions were still at odds, leading to a stalemate in the negotiations, and threatening the entire process. To put additional pressure on the Europeans, the USA and its allies took the decision not to negotiate on any other aspect of the Round until the agricultural issue was resolved.

A radical shift in policy: the MacSharry reform

The 1990 GATT crisis provided an opportunity for European reformers, who saw a radical CAP reform as the only solution. At this point the Commission, led on this issue by the Irish Agricultural Commissioner, Ray MacSharry, decided to launch a project that it had been preparing secretly for some months. Using its right of initiative, the Commission delivered its radical CAP reform proposal to the Agricultural Council in February 1991. The spirit of the reform was in line with international requirements, in that it would partly replace the system of agricultural price support with a system of direct support to farmers. In broad terms, the proposal revolved around a dramatic decrease in guaranteed prices for oilseeds, cereals, and beef. As this implied a serious loss of income for the farmers, the price cuts were to be compensated by individual direct payments. In addition, the Commission proposed a sliding scale of compensation for price decreases, for both equity and budgetary reasons. The biggest producers, it was felt, were strong enough to deal with competition in world markets and were therefore not compensated at all for the reduction in the level of prices. Small producers, on the other hand, who would not be able to cope with market pressures without public support, were to be fully compensated, in part on social grounds. Medium-sized farms would be only partially compensated.

The political decision to implement such a radical shift in policy instruments, agreed by the Council in May 1992, was taken initially by Helmut Kohl and François Mitterrand, the then leaders of Germany and France. Both were very keen to conclude the Uruguay Round. Germany had important interests in the non-agricultural part of the negotiations, and the German industrial policy community put intense pressure on the German government to resolve the impasse. In France, the pressures came from the biggest cereal growers, who had a direct interest in the reform. Thanks to the agreed price decreases, they would be able to gain the upper hand in the European animal food market over US cereal substitutes, which had been sold in the EC at world prices (that is, with a zero border tariff) since 1967. Their pressure was kept secret however, given the fact that the cereal growers were officially part of the FNSEA, which was vehemently opposed to any price decrease for the reasons mentioned before. Another important lobby was the aeronautical industry, so the outcome of what came to be known as the Blair House Agreement, concluding the Uruguay Round in 1993, was really as much about 'Airbus' as about agriculture.

However, although the political decision to reform the CAP was taken by the heads of government or state, negotiations on precisely how the reform would be implemented took place in the Agricultural Council over a period of 18 months. As a result of the sectoral brake mechanisms described before, the Commission's original proposal was largely rewritten. The price levels for crops (cereals and oilseeds) were reduced by 30 per cent and there was a 15 per cent decrease in the price for beef. But the sliding scale of compensatory direct payments that had been proposed by the Commission was rejected by the Council, largely due to UK and French opposition, driven by large arable farmers. Direct payments to farmers were finally calculated on the basis of the area of land cultivated and according to historical estimates of yields on the farm and/or in the region over a reference period (an average of the past three years). That meant that the redistributive effect of the policy among farmers remained exactly as it was in the old CAP. Other so-called 'flanking measures' were also adopted in the reform package proposal, though these remained very marginal from a budgetary point of view. They dealt mainly with agri-environmental issues, early retirement, and forestry.

In sum, the outcome of the 1992 reform was not quite as innovative as it might have been, but the deal that was finally concluded on 21 May 1992 was still regarded in many quarters as historic (see *Financial Times*, 22 May 1992: 1–3).

KEY POINTS

- An agricultural learning process, at the international level, led to a profound shift in knowledge, beliefs, and ideas about agricultural policy.
- The inclusion of agriculture in the Uruguay Round of the GATT in 1986 placed an important political constraint on European governments which led to the reform of the CAP.
- The European Commission used this opportunity to advance its own proposals and the CAP was subject to a radical shift in 1992, with a reform based on a decrease of the guaranteed price levels replaced by direct individual payments to farmers (decoupling).

An ongoing reform process

The MacSharry reform marked the point of departure of a deeper CAP reform process after 1999. In many respects this reform was similar to the earlier one; included further international pressure to 'decouple' agricultural support; interrelated international trade bargains and interests; freeriding strategies by big farmers organizations; and brake mechanisms in the Agricultural Council which slowed down the pace of reform.

Agenda 2000 and the 1999 Berlin compromise

A further CAP reform was agreed in March 1999 at the Berlin European Council, and was incorporated into the Commission's *Agenda 2000* plans (see Box 21.3). On the basis of this document, 10 new regulations were adopted, which were expected to come into force from 2000. The Berlin Agreement continued the reform initiated in 1992 for various products, with price reductions in the form of progressive decreases for cereals and dairy products (15 per cent by 2006), and beef (20 per cent), partially compensated for by direct income payments to the farmers affected. As a response to calls for the decentralization of the policy, some of these direct payments took the form of 'national envelopes' (de facto national allocations), paid to the member states from the EC budget, and which each state could distribute to its farmers to target specific national and/or regional priorities.

CASE STUDY 21.3

Eastern enlargement and the CAP

A first crucial issue regarding EU enlargement and agriculture was the extent to which the CAP would be applied to the 10 member states who joined in 2004, and whether CAP instruments would have to be adapted. This raised the question of the economic consequences that applying CAP to the new members would have on the general structure of farming. Moreover, the question of how the CAP would be financed in future was also of major concern.

The European Commission presented its strategy for dealing with these questions at the beginning of 2002. Its proposal involved offering direct payments to farmers and introducing production quotas for new member countries after they joined. To ease transitional problems in rural areas, and to encourage the restructuring of agricultural sectors, the Commission also proposed complementing its financial support with an enhanced rural development policy. Given that the immediate introduction of 100 per cent direct payments would have frozen existing structures and hampered modernization (and bankrupted the EU), the Commission favoured a gradual introduction over a transition period of 10 years, covering 25 per cent in 2004, 30 per cent in 2005, and 35 per cent in 2006, ultimately reaching 100 per cent in 2013.

For existing member states, the northern Europeans had argued that the proposal was too costly, and that there should be no direct aid to the Central and East Europeans in the first few years after accession. The Dutch government pointed out that no direct aid for new members was assumed in the *Agenda 2000* agreement of 1997. The Swedes argued that direct aid for the new member states would actually discourage much needed agricultural restructuring. Germany was more concerned about predictions that its net contribution to the agricultural budget would grow after enlargement and, as a result, that its budgetary return would decrease. France, always concerned to keep its own budgetary returns on CAP as high as possible, expressed concern about the cost of the Commission's strategy, but firmly opposed the suggestion by some members that a more profound reform of the CAP needed to take place before enlargement.

For their part, most of the candidate countries reacted by saying that the Commission's proposal did not offer them enough, and that they needed 100 per cent of direct aid paid from the beginning, not just for sectoral, but also for political reasons, in order to convince their publics to agree to EU membership in the first place.

At the Brussels Summit on 25 October 2002, the EU heads of government finally adopted the main lines of the Commission's proposal on CAP and enlargement. In order to address some national concerns (those of Germany in particular), they placed their decision in a framework of financial stability from 2007 to 2013. More specifically, this meant that total annual expenditure on CAP direct payments and market-related expenditure for a Union of 25 members would not exceed the corresponding combined ceilings for 2006.

The 1999 reform was remarkable in that it placed a renewed emphasis on the environment and on sustainability. Three possible avenues were proposed to the member states in this regard: (i) direct payments explicitly dedicated to agri-environmental issues (the old 'agri-environment measures' of the MacSharry reform); (ii) direct payments conditional upon the observance of generally applicable environmental requirements; or (iii) direct payment attached to specific environmental conditions. However, this was to be implemented on a voluntary basis by member states, with maximum levels on direct aid by farmer permitted. National difficulties and conservative pressures prevented widespread implementation of these optional measures by the member states. As a consequence, no real radical change took place regarding the redistributive effects of the policy. Although rural development was newly presented as the 'second pillar' of the CAP (nothing to do with the three pillars of the EU), intended to enhance the **multifunctionality** of European agriculture (see Box 21.4), only 10.5 per cent of total CAP expenditure was allocated to it, as against 89.5 per cent for the market measures of the first pillar.

With the concept of multifunctionality, European policy-makers were not only seeking for new ways to legitimize the CAP within the EU, however. They also had the forthcoming WTO round in mind. When the Uruguay Round was

CASE STUDY 21.4

The multifunctionality of agriculture

The concept of 'multifunctionality' signals that agriculture is not just about production, it also incorporates 'non-production' aspects of farming: the social, cultural, territorial, and environmental dimensions. It was initially introduced by the EU as a defensive argument to respond to international pressure and prevent the CAP from being dismantled under WTO rules. Other countries with protectionist traditions in the agricultural field, like Japan and Norway, traditional allies of the EU in international trade negotiations, soon joined the EU in claiming the merits of multifunctionality. For countries with a more liberal approach to agriculture, however, the concept was little more than a rhetorical device used to justify domestic production support and export subsidies. With multifunctionality potentially being used as a basis for distinguishing between permitted and prohibited types of agricultural support, the stakes became high over finding a common definition of the concept at the international level.

In this context, new studies were launched by the OECD states in March 1998. Since that time the OECD Secretariat-General has worked on a common definition of multifunctionality, notably through the building of an economic framework to evaluate 'jointness in production', that is, the extent to which commodity (food and fibre) and non-commodity (landscape, environment, rural development, or food security) outputs are linked. This research attempted to 'fill a void' in the debate and to 'help governments to develop efficient and effective policies to internalise the external effects of agriculture and reduce the risk of conflict between domestic policies in pursuit of multi-functionality and further agricultural trade liberalisation' (Cahill 2001). As was the case a decade earlier with the agriculture and trade issue, OECD thinking has fostered a new international learning process in the agricultural policy field. Multifunctionality is now widely accepted as a characteristic of agriculture. However, the degree to which policies enhance production or non-production goals is still a point of strong controversy, notably dealt with through political bargaining in the WTO arena.

concluded in 1994, the Agreement on Agriculture (AoA) defined three 'boxes' used to distinguish between support policy programmes that directly stimulate production and consequently distort trade, and those that were considered to have no direct effect on production and trade. Domestic measures with a direct effect on production were placed in the amber box; they had to be cut. Measures considered to be 'decoupled from production', with no linkage between the amount of payment and the production process, agricultural prices, or factors of production, were placed in the green box and could be freely used. Payments linked to programmes aiming at limiting production went in the blue box and did not need to be reduced as long as certain conditions were met. In the AoA, the post-1992 CAP compensatory payments were classified in the blue box, which meant that the Europeans were exempt from any commitment to reduce these subsidies. And in view of the forthcoming international trade negotiations, the strategy decided by the Agricultural Council in October 1999 involved 'securing' CAP payments in the blue box, by arguing that the CAP could not be challenged because it pursued multifunctionality, meaning non-production as well as production goals (see Box 21.4).

The 'Mid-term Review' of June 2003

However, in the 2001 World Trade Organization (WTO) Round (see Box 21.5), the fate of the blue box became uncertain, and the Council's position appeared more and more unsustainable. In this context, the European Commission issued a new CAP reform plan in July 2002 that proposed a substantial reshaping of the policy by furthering reform for crops and meat and extending it to new commodities like milk products (European Commission 2002c). The official argument was that public expenditure for the farm sector had to be better justified, and that as well as supporting farm incomes, it had to do more to ensure high-quality food and animal welfare, preservation of the environment, landscapes, and cultural heritage, and social welfare and equity. But the real reason was that the EU could secure CAP payments to European farmers in the WTO negotiations only by further 'decoupling' them from production, thereby transferring them to the green box.

While initially supported by the UK, Germany, and other 'northern' governments, the proposal faced very strong French opposition. The French government refused to reduce its support for its larger cereal growers and wanted reform postponed until 2006. After 11 months, the Agricultural Council reached a final compromise in June 2003. The 2003 'Mid-term Review' (MTR) of the CAP (so called because it was foreseen in the 1999 Berlin Agreement as a simple reviewing exercise) is considered as a second revolution (after the 1992 reform) by some commentators.

The June 2003 reform continues that of 1992 and 1999, with a further decrease in the intervention price of cereals and similar measures for durum wheat, rice, dried fodder, protein crops, and nuts. But a new element was to be introduced through the Single Farm Payment (SFP), a unique CAP direct payment aimed at achieving a complete decoupling between support and production. Even a farmer who decides to grow nothing is eligible to receive it, as long as he complies with environmental, food safety, animal welfare, and occupational safety standards. In addition, 3 per cent of direct payments (market policy or 'first pillar') were to be shifted each year towards EU rural development measures

CASE STUDY 21.5

The Doha Round and the CAP

In 1995, the GATT became the World Trade Organization (WTO). After a first failed attempt in Seattle in November 1999, a new round of negotiations, the 'Doha Development Round', was finally launched in November 2001. The negotiations were initially to be concluded by December 2005, but as of early 2006 they are still under way.

The Doha Round agricultural negotiations comprise three elements: market access (aiming at reduction of tariff and non-tariff barriers); export competition (reducing export subsidies); and domestic agricultural support (reducing trade distorting – coupled – domestic measures). The EU's position, as proposed by Trade Commissioner Peter Mandelson in October 2005, included:

1. Regarding domestic support, important cuts (of 65 to 70 per cent) in distorting measures (amber box) and some possible further cuts (blue box). The latter was made possible by the transfer of most agricultural spending into the green box at the time of the 2003 reform.

2. Regarding market access, four tariff bands with higher cuts for higher tariffs, and a maximum tariff for developing countries.

3. Regarding export competition, a reiterated offer to end all exports subsidies (under the condition of reciprocity by other players, the USA in particular).

The Trade Commissioner seems to be prepared to be flexible in the agriculture negotiations in order to get market access for European transnational companies in services and industrial products. Mandelson has made it quite clear to the services and manufacturing industries that his priority in this round is to fight for substantial market access for both sectors. The aggressive proposals by the EC in both areas, services and non-agricultural market access, seem to reflect this priority. This approach has generated tensions between the Commission and some EU member states (in particular with France), however. Thirteen EU members wrote a 'Memorandum concerning WTO agricultural negotiations' (7 October 2005) to the Agricultural Commissioner Mariann Fischer Boel to 'express their deep concern regarding the state of the negotiations in agriculture' and underline 'obvious imbalances in these negotiations'. This case illustrates once again the difficult position of the European Commission where it must negotiate without departing too much from the mandate provided by the member states in the Council (see also Chapter 14).

('second pillar'). Such a decision (called **modulation** in the CAP jargon) was intended to improve the balance between the two CAP pillars.

Implementation of the reform was to begin in the member states in 2006. Schematically, the SFP is to be calculated on a historical basis (based on the total payments received for all products in previous years). However, in almost all the member states individual SFPs are calculated on a regional basis, to redress the imbalances between big and small farmers – other than in France and the UK, where the payment is made on an individual basis after pressure from large-scale cereal growers and landowners.

Further reforms have been decided on the same model since the MTR, for Mediterranean products (olive oil, cotton, tobacco) in 2003 and 2004, and for sugar in December 2005.

KEY POINTS

- A further CAP reform was agreed in December 1999, in light of forthcoming enlargements. The 1999 reform introduced the concept of multifunctionality.
- The policy was further reformed in June 2003 to avoid a clash with the WTO.
- The introduction of the Single Farm Payment (SFP), completely decoupled from production in the 2003 reform, can be seen as a second 'revolution' in the policy.

New challenges and debates for the CAP

While new ideas often run ahead of policies, sometimes new policies induce new debates. The CAP provides a good example of how reform can feed back into discussions about the very purpose of the policy. The shift from an opaque set of instruments (guaranteed price mechanism) to a more transparent system of direct payment led to further debates about the CAP and desirable models of agriculture.

The emergence of the environmental issue

The environment and, more broadly, issues of sustainable development, have progressively found their way into the agricultural policy debate since the 1980s. The negative effects of modern farming were initially denounced by environmental groups. Problems identified included soil erosion in areas of intensive crop production, pollution by pesticides, water pollution caused by nitrate fertilizers in areas of intensive livestock production, and homogenization of the rural landscape. During the same period, public health problems linked to intensive farming were also multiplying, as dioxins in poultry, 'mad cow' disease (BSE), and genetically modified organisms (GMOs) hit the headlines. But initially, due to the opacity of the guaranteed price mechanism, the link between environmental concerns in rural areas and the CAP (which provided incentives to farmers to intensify farming practices, exacerbating environmental degradation) was not easy to explain to the public. With CAP support becoming more transparent in 1992, 1999, and 2003, the situation became clearer and environmentalists could enter the agricultural policy debate more directly. They called for the establishment of a direct link between the amount of support provided to farmers through the CAP and their environmental performance, or at least their compliance with a minimum set of environmental requirements.

While remaining very marginal in the CAP budget, the new environmental measures did seem to be having an impact on behaviour on the ground. By importing new values and beliefs, and new ways of doing things into the agricultural policy community, they pushed traditional communities a little further in the direction of environmental consciousness. They also contributed to a better recognition of farmers who had been involved in environmentally friendly modes of farming for years without any public support, and who were most often rejected by the broader farming community, like organic farmers (see Box 21.6). This process has not been an easy one, and is often resisted by both farmers and farmers' unions.

CASE STUDY 21.6

Alternative ways of farming

Without public support and in opposition to 'conventional' models of agriculture, 'alternative' farmers have been proving that it is possible to farm differently. Organic farming is the best known example, but there are others. These farmers have proved that farming can be friendlier to the environment, and that it need not contribute to intensification, pollution, and the destruction of soil and landscape, and that it can also offer better working conditions and quality of life for the farmer, providing a similar or even better income. Whereas this sort of farming used to be denounced as old-fashioned and out of line with modernity and technical progress, thanks to an opening of the agricultural debate to incorporate environmental and sustainability issues, alternative farming is gaining much more attention at both national and EU levels. These farmers are also more active politically. For example, in April 2002 the International Federation of Organic Agricultural Movements published a position paper on CAP reform entitled 'A Sustainable Agriculture Policy for Europe' (available at www.ifoam.org). As a consequence, some steps have been taken to move beyond rhetorical support for alternative modes of farming. For example, in 1991 the Agricultural Council voted to harmonize production norms for organic vegetal products. This has been operational since 1993. Alternative farming is also considered under the CAP's agri-environmental measures, with member states now authorized to support alternative models of agriculture under the EU's co-financing procedures. However, it seems that - policy-makers do not yet consider these models as real alternatives to the 'modernist agriculture' model, based on principles of intensification and productivity.

Social concerns: old stakes and new items in the agricultural policy debate

Another dimension to reform since the mid-1990s relates to social justice and equity. As already mentioned, the old guaranteed price system was deeply inequitable, with the highest level of support provided to the biggest farmers (for example, the 'classical' argument of 80 per cent of CAP support going to 20 per cent of farmers). But due to its opacity, the system did not allow a real debate to take place in the farming community. Under the reformed CAP, the inequities remain (the calculation of compensatory direct payments is based on historic criteria) but became visible. Farmers could see that most of the agricultural support granted in the EU is given to the biggest and often the wealthiest farmers. In some member states, the amounts and the end beneficiaries have been publicized: it came as a surprise when they discovered that huge CAP payments were allocated to the late British Queen Mother or Prince Rainier of Monaco! In France (as in the UK), data on individual payments are secret, but a list of the main beneficiaries of the CAP was recently published (see *La Tribune*, 3 November 2005: 2–3), revealing for instance that the first on the list is a farmer in the south of France who in 2004 was allocated more than €850,000 to produce rice; and the second almost the same for 1,500 hectares of irrigated maize in the south-west of France (one of the less environmental friendly crops in this area). Other studies show that huge disparities also exist among European regions (Shucksmith *et al.* 2005).

In sum, with the distribution of CAP support suddenly becoming more visible, the question of social justice has been raised both from an inter-individual and from an inter-regional point of view. This shift in the debate not only allowed left-wing farmers' unions to gain additional support, it also created tension between producers (for example intensive crop growers versus extensive cattle raisers) and regions and, to some extent, a shift in the balance of power within traditional farmers' unions. Similar tensions have also appeared within COPA, which represents European farmers in Brussels. To deal with these 'new' issues, it seems that European policy-makers have finally decided to reinforce rural development aspects of the CAP (see Box 21.7).

KEY POINTS

- CAP reforms have had a deep impact on the shape of the agricultural policy community in the EU.
- New actors, and with them new issues, such as the environment, social redistribution, and rural development, entered the agricultural policy debate.
- However change is still resisted by some member states in the Council, who continue to support large payments to big farmers.

CASE STUDY 21.7

The long road towards rural development

Since the beginning of the CAP, the European Commission has tried to introduce a socio-economic dimension into the policy. The very first attempt of this kind was made by the Dutch Agricultural Commissioner, Sicco Mansholt, in the late 1960s, who proposed a radical revision of the CAP's market measures, together with an active structural agricultural policy at European level, intending to help restructure the sector. Strongly rejected by the Council, the proposal gave birth to a timid structural policy in 1972, providing funds for such things as new technologies and equipment and financed by the so-called 'Guidance' section of the Agricultural Fund through fixed, multi-annual budgetary 'envelopes' co-financed by member states. Despite an increase in allocations since the mid-1980s, EU structural farm policy has always represented an extremely small part of the European agricultural budget if compared to market (production-) related expenditures.

Since the beginning of the 1990s, the European Commission has made various attempts to promote rural development as a parallel approach to agricultural policy. Its Directorate-General for 'Agriculture' was renamed 'Agriculture and Rural Development', and its publications promoting a 'sustainable rural development' strategy multiplied. A first important event organized in line with this perspective was the European Conference on Rural Development (Cork, Ireland, 7–9 November 1996), initially planned as a way of building an ambitious 'integrated' approach to the countryside. The Cork Declaration invited European policy-makers to switch their public support from financing market measures to assisting rural development and agri-environmental programmes. The member states remained reluctant to adopt such an approach however.

Some progress was made in pursuing this agenda in 1999, with structural measures converted into the 'second pillar' together with agro-environmental measures, but this new 'pillar' remained very marginal from a budgetary point of view. Some commentators then expected the Eastern enlargement to provide an opportunity to reinforce rural development measures in the CAP, but this did not really occur (see Box 21.3). In sum, the 'modulation' measure decided in 2003, which will transfer 3 per cent of the first pillar to the second annually, is certainly the most concrete measure ever taken in this direction, and may progressively lead to a stronger rural development and agri-environment policy in the EU.

Conclusion: the CAP at a crossroads

Originally intended to make Western Europe self-sufficient in food, the CAP was equipped with 'productivist' instruments that led to an overproduction of agricultural produce and serious budgetary problems for the EC. In the 1980s, the first reforms introduced supply control measures, such as quotas. At the beginning of the 1990s, due to international developments, new policy beliefs inspired the 'decoupling' of farm support from production. This provoked a radical reform of the CAP in 1992, which shifted policy instruments from market or price support to direct income support. This decreased centrally planned prices, compensating for these cuts through direct payments to farmers. This new path has continued in subsequent CAP reforms, with further decoupling for an increasing number of products, and attention paid to the environmental and social dimension of the CAP. These concerns are reflected in the concept of multifunctionality, which is presented as the core element of a 'European model of agriculture'.

The evolution of the CAP since the 1980s is an excellent illustration of the complexity of the links that exist between national, European, and international political arenas. Intersectoral deals that are not easily understood at national level become even more complicated when various governments, coalitions of interests, and European and international institutions enter the game. Caught in the crossfire between national interest and international bargains, the EU's political system is a complex, intricate, and competitive system. It is possible to deconstruct this complexity only by examining the actors involved in the policy process and the nature of the political exchanges that take place amongst them.

? QUESTIONS

1. Why did the CAP originally seek to maintain high prices for agricultural produce?
2. What were the negative consequences of the CAP's price support mechanism?
3. How did European policy-makers try to deal with the problems of overproduction and increasing budgetary costs in the 1980s?
4. Why did the 1992 reform happen?
5. What have the 1992, 1999, and 2003 CAP reforms in common?
6. To what extent does the current round of international trade negotiations pose a threat to the CAP?
7. What is multifunctionality? What implications does it have for agricultural policy?
8. Why did new issues enter the agricultural policy debate from the late 1990s on?

GUIDE TO FURTHER READING

- **Jones, A., and Clark, J.** ***The Modalities of European Union Governance: New Institutionalist Explanations of Agri-environmental Policy*** **(Oxford: Oxford University Press, 2001).** An excellent study of the relationship between agricultural and environmental policy in the EU, exploring in the process many of the intricacies of the CAP.

■ **Moyer, W., and Josling, T.** ***Agricultural Policy Reform: Politics and Process in the EU and US in the 1990s*** **(London: Ashgate, 2002).** This book provides a detailed, accurate, and well-informed presentation of agricultural policy reforms in the 1990s in the USA, EU, and the GATT/WTO. The comparative approach used makes it a unique enterprise in the recent literature on agricultural policies, following an earlier similar book by the same authors covering the 1980s.

■ **Shucksmith, M., Thomson, K., and Roberts, D. (eds)** ***CAP and the Regions: The Territorial Impact of the Common Agricultural Policy*** **(Wallingford: CABI Publishing, 2005).** Through detailed statistical analysis and case studies, this book assesses the regional impact of the EU's CAP and rural development policy, and asks how far these policies are compatible with more general objectives of territorial cohesion across the enlarged EU.

IMPORTANT WEBSITES

● **http://www.defra.gov.uk** The official homepage of the UK's Department for the Environment, Food and Rural Affairs (incorporating what was formerly the Ministry of Agriculture, Fisheries and Food).

● **http://europa.eu.int/comm/commission_barroso/fischer-boel/index_en.htm** Mariann Fischer Boel's web page, with lots of information on ongoing works on CAP reforms.

● **http://europa.eu.int/comm/agriculture/index_en.htm** The homepage of the European Commission's Directorate-General for Agriculture.

● **http://commonagpolicy.blogspot.com/** Professor Wyn Grant's blog on the CAP, with lots of useful information on the CAP, very frequently updated.

● **http://www.farmsubsidy.org** An interesting website managed by a group of journalists and researchers gathering both general information and detailed figures on CAP subsidies.

Visit the Online Resource Centre that accompanies this book for lots of interesting additional material. http://www.oxfordtextbooks.co.uk/orc/cini2e/

PART FIVE

Issues and Debates

22 Democracy and the European Polity

DIMITRIS N. CHRYSSOCHOOU

Chapter Contents

Reader's Guide

This chapter examines the notion of a **democratic deficit** in the European Union (EU) and explores its various meanings. It differentiates between divergent proposals for rectifying the deficit by distinguishing between its institutional and socio-psychological perspectives. While the former focuses attention on power-sharing both at the EU level and nationally, the latter addresses the absence of a European **demos** (a European civic body). Although these perspectives imply different strategies for democratic reform, there is no consensus over the future of the EU polity. The chapter emphasizes this point by identifying five models of democracy – the parliamentary, **consociational**, **federal**, **confederal**, and republican – and asks which of these models best reflects the existing characteristics of the EU, and which is likely to be the most appropriate model for the future. Finally, it considers whether recent treaty reforms have begun to address the democratic deficit.

Introduction

What is the democratic deficit? In general, it points to a negative side effect of European integration – the growing dissonance between the requirements of democratic rule and the actual conditions upon which the management of EU affairs is largely based. To be more specific than that is to pre-empt the discussion below which stresses the contested nature of the democratic deficit (see Box 22.1). Not only does the debate revolve around how to resolve the deficit in question, but it also concerns its nature.

The chapter begins by explaining what the democratic deficit is. The first section distinguishes between institutional and socio-psychological perspectives. Whereas the former focus attention on power-sharing and on institutional reform as a solution to the perceived problems of EU democracy, the latter are concerned with questions of European identity and demos formation. As the debate raises fundamental questions about the future form of the EU, the chapter goes on to consider five models of democratic governance each of which is judged not only in light of what it can tell us about today's EU, but also as a possible future for the European polity. Moreover, the chapter examines recent reforms and considers whether these have helped to democratize the EU. It concludes that the Amsterdam and Nice Treaties have failed to enhance the democratic properties of the EU in any fundamental way, and that the EU still remains closer to a *system* of democracies.

KEY CONCEPTS AND TERMS 22.1

Definitions of the democratic deficit

The idea behind the notion of a 'democratic deficit' is that decisions in the EU are in some ways insufficiently representative of, or accountable to, the nations and people of Europe (Lord 2001: 165).

It has become a received wisdom that the EU suffers from a 'democratic deficit'. It suffers from deficiencies in representation, representativeness, accountability and support. The problem is not merely that of the establishment of an additional layer of governance, further removed from the peoples of Europe. It is also that this process contributes to the transformation of the Member States, so that each Member State can no longer claim to be the source of its own legitimacy (Eriksen and Fossum 2000: 401).

The limited ability of Europeans to influence the work of the major EU institutions is a problem that has become so entrenched as to merit its own label: the democratic deficit (McCormick 1999: 147).

The democratic deficit is

the combination of two phenomena: (a) the transfer of powers from the Member States to the European Community; and (b) the exercise of those powers at the Community level by institutions other than the European Parliament, even though, before the transfer, the national parliaments held power to pass laws in the areas concerned (European Parliament 1988: 10–11, quoted J. Smith 1999: 13).

Understanding the 'democratic deficit'

When the integration process began in the late 1950s no one gave much thought to its democratic credentials. For decades since, the European Community (EC) rested on a 'permissive consensus', the tacit agreement of the member state citizens. The legitimacy of the EC came from elsewhere, that is, the peace and prosperity that integration would bring to Western Europe, rather than from its aspirations to become a democracy (Newman 2001: 358). But since the early 1990s and the ratification crisis of the Maastricht Treaty, such a consensus is said to have broken down. In its place have arisen new discourses which offer conflicting solutions to the problem of democratizing the EU.

KEY CONCEPTS AND TERMS 22.2

What is democracy?

Democracy is a method of organizing public life that allows the concerns and interests of citizens to be articulated within government. Democracy's defining properties are its institutional controls, the peaceful resolution of conflicts in society, meaningful legislative representation, as well as civic inclusion and political participation. Important in understanding democracy is the concept of the **demos**, which is more than simply the people, as it also represents the idea of a political community of shared values and identities. One possible model of democracy involves the demos participating in the making of decisions that affect its members (Arblaster 1987: 105). Democracy may be defined as an institutional arrangement for arriving at publicly binding decisions, with the legitimacy of those decisions resting on competitive elections. This suggests that the institutions of democracy are ends in themselves. But democracy may be viewed as a means of realizing the common good through the electoral process. Here, institutions are merely means to much deeper ends. Democracy may also be defined in terms of active civic involvement in the affairs of the polity (democracy in input) or by focusing more on policy outcomes (democracy in output) (Scharpf 1999). Whatever the definition, democracy comprises a mixture of an ideal and a procedural arrangement. As such, it involves principles, norms, and values that are shared amongst citizens, and which provide the institutional means through which ideals are embodied in political institutions and through which the demos engages actively to arrive at publicly binding decisions, whilst holding government to account for its actions or lack of action.

In a period when transnational pressures are challenging both intra- and inter-state relations, it may no longer be enough to confine democracy within the territorial boundaries of the nation state in order to deal with the implications of new forms of polity and governance.

This understanding raises new questions such as how it might be possible to hold EU decision-makers to account to citizens who belong to different political systems. Questions of this kind reflect democratic concerns that have grown as the EU has evolved away from being merely a diplomatic forum for interstate bargaining and towards a fully fledged political system. This has led to scholarly interest in the idea that the EU might one day transform itself into a democratic **polity**. While there is some measure of agreement that the EU system is not democratic, there is no consensus on how the EU might become so. Indeed, there are two quite different understandings of what the democratic deficit is.

The first focuses on its institutional characteristics, arguing that the problem of EU democracy is tied to the flawed interinstitutional relationships that characterize the EU. Here, proposals for reform speak of the EU's 'institutional imbalance', and of the need to enhance the accountability and representative nature of EU policy-makers. The second understanding of the democratic deficit focuses on socio-psychological factors, arguing that it occurs because of the absence of a European demos. As a consequence, this second perspective is more interested in European civic identity and the extent to which there is a feeling of community amongst Europeans. Acknowledging that the absence of a demos is a barrier to a democratic EU, proposals for reform tend to suggest paths to EU demos formation. The subsections that follow look in more detail at these two perspectives.

The democratic deficit: an institutional perspective

The orthodox view of the EU's 'democratic deficit' is that the transfer of legislative powers from national parliaments to the EU institutions has not been matched by an equivalent degree of democratic accountability and legislative input on the part of the European Parliament (EP), the only directly elected institution at EU level. This has been the dominant view of the democratic deficit since the first EP elections of 1979, and one which has become more convincing since the **Single European** Act extended the scope of EU competences and the use of **qualified majority voting** (QMV) in the Council. Although greater majority rule in the Council has increased decision-making *efficiency*, it has exacerbated the already marginal role that national parliaments enjoy within the integration process. This is because there is no guarantee that the scrutiny of national parliaments will matter when national governments may be outvoted in the Council.

The orthodox view also brings together two forms of institutional democratic deficit. The first refers to the 'de-parliamentarization' of national political systems and the growing influence of the executive (Chryssochoou *et al.* 2003). The second focuses on the transfer of decision-making authority from the national (or subnational) to the European level. Implicit in this reading of the democratic deficit is that the shift from national to EU level has, *at the same time*, benefited executive decision-makers at the expense of parliamentarians. This weakens the link between the electorate and de facto legislators. Shifting control of the integration process from national governments, from the national civil servants who support them and, indeed, from the unelected European institutions, seems to provide an obvious solution to the democratic deficit. Thus, the most familiar argument is that a loss of control by national parliaments must be compensated for by a process of parliamentarization at EU level. In other words, the EP must be given more powers if it is to perform the functions of a 'real' parliament. This usually implies a move towards a bicameral system – of direct and popular representation within the EP and indirect, territorial representation within the Council.

Yet the Parliament, and others who argue for an extension of the parliamentary system to the EU (see below), recognize that the EP's gains have not entirely compensated for losses at national level, and that integration remains very much controlled by national and EU-level executives. As a consequence, measures to extend further the EP's involvement both in the legislative process and in scrutinizing the executive have been proposed – for example in the form of an extension of the codecision procedure so that all provisions falling under codecision also operate on the basis of QMV in the Council, and in extending the EP's involvement in the appointment of the Commission, possibly by allowing MEPs to choose the President of the Commission from a shortlist put forward by the European Council. But there is also growing support for increasing the involvement of national parliaments (rather than just the EP) in the EU policy process. National MPs already have an important role to play in scrutinizing EU legislation, though in practice they are often unable to perform that function very effectively.

Since Nice (2001), there has been a renewed interest in giving national parliaments more of a formal role in the EU's legislative process. One suggestion is that national parliaments should have a say over whether EU legislation has been made on the basis of the subsidiarity principle. In other words, they should decide whether decisions are being taken at the most appropriate level. Others have sought to reinstate national parliamentary assizes, by adding a second chamber to the EP even if critics note that a similar experiment was attempted in 1990 with little success. The political agenda of those who favour a greater role for national parliaments sometimes stretches to support for the de facto renationalization of EU policies. For this group, arguments about the democratic deficit may mask a more general hostility to the EU project as a whole. Alternatively, it may assume that the EU is incapable of substantive democratic reforms and that the only viable solution to its democratic deficit is for the EU institutions to play much less of a role in domestic politics and for the EU to become more intergovernmental than it currently is.

As European integration is said to privilege executives at the expense of directly elected legislatures, the criticism is not just that parliaments do not have sufficient powers, but that non-elected bodies possess too many. In this vein, many in the past have attacked the European Commission for being the archetypal undemocratic institution, in that it is a civil service composed of appointed members that possess substantive policy-making, if not legislative, powers (see Chapter 9). There are various possible perspectives on such criticisms. Perhaps the most relevant has been that this issue is really about **accountability** and institutional autonomy – the extent to which the Commission, as an executive body, is accountable to the European citizens; or the degree to which it has been able to break free from the control of national governments and parliaments, to act in an independent fashion, thereby directly influencing policy and integrative outcomes. While there has clearly been an extension to the scrutiny role of the EP over the Commission in the treaty revisions of the 1980s and 1990s, the Commission does retain a degree of discretion over how it performs its initiative function. But whether this is undemocratic or not is disputed.

It is not only the Commission that is subject to criticism of this kind. The European Court of Justice (ECJ) has also been attacked for its teleological pro-integrationist bias. While it has an obligation to interpret the Treaties, and has also been instrumental in pushing out the boundaries of European law, there is once again little agreement on the extent to which the Court really plays an autonomous role in the EU integration and policy process. But, as is clear from Chapter 12, the role played by the Court may be inventive, but it is also very much in line with the spirit of the Treaties that it was set up to interpret. Also, criticisms of the Council usually refer to the fact that it is the Council rather than the EP which still has the final say in legislative matters – at least on issues of vital importance. One reason why this criticism is deemed credible is that the Council is a somewhat secretive and arcane body, whose legislative decisions are taken behind closed doors.

Underpinning arguments that the non-parliamentary EU institutions need to be more open and accountable is a more general point – that the EC/EU has traditionally been a technocratic body, which has valued expertise (and effectiveness) much more than representation (and democracy). Since the early 1990s, the democracy debate within the EU has been extended, so that even where it remains institutionally orientated, it has become inextricably linked with issues of public participation in the EU policy process. Thus, democratizing the EU is not just about rejigging the institutional balance of the EU to give this or that institution more of a policy role. It is not solely reliant on the representative role of parliaments. It is also about bringing the EU closer to ordinary people, ensuring that the integration process is no longer simply an elite-driven process, distant or even irrelevant for the vast majority of European citizens. There are various dimensions to these arguments, ranging from the idea of strengthening the representation of regions and localities in the EU (see Chapter 18) to increasing transparency and simplification (Dinan 2000: 133). In the latter case, democracy is said to be facilitated through greater institutional openness, such as the availability of Council minutes or enhanced public consultation by the Commission in advance of legislative proposals.

The democratic deficit: a socio-psychological perspective

The problem with institutional approaches to the democratic deficit is that they leave the equally important socio-psychological dimension of this phenomenon unexplored. Such a dimension shifts the emphasis from the question of 'Who governs and how?' to the more demanding question of 'Who is governed?', thereby focusing more on the treatment of the disease than on its symptoms. The starting point is that at the heart of the EU's democratic deficit lies the absence of a European demos and, by extension, of 'civic we-ness' – that is, a sense of common identity amongst Europeans (Chryssochoou 2000a).

This perspective on the democratic deficit builds on the wider assumption that democracy, in the form of representative and responsible government, presupposes a popular infrastructure upon which certain basic properties, such as adherence to and acceptance of majority rule, apply in any given political community. A transnational demos can be defined as a composite citizen body, whose members share an active interest in the democratic governance of the larger polity, and who can direct their democratic claims to, and via, the central institutions. Thus it is the demos itself that endows the EU with legitimacy. It follows that the transformation of the EU 'from democracies to democracy' requires the positive feelings of the member publics to be stronger than any divisive issues that may arise as integration proceeds. As Cohen states, 'there can be no larger part unless the larger part and the smaller parts are indeed parts of one whole' (Cohen 1971: 46).

The more the EU relies on democratic credentials, the more important it is for citizens to have feelings of belonging to an 'inclusive' polity. In this context, the emergence of a European civic identity out of the democratic traditions that currently exist in the EU is imperative, not only for the viability of EU democracy, but also if the democratic integrity of the constituent populations is to be respected, and for cultural variation and multiple identity-holding to be fostered. For a European demos to exist, its members must recognize their collective existence. Merely being granted citizenship rights is far from adequate. This is a question of changes in the way that Europeans think about themselves and the way that they view the communities to which they belong.

As the polity of the EU cannot be detached from its constituent identities, transnational demos formation does not imply a melting-pot type of society in which pre-existing (mainly territorial) identities are assimilated into a new supranational identity. Rather, it projects an image of a pluralist polity, within which the civic demos emerges as the unchallenged unit of transnational authority and the ultimate focus of political purpose. 'Many people, one demos', rather than 'many demoi, one people', epitomizes this. Put differently, this implies 'a many turned into one without ceasing to be many'. A European demos can be said to exist when the constituent publics see themselves as part of a democratic whole, and are given the institutional means to mark their impact in EU governance, even though they retain their regional and national identities. It is thus possible to identify the following as necessary for EU demos formation: the democratic self-consciousness of citizens; adherence to shared democratic values; public awareness of the transnational polity; and a desire to shape democratically the future of a plurality of interrelated peoples, without endangering the very essence of that plurality, its diversity.

KEY POINTS

- The institutional perspective of the democratic deficit emphasizes the need for democratic power-sharing, which might give the EP or national parliaments more of a role in the EU policy process, or make other institutions accountable to elected bodies.
- The socio-psychological perspective of the democratic deficit stresses the absence of a European demos and identifies what it would take to construct a European civic body.

Models of European democracy

Resolving the democratic deficit is no easy task as it would require some form of agreement about the sort of model of democratic governance to which the EU should adhere. Up to now, the EC (and recently the EU) has evolved incrementally and, despite various reforms, there has been no consensus on its future shape. The Convention on the Future of Europe discussed these issues with a view to agreeing the Constitutional Treaty in 2004 (see Chapter 4). This section looks at five models that could guide the democratization of the EU – the parliamentary, consociational, federal, confederal, and republican.

The parliamentary model

The parliamentary model emphasizes the role of the elected assembly as legislator. Crucial within this model is the parliament's role within a representative and often majoritarian system that allows executives to govern as long as they have the confidence of a majority of the members of the assembly. The model draws attention to a number of features that relate to the EU: the use of QMV in EU decision-making; the role of the EP in law-making; and the role of national parliaments in the monitoring of legislation. But, despite having certain parliamentary characteristics, the EU is not a parliamentary system, as it is not based on the separation of powers between executive and legislative institutions. Neither is there a clear division of competences among different levels of governance.

Supporters of the parliamentary model stress the importance of democratically monitoring EU legislation through the institutional checks and balances offered by deliberative plenary sessions and specialized parliamentary committees. But there are important implications for EU legitimacy should a parliamentary system be established, as this implies that majority rule would be extended to all EU policy areas. The parliamentary model presupposes some form of social unity, which allows the minority to identify with the central institutions. Given the fragmented nature of the European citizenry, there would seem to be no such social unity of this kind within the EU. For the moment, QMV still applies to areas of EU action that are not prone to intense conflict, that is, in areas where the states want to see collective progress rather than to hold on to their national prerogatives (Taylor 1996: 85–8). Major policy initiatives and decisions on reform take place through formal treaty revision on the basis of unanimity (with each state holding a potential veto) (see Chapter 10). Where majority decisions *are* at issue, they are often subject to a lowest common denominator approach, with the informal norm of consensus usually overriding the idea of a decision at any cost. Indeed, no single state is prepared to be outvoted on a regular basis in the Council. Taylor summarizes the above discussion well: 'Majority voting merely cloaked the continuing need to obtain the assent of all states . . . In a system of sovereign states, it could not be otherwise' (Taylor 1996: 86).

The confederal model

Confederation involves the merging of distinct politically organized states into some form of Union, without losing either their national identity or their individual sovereignty. The confederal model emphasizes the intergovernmental properties of the EU, highlighting its treaty-based nature. This model suggests that democracy in the EU is better served by establishing a democratic society of European states, rather than by forging a new polity and EU democracy. The confederal model sees European integration as a predominantly interstate affair, and favours the diffusion of authoritative decision-making power to the segments (or member states), rather than to the regional centre (the EU level). The end-product of integration takes the form of a 'treaty-constituted body politic, rather than . . . [a] constituted unity of one *people* or *nation* (Forsyth 1981: 15–16).

Thus, confederation takes the form of a 'halfway house' between 'normal' interstate and 'normal' intrastate (or domestic) relations, with the constituent units reserving the right to revert to democratic self-rule. What this implies is that integration 'falls short of a complete fusion or incorporation in which one or all the members lose their identity as states' (Forsyth 1981: 1). The main characteristic of a confederation as 'a system of governments' is that it provides states with a variety of opportunities, enabling them to achieve mutually advantageous cooperation without resigning their individual sovereignty to a single common government, in the form of either a federal authority or a regional state.

Accordingly, the idea of power-sharing at the EU level, which involves the management of certain policies over which there is a form of joint sovereignty, provides an alternative to the creation of a new political centre 'beyond the nation state'.

Although the confederal model incorporates a wide range of institutional possibilities, including for example power-sharing arrangements among different actors, the larger political entity ultimately rests upon the separate constitutional orders of the member states which, by virtue of their sovereign nature, continue to act as 'Masters of the Treaties'. The fact that formal treaty revisions require the unanimous consent of the member governments alone makes this point all the more resonant, as does the understanding that it is the member states and not a self-conscious and politically active European demos that legitimizes the EU. In this model, as a consequence, resolving the democratic deficit might involve, not an attempt to create a European demos, but a renationalization of European policies.

The federal model

The federal model foresees the creation of a 'union of *people* in a body politic', as opposed to merely a 'union of *states* in a body politic' (see also Chapter 5). This task recognizes that individuals who come under the federal compact must be moved by such strong 'we-feelings' that it propels them not only to use but also to support federal policy outcomes. Students of democracy hold the view that federalism, by implying a diffusion of political power, moderates conflicts and offers a greater opportunity for 'political schooling', a condition for socializing minorities into a civic culture. From this view stems the importance of institutional arrangements, which allow each state to be represented in the federal polity, without disturbing the overall effectiveness of the system or indeed challenging its political legitimacy. Federalism aims to establish a cooperative democratic ethos in relations between the centre and the subunits. It seeks to reconcile the parallel demands for greater political union of the whole, at the same time as ensuring adequate constitutional guarantees for the autonomy of the parts, in order to establish unity without uniformity and diversity without anarchy. Thus an understanding of federation emerges as a living, pluralist order that builds itself from the ground upwards.

When this model is applied to the EU, a frequent criticism is that it places too much emphasis on the idea of a central constitutional settlement and, by extension, the need for a clear demarcation of competences between higher- (EU) and lower-level (national, subnational) authorities. In so doing, it ignores the inherently dynamic nature of European integration and the complexity of competence allocation (or 'Who does what?') within the EU. The making of a European political federation also presupposes the creation of a new sovereignty at the higher level and the establishment of a bicameral system in which the EP is given the power to initiate and codecide legislation with the Council. However, the democratic properties normally associated with federal polities, where a composite civic demos forms the 'constituting authority' of the federation – in other words, where the federal model is composed of one 'people' – seems absent from this EU version of federalism. In the absence of a European demos, it is difficult to imagine the qualitative transformation of the EU from a confederal to a federal-type organization and, hence, to a polity constituted by a unity of the people.

The consociational model

Consociationalism is a model of governance which has been used to cope with the need to govern effectively within territories inhabited by more than one distinct community or societal group. As such, consociationalism seeks to forge a community of territorial entities in order to provide an institutional defence against the abuse of minority rights. It has four main features: a grand coalition of elites; proportionality; segmental autonomy; and mutual vetoes. A *grand coalition*, or a 'cartel of elites' (Dahrendorf 1967: 267) is an institutional setting, within which decisions are taken and bargains are struck among the groups of elites. *Proportionality* implies that all societal forces or communities are represented within the government, in a way that reflects their size. *Segmental autonomy* means that each elite has control over its own particular territory, in areas that do not impinge on other elites within the consociation. Finally, the existence of *mutual vetoes* means that for important decisions unanimous approval of all elites is required, which means that the majority is unable to dominate the minority. These features of the consociational model can all be found within the present-day EU system.

The consociational model is particularly relevant to the case of the EU as it stresses the consensual nature of EU decision-making. Consociationalism is related to the politics of accommodation employed behind the closed doors of the Council and the European Council, resulting in carefully negotiated package deals among the elites. With the absence of a single European demos, majoritarian patterns of politics would imply serious exclusionary practices harmful to minorities. Thus the model avoids excluding minority interests by institutionalizing new ways of reaching mutually acceptable compromises. The EU already possesses certain features of a consociational democracy. *Grand coalitions* are found in the sectoral EU councils as well as in the European Council (see Chapter 10). *Proportionality* appears in the idea that states are assigned different votes in the Council according to their size and/or population, and in that all the member states are represented in the central institutions. *Segmental autonomy* exists in the way that EU states retain their distinctive features as separate constitutional entities so that they remain responsible for dealing with issues that are exclusive to their jurisdiction. And finally, *mutual vetoes* allow EU states to block decisions of which they strongly disapprove, especially where their vital national interests are at stake.

According to the consociational model, the EU represents a compound polity whose units are bound in a consensual form of union. Its aim is to further certain common ends without sacrificing collective national identities or resigning individual sovereignty to a higher authority. Central to the workings of this consociation is the practice of political codetermination – the common management of separate sovereignties through means and objectives that have been agreed in advance. The result is a system of considerable interconnectedness coexisting with high levels of autonomy. In this consociation, the dominant elites resist the strengthening of horizontal links among their respective publics, preferring instead to promote vertical integration so as to retain ultimate control within their own subcultures. This also allows national elites to exercise managerial control over integration, whilst deciding on the bases of acceptable behaviour within the larger system.

The advantage of this model is that it allows for a less rigid understanding of statehood than is found in the other models. In brief, national and collective systems of governance are bound together in a symbiotic relationship that accommodates divergent expectations in joint decisions. As for democracy, in this model it is not so much an end in itself, but an institutional device used to arrive at mutually acceptable compromises among sovereign states. In this sense, the model is inherently elitist and, hence, not the most appropriate model for democratizing the EU through greater public involvement.

The republican model

Res publica means that which belongs to the public. Originating from the Latin term *res populi*, it literally means 'public thing', 'public property', or even 'public affairs'. A *res publica* has three primary objectives: justice through the rule of law; the common good through a mixed and balanced constitution; and liberty through active citizenship. Love for a virtue-centred life constitutes the raison d'être of the *res publica*, marking its impact in the search for 'the good polity' (Schwarzmantel 2003). Recently, republican perspectives have sought to nurture a paradigm of social and political organization for the EU, founded upon a new 'civic partnership' among a distinct politically organized people.

Republican conceptions of Europe reflect a wider concern with the search for a reliable *and* democratic theory of integration able to capture the relationship between the component public spheres and the functioning of a mixed sovereignty regime at EU level. The point here is that, absent a formal European constitution, and given the inchoateness of a European civic demos, there is urgent need for greater civic participation in European affairs. This philosophy accords with a civic conception of the European polity that aims to assess the relationship between the EU and 'the civic'. This recent refurbishment of republican thought has given rise to a 'normative turn' in EU studies (Chryssochoou 2000b, 2001, 2002). The recent paradigm shift 'from policy to polity' illustrates this point well, in that there is increasing scholarly focus on the capacity of the EU as a polity to reach publicly binding decisions as well as to allocate values in European society.

Since the mid-1990s, the development of the EU has raised questions of social legitimation in connection with the making of a transnational public sphere. This 'normative turn', drawing largely from constructivist discourses in international relations theory (Checkel 1998; Wendt 1999; Christiansen *et al.* 1999), has also opened the way for novel conceptualizations of the EU as 'an entity of interlocking normative spheres' (Bankowski *et al.* 1998) from a post-statist angle. This conception of the EU as an ordered political arrangement for diverse communities and arenas for action – a 'heterarchical space' – transcends pre-existing forms of allegiance and affiliation, and projects a form of authority that accords with its composite nature.

Bellamy and Castiglione (2000: 181) capture the complexity and pluralism of the EU through a theory of 'democratic liberalism', founded upon 'a pre-liberal conception of constitutionalism that identified the constitution with the social composition and form of government of the polity'. This amounts to 'a political system that disperses power within civil society . . . and encourages dialogue between the component parts of the body politic' (Bellamy and Castiglione 2000: 172). The point Bellamy and Castiglione (2000: 182) make is that, '[i]nstead of the constitution being a precondition for politics, political debate becomes the medium through which a polity constitutes itself'. Democratic liberalism brings the members of the polity into an equilibrium with one another, and aims 'to disperse power so as to encourage a process of controlled political conflict and deliberation' (Bellamy and Castiglione, 2000: 181). Within this pluralist polity, there can be different forms of representation for different purposes. Differentiation is crucial for it links together justice, the rule of law, and the democratic dispersal of political power, whilst providing a balanced mix of social forces and levels of governance.

Similarly, by reviving the usage of an eighteenth-century term, MacCormick (1997) conceptualizes the 'EU order' as a 'mixed commonwealth', within which the subjects of the 'constitution' represent a mixture of agents that share in the sovereignty of the larger unit. Bellamy and Castiglione (1997: 443) explain: 'The polycentric polity . . . is a definite departure from the nation state, mainly because it implies a dissociation of the traditional elements that come with state sovereignty: a unified system of authority and representation controlling all functions of governance over a given territory'. MacCormick's notion of a lawfully constituted European commonwealth of post-sovereign states allows the EU to conduct itself as a 'community of law'. Here, the rule of law emerges as the most fundamental constitutional guarantee of the system, 'as all other [legal] values depend on it, for them to be upheld at all' (Piris 2000: 12). Here, political authority is neither proportionately nor symmetrically vested in a single decision-making centre. Rather, it is distributed through overlapping arrangements, with the polity being characterized by various degrees of decentralization and sources of loyalty-holding.

Republican theory embodies a normative commitment to civic deliberation for the promotion of the public interest and to the setting up of a particular kind of constitutional ordering founded on the notion of 'balanced government'. Such ordering is committed to offering citizens 'undominated' (or quality) choice. But it is not the latter that causes liberty. Instead, liberty is constituted by the legal institutions of the human association – the republican state (Pettit 1997: 106–9). Brugger explains: 'whereas the liberal sees liberty as essentially pre-social, the republican sees liberty as constituted by the law which transforms customs and creates citizens' (1999: 7). Active civic participation is not taken as a democratic end in itself, but as a means of ensuring a dispensation of non-domination by others (non-arbitrary rule). In short, the rule of law, opposition of arbitrariness, and the republican constitution are constitutive of civic freedom itself.

Central to republicanism is the idea of 'balanced government'. This is forged in two related ways: negatively, by associating the constitution of 'a proper institutional balance' with the prevention of tyranny (and other forms of authoritarian rule); and positively, by ensuring a deliberative mode of democratic public engagement, 'within which the different "constituencies" which made up civil society would be encouraged to treat their preferences not simply as givens, but rather as choices which were open to debate and alteration' (Craig 1997: 114). Liberty was expected to be best preserved under a mixed form of governance through certain constitutional guarantees, with no single branch of government being privileged over the others. Such issues are of relevance to the distribution of political authority within the EU (Craig 1997: 115). Here, republicanism claims to strike a balance between civic participation and the attainment of the public good, by allowing for 'a stable form of political ordering for a society within which there are different interests or constituencies' (Craig 1997: 116). A 'balanced constitution' is reflected in the Commission's exclusive right to initiate legislation and its interaction with civil society; the EP's codecision rights in fostering deliberative outcomes; the political activism of the ECJ in interpreting European law; and the relation between the indirect mandate of the Council and the fact that the 'EU order' rests on an international treaty.

Lavdas (2000, 2001) draws from Pettit's (1997) seminal study on freedom as non-domination – as opposed to a negative conception of liberty as non-interference, or a positive one as self-mastery – to argue that the EU may develop democratic forms of deliberation and a corresponding concern with active citizenship, which are necessary, but not sufficient, conditions for EU democracy-building. Given the absence of an engaging European civic demos, republicanism emanates as a means of disentangling 'the issue of participation in an emerging polity from the cultural and emotional dimensions of citizenship as pre-existing affinity and a confirmation of belonging' (Lavdas 2001: 4).

What conclusions might we draw from these five models of democracy? First, the EU is a hybrid form of polity, in that elements of all five models are currently reflected in its workings. Secondly, the models that reflect the EU's character most closely are the confederal and consociational models. As the confederal model assumes that democracy will be located at the national level, the democratic deficit could be resolved only by a shift in an intergovernmental direction. Moreover, the elitist character of the consociational model also seems to preclude any possibility of democratization transnationally. Hence the need to invest in the civic dimension of European polity-building. The section that follows asks whether recent treaty reforms demonstrate evidence of the beginnings of such a shift.

KEY POINTS

- There are at least five models of democratic governance that resonate with the EU.
- Despite some parliamentary features, the EU does not fit the parliamentary model.
- The absence of a demos would seem to preclude the application of a federal model.
- Relevant as they may be in the EU of today, the confederal and consociational models do not provide an avenue for democratizing its political system.
- Republican notions of the EU project a participatory model of European citizenship.

Democracy and treaty reform

As the Amsterdam Treaty (1997) was an attempt to rectify the deficiencies of the Maastricht Treaty (1992), this would seem to provide a fitting start for an assessment of democratic reform in the EU. Although Maastricht preserved the confederal nature of the EU, it also introduced federal-like principles such as codecision, subsidiarity, and proportionality. According to Taylor, however, what this treaty revision brought about was a 'symbiotic consociation' (Taylor 1996) and with it an informal culture of consensus-building at the highest level. Taylor argues that after the Maastricht Treaty the EU and the member states became increasingly locked together in a mutually reinforcing relationship that left much to be desired from a democratic standpoint. That the issue of democracy was to occupy a more prominent position in the Amsterdam negotiations was a reflection of increasing public concern. Thus a widespread consensus emerged during these negotiations that the EU had to find ways of developing closer links with its citizens. However, this consensus did not leave much of a mark on the Treaty.

Hailed by some as a 'reasonable step', but criticized by others as 'lacking ambition', the Amsterdam Treaty consolidated state competences by preserving the EU's three-pillar structure (see Chapter 4). As Devuyst put it: '[r]ather than focusing on pre-emptive institutional spillover in preparation for enlargement, the Amsterdam negotiation was characterized by a "maintaining national control trend" ' (Devuyst 1998: 615).

One of the most important questions to be addressed at Amsterdam concerned the institutional structure that would permit the future enlargement of the EU to take place. It was agreed that, after the first enlargement, the big states would lose their second commissioner, provided that they were compensated through a reweighting of votes in the Council, although a final decision must be taken at least a year before EU membership exceeds 20. Although the Amsterdam Treaty increased the role of the EP by extending the scope of the codecision procedure and by simplifying the conciliation process, the reform did not address more fundamental issues of parliamentary involvement in EU decision-making. For example, the Treaty failed to agree that codecision would always be used with QMV in the Council, and it did not extend the EP's involvement in third-pillar issues (police and judicial cooperation) to cover the financial implications of such policies.

The largest deficiency of the Amsterdam process was that it prioritized specific policy issues over broader questions relating to the EU's future. On the basis of its incomplete outcome, the treaty revision reflected a member state preference for a managerialist type of reform which would improve the *effectiveness* of policy output rather than its democratic character. Those who had hoped that the Amsterdam process would forge a new democratic EU polity had no grounds for celebration as political pragmatism won the day. It is not overstating the case to argue that Amsterdam was characterized by a profound lack of democratic vision about the future of Europe.

Similarly, the Treaty of Nice, signed in 2001, provides a good example of the limits of EU polity-building. As *The Guardian* put it: 'At every stage of the prolonged negotiation, raw national interest has overshadowed the broader vision'. For example, the 'declaratory' Charter of Fundamental Rights, signed at Nice, but not incorporated into the Treaty, seemed a missed opportunity for EU democracy. The institutionalization of fundamental rights within the EU is likely to have strengthened the credibility of national commitments to protect the rights of persons residing within their territory, while empowering the ECJ to ensure that principles underpinning the Charter were respected. It is also likely to have advanced the fight against various forms of discrimination within the EU, contributing to the preservation and further development of shared values, while respecting and protecting the diversity of constituent cultures, traditions, and identities.

Nice was intended to deal with the so-called 'Amsterdam left-overs', those issues that remained unresolved in the last round of treaty reforms. After four days of marathon talks in December 2000, an agreement was reached that the larger states would retain their second commissioner until 2005, whilst each state would nominate one commissioner until the EU expands to 27 members. It was also agreed that the four largest states would each have 29 instead of 10 votes in the Council, which meant that three large states and a small one could now form a blocking minority, while the small and medium-sized members would each have between three and 13 votes (which meant that while the larger states' votes have increased threefold, those of the smaller states have only doubled). The threshold of seats in the EP was raised to 732 and QMV was extended to a number of relatively non-controversial areas. Finally, the states agreed to yet another round of constitutional reforms in 2004, covering questions of competence allocation, the status of the Charter, the simplification of the Treaties, and the future role of national parliaments.

What conclusion can we draw from the Nice process as regards EU democracy-building? Three points deserve our attention. First, although the EU has sought to create large-scale civil society, the development of a shared civic identity among its constituent publics has not yet materialized. Secondly, the EU is still characterized by its diversity and, moreover, by a lack of agreement on where integration will end. Despite the increase in substantive policy competences, the EU has not become a federation, and remains a consensual form of governance, albeit one that is comparable to many federal systems. Thirdly, by acknowledging how important it is that states retain ultimate control over treaty changes, the Nice reforms have revealed the limits of democratization in the EU. In failing to strengthen common citizenship rights and to decouple EU legitimacy from policy performance, Nice, like Amsterdam, has been a missed opportunity for EU democracy.

As far as the Constitutional Treaty is concerned, it is worth noting that the French rejected it on 29 May 2005, as did the Dutch a few days later, throwing the EU into a profound political crisis. The Constitutional Treaty has been described as a relatively modest but positive step toward the constitutionalization of earlier Treaties. Most analysts have asserted that the institutional changes proposed would have contributed to a more functional, viable, and balanced form of decision-making in an enlarged EU of 25 or so members, coupled by a strengthening of the EU's international role (see Chapter 4). Yet, there were mainly nationally driven causes for rejecting the new Treaty, which have produced an ideologically incoherent, yet discernible voting block against ratification. Were the Treaty to have been ratified by all its signatories, the EU would have still rested on an international treaty or, at best, on a quasi-constitutional system of checks and balances designed to organize political authority in a non-state polity.

Yet, the new Treaty was assigned the task of establishing a new constitutional order – albeit of a (much) less federalist kind. The following questions are in order. Did the Convention act as a 'constituent assembly'? Has the outcome of deliberating on a new Treaty been legitimized by European public opinion? Would the envisaged Treaty take the EU further down the road to federalization? The answer to these questions is closer to a 'no' than a 'yes'. First, the drafting process was characterized by a lack of a genuine European constituent power; let us recall that the Convention was composed of appointed delegates, albeit drawn from a wider socio-political spectrum than has previously been the case. Secondly, the outcome of the Convention was liable to change by the IGC that followed it, which retained the right to a final say over the end product through classical forms of intergovernmental bargaining. Thirdly, following the argument about the lack of a European constituent power, the outcome of the IGC failed to produce a Constitution 'proper' that derives its social legitimacy directly from a European demos.

The general assessment is that state-centrism seems to be the order of the day when it comes to bestowing the EU with a system of 'basic law' provisions. Nor does the unquestionably integrative nature of a Constitutional Treaty suffice to transform a constellation of national democracies into a democratic polity in its own right. Thus the Constitutional Treaty would have to be based as much on the constitutional orders of the member units as on a new kind of political ordering for the EU to retain its character as a composite polity. Thus, European constitutionalism can only follow the previous path of sovereign-conscious states wishing to bring about a moderate reordering of the Treaties.

The Constitutional Treaty would not have endowed the EU with 'a new base of sovereignty' able to transcend the sovereignty of its parts. Instead of arguing that the EU is part of a federal process, one should argue that it is about the preservation of those state qualities that allow its members to survive as distinct polities, whilst engaging themselves in a polity-building exercise that transforms their traditional patterns of interaction.

KEY POINTS

- The Amsterdam Treaty was little more than a managerialist reform which aimed to increase policy effectiveness rather than democratic participation in EU decisions.
- After Nice, there was still no evidence of the emergence of a European civic identity.
- The rejection of the Constitutional Treaty by the French and Dutch publics threw the EU into a prolonged political crisis about the kind of Europe we want.

Conclusion

At a time when the EU retains its character as a *via media* between different forms of polity, the initial prospects for a smooth ratification of the Constitutional Treaty raised the expectations of endowing a fragmented European demos with a common civic identity. But such aspirations did not prove realistic enough. Even the new dialectic between sovereignty and integration, carrying the implication of an explicit right to political codetermination, failed to produce a credible commitment to democratizing the EU. What recent treaty reforms failed to produce was not only a common democratic vision per se, but also a belief that such a vision remains without reach, at least in the foreseeable future. This is justified further by perceiving their outcome as a product of a predominantly utilitarian calculus among the divergent preferences of the dominant national political elites. Therefore, it would seem fair to suggest that the exclusion of citizens from European governance is at the expense of elevating their status to a system-steering agency. It is against the interests of better equipping citizens to become the decisive agents of civic change within a nascent pluralist order composed of increasingly entangled arenas for action – or indeed against the aspirations of the EU qua polity to allocate authoritatively, rather than merely derivatively, civic rights and values in European society.

Anything less would perpetuate a predominantly elitist operation that is detrimental to legitimate forms of polity. It would also prevent the EU from acquiring a distinctive political subject, whose civic identity exists and manifests itself independent of national public spheres, but whose 'politics' extends to both European and national civic arenas, thus signalling a shift in the basis of legitimation from international treaty rules and managerial forms of executive elite governance to a transnational demos founded on more active and inclusionary virtues of belonging. Like any other polity that aspires to becoming a democracy, the EU has to engage itself in a constitutive process based on a new framework of politics that embraces the virtues of civic freedom, civic solidarity, and free public deliberation, by inventing and, where necessary, reinventing, a sense of *res publica*.

In conclusion, the discussion of EU democracy and the democratic deficit in this chapter is underpinned by a belief that it is increasingly important for the EU to address issues of democratic governance and to ensure that its decisions are informed by public discourse. The chapter began by distinguishing between two perspectives on the democratic deficit – institutional and socio-psychological. It went on to consider the relevance to the EU of five models of democracy. Although the EU is closer to confederal and consociational models of democracy than to the other models reviewed, this is deemed to be far from an ideal end state for the EU, as it is likely to hinder the development of a European demos. As the EU was founded and is still based on an international treaty, the transition to a participatory model of governance is likely to be neither easy nor linear. This is because the EU will continue to be confronted with the reality of multiple states and peoples as well as by the fact that its present institutional structure favours pragmatic and accommodationist reform rather than a fundamental constitutional transformation.

? QUESTIONS

1. What is the democratic deficit and how might one rectify it?
2. Why is democracy important for the making of a European polity?
3. Is a European demos necessary for European democracy?
4. Which model of European governance is most likely to democratize the EU?
5. What are the main weaknesses of the consociational model of democracy?
6. What merits does the republican model of democracy have for the EU?
7. To what extent have the Treaties of Amsterdam and Nice enhanced democracy in the EU?
8. What would the Constitutional Treaty have done to enhance democracy in the EU?

GUIDE TO FURTHER READING

- **Abromeit, H.** ***Democracy in Europe: Legitimizing Politics in a Non-state Polity*** **(Oxford: Berghahn Books, 1996).** Contributes to the theoretical debate about governance beyond the state.

- **Beetham, D., and Lord, C.** ***Legitimacy in the European Union*** **(London: Addison Wesley Longman, 1996).** Provides a synthesis and an original perspective on the issue of political legitimacy.

- **Bellamy, R., and Warleigh, A. (eds)** ***Citizenship and Governance in the European Union*** **(London: Continuum, 2001).** Offers a comprehensive account of the relationship between citizenship and governance in the EU, bringing together scholars from different disciplines.

- **Chryssochoou, D. N.** ***Democracy in the European Union*** **(London: I. B. Taurus, 2000).** Offers a rich analysis of the relationship between democracy and European integration and examines alternative approaches to understanding the democratic deficit.

■ **Eriksen, E. O., and Fossum, J. E. (eds)** *Democracy in the European Union* **(London: Routledge, 2000).** Takes a theoretical approach to understanding democracy and deliberation in the EU and assesses the prospects for EU-level democracy.

■ **Hoskyns, C., and Newman, M. (eds)** *Democratizing the European Union* **(Manchester: Manchester University Press, 2000).** Offers a fresh approach to understanding and resolving the democratic deficit by relating academic debates to practical politics.

■ **Lord, C.** *Democracy in the European Union* **(Sheffield: Sheffield Academic Press, 1998).** Offers an excellent assessment of the EU's democratic deficit and the problems associated with the construction of a transnational democracy.

■ **Newman, M.** *Democracy, Sovereignty and the European Union* **(London: Hurst, 1996).** Takes a critical look at democracy and sovereignty issues in the EU, presenting a strong case for a democratic Europe.

■ **Schmitter, P. C.** *How to Democratize the European Union . . . And Why Bother?* **(Lanham, MD: Rowman & Littlefield, 2000).** Explores the possibility and desirability of democratizing the EU through novel forms of citizenship, representation, and decision-making.

■ **Warleigh, A.** *Democracy in the European Union* **(London: Sage, 2003).** Contributes to a fresh understanding of the evolution of democratic reform in the EU, presenting a strong case against federalism and supporting a more participatory and flexible democratic model.

■ **Weale, A.** *Democratic Citizenship and the European Union* **(Manchester: Manchester University Press, 2005).** Explores the democratic potential of European citizenship from a political theory perspective.

IMPORTANT WEBSITES

- **www.statewatch.org** The website of the non-governmental organization, Statewatch.
- **http://europa.eu.int.comm/public_opinion/Eurobarometer** The EU's *Eurobarometer* website, which brings together surveys of public opinion on European issues.
- **http://european-convention.eu.int** The website of the European Convention.
- **http://conventionwatch.iue.it** Website hosted by the European University Institute in Florence on the European Convention.

Visit the Online Resource Centre that accompanies this book for lots of interesting additional material. http://www.oxfordtextbooks.co.uk/orc/cini2e/

23 Public Opinion and the EU

LAUREN M. MCLAREN

Chapter Contents

Reader's Guide

This chapter provides an overview of trends in public opinion toward the European Union. The chapter also discusses the key factors thought to explain differences in mass opinion regarding the EU. These include knowledge of the EU and **cognitive mobilization** (attentiveness to politics); **rational utilitarianism** (opinions stemming from calculations about the costs and benefits of the EU); perceptions of the national government; concerns about the loss of national identity and distrust of the EU institutions. Finally, the chapter provides a summary of opinion in the new Central and East European member states, and contends that concerns in these countries appear to mirror those in the older member states.

Introduction

The European Union began primarily as an elite-driven process. The early days of agreements and negotiations were seen as too complicated for the ordinary citizen, and so most decisions were taken outside of the public limelight. Hence, early observers of public opinion toward the European project remarked on what was perceived as a **permissive consensus** of public opinion (Lindberg and Scheingold 1970), whereby citizens generally held neutral opinions regarding what their governments were doing in Brussels, giving these governments considerable leeway to pursue policies outside of the purview of an attentive public. It was only after the addition of **Eurosceptic** member states (particularly Britain and Denmark) in the first enlargement (1973) that we finally saw the beginnings of consultation with mass publics on issues related to European integration. Even then, such consultation tended to be limited and was focused on referenda. In general, through the mid-1980s, EU member governments and bureaucrats can be said to have been interested in limited public involvement in the integration process. The **Single European Act** seems to have marked a turning point in this regard, as member state governments began selling their varying visions of a renewed European project that would contribute to further economic development of the member states. It is also at this point that more EU policies began to impinge upon national policy-making because of the increased level of economic coordination within the EC/EU.

Nowadays it would be difficult to argue that mass European publics are providing a 'permissive consensus' for EU-level policy-making. Referenda in the past decade or so have come very close to putting the brakes on European integration, and the recent referenda in France and the Netherlands on the European Constitution (see Boxes 23.1 and 23.2) highlight the important role that the mass public plays in the integration project in the modern day. Moreover, it is clear that public opinion plays a role in constraining integration outside of referenda settings as well. A key example of this is the constraint that the British public opinion placed on Prime Minister Tony Blair's promised referendum on joining the **eurozone**. There are, of course, other factors that are likely to have prevented the holding of such a referendum, such as Chancellor (finance minister)

CASE STUDY 23.1

The constitutional referendum in France

While the French are not overly Eurosceptic, trends in support for the EU indicate that positive feelings about the EU have been in decline since the early 1990s (see McLaren 2006). Thus, in considerable contrast to the Netherlands (see Box 23.2), the French 'No' vote was perhaps less of a surprise. Indeed, history indicates that even when feelings about the EU are generally positive, votes in EU referenda can be very close indeed (as was the case with the vote on the Maastricht Treaty on European Union, in which a bare majority of 51.05 per cent voted to support the Treaty). While there was some discussion of the vote in the French referendum being a vote on Turkey's eventual membership of the EU, in fact, the 'No' vote in France appears to be related to two key issues: the French economy and opposition to the government. Several concerns about France's future economic outlook developed during the referendum campaign. Amongst these were general worries about the state of unemployment in France, fears about the relocation French business and the decline of small business, and anxiety about decline of the French 'social model', along with the failure of the Constitutional Treaty to address the issue of 'social Europe'. At the same time, the national government – and French President Jacques Chirac in particular – was becoming increasingly unpopular, and for many French voters the referendum turned into a confidence vote on the government of the day. Thus, on 29 May 2005, 55 per cent voted against the treaty (with a 70 per cent voter turnout).

CASE STUDY 23.2

The constitutional referendum in the Netherlands

While referenda in France are relatively common nowadays, they are far less so in the Netherlands. In fact, the constitutional referendum held on 1 June 2005 was the first such referendum in modern Dutch history. As seen in this chapter, the Dutch are generally amongst the most enthusiastic EU supporters, and so it was widely expected that they would provide resounding support to the referendum ratifying the Constitutional Treaty. However, with a relatively high turnout of 62 per cent, 61.8 per cent voted against the treaty. While the referendum was to be consultative only, most major parties had pledged to respect the voters' wishes, whatever the outcome.

Given general widespread support of the EU and European integration in the Netherlands, the big question still being posed about the referendum result is 'Why?' One of the key explanations seems to be that Dutch citizens were unclear as to what they were being asked to approve. The referendum campaign got off to a very slow start, and media and politicians struggled to find ways to frame the debate about the referendum. Moreover, in the absence of clear information as to what that Constitution meant for the EU and for the Netherlands, many Dutch citizens relied on the sorts of cues discussed in this chapter – especially opposition to the government. In the case of the Netherlands, such opposition has spread beyond just hostility to the government of the day and now seems to extend to hostility to the political establishment in general, especially established political parties. All of the main political parties were, in fact, campaigning in favour of the referendum, thus presenting voters with a clear opportunity to cast protest votes against all of these parties. There may have been some EU-related reasons for the 'No' vote as well, however. One of these is connected to the budget contribution of the Netherlands; another may be connected to unhappiness with the Dutch government's adoption of the euro with little public debate and no opportunity for citizens to vote on this decision. Finally, as the EU has continued to expand, two fears have subsequently developed. One is whether this small (original) member state can continue to wield influence in the new Europe and the other is whether Dutch interests can still be protected within the EU.

Gordon Brown's opposition to the idea, but the public's clear opposition to joining the euro has at the very least bolstered the Brown camp's position. Thus, importantly, after promising in 1997 to take Britain into the eurozone, Blair seems likely to leave office without even taking the promised public consultation on the matter, in great part because it is fairly clear which way the public would vote.

Ultimately, then, it is difficult to argue that the European mass public is irrelevant in European-level decision-making nowadays. Indeed, the stated purpose of the **Constitutional Treaty** was to make an anxious public more comfortable with its European institutions. If public opinion is indeed important in the realm of European politics, the next question to ask is why some people feel hostile toward the EU, others are more positive about it, while others are still fairly neutral. This chapter outlines the leading explanations for differences of opinion regarding the EU. It begins, however, with an overview of general trends in the European public's opinions toward the EU.

General perceptions of the EU

Since the early 1970s, the European Commission has sponsored regular opinion polls that monitor public support for various aspects of the European project (along with a whole host of other topics). The regular reports – known as *Eurobarometer* polls – are published by the Commission and are freely available at http://europa.eu.int/comm/public_opinion/index_en.htm. Here, I will summarize the survey items found in *Eurobarometer* polls that are generally used in academic literature to describe the public's perceptions of the European project. These items are:

- Generally speaking, do you think that [OUR COUNTRY'S] membership of the European Union is a good thing, a bad thing, or neither good nor bad?
- Taking everything into consideration, would you say that [OUR COUNTRY] has on balance benefited or not from being a member of the European Union? (benefited, not benefited, don't know).

Trends for the first of these items indicate that in the run-up to the Maastricht Treaty ratification period there was a marked increase in levels of Euro-enthusiasm (see McLaren 2006; see also Chapter 3). By 1991, approximately 70 per cent of Europeans (on average across the EU, that is) were claiming that their country's membership of the EU was a good thing. Also of interest is that by the time of the signing of the Amsterdam Treaty in 1997, enthusiasm had waned and less than 50 per cent of European citizens were claiming that their country's EU membership was a good thing. While some of this trend can be explained by the entry of several Eurosceptic member states in 1995, the same sort of downward trend in enthusiasm can be found in the original six (Western Germany, France, Italy, and the Benelux Countries) and the 'southern enlargement' countries (Greece, Spain, and Portugal), groups of countries that can usually be counted amongst the most enthusiastic EU supporters.

In terms of country differences, it is also apparent that citizens in the original six countries generally tend to be more positive about their countries' EU memberships than citizens of other member states, although Germany and France were leaning in the Eurosceptic direction toward the late 1990s. Similarly, the 'southern enlargement' countries tend to be relatively enthusiastic about EU membership, but not to the same degree as many of the original six (particularly the Netherlands, Luxembourg, and Italy). On the other hand, citizens in the First and Eftan enlargement countries lean toward the Eurosceptic direction, with, for instance, approximately 30–40 per cent claiming that their country's membership of the EU had been a good thing by the late 1990s in countries like the UK, Finland, Austria, and Sweden. (The first enlargement included Britain, Denmark, and Ireland while the Eftan enlargement consisted of Austria, Sweden, and Finland.) Not surprisingly, Ireland is a clear exception to this pattern, as well as to the general EU pattern: while positive attitudes to the EU were dropping across other member states in the 1990, the Irish became more and more Euro-enthusiastic from the mid- to the late 1990s. This is generally attributed to the economic miracle in Ireland that is thought to have been stimulated by the budgetary outlays coming from the EU (to be discussed further below).

Another key survey item often investigated is the question of whether one's country has benefited from membership of the EC/EU. Cross-time trends in responses to this item exhibit the same enthusiasm followed by scepticism or ambivalence in the 1990s, but the cross-time changes are not nearly as dramatic (see McLaren 2006; see also Chapter 3). From the 1980s through to the present period, clearly the majority of EU citizens have believed that their country has benefited from EU membership. However, there are also clear country differences: citizens of the UK, Finland, Austria, and Sweden are consistently below the EU average for this item and, by the early twenty-first century, Germans are also considerably below the average.

The chapter now turns to some of the key explanations provided for individual differences in Euroscepticism. Our discussion will be focused upon theories that have been developed since the early 1970s to explain varying attitudes to European integration, and the data currently available to test these theories are from the EU15 (the pre-2004 CEE enlargement set of member states). The last section of this chapter will consider public opinion and the EU amongst the new CEE member states.

KEY POINTS

- Trends in public opinion toward the EU are collected through regular polls known as *Eurobarometer* polls.
- EU-enthusiasm was generally on the rise until 1991.
- Enthusiasm was considerably reduced by 1997.
- Citizens in the UK, Finland, Austria, and Sweden are amongst the most Eurosceptic mass publics, while the original six and southern enlargement member states, plus the Irish, are amongst the most enthusiastic.
- However, enthusiasm for the EU declined during the 1990s in every member state except Ireland.

Knowledge of the EU and cognitive mobilization

Early approaches to the study of attitudes to European integration conceptualized the project in terms of **cosmopolitanism** and contended that those who were more 'cognitively mobilized' would gravitate toward the new **supranational** organization. It was also contended that differences in opinion regarding the EC were likely to stem from familiarity with the project itself – the more people knew about it, the less fearful they would be of it and thus the more supportive they would be as well. Initially, the test of these ideas revolved around creating a combined index of education level and political discussion; it was argued that those who were better educated and talked politics with their friends and family more often were more cognitively mobilized and were the individuals who would be more supportive of the European project (see Inglehart 1970). Later research has used education as an indicator of another concept (see below) and has tended to focus on the political discussion component of cognitive mobilization (see Gabel 1998). Moreover, later analyses have pointed to the conclusion that knowledge of the EC/EU itself can have an independent effect on support for the project (see Karp, Banducci, and Bowler 2003). Here we examine a few simple tabulations to illustrate these relationships.

As indicated in Table 23.1, 66 per cent of those who claim to discuss politics with friends frequently also claim that their country's membership of the

Table 23.1 Attitudes to EU membership by political discussion (%)

	Frequently	Occasionally	Never	DK, NA
A good thing	66	58	47	49
Neither good nor bad	20	27	31	29
A bad thing	12	11	10	9
DK, NA	2	4	12	13
No.	2,173	8,863	4,864	112

Source: *Eurobarometer* 57(1) (Spring 2002).

Table 23.2 Attitudes to EU membership by self-reported knowledge of EU (%)

	Little knowledge (1–3)	Medium knowledge (4–8)	High knowledge (8–10)
A good thing	42	62	71
A bad thing	12	10	10
Neither good nor bad	33	25	18
DK	13	3	1
No.	5,609	9,015	1,204

Source: *Eurobarometer* 57(1) (Spring 2002).

EU is a good thing; on the other hand, 47 per cent of those who claim to never talk politics with friends would argue that EU membership is a good thing. However, as is apparent from the second and third rows of the table, those who never talk politics are not necessarily hostile to the EU – they simply tend to be more apathetic (giving the 'neither good nor bad' response). We see a similar relationship when we examine Euro-enthusiasm against self-professed knowledge of the EU (Table 23.2). While 42 per cent of those who claim little knowledge of the EU think their country's membership has been a good thing, 71 per cent of those with a great deal of knowledge of the EU are clearly EU-enthusiasts. Again, however, the key way in which lack of knowledge is expressed vis-à-vis the EU is through ambivalence; while only 18 per cent of those with a self-reported high level of knowledge of the EU claim that EU membership is neither good nor bad, 33 per cent of those with low levels of EU knowledge claim the same.

KEY POINTS

- People who discuss politics frequently are said to be *cognitively mobilized*.
- Cognitively mobilized Europeans are amongst the strongest supporters of the European project.
- In addition, those who know more about the EU (either self-professed or in a knowledge quiz) are also generally more enthusiastic.

Political economy and rationality

In the mid-1980s, the discipline of Political Science was becoming heavily influenced by rational, utilitarian approaches to the study of politics. More specifically, models of political behaviour were being developed around the assumption that individuals rationally pursue their self-interest. This approach has had a powerful impact on the study of attitudes to European integration. Some of these theories have been *egocentric* in nature – that is, individuals support or oppose the integration project because they personally have benefited (or will benefit) or have been harmed (or will be harmed) from it. Other approaches that would fit within this context are more *sociotropic* in nature: citizens of some of the EU member states are more supportive of the European project because their *countries* have benefited from the European project.

With regard to the egocentric utilitarian theories, the contention is that individuals from certain socio-economic backgrounds are doing far better economically than individuals of other backgrounds as a result of European integration. In particular, the opening up of the Single Market and the common currency are thought to benefit top-level business executives the most, as they no longer face trade barriers and exchange rate differences across (most of) the EU. Similarly, individuals with higher levels of education will be more likely than those with little education to feel that their knowledge and skills will serve them well in a wider EU market.

Furthermore, it is argued that those with higher incomes are more favourable toward European integration because of the freed capital markets and monetary union which make it more possible for such individuals to move capital across the EU to earn better interest rates. On the other hand, those with poor job skills, levels of education, and incomes are expected to be the most fearful of a common market and monetary integration. As business executives are free to look across the EU-wide market for lower-paid or higher-skilled workers, domestic *manual* workers in particular are likely to feel vulnerable to job loss. Moreover, without any Europe-wide social safety net and with member state governments being pressured by EU-wide agreements and the European Commission to reduce social welfare budgets (or increase taxation to fund these benefits), those at the lowest levels of occupational skill, education, and income are expected to be most economically vulnerable and hostile to the EU as a whole (see Gabel 1998).

As illustrated in Tables 23.3, 23.4, and 23.5, these theories are generally supported empirically. For instance, while 70 per cent of professionals and executives claim that their country's membership of the EU has been a good thing, only 48 per cent of manual workers would say the same; similarly, 46 per cent of the unemployed across the EU think that their country's membership of the EU has been a good thing. In addition, while 47 per cent of those with lower levels of education are happy about their country's membership of the EU, an overwhelming 66 per cent of those with higher levels of education claim that their country's EU membership is good. Finally, there are almost identical percentages for the income variable. As argued above, however, the lack of positive attitudes to the EU does not necessarily translate into negativity; in general, those who are not thought to do very well in an expanded market lean towards the neutral response more heavily than groups like professionals and executives. Thus, the potential losers from EU integration do not appear to perceive themselves as such and instead tend to be generally neutral about the project.

In addition to proposing the notion of egocentric utilitarianism, rational approaches have also focused upon the **sociotropic** costs and benefits that the EU brings. That is, the EU can provide economic benefits to member states in two realms: trade and budgetary outlays (see Eichenberg and

Table 23.3 Occupation and attitudes to EU membership (%)

	A good thing	A bad thing	Neither good nor bad	DK	No.
Professional	70	8	21	1	507
Executive	69	8	20	3	1,217
Manual worker	48	12	33	8	2,225
Unemployed	46	12	32	9	844
Retired	50	15	28	7	3,512
Small business owner	61	9	26	4	853
Farmer	57	17	24	2	226
Student	67	6	21	5	1,730
Housewife	51	8	31	11	1,897
Other	57	10	28	5	3,001

Source: *Eurobarometer* 57(1) (Spring 2002).

Dalton 1993). Analyses indicate that these factors do fairly consistently explain attitudes to integration. A country's EU budget balance in particular has a strong impact on the percentage in the country saying that EU membership is a good thing (see McLaren 2006; see also Chapter 3). The evidence indicates that key net contributors to the EU budget – Britain and Germany – have the smallest percentages of citizens claiming that their country's EU membership is good (at about 30 per cent in the UK and 40 per cent in Germany). On the other hand, citizens in countries that are the largest beneficiaries of the EU budget – particularly Spain and Ireland – are far more positive about their country's membership of the EU, with approximately 65 per cent in Spain and 75 per cent in Ireland claiming to feel positively about EU membership. Moreover, the trend across member states is fairly linear, in that attitudes to EU membership become more positive in proportion to the amount of money the member state contributes to or receives from the EU budget. The trend for trade benefits is not quite as clear, however (McLaren 2006). Thus, the most powerful of the sociotropic explanations appears to be that related to the budget balance.

Table 23.4 Education* and attitudes to EU membership (%)

	Up to age 15	16–19 years	Age 20 or more
A good thing	47	54	66
A bad thing	12	10	10
Neither good nor bad	32	29	22
DK	10	7	3
No.	4,325	6,829	4,794

*Education is measured by the age at which the survey respondent stopped his or her full-time education; because of the vast differences in education systems across the EU, this survey item has become the standard measure of education used in academic research.

Source: *Eurobarometer* 57(1) (Spring 2002).

Table 23.5 Income and attitudes to EU membership (%)

	Low	Low-mid	High-mid	High	DK
A good thing	47	51	56	64	58
A bad thing	13	13	10	10	8
Neither good nor bad	32	30	29	23	26
DK	8	6	4	3	8
No.	2,635	2,747	2,614	2,642	5,374

Source: *Eurobarometer* 57(1) (Spring 2002).

KEY POINTS

- *Egocentric utilitarianism* explains support for the European Union in terms of the economic costs and benefits of the European project to the individual.
- Those with higher levels of education, better job skills, and higher incomes are, it is argued, amongst the most supportive of European integration because their skills and incomes put them in a superior competitive position in a free market.
- However, those without such skills are not necessarily hostile to the project, but instead display indifference.
- *Sociotropic utilitarianism* explains support for the EU in terms of the benefits that the EU has brought to the country as a whole, specifically budgetary outlays and increased trade.

Attitudes to the national government

The arguments presented above assume that EU citizens are able to consider rationally the economic costs and benefits of EU membership to their own personal lives. The approaches discussed in this section and the next make very different arguments about how individuals come to feel the way they do about the EU. That is, these approaches argue that support for or opposition to integration may have very little to do with perceived economic gains or losses. This is because it is unlikely that most Europeans are able to calculate whether they have indeed benefited or not from European integration. That is, the egocentric utilitarian models in particular demand a great deal of knowledge of both the integration process and the economy, and for the ordinary European to come to any conclusion about whether he or she is going to be harmed by the process is likely to be extraordinarily difficult. Thus, many researchers have argued that because of the complexity of the integration process (and the EU institutions), the EU is often perceived in terms of *national* issues rather than European-level ones. This effect is seen most clearly in the context of referenda (Franklin, Marsh, and McLaren 1994), in that referenda on European issues often turn into a vote on the national government's popularity. For example, the French nearly voted against the Maastricht Treaty in 1992, not because of opposition to the components of that Treaty (for example, monetary integration) but because of unhappiness with the government of the day (see Box 23.1). Further, it is likely that the French and Dutch votes in the recent constitutional referenda were also driven to a considerable extent by unhappiness with the government of the day. Moreover, it has been argued that European elections are generally fought on national issues rather than European-level issues (van der Eijk and Franklin 1996).

Even outside of the context of referenda and elections, some have argued that general feelings about the EU are also driven to some extent by feelings about the national government. As argued by Christopher Anderson (1998), it is clear from survey after survey that few Europeans know much about the details of the European project and so they must be formulating their opinions toward this project from something else. Anderson's contention is that such attitudes are in part projections of feelings about the national government; that is, hostility to the national government is projected on to the EU level while positive feelings about one's national government also translate into positive feelings about the EU.

KEY POINTS

- Political economy approaches may require too much knowledge on the part of EU citizens.
- Most Europeans are unfamiliar with the details of the integration project.
- Referenda on European matters are often turned into referenda or confidence votes on the national government.
- Many EU citizens also project their general feelings about their national governments on to the EU.

Identity

The quest for rational explanations for individual-level feelings toward the EU was motivated by the assumption that the European project was mostly economic in nature. Such an assumption is not unreasonable, in that much of the integration that has occurred has indeed been in various sectors of the economy. However, the overriding goal of such integration has always been political – namely the prevention of war on the European continent. As the most recent of these sets of wars were motivated in part by nationalist expansion, one of the phenomena to be thwarted was therefore to be the roots of such expansion. And while the project as a whole has mostly been sold to Europeans as an economic one, particularly through the 1980s and 1990s, some are likely to perceive it not in economic terms but instead in terms of threat to one of their key identities.

The body of work known as social identity theory leads us to the firm conclusion that identities are terribly important for people and that in-group protectiveness can develop even in the context of seemingly meaningless laboratory experiments and even when individuals expect no material gain for themselves by maintaining such identity (Tajfel 1970). The reasons for such behaviour are still unclear, but the major explanations are that many people use in-group identity and protectiveness to bolster their self-esteem and that some people use these to help them simplify and understand the world (Turner 1985).

European integration may be perceived by Europeans as a potential threat to a basic identity that they have used for either (or both) of these purposes, namely their national identities. Table 23.6 explores the degree to which EU citizens do indeed worry that the European project will bring about a loss of national identity and culture. It is apparent from the figures presented here that concern about the loss of national identity as a result of European integration varies widely across the member states. In Britain, for instance, 60 per cent claim to be currently afraid of the loss of national identity and culture; similar figures can be found in Northern Ireland and Greece. On the other hand, only 28 per cent of Italians, 31 per cent of Belgians, 33 per cent of West Germans, 34 per cent of Spaniards, etc. are worried about this possibility.

To what degree do such fears impact general feelings about the EU? Table 23.7 provides the tabulation between fear of loss of national identity and feeling that EU membership has been a good thing. While 39 per cent of those who worry about the loss of their national identity due to European integration claim that EU membership is a good thing, 66 per cent who do not fear the loss of their national identity believe EU membership to be a good thing. As argued by Liesbet Hooghe and Gary Marks (2004), however, what may be important is the *exclusiveness* of national identity. Indeed, the figures in Table 23.7 indicate that many people who are afraid the EU will lead to a loss of their national identity and culture still think their country's membership of the EU is good nonetheless. Thus, the important distinction may be between those who conceptualize themselves in terms of multiple identities and those who feel that they identify only

Table 23.6 Fear that European integration means loss of national identity (%)

	Currently afraid of it	Not currently afraid of it	DK	No.
Belgium	31	64	6	1,045
Denmark	45	53	2	1,000
W. Germany	33	60	7	1,000
Greece	57	38	5	1,002
Italy	28	67	5	1,000
Spain	34	59	7	1,000
France	47	50	3	1,010
Ireland	46	49	5	984
N. Ireland	62	35	3	307
Luxembourg	41	55	4	602
Netherlands	40	55	5	997
Portugal	53	41	7	1,000
Great Britain	60	34	6	1,004
E. Germany	37	56	6	1,051
Finland	43	55	2	1,010
Sweden	49	49	2	1,000
Austria	36	60	4	1,000
EU15	*43*	*52*	*5*	*16,012*

Source: *Eurobarometer* 57(1) (Spring 2002).

Table 23.7 Fear of loss of identity and attitudes to EU membership (%)

	Currently afraid of it	Not currently afraid of it	DK
A good thing	44	66	38
A bad thing	17	6	7
Neither good nor bad	32	23	34
DK	7	5	21
No.	6,855	8,395	762

Source: *Eurobarometer* 57(1) (Spring 2002).

with their nationality. In fact, exclusively national identity seems to vary widely across the EU. Minorities in the original six countries, Spain, and Ireland tend to see themselves in exclusively national terms while clear majorities in the UK, Greece, Finland, and Sweden claim to identify exclusively as nationals. Table 23.8 also indicates that this factor does indeed seem to be important in explaining general feelings about the EU. However, both Tables 23.7 and 23.8 also indicate that while some of those who see themselves exclusively in national terms and those who fear the loss of national identity are openly hostile to the EU, it is more generally the case that such fears translate into ambivalence toward the EU rather than outright hostility.

Table 23.8 Exclusive national identity and attitudes to EU membership

	Nationality only	Nationality and European	European and nationality	European only	DK
A good thing	37	69	74	74	42
A bad thing	19	5	3	4	9
Neither good nor bad	35	23	20	18	32
DK	10	4	3	3	17
No.	6,656	7,375	1,056	559	366

Source: *Eurobarometer* 57(1) (Spring 2002).

KEY POINTS

- The ultimate goal of European integration is political rather than economic.
- A reduction in feelings of nationalism (particularly those that might lead to nationalist expansion) also seems to be one of the goals of European integration.
- *Social identity theory* points to the fundamental importance of identity to humans.
- European integration is perceived as a threat to one of the key identities of Europeans, their national identities.
- Worry about the loss of national identity varies considerably by country, however: clear majorities in the UK and Greece believe their national identities to be under threat by the EU, while roughly one-third of Italians, Belgians, Germans, and Spaniards worry about this possibility.
- *Exclusiveness* of identity may be more important in explaining hostility to the EU.

The perceived poverty of EU institutions

In contrast to the above two approaches, which contend that in the face of little specific knowledge of the EU, citizens are likely to use proxies such as their feelings about the national government of the day or to revert to concerns about the loss of national identities, other recent approaches to the study of public opinion and the EU assume that people are at least familiar with some aspects of the EU; in particular, people may perceive that EU institutions are deficient and become hostile to the project as a whole because of the poor quality of these institutions (Rohrschneider 2002). As illustrated in Table 23.9, levels of trust in the key policy-making institutions of the EU vary considerably across member states. For instance, only 34 per cent of the UK public trusts the European Parliament, while 30 per cent trusts the Commission, 21 per cent trusts the EU Council, and 35 per cent trusts the European Court of Justice. In contrast, in Italy and Luxembourg, trust in the EP is generally widespread, although trust in the other EU institutions is not quite as high. In general across the EU, roughly half of the public trusts each of the key EU institutions. Moreover, empirical analyses consistently

Table 23.9 Trust in EU institutions, 2002 (%)

	European Parliament	European Commission	Council of Ministers	European Court of Justice
France	55	50	42	43
Belgium	56	52	45	46
Netherlands	60	57	50	62
Germany	54	42	37	59
Italy	70	64	55	49
Luxembourg	70	66	59	70
Denmark	59	53	47	71
Ireland	63	58	47	54
UK	34	30	21	35
Greece	58	52	46	50
Spain	58	52	47	44
Portugal	59	57	52	51
Finland	54	52	45	58
Sweden	47	41	43	56
Austria	46	42	36	56
EU15	*56*	*51*	*45*	*54*

Source: *Eurobarometer* 57(1) (Spring 2002).

point to the conclusion that distrust of these institutions or perceiving that the EU institutions are deficient has a substantial effect on general attitudes to the EU, *even after very strict statistical controls* are put in place to minimize the possibility of spuriousness.

KEY POINTS

- Many Europeans are opposed to the EU because they do not trust European institutions.
- However, an overall majority of EU citizens does claim to trust these institutions.

Public opinion in the new member states

Most of the research that has been conducted on public support for the European Union or the European integration project has been based on the EU12 or EU15. Recent publications have, however, investigated attitudes to the EU amongst the member states that joined the EU in May 2004. One of the key points to note about public opinion regarding the EU in these countries is that it is – perhaps surprisingly – fairly lukewarm (see McLaren 2006; see also Chapter 26). The cross-time trends in the Central and East European *Candidate Barometers* indicate that even in the early 1990s – prior to entry to the EU – the overall image of the EU in Central and Eastern Europe was not very positive. Moreover, amongst many of the CEE candidates, citizens became less and less positive toward the EU during the mid-1990s, presumably as a result of the EU's initially hesitant response to the prospect of a CEE enlargement. It was only after the EU finally opened accession talks to these candidates in 1997 that its image received a bolster amongst the mass public. Moreover, when asked whether their country's membership of the EU would be a good thing (prior to entry in May of 2004, that is), the response was clearly mixed amongst the candidate countries (see McLaren 2006; and Chapter 26). Rather interestingly, citizens in the candidate countries that were not accepted for entry in 2004 – Bulgaria, Romania, and Turkey – are amongst the most positive about their country's EU memberships. At the low end of support for the EU, we find Estonia and Latvia, where only 30–40 per cent during the 1999–2004 period thought that their country's membership of the EU would be a good thing.

In terms of the explanations for differences in opinion regarding the EU, while the early studies mentioned above question the applicability of the utilitarian model, my own findings (McLaren 2006) indicate that this model may be just as applicable in the new member states as it is in the EU15, if not more so. That is, it is clear that feelings about the EU are driven in great part by perceptions of one's own financial situation. It is also clear that citizens of the new member states are worried about the financial cost of the EU to their own countries. In addition, as with citizens of the old EU15, a considerable portion of the citizenry in the new member states is worried about the impact of European integration on things like their national identity and culture. Thus, the explanations for opposition to the EU in the CEE member states are quite similar to those from the EU15. At the same time, however, feelings about the EU appear to be generally tied up with feelings about other reforms, particularly economic and political reforms after the collapse of communism (Christin 2005).

KEY POINTS

- Public opinion toward the EU in the new member states is generally lukewarm.
- The image of the EU declined amongst the new member states whilst they were still candidates, until accession talks were opened in 1997.
- The candidates that were not admitted in the 2004 enlargement – Turkey, Bulgaria, and Romania – include citizens who are the most positive about the EU.
- The Baltic countries, very much like their Scandinavian counterparts, are the least enthusiastic of the new member states about the EU.
- Citizens in the new member states are mostly concerned with the cost of the EU both to their own countries and to their own financial situations.
- Citizens of the new member states are also worried about the potential for loss of national identity and culture due to European integration at roughly the same levels as the EU15 citizens.

Conclusion

The analyses discussed above point to several conclusions. The first is that feelings about the EU seem to range from ambivalence to support. Only very small proportions across the EU are openly hostile to it. However, these proportions do vary by country, and hostility is far greater in countries like the UK, Sweden, Finland, and Austria.

This chapter also outlined the explanations for differences of opinions regarding the EU. Firstly, it was argued that higher levels of political discussion (or cognitive mobilization) and greater knowledge of the EU both appear to lead to more positive opinions about the EU. Those who do not talk politics much with friends and who do not know much about the EU tend to be far more ambivalent about the European project.

Secondly, it was argued that some of the difference in opinion regarding the EU was *utilitarian* in nature. It was argued that there were two components to this utilitarian approach to the EU: egocentric and sociotropic. Egocentric utilitarians support the EU because it has brought them or is likely to bring them economic benefits; others in this category are ambivalent toward the project because they have not received any benefits themselves. Sociotropic utilitarians support or oppose the project because of the budgetary outlays they have received from the EU, which have presumably increased economic development and growth, or because of the large amount that their country contributes to the EU budget.

Thirdly, part of the differences in attitudes to the EU is thought to be related to perceptions of the national government. That is, some individuals project their feelings about their own government on to the EU level; when they feel positively about the national government, the EU gets an extra boost of support, but when they feel negatively about the national government, the EU is punished.

Fourthly, it is argued that some portion of public opinion toward the EU is driven by concerns regarding the loss of national identity. More specifically, individuals who identify exclusively in national terms (vis-à-vis Europe) are either more hostile or in some cases more ambivalent to the EU.

Fifthly, Euroscepticism (ambivalence and hostility) seems to stem partly from perceived deficiencies in the EU institutions. Thus, it is not only academics who worry about the problem of democracy in the EU; ordinary citizens are also concerned about this issue.

Finally, the chapter turned to the new member states, and contended that citizens in these countries were very similar to their EU15 counterparts. Many of their concerns are also utilitarian and identity-based in nature, but they have additional concerns that confound the EU with the ongoing economic and political reforms.

Overall, then, we have a fairly good idea why some individuals are positive about the EU, some are negative, and many others are simply ambivalent. Still, even when we take all of the above-mentioned factors into account, it is also clear that there is room for improvement in our explanations. Thus, it is highly likely that research in this field will continue to develop further alternative theories in the near future.

QUESTIONS

1. To what extent is European public opinion still marked by a 'permissive consensus'?
2. To what extent are referenda on European issues and European elections about *Europe*?
3. To what extent are European citizens utilitarian in their approaches to the EU?
4. Why does cognitive mobilization contribute to positive feelings about the EU?
5. Is distrust in EU institutions widespread? What explains distrust in these institutions?
6. To what extent are citizens of the new member states similar to those of the EU15 in their attitudes to the EU?
7. Why are citizens in new member states so seemingly Eurosceptic?
8. What are some alternative explanations for differences in public opinion toward the EU?

GUIDE TO FURTHER READING

■ Gabel, M. J. *Interests and Integration: Market Liberalization, Public Opinion, and European Union* (Ann Arbor, MI: University of Michigan Press, 1998). This book provides an analysis of the utilitarian approaches to the study of public opinion and the EU.

■ McLaren, L. M. *Identity, Interests and Attitudes to European Integration* (Basingstoke: Palgrave, 2006). This book reanalyses the utilitarian approach and introduces the concepts of group conflict and identity to explain public opinion towards the EU.

■ Niedermayer, O., and Sinnott, R. (eds) *Public Opinion and Internationalized Governance* (Oxford: Oxford University Press, 1995). This edited volume provides chapters by separate authors on multiple topics related to the EU and public opinion.

European Union elections

■ Thomassen, J., and Schmitt, H. (eds) 'European Union' in H. Schmitt and J. Thomassen (eds), *Political Representation and Legitimacy in the European Union* (Oxford: Oxford University Press, 1999). This edited volume provides key analyses of voting behaviour and opinions amongst both the mass European public and members of the European Parliament.

■ van der Eijk, C., and Franklin, M. N. (eds) *Choosing Europe? The European Electorate and National Politics in the Face of Union* (Ann Arbor, MI: University of Michigan Press, 1996). This edited volume provides a convincing argument by the editors about the nature of voting in European elections, as well as country-by-country chapters that further elaborate this argument in each EU member state.

IMPORTANT WEBSITES

- **http://www.gesis.org/en/data_service/eurobarometer/** *Eurobarometer* data: the German Social Sciences Infrastructure Services is the key European archive for *Eurobarometer* data. Access to codebooks and data can be gained through this site.
- **http://europa.eu.int/comm/public_opinion/index_en.htm**. *Eurobarometer* reports: the Public Opinion unit of the European Commission writes regular reports on *Eurobarometer* and *Candidate Barometer* polls. These reports can be found at this web address.
- **http://www.europeanelectionstudies.net**. European Election Studies: the European Election Studies group has led the way in studying voting behaviour in European elections since 1979. This website provides information about the group's research activities.

Visit the Online Resource Centre that accompanies this book for lots of interesting additional material. http://www.oxfordtextbooks.co.uk/orc/cini2e/

24 Differentiated European Integration

KERSTIN JUNGE

Chapter Contents

Reader's Guide

'Differentiated integration' (or differentiation) describes methods of European integration that do not require all member states to participate in every integration project, or that allow member states to implement European policies at their own pace. This chapter explores the four key issues related to the differentiation of the European integration process: the relevance of differentiated integration in the EU of the early twenty-first century; the key methods of differentiation; hopes and concerns with regard to their application; and a brief discussion of the experience thus far of applying methods of differentiation in EU policies. The chapter concludes by summarizing the key points made and by giving a glimpse of future developments.

Introduction

Differentiated integration (or **differentiation**) is used in this chapter as a collective term that covers all methods of European Union (EU) integration that do not require member states to participate in every integration project, or that allow member countries to implement European policies at their own pace. Other terms frequently employed to describe these processes are flexibility or 'closer cooperation'.

Historically, uniform integration – the idea that all member states progress at the same time and speed towards an 'ever closer union' – was the only accepted (and indeed acceptable) method of developing the European Community and later European Union, as it symbolized the principles on which the organization was founded. However, consecutive enlargement rounds increasing the number of EU countries from six to 25 and bouts of deepening have shown that such joint progression is likely to become more difficult. As a result, member states appear to be warming to differentiation as an alternative integration concept supplementing – though not replacing – 'uniformity'. The inclusion of 'enhanced cooperation' into EU primary law with the **Treaty of Amsterdam**, enabling a subset of member states to progress faster than the rest with certain integration projects, and the subsequent development of the concept in the Nice Treaty and in the **Constitutional Treaty**, seem to be sanctioning this alternative mode of integration.

Against this background, this chapter explores, in the changed circumstances of differentiation in the early twenty-first century, the main methods of differentiation, discusses possible dynamics related to their application in the European integration process, and assesses some of the risks associated with these instruments. It finishes with a brief conclusion summarizing the main arguments made in the chapter.

The EU in the twenty-first century: flexibility as the norm?

At the beginning of the twenty-first century, flexibility is a much more integral part of the reality of the European integration process than it has ever been before. European integration was never a 'uniform' process. Directives are transposed by member states in accordance with their national law. They often contain minimum standards that member states are free to exceed (in particular in the fields of environmental and social policies where, arguably, differences between national policy preferences, approaches, and abilities are particularly pronounced). Countries joining the EU in the last five enlargement rounds have been granted transition periods: a period of time after accession to the EU when EU law is not fully applied in the new member states, either to give them more time to implement fully the ***acquis communautaire*** or to allow the existing member states to adjust to their accession. Crucially, however, these examples of flexibility in the European integration process have in common that the fundamental objectives of the policies to which they apply are not contested among member states. That is, all countries agree that a policy problem is best pursued at the European level and all countries participate in binding legislative agreements. This is the governance model originally foreseen by the founders of the EU. In this chapter, it is labelled 'the paradigm of uniformity': the idea that EU member states progress jointly towards an ever closer union.

In the late twentieth century and early twenty-first century, however, it is possible to observe a diluting of this paradigm of 'uniform integration'. While in previous decades European integration entailed a degree of de facto flexibility, now new modes of managing the integration process are being introduced into the Treaties (the so-called EU primary law) and applied. *De jure* flexibility is being established that diverges from the paradigm of uniformity as originally envisaged by the 'founding fathers' of the EU. A first concrete expression of this development was Economic and Monetary Union (EMU). The results of the negotiations to introduce a single currency, laid down in the Maastricht Treaty on European Union, stipulated economic competence as a precondition for full membership by requiring EU countries to comply with five convergence criteria before becoming full members of EMU (see Chapter 20). In doing so, member states accepted the possibility of a multi-speed Europe where countries complying with the convergence criteria are able to progress faster than those not complying. Importantly, EMU was also the first example of à la carte integration: both Britain and Denmark were granted an indefinite opt-out which exempts them from having to join even if they comply with the convergence criteria. While at the time, the EMU opt-outs of Britain and Denmark were widely regarded as exemptions, only a few years later the Treaty of Amsterdam introduced a clause into EU primary law which for the first time allowed a subset of countries to progress with an integration project without the remainder of the EU countries. These provisions on 'enhanced cooperation' were maintained and refined in the Treaty of Nice (see Box 24.1). They also found their way into the EU Constitution (see Box 24.2), where the threshold for establishing 'enhanced cooperation' has been significantly lowered and extended to new policies.

A further sign of the growing acceptability of flexible modes of integration is the inauguration by the 2000 Lisbon Council of what has been described as a 'new method of governance' (Regent 2002) for the EU: the **open method of coordination** (OMC). The OMC is an instrument of 'soft law' rather than a binding agreement; it is a mechanism for coordinating national policies, which focuses on benchmarking member states' policies and does not include any mechanisms of enforcement. The application of the OMC was originally restricted to employment and social exclusion policies, but has subsequently been extended to information society and enterprise policies. Thus, what appeared impossible only a few years ago is now apparently a reality of the European integration process: a potentially looser, more flexible Union. What is at the origin of these developments?

Arguably, these developments are an expression of a fundamentally changed reality of European integration in the twenty-first century compared to the earlier years. In the preamble to the 1957 Treaty of Rome, the six founding countries of what was then the EEC – France, Germany, Italy, Belgium, the Netherlands, and Luxembourg – declared that they intended to 'lay the foundations of an ever closer union among the peoples of Europe' and to 'ensure the economic and social progress of their countries by common action to eliminate the barriers which divide Europe'. These common political and economic objectives demanded the participation of all six member states in the policies set out in the Treaty. There was also a legal requirement for uniform integration, however. As Martenczuk (2000) points out, law is the instrument used to realize the objectives of the integration process. If the EU is to be deepened towards an ever closer union, European law must apply and be enforced in a uniform manner across the Union in the interest of consistency (see also Chapter 12). It is against this background that the European Court of Justice (ECJ), in its case law, has continually emphasized the importance of interpreting and applying Community law in a uniform way. The political and economic motives underlying the origins of the EEC, as well as the use of law as the instrument with which to achieve them, are thus responsible for making uniformity the dominant paradigm of European integration.

CASE STUDY 24.1

Enhanced cooperation in the Nice Treaty

The provisions on 'enhanced cooperation' in the Nice Treaty are divided into general (enabling) clauses and clauses specific to each pillar of the EU.

General clauses

Title VI 'Provisions on Enhanced Co-operation' of the Treaty on European Union (TEU) contains some general conditions for the use of the instrument. They are sometimes referred to as 'enabling clauses' because they give a general permission to interested member states to establish an 'enhanced cooperation' within the framework of the Treaties.

According to Article 43, member states may establish closer cooperation between themselves and may, to this end, make use of the EU institutions, procedures, and mechanism if the cooperation:

- is aimed at furthering the objectives of the Union and the Community, at advancing the integration process and at protecting and serving their interests;
- respects the Treaties, the single institutional framework, and the *acquis communautaire*;
- concerns Union or Community policies but not those that fall within the exclusive competence of the Community;
- does not undermine the internal market or economic and social cohesion;
- does not constitute a barrier to or discrimination in trade between the member states and does not distort competition between them;
- involves a minimum of eight member states;
- respects the competences, rights, and obligations of non-participating member states;
- does not affect the Schengen protocol; and
- is open to all member states.

According to Article 43a, enhanced cooperation may be used only as a last resort. Article 43b requires that enhanced cooperation is open to all member states as long as they comply with the conditions for participation; both Commission and participating member states shall encourage as many EU countries as possible to take part.

According to Article 44 (1), all member states take part in the deliberations on enhanced cooperation, but only the participating member states adopt the provisions.

Specific clauses

In addition to these general provisions, there are specific clauses for each EU pillar. They mostly concern decision-making procedures.

In the first (EC) pillar, EU institutions have more influence over the establishment of enhanced cooperation. According to the new Article 11, the Commission has the right to propose enhanced cooperation after interested member states have requested it to do so. Authorization for enhanced cooperation is given by the Council by a qualified majority on a proposal from the Commission and after consulting the EP. When enhanced cooperation is to be established in an area where the codecision procedure applies, the assent of the EP is required. A member state may also request that the matter be referred to the European Council for discussion. After the matter has been raised before the European Council, decision-making proceeds as outlined above.

The Treaty of Nice also introduces new clauses on enhanced cooperation in the second (Common Foreign and Security Policy) pillar. According to Articles 27a–e, enhanced cooperation may be used for joint actions or common positions, but not in matters having military or defence implications. Interested member states address a request to the European Council to authorize the cooperation. The Commission 'shall give its opinion particularly on whether the enhanced cooperation as proposed is consistent with Union policies' (Article 27c). Otherwise the Commission and the EP must only be informed about developments.

In the third (Justice and Home Affairs) pillar, member states wanting to establish enhanced cooperation may ask the Commission to submit a proposal. However, in contrast to the procedure for the first pillar, if the Commission refuses to do so, the interested member states may develop a proposal themselves and submit it to the Council for authorization. Authorization is given by a qualified majority and after consulting the EP. Again, a member state may request that the matter be referred to the European Council.

CASE STUDY 24.2

Flexibility in the EU's Constitutional Treaty

The EU Constitutional Treaty, signed in October 2004, but unratified as of mid-2006, introduces some significant changes to the provisions on enhanced cooperation of the Nice Treaty, in terms of both procedures and the policies to which enhanced cooperation applies.

Chapter III (Article I-44) lists the general conditions for enhanced cooperation which have been simplified and modified compared to the Nice provisions. The text reinstates that enhanced cooperation is to be used as a last resort 'when it has established that the objectives of such cooperation cannot be attained within a reasonable period by the Union as a whole' (Article I-44.2). One-third of member states must participate in the integration project and decisions must be taken by qualified majority representing 55 per cent of participating member states or 65 per cent of the populations of the participating member states. Decisions can be blocked by member states representing more than 35 per cent of the population of the participating member states.

Moreover, the Constitutional Treaty extends the applicability of enhanced cooperation to those matters 'having military or defence implications'. In the field of defence and security policy, the procedures for starting enhanced cooperation differ slightly from those in other policies. In the CFSP requests to this effect have to be addressed to the Council, not the Commission. Opinions have to be given by both the Union Minister for Foreign Affairs *and* the Commission. Moreover, voting takes place by unanimity (Article III-419.2 and 422.3).

In addition, the Constitutional Treaty introduces a new form of flexibility only applicable in the area of CFSP: *permanent structured cooperation* (Arts I-41.6 and III-312). Unlike enhanced cooperation, permanent structured cooperation does not require a minimum number of participating countries. Decisions can be taken by a qualified majority even if they concern CFSP. The conditions for embarking on this permanent structured cooperation are laid down in a Protocol attached to the Constitutional Treaty (n.23):

- further development of own military capabilities (at the national or multinational level);
- participation in 'the main European equipment programmes' and in the activities of the 'Agency in the field of defence capabilities development, research, acquisition and armaments';
- adequate involvement in the creation of the so-called EU 'battle-groups' for high-end military operations.

The Protocol also mentions the need for 'achieving approved objectives concerning the level of investment expenditure on defence equipment' and for 'harmonizing', 'pooling', and 'specializing' defence means and capabilities at the EU level. However, in contrast to what happened for instance with EMU, the Protocol does not list any specific figures to be attained or binding criteria to be met.

Source: http://europa.eu.int/constitution/en/ptoc9_en. htm.

In the early twenty-first century, however, the large economic integration projects that have occupied European policy-makers for most of the past decades have been achieved: the legislation necessary to establish the Single Market is overwhelmingly in place and a single European currency has been created. Further deepening towards an 'ever closer union' now often means Europeanizing policies of which member states are traditionally protective: most notably justice and home affairs or foreign and defence policy. This makes negotiations more difficult as, rather than about technicalities, they concern core functions of the modern nation state, over which sovereignty is not easily pooled. The larger size of the Union also makes it more difficult for all countries to agree on common policies. The 2004 enlargement round saw EU membership rise to 25, and (at the time of writing) further countries are heading towards membership: accession dates have been agreed with Bulgaria and Romania; Turkey and Croatia are candidate countries and a further four countries from the former Yugoslavia are potential candidate countries. These developments mean that the historic assumption of a progression towards an 'ever closer union' involving all member states can no longer be taken for granted. The deep split in positions of member states on the Iraq war, for instance, is only one example highlighting the difficulties of developing common policies in these sensitive areas.

Taken together, these two trends begin to explain the current trends towards looser forms of integration, with regard both to the underlying legal provisions and to the expectations on member states' participation.

KEY POINTS

- In the early twenty-first century, flexibility in the European integration process is becoming more acceptable to the member states.
- This interest in flexibility is an expression of the fundamentally changed reality of the European integration process compared to the 1950s and 1960s. There are now more member states than ever before while at the same time more policies are integrated more deeply than ever before.
- Flexibility is increasingly seen as a solution to managing integration under new circumstances.

Three methods of differentiation

Despite the inclusion of enhanced cooperation into the Treaties and several decades of debate on the topic, as well as increased efforts by various academics to shed light on the issue since the 1990s, the terminology of differentiation remains elusive. A large number of concepts have emerged, often being described with the same or similar words independent of similarities or differences between them. For instance, 'graduated integration', 'core Europe', 'flexible integration', 'variable geometry' tend to be used not only to describe specific methods but also as collective nouns to describe all methods of non-uniform European integration.

Since the 1990s, a number of academics have worked at developing a systematic categorization of differentiation concepts in an attempt to clarify the language of differentiated integration (Stubb 1996; Tuytschaever 1999). Nevertheless, a universally accepted standard terminology has not yet evolved. This section therefore introduces the three main methods of differentiation: multi-speed Europe; integration à la carte; and concentric circles.

Multi-speed Europe

Multi-speed Europe maintains the basic principles that have traditionally underpinned the European integration process. It could therefore be described as the least radical of the three types of differentiation mentioned above. Multi-speed Europe assumes that the EU member states are able to define the common goals of integration and that these goals are accepted and then implemented by all countries. However, proponents of multi-speed Europe acknowledge that 'objective' – that is, economic – differences between member states may make it impossible to achieve these goals at the same time. While all member states will eventually have to apply the agreed policy objectives, multi-speed integration allows countries to do so in their own time. Countries for which progression is economically feasible must thus go ahead, while member states unable to follow because of 'objective' difficulties are permitted to progress according to their abilities. The aim of multi-speed Europe is therefore to achieve, not permanently but merely temporarily, different degrees of integration. In contrast to transition periods or derogations, commonly used for the implementation of directives or to facilitate the adoption of the *acquis communautaire* by new member states, multi-speed integration does not involve fixed timetables for implementation. The different levels of implementation of a multi-speed policy are maintained for an indefinite period of time. However, in order to prevent a permanent separation of the faster from the slower member states, countries lagging behind in the implementation of a multi-speed policy are supported in the process of catching up with their more advanced peers. Multi-speed Europe thus maintains the legal and institutional structure of the EU as well as the objective of an ever closer union among all member states. Yet, it adapts the method of achieving this goal in response to the increasing (economic) heterogeneity of the Union. A good example of a recent application of multi-speed Europe is Economic and Monetary Union (EMU): only member states complying with the five convergence criteria may fully participate. Thus, the new member states from central and southern European that joined the EU in 2004 are not currently full members of the single European currency as none complies with all of the Maastricht criteria.

Europe à la carte

Europe à la carte could be described as the most radical method of differentiation with regard to underlying assumptions, method, and outcome. Europe à la carte allows member states to 'pick and choose' the European policies in which they participate. The current dominant paradigm of European integration, which also underpins multi-speed Europe, is based on the assumption that member states will find a common denominator that will allow them to progress together (uniform integration). By contrast, Europe à la carte assumes that this common denominator is missing: social, political, and economic differences between the member states become an insurmountable obstacle to the common progression towards an ever closer union. The most radical variant of Europe à la carte opens up all EU policies to picking and choosing. Most *à la carte* proposals, however, require a common base of policies in which all countries must participate if they want to become an EU member. This common base is usually the Single Market, but may also include some supporting policies such as certain elements of social and environmental policies. Independent of the extent to which picking and choosing is allowed, however, à la carte integration will produce numerous partnerships of varying membership and potentially different degrees of supranationality. Unlike multi-speed Europe, Europe à la carte thus allows for different degrees and forms of integration on a permanent basis and gives up on the idea of uniform progression towards a supranational, and possibly even an ultimately federal, political system. While a unified supranational system is not excluded as an end goal of the integration process, and the different partnerships are presumed to be open to those not initially involved, it is assumed that the predominance of national interests within this model will move the EU in the direction of a purely intergovernmental organization. The two most prominent examples for à la carte integration to date are the **Schengen** cooperation, started in 1986 with an initial subset six member states, and EMU which started without Britain and Denmark as they found it difficult to agree with this policy objective.

Concentric circles

The third and final category of differentiation methods is a Europe of concentric circles. In contrast to the two methods described above, which tend to focus on individual policies and the EU, the concentric circles idea tends to look at the European continent as a whole. It divides European countries into several concentric circles so that around the smallest central layer several other layers are arranged. These circles increase in size the further away they are from the centre. Conversely, the intensity of supranational integration increases from the largest inner (or bottom) layer to the outer (or top) layer. A member of a smaller circle is also a member of the wider circles. Membership of one circle is not permanent, however, and 'upward mobility' (or maybe we should say 'inward mobility') is possible as soon as the necessary (political, social, or economic) conditions are fulfilled, or when the political will for further integration is found. In contrast to the Europe à la carte approach, it will not be possible, using this method, to decide to deepen one policy alone. Rather, the different layers are made up of a set of policies: the more highly integrated a circle is, the more the policies within it are communitarized or Europeanized. The decision by a country to move towards or away from the centre of the circle implies an acceptance of all the policies in that chosen circle. Thus, the concentric circles method does not make single policies available for picking and choosing but limits the choice to different types of international organization or institutional arrangements. The geometric result of this method of differentiation resembles a wedding cake, looked upon from above, or perhaps the ripple effect of a stone thrown into water.

Differences and similarities

The sections above have described the 'ideal types' of the three main methods of differentiating the European integration process. Multi-speed integration, à la carte integration, and concentric circles thus vary greatly in terms of their method of differentiation and possible end product. In brief, multi-speed Europe differentiates by time, à la carte integration by policy, and concentric circles by space (Stubb 1996). The three methods also differ in terms of their outcome. A multi-speed integration is merely differentiated by time. It eventually produces a higher degree of integration for every member state. Europe à la carte, by contrast, results in permanently different degrees of integration, as member states participate in different policies. The concentric circles method, finally, creates a deeper form of integration across a wide range of issues for some member states, and lower levels of integration for others. This is the result of grouping member states into circles depending on their ability and willingness to progress.

As a result of their different potential impacts on the future shape of the EU, the three methods of differentiation have attracted different degrees of scepticism and support from the member states. While multi-speed integration tends to be regarded as largely unproblematic, à la carte integration was for a long time rejected as a model for European integration. It is here that the recent shift of opinion is most obvious, as the provisions on enhanced cooperation inserted into the Treaties since Amsterdam strongly resemble the kind of functional differentiation that à la carte integration implies.

KEY POINTS

- There are three main types of differentiation: multi-speed integration, à la carte integration, and concentric circles.
- The three methods differ in the kind of differentiation employed: multi-speed Europe uses time as the main variable of differentiation; à la carte integration differentiates by policy area; and concentric circles differentiates by space.
- 'Enhanced cooperation' spelt out in the Nice Treaty resembles à la carte integration. The Nice Treaty provisions were extended in the Constitutional Treaty, signed, but unratified.

Some possible problems of differentiation

Much of the scepticism against differentiating the European integration process is based on the fact that it appears to undermine some of the fundamental principles that have long underpinned the European integration process (Devuyst 1999):

- the gradual process towards ever closer union;
- the principle of solidarity among EU member states;

- non-hegemonic (consensual) decision-making;
- democratic decision-making.

Traditionally the European integration process has advanced by means of a gradual transfer of power to the EU level, resulting in an every closer union of all member states. Differentiated integration puts an end to this paradigm. A la carte integration and the concentric circles model allow for the permanent differentiation of the degree of integration in which member states are involved. Thus, rather than moving member states towards an ever closer union, these two methods of differentiation risk fragmenting the EU. If member states are allowed to pick and choose from a wide variety of EU policies or circles, and the EU continues to enlarge, the probability is that not all member states will participate in all EU policies. As a consequence, the EU might break up into subsystems, each with a different membership and each forming permanently different configurations of 'Europe'. While these disintegrating tendencies would obviously be most pronounced in the case of an à la carte Europe, the implementation of multi-speed integration could also produce similar outcomes. Although the method of temporal differentiation implied by the multi-speed model foresees all member states eventually catching up with the 'leaders', a number of factors might obstruct this dynamic. For instance, a change of government in a derogating member state could change that state's policy preferences. Changes in the economic situation might also result in a defection from previously agreed policies. Finally, the realization that policies opted into by a few do not really work or are expensive to operate may prevent a derogating country from making an effort to catch up.

Finally, a shift towards hegemonic decision-making might also cause problems for the democratic legitimacy of decisions adopted. If the more integration-minded member states are able to set the tone of policy content, countries joining late will have no choice but to comply with provisions adopted by others – they will have become 'decision-takers' rather than decision-makers (Andersen *et al.* 2005). Those governments cannot, therefore, be held accountable for the differentiated policy. Differentiated integration could thus exacerbate the democratic deficit of the EU.

Differentiation also challenges the principle of solidarity which is said to operate amongst member states. As Devuyst explains: Schuman insisted that Europe had to 'be built by practical actions whose first result will be to create a de facto solidarity. An extensive differentiation of the integration process threatens this principle . . . the risks are greatest if à la carte integration and concentric circles is extended' (1999: 112). However, temporal differentiation might have the same effects if the faster (and thus richer) member states decide against transfer payments to their poorer partners in order to avoid the double financial burden of implementing the new policies and helping the poorer countries to catch up. In all three instances the result of a loss of solidarity could thus be a two-class Community in which the poor and unwilling member states are left behind permanently, while the remaining ones create ever more sophisticated integration projects. A two-class community, however, will intensify the problems of decision-making and democratic legitimacy that risk being created by the use of differentiated integration in general.

Differentiation also risks putting an end to the principle of non-hegemonic decision-making, that is, the premise that the bigger member states should not be able to dominate the decision-making process and thus impose their preferences on the smaller members. Differentiated integration threatens this principle in two ways. A la carte integration and the concentric circles approach pose a direct threat to non-hegemonic decision-making. In both cases, a member state's abstention will result from a desire not to participate in further policy integration. In principle, it is therefore logical that those states should not be involved in setting up the cooperation, as this might dilute the provisions, rendering them less effective or even useless. These two methods of differentiation therefore assume that subgroups of member states will continue to deepen EU policies unilaterally without granting a say over this new cooperation to non-participants.

What this means is that if the initially unwilling countries decide to participate, they must comply with provisions into which they have had no input. In such cases, initially willing member states are able to dictate the provisions that might ultimately apply to the rest of the union. Even though the provisions on 'enhanced cooperation', which resemble in outlook the principle of à la carte integration, as included in the Treaties and the proposed Constitutional Treaty, somewhat reduce this danger for the first (EC) pillar, Sepos (2005) shows that hegemonic decision-making is still a threat to small member states in particular in the second and third pillars of the EU. In the third (PJCCM) pillar, enhanced cooperation can be invoked even if the Commission refuses to submit a proposal, making it much easier to differentiate a policy. In the second (CFSP/ESDP) pillar, both Commission and EP must only be informed of any plans member states may have on establishing enhanced cooperation. Moreover, the policy itself favours the dominance of the large member states because 'the sensitivity of the issue speaks in favour of limiting the participation only to actors that are instrumental' and larger member states 'enjoy a different international status in the eyes of the world as foreign policy actors, as opposed to smaller member states' (Sepos 2005: 9).

KEY POINTS

- Some of the major potential negative implications of using differentiated integration are that the EU could potentially break up into smaller subsystems; the democratic deficit could become aggravated; and solidarity between member states could be undermined.
- Overall, differentiated integration could threaten the fundamental principles on which the European integration process has been based thus far.

Differentiation: what impact on the EU?

While differentiation does in theory appear to offer a solution to the challenges faced by the European integration process in the twenty-first century, the potential risks involved in the use of these instruments are severe. However, the extent to which they will materialize will depend not only on the execution of methods of differentiation in practice but also on the impact of a differentiated policy on the EU system as a whole. These studies suggest that at least some of the traditional criticisms put forward in connection with differentiated integration may be unjustified.

A number of empirical studies have recently examined the impact of differentiation on the European integration process by examining the two most prominent cases of application: the Schengen agreement and EMU (Junge 2002; Kölliker 2001). These examples show – perhaps paradoxically – that the use of à la carte and multi-speed integration may have a deepening impact on the EU, including rather than (permanently) excluding those member states initially unable or unwilling to participate. Three processes can contribute to this development (Junge 2002).

Importantly, the differentiation of an EU policy can encourage those member states not participating from the beginning to join. On the one hand, the faster progression by some member states may attract those countries that are interested in participating but that were not originally in a position to participate fully. A good example of this is EMU. The convergence criteria established in the Maastricht Treaty meant that Greece, though in favour of the policy, was required to stay out of the single currency as it did not fulfil the economic conditions for participation. As did some of the other countries occasionally quoted as potential 'laggards' in the run-up to the introduction of the single currency (Italy, Spain, and Portugal), Greece embarked on an ambitious economic reform programme which meant it was able to become a full member of EMU in 2001. In addition to the original commitment of these countries to the project, the discourse of their leading politicians displayed a commitment to the European integration process more generally and showed a perceived need to be fully involved in it.

On the other hand, a differentiated policy may attract member states that originally opted out of participation altogether. The Schengen agreement is an example for such a process (see also Chapter 19): originally concluded between six member states only, it now counts almost all the EU member states as members. A discourse analysis of speeches by leading politicians highlights that concerns over status and de facto political influence in the EU are major concerns for countries not fully participating in key integration projects and provide a strong incentive for joining or at least considering doing so.

Kölliker (2001) also argues that differentiated integration can 'pull up' the level of integration in the EU using **public goods theory** to explain this phenomenon. He argues that the motivation of 'outsiders' to join a differentiated policy depends on the type of 'public good' the policy represents. Thus, if policies are differentiated that benefit from the participation of additional countries, the probability that initial laggards or non-participants will join is high. On the other hand, if a differentiated policy suffers from additional countries joining, the probability of differentiation leading to a general lifting of the integration process is reduced.

Fragmentation of the EU into different subsystems is therefore not an inevitable consequence of the use of differentiation. Rather, it would appear that if the 'right' policies for differentiation are chosen, potential fragmenting tendencies can be minimized. Moreover, if differentiated policies are based firmly on EU primary and secondary legislation, the foundations are laid for the eventual integration of à la carte cooperation into the Treaties. Such a process can already be observed in the Schengen agreement. While this was initially concluded as an agreement separate from the EU Treaties, the original six signatories included a number of clauses in their agreement which subordinated the Schengen provisions to Community law. A further process through which differentiation, and in particular à la carte Europe, deepens the policy field concerned is the opportunity it offers for interested, able, and willing member states to achieve high-level solutions: it reduces the degree of compromise necessary to achieve common decisions.

While the risk of fragmentation may have been overrated in previous critiques of differentiation, the impact on democratic decision-making is potentially serious. Thus, evidence is also emerging that differentiation can impact on EU policy-making even if not all member states join: differentiated solutions can serve as a blueprint for common initiatives in the same field or even accelerate the deepening of neighbouring policies (even those in which all member states participate). The Schengen cooperation illustrates this phenomenon. The agreement has clearly served as a blueprint for a number of key decisions taken by all member states in the field of immigration, visa, and asylum policies (for instance the Draft Convention on External Frontiers, common visa regulations, the firearms directive). By concluding an early agreement, a subset of member states has thus had the tools to make a significant impact on the content of provisions agreed to and adopted by all member states. The 'early adopters' have, to an extent, set the pace and the standards for further deepening, leaving only limited scope for those countries not part of the negotiations from the beginning to be heard. This example shows that the issue of 'hegemonic' decision-making is a potentially serious one: differentiated integration means that a subset of member states could be in a position to define not only the content of the differentiated policy without outside interference, but also that of neighbouring policies.

However, the provisions of the Nice Treaty go some way towards reducing (if not eliminating) this risk. By requiring that all member states participate in the negotiations of a differentiated policy (as has in effect happened in the case of EMU), it becomes less likely that a minority of member states' decisions are de facto imposed on countries not initially part of the differentiated policy. This means that while after the 2004 enlargement the 'quorum' of eight countries required to initiate an 'enhanced cooperation' no longer constitutes a majority, the need to involve all member states in the creation of the differentiated policy means that the risk of exclusion is minimized.

KEY POINTS

- The disintegration of the EU is not an inevitable consequence of applying modes of differentiation in EU policies. By being selective about policy areas and ensuring that any cooperation is based on EU law the Union can avoid such tendencies.
- At the same time, hegemonic decision-making is a clear risk as differentiated policy may be a blueprint for prospective common initiatives in neighbouring policy areas. The requirement under 'enhanced cooperation' that all member states should be involved in the decision-making of a differentiated policy is thus a useful way of maintaining democracy within the Union.

Conclusion

Flexibility is an important part of the European integration process of the twenty-first century. A larger membership than ever before, the completion of the major integration project, and the move into coveted competences of the nation state have all contributed to the traditional mode of uniform integration being systematically complemented with greater differentiation of integration between the member states.

It is clear that moving away from uniform integration towards greater flexibility is not without its risks. Differentiation raises the possibility of undermining fundamental principles on which the EU is based, and this may compound rather than solve some of the difficulties frequently experienced. At the same time, however, it is becoming increasingly clear that differentiation may offer genuine opportunities for further deepening that do not inevitably have to result in the break-up of the EU.

If the process is carefully managed, not only can the risk of fragmentation be reduced, but the use of differentiation may also provide a powerful motivation for countries not initially part of a differentiated policy to join. The clause on 'enhanced cooperation' in the Nice Treaty sets an important structural condition allowing this to happen: the requirement that all member states be involved in the negotiations leading to the setting up of a differentiated policy.

? QUESTIONS

1. What are the main methods of differentiation? What are their key features and how do they differ from each other?
2. Is the EU too large for uniform integration?

3. Is differentiation necessary and desirable?
4. Is 'enhanced cooperation', as in the (proposed) Constitutional Treaty, a useful instrument for addressing the challenges facing the enlarged Union in the twenty-first century?
5. What are the main opportunities and risks of using differentiation in the European integration process?
6. How has the Nice Treaty altered the way in which differentiation might operate in practice?
7. Has the 2004 enlargement made it more or less likely that some EU member states will pursue differentiation?
8. Is fragmentation an inevitable consequence of the application of differentiation amongst EU member states?

GUIDE TO FURTHER READING

- **Federal Trust, The** ***The Beginning of the End or the End of the Beginning? Enhanced Cooperation and the Constitutional Treaty*** **(European Policy Brief, Issue 7, 2004).** A summary of the main changes made to 'enhanced cooperation' in the unratified Constitutional Treaty.

- **Kölliker, A. 'Bringing Together or Driving Apart the Union? Towards a Theory of Differentiated Integration',** ***West European Politics*****, 24(4), October 2001, pp. 125–51.** This article works towards a theory of differentiation by linking it with public goods theory. In doing so, the author sets out to explain the effects of differentiation on the EU, its policies and members, as well as on individual policy areas.

- **Regent, S.** ***The Open Method of Coordination: A Supranational Form of Governance?*** **(Discussion Paper DP 137/2002, International Institute for Labour Studies, 2002).** This paper discusses the history and role of the OMC in the political system of the EU.

- **Sepos, A.** ***Differentiated Integration in the EU: The Position of Small Member States*** **(EUI Working Paper RSCAS 2005/17).** This working paper examines the impact of the different methods of differentiated European integration on the positions of smaller EU member states.

- **Tuytschaever, F.** ***Differentiation in European Union Law*** **(Oxford: Hart, 1999).** This book includes a discussion of differentiated integration from a legal perspective. The book categorizes some concepts of differentiated integration and gives examples of differentiation in EU law and policy.

- **Warleigh, A.** ***Flexible Integration: Which Model for the European Union?*** **(Contemporary European Union Studies 15) (Sheffield: Sheffield Academic Press, 2005).** This book examines why flexibility has become such an important feature in the EU. It develops a typology to explain the different models through which this concept might be understood. The author argues that there is ample scope for flexibility to make a positive contribution to the European integration process.

IMPORTANT WEBSITES

- **http://europa.eu.int/constitution/en/lstoc1_en.htm** This is the official EU website on the Constitutional Treaty which includes a link to Title IV, Chapter III on 'Enhanced Cooperation'.

- http://www.euractiv.com/Section?idNum=3750354 A website with comprehensive coverage of EU affairs. This section on the Constitutional Treaty gives news, interviews, and analytical dossiers on developments related to the EU Constitution as well as containing information on the referenda and the 2003/04 IGC.

Visit the Online Resource Centre that accompanies this book for lots of interesting additional material. http://www.oxfordtextbooks.co.uk/orc/cini2e/

25 Europeanization

LUCIA QUAGLIA, MARI NEUVONEN,
MACHIKO MIYAKOSHI, AND MICHELLE CINI

Chapter Contents

Reader's Guide

This chapter reviews some of the recent literature on **Europeanization**. It begins by identifying the different ways in which the concept is understood, and by clarifying how 'Europeanization' is undertood in this chapter. The second section examines a sample of theoretical work recently undertaken on Europeanization, giving a taste of how authors working in this field have tried to identify patterns and variations in its impact. The remainder of the chapter considers, in a more empirical manner, how (a) member state institutions, (b) domestic policies, and (c) party politics and representation at national level have been affected by membership or prospective membership of the European Union.

Introduction

Europeanization has become a fashionable concept, used frequently by researchers working on European Union politics. From the Europeanization of media discourse (Meyer 2005) to the Europeanization of party politics (Mair forthcoming 2006), a wealth of literature now exists on this relatively new dimension of EU research. Although there is still no agreement on how to define this term, it is clear that Europeanization research focuses as much on the domestic politics of the EU as on what goes on in Brussels. Indeed, the most widely accepted definition of Europeanization acknowledges not only the impact of the EU on national polities and politics, but also how the domestic level shapes European politics. Thankfully, there is now not only a wealth of empirical case studies, examining different dimensions of Europeanization, but also a burgeoning theoretical and conceptual literature, which tries to make sense of the patterns and variations that appear across time, across policies, institutions, and, indeed, cross-nationally. While there is no attempt in this chapter to tackle all aspects of Europeanization research, the objective is to give the reader an indication of the kind of work being done in this relatively new EU-related research field.

The chapter begins by considering the range of definitions of Europeanization that have been applied to this concept, acknowledging that the concept remains contested. The second section examines some of the theoretical work that has been undertaken on this topic. The remainder of the chapter examines three domains of Europeanization research: focusing first on member state institutions; second, on policies; and third, on party politics, party systems, and political representation.

Defining Europeanization

As a contested and multifaceted concept (Olsen 2002: 921), Europeanization is difficult to define. Its meanings vary according to the theoretical perspective adopted and the subject area chosen (see Boxes 25.1 and 25.2). However, like **globalization**, it provides a valuable vantage point from which to survey the significant changes that are taking place in the contemporary politics, society, and economy of Europe.

In the field of EU politics, there are four shorthand definitions of Europeanization (see Box 25.3). These broadly coincide with four perspectives that can be adopted when studying this topic. The first, which embodies a 'top-down approach', draws attention to the impact of the European Union on the EU's member states. This approach is interested in the effects that EU-level institutions, policies, and policy-making have on institutions, policies, policy-making, and politics at the domestic (national or subnational) level of governance.

The second perspective, which incorporates both a bottom-up and a top-down approach, involves two consecutive and interlinked phases, and also incorporates feedback effects: that is, the formation of institutions, policies, and policy-making at the EU level *and*, subsequently, their reverberation back into the domestic arena and hence on national (or subnational) institutions, policies, policy-making, politics, and polity. This perspective focuses attention on how member states *shape* EU policies and institutions by 'uploading' their own policies and institutions to the European level; and how the member states *adapt* to the EU, by 'downloading' EU policies and institutions into the domestic political arena (Börzel 2002: 193).

Given that the principal focus of these two perspectives is the European Union, there have been debates as to whether the word 'EU-ization' (Radaelli 2003: 27) might be an appropriate one to apply to these processes of change. After all,

 KEY CONCEPTS AND TERMS 25.1

Some broad definitions of Europeanization

Olsen (2002: 923–6) identifies five broad definitions of Europeanization:

- Changes in the external boundaries of Europe, especially of the EU, mainly through the process of enlargement. This definition conceptualizes 'Europe' as a geographical entity.
- Institution building and the development of common norms at the European level, especially, but not only, in the EU. This definition conceptualizes Europe as a distinct system of governance.
- Domestic impacts of European-level institutions and norms, thus the penetration of national systems of governance, feeding into the literature on multi-level governance. This definition considers the adaptation of national and subnational systems of governance to European institutions and norms.
- Exporting certain forms of political organization (institutions, norms) to political systems outside Europe. This definition contextualizes Europe into the international system, arguing that the spread of European models can take place in several different ways, such as persuasion and argumentation, but also coercion.
- A project of political unification, whereby Europe should be a unified and strong political entity. This definition of Europeanization is largely normative. It should also be noted that there are competing models for the building of a unified Europe.

 KEY CONCEPTS AND TERMS 25.2

A specific definition of Europeanization

Europeanization consists of processes of a) construction, b) diffusion and c) institutionalization of formal and informal rules, procedures, policy paradigms, styles, 'ways of doing things' and shared beliefs and norms which are first defined and consolidated in the EU policy process and then incorporated in the logic of domestic (national and subnational) discourse, political structures and public choices (Radaelli 2003: 30).

 KEY CONCEPTS AND TERMS 25.3

Four shorthand definitions of Europeanization in EU politics

The first definition adopts a 'top-down approach', concerning the impact of the European Union on the EU's member states (Börzel and Risse 2003). The second definition incorporates both a 'bottom-up' and a 'top-down' approach, considering both the formation of institutions, policies, and policy-making at the EU level *and*, subsequently, their reverberation back into the domestic arena of the member states (Börzel 2002). The third, albeit less common, definition is not EU centred, but is based on a horizontal approach, which sees change occuring from country to country, with little, if any, mediation or intervention from the EU institutions (Radaelli 2003). A fourth definition is largely synonymous with institution-building and policy-making at the EU level (Cowles *et al*. 2001), hence this can often substitute for the more established term 'European integration'.

'Europeanization' technically applies to the whole of Europe, and not just to the EU. Before the 2004 enlargement, the difference between the two was particularly significant. However, given the rather awkward composition of the word EU-ization, this more accurate term did not gain ground.

The distinction between EU-ization and Europeanization matters, however, when we turn to a third, albeit less common, definition of Europeanization. This definition is not EU centred, but is a horizontal approach, which sees change occurring from country to country, with little if any mediation or intervention from the EU institutions (see Radaelli 2003). This is a process by which institutions, policies, and policy-making in one member state (or in a subgroup of states) are transferred, replicated, imported, and/or exported to other member states, without any top-down involvement from the EU institutions. This definition is rooted in the literature on **policy transfer**, **institutional isomorphism** (DiMaggio and Powell 1991), and, more generally, on institutional and **policy convergence**.

A fourth perspective on Europeanization is synonymous with institution-building and policy-making at the EU level (Cowles *et al.* 2001). In this understanding of Europeanization, the term can often substitute for **European integration.** Although it may be *followed* by the institutional interpenetration of national and subnational levels (so-called 'Europeanization *effects*'), using Europeanization in this way can lead to some confusion, and is therefore avoided in this chapter. It is the first and second, and particularly the second, perspectives that are used in the rest of this chapter.

KEY POINTS

- There are at least four definitions of and perspectives on Europeanization.
- The most commonly used of these involves the impact of the EU on domestic politics, institutions, policies, policy-making, and polity.
- A broader, and more helpful, definition also incorporates a feedback loop from the domestic level to the European level, so that Europeanization involves the interplay between the EU and the domestic level of governance.

Theorizing Europeanization

Until the early 1990s the concept of Europeanization was seldom, if ever, used in mainstream research on the EU. From the mid-1990s onwards its use has increased substantially. Especially after 2000, Europeanization became an extremely fashionable concept for EU researchers, and this has led to a wealth of new EU studies. Whereas political scientists were the first to adopt the term, the concept has also entered the research agendas and the academic lexicons of sociologists, historians, lawyers, and economists (Featherstone 2003: 3).

The concept of Europeanization became prominent in EU studies as the primary focus of EU research switched from the process of European integration, institution-building, and policy-making *at the EU level*, to the *impact* of all these factors on the member states. As European integration deepened and the EU enlarged, it became evident that the Union exerted a crucial influence on domestic politics; and that a specific terminology, as well as suitable analytical tools, were necessary to enable researchers to investigate this phenomenon.

In order to situate Europeanization within the field of **integration theory** (see Chapters 6, 7, and 8), it is useful to distinguish between three historical phases, each of which has had a distinct empirical focus. The first generation of these theoretical studies dealt with what the European Community was – that is, whether it was an **intergovernmental** or a **supranational** regime; as well as what it did – that is, in which policy areas it was active and what role the European institutions possessed. These scholarly works were mainly rooted in international relations theories. The second-generation studies, associated with the **governance turn** in EU studies (Jachtenfuchs 2001), coincided with a deepening and widening of the scope of European integration in the 1990s. These analyses emphasized how the EU worked in different policy areas, drawing mainly on the field of public policy and comparative politics (Rosamond 2000). The third generation, which is associated with the subject matter of this chapter – Europeanization – examines how the EU level interacts with its member states. Theoretically the literature on Europeanization is eclectic, as it has borrowed concepts and analytical tools from international relations, comparative politics, public policy, and political economy. It has also been argued that Europeanization research has helped to bring EU studies into mainstream political science (Radaelli 2006).

There is no claim made here however that Europeanization is an irreversible process. Moreover, it is assumed to be incremental and irregular; and it does not necessarily lead to policy convergence. It is difficult to distinguish between its causes and effects, or indeed between the consequences of Europeanization and globalization (Featherstone 2003: 4). Moreover, many authors conceptualize Europeanization as a circular process (Goetz 2001: 4) in the sense that institution-building, policy-making, and the development of norms at the EU level have repercussions for institutions, policies, and norms at the national and subnational levels. This, consequently, affects member states' 'input' into the EU, which in turn affects the 'output' of the EU and its domestic reverberation with national arenas.

There are several *domains* of Europeanization. These are research objects to be studied and compared. The most conventional distinction is between policies, politics, and polity (Börzel and Risse 2003). Some authors (for example, Radaelli 2003) also consider domestic structures, both material (relating to institutions) and cognitive (relating to ideas). Others have investigated the *mechanisms* of Europeanization, that is, how Europeanization as a process of change operates (see Olsen 2002), arguing that the mechanisms of Europeanization vary according to the type of policy pursued.

Positive integration, through **market-shaping measures**, occurs when the EU prescribes a specific institutional model or policy template that the member states have to adopt. Examples of this kind of integration can be found in the fields of health and safety, consumer protection, environmental policy, and Economic and Monetary Union (Knill and Lehmkuhl 2002). In these cases the pressure for adaptation at the national level results from the degree of 'fit' or 'misfit' between EU and domestic policies, processes, and institutions (Börzel and Risse 2003; Cowles *et al.* 2001). The greater the misfit, the greater the vertical adaptational pressure on the member states from the EU. For example, in order to join EMU, the member states had to make their national central banks independent. Thus, the Banque de France, a central bank traditionally subordinate to the French government, had to be made fully independent, with the relevant national legislation revised to effect this change. This is an example of a misfit which put a fair amount of pressure on the French system. By contrast, the Bundesbank, the German central bank, had been independent from the Federal government from its inception. Because of this, it did not have to undergo significant changes.

Negative integration, through **market-making measures**, is promoted by EU rules that do not prescribe specific institutional or policy templates for the member states; market-making measures forbid certain behaviours (Bulmer and Radaelli 2005: Radaelli 2003), often removing barriers to trade or other forms of cooperation. In policy areas where negative integration predominates, EU rules are designed to promote the efficient functioning of the market and further market integration. The main example of negative integration in practice is the establishment of the Single Market (see Chapters 3 and 16), which was achieved though legislation to remove trade barriers and by encouraging the **mutual recognition** of national laws. The main mechanism of Europeanization in this case is **regulatory competition**, which is competition amongst national regulatory regimes. In other words, member states compete with each other in order to provide a favourable domestic regulatory environment, which promotes the competitiveness of the economic actors in their jurisdiction. For example, in the case of financial activities, all other things being equal, the expectation is that firms will prefer to be located in countries that have a 'light regulatory touch'.

Framing integration (which might also be called 'facilitated coordination') takes place in policy areas where national governments are the key players, and where there is little EU legislation. This contrasts with the previous two examples which rested on vertical relations between the EU and the member states and which were based on **hard law**, that is law which is legally enforceable (Bulmer and Radaelli 2005; Knill and Lehmkuhl 2002). **Soft law**, by contrast, is the main instrument of facilitated coordination. Paradoxically, soft laws are not really laws at all as they are not legally enforceable (and not surprisingly some even question whether the word 'law' should be used in this context). Soft laws are found where the open method of coordination is applied. This is a policy approach based on practices such as benchmarking and the diffusion of best practice, with examples found in the fields of pensions reform and employment policy. Minimalist directives, as in railways policy, and political declarations, such as in the Presidency Conclusions, which are published at the end of European Council meetings, are also examples of soft law. Other examples are found in the policies in the second (foreign affairs) and third (police and judicial cooperation) pillars of the EU (see Figures 3.1 and 3.2), which are largely intergovernmental in character, and where the main mechanisms of Europeanization are learning across countries. They might also involve convergence around particular policy paradigms, in conjunction with legitimation provided by the EU in order to justify certain domestic policy changes.

Moving on from this discussion of mechanisms, we turn to various responses to the effects or *outcomes* of Europeanization. The most common taxonomy comprises four variants that embody different degrees and direction of change (Radaelli 2003: 37). These are (1) inertia; (2) absorption; (3) transformation; and (4) retrenchment. *Inertia* is when no change occurs. This usually happens where there is substantial 'misfit': that is, where existing national policy, institutions, practices, and/or norms are very different from those promoted by the EU. However, in the long run, inertia probably cannot be sustained, at least where positive integration exists, and ultimately some kind of transformation will usually occur. The second outcome, *absorption*, denotes a limited form of adaptation. This comprises a marginal modification of national policy, institutions, and/or norms to accommodate EU requirements, but without any profound transformation. Because of the nature of absorption, it is not always easy to measure the degree of change. By contrast, the third outcome, *transformation*, implies a major domestic adjustment, for example a change of party system; revised macroeconomic policies; or the emergence of new cognitive structures (belief systems) held by groups of individuals. Finally, the fourth outcome, *retrenchment*, involves the empowering of a coalition of domestic actors who oppose EU-inspired changes. As in the case of inertia, there is at least some evidence to suggest that such coalitions will be able to resist Europeanization only for a limited period of time.

This kind of theoretical Europeanization research is not without its critics however. There are three main criticisms. First, some studies of Europeanization are neither coherent nor systematic in the way they tackle their subject matter. This is perhaps understandable, given that there is no one theory of Europeanization, and that the concept usually involves an eclectic approach to theorizing, borrowing, for example, from various subdisciplines in political science (Mair 2004: 339). Secondly, there is a danger that research into Europeanization is little more than a 'reinvention of the wheel' or a form of 'ad-hocism' (see Radaelli 2003: 28). In other words, researchers sometimes formulate explanations and concepts relating to Europeanization that cannot travel beyond the boundaries of a very narrow literature – in EU studies. Empirically, Europeanization, like globalization, is sometimes used as a 'default explanation for almost everything that cannot otherwise be explained at the domestic level' (Mair 2004: 339). Thirdly, many studies are formulated so as to detect Europeanization even where it is minimal or even completely absent (Radaelli 2003). In other words, if the researcher is specifically looking for signs of Europeanization without considering alternative explanations that might account for domestic change – such as the effects of international as opposed to purely EU factors, or the presence of home-grown domestic sources of change – the impact of Europeanization is likely to be overestimated.

On the positive side, however, Europeanization research has opened up a new phase in EU studies and European integration theory, facilitating a dialogue with other subdisciplines in politics (Featherstone and Radaelli 2003: 332–5) and within the social sciences more generally. It has drawn attention to the underresearched but increasingly salient issue of the impact of EU 'output' on the member states and to the circularity of the process, something which is acknowledged now in almost all approaches to the concept. Finally, in its most mature phase, it offers the opportunity of (re-) exporting empirical findings and analytical instruments to other literatures from which it borrowed in its initial stage (Featherstone and Radaelli 2003; Thatcher 2005). Having briefly reviewed and analysed the 'state of the art', this chapter now considers the kinds of empirical results (or 'findings') that have emerged as a consequence of this burgeoning field of research.

KEY POINTS

- Theoretical research on Europeanization has sought to distinguish different domains, mechanisms, and outputs (effects) of Europeanization.
- This research has been criticized on a number of grounds, not least for being unsystematic and for failing to consider other potential sources of domestic influence.
- However, Europeanization has helped to begin to open up EU research to the social sciences, allowing EU studies to influence other research fields.

Europeanization and state institutions

One branch of the Europeanization literature is devoted to research on state institutions, and in particular to the impact of the EU on national governments, their administrations, parliaments, courts, and regional bodies. Following the second definition of Europeanization above, the relationship between the EU and its member state institutions is usually understood as a 'two-way interaction', with member states having an incentive to 'upload' their policies to the European level to minimize the costs of 'downloading' them to the domestic level (Börzel 2002: 193). Much of this Europeanization research therefore examines how and why national governments have sought to coordinate policy towards the EU.

The effect of the EU on domestic institutions is complex and far-reaching, and varies significantly across the Union. While there is no suggestion of a convergence of institutional characteristics as a consequence of Europeanization, this does not mean that the effect has been negligible. Not only have institutions changed, but Europeanization has put pressure on member states to develop and present coherent positions in institutional fora in Brussels. The benefit to be had from getting things right at this level can be substantial, while getting things wrong may be costly both economically and politically (Kassim 2003: 84); and it is this that has led to changes in institutional structures and processes.

The extent to which domestic institutions are able to participate in EU policy-making also depends on domestic factors, such as the constitutional provisions that frame executive–legislative relations; the institutional culture of the state (or region); the nature of the party system; and parliamentary norms and practices. All these factors affect how member states are able to 'shape' and adapt to European policy outcomes.

National governments occupy the most privileged position in the EU, as they negotiate treaty changes, set the EU's medium-term goals, and adopt or reject European legislation in the EU Council. Because of this they have been able to increase considerably their own (domestic) position by strengthening their capacity to mobilize resources over a growing range of vital policy areas and over all phases of the policy cycle (Wessels *et al.* 2003: xv). Research in this field has shown that there is a broad and intensive Europeanization of national governments (Bulmer and Burch 2001: 76). Nowadays all central government departments are drawn into EU business to a greater or lesser extent, and member states have created national coordination systems so as to disseminate relevant EU information throughout this growing network of participants, and to facilitate the agreement of a single domestically approved position at the EU level (Bulmer and Burch 2001).

The main advantage for national governments in adapting to EU integration by creating sophisticated coordination systems at the national and EU level is to achieve goals collectively that would otherwise not be possible (Kassim 2005: 288). For example, governments can use the EU as a channel to influence policies pursued in the rest of the Union in a way that is more favourable to their own domestic preferences. They can do this by exporting their domestic models through Brussels. This can give their nationals a competitive advantage over their competitors at the European level (Börzel 2002: 194). For instance, in the EU's environmental policy, member states with high levels of regulation have succeed in harmonizing their higher environmental standards at the EU level and by doing this, have avoided environmental dumping by member states with low levels of regulation. Another benefit to governments arises out of the 'nesting' of the domestic arena inside the EU framework. What this means is that national governments can override domestic policy constraints by citing demands made by Brussels; and they may also use the EU as a scapegoat when things go wrong. Using environmental policy as an example again, we see that member states with little regulation are critical of the EU because they claim that it forced them to accept more expensive higher standards, reducing their competitive economic advantages in the process. However, there are also occasions where the autonomy of national governments is restricted by the need to share power over policy with other European governments, as well as, in some cases, with the EU institutions (Hix 1999: 25). Even if member states manage to frame policy proposals in line with domestic preferences, most major legislative proposals are subject to substantial intergovernmental bargaining in the EU Council. Many proposals also have to accommodate the European Parliament's position.

The Europeanization effect has also had an impact on human resources within the member states, and has led to the creation of new structures and posts within national administrations. The need to be present at more than 300 Council working groups places a considerable strain on government departments, not only because of the time spent in these meetings, but also on account of the need to prepare and coordinate national positions (Kassim 2005: 290). Moreover, national (and in some cases regional) administrations take primary responsibility for the implementation of EU policy in addition to their domestic responsibilities. Indeed, for many the boundaries between these national and Europeanization responsibilities in implementation are now so blurred that officials may not even be aware which of the tasks they perform relate to home-grown policy and which to European-level decision-making.

National parliaments are also important in EU action because they ratify treaty changes and implement legislation at the national level. Most of the existing literature considers national parliaments as the main losers in the European integration process (for example, Raunio 2001, 2004). The reasons for this are threefold, and can be summarized as (a) the distance issue, (b) executive dominance, and (c) the lack of transparency.

Firstly, national parliaments have lost much of their traditional legislative power to the EU (Norton 1996: 182). This means that a great deal of legislation is decided at the EU level rather than at the national level. This applies, for example, to all regulations relating to the internal market. Secondly, national parliaments have only an indirect role in the EU's policy process. They are able to influence the EU *through* national governments, but not directly and individually (Norton 1996: 192). They can try to convince their governments to adopt certain positions at the EU level and depending on their constitutional role can force governments to reject decisions if they are against the positions taken in parliament. The Danish Parliament is particularly influential and, though far from typical, is interesting as it presents a potential model for parliamentary influence that other national parliaments may wish to emulate (Damgaard and Jensen 2005: 396). The reliance of parliaments on their governments also means that their capacity to influence depends on specific political circumstances. Parliaments do not have the same kinds of resources as governments, such as recourse to the civil service, which might allow them to participate as effectively in the EU process (Wessels *et al.* 2003: 431).

The third problem is the *lack of transparency* in the EU's decision-making procedures. Much of the EU's decision-making takes place behind closed doors, and there are many complex legislative procedures and voting rules that only experts on European law understand (Rizzuto 2003: 97). Moreover, the timing and volume of the material involved in the European decision-making process makes it difficult for national parliaments to be involved in an effective manner (Kassim 2005: 297). Despite this, parliaments have developed methods which allow them to participate to greater effect in European-level decision-making (Norton 1996: 8; Rizzuto 2003:103). This has happened gradually as the EC/EU has grown. The Single European Act (passed 1986) resulted in a substantial amount of legislation which had to be passed and implemented by national parliaments. It also introduced qualified majority voting (QMV) as a decision-making model in the EU Council. This has meant that governments are no longer able to veto decisions in the Council (Rizzuto 2003:104). But, more significantly, it was the creation of the European Union in 1993 (by the Maastricht Treaty) that changed the situation for parliaments. Realizing that they were losing their traditional access and influence, parliaments reacted to this by creating Committees of European Affairs (EACs) (Norton 1996: 8). While these committees all deal with EU matters, *how* they do so varies greatly across the member states (Maurer 2001: 67). The Danish and Finnish EACs are good examples of parliamentary committees that are effective in influencing EU policy-making (Laursen 2005: 412). The creation of EACs has been recognized as the most important example of adaptation to EU integration that parliaments have made (Norton 1996; Wessels *et al.* 2003; Rizzuto 2003).

Domestic courts are participants in a continuous inter-institutional dialogue with the European Court of Justice (ECJ) (Stone Sweet 2003: 45–7). They are involved in controlling and implementing Community law at the end of the policy cycle. At the heart of the EU's legal order is a 'set of institutionalized dialogues' between supranational and national judges (Stone Sweet 1998: 305). In this system national courts act as an apex of European Court of Justice (ECJ) by ensuring member-state conformity with EU law (Stone Sweet 2003: 44–6). The ECJ applies a 'preliminary ruling procedure', which permits a national court to request the ECJ's Opinion when a case raises an issue that requires interpretation, and it has developed the principle of the supremacy of European over domestic law (see Chapter 12). Courts have expressed doubts about this principle: as during the Irish ratification of the Single European Act (see Chapter 3), and when the German Constitutional Court ruled that it did not accept the principle of supremacy. However, the supremacy of Community law has generally been accepted (Wessels *et al.* 2003: 436). As a consequence of the EU's legal framework, the ECJ and national courts are integrated into a unitary legal system of judicial review with the ECJ relying heavily on the willingness of national judges to follow its rulings. This interchange is crucial as national courts have frequently asked questions that have enabled the ECJ to comment on national policy and to expand the reach of European law (Kassim 2005: 310).

As the range of policies dealt with by the EU has widened, so the rights and competencies of regional as well as local bodies have been affected to an increasing extent. This is because some regions in some EU states have specific, sometimes even autonomous, rights and responsibilities to implement EU legal acts. This especially applies in fields such as education, culture, research, health, environment, agriculture, and fisheries (Wessels *et al.* 2003: 436). Subnational actors too now operate within a broader political system that transcends national borders and in which they are able to develop and pursue projects independent of national capitals by making direct contacts with their counterparts abroad as well as with EU institutions (Kassim 2005: 303).

In sum, the impact of the EU on state institutions has been considerable. The demands and challenges faced by national institutions have grown heavily. The impact of integration has not been uniform, however, and there is no sign of an 'ever greater convergence' of national political systems. The most powerful actors in the EU are still national governments and, though affected by the EU, they also have greater opportunities to pursue their preferences at the EU level than other national or subnational bodies.

KEY POINTS

- The effect of the EU on domestic institutions has been far-reaching and complex and there is substantial variation in impact across the EU.
- Governments and national administrations have changed in different ways as a consequence of EU membership, and have sought to shape as well as be shaped by the EU.
- The impact on and of parliaments, courts, and regional actors, though far from negligible, is more limited.

The Europeanization of domestic policy

Since the mid-1990s, there has been a substantial increase in research on the Europeanization of domestic public policy. This research examines domestic change deriving from the EU in specific policy areas, and a great deal has been published on the topic. This reflects the fact that the scope of the Europeanization of domestic policy has expanded as the EU has become involved in new activities beyond the economic sphere. Whereas the effect of the EU in the fields of trade, industrial, and monetary policy is well reported, an impact can also be detected in the domains of health and social care for instance, areas which have traditionally been untouched by EU intervention (Geyer 2000; Hantrais 2000). Cross-national and cross-sectoral comparisons are common tools for identifying trends in policy convergence (Jordan and Liefferink 2004) and differentiation (Héritier *et al.* 2001). As we have already seen, European policies can be categorized as examples of positive integration, for example in environment policy, EMU, and the CAP; negative integration, in the areas of the Internal Market; and framing integration (or 'coordination'), as in the fields of CFSP, social inclusion, and asylum policy. It is fair to say that Europeanization, in these different types of policy domain, has produced varied empirical patterns. However, there is also evidence to suggest that variation exists even within these policy types. The rest of this section gives a taste of the range of findings presented in the empirical literature on the Europeanization of domestic policy.

Surprisingly, perhaps, there is little conclusive research evidence on what might be considered the most integrated of all European policy areas – agriculture. However, it has been argued that in the early years, the Community served to 'freeze' pre-membership agricultural systems, rather than forcing any adaptation of them. However, the situation has changed since the 1990s, and there is increasing evidence that shifts at EU level are shaping changes in core–periphery relations in farming domestically, and challenging the balance of power between farm and non-farm (including environmental) interests in agriculture (Roederer-Rynning forthcoming 2006; see also Chapter 21).

As with agricultural policy, the economic policy effects of Europeanization are relatively recent, even though the trajectory of the policy's development is very different. However, these effects are important all the same, particularly in those countries that form part of the eurozone. The main focus of research has been on monetary, exchange-rate, and fiscal policies, and how they have impacted on interest rates and price stability. Interesting, too, is the displacement effect that has been provoked by the setting up of EMU. As the scope for autonomy at national level has decreased in monetary policy and exchange-rate adjustment, governments have tried to compensate for this loss by using other instruments to attain similar ends, such as social policies on labour market flexibility. The Europeanization of economic policy has thus involved an adjustment to a loss of domestic control, which may have had unforeseen consequences for other policy areas (Dyson forthcoming 2006).

Telecommunications policy is regarded as one of the most successful examples of European standard-setting (Sandholtz 1998; Thatcher 2004). It is also an area where there have been dramatic changes since the European integration process began. However, Europeanization in this policy area may be considered as the result of international (or globalization) factors, such as the policy's connection with transnational business and its dependence on advanced technologies, rather than as driven by the EU. The telecoms sector exemplifies the difficulties involved in divorcing globalization from Europeanization effects. As there is much variation in the extent of EU regulation in this policy area, it also alerts scholars of Europeanization to the dangers of generalization (Schneider and Werle forthcoming 2006).

In social policy, one might expect to find little evidence of Europeanization. However, Falkner (forthcoming 2006) claims that there are few aspects of domestic social policy that are untouched by EU influence, even if social policy was a latecomer to EU regulation. By contrast, in the environmental field, where one might expect evidence of dramatic findings of Europeanization, Börzel claims that domestic impacts are more subtle, indirect, and limited than one might expect (Börzel forthcoming 2006). The substantial research in the area of cohesion policy indicates that there have been some rather dramatic Europeanization effects, contributing to changes in the way in which traditionally centralized states organized themselves internally (see also above on state structures). It is suggested that these changes have come about as a consequence of a process of social learning, driven by a cooperative European approach, which has reduced resistance to change, rather than by means of a prescriptive EU strategy.

This theme of social learning is strong in much of the literature on Europeanization. In areas such as transport (Héritier *et al.* 2001; Kassim and Stevens 2005), electricity (Bulmer *et al.* 2003), and financial regulation (Busch 2004), it has been argued that discursive and institutional factors have led to *regulatory* changes. Foreign policy cooperation has, moreover, produced *shared norms*, alongside a limited number of common rules (Tonra 2001); and *common concepts* have also been developed in environment policy (Jordan and Liefferink 2004) and in taxation and fiscal policy (Radaelli 1997; Dyson 2000; Sbragia 2001). In the field of refugee policy, too, debates about what a refugee is, and what protection is appropriate for refugees, have had an important ideational impact (Lavenex 2001).

It is clear then that the literature on the Europeanization of domestic policy tells us a great deal about the variation across and within policy areas. Much of this research comprises individual case studies, rather than comparisons across policies and countries and, as such, it can be difficult to identify patterns. As we saw in an early section of this chapter, theorists are doing their best to work with this material to that very end, but this is still very much work-in-progress.

CASE STUDY 25.4

Europeanization and enlargement

It is only since the start of negotiations leading up to the 2004 enlargement that researchers have examined enlargement in the light of Europeanization processes. This research has begun to ask whether the impact of the EU on candidate states is comparable to the impact in existing member states. Although there was some scepticism about this research agenda at the outset, there is now a consensus emerging that it is relevant to apply the Europeanization literature to non-members. This is because these countries are already subject to much the same pressures to adapt to EU policies as are existing member states. Moreover there was a particularly strong link between the 2004 enlargement and Europeanization because the negotiations were largely about rule transfer.

There is now substantial evidence to support the view that Europeanization effects are felt beyond the current member states. The relationship between the EU and the applicant states can appear akin to that of David and Goliath, albeit with the former having no effective sling. If one accepts this premise, then the interesting questions are: '*How* does the EU matter in candidate countries?' and 'How does this differ from the EU's impact on existing member states?'

Conditionality is the core strategy of the EU that begins to take effect even before candidate countries enter the EU, as they have to take on the obligations of EU membership. It includes respect for human rights and other key components of liberal democracy (political conditionality); and the capacity to meet the demands of a functioning market economy (economic conditionality). It also requires candidates to adapt to the existing body of EU laws and norms, the *acquis communautaire*; and to develop the institutional capacity to operate effectively once in the Union.

The main problem with these criteria is that the EU has a substantial degree of discretion over deciding whether and when the watershed has been reached. For this reason EU conditions may vary significantly between candidate countries. One example of this occured in the field of minority rights protection. Moreover, the political and economic criteria are so vaguely and broadly defined that governments have had difficulty in knowing precisely which changes are required of them. This results in a high degree of uncertainty being built into the accession processes. As a result, paradoxically, the reach of EU influence in candidate countries stretches beyond the Community's competence within the existing member states.

Therefore, the fundamental difference between the EU member states and the candidate countries is that the latters' experience of 'Europeanization' is derived from the asymmetrical relationship between the EU and those states that wish to join the Union. Candidate states cannot influence EU policy-making from the inside in the same way that members can. They can participate only at the 'second' stage, during the implementation of EU rules. Because they wish to gain accession to the EU, they have a stronger incentive than existing member states to implement EU policies, even if they often face difficulties in translating this motivation into practical results. As a consequence of this asymmetry the EU candidates are primarily 'downloaders' of EU law, policies, and practices, with only limited opportunities for 'uploading' country-specific preferences and priorities. Moreover, the experiences of the southern enlargement in the 1980s and after suggest that the capacity of new member states to 'upload' their preferences to the EU level are limited for quite some time after they join, with accession serving only as a point of departure for this new relationship.

KEY POINTS

- There is more research done on the Europeanization of domestic policy than on any other aspect of Europeanization.
- The impact of the EU on domestic policy has been variable.
- Although it is helpful to distinguish between positive, negative, and framing policies, variation exists within these categories, and even within individual policies.

The Europeanization of parties, party systems, and political representation

Although there is a longer-standing literature on the impact of the EU/EC on party manifestos, ideology, and competition at national level, it is only recently that there has been any attempt to study in a systematic fashion the impact of the EU on national political parties and party systems (see Ladrech 2002). One of the reasons for the lack of interest in this area was the limited effect that the EU seemed to have on this aspect of domestic life. Some feel this is not accidental; rather that 'parties have done much to insulate themselves from European encroachment into the domestic arena' (Mair forthcoming 2006).

But in what ways might the EU impact upon parties, party systems, and, indeed, upon political representation more generally? Clearly, the impact may be direct or indirect. The most obvious direct impact is by causing the formation of new political parties. In theory, these could be parties that mobilize in support of or against the EU. But, in practice, new parties have only really appeared as a negative response to European integration, in the Denmark and the UK.

A more direct effect of Europeanization can be identified on existing political parties. Important in this respect is the way in which alignments on the issue of Europe overlap with or run counter to other political cleavages (van der Eijk and Franklin 2004; Marks and Wilson 2000). Until recently dramatic changes in party politics as a consequence of European integration seemed few and far between. 'Europe', as an issue, was not politicized at the domestic level in most European countries (van der Eijk and Franklin 2004) – the UK may be an exception here, but even in the UK mainstream parties preferred not to raise the issue during election campaigns. As a cross-cutting cleavage in most European states, the European issue could serve only to emphasize internal party disunity. Perhaps as a consequence, Europe seemed to impact only marginally on national electoral politics. Yet in recent years 'Europe', as an issue, has been having a much greater resonance in political debate at the national level, and national political parties are starting to differentiate themselves in terms of their stance on the EU, or on specific European policies. But, even here, the impact seems more apparent at the margins of politics (including at the margins of the mainstream political parties), and often takes the particular form of Euroscepticism. Mainstream parties remain less convinced of the benefits to be had from raising the Europe issue.

The literature on the Europeanization of parties and political representation tends to emphasize the importance of the direct effects of Europeanization. But, as Mair (forthcoming 2006) argues, it is likely to be the indirect effects that have more of an impact. First, the EU restricts the arena in which political competition is played out, by harmonizing policies, restricting national political actors' freedom of manoeuvre in decision-taking. Secondly, the EU also limits the range of policy instruments at the parties' disposal. Dominated as it still is by regulatory politics (at least in the core functions of the Single Market), the EU tends to rest on a process of delegation to non-majoritarian institutions, which base their legitimacy on expertise and effectiveness rather than on their representativeness. Parties, and political actors, are excluded. Thirdly, European integration, through its promotion of the Single Market, limits the range of policies that national political parties can implement. Policy decisions that interfere with the free market are prohibited, restricting what public bodies at the domestic level can do. All this serves to 'reduce the stakes of competition between political parties, and to dampen down the potential differences wrought by successive governments' (Mair forthcoming 2006).

Moreover, there is little in the way of compensation at the European level. Negative views about the EP could spill over into disregard for national parliamentary institutions (though this learning effect should not be overstated, and there is no hard evidence of this actually happening). Where the EU aims to redress this balance, it often does so by encouraging the participation of civil society and interest organizations, rather than by using more traditional channels of political representation, and limiting the role that parties can play in European governance (Mair forthcoming 2006). Over time, legitimacy derived from non-party sources is likely to come to be valued more than party-political sources, even at national level, as citizens become socialized into accepting this as 'normal'. 'In this sense, there remain major questions that can be asked about the indirect impact of Europe on the declining legitimacy of traditional actors in national politics' (Mair forthcoming 2006; see also Bartolini 2005).

Europe has often been seen as a challenge to parties and to political leaders, forcing them to change their behaviour in ways that they would not otherwise entertain. However, it may be that European integration (and the depoliticization of decision-making that accompanies it) provides opportunities for political actors to 'externalize their political costs and seek to evade accountability and responsibility' (Mair forthcoming 2006), constructing barriers which allow them to defend the position of their party and their own positions in public office. They can then say that this has been forced upon them by the EU, denying that it is a conscious strategy.

Mair (forthcoming 2006) is critical of the literature on the Europeanization of party politics and political representation because it relies too much on quantifiable variables, and not enough on the softer case studies, which might tell us more about why political actors respond to Europe in the way that they do. He points to research that draws on expert judgements (Marks *et al.* 2004) and on the contents of party programmes (Gabel and Hix 2002). Mair, by contrast, advocates a comparative study of the political discussions that occur at national level, possibly focusing on parliamentary debates or on the discussions around the time of referenda or election campaigns. In other words, what is needed is more understanding about how Europe affects national political discourse. Do parties see Europe as a constraint or an opportunity? Or do they simply see it as irrelevant? Given the current state of research, Mair claims that it is impossible to answer these questions definitively.

KEY POINTS

- The Europeanization of political parties has taken the form of the creation of new parties that are almost exclusively anti-European (Eurosceptic).
- Party systems have also changed as a consequence of participation in the EU, with new coalitions, alignments, and political cleavages emerging.
- There have also been more indirect effects on political representation at the domestic level, as the EU limits both the arena within which political competition is played out at national level, and the instruments available to political actors.

Conclusion

This aim of this chapter has been to introduce readers to the concept of Europeanization, and to review some of the research that has been undertaken thus far on this topic. One thing is clear: Europeanization is a concept that is here to stay. The chapter began by offering a non-exclusive range of definitions of Europeanization, whilst at the same time expressing a preference for an understanding of the term which involves both the impact of the EU on domestic politics (and institutions, policies, and so on), and a feedback loop, which expects domestic actors and institutions to shape or seek to shape politics across the EU and at the European level.

The chapter focused attention on some of the theoretical literature. It also acknowledged the wealth of empirical material that now exists. Here we have seen how the EU has contributed to changing structures, processes, and behaviour in national and subnational arenas. There is even some suggestion that EU membership has also changed identities, though a substantial body of evidence on that topic is still to be produced (Laffan forthcoming 2006). Ultimately, however, it is possible to conclude from all this that Europeanization research will continue to be an important – and some might say *the* most important and indeed cutting-edge – field of EU research for the foreseeable future. This does not mean that all EU research needs to fall under the rubric of 'Europeanization' (though sometimes it seems that way in practice); but it does mean that no one interested in EU affairs can now justifiably ignore the research that has been done using Europeanization as a point of departure.

? QUESTIONS

1. Why is Europeanization a difficult concept to define?
2. Which mechanisms of Europeanization are associated with (a) positive integration; (b) negative integration; and (c) framing integration (cooperation)?
3. What criticisms have been made of Europeanization research?
4. What positive effects has research on Europeanization produced?
5. To what extent is it possible to generalize about the Europeanization of state institutions?
6. How has the EU impacted upon domestic policy?
7. In what ways has there been a Europeanization of political parties, party systems, and political representation in Europe?
8. Is it appropriate to use the concept of Europeanization to analyse the impact of the EU on EU candidate countries?

GUIDE TO FURTHER READING

■ Börzel, T. 'Pace-setting, Foot-dragging and Fence-sitting: Member State Responses to Europeanisation', *Journal of Common Market Studies*, 40(2), 2002: pp.193–214. An interesting conceptualization of Europeanization using the case of EU environment policy, and focusing on possible responses to (or effects of) Europeanization.

■ Cowles, M., Caporaso, J., and Risse, T. (eds) *Transforming Europe: Europeanisation and Domestic Change* (Ithaca, NY: Cornell University Press, 2001). An edited book on Europeanization, which covers a wide range of policy areas and issues.

■ Featherstone, K., and Radaelli, C. M. (eds) *The Politics of Europeanisation* (Oxford: Oxford University Press, 2003). An excellent edited book, covering both theoretical and empirical perspectives on Europeanization.

■ Olsen, J. 'The Many Faces of Europeanisation', *Journal of Common Market Studies*, 40(5), 2002: pp. 921–52. A rich and challenging account of the different definitions of Europeanization, which also focuses on the mechanisms through which Europeanization operates.

■ Radaelli, C. M. 'Europeanisation: Solution or Problem?', in M. Cini and A. Bourne (eds) *Palgrave Advances in European Union Studies* (Basingstoke: Palgrave, 2006). An excellent, strongly recommended overview of Europeanization research.

IMPORTANT WEBSITES

- **http://www.qub.ac.uk/schools/SchoolofPoliticsInternationalStudiesandPhilosophy/Research/PaperSeries/EuropeanizationPapers/** A Europeanization research papers series published by Queen's University Belfast.

- **http://www.arena.uio.no/** The website of ARENA, a Norwegian institute devoted to research on Europeanization.

- **http://www.shef.ac.uk/ebpp/** A collection of research papers on Europeanization, focusing exclusively on the Europeanization of British politics and policy-making.

Visit the Online Resource Centre that accompanies this book for lots of interesting additional material. http://www.oxfordtextbooks.co.uk/orc/cini2e/

26 Enlargement

IAN BARNES AND PAMELA BARNES

Chapter Contents

- Introduction
- Why enlargement?
- The impact of enlargement on the EU
- Who can join the EU?
- What is the accession process?
- Conditionality
- Countries and regions
- Moving the border eastward
- Conclusion

Reader's Guide

This chapter deals with the process of enlargement which has seen the European Union grow from an organization of six member states in 1958 to 25 member states in May 2004. It is particularly concerned with why enlargement took place after 1989. The chapter begins by reviewing the process of enlargement, concentrating on the period after the disintegration of the Soviet Union. It then reviews the impact of enlargement on the European Union. The chapter deals in some depth with the criteria which determine whether prospective member states can join; the process of joining (the accession process); and the use of conditionality. This information will enable the reader to form judgements on the viability of further enlargement, especially with respect to the Western Balkans and Turkey.

Introduction

Prior to 1989, European borders appeared to be fixed. Since then, the borders of Europe and the membership of the European Union EU have become a source of constant debate. The EU has grown from six to 25 member states since the 1950s, and has become an attractive model of economic and political development for neighbouring states. Enlargement is the most successful foreign policy tool that the EU has at its disposal in terms of influencing the behaviour of neighbouring states. It is an indication of the EU's resilience that there is a queue of states wishing to join, despite the commitments that come with membership. The EU provides an exemplar for states seeking to develop market economies in a politically stable framework. This has not meant that the EU has taken over the role of the national governments. The EU remains a union of strong independent and sovereign states which cooperate and collaborate for their mutual benefit. Few of the new or aspiring members wish to sacrifice their newly found freedom to join a superstate. The EU has spread geographically to the north-east and south and has within it states at various stages of political and economic development. Enlargement has meant that the EU has become more heterogeneous. However, all states can claim that they have met certain standards in order to qualify for membership, including the requirement that they are liberal democratic market economies; that they respect human rights and the rule of law; and that they are European in a geographical sense.

Why enlargement?

Since its the creation the EU has experienced five phases of enlargement, moving in the process from six to 25 member states (see Box 26.1). This process was on the political agenda when the organization first came into existence and its aim has been to extend prosperity, peace, and democracy across the European land mass. The first enlargement in 1973 involved states who regretted that they had not joined the organization at its inception. The motive for other states joining is largely associated with changing political and economic circumstance. As for the EU, its motives for accepting new members have varied over time, but at its root is the wish to maintain and spread liberal democratic ideals and the market economy across the mainland of Europe. This was a particularly important motive after the collapse of communism in Central and Eastern Europe after 1989. There has also been a wish to see the EU grow bigger and stronger as a consequence of the enlargement process and at various times there has been an associated enthusiasm for deeper political and economic integration.

The enlargement process was given new impetus as a result of the collapse of communism in 1989. A number of states emerged, as peoples across Europe established their identity and escaped from the tyranny of the Soviet Union (for example Georgia and Ukraine) or broke away from the Yugoslav Federation (such as Slovenia and Croatia). The EU was not really prepared for these dramatic events or for a significant number of states that wanted to join their organization. In 1993, the Copenhagen European Council (22 June) set out very general terms of membership. These criteria were important because they set an agenda for transition and indicated that the EU was prepared to go much further than in the past to influence the domestic agenda of the applicant states.

CHRONOLOGY 26.1

Past enlargements

- 1973 The United Kingdom (UK) joined along with Denmark and Ireland. France had rejected the UK's application in 1962, but by the 1970s the UK's strong democratic credentials were regarded as being a major asset. At that time both the Irish and Danish economies were more closely tied to the UK (the first enlargement).
- 1981 Greece joins, followed by Portugal and Spain in 1986. In these cases, the need to consolidate emergent democracies after periods of right-wing dictatorships was the primary driving force (the second and third enlargements).
- 1995 Austria, Finland, and Sweden joined because they were no longer bound by the postwar political settlement. These states were in many ways ideal members as they were relatively affluent and had a tradition of stable democratic government (the fourth enlargement).
- 2004 Eight Central and Eastern European (CEE) states: the Czech Republic, Hungary, Estonia, Latvia, Lithuania, Poland, Slovakia, and Slovenia joined, along with two of the Mediterranean states, Malta and Cyprus. The CEE states were the first of the former communist states to join, although the German Democratic Republic had been absorbed into the Federal Republic of Germany as early as October 1990. This enlargement was motivated by the desire to end the historic divisions in Europe (the fifth enlargement).

Many citizens in the Central and Eastern European (CEE) states expected membership to be a speedy process, but it took nearly 15 years from the collapse of communism for some of these states to achieve membership, with others being held back in a queue which could stretch to another 15 years or more.

The accession negotiations started on 31 March 1998 with six applicant countries: Hungary, Poland, Estonia, the Czech Republic, Slovenia, and Cyprus. At that stage it appeared that the fifth enlargement would be a long drawn-out affair. However, on 13 October 1999, the Commission recommended to the EU's Council of Ministers that negotiations should commence with Romania, Slovakia, Latvia, Lithuania, Bulgaria, and Malta. All but Bulgaria and Romania achieved membership in 1 May 2004, though these two states have signed an Accession Treaty and are expected to join on 1 January 2007. This enlargement was a reflection of the profound changes taking place in all the applicant states, spurred on by the prospect of membership. Latvia and Lithuania, who appeared to be being left behind because of the slow pace of economic transition, were able to achieve market economy status. Slovakia looked as though it was to be excluded on political grounds because of the behaviour of Vladimir Meciar's government, but once this government lost power in 1998, the way to membership was open.

The pace of any future enlargement of the EU will depend upon the perceptions of the current members as to the capacity of the organization to absorb additional members. That is, the organization must maintain its ability to function. Also, any future members will need to be suitably qualified, which makes it unlikely that there will be a further enlargement involving a large number of states. Membership is not ruled out for any suitably qualified European state, although it is unlikely that the Russian Federation would be seriously considered because of its size. The likelihood is that the states of the West Balkans and Turkey will be considered in preference to those of Eastern Europe, largely because of the need to honour existing commitments.

KEY POINTS

- There have been five rounds of enlargement since the 1950s.
- The pace of enlargement depends upon the EU's capacity to absorb new members.
- The EU's model of the market economy and liberal democracy is widely accepted throughout Europe.

The impact of enlargement on the EU

The enlargement of any organization will inevitably have an impact upon both the joining party and the organization itself (see Table 26.1). The level of the impact will depend upon the scale of the event. When the German Democratic Republic merged with the Federal Republic of Germany, the impact upon the EU in an organizational sense was minimal. However, it did cause some stresses in certain policy areas, most notably in the progress towards monetary integration. The need to keep German inflation under control led to higher interest rates in Germany than might otherwise have been the case, which in turn caused the Deutschmark to rise in value and the European Monetary System (EMS) to come apart temporarily. German unification also led to even greater demands being placed upon the EU's Regional Development Fund. The 1995 enlargement, which brought Austria, Finland, and Sweden into the EU, was without significant complications, although the fact that the Norwegian people rejected membership in 1994 (for a second time) suggests negotiators do not always read public opinion effectively. Generally the process of negotiating enlargement tends to be kept well away from the people until the final decision is about to be made. Indeed the paradox is that although EU membership is meant to consolidate democracy, it is essentially a take-it-or-leave-it process. Any real involvement in EU policy-making does not really begin until membership is achieved.

The integration of the CEE states into the European economy started very soon after the fall of communism and thus had been in process for up to 14 years prior to the 2004 enlargement. Trade was quickly liberalized, in some cases too quickly, in order to meet the demands from the domestic consumers for more western goods. The CEE states' trade became dominated by imports and exports from the EU (with the exception of energy), largely because of the crisis in the Russian economy. Internal changes came more slowly, but those states that were most willing to reform the internal workings of their economies tended to be the most able to adapt to EU membership requirements. The immediate impact of the move towards a market economy tended to be negative, because many industries that had survived within the protected environment of the socialist economies were simply swept away. Some states did attempt to cushion the impact of the changes by protecting domestic industry, but generally this was to no avail, because the pace of change simply slowed down. It was not until 10 years after the collapse of communism that living standards started to compare favourably with those of communist era.

Over time, however, a combination of foreign direct investment and the growth of the service economy did lead to progress being achieved. At the time of the 2004 enlargement, the new members were achieving economic growth rates almost twice that of the EU15. This trend may well continue, as the new members continue to be an attractive low-cost destination for companies who wish to keep their manufacturing base in Europe. However, even if growth rates in the CEE economies are maintained at an annual rate of 2 per cent growth above those of the EU15, it will take between 25 and 60 years for these states to catch up with the EU average GDP. The achievement of this objective will depend upon how the CEE states perform relative to the rest of the EU. If the benefits of membership and access to the Single Market have already run their course, these states could remain permanently behind the rest of the EU. If this is the case, then there are likely to be continuing demands for additional transfers of resources to these members.

The EU has provided funding to assist the transition of the CEE countries as have the individual member states, but it was the willingness to implement the required market-orientated reforms that was one of the most significant drivers of success. The more individual CEE economies started to look like those of the EU15, the more attractive they were to foreign investors, especially if unfettered access to the Single Market was assured.

Table 26.1 Impact of enlargement

Enlargement	New members	Additional population (%)	Added GDP (PPP) (%)	GDP per capita of new members (% of existing)
1973	Denmark, Ireland, UK	33.4	31.9	95.5
1981	Greece	3.7	1.8	48.4
1986	Portugal, Spain	17.8	11.0	
1995	Austria, Finland, Sweden	6.3	6.5	103.6
2004	Cyprus, Czech Republic, Estonia, Hungary, Latvia, Lithuania, Malta, Poland, Slovakia, Slovenia	19.6	9.1	46.5
2007–8	Bulgaria	1.7	0.5	29.4
	Romania	4.8	1.5	29.8

Source: Adapted from data from Eurostat, the IMF, and the OECD.

BOX 26.2

Conditions applying to Romania's accession

If the Commission informs the Council of Ministers that Romania has manifestly failed to meet its membership obligations in the following areas, membership can be delayed by one year on the basis of a qualified majority vote. Seven of the requirements are in the Justice and Home Affairs field. They include:

- implementation of the Schengen Action Plan;
- improved border surveillance;
- reform of the judiciary;
- introduction of stronger anti-corruption legislation;
- monitoring the effect of the anti-corruption strategy;
- improvement of the legal framework for policing and increasing the size of the police force;
- development of a coherent anti-crime strategy.

The remaining four areas are in the domain of competition policy and include:

- effective control by the Competition Council of any potential state aid;
- strengthening of state aid enforcement;
- submission to the Commission of a revised steel restructuring plan by mid-December 2004;
- devoting adequate resources to the Competition Council to permit it to operate effectively.

The 2004 enlargement brought many countries into the EU, the majority of which were poorer than the existing members. If Bulgaria and Romania join as expected, this trend will continue. Croatia, with a population of around 4.5 million people, has an income per head of about 36 per cent of the EU average, but Turkish incomes are only 27 per cent of the current EU average in 2004, with a population of 70.7 million. The impact of these trends is that they make the existing members seem better off in a relative sense, but there is a disadvantage, in that any EU funding that is related to relative poverty will go to the new members. This has the effect of reducing some of the membership benefits to those states that were relatively poorer prior to the 2004 enlargement, such as Greece, Spain, and Portugal.

At the centre of the EU's policies is the Single (Internal) Market. This involves the harmonization of the legal and regulatory business framework, so that full advantage can be taken of a market of 453 million consumers. The free movement of people, goods, services, and capital has proved difficult to achieve and it will take some time before it is fully in place. In particular the four freedoms involve having secure borders and a Common Commercial Policy (CCP) dealing with international trade relations (see Chapter 14). Internally, Economic and Monetary Union (EMU) (see Chapter 20) and the Schengen regime (see Chapter 19) are thought to be the most important parts of the EU's policy to complete the market, as well as deepening integration generally.

KEY POINTS

- The EU's membership is much more diverse as a result of enlargement.
- Enlargement has had a significant impact on the running of the EU.
- The new members' economies did well in the period leading up to the 2004 enlargement.

Who can join the EU?

The European Union is on the verge of completing its fifth enlargement. At the time of the first enlargement in 1973 the process was relatively unsophisticated and the negotiations went ahead without a detailed structure in place. The processes were governed by Article 237 of the EEC Treaty which has now been replaced by Article 49 of the TEU. This Article simply says that any European state can apply for membership, addressing the membership application to the Council (for example, the government of the Former Yogoslav Republic of Macedonia (FYROM) presented its application during the European Council Summit of March 2004). For the application to be successful the Commission has to be consulted and the European Parliament has to support the application. The unanimous support of the Council is required and the ratification of membership is subject to the constitutional processes in place in the member states. This makes individual member states an important part of the process.

After 1989 the prospect of a large number of potential applicant states resulted in the introduction of measures to bring greater clarity into the formal application process and greater detail of the requirements of membership (see Box 26.3). It was during the Copenhagen European Council that the framework of political and economic conditions which would determine whether the CEE states might become member states of the EU was established. They must:

- have stable institutions guaranteeing democracy, the rule of law, respect for human rights, and the protection of minorities;
- have a functioning market economy capable of withstanding the competitive pressures of membership;
- have the ability to take on the obligations of political, economic, and monetary union;
- adopt the *acquis communautaire* (the body of law and regulation) of the EU.

In 1997 procedures for negotiations with the prospective candidate states of CEE were agreed and it is these procedures, together with the Copenhagen conditions, which continue to form the basis of the negotiations with prospective member states after 2004 (see Table 26. 2).

Table 26.2 Prospective member states after 2004

	Population 2004	GDP (2004) € per capita purchasing power†	Unemployment (%) 2004	Economic growth (%) 2004	Inflation (%) 2004
Albania	3.4	3,983	14.6	6.0	3.4
Bosnia and Herzegovina	4.3	4,895	40.0	5.0	0.9
Croatia**	4.4	5,400	18.0	2.2	3.8
FYROM*	2.0	5,200	36.7	2.5	0.9
Serbia and Montenegro	8.1	1,933	31.5	5.0	13.8
Kosovo	2.4	964	49.7	3.2	0.5
Bulgaria***	7.8	6,324	12.0	5.7	6.2
Romania***	21.7	7,000	6.8	8.3	11.9
Turkey**	70.7	4,952	10.0	8.0	12.0
EU25	*457.2*	*23,160*	*8.6*	*2.4*	*2.1*

* Former Yugoslav Republic of Macedonia candidate status awarded in December 2005.

** Negotiations began October 2005.

*** Accession Treaties signed April 2005.

† Purchasing power measures incomes against the prices of goods and services; incomes per head would appear to be far lower if current exchange rates were used.

Source: Eurostat.

BOX 26.3

Membership criteria

Article 49 of the Treaty on European Union (TEU) says that any European state can apply to become a member, provided it is prepared to abide by the organization's principles. Article 6 of the TEU says:

1. The Union is founded on the principles of liberty, democracy, respect for human rights and fundamental freedoms, and the rule of law, principles which are common to the Member States.
2. The Union shall respect fundamental rights, as guaranteed by the European Convention for the Protection of Human Rights and Fundamental Freedoms signed in Rome on 4 November 1950 and as they result from the constitutional traditions common to the Member States, as general principles of Community law.
3. The Union shall respect the national identities of its Member States.
4. The Union shall provide itself with the means necessary to attain its objectives and carry through its policies.

Article 49 then states that an application for membership shall be addressed to the Council, 'which shall act unanimously after consulting the Commission and after receiving the assent of the European Parliament, which shall act by an absolute majority of its component members'.

The application for membership does not have to be accepted; indeed this is just the first phase of a process to ensure that applicants are suitable. Because absolute majority voting applies, any one member state can veto membership of another.

What is the accession process?

The process of accession is a highly technical exercise which has to be completed by each applicant state and which is managed and coordinated for the European Union within the European Commission (Directorate-General for Enlargement). The main activity of the Commission is to establish timetables for the body of EU legislation to be both transposed and implemented by the prospective member states. Monitoring by the Commission of the progress made is a crucial element as each stage of the process must be completed before the applicant state may move to the next. Following the unanimous approval of an application by the national governments of the existing member states the Commission is invited to begin to prepare an opinion (*avis*) on the suitability of an applicant, against the conditions set out in Article 49 TEU. A questionnaire is forwarded from the Commission to the applicant government requesting information.

The Commission does not rely solely on the responses from the national governments. In the case of Croatia, for example, information was also sought from the EU member states, the Council of Europe, the Organization for Security and Cooperation in Europe (OSCE), the United Nations High Commission for Refugees (UNHCR), the International Criminal Tribunal for the Former Yugoslavia (ICTY), the International Monetary Fund (IMF), the World Bank, the European Bank for Reconstruction and Development (EBRD), the European Investment Bank (EIB), and representatives of international and national non-governmental organizations dealing with issues of minority representation. In addition the progress on the implementation of the Stabilization and Association Agreement (SAA) for Croatia was also reviewed as part of the Commission Opinion. The SAA is an important initial stage, which is used to establish that there is a sufficient degree of political and economic stability for the opening of negotiations. SAAs are part of the 'roadmap' to membership, prepared for each of the applicant states, outlining the concrete measures to be completed in preparation for accession. In short, 'Proper implementation of the Agreement is the best basis on which to assess a country's readiness to move to the next phases of candidate status and then accession negotiations' (European Commission 2005a: 10).

Following a favourable opinion and recommendation from the Commission to the European Council an applicant state, by unanimous vote, may be considered a candidate for accession to the EU. This is only the first stage, however, in what may be a protracted process. The candidate state has to demonstrate that the political criteria have been met (including full cooperation with the ICTY if relevant), that significant progress is being made on meeting the economic criteria and the obligations of membership. The monitoring of progress is done by the Commission and regular progress reports are prepared for the EU Council and the European Parliament. However, the whole process remains one which is essentially intergovernmentalist.

The confirmation of candidate status for an applicant state is a political acknowledgement of a closer relationship between the EU and the candidate state. But it also activates a number of supportive measures which are intended to assist the candidate state in the preparations for accession. The financial instruments of assistance are PHARE (Poland and Hungary Aid for Economic Reconstruction) for institution-building and economic and social cohesion, ISPA (Instrument for Structural Policies for Pre-Accession) for environment and transport infrastructures, and SAPARD (Special Accession Programme for Agriculture and Rural Development). In addition, regional support is provided through the CARDS (Community Assistance for Reconstruction, Development and Stability in the Balkans) regional programme (total funding for Croatia €105 million in 2005, and €140 million in 2006). Croatia was also able to participate in Community programmes. For

Turkey, pre-accession funding was €300 million for 2005 and €500 million for 2006.

The post-2004 enlargement is likely to become more complicated and diverse as parallel negotiations take place with Turkey, a large country with many unique and specific problems, and with a number of the smaller states of the Western Balkans. The negotiations are an open-ended process with an outcome which cannot be guaranteed beforehand: in other words, there is no irrevocable timeline or commitment. The speed of the negotiations depends on progress made by the state on the implementation of EU rules and standards – assessed and reported in annual progress reports. The introduction of 'safeguard clauses' and the prospect of a suspension of negotiations if insufficient progress is made may slow the process further. For Turkey, the pace of negotiations will be determined by Turkey's own merits, independent of other accession negotiations taking place at the same time. Indeed it may be that some of prospective applicant states in the Western Balkans become member states before Turkey.

Support for the technical process of accession is provided by the EU in the form of 'European Partnerships'. These are established to identify the short-term and medium-term priorities for each stage of the pre-accession process. In return, the candidate states are required to provide action plans to identify how these priorities will be met. The last technical step before the start of negotiations is the adoption in the Council of Ministers (by unanimity) of a negotiating framework. In the case of Turkey, this was proposed by the Commission on 29 June 2005, and was adopted by the Council on 3 October 2005. The adoption of the negotiating framework marks the formal convening of the Intergovernmental Conference for the conduct of the negotiations. For the European Union the negotiations are conducted by ministers or the members of COREPER, senior national civil servants based in Brussels. The Presidency of the Council is responsible for setting the negotiating agenda and for providing the Chair of the deliberations. Each applicant state provides a chief negotiator and an expert team. The Council Secretariat working with a secretariat from the candidate state provides support for the negotiations. The role of the Commission includes drafting the EU's common negotiating position and benchmarks for the unanimous approval of the existing member states.

Negotiations cover the adoption of the EU's *acquis* – broken down into policy areas known as chapters. For the 2004 enlargement 31 chapters were identified, whereas a preliminary list of 35 was identified in 2005 for the Turkish negotiations. The first stage of the negotiations involves a screening of the chapters. Screening is done in two stages. First, the Commission carries out a formal examination of each chapter to enable it to explain the chapter to the relevant authorities in the candidate states, to assess the preparations for the negotiations in each area, and to identify preliminary issues (analytical screening). The second stage of screening involves the applicant state explaining its laws (detailed or bilateral screening). In the Turkish case the screening of the chapters relating to the Customs Union began in 2000. Following the opening of negotiations in November 2005 the chapters concerned with science and research, education, and culture were dealt with very quickly, and screening next began on the right to establishment and freedom to provide services, free movement of capital, and public procurement. Chapters relating to agriculture, the budget, the environment, and free movement of workers were much more problematic and the screening process in these areas was due to continue throughout 2006.

Following the screening of the chapters, negotiations can begin in earnest. For each chapter benchmarks to determine legislative alignment are determined as a precondition for the opening and later for the provisional closure of the chapter. In addition, states have to demonstrate a satisfactory track record on implementation through the existence of adequate national administrative and judicial capacities. Each chapter has to be dealt with in turn, but any may be reopened if subsequent implementation is unsatisfactory. All chapters are considered to be only provisionally closed until the last stage of the

Table 26.3 Referenda on accession

	Date of referendum on EU membership	Turnout (%)	Yes (%)	No (%)
Cyprus	(Not held on membership)			
Czech Republic	15–16/06/03	55	77.3	22.6
Estonia	14/09/03	63	67	33
Hungary	12/04/03	45.6	83.7	16.4
Latvia	20/09/03	72	67	33
Lithuania	10–11/05/03	65	91	9
Malta	08/03/03	91	53.6	46.4
Poland	08/06/03	58.9	77.5	22.5
Slovakia	16–17/05/03	52.1	92.5	6.2
Slovenia	23/03/03	60	89.6	10.4

negotiations is reached. In contrast to other enlargement processes, where a simple statement of commitment has been enough to decide if benchmarks have been met, for Turkey there is an additional requirement that it must demonstrate *actual* implementation.

Transitional measures, that is, additional time to implement measures, may be requested during the negotiations, but the Commission expects that these will be limited. For example, during the 2004 enlargement negotiations there were a number of requests for transitional periods in the field of environmental policy. After initially indicating that the new member states would be required to implement all legislation without transitional periods, it was decided that these should be given in certain cases. Common to all the new member states were concerns about establishing appropriate infrastructures for waste management and water quality, and transitional periods were agreed for a number of directives in these areas.

Once they are concluded, the results of the negotiations are included in an Accession Treaty. For the accession process to be completed the Treaty has then to be approved by the European Parliament, and ratified by the appropriate procedures of all the existing member states and the acceding state. For the 2004 enlargement this final stage of the accession process included referenda in all the acceding states apart from Cyprus (see Box 26.3).

KEY POINTS

- Although all institutions of the EU are involved in the approval of membership applications, the process remains one that is based on intergovernmental decision-making.
- Accession negotiations are a highly technical exercise, managed for the EU by the Commission and by a team of negotiators from the applicant states.
- The purpose of the negotiations is to determine the readiness of the applicant state for accession to the EU and the EU's capacity to absorb a new member state.

Conditionality

It is a normal practice to expect that new members of an organization will believe in the purpose of the club and will agree to abide by its rules. The conditions of membership are therefore of importance to both the existing members and the new ones. Enlarging the EU (the 'Club Europe') operates in much the same way, but meeting the conditions of membership has grown more onerous over time because the process of deepening integration has made the rules of the organization more complex. At the same time, most of the states which fitted best with the EU's ideal-type membership have already become members. Those ideal-type states that have not joined such as Iceland, Norway, and Switzerland have made a conscious decision not to belong, but do work very closely with the EU. What is left, to both the south and east of the EU is a group of states that have found the process of change to be very difficult.

Conditionality describes the process of laying down and monitoring the conditions for new states to become members of the EU. This has become a source of power for the EU over states who wish to join the organization, but it is effective only if a really strong desire to become a member exists. Its effectiveness also depends on the degree of clarity that exists about what is required of those who wish to join. The present conditionality rules take the membership requirements beyond the rather vague 1993 Copenhagen Criteria and makes them more specific in terms of the actions that are required of the aspiring members. The process has built within it incentives such as enhanced funding to implement change and the ultimate prize of membership. There are also sanctions involved, including delay or even an outright refusal to proceed with accession.

The purpose of setting conditions is to ensure that states are prepared for membership, whilst reassuring existing members that new members will not undermine the organization. Admitting the former communist states to membership requires radical change, which goes against well-established domestic interests. For this reason, it is important that there is clarity about what is expected, if only to assist domestic politicians to move the reform process along. However, the more prescribed the membership process becomes, the more likely it is that ordinary citizens in the applicant states are distanced from the process. Citizens have to accept the EU's *acquis* and the process of achieving it, without much opportunity to debate the process. It is only once membership has been achieved that the EU's democratic mechanisms become relevant. So, for example, the reforms being pushed through in preparation for Turkey's eventual membership may well go too far for many of the country's citizens, and could ultimately be rejected by them.

For existing members, tough conditions, where they are fully enforced, help to overcome some of the feeling of 'enlargement fatigue' which has come from attempts to push the borders of the EU outward. Poverty-stricken countries with significant political and social problems tend to be poorly regarded in the wealthy states of the EU15 because they are a drain on resources and undermine the image of the organization. For example, the plight of the orphans in Romania abandoned to live in appalling squalor resulted in widespread criticism of that country over many years. Consequently there is a wish by many citizens not to be associated with such countries.

Not all member states are, however, fully convinced of the need for strict conditions, especially where they feel an affinity with the applicant state. The negotiations for Turkish membership were delayed in October 2005 by Austria, in part because it looked as if Croatia would be excluded because of its apparently poor record on cooperating on war crimes. Once it was agreed that Croatian negotiations could commence, discussions with Turkey were also able to begin.

In the lead-up to accession, the Commission produces regular progress reports which list the achievements of membership criteria and indicate where further progress needs to be made. The most important hurdles are those laid out in the 1993 Copenhagen Criteria, so for example the achievement of a functioning market economy is very important. Warning letters are sent in cases where there are shortfalls in the timetable. Once negotiations have been completed and the Accession Treaty has been signed, the EU has two types of safeguard clauses at its disposal. The first kind was used when the 10 new members joined in May 2004.

- An economic safeguard clause applies if markets are disrupted after enlargement. This can be applied where trade liberalization causes disruption to the economies of the new members or existing members. The Commission must agree to any restrictions and there is a time limit of three years. Protective measures can be introduced to protect the markets of one of the existing member states for a period of three years after membership.
- If the new members fail to implement legislation related to the Internal Market, Justice and Home Affairs, the EU can impose sanctions which may remove some of the benefits of membership. Any sanctions against the new members must be proportional and can result in funding being denied, for example. These sanctions can apply for a period up to and beyond three years if the shortfalls have not been remedied. The existence of these safeguards means that there is an incentive for new members to move quickly to achieve their specific membership commitments.

There was some evidence that progress with respect to adopting the *acquis* slowed down prior to the 2004 enlargement, once the Accession Treaty was signed. Therefore, more specific conditions were applied to Romania (see Box 26.2) and Bulgaria, which meant that if either of the two states was manifestly unprepared for membership in January 2007, the Commission could recommended a delay until January 2008. This would take effect if unanimously supported by the EU Council of Ministers. It should be remembered that both states had already failed to match the performance of the other CEE states that joined in May 2004. Finally, in order to secure a final agreement on Romania's accession, even tougher constraints were placed upon that country. These 'super safeguard' clauses also reflected concerns about the specific candidature of these states. Predictably the Romanians felt that they had been unreasonably singled out in the process, perhaps because they felt that they had more readily admitted to problems

Table 26.4 Impact of enlarging upon the EU

Positive	Challenges
EU becomes a more important global actor	EU becomes more diverse in terms of its culture, society, and economy
Increased size of the internal market	Institutions may find it more difficult to reach important decisions
Widening of the eurozone over time	Competition from cheaper labour in the new member states
Convergence in living standards over time	Demands on the structural funds
Relationships with the new members become more intense	Greater pressure on the Common Agricultural Policy

than had Bulgaria. But this special treatment reflects the heightened concerns felt by some member states about the willingness or ability of Romania to keep to its commitments. The threat of delaying accession means that the process of completing the *acquis* must continue without stop almost up to the time of accession.

The general qualifications for membership of the EU may be unlikely to change in the future, but the process of refining the detailed conditions for membership will continue, and may well involve differentiated treatment, as was the case between Bulgaria and Romania.

KEY POINTS

- Conditionality describes the process of laying down and monitoring the conditions for new states to become members of the EU.
- Conditionality helps to maintain the confidence of existing EU members.
- There is now more detailed monitoring of the conditions of membership.
- Membership of Bulgaria and Romania could have been delayed for up to one year if they had not met the conditions set out by the EU.

Countries and regions

The subsections that follow examine enlargement from specific country and regional perspectives.

The Western Balkans

The Western Balkans (known formerly as Yugoslavia) is an area where Islam and Christianity meet, and where, at the same time, Christianity is split between Catholic and Orthodox faiths. The break-up and division of Yugoslavia in 1991 led to wars which were calmed down only as a result of international intervention in Bosnia in 1995, Kosovo in 1999, and the Former Yugoslav Rebublic of Macedonia (FYROM) in 2001. Whilst nations were able to emerge from the chaos, these wars led to a considerable loss of life, the destruction of property, and the displacement of huge numbers of people. The overspill from this was felt throughout Europe as large numbers of displaced persons sought to escape the war zones.

The EU has a commitment to the rule of law and it will be difficult for the region to move forward unless the legacy of the past atrocities has been dealt with. Therefore, a condition of EU membership for all the states of the former Yugoslavia is that the atrocities which were committed by all sides during the upheavals of the 1990s are dealt with either domestically or via the United Nation's International Criminal Tribunal for the Former Yugoslavia (ICTY). The prospect of EU membership has helped the stabilization of the region. Slovenia became an EU member in 2004. Croatia began negotiating accession in October 2005 and the FYROM, having applied for membership in 2004, was recommended for candidate status in November 2005. Applications for membership are eventually expected from Bosnia Herzegovina and Serbia and Montenegro. Albania, which was not part of Yugoslavia, is also expected to apply, as is Kosovo, as soon as its long-term status is defined.

A meeting of foreign ministers on 10 June 1999 in Cologne led to the adoption of the Stability Pact for South Eastern Europe. This initiative was led by the EU but had representation from over 40 interested parties. The pact is a political declaration and an agreement on international cooperation. It is not a new international organization: nor does it have independent financial resources. As part of this initiative to stabilize the region and bring to it both democracy and the benefits of the market economy, the EU has offered the prospect of eventual membership on the proviso that membership conditions are met. This has been a considerable stimulus for change in the region in order to meet the EU's criteria for membership. Each state will determine its own pace of reform, but Croatia has made most progress towards achieving membership in the post-2004 period.

The economies of the Western Balkans suffered significant damage as a result of the wars in the 1990s, although greater political stability in the region after the millennium has permitted some economic recovery, with annual growth rates in excess of those within the EU. The most prosperous of the states (apart from Slovenia which is now in the EU) is Croatia with an income per head about 36 per cent of the EU25 average. The remaining territories have income of less than half of that.

Croatia

Croatia declared independence from Yugoslavia in June 1991. This led to a war with the remainder of Serbian-dominated Yugoslavia and ethnic Serbs within Croatia which ended in 1995. Since that time the economy has been reformed and the Commission believes it to have a functioning market economy, which is a major prerequisite to membership. Croatia has a vibrant tourist trade and is a popular low-cost destination for many European holiday-makers.

The problems associated with Croatia's accession have been largely political and were centred on the autocratic style of the late President Tudjman. This led to the country being isolated at the end of the war because of the suppression of the media, human rights abuses, and the slowness to implement the Bosnian peace treaty, which delayed the return of Serb refugees. President Tudjman's death and parliamentary elections in January 2000 saw a return to a more acceptable political style in the country. However, right up to the start of accession negotiations, the international community was still concerned about the apparent lack of cooperation with respect to the capture of war crimes suspects such as General Ante Gotovina. Not surprisingly, the capture of Gotovina in December 2005 was regarded as very helpful development. The treatment of the country's Serbian minority still remains a problem. Only one-third of the country's 300,000 ethnic Serbs who fled the country during the 1991–5 period have returned home, and many of the homes of the exiles have been taken over by Croatians. The fact that membership negotiations finally got under way in October 2005 suggests that Croatia could move towards EU membership.

The Former Yugoslav Republic of Macedonia (FYROM)

The FYROM declared its independence in 1991 and applied for EU membership on 22 March 2004, gaining candidate status in December 2005. The lengthy title for this state derives from the contested nature of its name. Greece has a region called Macedonia and it felt that the newly emergent state with the same name posed a threat to its sovereignty. It is an ethnically diverse country with Macedonians comprising 64.2 per cent of the population and Albanians 25.2 per cent. There is a corresponding religious split between Orthodox (70 per cent) and Muslim (29 per cent). Following unrest in 2001, the rights of the Albanian minority have improved.

The economy enjoys price stability, bolstered by the tying of the Macedonian denar (MKD) to the euro. However, the country's isolation and its generally poor business climate have led to stagnation and recorded unemployment of about 40 per cent of the workforce. The country has a significant 'grey' economy, which might suggest that actual unemployment is lower than the recorded figure. No date for membership negotiations was set at the time candidate status was granted, because of a fear that accession by the FYROM would place an undue burden on EU finances.

Bosnia and Herzegovina

Bosnia and Herzegovina declared independence from Yugoslavia in 1992. This sparked a war which was halted only by the Dayton Agreement of 21 November 1995. The agreement retained the boundaries of the country and put in place a multi-ethnic government. A second tier of government was established which divided the country in two, creating the Bosniak/Croat Federation of Bosnia and Herzegovina and the Bosnian Serb-led Republika Srpska. The overall responsibility for the country was placed in the hands of the UN High Representative and the EU Special Representative, who was given extensive powers, for example to dismiss politicians who were considered to be corrupt. Ten years after the war, the multicultural relations between the communities, which had been a feature of the prewar period, had not been restored and over 90 per cent of people were living in religious and ethnic enclaves. Central institutions were created to overarch the separate communities, including a common currency, customs service, and tax regime. But efforts to reform the police system proved difficult. Yet a unified policing system is an essential prerequisite for the country's unification. There are still many refugees in Bosnia Herzegovina, corruption is still a problem as is the bringing to justice of war criminals. With these many difficulties facing the country membership is unlikely before 2015.

Serbia and Montenegro

When the Socialist Federal Republic of Yugoslavia broke up in 1992, Serbia and Montenegro remained tied to each other as the Federal Republic of Yugoslavia (FRY). This was replaced in 2003 by the loose federation of Serbia and Montenegro. Serbia was generally thought to be an aggressor in the wars in the region and the state was not readmitted into the United Nations until 2000. Kosovo is also a part of the territory but, as a result of a conflict between ethnic groups, the UN placed the province under an interim international civil and military administration. In October 2005, five years after the overthrow of Slobodan Milosevic, it was decided that negotiations with the EU to establish the country's Stabilization and Association Agreement (SAA) could begin. Milosevic was arrested in 2001 and faced trial before the UN War Crimes Tribunal for the Former Yugoslavia. He died in March 2006 before the trial could be completed.

Whilst the economy of these two joined states has the potential to achieve market economy status, the major issues are the pursuit of war criminals and the sovereignty of Kosovo. Achieving full democratic control of the military is essential and it is important to reduce the levels of corruption. It is estimated that it will be at least 2012 before membership of the EU can be considered a realistic prospect.

Kosovo

Kosovo is a region to the south of Serbia with a population largely made up of ethnic Albanians. Attempts to bring the region under the control of the Serbian government in Belgrade eventually led to open conflict in 1998, with huge numbers of people being displaced. The intervention of the international community led to the region being separated from Serbia, and since 1999 it has been governed by the United Nations Interim Administration Mission in Kosovo (UNMIK), supported by a NATO-led peacekeeping force. The region's internal security has improved significantly since that time. The EU has been the major external financial backer for the region. A market economy operates in Kosovo, underpinned by the use of the euro. At some stage the formal separation of this region will have to take place, so that it can either join the EU in its own right or choose to be absorbed by another state.

Albania

Albania was the most isolated and Stalinist of the European states to fall into the grip of communism. The price paid for this by its people was a life of great hardship and deprivation. The fall of communism in 1991 led to a difficult transition period, with reforms slow to take place. The process was hindered by financial scandals and the threat that law and order would break down.

The EU's involvement with Albania began on a formal basis in 1991, and a year later a Trade and Co-operation Agreement was signed, making it eligible for funding under the PHARE programme. In the period to 2005, Albania received at least €1 billion in aid from the EU. It started negotiating its Stabilization and Association Agreement (SAA), a precursor to membership, with the EU in January 2003. The main challenge facing Albania, now that the country is broadly stable, is the fight against corruption and organized crime, the establishment of a fair judiciary, and the embedding of democratic practices. Externally, relations with ethnic Albanians in Kosovo and the FYROM will remain an issue. Membership is unlikely to be achieved before 2015.

Turkey

Turkey is a secular democracy that lies at the very edge of what many consider to be the boundaries of Europe. It has a predominantly Muslim population of over 70 million. The country has been a member of the Council of Europe since 1949, NATO since 1952, and an Associate Member of the Western European Union since 1992. Turkey's membership of the EU is one of the organization's longest-running sagas. It originally applied for associate member status in 1959 and in 1963 this was agreed via the Ankara Agreement, with the long-term aim of EEC membership. The invasion of Northern Cyprus in 1974 and a military *coup d'état* on 12 September 1980 held back relations for many years. In 1987 Turkey unsuccessfully applied to join the EEC. In 1995 a customs union was agreed and this entered into force in 1996.

On 3 October 2005 accession negotiations began, despite reservations about Turkey's suitability for membership. One alternative proposed by leaders in Austria and Germany was a 'privileged partnership', although the precise status of this partnership has never been clear. It was favoured because of concerns that the EU would be overreaching itself, with its geographical borders reaching as far as Iraq and Iran. There were concerns about Turkey's relative poverty and the strain that would be placed upon the EU's budget because of the need for significant resource transfers. The potential for significant migration into the existing member states was also a concern, even if this migration might offer a solution to the problem of an ageing and declining population facing many EU members. Finally, Turkey's application has had only limited support from the public because of perceived cultural incompatibilities and discomfiture about the role of Islam.

The Commission believes that Turkey has a functioning market economy, but there are many internal reforms that must take place before the country can achieve membership. This suggests that it cannot take place before 2015. Most notable amongst the necessary reforms is the issue of respect for human rights and the elimination of police torture. Respect for the Kurds and other minorities is a related issue, as is the occupation of Northern Cyprus.

KEY POINTS

- The Western Balkans is the area that used to be known as Yugoslavia.
- If the states of the Western Balkans meet the EU's conditions, they may become members.
- Croatia is likely to become the next EU member after Bulgaria and Romania.
- The status of Kosovo needs to be determined for the territory to move forward.
- Turkey is unlikely to achieve EU membership until 2015 at the earliest.

CHRONOLOGY 26.4

Some landmark dates

Date	*Event*
14 April 1987	Turkey applies for membership of the EEC
19 December 1989	The PHARE programme is established to provide financial and technical assistance to the Central and Eastern European (CEE) states
3 and 16 July 1990	Cyprus and Malta apply for EU membership
22 June 1993	The Copenhagen European Council establishes the criteria for joining the European Union
31 March and 5 April 1994	Hungary and Poland apply for EU membership
1995	Applications for membership are received from Slovakia (21 June); Romania (22 June); Latvia (13 October); Estonia (24 November); Lithuania (8 December); and Bulgaria (14 December)
1996	Applications for membership are received from the Czech Republic (17 January); and Slovenia (10 June)
12–13 December 1997	The Luxembourg European Council commits to launching the enlargement process
10–11 December 1999	The Helsinki European Council agrees that accession talks will be held with 12 candidate countries. Turkey is considered to be a candidate country 'destined to join the Union'
13 December 2002	Agreement is reached with 10 candidate countries that they may join the EU on 1 May 2004 (Bulgaria and Romania are to join later)
21 February 2003	Croatia applies for EU membership
16 April 2003	The 10 accession treaties are signed in Athens
22 March 2004	The Former Yugoslav Republic of Macedonia (FYROM) applies for EU membership
1 May 2004	The 10 states join the EU
17 December 2004	The Brussels European Council endorses the closure of negotiations with Bulgaria and Romania
	The Council also defines conditions for the opening of accession negotiation with Croatia and Turkey
25 April 2005	Accession Treaties with Bulgaria and Romania are signed in Luxembourg
3 October 2005	Croatia and Turkey begin membership negotiations
16 December 2005	FYROM given candidate status by the European Council but no date given for the start of negotiations
26 September 2006	Bulgaria and Romania given the go-ahead to join the EU on 1 January 2007

Moving the border eastward

Georgia, Moldova, and Ukraine lie to the east of the EU and could be considered for membership at some time in the future. All have experienced a democratization process after the millennium and have moved away from the direct political influence of the Russian Federation. These states represent a low priority on the enlargement agenda because of the impact on the EU's budget, the poor state of their economies, and the need to consolidate the political reforms that have taken place. Whilst the

EU is likely to continue to provide a significant function via the European Neighbourhood Policy, the main concerns will be maintaining good relations and securing borders.

The next target for the democratization process is Belarus, a state which is closely tied to the Russian Federation. There is evidence of civil rights abuses there and the economic system has hardly progressed since the Soviet era. President Lukashenka won a third term in 2006, amid accusations of electoral irregularities, and this event may prove to be a watershed. If there is a shift towards greater democracy and economic change, Belarus could join other states in establishing the EU's permanent eastern border.

Conclusion

No enlargement of the EU has been unproblematic, but the process has been successful in most cases (see Box 26.4). However, the development gap between the existing members and potential candidates has widened as the EU moves forward with its own internal agendas. Those countries most obviously qualified to join have now become members, leaving states who have chosen not to join or who have left the process of reform until very late in the day.

Whilst enlargement is a very powerful tool of EU foreign policy, the EU's primary concern will surely be its own internal survival. This ultimately depends upon ensuring that post-enlargement decision-making is effective, and that coherent policies can be agreed upon. There is also a need to ensure that the general public are happy with developments. The failure of the referenda on the European Constitution in 2005 illustrates the problem of leaving negotiations in the hands of an elite. Only half the population of the EU surveyed in May–June 2005 supported the idea of further enlargement, with only 33 per cent of Germans being in favour and only 32 per cent of French. It was the new members who joined in May 2004 who were most enthusiastic (*Eurobarometer* 63, July 2005).

There is a limit to the size of the EU. In theory this is based upon perceptions of where Europe ends and other continents begin. Whilst enlargement does create a dynamic to the European project, it also creates significant stresses within it. With each additional member, there comes a new point of view to accommodate and the organization becomes more diverse. The federalist aspiration of a highly integrated United States of Europe (see Chapter 5) is unlikely to be realized. Indeed the problem of a significantly enlarged EU is more likely to be a feeling of a lack of identity and an absence of a sense of purpose. Moreover, if there is further enlargement to the east, there will inevitably be competition with Russia.

The issues that govern the future of enlargement are those relating to the EU itself (see Box 26.4). Enlargement does create tensions about the allocation of resources, especially as the need to respond to the budgetary demands of the poorer states will mean some states that are only slightly better off will lose out. Agricultural spending, which dominates the EU budget, will remain a prominent issue, as poorer countries seek to gain the same benefits as the richer ones. The migration of workers will also remain a controversial issue if unemployment is unacceptably high within the more affluent EU states. An enlarged EU will also be faced with the prospect of ever more complex ethnic relationships, especially in the border areas. Finally, there is a concern that the EU will become more inward looking generally as it tries to cope with enlargement. Issues such as relations with the developing world, with North Africa, and the USA may all have to take second place.

QUESTIONS

1. Why has the European Union enlarged since 1989?
2. What is meant by the term 'enlargement fatigue'?
3. Why does the Western Balkans pose major problems for the enlargement process?
4. What role does conditionality play in the enlargement process?
5. Why does the EU continue with the enlargement process?
6. What are the key policy issues facing the EU in the next round of enlargement?
7. How has the enlargement process changed the EU?
8. Why are the accession criteria important?

GUIDE TO FURTHER READING

■ **Cameron, F. (ed.)** ***The Future of Europe: Integration and Enlargement*** **(London: Routledge, 2004).** A useful guide to enlargement issues just prior to the 2004 enlargement.

■ **Cremona, M. (ed.)** ***The Enlargement of the European Union*** **(Oxford: Oxford University Press, 2004).** An examination of the enlargement process and its impact upon the EU and the candidate states.

■ **European Commission** ***2005 Enlargement Strategy Paper,*** **COM (2005) 56 (Brussels: European Commission, 9 November 2005).**

■ **Schimmelfennig, F., and Sedelmeier, U. (eds)** ***The Politics of European Union Enlargement: Theoretical Approaches*** **(London: Routledge, 2005).** The strength of this volume is its application of theoretical issues to enlargement.

IMPORTANT WEBSITES

● **http://europa.eu.int/comm/enlargement/index_en.html** The European Commission's website is a very good starting point for key policy documents and country reports.

● **http://www.one-europe.ac.uk** The British Economic and Social Research Council's One Europe or Several? programme finished at the end of April 2003. This site contains access to a series of high-quality monographs.

● **http://www.euractiv.com** The Euractiv website is constantly being updated and contains dossiers on enlargement themes and on candidate and applicant states.

● **http://www.europarl.eu.int/enlargement/default_en.htm** The European Parliament's website has details of the Parliament's role in the process as well a clear description of the main events.

● **http://europa.eu.int/comm/economy_finance/publications/enlargementpapers_en.htm** European Economy Enlargement Papers provide information on the economies of the candidate countries and on the economic implications of enlargement.

- http://europa.eu.int/comm/enlargement/communication/archives/index.htm European Commission PowerPoint slides covering enlargement with excellent maps covering the different enlargements. At this site click on the PowerPoint Presentations (PPT) on the right-hand banner.

Visit the Online Resource Centre that accompanies this book for lots of interesting additional material. http://www.oxfordtextbooks.co.uk/orc/cini2e/

27 Conclusion: The Future of the European Union

ALEX WARLEIGH-LACK

Chapter Contents

Reader's Guide

This chapter is an informed personal view of the EU's evolution in the coming years. This is a subject about which opinions differ for many reasons, and so this chapter is best understood as one contribution to the debate rather than as a definitive discussion. The chapter discusses recent literature on the future of the EU in order to consider what kind of entity the EU is, or could become, and what kind of role in world affairs the EU might play as a result. The chapter also investigates a range of variables which are likely to shape the evolution of the EU significantly, and argues that the key issue for the Union will be how it can manage its increasing diversity by adopting a more flexible approach to its politics and organizational structure.

Introduction: the EU in crisis – again

The European Union has had a turbulent time in recent years. Problems such as the failure to agree a **Constitutional Treaty** in December 2003 set a morose tone for the integration process; even though such large difficulties have proved capable of resolution (Miles 2005), others come to take their place. In 2006, it seems that the Constitutional Treaty, having finally been agreed, has been killed off by the voters of France and the Netherlands, leaving the EU's reform process. Citizens continue to disengage from the EU institutions, including what is ostensibly 'their' Parliament (Greffet 2005); the richer member states are seeking to reduce their contribution to the EU budget rather than increasing it to allow equitable treatment of the 2004 entrants in cohesion and agricultural aid (Devuyst 2005); policy reform is difficult, since both vested interests (powerful groups which want to shape public policy according to their own needs) and short-term concerns in domestic politics often encourage member states to reject changes which, from the perspective of the 'European interest', seem eminently sensible – witness, for example, the still very incomplete process of reform in agricultural policy. No actor, state, or institution has yet come forward to provide leadership; and the official response to the Treaty ratification crisis – to declare a 'year of reflection', and prepare a so-called **Plan D** (democracy, dialogue, and debate) – has so far proved vacuous.

Of course, the EU remains in place. The Single Market and the euro continue to function; the Nice Treaty of 2000 remains in force; the enlargement process continues, with Croatia and Turkey added to the list of official candidates; and joint action in immigration policy and criminal investigations is arguably deepening, with progress towards the **European Arrest Warrant** and further cooperation in matters of personal data exchange and pursuit of criminals across borders. Is it possible, then, that just as the 1970s was only superficially a period of stagnation in European integration (Weiler 1991), the Union's current travails will retrospectively appear of exaggerated importance? Such must remain a possibility: nothing about the future is certain. However, the EU must now be the subject of a searching enquiry about its key purpose in the twenty-first century, and about how it uses power for the good of its citizens. There is a significant difference between the current crisis and the 1970s equivalent, **Eurosclerosis** (a period when political integration in Europe stalled). Eurosclerosis was primarily the result of government decisions in member states, and there was very little public concern about the condition of European integration. The EU's current drama is being played out against a background of over a decade of public disquiet about the Union's **legitimacy**, and is thus at least as deeply an issue of mass politics as it is of **diplomacy** and **statecraft** (that is, dealings between member governments). Moreover, because the EU is now inherently controversial, it will be impossible to find a sustainable way out of the crisis – as opposed to a tired acceptance of the impasse – without articulating different ways forward for the Union and subjecting them to public debate. From this crisis, however, may thus eventually come the very legitimacy that the Union has so often been seen to lack.

In this chapter I will attempt to address three issues. First, I will categorize the recent literature on the future of the EU, which falls into three approaches (those which expect the EU to become a federal-state kind of superpower; those which anticipate a novel kind of network-based but powerful Euro-polity; and those which see the EU as a junior partner of the USA). These scenarios are about two major issues: first, the kind of entity that the EU is, or could become, and thus how it works and the kind of policies it can make. Secondly, the kind of role that the EU could play in world politics. After presenting these scenarios I will set out the factors that appear the most relevant in determining in which direction the EU will travel in the immediate future. Finally, I will argue that the 'future of Europe' depends ultimately on one key variable – the degree to which member states are willing to adopt a flexible model of integration to address the fact that they do not share the same preferences for European integration at either macro or micro levels (that is, regarding either the 'big picture' or individual policies), and are also very short on the kind of solidarity which would allow the creation of a more uniform political community. Hence the EU must choose between flexibility and stagnation.

Euro-visions: superpower or subordinate?

The following paragraphs set out three visions of the EU's future that can be found in recent literature. These visions offer different understandings of the kind of structures and institutions the EU has, or needs. They also offer a range of understandings about the kind of role that the EU can, could, or should play in global politics. Taken together, they comprise an intriguing range of ways in which the EU's future can be imagined.

Europe as federal superpower

Several authors have recently argued that the EU is, or should become, a federal state and superpower, the equal of the USA, and even the saviour of the world political economy as the author of a softer form of capitalism which is more open to social and environmental concerns (Coffey 2003) (see Box 27.1). These heady visions, based on observations of the EU's increasing competences and geographical size since the early 1990s, have often been written by commentators struck by the difference between 'European' and US world views, social philosophies, interests, and understandings of power (Haseler 2004; Reid 2004). Seen in this light, in the USA, general opinion supports a minimal approach to social policy at home and the extensive use of the USA's military might abroad whenever necessary, whereas in the EU, general opinion is in favour of a welfare state (that is, a guarantee by the government to meet basic social needs, such as education, health care, and social security), which provides more generous support for the poorest and weakest citizens, and an approach to foreign policy which is more rooted in

KEY CONCEPTS AND TERMS 27.1

Federal superpower Europe

The idea of the EU as a federal superpower is an old one. Many people have wanted the EU to become a federation in its own right, that is, to become a new single state based on a written constitution and a clear division of powers between the new centre of government (presumably Brussels) and the member states. Others have strongly opposed this idea, because it would mean the member states ceased to exist as independent, or 'sovereign' units. Recently, it has been suggested that the EU is about to become such a federation in order to play a strong role in world politics, which is necessary because the established partnership with the USA is breaking down. In this view, the EU will become a federal state because it is the only way the EU can defend its own interests and values in the world where US power is obvious, and where, essentially, the USA and the EU no longer want the same things. This has increased a sense of 'Otherness' or basic difference, between the EU and the USA, whose respective views of the world are increasingly divergent. Thus, in order to advance their own interests and stand up to the power of the USA, the member states of the EU will simply have to sacrifice their independence and pool their sovereignty in a new, EU, state.

Sources: Haseler (2004); Reid (2004).

international law and diplomacy than in the use of military power.

In this perspective, the EU has stealthily reached the point at which its economic power and diplomacy poses a fundamental challenge to US **hegemony** (or dominance), which US actors fail to understand because they are wedded to outdated notions of power based on military might. For Haseler and Reid, the EU, by creating a Single Market for its own benefit, has evolved a way of working which is more in keeping with contemporary global governance than that of the USA, and has developed an extremely powerful tool to use in its external policy: controlling market access. By creating the world's biggest market, the EU has also begun to act like a magnet, because businesses and producers who want to access this vast number of consumers in order to make a larger profit have to play by the rules set by the EU. These rules can often be very extensive, and require businesses to work in ways that they otherwise would not, and even to change their products to meet EU standards. Thus, although the EU cannot match the military power of the USA, it has a great influence on what states and business do throughout the world, every day.

Furthermore, the EU is destined to integrate more deeply. Propelled by an ever more profound sense of difference from the USA, catalysed by the US-led war on Iraq begun in 2003 and pride in a general attachment to the welfare state which is not part of US political culture, Europeans will be increasingly supportive of joint action to protect themselves in the global economy and assert their strategic interests independently of Washington. This will be underpinned by the rise and progeny of what Reid calls 'Generation E': the younger citizens of the member states, who increasingly travel and work across the continent, united by a common tongue (English) and the good offices of EasyJet and RyanAir. Thus, Europeans are becoming increasingly aware of a shared identity and difference from the inhabitants of other parts of the globe, which sense of 'Otherness' will underpin a cycle of deepening integration and soon produce a fully-fledged European federation.

Careful consideration of EU politics, not to mention EC law, can indeed reveal evidence of EU movement in a federal direction, as analysis of the contents of the 2003 version of the Constitutional Treaty demonstrates (Føllesdal 2005). However, it is also clear even for those committed to European **federalism** that the EU is not currently a federal state: neither version of the Constitutional Treaty has (yet) been ratified, and even if the first, and more ambitious, of these documents had become the EU's basic law there would have remained shortcomings in EU powers from a federalist perspective (Trechsel 2005). Moreover, even if we overlook the **ratification** problems of the Constitutional Treaty, there are problems with the diagnosis of the EU as a federal superstate. For example, Reid makes too swift a leap from observing EU citizens' increased freedom of personal movement to assuming, first, the deepening of European identity, and, secondly, that this change in identity would automatically translate into an attachment to the EU (Warleigh 2003: 11–14). Haseler (2004: 118) fails to comprehend that the 'European rescue of the nation state' has been about preserving that tool of government by means of its transformation, not a means of doing away with it. Both commentators also exaggerate the extent to which the EU political system, with its complex sharing and network system of power, can really be judged as analogous to a federal state, and make false assumptions that there is a single 'European social model' that serves as a conscious source of European pride and pan-continental identity, rather than often very different *national* social policies and significant controversy about the way in which they should evolve in the context of Europeanization (Castle-Kanerova and Jordan 2001). Hence, Coffey (2003: 123) argues that implementing the federal model of European integration, which he finds normatively attractive, will have to remain a long-term goal.

Europe as network power

The second set of perspectives on the future of the EU foresees a great future for the Union as a new kind

KEY CONCEPTS AND TERMS 27.2

Network power Europe

An alternative view of how the EU might become a powerful entity and shape world politics is the idea of a 'network power Europe'. In this view, the EU can typify the new kinds of politics and power that are necessary in the twenty-first century. This is seen to be a world in which international law, globalization, and human rights norms have created a climate in which states are interdependent. This means that the international system is no longer a 'state of nature', in which states have to be prepared to fight each other for their survival, but is rather a place that is structured by rules, laws, and habits of negotiation. Because this matches the way in which the EU itself works, and because it means military power is less necessary than diplomatic skill to achieve influence and promote one's interest, the EU is better placed to be a powerful actor than others such as the USA or Russia, which reflect outdated understandings of how power works. Thus, in this view, the complicated nature and structures of EU decision-making are not barriers to its progress, but rather evidence of its ability to adapt to a changed global context, and the way in which the EU's member states share power with each other while retaining their core independence is a model for the rest of the world.

Source: Leonard (2005).

of political entity able dextrously to exploit the structures of the interdependent global polity, and foster European unity as both a cause and a consequence of this power. Although they share some of the ideas of the federalists discussed above – notably the beliefs that the EU has, or is, a distinctive model of social market capitalism, and that it seeks to use its external influence for altruistic as much as self-interested reasons (Manners 2002) – commentators in this school of thought are much more optimistic about the ability of the EU to use and develop its existing complex structure as an organizational asset (Schmitter 1996; Grant 2000; Leonard 2005) (see Box 27.2).

Considered from this perspective, both EU federalists and advocates of hard power such as the US neo-conservatives (the group of strongly right-wing Republicans in the entourage of President George W. Bush) misapprehend what is required for both European unity and influence on the world stage. To work together, Europeans do not need to create a new state: instead, the novel legal structures that the ECJ has created under member state acceptance of the principle of the rule of law, together with the complex but member-state-dependent political structures of the EU, are enough to provide a working Euro-polity even if certain reforms to increase **efficiency** and **transparency** would be beneficial (Grant 2000: 21–2). If the contemporary world is one of rules, laws, and international organizations, economic power, law, and negotiation are usually more useful foreign policy tools than hard power (Leonard 2005): the federalist diagnosis that the EU can be an independent actor only when it has its own hard power, made by such as Haseler (2004: 7), fails to understand both how the nature of power in international politics has changed and how the EU can be an effective foreign policy actor with minimal hard power (that is, without armed forces which are capable of aggressive deployment). The EU's primary asset, indeed, is that it has understood this shift in power, and provided a model of how it can be employed; this model, coupled with the EU's emphasis on the social market, provides the blueprint for emerging world powers such as India, South Africa, Brazil, and China (Leonard 2005: 4–7) and will provoke a rush to emulate the EU's approach to region-building in other parts of the world (Leonard 2005: 135–43).

This view of the EU's future has several strengths. First, it understands how the EU is already influential both internally and externally through the process of 'Europeanization': the EU can shape policies and structures around a new standard or approach of its choosing not only in its current member states, but also in non-member states which want access to the Single Market or even to join the Union. The idea of the Union as a network power also appreciates how the EU can have influence in the wider world through its use of development aid and direct investment, and the use of conditionalities (requirements for reform) as the price to be paid for receipt of such sums. If the international environment really has moved away from a **Hobbesian state of nature**, then the EU may offer new ways of understanding how power can be exercised in global politics. The 'network Europe' approach also understands the effectiveness of the existing complex structures of governance which engineer day-to-day policy-making success in the present-day Union, that is, the multi-level policy networks and negotiation processes involving the EU and member state institutions plus a constellation of non-state actors. Thus, in this approach, there is less to be said for the kind of federally inspired 'tidying up' of EU governance processes than meets the eye, not least because such a process would be superfluous. The approach also has a certain **normative** attractiveness for pro-Europeans of a social democratic persuasion: it offers a means by which Europe can enjoy power and influence while claiming with at least some justification to have an ethical foreign policy and to be preserving, rather than replacing, its member states.

Of course, this perspective on the future of Europe can also be criticized. First, if the USA is an imperial power (Bacevich 2002), then the claims about the potential external influence of the EU made by such commentators as Leonard and Grant must require dilution. An imperial USA will structure the international system according to its own perception of its interests and understanding of power; although as a result of its own governance structures and norms the EU may grasp the complexities of international law and rules more quickly than the USA, this does not remove US ability to structure those rules in the first place or simply ignore them should it so choose. Moreover, it is a mistake to assume that the EU provides a 'model' that processes of region-building in other parts of the globe will automatically emulate. Indeed, the EU has often been explicitly refused as a model for other regional blocs, which reject what they see as normatively unacceptable founding principles or excessively institutionalized governance structures (Acharya 2002; Hettne 2002).

Additionally, while the 'network Europe' model rightly claims that the existing approach to decision-making can be more effective than is often understood, it underestimates both the need for, and the possibilities of, meaningful reform in EU governance. Thus, even ostensibly modest proposals for EU reform such as those contained in Grant (2000) are currently beyond reach; Schmitter's (1996: 125) prediction of the levels of integration that would be achieved by 2001 in foreign and defence policies, but also in macro-economics, citizenship, and education and research, are still far off. Instead, as a collective, the member states remain unwilling to make significant reform of the EU either to deepen its democratic foundations (Warleigh 2002b) or to experiment more radically with its decision-making processes (Warleigh 2005). Thus, while the diagnosis of the EU as a network form of governance is accurate, it may be premature to understand the EU as anything but a putative, or partly realized, 'network power'.

Europe as subordinate power

The final recent view of the EU's future is one which places it as a subordinate to the USA. Although they differ in their analyses of the likely influence of the EU, both David Calleo and Robert Kagan have latterly argued that Europe cannot have a future as a major world power, and will instead be a regional governance system reliant upon the USA for its military security – if indeed the USA continues to want to provide this (see Box 27.3).

Calleo argues that there are natural limits to the possibilities for European integration, as certain states which are geographically in Europe are simply unable to fit EU requirements and norms, 'economically, militarily, or politically' (Calleo 2001: 351). Furthermore, the EU is more fittingly seen as, at best, a confederation of nation states rather than a potential federation or new kind of polity; defence of national sovereignty will prevent the EU becoming a federation, and as a result its external influence will be limited to its very near abroad. Thus, the future for the EU is to be part of a 'tri-polar Europe', in which the EU and the USA become more equal

KEY CONCEPTS AND TERMS 27.3

Subordinate Europe

This perspective takes a rather different understanding of the EU's status as a 'network', drawing on neo-realist theory in international relations. This theory holds that the international system consists of states struggling for power, and where the most powerful states – in our period, the USA – are able to dominate the others through a process of *hegemony*. States in this international system have to put up with it if they are too weak to fight; and because they must protect themselves against rivals, states will retain whatever power they can to defend themselves. States may cooperate with each other, but they will never form an alliance that goes so deep as to create a new federation. Instead, states will withdraw from alliances when they have served their purpose. Thus, the EU is a network not because it wants to be, or because this is the key to successful organization in the twenty-first century, but because it has no choice. The member states are weak enough to want to cooperate across a range of issues, but they will refuse to give up their sovereignty, so there are clear limits to the powers that the EU can acquire. Furthermore, because of this refusal deeply to integrate key aspects of policy, such as security and defence, the member states will make the EU depend on the USA for its defence. This means that Washington will have great influence over what the EU does, and how it does it, and in turn that the EU will be a limited organization with a constrained role in world affairs.

Source: Kagan (2004).

partners (because the EU will shoulder a greater share of responsibility), and in which they both develop a more functional working relationship with Russia but keep that country as much at arm's length as possible (Calleo 2001: 348). The USA will tolerate this increase in EU influence in pan-European politics out of concern for stability, and because it could allow strategically useful diplomatic deployment of the Union as the 'good cop' to partner the USA's more heavy-handed approach to being the world's 'police force'.

Robert Kagan's contribution to the debate is essentially an analysis of the relative power and capacity to shape global politics of the EU and the USA, written in the context of the transatlantic tensions that arose immediately before and after the US-led invasion of Iraq. His 2004 book *Paradise and Power* argues that the EU has actually made itself ineligible for a world power role as a result of its status as a network polity. To this extent, Kagan agrees with the federalists that the EU would have to become a federation and acquire a greater military capacity to have an important global role. However, he differs fundamentally from the federalists in his view of the possibility of such a transformation. For Kagan, the EU has been able to develop its novel system of governance only because it has enjoyed the military protection of the USA, and was thus able to concentrate its resources on non-military expenditure. Furthermore, this isolation from the harsher realities of international politics, which Kagan sees as red in tooth and claw, has led the EU to develop a misleading view that its own rule-and-negotiation-based internal governance style can be applied to the rest of the world. This naivety hobbles the EU and makes it incapable of doing the dirty work, or undertaking the kind of external policy, required of a great power. The USA, on the other hand, sees the international system as characterized by anarchy, and seeks aggressively to defend its interests where it feels the need. The EU's task is thus to prevent a further slide behind the USA in terms of military capacity (in which it is likely to fail as a result of its governing norms), and to seek to ensure it continues to receive US military protection despite the growing sense of different values and world views on each side of the Atlantic.

This understanding of Europe's subordinate future mixes two concepts familiar in (neo-)realist International Relations theory, namely the determination (and duty) of nation states to preserve their sovereignty and the ultimate importance of military power. Calleo's perspective is perhaps more old-fashioned, drawing on concepts of 'great powers' and 'spheres of interest', but also on the idea that the pursuit of stability is of prime importance in determining great powers' international policies. He argues that both the EU and the USA have an interest in global stability, and in stability on the

European flank in particular. The two actors will have to treat with the other likely regional power, Russia, but will benefit from sharing the burden of providing security even if the USA's superior military power makes it very much the senior partner. Kagan, writing at the height of the first term of office of George W. Bush, argues that transatlantic tensions are deep and chronic, and that although the EU needs the USA, the USA may decide it doesn't need the EU. This is a challenge to Cold War strategic 'certainties' which is very much in keeping with the US unilateralism of the time.

This 'subordinate Europe' approach helpfully reminds us that the EU, as a network-based polity, has limits that would not be apparent in political systems or states of a more traditional kind. It also reminds us of the importance of the USA in determining EU foreign policy capability: not for nothing does the EU's **Rapid Reaction Force** have to operate through, and with the permission of, US-dominated NATO. When hard power is required, the EU has little capability, and even its best-armed member states are militarily puny in comparison with the USA. Calleo helpfully recalls that the EU must thus be seen as only one set of institutions in European governance, and by no means always the most powerful of them, and in this respect he is open to the kind of view of European governance that might be called the *condominio* – an overlapping set of institutions and networks which collectively govern the continent (Schmitter 1996).

Nonetheless, Calleo fails to appreciate the nature of the EU as a polity: for him it is and must remain a confederation of nation states, but one which is much weaker, and much less open to intrusive, if often 'light', governance structures and processes than Coffey would understand by the same term (Coffey 2003: 123). He also fails accurately to assess the capacity of the EU for enlargement, not to mention its strategic interest in pursuing this policy. As a result, Calleo misreads the nature of the EU and one of its most important policies. Kagan, on the other hand, better appreciates the network governance style of the EU, but also sees in this very governance style the lack of ability to act coherently on the world stage. This emphasis on hard power underestimates the Union's ability both to influence third parties and to intervene militarily, even if such action is limited to humanitarian and peacekeeping functions. Thus, Kagan misrepresents the likelihood of the EU achieving foreign policy *powers* if not its chances of becoming a foreign policy *power* (Hill and Smith 2005).

Thus, there are three very different perspectives seeking to persuade us about the future possibilities for the European Union. In the next section of the chapter, I investigate the principal factors which are likely to shape the manner in which the EU evolves in the coming years, and in the subsequent and final section I assess which of these three models is the most likely to be realized.

KEY POINTS

- The idea of the EU as a federal superpower has recently been put forward as a response to US power in world politics.
- A 'federal superpower Europe' would see the EU rival the USA as one of two major global powers, with the EU acting as an advocate for an alternative, gentler form of capitalism and a world system with a greater respect for international law.
- In the 'network power Europe' scenario, the EU is seen as a successful if untidy model for dealing with a very interdependent global political and economic system.
- The view of Europe as a 'subordinate power' rests on the idea that the EU has major inherent weaknesses. These are that national sovereignty will prevent the EU federating, and yet without federating the EU cannot hope either to function well domestically or to be influential in the wider world.

Determining the future of the EU

Can the Union move forward? It is legitimate to doubt this, given the scale of the challenges that confront the EU and the degree of commitment so far shown by the member states to finding a solution: although it may not have been possible to predict the exact shape of the current impasse, something like it has been foretold by scholars for over a decade, and yet there has been no substantial democratic reform of the EU (Warleigh 2005). That said, there is certainly a far greater acceptance of the need for significant change in the functioning and structures of the EU now than in the past, and it is from this momentum that change may come.

Elsewhere (Warleigh 2004: 94–109) I have developed four scenarios for the medium-term future of the EU, which range from collapse to federation (see Box 27.4). I here suggest that the principal factors which will impact on the evolution of the EU, and thus determine towards which of these scenarios it moves, can be grouped into three categories: external factors; member state factors; and issues at the EU level. In what follows, I address each of these categories in turn.

BOX 27.4

Shaping the EU's future

There are many issues which will be important in determining how the EU develops. Some of these issues involve external affairs, in particular relations with important other players in world politics such as the USA, which is the most powerful entity in world politics, and Russia, which has an increasing role in the EU's energy supply and an extensive border with the EU. Other issues relate to domestic politics in the EU's member states, where what citizens and key interest groups want their governments to prioritize in terms of EU reform will be crucial. Thus, it will be necessary to watch whether domestic politics shifts in favour of 'more Europe' or 'less Europe', and which policy issues are prioritized here. A third set of issues relates to EU-level politics. At this level, the most important question is what will happen to the Treaty Establishing a Constitution for Europe: is it dead? Can a replacement for it be found? However, other matters such as structural reform to boost economic growth and the ability to manage the increasing diversity of the EU will also be significant. Can the increasingly large EU find a way to make all its member states agree a common way forward, or will it have to allow groups of states to cooperate in certain policies, while other states remain outside that particular initiative? The action that the EU takes on all these matters, and more, will indicate the kind of entity that its member states wish it to become, and also what sacrifices they are willing to make – if any – in order to reach this goal.

Source: Warleigh (2004: chapter 6).

External factors

Relations with two particular states are crucial here. First, the USA. The EU and the USA are currently the world's major economic powers. If they act in concert, and possibly deepen the plans for a transatlantic free trade area, this will lock the two actors together more deeply and ensure that their economic rivalry is constrained. If the two pursue their own economic interests more aggressively, economic rivalry is more probable, and the number of trade wars between the two is likely to escalate. Security issues are also paramount here. In the past, the EU (and its member states) have relied heavily on the USA for their security. If the USA continues to wish to provide this security guarantee, the EU may continue to accept it; there are also opportunities for the relationship to become more balanced, particularly regarding security in the continent of Europe and its near abroad, if the EU increases its military capacity. However, the USA may prefer to concentrate its resources in other parts of the world which it considers more of a strategic priority. If Washington takes this course of action, the EU will have to decide how much it wishes to invest in a common security force, and also recalibrate its foreign policy to take account of US withdrawal. As a background to these issues, and one which may be capable of shaping decisions made about them, is the question of identity. Will the USA be increasingly seen as Europe's 'Other'? If so, will this be enough to persuade EU leaders to develop a more independent security policy?

The second crucial relationship is with Russia. The 2004 enlargement brought inside the EU eight states which had formerly been part of the Soviet bloc during the Cold War, and future enlargements will increase this number further. These states are already ensuring that the EU is more involved in the politics of its eastern flank than before, as demonstrated by the EU intervention in the 2004 Ukrainian presidential election. **Kaliningrad** has already been a matter of controversy in Russia–EU relations, albeit one which now appears to have been resolved. The EU is deepening its links with Russia in terms of energy supply, which is likely to create a certain dependency of the Union on Russian oil and gas. As Russia addresses its own issues of economic and social reform, not to mention its foreign policy/secession problems such as Chechnya, it may seek to develop its relationship with the EU as a potential alternative to the USA; Russian policy on the Kyoto Protocol and on Iranian nuclear energy/weapons technology indicates the possibilities here. Thus, relations with Russia will be important for the EU in terms of internal, near abroad, and global policies. Will relations with the USA and/or Russia oblige the Union to deepen its foreign and security policy capabilities?

Global economics will also be a major factor, in particular the EU's response to the growing challenge of China and India. As these two countries garner greater shares of the world economy, the EU will need to develop strategies for economic growth which are environmentally sustainable and play to the EU's comparative advantage. In this respect, the **Lisbon Agenda** to turn the EU into the world's leading knowledge economy by 2010 is a crucial plank of its external policy. Currently, this target is extremely unlikely to be met, given the limited progress in economic reform in the member states and the problems in completing the Single Market.

Member state politics

Here, the principal issue is how each member state decides to shape its preferences regarding the EU. These are partly determined by long-standing issues of political culture (popular values and understandings of what politics should be about, and how political systems should work) and 'big picture' views of the national interest, but they are also shaped by complex bundles of issue-specific factors, which in turn rely on both negotiations between the members of the EU25 and the shifting patterns of domestic politics within each member state. For example, the French '*Non*' to the Constitutional Treaty motivated President Chirac to oppose further **liberalization of services** in the Single Market (a major EU policy, the so-called Bolkestein Directive), a measure of which he had previously been in favour. Hence, what is seen by a given member state to be possible or desirable at the EU level can change for reasons of domestic electoral politics, or even, in the case of a new government, a shift in ideology. Hence, understanding what will happen to and in the EU requires us to pay close attention to the politics of its member states.

EU-level politics

At this level, the first and overarching issue is the fate of the Constitutional Treaty. If it really is dead, what are the prospects for institutional change and reform? What will Plan D yield in terms of reform proposals? If there is no prospect of meaningful reform on issues such as qualified majority voting in the Council, will the EU system be able to continue functioning? In addition, what kind of policy style (or understanding of the best way to make policy) do the member states want the EU to adopt? Recent years have seen a trend towards soft policy, which seeks to set standards and targets, or measure best practice so that member states can learn from each other, while avoiding making binding legislation that forces states to comply (Wallace 2000). Will this preference continue and, if so, will it yield effective policy outputs?

The next three issues are financial and economic. First, what will happen to the EU budget? Will the 2005 budget deal aid subsequent policy reform on the ground that, for example, the Common Agricultural Policy can no longer be afforded? If not, will the EU go bankrupt? Secondly, how will the euro fare? Will it become a rival world currency to the US dollar, or collapse because either the member states cannot follow their own policy rules or because the EU's powers to make monetary policy are not balanced by powers in other areas of macro-economics, such as tax? A key issue here is reform of the **Stability and Growth Pact** (SGP), or its replacement with a new set of policy norms for the single currency. Thirdly, will the EU economies grow sufficiently to generate the elusive 'feel-good factor' and allow more money to enter the EU coffers in order to pay for policy innovation and expansion?

How will the 2004 enlargement round, and any future enlargements, impact upon EU politics? Certainly, such enlargements increase the diversity of the EU, but will they make it ungovernable under the existing decision rules? Or will they be the necessary catalyst for reform? The 2004 enlargement has already shifted EU foreign policy concerns eastwards, and shown that institutional reform in the context of an EU25 can be very difficult (it was Poland, and also Spain, which blocked ratification of the first draft of the Constitutional Treaty). In the medium term, if Turkey's accession negotiations are successful, how will the EU adjust to having a culturally Islamic, relatively poor, and heavily populated new member state that would deserve to be, in terms of the current voting system, the second most powerful EU member?

The final major issue is the democratic deficit. Although this issue can be misunderstood and exaggerated (Majone 2005), it is nonetheless of crucial importance. Many, if not most, EU citizens have great worries about its legitimacy. These simply cannot go unaddressed any longer; and yet the EU's capacity to respond to these concerns is arguably reduced by the rejection of the Constitutional Treaty, which contained measures to increase EU transparency and render the EU decision-making process more participatory. Allied to this issue of democracy is that of diversity. In an EU of 25 member states, and in which issues at the heart of national sovereignty (the ability of a state to determine its own independent course of action) are moving higher on the EU agenda, it is increasingly difficult both to present the Union as a solely economic enterprise and to generate a common understanding about what the EU should do in a given policy area, or whether it should acquire new powers in certain policies.

How can these differences be reconciled? How can those member states which wish to deepen integration in a particular policy area coexist with those which do not? This problem is made more complex by the fact that these preferences about integration cannot be simply divided along a binary more/less Europe line. Instead, member states have different preferences according to the issue at hand: for example, Ireland is happy to participate in the single currency, but as a neutral state has reservations about participating in a deeper security policy; the UK wants to stay out of the euro, but is happy to participate in a pro-USA form of defence integration; and France wants both the euro and an EU defence capacity, independent of the USA. Managing this diversity, which is made more complex by the issue of policy capacity (a state may wish to adopt a particular EU policy, but be technically incapable of so doing), will be a most intricate dance for the Union, and the tools which it has available to use in this process will have to be a key agenda item in any future institutional reform negotiations.

KEY POINTS

- The EU's future will be shaped by events in the wider world, the domestic politics of its member states, and by developments in EU policy. It is thus complex to predict.
- Key external relationships are with the USA and Russia.
- Domestic politics, particularly regarding the future of the welfare state and the role that the EU can or should play in its transformation, will be a crucial factor.
- The main EU-level events which are likely to impact upon its near future are the crisis over the ratification – or otherwise – of the Constitutional Treaty, the drive (so far only moderately successful) for economic reform, and the crisis of legitimacy which has both led to, and results from, these problems.
- An issue undercutting all the above is the increased, and increasing, diversity of the EU, which has the potential to make the securing of common policies and understandings even more difficult than in the past.

Conclusions: a flexible future for Europe?

How can the immediate future of the EU best be understood? At the time of writing, the problems of European integration are far more obvious than their solutions. At elite level, there is clearly insufficient solidarity and mutual trust to produce a far-reaching and deep constitutional settlement (H. Wallace 2005). At popular level, the EU is increasingly (if not always fairly) considered illegitimate, and, more importantly, popular views about how the EU should proceed do not appear to be coalescing around a shared perspective. The French referendum of 2005, for example, showed a bitter divide between those in favour of a more economically liberal Europe (where the national states and the EU would leave as much as possible to the market) and advocates of a social democratic Europe (where the state and/or the EU would actively intervene to promote greater social equality). The Dutch referendum of the same year revealed, inter alia, concerns about immigration and cultural change, as well as the balance of power between small and large states within the Union. Beyond the debate about whether or not the EU should have a deeper foreign and security policy, further divisions between those who see the EU as an active player in world affairs persist: should the EU be a global peacemaker, or a power with the ability to wage war?

A way forward could be to draft several new constitutions, and put them all to a multiple-choice kind of referendum in each member state: this should at least make clear what the majority of citizens of each state want from and for the EU, and thus provide a basis for (re-)negotiating national participation in the Union. However, such an exercise might not generate a pan-EU majority in favour of any one vision of Europe, as the member states, and their peoples, continue to demonstrate differing perceptions of the role of the EU and its key purposes/strategic interests. Federalist proposals to remove the veto on decisions about Treaty change (for example, Trechsel 2005) also run into this problem: even a qualified majority of, say, 20 of the 25 member states in favour of a particular constitutional plan would still oblige five member states either to accept an EU constitutional settlement with which they are unhappy or leave the EU.

In the absence of consensus, it may be that the only way forward for the EU is to embrace **differentiated integration**, or flexibility (Warleigh 2002a; Majone 2005; see also Chapter 24). This approach, whereby the EU makes policy with and for only a 'coalition of the willing', has already shown its worth with regard to establishing key new policy initiatives: neither the single currency nor the **Schengen** agreements could have been realized without allowing reluctant member states to opt out from, rather than veto, the relevant legislation. However, there has so far been no use of the Treaty provisions on **enhanced cooperation**, which would allow the Union to make policy for a vanguard grouping of states more regularly. This reluctance to embrace a differentiated EU will have to be overcome if consensus on a single way forward is not found, or if the member states wish to change the balance between those who want to move forward, and those who do not. (In the current system, the latter are often more powerful since they can veto progress either singly or by assembling a blocking minority.) The price to be paid for a flexible Union, however, is the recognition that *both* a federal future *and* a minimalist, free trade area future for the entire EU are unlikely. A further requirement of flexibility is the recognition that member states of the EU can, and will, differ legitimately about what they *want* from European integration, not just what they are capable of contributing to it at any given time. Thus, flexibility challenges orthodox conceptions of both pro- and anti-Europeans, and as a result it may be ideationally too radical to be adopted (Warleigh 2002a, 2002b, 2005).

Finally, it is appropriate to assess which of the three models of the EU's future set out earlier in the chapter currently appears most likely to be realized. The idea of a 'superpower Europe' would seem far-fetched: unless a major unanticipated event (such as massive environmental change or sustained terrorist attacks) should affect Europeans deeply and shift their calculations of what they are prepared to countenance in the way of transfer of sovereignty to the EU, a United States of Europe is fantasy. 'Subordinate Europe' remains a possibility: if the Union cannot find a way out of its constitutional crisis, then it will have no choice but to accept US leadership and resign itself to both a smaller role in global affairs than it might like and the probability of regular paralysis in its decision-making system. 'Network Europe', however, is also a possible EU future, albeit one which requires a new constitutional settlement to be agreed and reform of EU decision-making in order to allow the normative vision of commentators such as Leonard to be operationalized: as it stands, the EU is only partially a model for other global regions and powers, since its clever use of soft power is constrained by its chronic (and now severe) decision-making problems and legitimacy deficit. The 'Future of Europe', as the debate on the EU's draft constitutional settlement in 2003–4 was grandly called, is still to play for, and the coming years will indicate whether the Union's states are imaginative enough to elaborate flexible means of cooperation or would rather settle for increasing irrelevance.

? QUESTIONS

1. Why is the EU's future development so controversial?
2. What are the arguments in favour of a European federation?
3. How likely is it that a 'network Europe' could be effective in making policy for the EU?
4. Is it likely that the EU will become less integrated in the near future?
5. What are the main issues that are likely to shape the EU's development in the next five years?
6. What kind of future do you think the EU *should* have, and why?
7. What role are national governments likely to play in the future of the EU?
8. How important is flexibility in determining the future development of the Union?

GUIDE TO FURTHER READING

In addition to the key texts outlined in the various boxes for this chapter, the following are useful sources of information and ideas:

- **Bertrand, G., Michalski, A., and Pench, L.** ***Scenarios Europe 2010: Five Possible Futures for Europe*** **(Brussels: European Commission Forward Studies Unit, 1999 available at www.europa.eu.int/comm/cdp/scenario/index_htm).** This is a study undertaken by officials working for the EU Commission. It is complex and detailed, investigating issues of economic policy, welfare policy, demographic change, and political trends in the member states. It is a little out of date, but very much worth reading.

- **Grant, C.** ***EU 2010: An Optimistic Vision of the Future*** **(London: Centre for European Reform, 2000, available at www.cer.org.uk/publications/19x.html).** This is an analysis produced by a left-of-centre think tank, seeking to chart the development of the EU and speak in particular to the role of the UK as a member state. It includes a detailed set of recommendations for reform, and is accessibly written.

- **Schmitter, P. 'Imagining the Future of the Euro-polity with the Help of New Concepts' in G. Marks** ***et al. Governance in the European Union*** **(London: Sage, 1996).** This is a conceptual exercise drawing on integration theory to develop a range of models for the EU's future. Although a decade old, it remains an interesting and thought-provoking piece.

IMPORTANT WEBSITES

The best weblinks for this issue are usually those of think tanks or activist groups concerned with EU policy. Here are a few of the most useful think tank sites:

- **www.ceps.be** Centre for European Policy Studies (Brussels-based independent think tank).
- **www.europe2020.org** Europe 2020 (Paris-based think tank, focused on serving 'the generations born since the Treaty of Rome').
- **www.ose.be** L'Observatoire Social Européen (Brussels-based research centre with a strong social policy interest, but also of general use).
- **www.theepc.net** The European Policy Centre (Brussels-based think tank).
- **www.iiea.com** The Institute of European Affairs (Dublin-based organization with educational and political aims).
- **www.fedtrust.co.uk** The Federal Trust (UK-based organization which lobbies for a federal EU).
- **www.cer.org.uk** The Centre for European Reform (a left-of-centre think tank).
- **www.notre-europe.asso.fr** Notre Europe ('Our Europe', a pro-European think tank established by former Commission President, Jacques Delors).
- **www.brugesgroup.com** The Bruges Group (an anti-federalist, neo-liberal organization).

Visit the Online Resource Centre that accompanies this book for lots of interesting additional material. http://www.oxfordtextbooks.co.uk/orc/cini2e/

Glossary

Accession: in a general sense, 'increasing by addition', meaning membership or the process of joining (the EU).

Accountability: the requirement for representatives to answer to the represented on how they have performed their duties and powers, and for them to act upon criticisms made of them and accept responsibility for failure, incompetence, or deceit.

Acquis (communautaire): the *acquis* is the Community patrimony, the body of common rights and obligations which bind the member states together. It includes the content of the Treaties, legislation, international agreements, and other measures.

Adenauer, Konrad: first Chancellor of the Federal Republic of German after the end of the Second World War. Adenauer (1876–1967) held office for 14 years, and was responsible for overseeing the reconstruction of Germany in the 1950s, particularly in the context of European integration, of which he was a key supporter.

Agenda 2000: an influential action programme adopted by the Commission on 15 July 1987, which set out the reforms needed for the EU to enlarge.

Agenda-setting: the process by which an issue or problem emerges on to the political scene and is framed for subsequent debate.

A la carte: a non-uniform method of integration which would allow member states to select policies as if from a menu.

Amsterdam (Treaty of): signed in October 1997, and in force from 1 May 1999, the Treaty amended certain provisions of the Treaty on European Union and the European Community Treaties.

'Anoraks': a British English slang term for a 'geek' or a 'nerd', drawn from the coats worn by trainspotters, implying someone who spends a large amount of time collating information on a very specfic subject.

Assent: a legislative procedure in which the Council must first obtain the European Parliament's assent before certain important decisions can be taken. It applies to the accession of new members to the European Union.

Asymetric military threats: usually refers to chemical, biological, or cyber terrorism or the potential for less powerful actors/states to attack effectively those who are ostensibly more powerful.

Authority: the right or capacity (or both) to have proposals, prescriptions, or instructions accepted without recourse to persuasion, bargaining, or force; more simply, the power or right to control, judge, or prohibit the actions of others.

Barriers to trade: protectionist technical and fiscal rules, and more physical constraints that carve up or prevent the creation of the Internal Market.

Benelux: short for 'Belgium, Netherlands, and Luxembourg'. The term originally related to the 1944 Customs Union between these three countries, and is said to have been coined by the Brussels correspondent of *The Economist* in 1947.

Bicameral: involving two chambers. Usually refers to parliaments divided into an upper and lower house.

Bolkestein Directive: named after the former Dutch EU internal market Commissioner, Fritz Bolkestein, it aimed to liberalize services across Europe, allowing service providers (from insurance companies to dentists) to trade across national borders.

Bretton Woods: agreement signed by 44 countries in July 1944 to support an international monetary system of stable exchange rates. The aim of the Agreement was to make national currencies convertible, to encourage multi-lateral world trade, and to avoid disruptive devaluations and financial crashes.

Budgetary deficits: governmental shortfalls of current revenue over current expenditure.

Capabilities Catalogue: a document listing the military capabilities necessary to carry out the Petersberg tasks.

Central banks: bankers to the government and to commercial banks. They manage public debt, control the money supply, and regulate the monetary and credit system.

Civic identity: a feeling of community amongst citizens within a particular territory.

Civil society: an intermediate realm between the state and the individual or family; or a particular type of political society rooted in principles of citizenship.

Closer cooperation: established by the Amsterdam Treaty, it introduces instruments which allow groups of states that wish to integrate further than provided for in the Treaties to do so. It was renamed 'enhanced cooperation' at Nice.

Codecision (procedure): a complicated three-stage decision-making procedure that involves both the EU Council and the European Parliament in making European legislation, thereby enhancing the role of the Parliament in the legislative process. It was introduced in the Treaty on European Union at Maastricht (Article 251, ex 189b) and simplified in the subsequent Amsterdam Treaty. Codecision refers to decision-making jointly by the Parliament and the Council.

Codetermination: employee participation in a firm's decision-making, through, for example, works councils.

Cognitive mobilization: the capacity to articulate basic implications of a value system and act accordingly.

Cohesion: regional economic and social policy; a principle which favours the reduction of regional and social disparities across the European Union.

Collective bargaining: an agreement negotiated by trade unions and employers or their associations on incomes or on the working conditions of employees.

Collective goods: goods or elements (such as 'fresh air') freely available to all. Those who do not pay for a collective good cannot be excluded from sharing or using it.

Collegiality: a principle which implies that decisions taken by one are the collective responsibility of all.

Comitology: refers to the network or procedures of committees designed to oversee the agreement of implementing measures taken by the EU's executive bodies.

Common external tariff: a central element of any customs union. A set of common tariffs, agreed by all members, imposed on goods coming into the union from the outside its borders.

Common market: an economic agreement that extends cooperation beyond a customs union, to provide for the free movement of goods, services, capital, and labour.

Common market organization: a system operating for individual items of agricultural produce, which involves public intervention, a price guaranteed for farmers, and levies at the EU's borders.

Common strategy: overall policy guidelines for EU activities within individual non-member countries.

Community method: the use of the 'established' process of EC decision-making, which involves a Commission legislative initiative being agreed by the Council, and now usually the European Parliament. It also implies that the Court of Justice will have jurisdiction over any decision taken.

Community preference: the fact that EU agricultural products are given a preference and price advantage over imported products.

Competence: legal capacity to deal with a matter (also competency).

Concentric circles: a concept which envisages a Europe structured out of subsets of states which have achieved different levels of integration.

Conciliation (process): the third stage of the codecision procedure, at which point an equal number of representatives of the Parliament and Council get together to try to work out an agreement acceptable to all.

Conditionality: the principle that applicant states must meet certain conditions before they can become members of the European Union.

Confederal: see Confederation.

Confederation: a political model which involves a loose grouping of states, characterized by the fact that the centre has fewer powers than the states or regions.

Consensual: type of decision-making which involves the agreement of all, even where this is not formally a requirement.

Consociational(ism): a political model which brings together distinct communities in shared decision-making, whilst protecting the interests of the minority.

Constitutional Treaty: the Treaty sometimes known as the EU Constitution, which was signed on 24 October 2004, but which has not been ratified, not least because of 'No' votes in referenda in France and the Netherlands in 2005.

Constitutionalization: the formalization of the rules of the game, which in an EU context might involve a process whereby the Treaties become over time – *de jure* or just *de facto* – a Constitution.

Constitutive tradition: an understanding of the world which problematizes the relationship between theory and reality, which are deemed to be tied closely one to the other.

Constructive abstention: allows member states to abstain in the Council on Common Foreign and Security Policy decisions, without blocking a unanimous agreement.

Constructivism: or 'social constructivism'. A theoretical approach which claims that politics is affected as much by ideas as by power. It argues that the fundamental structures of political life are social rather than material.

Consultation: the original EC decision-making procedure, which gave the Commission the exclusive right of initiative and the Council the ability to take the decision, but which only allowed the Parliament a consultative role in the legislative process.

Convention (on the Future of Europe): a body set up in 2002 to debate alternative models and visions of the European Union, and to prepare a draft Constitution which could be used as the basis of discussion in the Intergovernmental Conference of 2004.

Convergence criteria: the rules that member states had to meet before they could join Economic and Monetary Union in 1999.

Convertibility: where one currency is freely exchangeable into other currencies.

Cooperation: usually implies government-to-government relations (with little supranational involvement).

Cooperation procedure: a legislative procedure introduced in the Single European Act (Article 252, ex 198c), which allows the European Parliament a second reading of draft legislation. Since Amsterdam, it is now very little used, as most policies originally falling under cooperation now come under the codecision procedure.

Copenhagen Criteria: the criteria which applicant states have to meet in order to join the EU. They were agreed at the Copenhagen European Council meeting in 1993.

Core Europe: or 'hard core': the idea that a small group of countries able and willing to enter into closer cooperation within one another might 'leave behind' the less enthusiastically integrationist members of the Union.

Cosmopolitanism: relating to 'citizenship of the world'.

Council of Europe: a European political organization with 49 members, distinct from the EU, set up in 1949. It has been particularly involved in assisting post-communist states to democratize after 1989.

Credit conditions: the conditions under which money is available for borrowing.

Customs union: an economic association of states based on an agreement to eliminate tariffs and other obstacles to trade, and which also includes a common trade policy vis-à-vis third countries, usually by establishing a common external tariff on goods imported into the union.

Davignon Report: a document issued by EC foreign ministers in 1970, outlining how the Community might develop its own foreign policy, and setting out some initial steps to that end.

Decoupling: divorcing the grant of direct aid to farmers from production.

Deepening: the integration dynamic; a term usually describing an intensification of integration processes and structures.

de Gaulle, Charles: President of France, 1959–69. Responsible for keeping the UK out of the EC in the 1960s, and for the 'empty chair policy' which is said to have slowed down the European integration process after 1966.

Delegated legislation: legislation usually made by executive bodies on behalf of legislatures. It often involves the making of administrative rules, and the filling in of gaps in existing legislation.

Delegation: an act which allows a legitimate political institution to hand powers over to a body which then acts on its behalf.

Delors Report: the Report drafted by central bankers in 1989, which later formed the basis of the monetary union section of the Treaty on European Union. The Committee that produced the Report was chaired by Jacques Delors, then Commission President.

Democratic deficit: the loss of democracy caused by the transfer of powers to the European institutions and to member state executives arising out of European integration. It implies that representative institutions (parliaments) lose out in this process.

Demography: the scientific study of human population.

Demos: the people of a nation as a political unit; a politically defined public community.

Dependent variable: the object of study; the phenomenon one is trying to explain.

Derogations: temporary exceptions to legislation.

Differentiated integration: see Differentiation.

Differentiation: the idea that subsets of member states might engage in European integration projects that do not involve all existing members; contrasts with the notion of the EU as a uniform Community.

Diplomacy: the art and practice of conducting (international) negotiations by accredited persons.

Direct actions: cases brought directly before the European Courts.

Direct implementation: the putting into effect of European legislation by the European institutions (rather than by national governments).

Direct support: agricultural subsidies given directly to farmers, decoupled from production.

Directives: legislative instruments that specify the aims to be achieved, but which generally leave the question of how to achieve those ends up to national governments or their agents.

Directly effective: having a quality which allows provisions of Community law to be enforced in national courts, these being provisions which impose obligations on those against whom they are enforced.

***Dirigisme/dirigiste*:** see Interventionist.

Dumping: selling at below cost, often to force competition out of the market.

ECOFIN: the EU Council of Economics and Finance Ministers.

Efficiency: the ratio of output to input of any system.

Eftan: relating to the countries of EFTA, the European Free Trade Association.

Enforcement: the process of ensuring that (Community) rules are implemented. It may involve taking action in the European Courts.

Enhanced cooperation: see Closer cooperation.

Enlargement: the expansion of the European Union to include new member states.

Epistemology: theory of knowledge, which accounts for the way in which knowledge about the world is acquired.

Euro area: that part of the EU which uses the single currency. See Eurozone.

***Eurobarometer*:** a Europe-wide public opinion survey of attitudes, including towards the EU.

Eurogroup: an informal group comprising those member states of the ECOFIN Council that are members of the single currency.

European Arrest Warrant: replaces the lengthier extradition procedures amongst EU member states, simplifying the arrest and return of suspected criminals across the Union. Introduced after 11 September 2001.

European Central Bank (ECB): established in Frankfurt in 1999, the ECB is responsible for the single monetary policy of the 'Eurozone'.

European Coal and Steel Community (ECSC): established by six states in April 1951 by the Treaty of Paris, the ECSC allowed for the pooling of authority over coal and steel industries. As it was based on a 50-year treaty, the ECSC ceased to exist on 23 July 2002.

European Currency Unit (ECU): the unit of account under the European Monetary System, composed of a 'basket of currencies'. Was replaced by the 'euro'.

European Free Trade Association (EFTA): an international organization set up in 1960 to promote free trade amongst its members. Most of its original members have since joined the European Union.

European integration: various definitions, one of which is 'the process of political and economic (and possibly also cultural and social) integration of the states of Europe into a unified bloc'.

European Monetary System (EMS): a regulated exchange rate system established in the EC in 1979 after failures to set up an Economic and Monetary Union earlier in the decade. The EMS aimed to promote monetary cooperation and exchange rate stability.

European Political Cooperation (EPC): foreign policy cooperation prior to Maastricht, set up after 1970 and formalized by the Single European Act.

European System of Central Banks (ECSB): the national central banks together with the European Central Bank.

Europeanization: defined in various ways (see Chapter 25). For example, it may refer to the process of European integration itself, or may be shorthand for 'Europeanization of domestic institutions, politics and identities'.

Eurosceptic: someone who is opposed to European integration, or is sceptical about the EU and its aims.

Eurosclerosis: a word used to characterize the period of EC history between 1966 and the early 1980s, when the process of integration appeared to have slowed down, and when the Common Market objective within the Treaty of Rome was not implemented.

Eurozone: the economic area which covers the 12 countries that have so far joined the EU's single currency.

Excessive Deficit Procedure: the EMU procedure which has the potential to sanction those member states who fail to control their budget deficits.

Exchange Rate Mechanism (ERM): the main element of the European Monetary System – a mechanism which aimed to create a zone of monetary stability within Western Europe.

Executive(s): branch of government, responsible for implementing laws taken by parliament; the administration.

Federal: see Federalism.

Federalism: an ideological position which suggests that everyone can be satisfied by combining national and regional/territorial interests in a complex web of checks and balances between a central government and a multiplicity of regional governments. In a EU context it tends to imply an ideological approach which advocates the creation of a federal state in Europe.

Federalist: promoting federal ideas or ideology.

Federation: a way of organizing a political system which involves the constitutionally defined sharing of functions between a federal centre and the states. A federation will usually have a bicameral parliament, a constitutional court, and a Constitution.

Finalité politique: the EU's final constitutional settlement.

Financial Perspective: the EU's multi-annual spending plan.

First pillar: see Pillar.

Fortress Europe: a term which is often used pejoratively to refer to the idea of creating a European Union which keeps out non-EU goods, businesses, and nationals.

Fouchet Plan: a plan proposed in 1961 and pushed by the French government, which would have led to the creation of a European intergovernmental defence organization, but which was rejected by the EC's member states.

Framing integration: integration which does not involve legally enforceable rules, but which rests on mechanisms such as sharing ideas, benchmarking, and 'naming and shaming'.

Franco-German axis: see Paris–Bonn axis.

Free trade area: a group of countries who agree progressively to reduce barriers to trade, such as quotas and tariffs, which are often imposed at borders.

Freeride: to freeride is to reap the benefits of a collective agreement without having participated in efforts to forge the agreement or to implement it. See also 'collective goods'; a freerider is someone who benefits from collective activity without participating in it.

Functional spillover: the knock-on effect of integration in one sector, which is said by neo-functionalists to provoke integration in neighbouring sectors.

Globalization: a contested concept, which usually refers to the growing economic independence of states and non-state actors worldwide. Often associated with increased capital mobility, the spread of neo-liberal ideas, for example. Implies that market authority is enhanced at the cost of formal political authority.

Governance turn: the shift in interest in EU studies which included the increased application of theories of governance, comparative politics, and public policy, as well as the shift towards the study of the EU as a political system in its own right.

Grand theory: a theory which tries to explain the entirety of a political process, such as European integration.

Gross National Product: a measure of the country's total economic activity.

Guarantee price: the (agricultural) price at which member states intervene in the market to buy up produce (also known as the 'intervention price').

Hard law: another way of saying 'the law', emphasizing its enforceability.

Harmonization: the act of setting common European standards from which states are unable to deviate (either upwards or downwards).

Headline Goal: initially a political commitment agreed at the Helsinki European Council in 1999 that states must by 2003 be capable of deploying within 60 days between 50,000 and 60,000 troops, sustainable for a year (a Rapid Reaction Force) to meet the requirements of the Petersberg tasks. The original commitment has since been superseded by a new headline goal.

Hegemony: power, control, or influence exercised by a leading state over other states.

Hobbesian state of nature: Thomas Hobbes' 'war of all against all': the contention that in a state of nature humans would act badly towards each other.

Independent variable: a factor contributing to an explanation of some phenomenon (to a dependent variable).

Individual direct payments: agricultural subsidies paid directly to individual farmers.

Inflation: a rate of increase in the general price of all goods and services.

Infringement proceedings: the act of initiating a procedure for breach of European law which may result in a court case.

Institutional isomorphism: a term used by diMaggio and Powell (1991) to denote the tendency for institutions within a similar environment to come to resemble each other.

Institutional theory: this explains how structures (including rules, norms, routines, etc.) become guides for social behaviour. The theory explains how these structures are introduced, evolve, adapt, and disintegrate over time. The theory generally emphasizes stability and order in social life. Some work in this field also places emphasis on explaining social change.

Integration: a general concept which implies the act of combining parts to make a unified whole – a dynamic process of change. European integration is usually associated with the intensely institutionalized form of cooperation found in Western Europe after 1951.

Integration theory: sometimes used generally as shorthand for all theoretical and conceptual approaches that discuss European integration; otherwise, it refers more specifically to supranational (especially neo-functionalist) theories of European integration.

Interdependence: a condition in which the actions of one state impact upon others.

Interest intermediation: the process of translating interests into policy, through the medium of interest organizations.

Interest rate: the rate of return on savings, or the rate paid on borrowings.

Intergovernmental Conference (IGC): structured negotiations among the EU's member states, which usually lead to a treaty revision.

Intergovernmental (cooperation): cooperation that involves sovereign states, and which occurs on a government-to-government basis, rather than implying the extensive involvement of supranational actors.

Intergovernmentalism: a theory of European integration which privileges the role of states.

Intergovernmentalist: see Intergovernmentalism.

Interlocutory: rulings that are interlocutory are made during the course of a court case, rather than at its end.

Intervention price: see Guarantee price.

Interventionist: interventionism occurs where governments involve themselves in the regulation of markets, through government policy, rather than leaving markets to regulate themselves.

Joint Action: coordinated action by member states to commit resources for an agreed (foreign policy) objective.

Joint-decision trap: the idea promoted by Fritz Scharpf in 1988 that while it might be increasingly difficult in future for further integration to take place, it will also be impossible for states to go back on agreements already made. This meant that states were 'trapped' within the European integration process.

Judicial review: the right of a court to review a law or other act for constitutionality or its violation of some fundamental principle.

Kaliningrad: a Russian enclave between Poland and Lithuania on the Baltic Sea. The issue of overland access to the city from Russia was particularly contentious in the 1990s.

Keynesian: a position held which supports the economic theory of J. M. Keynes (1883–1946), and which has as its starting point the assumption that state finances should be used to counteract cyclical economic downturns. The argument implies that governments should focus on issues of employment and economic growth, rather on variables such as inflation.

Laissez-faire: an economic position which argues that the state (governments) should play only a minimal regulatory role in economic affairs, with decisions left mainly to the market.

League of Nations: an international organization set up in 1922 which had as its rationale the maintenance of peace in Europe. Replaced after the Second World War by the United Nations.

Legal basis: see Treaty basis.

Legitimacy: the idea that a regime's procedures for making and enforcing laws are acceptable to all its subjects; the right to rule.

Liberal-democratic: a system of representative government which has universal adult suffrage, political equality, majority rule, and a constitutional check on the power of rulers.

Liberal intergovernmentalism: Andrew Moravcsik's update on classical intergovernmentalism (see Chapter 7).

Liberalization of capital markets: the removal of exchange controls by states, allowing capital to flow freely across state borders.

Liberalization of services: the removal of barriers to the establishment and provision of services across state borders.

Lisbon Agenda: The EU's strategy to make the Union the most competitive and dynamic economy in the world by 2010.

Lock-out: a situation where employers lock employees out of their place of work as a consequence of a labour dispute.

Maastricht (Treaty): see Treaty on European Union.

Macroeconomic policies: economic policies which deal with aggregates such as national income and investment in the economy.

Majoritarian: application of majority rule. The principle that the majority should be allowed to rule the minority.

Market citizenship: the concept introduced to the EC in the 1950s whereby citizens of member states became endowed with certain rights as workers within the European Community.

Market integration: the breaking down of barriers to trade amongst the EU's member states, plus any regulation necessary to ensure the smooth running of the Single Market. It does not involve an explicitly political dimension.

Market-making measures: involving the prohibition of certain types of market behaviour.

Market-shaping measures: involving the laying down of an institutional model which shapes market behaviour.

Market unity: the removal of protection across the Union, allowing agricultural produce to move freely across borders.

Middle-range theories: theories that aim to explain only part of a political process and that do not have totalizing ambitions.

Minilateral: commercial interstate agreements, such as free trade agreements, amongst a small number of countries.

Modulation: the transfer of agricultural subsidies to agrienvironmental and other rural development projects.

Money supply: the stock of liquid assets in an economy that can be freely exchanged for goods and services.

Monnet, Jean: one of the founders of the European integration project. The driving force behind the 1950 Schuman Plan which led to the establishment of the European Coal and Steel Community, Monnet (1888–1979) became the first head of the ECSC's High Authority. He continued to play an active role in European integration throughout his life, though often behind the scenes.

Monnet method: see Community method.

Multifunctionality: the notion in agricultural policy that the policy can be used to serve a range of functions, including environmental protection and rural development.

Multi-level governance: an approach to the study of EU politics which emphasizes the interaction of the many different actors who influence European policy outcomes.

Multi-speed (Europe): a method of differentiated integration whereby common objectives are pursued by a group of member states, able and willing to advance further than others in the integration process.

Mutual recognition: the principle that an economic product sold in one member state should not be prohibited from sale anywhere in the EU. This was upheld in the famous *Cassis de Dijon* case (1979) brought to the European Court of Justice. Exceptions can be made in cases of public health and safety however.

Negative integration: a form of European integration which involves the removal of barriers between the member states.

Neo-corporatism: a model of policy-making which links producer interests to the state, and where interest organizations are incorporated into the system. The neo- prefix was added in the 1970s to distinguish this from the corporatism of the past – particularly in the fascist era.

Neo-functionalism: a theory of European integration which views integration as an incremental process, involving the spillover of integration in one sector to others, ultimately leading to some kind of political community.

Neo-functionalist: see Neo-functionalism.

Neo-liberalism: an economic school which advocates the reduction of state influence in the market, the liberalization of the economy, the privatization of state-owned firms, and tight control of money supply, and supports a general trend towards deregulation.

Neo-realism: an International Relations theory, associated with the work of Kenneth Waltz, which claims that the international state system is anarchic, thereby making state uncertainty a given. States will want to maintain their independence, and survival will be their primary objective, but they may nevertheless engage in European integration if this serves their ends.

Net contributors: those countries that get less out of the EC budget than they contribute.

Net recipients: those countries that get more out of the EC budget than they contribute.

New institutionalism: a conceptual approach to the study of politics which restates the importance of institutional factors in political life. It takes a number of very different forms, from rational institutionalism and historical institutionalism to sociological institutionalism.

Nice Treaty: Treaty revision agreed at Nice in December 2000, signed February 2001, and ratified in 2002. It introduced a number of institutional reforms which paved the way for the enlargement of the Union in 2004 or after.

Non-state actors: usually any actor that is not a national government. Often refers to transnational actors, such as interest groups (rather than to international organizations).

Non-tariff barriers: see Barriers to trade.

Normative: refers to value judgements, 'what ought to be', as opposed to positive statements about 'what is'.

Ontology: relates to the nature of being; an underlying conception of the world; that which is being presupposed by a theory.

Open method of coordination: an approach to EU policy-making which is an alternative to regulation and which involves more informal means of encouraging compliance than 'hard' legislation.

Optimum currency area (OCA): a theoretical notion which implies that monetary union will work effectively only when the states participating are economically very similar.

Paris–Bonn axis: the relationship between France and Germany, which is often said to lie at the heart of the European integration process.

Parity: equality in amount, status, or character.

Parsimony: a theory which is parsimonious is a theory which provides an extremely simplified depiction of reality.

Path dependence: the idea that decisions taken in the past limit the scope of decisions in the present (and future).

Peace dividend: a political term denoting the economic benefit of reducing defence spending.

Permissive consensus: the political context which allowed elites in the post-1945 period to engage in European integration, without involving Europe's citizens.

Petersberg tasks: these tasks were established in June 1992 at the Petersberg Hotel near Bonn in Germany. On this occasion, the West European Union (WEU) member states declared their readiness to make available military units for tasks conducted under the authority of the WEU. Apart from contributing to the collective defence, military units may be employed for humanitarian and rescue tasks; peacekeeping tasks; and tasks of combat forces in crisis management, including peacemaking.

Pillar: one of three parts of the European Union, which since its inception at Maastricht has been divided into Pillar 1 (the EC pillar), Pillar 2 (foreign and security policy), and Pillar 3 (formerly justice and home affairs, now just police and judicial cooperation in criminal matters).

Plan D: Commissioner Margot Wallstrom's communication strategy, emphasizing democracy, dialogue, and debate (launched in October 2005).

Pluralist: pluralism is a general approach which implies that organized groups play an important role in the political process.

Policy convergence: the tendency for policies (in different countries) to begin to take on similar forms over time.

Policy style: sets of characteristics which descibe different ways of making policy (for example, in a particular sector, or across a particular country).

Policy transfer: the replication of policies pursued in one context (country sector) to others.

Political opportunity structure: describes the various characteristics of a political system which influences elements within it such as social movements, organizational forms, and the way in which political actors behave.

Polity: a politically organized society.

Positive integration: a form of integration which involves the construction of policies and/or institutions.

Positive-sum outcomes: outcomes that constitute more than the sum of their parts. Often talked of in EU terms as an 'upgrading of the common interest'.

Power: the ability to control outcomes. The capacity for A to force B to do something in A's interest.

Preliminary rulings: acts of the European Court, which arise as responses to questions of European law posed in domestic courts.

Presidency: the EU Presidency is held on a six-monthly basis by member states in rotation. The Presidency performs various functions, for example, presenting a programme for the period concerned, and chairing European Council and EU Council meetings.

Price support: the system of agricultural support which involves keeping food prices higher than the market price so as to give farmers a higher and more stable income.

Proportionality: a principle which implies that the means should not exceed the ends – applies to decision-making/the legislative process.

Public debts: the amount of money owed by the state.

Public goods theory: a branch of economics that studies how voters, politicians, and government officials behave from the perspective of economic theory.

Qualified majority voting (QMV): system of voting in the EU Council, which attributes a number of votes to each member state (very roughly related to their size). A majority of these votes (currently 71 per cent) is needed for legislation to be agreed in the Council, implying that some states will be outvoted, but will have to apply the legislation all the same.

Rapid Reaction Force: a transnational military force managed by the European Union.

Ratification: formal approval. In the EU context, it implies approval of treaty revisions by national parliaments and sometimes also by popular referendum.

Ratification crisis (1992): the crisis provoked by the Danish 'No vote' in their 1992 referendum on the Maastricht Treaty.

Rational choice: see Rationalist.

Rational utilitarianism: where opinions stem from calculations involving the weighing up of costs and benefits.

Rationalist: theories that are rationalist assume that individuals (or states) are able to make rank orderings of their preferences and to choose the best available preference.

Realism: a rationalist theory of International Relations.

Realist: see Realism.

Rebate: an 'abatement' or reimbursement negotiated by the UK in 1984 to compensate the UK for the fact that even though it had one of the weakest European economies at the time, it was about to become a net contributor to the Community Budget because of the way in which the Common Agricultural Policy operated.

Recession: a temporary depression in economic activity or prosperity.

Redistributive: policy which transfers wealth from one group to another.

References: see Preliminary rulings.

Reference value: a baseline. A measure from which an assessment of economic process can be made.

Reflection group: a group established prior to an intergovernmental conference to prepare preliminary papers on relevant issues.

Regime: principles, norms, rules, and decision-making procedures around which actors' expectations occur. An international regime is usually considered to take the form of an international organization. It is a concept associated with neo-realism.

Regulation: the act of making rules or legislation in order to provoke certain policy outcomes.

Regulations: one of the legislative instruments used by the EU. Regulations are directly effective, spelling out not just the aims of legislation, but what must be done and how.

Regulatory competition: a situation where regulators try to offer a regulatory environment to attract business from abroad. This may involve deregulation.

Representation: the principle by which delegates are chosen to act for a particular constituency (group of electors).

Republican: a state or nation in which supreme power rests with voters, and in which the head of state has been elected.

Right of association: the democratic right of people to form groups such as trade unions.

Schengen: a 1985 agreement to create a border-free European Community. It was originally outside the EC, but was incorporated into the EU in 1997 when the Amsterdam Treaty was signed.

Schuman Plan: signed on 9 May 1950, it led to the setting up of the European Coal and Steel Community.

Schuman, Robert: (1886–1963) French foreign minister and one of the 'founding fathers' of the European Coal and Steel Community, through his 'Schuman Plan' of 1950.

Sectoral integration: a description of or strategy for integration which involves an incremental sector-by-sector approach. See also Spillover.

Separation of powers: a condition of democratic political systems where the executive, legislature, and judiciary are separate, and which provide checks and balances which serve to prevent abuses of power.

Single European Act (SEA): the first of the large-scale Treaty revisions, signed in 1986. It came into force in 1987, and served as a 'vehicle' for the Single Market programme.

Single Market: the idea of having one unified internal EU market, free of (national) barriers to trade. While the idea was included in the Treaty of Rome, the Single Market is usually associated with the revitalization of the Community from the mid-1980s.

Snake: a system aimed to stabilize exchange rates within the EC in the 1970s.

Social Chapter: agreed at Maastricht, the Social Chapter establishes minimum social conditions within the EU. Until Amsterdam, the Chapter was annexed to the Treaty, as the UK Conservative government had decided not to sign up to it.

Social dialogue: joint consultation procedure involving social partners at EU level, to discuss and negotiate agreements where relevant.

Social dumping: the undercutting of social standards in order to improve competitiveness.

Social learning: learning that occurs as a function of observing, retaining, and replicating behaviour observed in others.

Social partner(s): refers to labour (the unions) and capital (employers) acting together. The two sides of industry.

Sociotropic: relating to voting behaviour which maximizes social welfare (implying solidarity).

Soft law: documents that are not formally or legally binding but which may still produce political effects.

Sovereignty: a condition in which states are not subject to any higher authority; supreme, unrestricted power (of a state).

Spillover: a mechanism identified by neo-functionalist theorists who claimed that sectoral integration in one area would have knock-on effects in others, and would 'spill over', thereby increasing the scope of European integration.

Spinelli, Altiero: an important federalist thinker and politician (1907–86), responsible for the influential Ventotene Manifesto of 1941, and for the European Parliament's Draft Treaty on European Union (1984), which helped to shape the European political agenda of the late 1980s.

Stability and Growth Pact: an agreement of the EU member states concerning conduct over their fiscal policy, which aimed to ensure that the constraints on member states prior to the introduction of the single currency would continue after EMU was in place.

State-centrism: a conceptual approach to understanding European integration which gives primacy to the role of state actors within the process.

Statecraft: wisdom in the management of public affairs.

Statehood: the condition of being a state. See Stateness.

Stateness: the quality of being a state, that is, a legal territorial entity with a stable population and a government.

Strong currency: a situation arising out of relative levels of exchange rate whereby the value of national money is increased. This has the effect of lowering the price of imports (making imported goods cheaper), but also of increasing the price of exports, making exports less competitive in international markets.

Subsidiarity: the principle that tries to ensure that decisions are taken as close as possible to the citizen.

Superstate: a political term, which implies that the aim of supporters of European integration is to turn the EU into a (national?) state, writ large, with connotations of the detachment of elites and the European institutions from ordinary citizens.

Supranational(ism): that which is above the national level. It may refer to institutions, policies, or a particular 'type' of cooperation/integration; or an approach to the study of the EU, which emphasizes the autonomy of the European institutions and the importance of common European policies.

Supranational governance: a theory of European integration proposed by Wayne Sandholtz and Alec Stone Sweet which draws on neo-functionalism, and provides an alternative approach to Moravcsik's liberal intergovernmentalism.

Sustainability: or 'sustainable development'. The ability to meet the needs of the present without compromising the needs of future generations.

Tampere: city in Finland at which a summit meeting in 1999 agreed to create an 'area of freedom, security and justice' in Europe.

Third-country nationals: citizens of countries outside the European Union.

Third pillar: that part of the European Union that deals with police and judicial cooperation in criminal matters. From Maastricht to Amsterdam this pillar was labelled Justice and Home Affairs.

Transfer payments: payments not made in return for any contribution to current output. Usually refers to agricultural subsidies.

Transparency: a term used in the EU to refer to the extent of openness within the EU institutions.

Transposed: see Transposition.

Transposition: the translation of European law (directives) into domestic law.

Treaty base game: the act of selecting a treaty basis (in a 'grey area') for political ends.

Treaty basis: the provision of the Treaty which underpins a particular piece of European legislation.

Treaty of Rome: signed in 1957. The Rome Treaty formally established the European Economic Community (EEC) and EURATOM, the European Atomic Energy Community.

Treaty on European Union: (also known as the Maastricht Treaty) came into force in November 1993. It introduced a range of institutional and policy reforms, including the introduction of the three EU pillars (see Figure 3.1).

Trevi (Group): a forum for internal security cooperation, which operated from the mid-1970s until 1993.

Troika: (i) the country holding the Presidency together with the previous Presidency and the forthcoming Presidency; (ii) in CFSP: the Presidency, the High Representative for CFSP, and the Commission.

Unanimity: a method of voting which means that all member states in the Council must be in agreement before a proposal can be adopted (and which permits all member states to veto decisions).

Utilitarian theories: theories that relate to choosing the greatest good for the greatest number of people.

Variable geometry: an image of the European Union which foresees the breakdown of a unified form of cooperation, and the introduction of a 'pick and choose' approach to further integration.

Western European Union: a collaborative defence agreement and extension of the 1948 Treaty of Brussels, signed in 1955. It was designed to allow for the rearmament of West Germany. It was revitalized in the 1980s, and subsequently served as a bridge between NATO and the EU. Its functions have lately been subsumed within the European Union.

Widening: generally refers to the enlargement of the EU, but may also be used to denote the increasing scope of Community or Union competences.

Zero-sum game: a game played (by states) in which the victory of one group implies the loss of another.

Zollverein: a customs union between German states in the eighteenth century under Bismarck. The economic basis for German unification.

References

Abromeit, H. (1996), *Democracy in Europe: legitimizing politics in a non-state polity* (Oxford: Berghahn Books).

Acharya, A. (2002), 'Regionalism and the emerging world order: sovereignty, autonomy, identity' in S. Breslin, C. Hughes, N. Phillips, and B. Rosamond (eds), *New regionalisms in the global political economy* (London: Routledge).

Allen, D. (2000), 'Cohesion and the Structural Funds: transfers and trade-offs' in H. Wallace and W. Wallace (eds) *Policy-making in the European Union* (Oxford: Oxford University Press).

Allen, D. (2002), 'The common foreign and security policy' in J. Gower (ed.) *The European Union handbook* (London: Fitzroy Dearborn Publishers).

Allen, D. (2005), 'Cohesion and Structural Funds: competing pressures for reform?' in H. Wallace, W. Wallace, and M. Pollack (eds) *Policy and policy-making in the European Union* (Oxford: Oxford University Press).

Amin, A. and J. Tomaney (1995), *Behind the myth of European Union: prospects for cohesion* (London: Routledge).

Andersen, S. *et al.* (2005), *Differentiated integration: how much can the EU accommodate*? 37th World Congress of the International Institute of Sociology, Stockholm, 2005.

Anderson, C. J. (1998), 'When in doubt, use proxies: attitudes toward domestic politics and support for European integration', *Comparative Political Studies* 31/5: 569–601.

Anderson, J. (1990), 'Skeptical reflections on a Europe of the regions: Britain, Germany and the ERDF', *Journal of Public Policy*, 10/4: 417–47.

Arblaster, A. (1987), *Democracy* (Minneapolis, MN: University of Minnesota Press).

Armstrong, H. and J. Taylor (2000), *Regional economics and policy*, 3rd edn (Oxford: Blackwell).

Armstrong, K. and S. Bulmer (1998), *The governance of the Single European Market* (Manchester: Manchester University Press).

Arnull, A. (1999), *The European Union and its Court of Justice* (Oxford: Oxford Unversity Press).

Arnull, A. and D. Wincott (eds) (2002), *Accountability and legitimacy in the European Union* (Oxford: Oxford University Press).

Aron, R. and D. Lerner (eds) (1957), *France defeats EDC* (New York: Praeger).

Arter, D. (1993), *The politics of European integration in the twentieth century* (Aldershot: Dartmouth).

Aspinwall, M. and J. Greenwood (1998), 'Conceptualising collective action in the European Union: an introduction' in J. Greenwood and M. Aspinwall (eds), *Collective action in the European Union: interests and the new politics of associability* (London: Routledge).

Aspinwall, M. and G. Schneider (2001a), 'Institutional research on the European Union: mapping the field' in M. Aspinwall and G. Schneider (eds) *Rules of integration: institutionalist approaches to the study of Europe* (Manchester: Manchester University Press).

Aspinwall, M. and G. Schneider (eds) (2001b), *The rules of integration: institutionalist approaches to the study of Europe* (Manchester: Manchester University Press).

Axelrod, R. (1984), *The evolution of co-operation* (New York: Basic Books).

Bacevich, A. (2002), *American empire: the realities and consequences of US diplomacy* (Cambridge, MA: Harvard University Press).

Bache, I. (1999a), 'The extended gate-keeper: central government and the implementation of EC regional policy in the UK', *Journal of European Public Policy*, 6/1: 28–45.

Bache, I. (1999b), *The politics of European Union regional policy: multi-level governance or flexible gatekeeping* (Sheffield: Sheffield Academic Press).

Bachtler, J. and F. Wishlade (2005), *From building blocks to negotiating boxes: the reform of EU cohesion policy*, European Policy Research Paper, University of Strathclyde, no. 57, November.

Bailey, D. and L. de Propris (2004), 'A bridge too Phare? EU pre-accession aid and capacity-building in the candidate countries', *Journal of Common Market Studies*, 42/1: 77–98.

Balme, R., D. Chabanet, and V. Wright (eds) (2002), *L'action collective en Europe/Collective Action in Europe* (Paris: Presses de Sciences Po).

Bankowski, Z., A. Scott, and F. Snyder (1998), 'Guest editorial', *European Law Review*, December: 227–40.

Barber, L. (1995), 'The men who run Europe', *Financial Times*, 11–12 March, Section 2: 1–2.

Barnard, C. (2000), 'Regulating competitive federalism in the European Union? The case of EC social policy' in J. Shaw (ed.), *Social law and policy in an evolving European Union* (Oxford: Hart).

Barry, F. and I. Begg (2003), 'EMU and cohesion: introduction', *Journal of Common Market Studies*, 41/5: 781–96.

Bartolini, S. (2005), *Re-structuring Europe: centre formation, system building and political structuring between the nation state and the European Union* (Oxford: Oxford University Press).

Baumgartner, F. and B. Leech (1998), *Basic interests: the importance of groups in politics and political science* (Princeton, NJ: Princeton University Press).

Baun, M. J. (1996), *An imperfect Union: the Maastricht Treaty and the new politics of European integration* (Boulder, CO: Westview).

Baun, M. (1999), 'Enlargement' in L. Cram, D. Dinan, and N. Nugent (eds) *Developments in the European Union* (Houndsmills: Macmillan).

Baylis, J. and S. Smith (eds) (2005), *The globalization of world politics: an introduction to international relations*, 3rd edn (Oxford: Oxford University Press).

Beetham, D. and C. Lord (1996), *Legitimacy in the European Union* (London: Addison Wesley Longman).

Begg, I. and F. Heinemann (2006), 'New budget, old dilemmas', Briefing note, Centre for European Reform, 22 February.

Bellamy, A. (2002), *Kosovo and the international society* (New York: Palgrave).

Bellamy, R. and D. Castiglione (1997), 'Building the Union: the nature of sovereignty in the political architecture of Europe', *Law and Philosophy*, 16/4: 421–45.

Bellamy, R. and D. Castiglione (2000), 'Democracy, sovereignty and the construction of the European Union: the republican alternative to liberalism' in Z. Bankowski and A. Scott (eds), *The European Union and its order* (London: Blackwell).

Bellamy, R. and A. Warleigh (eds) (2001), *Citizenship and governance in the European Union* (London: Continuum).

Benz, A. (1998), 'Politikverflechtung ohne Politikverflechtungsfalle – Koordination und Strukturdynamik im europäischen Mehrebenensystem', *Politische Vierteljahresschrift*, 39/4: 558–89.

Berger, S. and R. Dore (1996), *National diversity and global capitalism* (Ithaca, NY: Cornell University Press).

Bergman, T. and T. Raunio (2001), 'Parliaments and policy-making in the European Union' in J. Richardson (ed.) *European Union: power and policy-making*, 2nd edn (London: Routledge).

Bertrand, G., A. Michalski, and L. Pench (1999), *Scenarios Europe 2010: five possible futures for Europe* (Brussels: European Commission Forward Studies Unit, available at www.europa.eu.int/comm/cdp/scenario/index_htm).

Bertrand, R. (1956), 'The European common market proposal', *International Organization*, 10/4: 559–74.

Bieber, R. and J. Monar (eds) (1995), *Justice and home affairs in the European Union: the development of the third pillar* (Brussels: European Interuniversity Press).

Blondel, J., R. Sinnott, and P. Svensson (1998), *People and parliament in the European Union: participation, democracy and legitimacy* (Oxford: Clarendon Press).

Börzel, T. (2002), 'Pace-setting, foot-dragging and fence-sitting: member state responses to Europeanisation', *Journal of Common Market Studies*, 40/2: 193–214.

Börzel, T. A. (forthcoming 2006), 'Environmental policy' in P. Graziano and M. Vink (eds) *Europeanization: new research agendas* (Basingstoke: Palgrave-Macmillan).

Börzel, T. A. and T. Risse (2000), 'When Europe hits home: Europeanization and domestic change, *European Integration Online Papers*, 27, 29 November.

Börzel, T. A. and T. Risse (2003), 'Conceptualising the domestic impact of Europe' in K. Featherstone and C. M. Radaelli (eds) *The politics of Europeanisation* (Oxford: Oxford University Press).

Bourne, A.K. (2002), 'Defending Basque taxation devolution in the European Union: the price of European integration', *International Journal of Iberian Studies*, 15/2: 103–14.

Bourne, A. K. (2003), 'The impact of European integration on regional power', *Journal of Common Market Studies*, 41/4: 597–620.

Breyer, S. G. (1982), *Regulation and its reform* (Cambridge, MA: Harvard University Press).

Brown, L. and T. Kennedy (2000), *The Court of Justice of the European Community*, 5th edn (London: Sweet & Maxwell).

Brugger, B. (1999), *Republican theory in political thought: virtuous or virtual?* (London: Macmillan).

Buiter, W. (2000), 'Optimal currency areas: why does the exchange rate regime matter?' *Scottish Journal of Political Economy*, 47: 213–50.

Bulmer, S. (1983), 'Domestic politics and European Community policy-making', *Journal of Common Market Studies* 21/4: 349–63.

Bulmer, S. and M. Burch (2001), 'The "Europeanization" of central government' in M. Aspinwall and G. Schneider (eds), *The rules of integration: institutionalist approaches to the study of Europe* (Manchester: Manchester University Press).

Bulmer, S. and C. M. Radaelli (2005), 'The Europeanisation of public policy?' in C. Lesquene and S. Bulmer (eds) *The member states of the European Union* (Oxford: Oxford University Press).

Bulmer, S. and W. Wessels (1987), *The Council: decision-making in the European Community* (London: Macmillan).

Bulmer, S., D. Dolowitz, P. Humphreys, and S. Padgett (2003), 'Electricity and telecommunications: fit for the European Union?' in K. Dyson, S. J. Bulmer, and K. Goetz (eds) *Germany, Europe and the politics of constraint* (Oxford: Oxford University Press, for the British Academy).

Burgess, M. (1995), *The British tradition of federalism* (London: Cassell).

Burgess, M. (2000), *Federalism and the European Union: building of Europe, 1950–2000* (London: Routledge).

Burgess M. and A.-G. Gagnon (1993) (eds), *Comparative federalism and federation* (Hemel Hempstead: Harvester Wheatsheaf).

Burley, A. M. and W. Mattli (1993), 'Europe before the court: a political theory of legal integration', *International Organization*, 47: 41–76.

Busch, A. (2004), 'National filters: Europeanisation, institutions, and discourse in the case of banking regulation', *West European Politics*, 27/2: 310–33.

Busch, K. (1988), *The corridor model: a concept for further development of an EU social policy* (Brussels: European Trade Union Institute).

Cahill, C. (2001), 'The multifunctionality of agriculture: what does it mean?, *Euro choices*, Spring: 36–40.

Calleo, D. (2001), *Rethinking Europe's future* (Princeton, NJ: Princeton University Press).

Cameron, D. (1992), 'The 1992 initiative: causes and consequences' in A. Sbragia (ed.) *Europolitics* (Washington, DC: Brookings).

Cameron, F. (ed.) (2004), *The future of Europe: integration and enlargement* (London: Routledge).

Camps, M. (1956), *The European Common Market and American policy* (Princeton, NJ: Center for International Studies).

Caporaso, J. A. (1974), *The structure and function of European integration* (Pacific Palisades, CA: Goodyear Publishing Company).

Carney, F. S. (1964), *The politics of Johannes Althusius* (London: Eyre & Spottiswoode).

Castle-Kanerova, M. and B. Jordan (2001), 'The social citizen' in R. Bellamy and A. Warleigh (eds) *Citizenship and governance in the European Union* (London: Continuum).

Chatham House (2004), *Unfinished business: making Europe's Single Market a reality* (London: Chatham House/RIIA).

Checkel, J. T. (1998), 'The constructivist turn in international relations theory', *World Politics*, 50: 324–48.

Checkel, J. T. (2001), 'A constructivist research programme in EU studies', *European Union Politics*, 2/2: 219–49.

Christiansen, T. (1996), 'Second thoughts on Europe's "third level": the European Union's Committee of the Regions', *Publius – The Journal of Federalism*, 26/1: 93–116.

Christiansen, T., K. E. Jørgensen, and A. Wiener (1999), 'The social contruction of Europe', *Journal of European Public Policy*, 6/4: 528–44.

Christiansen, T., K. E. Jørgensen, and Wiener, A. (eds) (2001), *The social construction of Europe* (London: Sage).

Christin, T. (2005), 'Economic and political basis of attitudes towards the EU in Central and East European countries in the 1990s', *European Union Politics*, 6/1: 29–57.

Chryssochoou, D. N. (2000a), *Democracy in the European Union* (London: I. B Taurus).

Chryssochoou, D. N. (2000b), 'Metatheory and the study of the European Union: capturing the narrative turn', *Journal of European Integration*, 22/2: 123–44.

Chryssochoou, D. N. (2001), *Theorizing European integration* (London: Sage).

Chryssochoou, D. N. (2002), 'Europe's republican moment', *Journal of European Integration*, 24/4: 341–57.

Chryssochoou, D. N., M. J. Tsinisizelis, S. Stavridis, and K. Infantis (2003), *Theory and reform in the European Union* (Manchester: Manchester University Press).

Church, C. H. (1996), *European integration theory in the 1990s*, European Dossier Series (London: University of North London).

Church, C. H. and D. Phinnemore (2002), *The Penguin guide to the European treaties: from Rome to Maastricht, Amsterdam, Nice and beyond* (London: Penguin).

Church, C. H. and D. Phinnemore (2005), *Understanding the European constitution: an introduction to the EU constitutional treaty* (London: Routledge).

Cini, M. (1996), *The European Commission: leadership, organisation and culture in the EU administration* (Manchester: Manchester University Press).

Cini, M. and A. K. Bourne (eds) (2006), *Palgrave advances in European Union studies* (Basingstoke: Palgrave).

Clark, A. (1993), *Diaries* (London: Weidenfeld & Nicolson).

Coen, D. (1997), 'The evolution of the large firm as a political actor in the European Union', *Journal of Public Policy*, 4/1: 91–108.

Coen, D. (1998), 'The European business interest and the nation state: large firm lobbying in the European Union and member states', *Journal of European Public Policy*, 18/1: 75–100.

Coffey, P. (2003), *The future of Europe – revisited* (Cheltenham: Edward Elgar).

Cohen, B. J. (1971), *The future of sterling as an international currency* (London: Macmillan).

Cohen-Tanugi, L. (2005), 'The end of Europe?', *Foreign Affairs*, 84/6: 55–67.

Constantelos, J. (1996), 'Multi-level lobbying in the European Union: a paired sectoral comparison across the French–Italian border', *Regional and Federal Studies*, 6/3: 28–55.

Coombes, D. (1970), *Politics and bureaucracy in the European Community: a portrait of the Commission of the E.E.C.* (London: George Allen & Unwin).

Corbett, R. (1998), *The European Parliament's role in closer EU integration* (London:Macmillan).

Cosgrove Twitchett, C. (1981), *Harmonisation in the EEC* (London: Macmillan).

Cowles, M. G. (1995), 'Seizing the agenda for the new Europe: the ERT and EC 1992', *Journal of Common Market Studies*, 33/4: 501–26.

Cowles, M. G (1997), 'Organizing industrial coalitions: a challenge for the future?' in H. Wallace and A. R. Young (eds) *Participation and policy-making in the European Union* (Oxford: Clarendon Press).

Cowles, M. G. (2001), 'The transatlantic business dialogue and domestic business–government relations' in M. G. Cowles, J. A. Caporaso, and T. Risse (eds) *Transforming Europe: Europeanization and domestic change* (Ithaca, NJ: Cornell University Press).

Cowles, M. G., J. A. Caporaso, and T. Risse (2001) (eds), *Transforming Europe: Europeanization and domestic change* (Ithaca, NJ: Cornell University Press).

Craig, P. P. (1997), 'Democracy and rule-making within the EC: an empirical and normative assessment', *European Law Review*, 3/2: 105–30.

Craig, P. P. and G. De Búrca (2002), *EU law*, 3rd edn (Oxford: Oxford University Press).

Cremona, M. (ed.) (2004), *The enlargement of the European Union* (Oxford: Oxford University Press).

Crombez, C. (2001), 'The treaty of Amsterdam and the co-decision procedure' in M. Aspinwall and G. Schneider (eds) *The rules of integration: institutionalist approaches to the study of Europe* (Manchester: Manchester University Press).

Curtin, D. (1993), 'The constitutional structure of the Union: a Europe of bits and pieces', *Common Market Law Review*, 30/1: 17–69.

Dahrendorf, R. (1967), *Society and democracy in Germany* (London: Weidenfeld & Nicolson).

Damgaard, E. and H. Jensen (2005), Europeanisation of executive–legislative relations: Nordic perspectives', *Journal of Legislative Studies*, 11/3–4: 394–411.

Dashwood, A. (1983), 'Hastening slowly the Community's path towards harmonisation' in H. Wallace *et al.* (eds) *Policy-making in the European Community*, 2nd edn (Chichester: John Wiley) .

Dassu, M. and A. Missoroli (2002), 'More Europe in foreign and security policy: the institutional dimension of CFSP', *The International Spectator*, 37/2: 79–88.

Davis, S. R. (1978), *The federal principle: a journey through time in quest of a meaning* (London: University of California Press).

de Bassompierre, G. (1988), *Changing the guard in Brussels: an insider's view of the EC Presidency* (New York: Praeger).

Dedman, M. (1996), *The origins and development of the European Union, 1945–95: a history of European integration* (London: Routledge).

De Grauwe, P. (2005), *The economics of monetary union*, 6th edn (Oxford: Oxford University Press).

de Grieco, J. M. (1995), 'The Maastricht Treaty, Economic and Monetary Union and the neo-realist research programme', *Review of International Studies*, 21/1: 21–40.

de Grieco, J. M. (1996), 'State interests and international rule trajectories: a neorealist interpretation of the Maastricht Treaty and European Economic and Monetary Union', *Security Studies*, 5/2: 176–222.

de la Porte, C. and P. Pochet (2002), *Building social Europe through the open method of co-ordination* (Berlin: PIE Lang).

Den Boer, M. and J. Monar (2002), 'Keynote article: 11 September and the challenge of international terrorism to the EU as a security actor', *Journal of Common Market Studies*, 40/1: 11–28.

de Villiers, B. (1995), *Bundestreue: the soul of an intergovernmental partnership*, Occasional Paper, March (Johannesburg: Konrad Adenauer Foundation).

Devuyst, Y. (1998), 'Treaty reform in the European Union: the Amsterdam process', *Journal of European Public Policy*, 5/4: 615–31.

Devuyst, Y. (1999), 'The Community method after Amsterdam', *Journal of Common Market Studies*, 37/1, 109–20.

Devuyst, Y. (2005), *The European Union transformed: Community method and institutional evolution from the Schuman Plan to the Constitution for Europe* (Brussels: Peter Lang).

Diebold, W. (1959), *The Schuman plan* (New York: Praeger).

DiMaggio, P. and W. Powell (1991), 'The iron cage revisited: institutional isomorphism and collective rationality in organizational fields', in P. DiMaggio and W. Powell (eds) *The new institutionalism in organizational analysis* (Chicago: University of Chicago Press).

Dimitrakopoulos, D. (ed.) (2004), *The changing European Commission* (Manchester: Manchester University Press).

Dinan, D. (1992), 'Institutions and governance 2001–02: debating the EU's future', *Journal of Common Market Studies*, 40/1: 29–43.

Dinan, D. (2000), *Encyclopedia of the European Union* (Basingstoke: Macmillan).

Dispersyn, M, P. van der Vorst, *et al.* (1990), 'La construction d'un serpent social européen', *Revue de Sécurité Sociale*, 12.

Dobson, L. and A. Føllesdal (eds) (2004), *Political theory and the European constitution* (London: Routledge).

Dølvik, J. E. (1997), *Redrawing boundaries of solidarity? ETUC, social dialogue and the Europeanization of trade unions in the 1990s*, ARENA report no 5, Oslo.

Douglas-Scott, S. (2002), *Constitutional law of the European Union* (London: Longman)

Douglas-Scott, S. (2004), 'The Charter of Fundamental Rights as a constitutional document', *European Human Rights Law Review*, Issue 1: 37–50.

Dover, R. (2004), 'The Europeanisation of British defence policy 1997–2001: a critical evaluation of liberal intergovernmentalism', unpublished PhD thesis, University of Bristol.

Dover, R. (2005), 'The prime minister and the core executive: a liberal intergovernmentalist reading of UK defence policy formulation', *British Journal of Politics and International Relations*, 7/4: 508–25.

Dowding, K. (2000), 'Institutionalist research on the European Union: a critical review', *European Union Politics*, 1/1: 125–44.

Duchêne, F. (1994), *Jean Monnet: the first statesman of interdependence* (London: W.W. Norton & Co.).

Duff, A. (1994), 'Building a parliamentary Europe', *Government and Opposition*, 29: 147–65.

Duignan, P. and L. H. Gann (1994), *The United States and the new Europe 1945–1993* (Oxford: Blackwell).

Dyson, K. (2000), 'EMU as Europeanization: convergence, diversity and contingency', *Journal of Common Market Studies*, 38/4: 645–66.

Dyson, K. (forthcoming 2006), 'Economic policy' in P. Graziano and M. Vink (eds) *Europeanization: new research agendas* (Basingstoke: Palgrave-Macmillan).

Dyson, K. and K. Featherstone (1999), *The road to Maastricht: negotiating Economic and Monetary Union* (Oxford: Oxford University Press).

Edwards, G. and D. Spence (eds) (1997), *The European Commission*, 2nd edn (London: Cartermill).

Eeckhout, P. (2004), *External relations of the European Union: legal and constitutional foundations* (Oxford: Oxford University Press).

Egan, M. (2001), *Constructing a European market: standards, regulation and governance* (Oxford: Oxford University Press).

Egeberg, M. (1996), 'Organization and nationality in the European Commission services', *Public Administration*, 74/4: 721–35.

Egeberg, M. (ed.) (2006), *Multilevel Union administration: the transformation of executive politics in Europe* (Basingstoke: Palgrave).

Egeberg, M., G. F. Schaefer, and J. Trondal (2003), 'The many faces of EU committee governance', *West European Politics*, 26/3: 19–40.

Eichenberg, R. C. and R. J. Dalton (1993), 'Europeans and the European Community: the dynamics of public support for European integration', *International Organization*, 47/4: 507–34.

Eising, R. (1999), 'Reshuffling power: the liberalization of the EU electricity markets and its impact on the German governance regime' in B. Kohler-Koch and R. Eising (eds) *The transformation of governance in the European Union* (London: Routledge).

Eising, R. (2004), 'Multi-level governance and business interests in the European Union,' *Governance*, 17/2: 211–46.

Eising, R. (2005), 'The access of business interests to European Union institutions: notes towards a theory', *ARENA Working Paper*, no. 29.

Eising, R. and N. Jabko (2001), 'Moving targets: national interests and European Union electricity liberalization', *Comparative Political Studies*, 34/7: 242–67.

Elazar, D. J. (1987), *Exploring federalism* (Tuscaloosa, AL: University of Alabama Press).

Elazar, D. J. (1989), 'Federal-type solutions and European integration' in C. L. Brown-John (ed.) *Federal-type solutions and European integration* (Lanham, MD: University Press of America).

Eriksen, E. O. and J. E. Fossum (eds) (2000), *Democracy in the European Union* (London: Routledge).

Eriksen, E. O., J. E. Fossum and A. J. Menendez (eds) (2005), *Developing a constitution for Europe* (London: Routledge).

ESC (Economic and Social Committee) (2004), *Final report on the ad hoc group on structured cooperation with European civil society organisations and networks* (Brussels: CESE 1498/2003, 17 February).

European Commission (1985), *Completing the internal market: white paper*, COM (85) 310 final,14 June.

European Commission (1992a), *The internal market after 1992: meeting the challenge* (the Sutherland report), SEC (92) 2044, Brussels, October.

European Commission (1992b), *An open and structured dialogue between the Commission and special interest groups*, SEC (92) 2272 final, Brussels.

European Commission (1996), *First Cohesion Report* (Luxembourg: Office for Official Publications).

European Commission (1997), *Agenda 2000*, COM (97) 2000, 15 July, Brussels.

European Commission (1999), *The Commission and non-governmental organisation: building a stronger partnership*, Commission discussion paper presented by President Prodi and Vice-President Kinnock, COM (2000) 11 final, 18 January, Brussels.

European Commission (2001a), *European governance: a white paper*, COM (2001) 428 final, Brussels, 25 July.

European Commission (2001b), *Proposal for a Council framework decision on combating terrorism*, COM (2001) 521 final, Brussels.

European Commission (2001c), *Making a success of enlargement*, Strategy paper and report of the European Commission on the progress towards accession by each of the candidate countries, Brussels, http://europa.eu.int/comm/enlargement/report2001/strategy _ en.pdf.

European Commission (2002a), *A project for the European Union*, COM (2002) 394 final, Brussels.

European Commission (2002b), *Communication from the Commission – towards a reinforced culture of consultation and dialogue: general principles and minimum standards for consulting of interested parties by the Commission*, COM (2002) 704 Final, 11 December 2002, Brussels.

European Commission (2002c), *Mid-term review of the Common Agricultural Policy* COM (2002) 394 final, Brussels.

European Commission (2004), *Communication from the Commission and the European Parliament: area of freedom, security and justice. Assessment of the Tampere programme and future orientations*, Brussels.

European Commission (2005a), *Enlargement strategy paper,* COM (2005) 56, Brussels, 9 November.

European Commission (2005b), *Third progress report on cohesion: towards a new partnership for growth, jobs and cohesion,* COM (2005) 192, 17 May.

European Commission (2005c), *Second report on the practical preparations for the future enlargement of the euro area,* SEC (2005) 1397, Brussels.

European Council (1996), *The European Union today and tomorrow, adapting the European Union for the benefit of its peoples and preparing it for the future: a general outline for the draft revision of the treaties* (Brussels: EU Council).

European Council (2001), *Declaration by the heads of state or government of the European Union and the president of the Commission: follow-up to the September 11 attacks and the fight against terrorism,* SN 4296/2/01 Rev 2, Gent.

European Council (2004a), *The Hague programme: strengthening freedom, security and justice in the European Union,* Brussels.

European Council (2004b), 'Treaty establishing a constitution for Europe', *Official Journal of the European Communities,* 47, C310.

European Parliament (1997), *Note on the European Parliament's priorities for the IGC and the new Amsterdam treaty: report and initial evaluation of the results,* http://www.europarl.eu.int/topics/treaty/report/part1_en.htm.

European Parliament (2001), *EP resolution on the Commission white paper on European governance,* A-5-0399/2001.

European Union (1997), 'Treaty on European Union', *Official Journal of the European Communities,* C340: 145–172.

Falkner, G. (1998), *EU social policy in the 1990s: towards a corporatist policy community* (London: Routledge).

Falkner, G. (2000a), 'The Council or the social partners? EC social policy between diplomacy and collective bargaining', *Journal of European Public Policy,* 7/5: 705–24.

Falkner, G. (2000b), 'EG-Sozialpolitik nach Verflechtungsfalle und Entscheidungslücke: Bewertungsmaßstäbe und Entwicklungstrends', *Politische Vierteljahresschrift,* 41/2: 279–301.

Falkner, G. (forthcoming 2006), ' Social policy' in P. Graziano and M. Vink (eds), *Europeanization: new research agendas* (Basingstoke: Palgrave-Macmillan).

Falkner, G., M. Hartlapp, S. Leiber, and O. Treib (2004), 'Non-compliance with EU directives in the member states: opposition through the backdoor?', *West European Politics,* 27/1: 2–73.

Falkner, G., O. Treib, M. Hartlapp, and S. Leiber (2005), *Complying with Europe: EU minimum harmonisation and soft law in the member states* (Cambridge: Cambridge University Press).

Featherstone, K. (2003), 'Introduction: in the name of "Europe" ', in K. Featherstone and C. M. Radaelli (eds) *The politics of Europeanisation* (Oxford: Oxford University Press).

Featherstone, K. and C. M. Radaelli (eds) (2003), *The politics of Europeanisation* (Oxford: Oxford University Press).

Federal Trust, The (2004), 'The beginning of the end or the end of the beginning? Enhanced cooperation and the Constitutional Treaty' *European Policy Brief,* 7.

Fisher, C. (1994), 'The lobby to stop cosmetics testing on animals' in R. H. Pedler and M. C. P. M van Schendelen (eds) *Lobbying the European Union: companies, trade associations and issue* groups (Aldershot: Dartmouth).

Føllesdal, A. (2005), 'Towards a stable *finalité* with federal features? The balancing acts of the Constitutional Treaty for Europe', *Journal of European Public Policy,* 12/3: 572–89.

Foreign and Commonwealth Office (2005), 'Treaty establishing a constitution for Europe: commentary', Cm 6459, London, 26 January.

Forster, A. (1998), 'Britain and the negotiation of the Maastricht Treaty: a critique of liberal intergovernmentalism', *Journal of Common Market Studies,* 36/2: 347–68.

Forster, A. (2002), *Euroscepticism in contemporary British politics* (London: Routledge).

Forsyth, M. (1981), *Union of States: the theory and practice of confederation* (Leicester: Leicester University Press).

Franklin, M. N., M. Marsh, and L. M. McLaren (1994), 'The European question: opposition to unification in the wake of Maastricht', *Journal of Common Market Studies,* 32/4: 455–72.

Fraser, C. (1999), *The foreign and security policy of the EU: past, present and Future* (Sheffield: Sheffield Academic Press).

Fursdon, E. (1980), *The European Defence Community* (Basingstoke: Macmillan).

Gabel, M. J. (1998), *Interests and integration: market liberalization, public opinion, and European Union* (Ann Arbor, MI: University of Michigan Press).

Gabel, M. J. and S. Hix (2002), 'Defining the EU political space: an empirical study of the European election manifestos 1979–99', *Comparative Political Studies,* 35/8: 934–64.

Gaffney, J. (2004), *Whither ESDP?: trends and challenges* (New York: RAND Corporation).

Galloway, D. (1999), 'Keynote article: agenda 2000 – packaging the deal', *Journal of Common Market Studies Annual Review,* 37: 9–35.

Galloway, D. (2001), *The Treaty of Nice and beyond* (Sheffield: Sheffield Academic Press).

Garrett, G. (1992), 'International cooperation and institutional choice: the European Community's internal market', *International Organization,* 46/2: 533–60.

Garrett, G. and G. Tsebelis (1996), 'An institutionalist critique of intergovernmentalism', *International Organization,* 50/2: 269–99.

Geddes, A. (2000), *Immigration and European integration: towards fortress Europe?* (Manchester: Manchester University Press).

Geddes, A. (2003), *The politics of migration and immigration in Europe* (London: Sage).

George, S. (1996), *Politics and policy in the European Union* (Oxford: Oxford University Press).

George., S. and I. Bache (2001), *Politics in the European Union* (Oxford: Oxford University Press).

Geyer, R. R. (2000), *Exploring European social policy* (Cambridge: Polity Press).

Goetschy, J. (2001), 'The European employment strategy from Amsterdam to Stockholm: has it reached its cruising speed yet?', *Industrial Relations Journal* 32/5: 401–18.

Goetz, K. (2001), 'Making sense of post-communist central administration: modernization, Europeanization or latinization?', *Journal of European Public Policy*, 8/6: 1032–51.

Gomez, R. and J. Peterson (2001), 'No one is in control: the EU's impossibly busy foreign ministers', *European Foreign Affairs Review*, 6/1: 53–74.

Gorges, M. J. (1996), *Euro-corporatism? Interest intermediation in the European Community* (London: University Press of America).

Grabbe, H. (2000), 'The sharp edges of Europe: extending Schengen eastwards', *International Affairs*, 76/3: 519–36.

Grande, E. (1994), *Vom Nationalstaat zur europaischen Politikverflechtung. Expansion und Transformation moderner Staatlichkeit – undersucht am Beispiel der Forschungs- und Technologiepolitik* (Universität Konstanz. Habilitationschift).

Grant, C. (2000), *EU 2010: An optimistic vision of the future* (London: Centre for European Reform).

Greenwood, J. (2003), *Interest representation in the European Union* (Basingstoke: Palgrave).

Greffet, F. (2005), 'Abstention' in Y. Déloye (ed.) *Dictionnaire des elections Européennes* (Paris: Economica): 1–6.

Grin, G. (2003), *Battle of the Single European Market: achievements and economic thought 1985–2000* (London: Kegan Paul).

Gros, D. and N. Thygesen (1998), *European monetary integration: from the European Monetary System to European Monetary Union*, 2nd edn (Harlow: Longman).

Grote, J. R. and A. Lang (2003), 'Europeanization and organizational change in national trade associations: an organizational ecology perspective' in K. Featherstone and C. M. Radaelli (eds) *The politics of Europeanization* (Oxford: Oxford University Press).

Guay, T. R. (1996), 'Integration and Europe's defence industry: a "reactive spillover" approach', *Political Studies Journal*, 24/3: 404–16.

Guay, T. R. (1999), *The European Union and the United States: the political economy of a relationship* (Sheffield: Sheffield University Press).

Haas, E. B. (1958), *The uniting of Europe: political, social and economic forces, 1950–1957* (Stanford, CA: Stanford University Press).

Haas, E. B. (1971), 'The study of regional integration: reflections on the joy and anguish of pretheorizing' in L. N. Lindberg and A. Scheingold (eds) *Regional integration: theories and research* (Harvard: Harvard University Press).

Haas, E. B. (1975), *The obsolescence of regional integration theory*, Research studies 25 (Berkeley, CA: Institute of International Studies).

Haas, E. B. (1976), 'Turbulent fields and the theory of regional integration', *International Organization*, 30/2: 173–212.

Haas, E. B. (2001), 'Does constructivism subsume neo-functionalism?' in T. Christiansen, K. E. Jørgensen, and A. Wiener (eds) *The social construction of Europe* (London, Sage).

Haas, E.B. (2004), 'Introduction: institutionalism or constructivism?' in his *The uniting of Europe: political, social and economic forces, 1950–1957*, 3rd edn (Notre Dame, IN: University of Notre Dame Press).

Haas, E. B. and P. C. Schmitter (1964), 'Economic and differential patterns of political integration: projections about unity in Latin America', *International Organization*, 18/3: 705–38.

Hall, P. (1986), *Governing the economy: the politics of state intervention in Britain and France* (Cambridge: Polity Press).

Hall, P. and D. Soskice (2001), *Varieties of capitalism* (Oxford: Oxford University Press).

Hall, P. and R. Taylor (1996), 'Political science and the three new institutionalisms', *Political Studies*, 44/5: 936–57.

Hamilton, D. and J. Quinlan (eds) (2005), *Deep integration: how transatlantic markets are leading to globalization* (Brussels: Centre for Transatlantic Relations/Centre for European Policy Studies).

Hantrais, L. (2000), *Social policy in the European Union*, 2nd edn (Basingstoke: Macmillan).

Harrison, R. J. (1974), *Europe in question* (London: George Allen & Unwin).

Hartley, T. (2003), *The foundations of European Community law*, 5th edn (Oxford: Oxford University Press).

Harvey, B. (1993), 'Lobbying in Europe: the experience of voluntary organizations' in S. Mazey and J. R. Richardson (eds) *Lobbying in the European Community* (Oxford: Oxford University Press).

Haseler, S. (2004), *Super-state: the new Europe and its challenge to America* (London: I. B. Taurus).

Hayes-Renshaw, F. and H. Wallace (1997), *The Council of Ministers* (New York: St Martin's Press).

Hayes-Renshaw, F. and H. Wallace (2006), *The Council of Ministers, 2nd edn* (New York: St Martin's Press).

Heinelt, H. (1998), 'Zivilgesellschaftliche Perspektiven einer demokratischen Transformation der Europäischen Union', *Zeitschift für Internationale Beziehungen*, 5/1: 79–107.

Héritier, A. (1996), 'The accommodation of diversity in European policy-making and its outcomes: regulatory policy as patchwork', *Journal of European Public Policy*, 3/2: 149–67.

Héritier, A., D. Kerwer, C. Knill, D. Lehmkuhl, M. Teutsch, and A.-C. Douillet (2001), *Differential Europe: the European Union impact on national policymaking* (Lanham, MD: Rowman & Littlefield).

Hettne, B. (2002), 'The Europeanisation of Europe: endogenous and exogenous dimensions', *Journal of European Integration*, 24/4, 325–40.

Hey, C. and U. Brendle (1994), *Unweltverbände und EG: Strategien, politische Kulturen und Organisationformen* (Opladen: Westdeutscher Verlag).

Hill, C. and M. Smith (eds) (2005), *International relations and the European Union* (Oxford: Oxford University Press).

Hirst, P. and G. Thompson (1996), *Globalization in question: the international economy and the possibilities of governance* (Cambridge: Polity Press).

Hix, S. (1994), 'The study of the European Union: the challenge to comparative politics', *West European Politics*, 17/1: 1–30.

Hix, S. (1999), *The political system of the European Union* (Basingstoke: Macmillan).

Hix, S. (2002), 'Parliamentary behaviour with two principals: preferences, parties and voting in the European Parliament', *American Journal of Political Science*, 46/3: 688–98.

Hix, S. (2005), *The political system of the European Union* (Basingstoke: Macmillan).

Hix, S. and R. Scully (eds) (2003), *The European Parliament at Fifty*. Special issue of the *Journal of Common Market Studies*, 41/2.

Hix, S., A. Noury, and G. Roland (2006), *Democracy in the European Parliament* (Cambridge: Cambridge University Press).

Hoffmann, S. (1966), 'Obstinate or obsolete? The fate of the nation-state and the case of western Europe', *Daedalus*, 95/3: 862–915.

Hoffmann, S. (ed.) (1995), *The European Sisyphus: essays on Europe 1964–94* (Oxford: Westview).

Hogan, M. J. (1987), *The Marshall Plan* (Cambridge: Cambridge University Press).

Holland, M. (2002), *The European Union and the third world* (Basingstoke: Palgrave Macmillan).

Hooghe, L. (ed.) (1996), *Cohesion policy and European integration: building multi-level governance* (Oxford: Oxford University Press).

Hooghe, L. (1999), 'Supranational activists or intergovernmental agents?', *Comparative Political Studies*, 32/4: 435–63.

Hooghe, L. (2001), *The European Commission and the integration of Europe: images of governance* (Cambridge: Cambridge University Press).

Hooghe, L. and G. Marks (1997), 'The making of a polity: the struggle over European integration', *European integration online Papers* (EIoP), 1/4, http://eiop.or.at/eiop/texte/1997-004a.htm.

Hooghe, L. and G. Marks (2001), *Multi-level governance and European integration* (Boulder, CO: Rowman & Littlefield).

Hooghe, L. and G. Marks (2003), 'Unravelling the central state, but how? Types of multi-level governance', *American Political Science Review*, 97/2: 233–43.

Hooghe, L. and G. Marks (2004), 'Does identity or economic rationality drive public opinion on European integration?', *PS*, 37/3: 415–20.

Hoskyns, C. (1996), *Integrating gender* (London: Verso).

Hoskyns, C. and M. Newman (eds) (2000), *Democratizing the European Union* (Manchester: Manchester University Press).

Hosli, M. O. (2005), *The euro: a concise introduction to European monetary integration* (Boulder, CO: Lynne Rienner).

Howarth, J. (2000), 'Britain, NATO, CESDP: fixed strategies, changing tactics', *European Foreign Affairs Review*, 16/3: 1–2.

Howarth, J. and J. T. S. Keeler (2003), *Defending Europe: the EU, NATO and the quest for European autonomy* (New York: Palgrave).

Hueglin., T. O. (1999), *Early modern concepts for a late modern world: Althusius on community and federalism* (Waterloo, ONT: Wilfrid Laurier University Press).

Hughes, J., G. Sasse, and C. Gordon (2004), 'Conditionality and compliance in the EU's eastward enlargement: regional policy and the reform of subnational government', *Journal of Common Market Studies*, 42/3: 523–51.

Hurrell, A. and A. Menon (1996), 'Politics like any other? Comparative politics, international relations and the study of the EU', *West European Politics*, 19/2: 386–402.

Imig, D. and S. Tarrow (eds) (2001), *Contentious Europeans: protest and politics in an emerging polity* (Lanham, MD: Rowman & Littlefield).

Inglehart, R. (1970), 'Cognitive mobilization and European identity', *Comparative Politics*, 3/1: 45–70.

Jachtenfuchs, M. (1997), 'Conceptualizing European governance' in K. E. Jørgensen (ed.) *Reflective approaches to European governance* (Basingstoke: Macmillan).

Jachtenfuchs, M. (2001), 'The governance approach to European integration', *Journal of Common Market Studies*, 39/2: 245–64.

Jachtenfuchs, M. and B. Kohler-Koch (2004), 'Governance and institutional development' in A. Wiener and T. Diez (eds) *European integration theory* (Oxford: Oxford University Press).

Jacobs, F., R. Corbett, and M. Shackleton (2005), *The European Parliament*, 5th edn (London: John Harper).

Jeffrey, C. (2004), 'Regions and the EU: letting them in and leaving them alone', *Federal Trust Online Paper*, XX04.

Jeffrey, C. and R. Sturm (1993) (eds), *Federalism, Unification and European Integration* (London: Frank Cass).

Jensen, C. S. (2000), 'Neofunctionalist theories and the development of European social and labour market policy', *Journal of Common Market Studies*, 38/1: 71–92.

John, P. (1996), 'Centralisation, decentralisation and the European Union: The dynamics of triadic relationships', *Public Administration*, 74: 293–313.

Jones, A. and J. Clarke (2001), *The modalities of European Union governance: new institutionalist explanations of agri-environmental policy* (Oxford: Oxford University Press).

Jordan, A. and D. Liefferink (eds) (2004), *Environmental policy on Europe: the Europeanization of national environmental policy* (London: Routledge).

Jørgensen, K. E. and B. Rosamond (2002), 'Europe: regional laboratory for a global polity?' in M. Ougaard and R. Higgott (eds) *Towards a global polity* (London: Routledge).

Junge, K. (2002), 'Does differentiation work', unpublished PhD thesis, University of Birmingham.

Kagan, R. (2004), *Paradise and power: America and Europe in the new world order* (London: Atlantic Books).

Karp, J. A., S. A. Banducci, and S. Bowler (2003), 'To know it is to love it? Satisfaction with democracy in the European Union', *Comparative Political Studies* 36/3: 271–92.

Kassim, H. (1994), 'Policy networks and European Union policy making: a sceptical view', *West European Politics*, 17/4: 12–27.

Kassim, H. (2003), 'Meeting the demands of EU membership: the Europeanization of national administrative systems' in K. Featherstone and C. Radaelli (eds) *The politics of Europeanization* (Oxford: Oxford University Press).

Kassim, H. (2005), 'Europeanization of member state institutions' in S. Bulmer and C. Lequesne (eds) *Member states and the European Union* (Oxford: Oxford University Press).

Kassim, H. and H. Stevens (2005), *The Europeanization of air transport and its limits* (Basingstoke: Palgrave).

Katzenstein, P. (1996), 'Introduction', in P. Katzenstein (ed.) *The culture of national security: norms and identity in world politics* (Ithaca, NY: Columbia University Press).

Katzenstein, P. J. (1997), 'United Germany in an integrating Europe' in P. J. Katzenstein (ed.) *Tamed power: Germany in Europe* (Ithaca, NY: Cornell University Press).

Katzenstein, P. J., R. O. Keohane, and S. D. Krasner (1998), 'International organization and the study of world politics', *International Organization*, 52/4: 463–85.

Keane, R. (2004), 'The Solana process in Serbia and Montenegro: coherence in EU foreign policy', *International Peacekeeping*, 11/3: 491–507.

Keating, M. (2000), *New regionalism in western Europe* (Cheltenham: Edward Elgar).

Keating, M. (2004), 'Regions and the Convention on the Future of Europe', *South European Society and Politics*, 9/1: 192–207.

Keohane, D. and H. Brady (2005), *Fighting terrorism: the EU needs a strategy not a shopping list* (London: Centre for European Reform).

Keohane, R. O. (1988), 'International institutions: two approaches', *International Studies Quarterly*, 32/4: 379–96.

Keohane, R. O. (1989), *International institutions and state power: essays in international relations theory* (Boulder, CO: Westview).

Keohane, R. O. and S. Hoffmann (eds) (1991), *The New European Community: decision making and institutional change* (Boulder, CO: Westview).

Keohane, R. O. and J. Nye (1975), 'International interdependence and integration' in F. Greenstein and N. Polsby (eds) *Handbook of political science* (Andover, MA: Addison-Wesley).

Keohane, R.O. and J. Nye (1976), *Power and interdependence: world politics in transition* (Boston, MA: Little Brown).

King, P. (1982), *Federalism and federation* (London: Croom Helm).

Knill, C. and D. Lehmkuhl (2002), 'The national impact of European Union regulatory policies: three Europeanisation mechanisms', *European Journal of Political Research*, 41/2: 255–80.

Kohler-Koch, B. (1996), 'Catching up with change: the transformation of governance in the European Union', *Journal of European Public Policy*, 3/3: 359–80.

Kohler-Koch, B. (1997), 'Organized interests in the EC and the European Parliament', *European integration online papers*, 1/9, http://eiop.or.at/eiop/_texte/1997-009.htm.

Kohler-Koch, B. (1999), 'The evolution and transformation of European governance' in B. Kohler-Koch and R. Eising (eds) *The transformation of governance in the European Union* (London: Routledge).

Kohler-Koch, B. and R. Eising (eds) (1999), *The transformation of governance in the European Union* (London: Routledge).

Kölliker, A. (2001), 'Bringing together or driving apart the Union? Towards a theory of differentiated integration', *West European Politics*, 24/4: 125–51.

Kreppel, A. (1999), 'What affects the European Parliament's legislative influence? An analysis of the success of EP amendments', *Journal of Common Market Studies*, 37: 521–37.

Kreppel, A. (2002), *The European Parliament and the supranational party system: a study in institutional development* (Cambridge: Cambridge University Press).

Ladrech, R. (2002), 'Europeanization and political parties: towards a framework for analysis', *Party Politics*, 8/4: 389–404.

Laffan, B. (1999), 'Becoming a "living institution": the evolution of the European Court of Auditors', *Journal of Common Market Studies*, 37/2: 251–68.

Laffan, B. (forthcoming 2006), 'Core executives' in P. Graziano and M. Vink (eds) *Europeanization: new research agendas* (Basingstoke: Palgrave).

Laffan, B. and M. Shackleton (2000), 'The budget: who gets what, when and how' in H. Wallace and W. Wallace (eds) *Policy-making in the European Union* (Oxford: Oxford University Press).

Laffan, B., R. O'Donnell, and M. Smith (2000), *Europe's experimental union: rethinking integration* (London: Routledge).

Lasok, K. P. E. and T. Millet (2004), *Judicial control in EU: procedures and principles* (Richmond: Richmond Law and Tax).

Lasswell, H. D. (1950), *Politics: who gets what, when, how* (New York: Peter Smith).

Laurent, P. H. (1970), 'Paul-Henri Spaak and the diplomatic origins of the common market, 1955–56', *Political Science Quarterly*, 35/3: 373–96.

Laursen, F. (2005), 'Denmark and the Constitutional Treaty: a difficult two level game', paper presented at the EUSA Conference, Austin, TX, 31 March–2 April.

Lavdas, K. A. (2000), *Mixed government and fragmentation in the European polity: a republican interpretation*, UWE papers in politics, 6 February.

Lavdas, K. A. (2001), 'Republican Europe and multi-cultural citizenship', *Politics*, 21/1: 1–10.

Lavenex, S. (2001), 'The Europeanization of refugee policy: normative challenges and institutional legacies', *Journal of Common Market Studies*, 39/5: 825–50.

Lavenex, S. and E. M. Uçarer (eds) (2002), *Migration and the externalities of European integration* (Lanham, MD: Lexington Books).

Lavenex, S. and E. M. Uçarer (2004), 'The external dimension of Europeanization: the case of immigration policies', *Cooperation and Conflict*, 39/4: 417–43.

Lavenex, S. and W. Wallace (2005), 'Justice and home affairs: towards a "European public order" ' in H. Wallace, W. Wallace, and M. Pollack (eds) *Policy-making in the European Union*, 5th edn (Oxford: Oxford University Press).

Le Galès, P. and C. Lequesne (eds) (1998), *Regions in Europe* (London: Routledge).

Lehmkuhl, D. (2000), *The importance of small differences: the impact of European integration on road haulage associations in Germany and the Netherlands* (Amsterdam: Thela Thesis).

Leibfried, S. and P. Pierson (1995), 'Semisovereign welfare states: social policy in a multitiered Europe', in S. Leibfried and P. Pierson (eds) *European social policy: between fragmentation and integration* (Washington, DC: The Brookings Institution) .

Leibfried, S., and P. Pierson (2000), 'Social policy: left to court and markets?' in H. Wallace and W. Wallace (eds) *Policy-making in the European Union* (Oxford: Oxford University Press).

Leinen, J. and I. Méndez de Vigo (2001), 'Report on the Laeken European Council and the future of the Union', *European Parliament report*, A5–0368/2001, Brussels, 23 October.

Lenaerts, K. and P. Van Nuffel (2004), *Constitutional law of the European Union* (London: Sweet & Maxwell).

Leonard, M. (2005), *Why Europe will run the 21st century* (London: Fourth Estate).

Lewis, J. (2005), 'Is the Council becoming an upper house?' in C. Parsons and N. Jabko (eds) *With US or against US? The state of the European Union, volume 7* (Oxford: Oxford University Press).

Lindberg, L. N. (1963), *The political dynamics of European economic integration* (Stanford, CA: Stanford University Press).

Lindberg, L. N. and S. A. Scheingold (1970), *Europe's would-be polity: patterns of change in the European Community* (Upper Saddle River, NJ: Prentice-Hall).

Lindberg, L. N. and S. A. Scheingold (eds) (1971), *Regional integration: theory and research* (Harvard: Harvard University Press).

Lord, C. (1998), *Democracy in the European Union* (Sheffield: Sheffield Academic Press).

Lord, C. (2001), 'Democracy and democratization in the European Union' in S. Bromley (ed.) *Governing the European Union* (London: Sage).

Loughlin, J. (1996), ' "Europe of the Regions" and the federalisation of Europe', *Publius: the Journal of Federalism*, 24/4: 141–62.

Loughlin, J. (1997), 'Representing regions in Europe: the Committee of the Regions', *Regional and Federal Studies*, 6/2: 147–65.

Lynch, P., N. Neuwahl, and W. Rees (2000) (eds), *Reforming the European Union from Maastricht to Amsterdam* (London: Longman).

McCarthy, R. (1997), 'The Committee of the Regions: an advisory body's tortuous path to influence', *Journal of European Public Policy*, 4/3: 439–54.

McCormick, J. (1999), *Understanding the European Union* (Basingstoke: Macmillan).

McCormick, J. (2002), *Understanding the European Union*, 2nd edn (Basingstoke: Palgrave).

MacCormick, N. (1997), 'Democracy, subsidiarity and citizenship in the "European commonwealth" ', *Law and Philosophy*, 16/4: 331–56.

MacCormick, N. (2005), *Who's afraid of a European constitution?* (Exeter: Imprint Academic).

McKay, D. (2001), *Designing Europe: comparative lessons from the federal experience* (Oxford: Oxford University Press).

McLaren, L. N. (2006), *Identity, interests and attitudes to European integration* (Basingstoke: Palgrave).

Mair, P. (2004), 'The Europeanisation dimension', *Journal of European Public Policy*, 11/2: 337–48.

Mair, P. (forthcoming 2006), 'Political parties and party systems' in P. Graziano and M. Vink (eds) *Europeanization: new research agendas* (Basingstoke: Palgrave-Macmillan).

Majone, G. (1994), 'The rise of the regulatory state in Europe', *West European Politics*, 17/3: 77–101.

Majone, G. (1995), *The development of social regulation in the European Community: policy externalities, transaction costs, motivational factors* (Florence: EUI Working Paper).

Majone, G. (1996), *Regulating Europe* (London: Routledge).

Majone, G. (2005), *Dilemmas of European integration: the ambiguities and pitfalls of integration by stealth* (Oxford: Oxford University Press).

Mandelkern Group Report (2001), Final Report, Brussels, 13 November.

Manners, I. (2002), 'Normative power Europe: a contradiction in terms?', *Journal of Common Market Studies*, 40/2, 235–58.

Marks, G. (1992), 'Structural policy in the European Community' in A. Sbragia (ed.) *Europolitics: institutions and policy-making in the 'new' European Community* (Washington, DC: Brookings Institute).

Marks, G. and D. McAdam (1996), 'Social movements and the changing structure of political opportunity in the European Union', *West European Politics*, 19/2: 249–78.

Marks, G. and C. Wilson (2000), 'The past in the present: a cleavage theory of party positions on European integration', *British Journal of Political Science*, 30: 433–59.

Marks, G., L. Hooghe, and K. Blank (1996), 'European integration from the 1980s: state-centric v. multilevel governance', *Journal of Common Market Studies*, 34/5: 341–78.

Marks, G., L. Hooghe, M. Nelson, and E. Edwards (2004), 'Mapping party support for European integration in a United Europe: all in the family?' Mimeo.

Marshall, T. H. (1975), *Social policy* (London: Hutchinson).

Martenczuk, B. (2000), 'Die differenzierte Integration und die föderale Struktur der Europäischen Union', *Europarecht*, 35/3: 351–64.

Martin, A. and G. Ross (1999), 'In the line of fire: the Europeanization of labor representation' in A. Martin, G. Ross *et al.* (eds) *The brave new world of European labor. European trade unions at the millennium* (New York: Berghahn).

Mattli, W. (2005), 'Ernst Haas's evolving thinking on comparative regional integration: of virtues and infelicities', *Journal of European Public Policy*, 12/2: 327–47.

Maurer, A. (2001), *National parliaments after Amsterdam: adaptation, recalibration and Europeanisation by process*, Paper for Working Group Meeting, XXIVth COSAC, 8–9 April.

Mazey, S. (1998), 'The European Union and women's rights: from the Europeanisation of national agendas to the nationalisation of a European agenda?' in D. Hine and H. Kassim (eds) *Beyond the market: the EU and national social policy* (London: Routledge).

Mazey, S. and J. R. Richardson (2001), 'Institutionalising promiscuity: Commission–interest group relations in the EU' in A. Stone Sweet, W. Sandholtz, and N. Fligstein (eds) *The institutionalisation of Europe* (Oxford: Oxford University Press).

Mearsheimer, J. J. (1990), 'Back to the future: instability in Europe after the Cold War', *International Security*, 15/1: 5–56.

Mendes, M. J. and N. Gall (2000), *What is federalism?* Braudel Papers, 23.

Messerlin, P. (2001), *Measuring the costs of protection in Europe* (Washington, DC: IIE).

Metcalfe, L. (1996), 'Building capacities for integration: the future role of the Commission', *Eipascope*, 2: 2–8.

Meyer, C. (2005), 'The Europeanization of media discourse: a study of quality press coverage of economic policy coordination since Amsterdam', *Journal of Common Market Studies*, 43/1: 121–48.

Michalski, A. (ed.) (2004), *The political dynamics of constitutional reform: reflections on the Convention on the Future of Europe* (The Hague: Netherlands Institute of International Relations).

Miles, L. (2005), 'Editorial: a fusing Europe in a confusing world?', *Journal of Common Market Studies*, (Annual Review), 43/1: 1–9.

Milward, A. S. (1984), *The reconstruction of western Europe, 1945–51* (London: Methuen & Co.).

Milward, A. S. (1992), *The European rescue of the nation state*, 2nd edn (London: Routledge).

Molitor, B. *et al.* (1995), *Report of the group of independent experts on legislation and administrative simplification*, Brussels, COM (95) 288, 21 May 1995.

Monar, J. (2001), 'The dynamics of justice and home affairs: laboratories, driving factors and costs', *Journal of Common Market Studies*, 39/4: 747–64.

Monar, J. and W. Wessels (eds) (2001), *The European Union after the Treaty of Amsterdam* (London: Continuum).

Monnet, J. (1978), *Memoirs* (New York: Doubleday & Co).

Moravcsik, A. (1991), 'Negotiating the Single European Act: national interests and conventional statecraft in the European Community', *International Organization*, 45/1: 19–56.

Moravcsik, A. (1993), 'Preferences and power in the European community: a liberal intergovernmentalist approach', *Journal of Common Market Studies*, 34/4: 473–524.

Moravcsik, A. (1998), *The choice for Europe: social purpose and state power from Messina to Maastricht* (London: UCL Press).

Moravcsik, A. (2001), 'A constructivist research programme for EU studies', *European Union Politics* 2/2: 219–49.

Moravcsik, A. (2005), 'The European constitutional compromise and the neofunctionalist legacy', *Journal of European Public Policy*, 12/2: 349–86.

Morgenthau, H. (1985), *Politics among nations: the struggle for power and peace*, 6th edn (New York: Knopf).

Moser, P. (1996), 'The European Parliament as a conditional agenda setter: what are the conditions? A critique of Tsebelis (1994)', *American Political Science Review*, 90: 834–8.

Moyer, W. and T. Josling (2002), *Agricultural policy reform: politics and process in the EU and US in the 1990s* (London: Ashgate).

Neill, P. (1995), *The European Court of Justice: a case study in judicial activism* (London: European Policy Forum).

Neunreither, K. (2000), 'Political representation in the European Union: a common whole, various wholes, or just a hole?' in K. Neunreither and A. Weiner (eds) *European integration after Amsterdam: institutional dynamics and prospects for democracy* (Oxford: Oxford University Press).

Newman, M. (1996), *Democracy, sovereignty and the European Union* (London: Hurst).

Newman, M. (2001), 'Democracy and accountability in the EU' in J. Richardson (ed.) *European Union: power and policy making* (London: Routledge).

Nicholson, F. and R. East (1987), *From the six to the twelve: the enlargement of the European Communities* (London: Longman).

Niedermayer, O. and R. Sinnott (1995), 'Democratic legitimacy and the European Parliament' in O. Niedermayer and R. Sinnott (eds) *Public opinion and institutionalized governance: beliefs in government*, vol. 2 (Oxford: Oxford University Press).

Noël, E. (1967), 'The Committee of Permanent Representatives', *Journal of Common Market Studies*, 5/3: 219–51.

Norman, P. (2001), 'Solana hits out at EU foreign strategies', *Financial Times*, 23 January: 9.

Norman, P. (2005), *The accidental constitution: the making of Europe's constitutional treaty* (Brussels: Eurocomment).

Norton, P. (1996), *National parliaments and the European Union* (London: Frank Cass).

Nugent, N. (1999), *The government and politics of the European Union*, 4th edn (Basingstoke: Macmillan).

Nugent, N. (2000), *The European Commission* (Basingstoke: Palgrave).

Nuttall, S. (1992), *European political cooperation* (Oxford: Oxford University Press).

Nye, J. S. (1971), 'Comparing common markets: a revised neo-functionalist model' in L. N. Lindberg and S. A. Scheingold (eds) *Regional integration: theory and research* (Cambridge, MA: Harvard University Press).

Obradovic, D. (2005), 'Civil society and the social dialogue in European governance' NEWGOV new modes of governance, Project no CIT1-CT-2004-506392.

Olsen, J. (2002), 'The many faces of Europeanisation', *Journal of Common Market Studies*, 40/5: 921–52.

O'Neill, M. (1996), *The politics of European integration: a reader* (London: Routledge).

Page, E. C. (1997), *People who run Europe* (Oxford: Oxford University Press).

Pearce, J. and J. Sutton (1983), *Protection and industrial policy in Europe* (London: Routledge).

Pelkmans, J. (1987), 'The new approach to technical harmonization and standardization', *Journal of Common Market Studies*, 25: 249–69.

Pelkmans, J. (1997), *European integration, methods and economic analysis* (London: Longman).

Pelkmans, J. and A. Winters (1988), *Europe's domestic market* (London: Royal Institute of International Affairs).

Pentland, C. (1973), *International theory and European integration* (New York: The Free Press).

Peterson, J. (1995), 'Decision making in the European Union: towards a framework for analysis', *Journal of European Public Policy*, 2/1: 69–93.

Peterson, J. (2004a), 'Keynote article: Europe, America and Iraq: worst ever, ever worsening', *Journal of Common Market Studies*, 42/1: 9–26

Peterson, J. (2004b), 'Policy networks' in A. Wiener and T. Diez (eds) *European integration theory* (Oxford: Oxford University Press).

Peterson, J. and E. Bomberg (1999), *Decision-making in the European Union* (Basingstoke: Macmillan).

Pettit, P. (1997), *Republicanism: a theory of freedom and government* (Oxford: Clarendon Press).

Pierre, J. (ed.) (2000), *Debating governance: authority, steering and democracy* (Oxford: Oxford University Press).

Pierson, P. (1998), 'The path to European integration: a historical institutionalist analysis' in W. Sandholtz and A. Stone Sweet (eds) *European integration and supranational governance* (Oxford: Oxford University Press).

Pinder, J. (1998a), *European Community: building of a union* (Oxford: Oxford University Press).

Pinder, J. (ed.) (1998b), *Altiero Spinelli and the British federalists* (London: The Federal Trust).

Piris, J.-C. (2000), 'Does the European Union have a constitution? Does it need one?' Harvard Jean Monnet Working Paper, No. 5/00, Harvard Law School.

Pochet, P. and C. de la Porte (2004), 'The European employment strategy: existing research and remaining questions', *Journal of European Social Policy*, 14/1: 71–9.

Poidevin, R. and D. Spierenburg (1994), *The history of the High Authority of the European Coal and Steel Community* (London: Wiedenfeld & Nicolson).

Pollack, M. (1995), 'Regional actors in an intergovermental play: the making and implementation of EC structural funds' in S. Mazey and C. Rhodes (eds) *State of the European Union, vol. 3: building a European polity* (Boulder, CO: Lynne Rienner).

Pollack, M. (1997), 'Delegation, agency and agenda-setting in the European Community', *International Organization*, 51/1: 99–134.

Pollack, M. A. (2002), *The engines of integration: delegation, agencies and agenda-setting in the EU* (Oxford: Oxford University Press).

Pollack, M. A. (2004), 'New institutionalism' in A. Wiener and T. Diez (eds) *European integration theory* (Oxford: Oxford University Press).

Pryce, R. (ed.) (1987), *The dynamics of European Union* (London: Croom Helm).

Puchala, D. (1971), *International politics today* (New York: Dodd Mead).

Putnam, R. (1988), 'Diplomacy and domestic politics: the logic of two-level games', *International Organization*, 42/3: 427–60.

Radaelli, C. M. (1997), 'How does Europeanization produce domestic policy change? Corporate tax policy in Italy and the United Kingdom', *Comparative Political Studies*, 30/5: 553–75.

Radaelli, C. M. (1998), *Governing European regulation: the challenge ahead*, RSC policy paper no. 98/3, European University Institute, Florence.

Radaelli, C. M. (2003), 'The Europeanization of public policy' in K. Featherstone and C. M. Radaelli (eds) *The politics of Europeanization* (Oxford: Oxford University Press).

Radaelli, C. M. (2006), 'Europeanisation: solution or problem?' in M. Cini and A. Bourne (eds) *Palgrave advance in European advances in Union studies* (Basingstoke: Palgrave)

Rasmussen, H. (1986), *On law and policy in the European Court of Justice* (Dordrecht: Nijhoff).

Raunio, T. (1997), *The European perspective: transnational party groups in the 1989–1994 European Parliament* (London: Ashgate).

Raunio, T. (2001), 'The Parliament of Finland: a model case for effective scrutiny?' in A. Maurer and W. Wessels (eds) *National parliaments in their ways to Europe: losers or latecomers*? (Baden-Baden: Nomos).

Raunio, T. (2004), 'Towards tighter scrutiny? National legislatures in the EU constitution', *The Federal Trust Online Paper*, 16/04. London, August 2004.

Rees, W. and R. J. Aldrich (2005), 'Contending cultures of counter-terrorism: transatlantic divergence or convergence?', *International Affairs*, 81/5: 905–23.

Regent, S. (2002), *The open method of coordination: a supranational form of governance?* (Discussion Paper DP 137/2002, International Institute for Labour Studies).

Reid, T. (2004), *The United States of Europe – The new superpower and the end of American supremacy* (New York: Penguin).

Rhodes, M. (1995), 'A regulatory conundrum: industrial relations and the "social dimension" ' in S. Leibfried and P. Pierson (eds) *Fragmented social policy: the European Union's social dimension in comparative perspective* (Washington, DC: The Brookings Institution).

Rhodes, M. and B. van Apeldoorn (1998), 'Capital unbound? The transformation of European corporate governance', *Journal of European Public Policy*, 5/3: 407–28.

Richardson, J. (2001), 'Policy-making in the EU: interests, ideas and garbage can of primaeval soup' in J. Richardson (ed.) *European Union: power and policy-making* (London: Routledge).

Riley, P. (1973), 'Rousseau as a theorist of national and international federalism', *Publius: The Journal of Federalism*, 3/1: 5–18.

Riley, P. (1976), 'Three seventeenth century theorists of federalism: Althusius, Hugo and Leibniz', *Publius: The Journal of Federalism*, 6/3: 7–42.

Riley, P. (1979), 'Federalism in Kant's Political Philosophy', *Publius: The Journal of Federalism*, 9/4: 43–64.

Risse, T. (2004), 'Social constructivism' in A. Wiener and T. Diez (eds) *European integration theory* (Oxford: Oxford University Press).

Risse, T. (2005), 'Nationalism, European identity and the puzzles of European integration', *Journal of European Public Policy*, 12/2: 291–309.

Risse-Kappen, T. (1996), 'Exploring the nature of the beast: international relations theory and comparative policy analysis meet the European Union', *Journal of Common Market Studies*, 34/1: 54–81.

Rittberger, B. (2000), 'Impatient legislators and new issue dimensions: a critique of Garrett and Tsebelis' 'standard version' of legislative politics', *Journal of European Public Policy*, 7: 554–75.

Rittberger, B. (2005), *Building Europe's Parliament: democratic representation beyond the nation state* (Oxford: Oxford University Press).

Rizzuto, F. (2003), *The new role of national parliaments in the European Union*, The Federal Trust, 19/3, June, London.

Roederer-Rynning, C. (forthcoming 2006), 'Agricultural policy' in P. Graziano and M. Vink (eds) *Europeanization: new research agendas* (Basingstoke: Palgrave-Macmillan).

Rohrschneider, R. (2002), 'The democracy deficit and mass support for an EU-wide government', *American Journal of Political Science*, 46/2: 463–75.

Rosamond, B. (2000), *Theories of European integration* (Basingstoke: Palgrave).

Rosamond, B. (2005a), 'The uniting of Europe and the foundations of EU studies: revisiting the neofunctionalism of Ernst B. Haas', *Journal of European Public Policy*, 12/2: 237–54.

Rosamond, B. (2005b), 'Conceptualising the EU model of governance in world politics', *European Foreign Affairs Review*, 10/4: 463–78.

Rosenau, J. N. and M. Durfee (1995), *Thinking theory thoroughly: coherent approaches in an incoherent world* (Boulder, CO: Westview).

Ross, G. (1995), 'Assessing the Delors era and social policy' in S. Leibfried and P. Pierson (eds) *European social policy: between fragmentation and integration* (Washington, DC: The Brookings Institution).

Ruggie, J. G. (1998), *Constructing the world polity: essays on international institutionalization* (London: Routledge).

Ruggie, J. G., P. J. Katzenstein, R. O. Keohane, and P. C. Schmitter (2005), 'Transformation in world politics: the intellectual contribution of Ernst B. Haas', *Annual Review of Political Science*, 8: 271–96.

Rutten, M. (2002), *From Saint Malo to Nice: European defence*, Core Documents (Paris: Institute for Security Studies).

Sabatier, P. A. and H. C. Jenkins-Smith (eds) (1993), *Policy change and learning: an advocacy coalition approach* (Boulder, CO: Westview Press).

Sandholtz, W. (1998), 'The emergence of a supranational telecommunications regime' in W. Sandholtz and A. Stone Sweet (eds) *European integration and supranational governance* (Oxford: Oxford University Press).

Sandholtz, W. and A. Stone Sweet (eds) (1998), *European integration and supranational governance* (Oxford: Oxford University Press).

Sandholtz, W. and J. Zysman (1989), '1992: recasting the European bargain', *World Politics*, 42: 95–128.

Sbragia, A. (2001), 'Italy pays for Europe: political leadership, political choice, and institutional adaptation' in M. G. Cowles, J. A. Caporaso, and T. Risse (eds) *Transforming Europe: Europeanization and domestic change* (Ithaca, NY: Cornell University Press).

Schaefer, G. F., M. Egeberg, S. Korez, and J. Trondal (2000), 'The experience of member states officials in EU committees: a report on initial findings of an empirical study', *Eipascope*, 3: 29–35.

Scharpf, F. W. (1988), 'The joint-decision trap: lessons from German federalism and European integration', *Public Administration*, 66: 239–78.

Scharpf, F. W. (1999), *Governing in Europe* (Oxford University Press).

Scharpf, F. W. (2002), 'The European social model: coping with the challenges of diversity', *Journal of Common Market Studies*, 40/4: 645–70.

Schimmelfennig, F. and Sedelmeier, U. (eds) (2005), *The politics of European Union enlargement: theoretical approaches* (London: Routledge).

Schmitt, H. and J. Thomasson (eds) (1999), *Political representation and legitimacy in the European Union* (Oxford: Oxford University Press).

Schmitter, P. (1969), 'Three neofunctional hypotheses about international integration', *International Organization*, 23/1: 161–6.

Schmitter, P. C. (1996), 'Imagining the future of the euro-polity with the help of new concepts' in G. Marks, F. W. Scharpf, P. C. Schmitter, and W. Streeck (eds) *Governance in the European Union* (London: Sage).

Schmitter, P. C. (2000), *How to democratize the European Union and why bother?* (Lanham, MD: Rowman & Littlefield).

Schmitter, P. C. (2005), 'Ernst B. Haas and the legacy of neo-functionalism', *Journal of European Public Policy*, 12/2: 255–72.

Schneider, V. and R. Werle (forthcoming 2006), 'Telecommunications policy' in P. Graziano and M. Vink (eds) *Europeanization: new research agendas* (Basingstoke: Palgrave-Macmillan).

Schwarzmantel, J. (2003), *Citizenship and identity: towards a new republic* (London: Routledge).

Scott, J. (1995), *Development dilemmas in the European Community* (Buckingham: Open University Press).

Scully, R. (1997a), 'The European Parliament and the co-decision procedure: a reassessment', *Journal of Legislative Studies*, 3: 58–73.

Scully, R. (1997b), 'The European Parliament and co-decision: a rejoinder to Tsebelis and Garrett', *Journal of Legislative Studies*, 3: 93–103.

Scully, R. (2000), 'Democracy, legitimacy and the European Parliament' in M. Green Cowles and M. Smith (eds) *The state of the European Union*, vol. 5 (Oxford: Oxford University Press).

Scully, R. (2005), *Becoming Europeans? Attitudes, behaviour and socialisation in the European Parliament* (Oxford: Oxford University Press).

Scully, R. (2006), 'Rational institutionalism and liberal intergovernmentalism' in M. Cini and A. K. Bourne (eds) *Palgrave advances in European Union studies* (Basingstoke: Palgrave).

Sepos, A. (2005), *Differentiated integration in the EU: the position of small member states*, EUI Working Paper RSCAS 2005/17.

Shackleton, M. (2000), 'The politics of co-decision', *Journal of Common Market Studies*, 38: 325–42.

Shapiro, M. (1992), 'The European Court of Justice' in A. Sbragia (ed.) *Europolitics* (Washington, DC: The Brookings Institution).

Shaw, J. (ed.) (2000), *Social law and policy in an evolving European Union* (Oxford: Hart).

Shucksmith, M., K. Thomson, and D. Roberts (eds) (2005), *CAP and the regions: the territorial impact of the Common Agricultural Policy* (Wallingford: CABI Publishing).

Simonian, H. (1985), *The privileged partnership* (Oxford: Clarendon Press).

Smismans, S. (2003), 'European civil society: shaped by discourses and institutional interests', *European Law Journal*, 9/4: 482–504.

Smismans, S. (ed.) (forthcoming 2006), *Civil society and - legitimate European governance* (Cheltenham: Edwrd Elgar).

Smith, A. (ed.) (2004), *Politics and the European Commission: actors, interdependence, legitimacy* (London: Routledge).

Smith, H. (2002), *European Union foreign policy: what it is and what it does* (London: Pluto Press).

Smith, J. (1999), *Europe's elected Parliament* (Sheffield: Sheffield Academic Press).

Smith, M. (2001a), 'The EU as an international actor' in J. Richardson (ed.) *European Union: power and policy-making*, 2nd edn (London: Routledge).

Smith, M. (2001b), 'The common foreign and security policy' in S. Bromley (ed.) *Governing the European Union* (London: Sage).

Smith, S. (2001), 'Reflectivist and constructivist approaches to international theory' in J. Baylis and S. Smith (eds) *The globalization of world politics: an introduction to international relations*, 2nd edn (Oxford: Oxford University Press).

Sørensen, G. (2004), *The transformation of the state: beyond the myth of retreat* (Basingstoke: Palgrave-Macmillan).

Spaak, P.-H. (1956), *The Brussels report on the general common market* (the Spaak Report), Brussels, June.

Spencer, C. (2001), 'The EU and common strategies: the revealing case of the Mediterranean', *European Foreign Affairs Review*, 6/1: 31–51.

Statewatch (2001), *The 'conclusions' of the special justice and home affairs council on 20 september 2001 and their implications for civil liberties*, http://www.statewatch.org/observatory2.htm.

Steunenberg, B. and J. Thomassen (eds) (2005), *The European Parliament on the move: towards parliamentary democracy in Europe?* (London: Rowman & Littlefield).

Stevens, A. (with H. Stevens) (2001), *Brussels bureaucrats? The administration of the European Union* (Basingstoke: Palgrave).

Stirk, P. M. and D. Willis (eds) (1991), *Shaping Postwar Europe* (London: Pinter).

Stone Sweet, A. (1998), *The European Courts and national courts: doctrine and jurisprudence* (Oxford: Hart).

Stone Sweet, A. (2003), 'European integration and the legal system' in T. Börzel and R. Cichowski (eds) *The state of the European Union*, vol. 6 (Oxford: Oxford University Press).

Stone Sweet, A. (2004), *The judicial construction of Europe* (Oxford: Oxford University Press).

Stone Sweet, A. and T. L. Brunell (1998), 'Constructing a supranational constitution: Dispute resolution and governance in the European Community', *The American Political Science Review*, 92/1: 63–81.

Stone Sweet, A. and T. Brunell (2004), *Constructing a supranational constitution: the judicial construction of Europe* (Oxford: Oxford University Press).

Stone Sweet, A. and J. Caporaso (1998), 'From free trade to supranational polity: the European Court and Integration' in W. Sandholtz and A. Stone Sweet (eds) *European integration and supranational governance* (Oxford: Oxford University Press).

Stone Sweet, A. and W. Sandholtz (1998), 'Integration, supranational governance, and the institutionalization of the European polity' in W. Sandholtz and A. Stone Sweet (eds) *European integration and supranational governance* (Oxford: Oxford University Press).

Streeck, W. and P. C. Schmitter (1991), 'From national corporatism to transnational pluralism: organized interests in the single European market', *Politics & Society*, 19/2: 133–65.

Streeck, W., J. Grote, V. Schneider, and J. Visser (eds) (2005), *Governing interests: business associations facing internationalism* (London: Routledge).

Stuart, G. (2003), *The making of Europe's constitution* (London: Fabian Society).

Stubb, A. C.-G. (1996), 'A categorisation of differentiated integration', *Journal of Common Market Studies*, 34/2: 283–95.

Sun, J. M. and J. Pelkmans (1995), 'Regulatory competition in the Single Market', *Journal of Common Market Studies*, 33/1: 67–89.

Tajfel, H. (1970), 'Experiments in intergroup discrimination', *Scientific American*, 223: 96–102.

Taylor, P. (1975), 'The politics of the European Communities: the confederal phase', *World Politics*, April: 335–60.

Taylor, P. (1990), 'Regionalism and functionalism reconsidered' in P. Taylor and A. J. R. Groom (eds) *Frameworks for international cooperation* (London: Pinter).

Taylor, P. (1993), *International organization in the modern world: the regional and the global process* (New York: Pinter).

Taylor, P. (1996), *The European Union in the 1990s* (Oxford: Oxford University Press).

Thatcher, M. (2004), 'Winners and losers in Europeanisation: reforming the national regulation of telecommunications', *West European Politics*, 27/2: 284–309.

Thatcher, M. (2005), 'Europeanisation and varieties of capitalism: EU regulation of markets and institutional reform', paper presented to APSA conference, Washington, DC, September 2005.

Tömmel, I. (1998), 'Transformation of governance: the European Commission's Strategy for creating a "Europe of the regions"', *Regional and Federal Studies*, 8/2: 52–80.

Tonra, B. (2001), *The Europeanization of national foreign policy: Dutch, Danish and Irish foreign policy in the European Union* (Ashgate: Aldershot).

Tonra, B. (2006), 'Conceptualising the European Union's global role' in M. Cini and A. K. Bourne (eds) *Palgrave advances in European Union studies* (Basingstoke: Palgrave).

Tranholm-Mikkelsen, J. (1991), 'Neo-functionalism: obstinate or obsolete? A reappraisal in the light of the new dynamism of the EC', *Millennium: Journal of International Studies*, 20/1: 1–22.

Trechsel, A. (2005), 'How to federalise the EU . . . and why bother?', *Journal of European Public Policy*, 12/3: 401–18.

Trondal, J. (2005), 'Contending decision-making dynamics within the European Commission: the case of seconded national experts', Paper presented at the ECPR Conference in Budapest, 8–10 September.

Truman, D. B. (1951/1993), *The governmental process: political interests and public opinion* (New York: Alfred A. Knopf. Reprinted Institute of Governmental Studies, University of California, Berkeley.)

Tsebelis, G. (1994), 'The power of the European Parliament as a conditional agenda setter', *American Political Science Review*, 88/1: 128–42.

Tsebelis, G. and G. Garrett (1997), 'Agenda setting, vetoes and the European Union's co-decision procedure', *Journal of Legislative Studies*, 3: 74–92.

Tsebelis, G., C. B. Jensen, A. Kalandrakis, and A. Kreppel (2001), 'Legislative procedures in the European Union: an empirical analysis', *British Journal of Political Science*, 31/4: 573–99.

Tsoukalis, L. (1977), *The politics and economics of European monetary integration* (London: Allen & Unwin).

Tsoukalis, L. (1997), *The new European economy revisited* (Oxford: Oxford University Press).

Turner, J. C. (1985), 'Social categorization and the self-concept: a social cognitive theory of group behavior', *Advances in Group Processes*, 2: 77–122.

Tuytschaever, F. (1999), *Differentiation in European Union Law* (Oxford: Hart Publishers).

Uçarer, E. M. (2001a), 'From the sidelines to center stage: side-kick no more? The European Commission in justice and home affairs', *European Integration online Papers* (EIoP), 5/5: http://eiop.or.at/eiop/texte/2001-005a.htm.

Uçarer, E. M. (2001b), 'Managing asylum and European integration: expanding spheres of exclusion?', *International Studies Perspectives*, 2/3: 291–307.

Urwin, D. W. (1995), *The community of Europe* (London: Longman).

Urwin, D. W. (1997), *A political history of western Europe since 1945* (London: Longman).

Usherwood, S. (2005), 'Realists, sceptics and opponents. Opposition to the EU's constitutional treaty', *Journal of Contemporary European Research*, I/2: 4–12.

van der Eijk, C. and M. Franklin (eds) (1996), *Choosing Europe? The European electorate and national politics in the face of Union* (Ann Arbor, MI: University of Michigan Press).

van der Eijk, C. and M. Franklin (2004), 'Potential for contestation on national matters at national elections in Europe' in G. Marks and M. Steenbergen (eds) *European integration and political conflict* (Cambridge: Cambridge University Press).

van der Klaauw, J. (1994), 'Amnesty lobbies for refugees' in R. H. Pedler and M. P. C. M van Schendelen (eds) *Lobbying the European Union: companies, trade associations and issue groups* (Aldershot: Dartmouth).

van Selm, J. (2002), 'Immigration and asylum or foreign policy: the EU's approach to migrants and their countries of origin', in E. M. Uçarer (ed.) *Migration and the externalities of European integration* (Lanham, MD: Lexington Books).

van Thiel, S. *et al.* (eds) (2005), *Understanding the new European constitutional treaty* (Brussels: VUB).

Verdun, A. (1996), 'An "asymmetrical" Economic and Monetary Union in the EU: perceptions of monetary authorities and social partners', *Journal of European Integration*, 20/1: 59–81.

Verdun, A. (2000), *European responses to globalization and financial market integration: perceptions of Economic and Monetary Union in Belgium, France and Germany* (Basingstoke: Palgrave-Macmillan).

Verdun, A. (2002), *The euro: European integration theory and Economic and Monetary Union* (Lanham, MD: Rowman & Littlefield).

Wæver, O. (2004), 'Discursive approaches' in A. Wiener and T. Diez (eds) *European integration theory* (Oxford: Oxford University Press).

Wallace, H. (1996), 'The institutions of the EU: experience and experiments' in H. Wallace and W. Wallace (eds) *Policy-making in the European Union*, 3rd edn (Oxford: Oxford University Press).

Wallace, H. (2000), 'The institutional setting: five variations on a theme' in H. Wallace and W. Wallace (eds) *Policy making in the European Union*, 4th edn (Oxford: Oxford University Press), 3–37.

Wallace, H. (2002), 'The Council: an institutional chameleon', *Governance*, 15/3: 325–44.

Wallace, H. (2005), 'An institutional anatomy and five policy modes' in H. Wallace, W. Wallace, and M.A. Pollack (eds) *Policy-making in the European Union*, 5th edn (Oxford: Oxford University Press).

Wallace, W. (1982), 'Europe as a confederation: the Community and the nation state', *Journal of Common Market Studies*, 21/1: 57–68.

Wallace, W. (2005), 'Post-sovereign governance: the EU as a partial polity' in H. Wallace, W. Wallace, and M. Pollack (eds) *Policy-making in the European Union*, 5th edn (Oxford: Oxford University Press).

Waltz, K. (1979), *Theory of international politics* (New York: McGraw Hill).

Warleigh, A. (2001), 'Europeanizing civil society: NGOs as agents of political socialization', *Journal of Common Market Studies*, 39/4: 619–39.

Warleigh, A. (2002a), *Flexible integration: which model for the European Union?* (London: Continuum).

Warleigh, A. (2002b), 'Towards network democracy? The potential of flexible integration' in M. Farrell, S. Fella, and M. Newman (eds) *European integration in the twenty-first century* (London: Sage).

Warleigh, A. (2003), *Democracy in the European Union: theory, practice and reform* (London: Sage).

Warleigh, A. (2004), *European Union: the basics* (London: Routledge).

Warleigh, A. (2005), 'Enlargement and normative reform in the European Union: the example of flexibility', *International Journal of Organization Theory and Behaviour*, 8/1: 103–23.

Warleigh, A. (2005), *Flexible integration*: which model for the European Union? (Sheffield: Sheffield Academic Press).

Warleigh, A. (2006), 'Learning from Europe: EU studies and the rethinking of international relations', *European Journal of International Research*, 12/1: 31–51.

Watts, R. L. (1999), *Comparing federal systems*, 2nd edn (Montreal: McGill-Queen's University Press).

Weale, A. (2005), *Democratic citizenship and the European Union* (Manchester: Manchester University Press).

Weiler, J. (1991), 'The transformation of Europe', *Yale Law Review*, 100: 2403–83.

Wendt, A. (1999), *Social theory of international politics* (Cambridge: Cambridge University Press).

Wessels, W. (1997), 'Ever closer fusion? A dynamic macropolitical view on integration processes', *Journal of Common Market Studies*, 35/2: 267–99.

Wessels, W. and D. Rometsch (1996), 'Conclusion: European Union and national institutions' in D. Rometsch and W. Wessels (eds) *The European Union and member states: towards institutional fusion?* (Manchester and New York: Manchester University Press).

Wessels, W. *et al.* (eds) (2003), *Fifteen into one? European Union and its members states* (Manchester: Manchester University Press).

Westlake, M. and D. Galloway (2004), *The Council of the European Union*, 3rd edn (London: Cartermill).

Wiener, A. (2006), 'Constructivism and sociological institutionalism' in M. Cini and A. K. Bourne (eds) *Palgrave advances in European Union studies* (Basingstoke: Palgrave).

Wiener, A. and T. Diez (eds) (2004), *European integration theory* (Oxford: Oxford University Press).

Wincott, D. (1994), 'Human rights, democratization and the role of the Court of Justice', *Democratization*, 1: 251–71.

Wincott, D. (1995), 'Institutional interaction and European integration: towards an everyday critique of liberal intergovernmentalism', *Journal of Common Market Studies*, 33/4: 597–609.

Young, A. R. (1997), 'Consumption without representation? Consumers in the single market' in H. Wallace and A. R. Young (eds) *Participation and policy-making in the European Union* (Oxford: Clarendon Press).

Young, A. (2002), *Extending European cooperation: the European Union and the 'new' international trade agenda* (Manchester: Manchester University Press).

Zeitlin, J. and P. Pochet, with L. Magnusson (eds) (2005), *The open method of co-ordination in action: the European employment and social inclusion strategies* (Brussels: P.I.E.-Peter Lang).

Zysman, J. (1994), 'How institutions create historically-rooted trajectories of growth', *Industrial and Corporate Change*, 3/1: 243–83.

Index

The following abbreviations have been used in this index:

CAP Common Agricultural Policy
CFSP Common Foreign and Security Policy
EMU Economic and Monetary Union
EU European Union
JHA Justice and Home Affairs

Page numbers followed by an asterisk indicate material in the glossary

D

E

J

K

L

M

N

O

P

Q

R

Y

Z